CONSUMER BEHAVIOR

McGRAW-HILL SERIES IN MARKETING

Consulting Editor
CHARLES SCHEWE
University of Massachusetts

DAVID L. LOUDON

ALBERT J. DELLA BITTA

College of Business Administration
University of Rhode Island

CONSUMER BEHAVIOR

CONCEPTS AND APPLICATIONS

McGRAW-HILL BOOK COMPANY

New York   St. Louis   San Francisco
Auckland   Bogotá   Düsseldorf
Johannesburg   London   Madrid
Mexico   Montreal   New Delhi
Panama   Paris   São Paulo
Singapore   Sydney   Tokyo   Toronto

CONSUMER BEHAVIOR: CONCEPTS AND APPLICATIONS

4567890DODO783210

This book was set in Helvetica by Black Dot, Inc. (ECU).
The editors were John F. Carleo and James B. Armstrong;
the designer was Nicholas Krenitsky;
the production supervisor was Dominick Petrellese.
The drawings were done by J & R Services, Inc.
R. R. Donnelley & Sons Company was printer and binder.

Library of Congress Cataloging in Publication Data

Loudon, David L
    Consumer behavior.

    (McGraw-Hill series in marketing)
    Includes index.
    1. Consumers. 2. Consumers—Case studies.
I. Della Bitta, Albert J., joint author. II. Title.
HF5415.3.L68   658.8'34   78-11083
ISBN 0-07-038753-2

TO

Carol, Bobby, and Susan

Margaret, Michael, and David

Our Parents

CONTENTS

PART FOUR
INDIVIDUAL DETERMINANTS OF CONSUMER BEHAVIOR

PART FIVE
CONSUMER DECISION PROCESSES

PREFACE

This book is written for the beginning student of consumer behavior, whether at the undergraduate or the graduate level, with the purpose of blending both concepts and applications from the field of consumer behavior.

No special assumptions have been made regarding student preparation for this text. Although many will have had previous exposure to some of the behavioral concepts discussed, all can benefit from a review of these topics and from an examination of them from a managerial perspective. Thus the concepts presented here are regarded as extremely valuable for the career-oriented student in general and indispensable for the marketing major.

Considerable effort has been made to present the material clearly and in a style that is readable, interesting, and motivating to students. Unnecessary jargon has been avoided, and behavioral concepts have been defined in simple language. In addition to topical examples, a large number of graphics and other visuals help to clarify and reinforce text material. Each chapter also has a brief introduction and a summary, the first to prepare the reader and the second to reinforce major points.

As the title indicates, the book not only presents theoretical concepts of consumer behavior but also stresses the application of this conceptual material to marketing strategies and decision making in the private, public, and nonprofit sectors. At the conceptual level, it seeks to present an integrated framework around which the major areas of consumer-behavior knowledge can be discussed. The book is thoroughly documented and provides ample opportunity for the reader to pursue a particular area of interest in greater detail. The explosion of consumer research, however, has made it impossible to cite every study relevant to a specific topic. In addition, such an approach tends to confuse the introductory student through information overload and often contradictory findings. Therefore, we have emphasized what is known about consumers rather than dwell on the present uncertainty and its implications for future research. Nevertheless, controversial areas still exist and will continue to exist for quite some time, and the student is made aware of this fact.

For too long consumer behavior texts have been crammed with theories and research findings while giving little attention to their pragmatic application in the marketplace. Our teaching experience has been that students, especially at the introductory level, are highly interested in discussions of potential and *actual* applications of these concepts. In addition to its motivating benefit, such an approach also allows students to gain a much greater appreciation of the conceptual material. Rather than just paying token attention to this, the text thoroughly incorporates marketing realism in several ways. First, throughout each chapter frequent reference is made to actual or potential applications of the concepts being discussed. Second, questions and exercises following each chapter offer opportunities for experiential learning. Here research may be conducted, decisions made, or other creative activities undertaken, bringing students closer to the real world of marketing. Third, cases at the end of each part offer opportunities for more extensive discussion and for decision making through application of text material.

The book is organized into five major sections.

Part One, *Studying Consumer Behavior*, introduces the reader to the discipline of consumer behavior by defining and describing its scope and importance, discussing the marketing function, and providing numerous examples of consumer-behavior relevance in managerial decision making. Traditional and contemporary models of consumer behavior are presented along with the authors' simplified framework, all of which serve as a foundation for studying and understanding the subject of consumer behavior.

Part Two, *Understanding Consumers and Market Segments*, begins with a brief treatment of some aspects of consumer research. This helps prepare students for the discussion of specific studies and stresses the importance of consumer research as a prerequisite to many marketing decisions. Because of the growing attractiveness of consumer behavior to nonmarketing majors, some students may be unfamiliar with major characteristics of the consumer market and the concept and methods of market segmentation. Consequently, consumer characteristics are discussed with a view toward selecting target markets and developing marketing programs.

Part Three, *Environmental Influences on Consumer Behavior*, examines the sociocultural influences on consumers and presents them in hierarchial order ranging from the broadest to the most immediate. The roles of culture, subculture, social class, social groups, family, and interpersonal influences are examined.

Part Four, *Individual Determinants of Consumer Behavior*, deals with the consumer's internal variables. Coverage includes the concepts of motivation, perception, learning, personality and self-concept, attitudes, and attitude change. These variables strongly influence each consumer's unique reaction to the environment.

Part Five, *Consumer Decision Processes*, concludes the book by describing the way in which consumers make purchase decisions based on their environmental influences and individual determinants. A four-stage model of consumers' decision processes (consisting of problem recognition, information search and evaluation, purchasing processes, and postpurchase behavior) is described.

Instructors desiring alternative orders in material coverage will find the book very flexible. For example, if students have had an introductory course in marketing and marketing research, Chapters 3–5 may be minimized or eliminated. Those who prefer to discuss individual determinants of consumer behavior prior to environmental variables can simply reverse Parts Three and Four. Finally, instructors facing time constraints will find the book quite flexible in regard to topics that can be covered over varying course lengths.

We are indebted to a number of people who helped us during the preparation of this text. First, Dean Richard R. Weeks and Professor Aaron J. Alton, both of the University of Rhode Island, were highly supportive and offered much administrative assistance. Second, we gratefully acknowledge the contribution of Professor M. Wayne DeLozier (University of South Carolina) who provided us with drafts of Chapters 16, 17, and 18. Third, Professors Beverlee B. Anderson (Wright State University), George W. Brooker, Jr. (SUNY–Albany), Robert Mittelstaedt (University of Nebraska), Colin F. Neuhaus (Eastern Michigan University), Richard C. Reizenstein (University of Tennessee), and W. Bruce Weale (Florida State University) reviewed sections of the manuscript and offered many helpful suggestions. Consulting Editor Charles D. Schewe (University of Massachusetts) also critically evaluated the entire manuscript, providing valuable comments and additional assistance. Our editors at McGraw-Hill, Bill Kane, John Carleo, and Jim Armstrong, provided considerable encouragement and support. In addition, Norma Pirhonen, Linda Hemphill, and Kristina Felbeck ably helped with numerous aspects of the manuscript's preparation. Finally, and most importantly, our wives and children deserve a medal for their patience, understanding, and encouragement.

David L. Loudon
Albert J. Della Bitta

CONSUMER BEHAVIOR

STUDYING CONSUMER BEHAVIOR

1. INTRODUCTION TO CONSUMER BEHAVIOR   2. A FOUNDATION FOR STUDYING CONSUMER BEHAVIOR   Cases for Part One

INTRODUCTION TO CONSUMER BEHAVIOR

DEFINING CONSUMER BEHAVIOR Ultimate Consumer; Individual Buyer; Decision Process; A Subset of Human Behavior WHY STUDY CONSUMER BEHAVIOR? A Part of Our Lives; Application to Decision Making APPLYING CONSUMER BEHAVIOR Consumer Behavior and Marketing Management; Consumer Behavior and Social Marketing; Consumer Behavior and Governmental Decision Making; Consumer Behavior and Demarketing; Consumer Behavior and Consumer Education

Welcome to the fascinating field of consumer behavior. There is probably no better way to begin our study than by examining several actual case histories that orient us to the nature and scope of consumer behavior.

Sayonara, Steve When Steve Scout, an all-American-looking, Boy Scout-type doll, was introduced to the market in 1974, Kenner Products had high hopes for its success. At stake was a share of the $175-million-a-year market for male "action figures." However, a merit badge was just not in the offing for Steve. His sales were so disappointing that in 1975 Kenner sent him to that big jamboree in the sky. An autopsy revealed that Steve was a failure because of his inability to generate fantasy among young children. Dolls such as Pulsar and the Six Million Dollar man, with his power arm and bionic parts, clearly represent what children can never become. These figures are able to nurture and focus children's fantasy potential, generating adventure and excitement. Steve Scout, on the other hand, represented something that most children could easily be and therefore was not intriguing enough to capture their fantasies and interest.[1]

Mad Monday In 1976 a program was instituted in Los Angeles, California, to encourage efficient transportation, save fuel, and curb air pollution. During rush hours, one lane in each direction of the eight-lane Santa Monica Freeway was designated by a diamond symbol as an express lane for exclusive use by buses and cars carrying three or more persons. In this city, where citizens have long cherished their "right" to buzz along solo on smooth, wide-open pavement, the diamond lanes were greeted unenthusiastically.

The system was implemented on what has become known as "Mad Monday," and then the fun really began. The result was mind-boggling traffic jams on the freeway and alternate routes, but little traffic in the diamond lanes. While some citizens lodged legal suits, others showed serious resistance by scattering the lanes with nails and throwing paint on the diamond markers. Recognizing an opportunity, one astute individual started a "rent-a-rider" business so motorists could actually buy their way onto the express lanes. Other drivers began carrying objects such as mannequins and tennis rackets disguised as passengers. One quick-talking hearse driver even argued that a passenger plus the corpse he was carrying should qualify him for use of the diamond lane.[2]

Melodic watts To Arne, a college junior, a stereo system was more than something that merely provided music. "Good sounds" enhanced his studies and entertainment, and even provided a type of natural "high." He was therefore understandably disappointed when the system in his dorm room was "ripped off." Because of the risk of future thefts, the small size of his dorm room, and improvements he expected for stereos in the near future, Arne decided that a modestly priced system would best suit his present needs.

While home on vacation, Arne noticed a component system being featured by a Lafayette franchise store. He was impressed with this store's reputation; and his understanding that Lafayette serviced what they sold, instead of returning it to the manufacturer, favorably influenced him.

The system on special included a LR-100 receiver, a Garrard turntable with a Shure cartridge, and Lafayette HLX speakers. His dormmate owned a LR-100 receiver, and Arne had always thought highly of it. These feelings were confirmed when he found that *Consumer Reports* had given the model a very favorable rating. His family owned a Garrard turntable with a Shure cartridge, and Arne was impressed with its performance and durability. The HLX speakers were slightly more expensive than another brand that he was considering as a substitute. However, after some time spent listening to the two brands in Lafayette's sound room, Arne decided that he preferred the HLX speakers. In addition, he was also persuaded by the knowledge that the HLXs employed an air suspension design like that used on the prestigious KLH brand of speakers.

The entire system carried a regular retail price of $335, but was presently reduced to $265. Arne knew that if he did not act before returning to college he would miss out on the special price. He discussed the purchase with his brother, who offered no negative comments on the system; and the next day, with that funny feeling in his stomach that accompanies big decisions, Arne purchased the system. Returning to school, the set was used for a while before a transistor malfunctioned. It was replaced free of charge in a matter of days. After two years of use, Arne was convinced that his stereo produced sound rivaling that of much higher-priced units.[3]

Have it your way A problem of national scope is how to provide low-cost school lunches that are nutritious and also appetizing to school children. Realizing that to qualify as "nutritious" a lunch must end up in the child's stomach, not in the garbage can, personnel of the Clark County, Las Vegas, school food service undertook to turn 70,000 students on to nourishing food. Their solution? To duplicate aspects of the menu and atmosphere of highly successful fast-food chains and, where necessary, fortify the foods so that they meet federal standards of nutrition. This resulted in a large number of menu items, including low-cholesterol pizza and hot dogs, natural corn tacos, roast beef on a bun, and tossed salads; hamburgers prepared with a specially enriched dressing; french fries fortified with vitamin C; and milk shakes made from low-fat milk fortified with protein and vitamins, and with no ice cream.

To further ensure the program's success, brightly colored food wrappers and menu posters are employed, the food service is promoted as "A Fun Place to Eat," and students order their lunches at fast-order counters just as they would at Burger King or McDonald's. Response has been tremendous, with a more than five-fold increase of participation in the program. In fact, the success has been somewhat embarrassing, since in one year the non-profit-oriented food service turned a $200,000 deficit into a $100,000 surplus![4]

These examples are quite diverse in nature, involving the successes and failures of products and services from profit and non-profit-oriented organizations, as well as the implementation of public policy. In addition, they span the spectrum from decision making of single individuals to that of group behavior. One theme common to each of these examples, however, is that they all involve the behavior of consumers. Thus, whether we are aware of it or not, consumer behavior is actually occurring all around us. This might not always be very apparent, because many aspects of consumer behavior are actually quite subtle in nature and hard to detect.

Studying consumers usually proves to be highly interesting to students. It is an exciting field, but for two reasons it is also one that requires serious study. First, consumer behavior can be quite subtle in nature, making it difficult to understand fully. Second, because consumer behavior is so prevalent, it significantly affects our lives through either our own actions or those of others in their roles as consumers. Therefore, it has a great deal of practical relevance to our daily lives.

To better appreciate the nature and scope of consumer behavior, the remaining sections of this chapter focus on two very basic questions:

1. What is the nature of consumer behavior?

2. Why should we study consumer behavior?

This material will provide a basis from which we can build an adequate understanding and appreciation of consumer behavior.

DEFINING CONSUMER BEHAVIOR

Before continuing, it is appropriate to offer a definition in order to clarify the focus of our study. Consumer behavior may be defined as:

the decision process and physical activity individuals engage in when evaluating, acquiring, and using economic goods and services.

Several aspects of this statement need emphasis and elaboration so that their meaning can be more fully appreciated.

Ultimate Consumer

Our primary attention will be directed toward *ultimate consumers*—those individuals who purchase for the purpose of private individual or household consumption. Some have argued that studying ultimate consumers also reveals much about industrial or intermediate buyers and others involved in purchasing for business firms and institutions.[5] While not denying this, we must recognize that much industrial purchasing behavior is unique because it often involves different buying motives and the influence of a large variety of people.[6] Therefore, for the sake of simplicity we will focus only on ultimate consumer behavior and will not become involved in drawing comparisons with industrial purchasing situations.

Individual Buyer

The most commonly thought of consumer situation is where an individual makes a purchase with little or no influence from others. However, in some cases a number of people are jointly involved in a purchase decision. For example, planning a vacation or deciding on a new car can involve an entire family. In other cases the purchaser may just be acquiring a product for someone else who has specified exactly what was wanted. These situations suggest that people can take on different roles in what we have defined as consumer behavior. Table 1-1 presents one way to classify these roles.

Some purchase situations involve at least one person in each of these roles, while in other circumstances a single individual can take on several roles at the same time. For example, in one situation a wife (initiator and influencer) may ask her husband (buyer) to pick up a particular cereal on his shopping trip because their child (user) said she wanted it. At another time the husband could act as the initiator, buyer, and user by purchasing the cereal for himself.

Any study of consumer behavior would be incomplete if it treated only one consumer role. However, an emphasis on one role, while still devoting adequate treatment to the others, can actually facilitate and simplify our study. The focus of our study of consumer behavior will rest on the *buyer*—the individual who actually makes the purchase. This approach is useful because even when told what to purchase the buyer often makes decisions regarding purchase timing, store choice, package size, and other factors. Therefore, focusing on the buyer, while allowing for the influence of others on the purchase decision, appears to be the most appropriate general approach to studying consumer behavior.

Decision Process

The way in which our definition views "behavior" also deserves special attention. That is, consumer behavior is seen to involve a *mental decision*

TABLE 1-1

VARIOUS CONSUMER BEHAVIOR ROLES

Role	Description
Initiator	The individual who determines that some need or want is not being met and authorizes a purchase to rectify the situation
Influencer	A person who by some intentional or unintentional word or action influences the purchase decision, the actual purchase, and/or use of the product or service
Buyer	The individual who actually makes the purchase transaction
User	The person most directly involved in consumption or use of the purchase

Source: Gerald Zaltman and Philip C. Burger, *Marketing Research: Fundamentals and Dynamics,* The Dryden Press, (A division of Holt, Rinehart and Winston), New York, copyright © 1975, by The Dryden Press, p. 142. Adapted by permission of Holt, Rinehart and Winston.

process as well as *physical activity.* The actual act of purchase is just one stage in a series of mental and physical activities that occur over a period of time. Some of these activities precede the actual purchase, while others follow it. However, since all are capable of influencing the purchase they will be considered as part of the consumer's behavior.

An example will illustrate the benefits of this viewpoint. Suppose a photographer who has been regularly purchasing one brand of film suddenly switches to a competing product. There has been no change in either the films or their prices. What has caused this shift in loyalty? Just noting that the individual's purchase behavior has changed does little to help our understanding of the situation. Perhaps the competing film received a strong recommendation by a friend, or possibly the photographer switched because he has developed an interest in new subject matter and believes the competing brand best captures its colors. On the other hand, his decision may have been caused by a general dissatisfaction with results from his regular film or recent exposure to an advertisement for the competing brand.

This example suggests the complexity of consumers' decision processes and demonstrates the limitations of viewing consumer behavior as just the act of purchasing. Therefore, to understand consumers adequately we should stress that, in addition to physical activities, their behavior involves a mental decision process that takes place over time.

A Subset of Human Behavior

Viewing consumer behavior in such a broad context suggests that it is actually a subset of human behavior. That is, factors that affect individuals in their daily lives also influence their purchase activities. Internal influences, such as learning and motives, as well as external factors, such as social expectations and constraints, affect us in our role as consumers as well as in our other capacities. In fact, it is often difficult to draw a distinct line between consumer-related behavior and other aspects of human behavior. For example, next-door neighbors might find lawn problems a convenient topic for striking up a conversation. However, this can quickly lead to a serious discussion of the merits of Scott fertilizers and Sears riding mowers.

The fact that consumer behavior is a subset of human behavior presents us with an advantage. The several disciplines collectively referred to as the *behavioral sciences* have studied human behavior for some time, and we may draw upon their contributions for understanding consumer behavior. This borrowing is quite extensive and includes not only theories used in explaining behavior but also methods useful in investigating it. In fact, this borrowing is so extensive that consumer behavior is often said to be *multidisciplinary* in nature. The behavioral science disciplines that have most contributed to our understanding of consumers are:

1. *Psychology*—the study of the behavior and mental processes of individuals

2. *Sociology*—the study of the collective behavior of people in groups

3. *Social Psychology*—the study of how individuals influence and are influenced by groups

4. *Economics*—the study of peoples' production, exchange, and consumption of goods and services

5. *Anthropology*—the study of people in relation to their culture

WHY STUDY CONSUMER BEHAVIOR?

Understanding the reasons for studying a particular discipline increases our ability to appreciate it. That is, such a perspective enables us to better evaluate the usefulness of the contributions that the field has to offer.

A Part of Our Lives

In a general sense, the most important reason for studying consumer behavior is the significant role it plays in our lives. Much of our time is spent directly in the marketplace shopping or engaging in other activities. A large amount of additional time is spent thinking about products and services, talking to friends about them, and seeing or hearing advertisements about them. In addition, the goods we purchase and the manner in which we use them significantly influence how we live our daily lives. These general concerns alone are enough to justify our study. However, many seek to understand the behavior of consumers for what are thought to be more immediate and tangible reasons.

Application to Decision Making

Most seek to understand consumer behavior for the purpose of applying their knowledge to problems or situations involving consumers. For this reason consumer behavior is said to be an *applied discipline*. Such applications can exist at two different levels of analysis. The *macro* perspective applies knowledge of consumers to aggregate-level problems and to situations faced by society as a whole. The *micro* perspective seeks application of this knowledge to problems faced by the individual firm or organization.

MACRO PERSPECTIVE On the macro, or aggregate, level we know that consumers collectively influence economic and social conditions within an entire society. In market systems based on individual choice, consumers strongly influence what will be produced, for whom it will be produced, and what resources will be used to produce it. Consequently, the collective behavior of consumers has a significant influence on the quality and level of our standard of living.[7] For example, consider the overall impact of American consumers' strong desire for private automobile transportation. Vast amounts of resources have been used to produce cars, highway systems, and petroleum products used in their operation. It has also strongly influenced where many of us live (e.g., the suburbs) and how we run our daily lives (e.g., what we eat, where we shop, and how we are entertained). Further, this collective desire not only has led to the development of a strong transportation network but also has significantly contributed to our pollution problems.

As this example illustrates, understanding consumer behavior from a macro perspective can provide insight into aggregate economic and social trends and can perhaps even predict such trends. In addition, this understanding may suggest ways to increase the efficiency of the market system and improve the well-being of people in our society.

MICRO PERSPECTIVE Viewing consumer behavior applications from a micro perspective involves understanding consumers for the purpose of helping a firm or organization accomplish its objectives. Advertising managers, product designers, and many others in profit-oriented businesses are interested in understanding consumers in order to be more effective at their tasks. In addition, managers of various nonprofit organizations have benefited from the same knowledge. For example, the United Way and the American Cancer Society have been very effective in applying an understanding of consumer behavior concepts to their activities.

APPLYING CONSUMER BEHAVIOR

The following selections have been made from a variety of practical applications in the field of consumer behavior. Some involve a macro perspective while others illustrate a micro viewpoint. Together they underscore the importance of understanding consumers in solving a variety of contemporary problems.

Consumer Behavior and Marketing Management

Effective business managers realize the importance of marketing to the success of their firm. *Marketing* may be defined as "human activity directed at satisfying needs and wants through exchange processes."[8] Such exchanges may involve products, services, or even social ideas.

A sound understanding of consumer behavior is essential to the long-run success of any marketing program. In fact, consumers and their wants and needs are seen as a cornerstone of the *marketing concept,* an important orientation or philosophy of many marketing managers. The essence of the marketing concept is to achieve the company's objectives by directing a coordinated marketing effort at identifying and satisfying consumers' wants and needs. Therefore, emphasis is placed on the following three orientations.

Consumers' wants and needs—this focus is on identifying and satisfying the wants and needs of consumers. The purpose of the firm is not seen as merely providing goods and services. Instead, want and need satisfaction is viewed as the purpose, and providing products and services is the means to achieve that end.

Company objectives—since consumers' wants and needs are so numerous, a firm most effectively uses its resources by seeking to satisfy only a small portion of them. The company's objectives and unique capabilities are used as criteria to select which wants and needs are to be aimed at.

Integrated strategy—an integrated effort is most effective in achieving a firm's objective through consumer satisfaction. For maximum impact this requires that marketing efforts directed at consumers be closely coordinated and compatible with other activities of the firm.

Limitations of the marketing concept have been noted on several fronts, especially in regard to the degree to which attempting to satisfy consumers' wants and needs can generate negative consequences for society.[9] For example, development of convenience packaging for consumers has, to a large extent, contributed to a solid waste disposal problem for society. Adjustments to the marketing concept which incorporate societal objectives have been suggested to alleviate such shortcomings.[10] However, the basic need to understand consumer behavior is still fundamental to these revised schemes.

Several major activities can be undertaken by a firm that is marketing oriented. These include market-opportunity analysis, target-market selection, and determination of the marketing mix, which includes decisions on the proper combination of marketing variables to offer consumers. Each of these is briefly discussed below with examples to illustrate the relevance of consumer behavior to their accomplishment.

MARKET-OPPORTUNITY ANALYSIS This activity involves examining trends and conditions in the marketplace to identify consumers' needs and wants that are not being fully satisfied. The analysis begins with a study of general market trends, such as consumers' life-styles and income levels, which may suggest unsatisfied wants and needs. More specific examination involves assessing any unique abilities the company might have in satisfying identified consumer desires.

A variety of recent trends have resulted in many new product offerings for consumer satisfaction. For example, companies attuned to the energy crisis have been quick to offer such new products as triple-paned replacement windows, water-saving shower heads, and light-activated thermostats that automatically reduce energy consumption at night. In the health care field, companies sensing consumers' unmet medical needs have offered accurate coin-operated blood pressure testing machines at shopping centers and other convenient locations. Also, low-priced surgical centers featuring neither meals nor overnight accommodations are now available for those seeking to minimize the costs of minor surgery, and a new device allows consumers the convenience of taking precisely calibrated medical doses at home instead of in the hospital.

TARGET-MARKET SELECTION The process of reviewing market opportunities often results in identifying distinct groupings of consumers who have unique wants and needs. This can result in a decision to concentrate company efforts on serving one or several of these target markets.

An excellent example of this has occurred in the bath soap market. By segmenting consumers according to their patterns of life-style and personalities, the Colgate-Palmolive company was able to identify a grouping of consumers who were quite unusual and who had distinct wants for a deodorant soap. Development of Irish Spring for this target group led to the capturing of 15 percent of the deodorant soap market within 3 years of introduction. This represents a highly significant success in a very competitive market where the leader, Dial soap, held only a 33 percent market share.[11]

DETERMINING THE MARKETING MIX This stage involves developing and implementing a strategy for delivering an effective combination of want-satisfying features to consumers within the target markets. A series of decisions are made on four major ingredients frequently referred to as the marketing mix variables: product, price, place, and promotion. The following characterizes each area and provides a small sampling of how knowledge of consumer behavior provides useful data for decision making.

Product The nature of the physical product and service features are of concern here. Among the decisions that are influenced by consumer behavior are:

What should be the size, shape, and color of the product?

What type of accessories or features should it have?

How should it be packaged?

How many different models should be offered in the product line?

What type of warranty should be offered?

The Gillette Company illustrates how consumer study helps provide answers to product decisions.[12] Each year Gillette spends about $1 million for shave-testing programs involving over 10,000 people in a variety of countries. Results from this program, and other consumer studies, serve as data for various razor designs. Relevant findings from this consumer research include:

The average person exerts a force of between one-third of a pound and two pounds while shaving.

Beard preparation and type as well as sensitivity to pain govern the number of comfortable shaves that can be obtained from a razor. However, most shavers discard blades at regular intervals out of habit, regardless of blade condition.

Some men hold their razor at an angle that negates the effect of the Trac II razor system. This appears to be an important reason for introducing the Atra model with its swivel-head modification.

Price The marketer must make decisions regarding both the price to charge for the company's product/service offerings and any modification to those prices. These decisions will determine the amount of revenues the firm will generate. A few of the factors involving consumer behavior input are:

What base price should be charged for each model in the product line?

What should be charged for accessories and company services?

How large a discount should be offered for new-product introductions and sales promotions?

What size discount should be given to those who pay with cash?

The situation faced by Procter & Gamble for Pampers, the disposable baby diaper, reveals the importance of understanding consumers' price reactions.[13] In early market testing the price was set at about 10 cents per diaper—more than the cost of using and washing regular cloth diapers. Surprisingly, the product "bombed"—apparently because consumers were unwilling to incur the extra cost for the convenience of using a disposable diaper. Over a four-year period the company was able to reduce the price in several stages due to cost-cutting programs. Three successive market tests in this period of declining prices suggested a significantly larger potential market. Finally the company was able to reduce the price to 6 cents per diaper, and sales skyrocketed. Pampers is now one of Procter & Gamble's best selling brands.

Place This variable involves consideration of where and how to offer products and services for sale and concerns the mechanisms involved in transferring goods and their ownership to consumers. Decisions influenced by consumer behavior include:

What type of retail outlets should sell the firm's offering?

Where should they be located, and how many should there be?

What arrangements are needed to distribute products to retailers?

To what extent is it necessary for the company to maintain tight control over activities of firms in the channel of distribution?

Selecting sites for McDonald's restaurants provides a good example of how consumers' activities affect the location decision. At one time, the corporation followed a rule that potential new store sites had to contain at least 50,000 residents within a 3-mile radius. Recent studies, however, have revealed that the majority of customers stop to eat in conjunction with other activities that draw them away from their homes. Consequently, new store sites are also chosen on the basis of consumer activity patterns. In some cases this can result in locating one McDonald's in a shopping mall and another across the street to capitalize on different activity patterns of potential customers.[14]

Promotion Of concern here are methods of communicating aspects of the firm and its offerings to target consumers. Consumer-related decisions include:

In which type of media should promotions be placed?

What are the most effective means for gaining consumers' attention?

What are the most effective methods for conveying the intended message?

Promotion is credited with much of the success of the highly profitable Revlon cosmetic line. A large portion of this success is attributable to founder Charles Revson's almost uncanny understanding of the mood of the sexual revolution, which the company's advertisements have reflected and sometimes influenced over the last 20 years. Revlon's advertisements have encouraged strong identification with the company's products among fashion-conscious women. As values in the United States changed, the healthy "American girl" image of the 1940s gave way to subtle sexual suggestiveness and then more openly erotic advertising themes of the 1950s. Promotions of the 1960s treated sexual themes frankly, with emphasis on removing guilt inhibitions about sex, and in the early 1970s this yielded ground to the liberated woman who uses Revlon products not as come-ons for males but to satisfy her own needs and wants.

In 1973, the highly successful Charlie product line was introduced and accompanied by extensive promotional efforts. Charlie is portrayed as a modern, confident, liberated career woman who has made it and is enjoying an active life to its fullest. As such, she typifies what many women today yearn to be and can easily identify with. As one reviewer wrote, "Women buy the line more to *live* like Charlie than to *look* or *smell* like her."[15]

These examples indicate the relevance of consumer behavior to marketing-management decision making. However, it is useful to also consider other areas where knowledge of consumers has significant practical application.

Consumer Behavior and Social Marketing

Can crime prevention or the concept of family planning be sold to people in much the same way that some business firms sell soap? Recently, a number of writers have suggested that a variety of social and nonprofit organizations can be viewed as having services or ideas which they are attempting to market to target groups of "consumers."[16] Such organizations include governmental agencies, religious groups, universities, and charitable institutions. Often these groups must appeal to the public for support in addition to attempting to satisfy some want or need in society. Clearly, a sound understanding of consumer decision processes can assist their efforts.

Consider, for example, the benefits such knowledge would have to administrators of the American Cancer Society. Two major tasks of this organization are (1) to solicit contributions from the public for support of cancer research and (2) to encourage regular physical examinations for early detection of the disease. Regarding the first task, fundamental information, such as the characteristics of potential contributors, what motivates their generosity, and how these motives can be most effectively appealed to, would be highly useful. Similarly, a sound basis for encouraging regular physical examinations would include specific knowledge of reasons why the exams are avoided—the expense, the time involved, the fear of learning about an illness, or some other reason.

A wide variety of other examples demonstrate the fundamental role consumer orientation plays in social-marketing endeavors.

Political positions—Many political candidates now base much of their platforms on results of public opinion polls. In addition, they often commission studies to determine their public image and use these findings to determine appropriate actions to improve their image.[17]

Preventing forest fires—Over 30 years of media exposure involving millions of dollars have made Smokey the Bear a nationally recognized symbol of forest-fire prevention. However, the U.S. Forest Service has recently decided that Smokey's nice-guy image impedes his effectiveness. Therefore, in 1977 Smokey got tough in order to have a greater impact on forest-fire prevention. Part of his angry song in one television advertisement is: "Wipe out your campfire, beat out the embers, drown it with water all the way through./Get all the red out; make sure it is dead out. Or Smokey the Bear will break you in two."[18]

Crime prevention—In Florida, business leaders contributed over $1 million to promote a reduction in armed robberies. One aspect of this effort involves outdoor billboards that show a handgun and the message: "Three years to life." Spot television announcements also remind viewers of the mandatory jail sentence for conviction of armed robbery.[19]

A wide variety of other cases of consumer-oriented social marketing exist. One example is shown in Exhibit 1-1. Not all these efforts have met with significant success. For example, congressional hearings revealed that in 1969 advertising valued at over $11 million was donated by media to encourage contributions for Radio Free Europe. However, the effort was reported to have generated only $100,000 in revenues for the organization![20] This underscores the need for a sound understanding of consumers' decision processes as the basis for more effective social marketing.

Consumer Behavior and Governmental Decision Making

In recent years the relevance of consumer-behavior principles to governmental decision making has become quite evident. Two major areas of government activity have been affected:

1. Government policies that provide services to the public or result in decisions that influence consumer behavior

2. The design of legislation to protect consumers or to assist them in evaluating products and services

There is evidence available at many levels that government policies can benefit from greater knowledge of consumer behavior. Numerous analysts have noted that our frequently failing mass-transportation systems will not be viable alternatives to private automobile travel until government planners fully understand how to appeal to the wants and needs of the public.[21] In other cases, state and municipal planners must make a variety of decisions, including where to locate highways, what areas to consider for future commercial growth, and the type of public services (such as health care and

EXHIBIT 1-1   **15**

INTRODUCTION
TO CONSUMER
BEHAVIOR

RELIGION INC.

The pews of the glass-walled church are full, and the overflow spills onto folding chairs outside, the worshipers fanning themselves in the heat. A 90-voice choir is singing, but the people are waiting for something else.

Just outside are scores of automobiles in a special drive-up worship area, their hoods pointed expectantly at the building. The people in the cars have tuned in their radios to 540 on the AM dial. They, too, are waiting.

The TV cameramen are already panning around the church while they wait for the central figure to appear. What the cameras pick up will be beamed several weeks later to almost three million people by 94 TV stations.

As the choir finishes, a tall man wearing robes, with silver hair so carefully coifed it looks sculpted, steps to the pulpit and presses two buttons. A dozen fountains outside send columns of water skyward. Two big glass wall sections roll aside, giving the auto congregation a clearer view. Raising his arms, the minister booms, "This is the day God has made. Let us rejoice and be glad in it!"

So begins another "Hour of Power" at Garden Grove Community Church, an event seen and heard by more people than any other regular Sunday service and the showcase of a growing religious conglomerate. Its founder, chief executive and prime attraction is the pastor of Garden Grove, the Rev. Robert Schuller, a bubbly, dynamic preacher who has turned a relentlessly positive-thinking theology and shrewd marketing into a plenteous harvest of souls—and cash.

Mr. Schuller is unabashed about the cash. A church is a business, he says, and his 22-acre complex here, two miles from Disneyland, is "a shopping center for God; it's part of the service industry."

Source: William M. Abrams, "Religion Inc., 'Possibility Thinking' and Shrewd Marketing Pay Off for a Preacher," *The Wall Street Journal,* August 26, 1976, p. 1. Reprinted with permission of *The Wall Street Journal,* © Dow Jones and Company, Inc., 1976. All rights reserved.

libraries) to offer. The effectiveness of these decisions will be influenced by the extent to which they are based on an adequate understanding of consumers.

A wide variety of agencies at all levels of government are involved with regulating business practices for the purpose of protecting consumers' welfare. In addition, over thirty federal agencies, including the Department of Commerce, the Food and Drug Administration (FDA), and the Federal Trade Commission (FTC), are taking a more active role by providing consumers with information relevant to their purchases. The goal of these information programs is to allow consumers to make more informed purchase decisions. Such efforts are also occurring throughout the country on the state level.

Unfortunately, it appears that the effect of many of these efforts has been considerably less than expected, and in some cases they may actually have had negative consequences for consumers.[22] Often this occurs because officials have based their decision on an inadequate understanding of consumers and how they process information.[23] The following case histories illustrate this point.

Mileage ratings   The U.S. Environmental Protection Agency (EPA) tests automobiles for fuel economy and publishes its mileage ratings on the window sticker of all new cars. Because its method of testing involves simulating only certain aspects of actual driving conditions, the resulting mileage estimates tend to be significantly higher than many customers actually experience. Feeling that they have been misled by the very government agency that is attempting to assist their purchase decisions, buyers have complained by the thousands. Apparently, they do not fully understand how to interpret EPA mileage figures and therefore are surprised when their actual mileage is considerably less than expected. Some EPA officials now are worried that their information program is beginning to lose credibility and will soon be ignored by consumers.[24]

Beef grading The U.S. Department of Agriculture (USDA) employs a nine-level grading system for classifying beef. Many have noted that this can provide consumers with useful information regarding their purchase of cuts of meat. One study, found, however, that many were not familiar with the grading system, and in actual taste tests consumers showed no preference for a "choice" grade of beef over a lower-graded cut. Also, few consumers are aware that the grading system is primarily determined by the fat content of meat (fat within the muscle) which influences tenderness. Generally, the highest, most tender grade (prime) has the greatest fat content and provides the most calories but offers the least amount of protein per serving. Consequently, some have argued that the grading system is inadequate and should be improved in order to promote more nutritional eating habits on the part of consumers.[25]

Similar problems with other government information and consumer protection programs has led to a greater awareness of the need to base such efforts on an adequate understanding of consumer behavior. For example, in 1971 the Commissioner of the Federal Trade Commission made a plea to researchers to provide information about consumers which is relevant to the agency's efforts.[26] Since then, the agency has used actual studies of consumers as the basis for some decisions and has relied less on arbitrary assumptions about their behavior.[27] This demonstrates that valid information regarding the behavior of consumers can serve as the foundation for effective regulatory practices and consumer information programs.

Consumer Behavior and Demarketing

United States history has long been characterized by the intensive efforts of private enterprise to stimulate the public to greater levels of consumption. Various government policies have supported such efforts because of their favorable effect on economic development. Recently, however, it has become increasingly clear that we are entering an era of scarcity in terms of some natural physical resources. For example, the limited remaining amounts of many basic resources, such as oil, natural gas, and even water, are frequently reported in the media.

Present and future scarcities have suggested the need for encouraging consumers to reduce their use of certain goods and services. These efforts, which have been termed "demarketing," can play an important role in conserving dwindling natural resources. A number of such attempts have been made by both private enterprise and the public sector. For example, various promotional campaigns have encouraged consumers to use less electricity, drive less, use car pools, and recycle various products. In other cases, electricity rates have been reduced during nonpeak hours, smaller, lighter cars are increasingly available, and tax rebates for home insulating efforts have been provided.[28] However, few of these efforts have been highly successful in changing long-established consumption patterns. It is quite clear from such experiences that successful demarketing programs must be based on a sound understanding of consumers' motives and their historically established consumption behavior.

Consumer Behavior and Consumer Education

Consumers themselves also stand to benefit directly from orderly investigations into the behavior of consumers. This can occur on an individual basis or as part of more formal educational programs. As we study what has been discovered about the behavior of others, we can gain insight into our own interactions with the marketplace. For example, when we learn that a large proportion of the $153 billion spent annually on grocery products is used for impulse purchases, and not spent according to preplanned shopping lists, we may be more willing to plan our purchases in an effort to save money. In general, as we discover the many variables that can influence consumers' purchases, we have the opportunity to better understand how they affect our own behavior.

What is learned about consumer behavior can also directly benefit consumers in a more formal sense. The knowledge we generate by studying consumers can serve as data for educational programs designed to improve their decision-making abilities regarding products and services.[29] Such courses are now available at the high school and college level and are becoming increasingly popular. To be most effective, these educational programs should be based on a clear understanding of the important variables influencing consumers.

SUMMARY

The purpose of this chapter was to serve as a brief introduction to the field of consumer behavior. After several orienting examples, discussion centered on defining consumer behavior and describing the focus we will take in studying it. This approach is to view consumer behavior as a decision process of those individuals purchasing for the purpose of individual or household consumption. Therefore, we recognize that in certain situations consumers will purchase products and services for use by other individuals. Also, we must realize that other individuals can have an influence on the consumer's decision process.

Discussion then turned to considering various reasons for studying consumer behavior. Most of our attention focused on the applied nature of the discipline. The relevance of consumer behavior to a variety of practical applications, including marketing management, social marketing, governmental decision making, demarketing, and consumer education was discussed.

With this introduction providing perspective, the next chapter lays additional groundwork for future chapters. It deals with factors influencing how we can best study consumer behavior.

DISCUSSION TOPICS

1. A marketer in the cosmetics industry once remarked: "In the factory, we make cosmetics, in the drugstore we sell hope." How does this relate to the marketing concept and the need for marketers to understand consumer behavior?

2. Review the activities undertaken by marketing-oriented firms and show the relevance of consumer behavior to each activity.

3. What action would you recommend to government officials interested in changing federal beef-grading methods so that they are more useful to consumers?

4. Every consumer is unique, and any study that concentrates on the "average" consumer is meaningless. Comment.

5. Describe at least two aspects of consumer behavior that are best understood from the decision-process viewpoint.

6. In what ways are the study of consumer behavior useful to consumer-advocate groups concerned with designing laws to assist and protect consumers?

7. Choose an actual nonprofit organization and suggest areas where knowledge of its "consumers" might improve the services it provides.

NOTES

1. Bernard Wysocki, Jr., "Disastrous Debuts: Despite High Hopes Many New Products Flop in the Market," *The Wall Street Journal,* March 23, 1976, pp. 1, 25.

2. Roy J. Harris, Jr., "To Drive Angelenos Wild, Try Pressing Them Not to Drive," *The Wall Street Journal,* May 5, 1976, p. 1.

3. Arne H. Sheets, "The Lafayette LR-100," unpublished paper, University of Rhode Island, 1974, 5 pp. Adapted with permission.

4. Len Fredrick, *Fast Food Gets an "A" in School Lunch,* Cahners Books International, Boston, 1977; "The Golden Key," *Cooking for Profit,* December 1976, pp. 29–31; and David Dearing, "Fast Food Lunches Big Hit in Schools," *Las Vegas Valley Times,* November 1975.

5. John A. Howard and Jagdish N. Sheth, *The Theory of Buyer Behavior,* Wiley, New York, 1969.

6. Jagdish N. Sheth, "A Model of Industrial Buyer Behavior," *Journal of Marketing,* **37**:50–56, October 1973.

7. W. T. Tucker, *Foundations for a Theory of Consumer Behavior,* Holt, New York, 1967, pp. 1–2.

8. Philip Kotler, *Marketing Management: Analysis, Planning, and Control,* 3d ed., Prentice-Hall, Englewood Cliffs, N.J., 1976, p. 5.

9. Martin L. Bell and C. William Emery, "The Faltering Marketing Concept," *Journal of Marketing,* **35**:37–42, October 1971; and Lawrence P. Feldman, "Societal Adaptation: A New Challenge for Marketing," *Journal of Marketing,* **35**:54–60, July 1971.

10. See James T. Rothe and Lissa Benson, "Intelligent Consumption: An Attractive Alternative to the Marketing Concept," *MSU Business Topics,* **22**:29–34, Winter 1974; George Fisk, "Criteria for a Theory of Responsible Consumption," *Journal of Marketing,* **37**:24–31, April 1973; and Kotler, *Marketing Management,* pp. 16–18.

11. "How Colgate's Brand Manager Applied Psychos to Market and Media for Irish Spring," *Media Decisions,* December 1976, pp. 70–71, 104–106.

12. Richard Martin, "Let's Face It: There is a Lot of Mystery about a Good Shave," *The Wall Street Journal,* April 23, 1976, p. 1.

13. Peter Vanderwicken, "P & G's Secret Ingredient," *Fortune,* July 1974, p. 78.

14. "The Fast-food Stars: Three Strategies for Fast Growth," *Business Week,* July 11, 1977, pp. 56–68.

15. "Revlon after Revson," *Forbes,* September 15, 1975, pp. 26–32.

16. Philip Kotler and Gerald Zaltman, "Social Marketing: An Approach to Planned Social Change," *Journal of Marketing,* **35**:3–12, July 1971; and F. Kelly Shuptrine and Frank A. Osmanski, "Marketing's Changing Role: Expanding or Contracting?" *Journal of Marketing,* **39**:58–66, April 1975.

17. A popular book addressing this topic is Joe McGinniss, *The Selling of the President 1968,* Trident Press, New York, 1969.

18. "No More Mister Nice Bear," *Time,* October 3, 1977, p. 27.

19. "Marketing Observer," *Business Week,* March 29, 1976, p. 59.

20. Leo Bogart, "The Marketing of Public Goods," *Conference Board Record,* November 1975, pp. 20–25.

21. See Arthur Schreiber, Paul Gatons, and Richard Clemmer, *Economics of Urban Problems,* Houghton Mifflin, Boston, 1976, and Rusk Loving, Jr., "Amtrak is About to Miss the Train," *Fortune,* May 1974, pp. 272–275 ff.

22. George S. Day, "Assessing the Effects of Information Disclosure Requirements," *Journal of Marketing,* **40**:42–52, April 1976, and Jacob Jacoby, Donald Speller, and Carol Kohn Berning, "Brand Choice Behavior as a Function of Information Load: Replication and Extension," *Journal of Consumer Research,* **1**:33–42, June 1974.

23. Jagdish N. Sheth and Nicholas J. Mammana, "Recent Failures in Consumer Protection," *California Management Review,* **16**:64–72, Spring 1974.

24. Patrick O'Donnell, "False Economy? New Car Owners' Ire Grows as Mileage Falls Below EPA Estimates," *The Wall Street Journal,* August 31, 1977, pp. 1, 25.

25. John A. Miller, David Topel, and Robert E. Rust, "USDA Beef Grading: A Failure in Consumer Information?" *Journal of Marketing,* **40**:25–31, January 1976; and Robert B. Choate, "The Consumer's Cookie Keeps Crumbling or Why There is a Crisis of Confidence in Our Food Supply," address to the 1971 Conference of the Food and Drug Law Institute, San Diego, Calif., March 29, 1971.

26. Mary Gardiner Jones, "The FTC's Need for Social Science Research," in David M. Gardner (ed.), *Proceedings of the Second Annual Conference of the Association for Consumer Research,* Association for Consumer Research, College Park, Md., 1971, pp, 1–9.

27. Michael T. Brandt and Ivan L. Preston, "The Federal Trade Commission's Use of Evidence to Determine Deception," *Journal of Marketing,* **41**:54–62, January 1977.

28. See, for example, "Flattening the Peaks," *Time,* September 6, 1976, p. 33.

29. Thomas S. Robertson and Scott Ward, "Toward the Development of Consumer Behavior Theory," in Boris W. Becker and Helmut Becker (eds.), *AMA Combined Proceedings,* American Marketing Association, Chicago, 1972, pp. 57–64.

A FOUNDATION FOR STUDYING CONSUMER BEHAVIOR

CHAPTER 2

Because the study of any subject is simplified when examined in an organized fashion, this chapter will lay the foundation for such an approach to the topic of consumer behavior. Our first task is to understand more fully what consumer behavior actually entails. This will lead to a discussion of basic approaches to studying behavior. Attention then will turn to several major models that have been offered to describe consumer behavior. After reviewing these models and their contributions to our study, the chapter ends by offering a framework helpful in integrating the variety of information presented in this text.

STUDYING CONSUMER BEHAVIOR

It is useful to consider consumer behavior as a part of human behavior because we can then study it by borrowing approaches that have been developed in the behavioral sciences. One such borrowed approach is consistent with viewing consumer behavior as a decision process involving considerable mental activity.[1] It treats the three classes of variables discussed below as essential to understanding behavior.

Classes of Variables

Three classes of variables having a significant role in understanding consumer behavior are stimulus variables, response variables, and intervening variables. The following paragraphs treat each in turn.

Stimulus variables exist in the individual's external environment (such as products, other people, and advertisements) and are also produced internally. For example, our stomachs produce certain stimuli when we desire food. The role of stimulus variables is to serve as inputs to consumers' behavior.

Response variables are observable activities of individuals that are initiated by stimulus variables. These include gesturing, arguing with a salesclerk, and changing the pitch of our voices slightly when we are not being truthful. In all such cases, the response is said to be *overt,* since it is observable or capable of being measured by some special instrument.

The third group of variables is termed *intervening variables* because they literally intervene between stimuli and overt responses. This suggests that stimuli do not directly affect responses but that their effects are modified by the influence of intervening variables. These variables are internal to the individual and include our motives, attitudes toward things or events, and how we perceive the world around us. Figure 2-1 graphically depicts the central role of intervening variables and how they can influence the effect of stimuli.

Intervening variables play a very important role in our study of consumer behavior. Because they exist, we cannot expect a given stimulus to produce the same response among all consumers. Even for the same individual, intervening variables can change over time and have different influences. Consider, for example, how a consumer's response might change toward some "old junk" found in a trash-and-treasure shop upon learning that it is actually an antique of great value.

The Process of Inference

It is essential for us to realize that intervening variables cannot be observed. For example, no one has ever seen, or will ever see, a consumer's attitude. Then how do we know that such aspects of consumer behavior exist, and how do we study them? Our answer involves the process of inference and can best be illustrated by the *black-box* concept first originated in electrical engineering.[2] Basically, as depicted in Figure 2-2, we imagine a black box hiding some variable or process from our observation. We can see the stimulus inputs to the box and outputs from it (observable responses), but we cannot see the intervening variables which connect these inputs and outputs.

Careful observation of inputs and associated responses enables a judgment to be made regarding the contents of the box. This process is referred to as *inference.* For example, in high school chemistry we inferred the existence and nature of invisible oxygen by employing the black-box concept and observing its effect on combustion and life. As another illustration, assume that we show a friend a magazine advertisement using a scantily clad model to attract readers' attention. Upon seeing it our friend frowns and says, "Disgusting." We might infer that this person has a negative attitude toward sexual exploitation in advertising.

These situations demonstrate that the names of intervening variables are actually invented (constructed) by the observer. For this reason they are often referred to as *hypothetical constructs.* We should not let this naming process bother us, however, since the nature of what we are studying is more important than its name.

FIGURE 2-1
A diagram of the relationship between stimulus, intervening, and response variables.

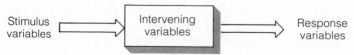

As the above discussion suggests, studying consumer behavior is not necessarily an easy undertaking. A number of factors too lengthy to review here contribute to this difficulty. However, it is useful to treat briefly several of the more important constraints.

Difficulty of Inference Process

Unfortunately, even experts frequently disagree about the exact nature of intervening variables. This occurs because the variables are unobservable, because they may have different aspects, and because they can change over time. Thus, if we observe the effect of a variable at two different points in time, and the variable is changing over time, we could easily reach two different inferences regarding its characteristics. The same would hold true if we happened to observe two different aspects of the same variable.

An important implication of this inference problem is that we must be prepared to face some uncertainty regarding the nature of variables that affect consumer behavior. We will even confront various definitions and contradictory conclusions about the nature of a given variable. Since such ambiguity is to be expected when dealing with complex unobservable behavior, it should be tolerated as we search for ways to minimize it.

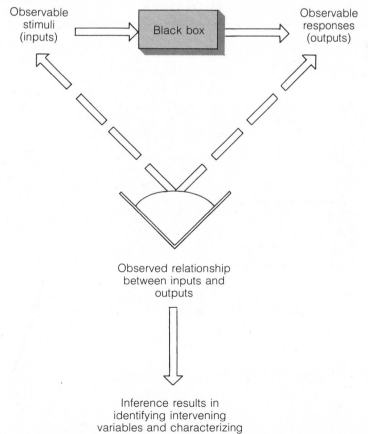

FIGURE 2-2
A diagram of black-box approach to inferring intervening variables.

Behavior Is Subjective

The experiences of individuals influence how they react to the world. Because the experiences of people differ, any given situation will probably be interpreted at least somewhat differently by each individual. Therefore, we must realize that consumers act on their own perceptions of the world, which are often considerably different from our own.

Unfortunately, there often is a strong tendency to overlook this subjective basis of behavior. Consequently, many marketing strategies are based on what managers *assume* are consumer preferences rather than on actual knowledge of these preferences. Researchers and consumer-protection advocates have also been misled by such faulty assumptions. We must therefore be constantly on guard against falling into a similar trap in our studies.

Many Input Variables

The variety of input variables that can potentially influence consumer behavior is astounding. Figure 2-3, which is based on the work of Kurt Lewin, summarizes the major categories of these variables, consisting of internal and external, past, present, and future dimensions.[3]

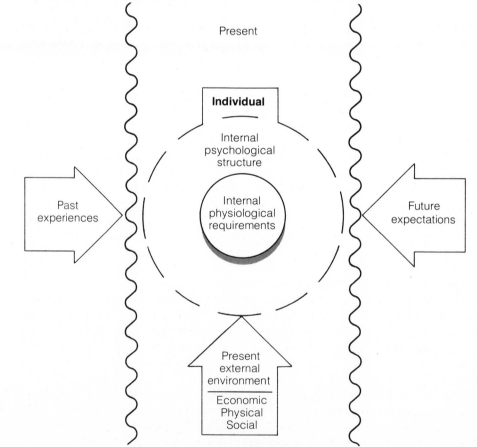

FIGURE 2-3
Summary of variable categories influencing the individual.

The individual is shown to exist within the present time frame as represented by the circular portion of the figure. The inner solid circle contains *physiological* variables which are *internal* to the individual and are only minimally influenced by his or her environment. Many basic needs and drives including nutrition, water, and sleep requirements exist here.

In addition to their internal physiological needs, individuals are also profoundly influenced by their internal *psychological structure.* This includes processes such as attitude formation, motives, perception, and learning, as well as the individual's subjective knowledge, values, and beliefs. For this reason, the psychological structure is often said to contain individual determinants of behavior.

As can be seen in the figure, the *external environment* is capable of influencing the individual's psychological condition and therefore his or her behavior. This external environment actually has three different aspects: present, past, and future influences on the individual. Particularly important aspects of the *present* environment are physical, economic, and social factors. Physical variables include distance to stores, weather, and available transportation. Economic variables include the individual's wealth, the cost of various products, and the economic climate of the country. Among others, social variables comprise the individual's social class and social group influences.

Aspects of the *past* environment are also influential. As we know, learning from experience can be useful in understanding and reacting to present situations. However, we also learn from some experiences so well that we often are not aware of their influence on our behavior.

Finally, expectations regarding the *future* can affect consumers' present behavior. To illustrate, expectations regarding future income, health, and job security can influence consumers' willingness to purchase capital goods (automobiles and washing machines, for example).[4]

The above paragraphs merely sample the types of specific variables relevant to studying consumer behavior. Many of these variables can go undetected because their influence is so subtle, and this can result in simple but incorrect explanations for complex behavior. Of course, the casual observer of consumers is in more danger of doing this than one who studies it in an organized fashion. We therefore must be constantly vigilant for additional variables influencing the behavior of consumers.

Variables Interact with Each Other
Not only do numerous variables affect consumers but they also frequently interact to magnify, cancel, or redirect each other's influence. For example, it seems that some advertisements may fail to persuade consumers to purchase because the announcer is not perceived as a believable source for the information.[5] In such cases, unfavorable perception of the announcer cancels out the positive effects of the message.

In addition, situations confronted by consumers can interact with other variables to modify their influence.[6] One study found that buyers of tableware were influenced by different sources of information depending on whether the tableware was being purchased as a gift or for personal use.[7] Such findings demonstrate the importance of being alert to the interactive effect of variables and their influence on the behavior of consumers.

While the four factors reviewed above in no way exhaust the list of constraints on studying consumer behavior, they do provide sufficient perspective for the reader. We now direct attention to models developed to facilitate our study.

MODELING BEHAVIOR

As just mentioned, studying consumer behavior can be quite complex, especially because of the many variables involved and their tendency to interact. Models of consumer behavior have been developed in an effort to overcome these difficulties.

Definition of a Model

A *model* can be defined as a simplified representation of reality. It simplifies by incorporating only those aspects of reality that are of interest to the model builder. Other aspects that are not of interest and only add to the complexity of the situation can be ignored. Thus an architect's model of a building may not show furniture arrangements if that is not important to the building's design. Similarly, in modeling consumers we should feel free to exclude any aspects that are not relevant to their behavior. Since we have defined consumer behavior as a decision process, models that focus on this process will be of most interest to us.

Types of Models

Any given property or process can be modeled in a variety of ways. For example, we could model something by verbally describing it, by representing it with mathematical symbols, or by characterizing it with some physical process such as electrical current. The most common consumer-behavior models are verbal.

Consumer-behavior models can also be classified in terms of scope. Some are designed to represent a very specific aspect of behavior, such as consumers' repetitive purchasing of the same brand over a period of time. Others are much more comprehensive because they attempt to accommodate the great variety of consumer behavior. These comprehensive models are necessarily less detailed in nature so that they may adequately represent diverse situations.

Uses of Models

Models are devised for a variety of uses, but the two purposes for developing most consumer models are (1) to assist in developing a theory that guides research on consumer behavior and (2) to facilitate learning what is presently known about consumer behavior. In both cases the model serves to structure systematic and logical thinking about consumers.[8] This entails (1) identifying the relevant variables, (2) indicating their characteristics, and (3) specifying their interrelationships, that is, how they influence each other.

DEVELOPING THEORY A *theory* is an interrelated set of concepts, definitions, and propositions that presents a systematic view of some phenomenon.[9] It presents a logical viewpoint that is useful in understanding some process or activity. More specifically, a theory has four major functions: description, prediction, explanation, and control. The *description* function involves characterizing the nature of something such as the steps consumers go through while deciding on a purchase. In its *predictive* role a theory is used to foretell future events, as when learning theory is used to predict which of two brand names will be the easier for consumers to remember. Theory can be used for *explanation* in order to learn the underlying *causes* of some event or activity. This would occur when we want to understand *why* a consumer regularly purchases the same brand of soup. Is it because of habit or loyalty to the brand? Although it is possible to predict events without understanding their causes, knowing why something happens greatly enhances our ability to predict its occurrence. *Control* is the ability to influence or regulate future events. This has been extremely difficult in the behavioral sciences because of the many variables involved and our lack of knowledge about them. Therefore, although marketers and others can sometimes influence consumers, we will find ample evidence that strict control of their behavior is far from a reality.

Models can assist theory development in any situation by clearly delineating the relevant variables and their influence on each other. In this way models can present a unified view of what is known about consumer behavior and help identify what remains to be explored. This allows researchers to advance knowledge by selecting the most important aspects of consumer behavior for analysis and testing.

FACILITATING LEARNING Our primary motivation for using models here is to serve as a learning aid. In this role, models provide a structure helpful for organizing knowledge about consumer behavior into a logical pattern that is easier to comprehend. They also remind us of the interrelationships between relevant variables. Therefore, as we concentrate on one particular variable, reference to the model will remind us to consider how it interacts with other variables to influence behavior.

MODELS OF CONSUMER BEHAVIOR

Comprehensive verbal models will be of most interest to us in our study of consumer behavior. A variety of such models exist, each taking a somewhat different view of consumer behavior. Those chosen for presentation here are quite well known and represent a broad perspective. The first two represent traditional approaches to the study of consumers while the remaining two portray a more contemporary view.

Traditional Models of Consumers

The earliest comprehensive consumer models were actually devised by economists seeking to understand the influence of consumers on economic systems. Economics involves the study of how scarce resources are allocated among unlimited wants and needs.[10] Its two major disciplines—macroeconomics and microeconomics—have each developed alternative views of consumers. Partially because they have undergone some modernization, these models still influence contemporary views of consumers.

MACROECONOMIC VIEWPOINTS Macroeconomics focuses on aggregate flows in the economy—the monetary value of goods and resources, where they are directed, and how they change over time.[11] From such a focus, the macroeconomist draws conclusions about the behavior of consumers who influence these flows. Although the discipline has not generated a fully unified model of consumers, it has offered a number of insights into their behavior.

One interest centers on how consumers divide their income between consumption and savings. This deals with two economic facts of life: higher-income families spend a smaller proportion of their disposable income than lower-income families, but as economic progress raises all income levels over time these proportions do not change. The *relative-income hypothesis* explains this apparent contradiction by arguing that peoples' consumption standards are mainly influenced by their peers and social groups and not absolute income levels.[12] Therefore, the proportion of a family's income devoted to consumption is expected to change only when an income change places it in a different social setting. This will not happen when all income levels are rising at the same time.

Another macroeconomic proposition, the *permanent-income hypothesis,* explains why consumers are slow to change their consumption patterns even when their incomes do suddenly change. It states that this occurs because consumers do not use actual income for any period to determine their consumption expenditures but instead are influenced by their estimate of some average, long-term amount that can be consumed without reducing their accumulated wealth.[13] Sudden increases or decreases in income are viewed as transitory, not permanent, income and therefore are expected to have little influence on consumption activity.

A variety of other variables have been suggested by macroeconomists as influencing consumption patterns. Included are consumers' previous income experiences, accumulated liquid assets, and variations in taxes or credits. Although useful, these suggestions represent rather traditional approaches to studying consumers, stressing economic variables while tending to ignore the influence of psychological factors. However, George Katona and the University of Michigan's Survey Research Center have pioneered studies emphasizing the importance of psychological variables. This research has resulted in two major conclusions:

1. Consumers' sentiment, future expectations, and aspirations have a profound influence on their consumption expenditures.

2. As a result of these factors, consumers strongly influence economic cycles to a greater degree than can be explained by changes in their income alone.[14]

Because of Katona and others, increased emphasis has been given to consumers' motives, expectations, and other psychological factors in explaining aggregate consumption patterns.[15] Although there still is some uncertainty about the usefulness of such variables in predicting aggregate consumer behavior, few would argue with the need to explore the area further in order to better understand consumers.[16]

The above paragraphs provide only a sampling of macroeconomic consumer studies. Since these efforts focus on aggregate economic activity, they can be useful in predicting total consumption patterns and the broad categories of goods that will be consumed. However, since this aggregate viewpoint can also overlook important details of consumers' behavior, there remains a need to understand how consumers choose between competing *brands.* Thus microaspects of behavior also need to be explored.

MICROECONOMIC MODEL The classical microeconomic approach, developed early in the nineteenth century, focused on the behavior of individual consumers. It involved making a series of assumptions about characteristics and goals of the "average" consumer and then developing a theory useful in explaining the workings of an economy made up of many such people. Focus was placed on the *act of purchase* which, of course, is only a portion of what we have defined as consumer behavior. Thus, microeconomists concentrated on explaining *what* consumers would purchase and in *what quantities* these purchases would be made. The tastes and preferences leading to these purchases were assumed to be given—that is, already known. Therefore, microeconomists chose to ignore *why* consumers develop a ranking of certain needs and preferences and *how* such an ordering develops.

The resulting theory was based on a number of assumptions about consumers. Primary among these were the following:

1. Consumers' wants and needs are, in total, unlimited and therefore cannot be fully satisfied.

2. Given a limited budget, consumers' goals are to allocate available purchasing dollars in a way that *maximizes* satisfaction of their wants and needs.

3. Consumers independently develop their own preferences without the influence of others, and these preferences are consistent over time.

4. Consumers have perfect knowledge of the utility of an item; that is, they know exactly how much want satisfaction the product can give them.

5. As additional units of a given product or service are acquired, the *marginal* (additional) satisfaction provided by the *next* unit will be less than the marginal satisfaction provided by previously purchased units. This is referred to as the *law of diminishing marginal utility.*

6. Consumers use the price of a good as the sole measure of the sacrifice involved in obtaining it. Price plays no other role in the purchase decision.

7. Consumers are *perfectly rational* in that, given their subjective preferences, they will always act in a deliberate manner to maximize their satisfaction.

Given these assumptions, economists argued that perfectly rational consumers would always purchase the good that provides them with the highest ratio of additional benefit to cost. For any given good this benefit/cost ratio can be expressed as a ratio of marginal utility to price (MU/P). Therefore, it can be shown that the consumer would seek to achieve a situation where the following expression holds for any number (n) of goods:

$$MU_1/P_1 = MU_2/P_2 = MU_3/P_3 = \ldots = MU_n/P_n$$

If any one product's ratio is greater than the others, the consumer can achieve greater satisfaction per dollar from it and will immediately purchase more of it. Purchasing will continue until its declining marginal utility reduces its MU/P ratio to a position equal to all other ratios. Additional purchasing of that good will then stop.

Although the microeconomic model has had an important influence on our understanding of consumers, it provides a severely limited explanation of consumer behavior, with a major deficiency being its highly unrealistic assumptions. For example, consumers frequently strive for acceptable and not maximum levels of satisfaction.[17] In addition, consumers lack perfect knowledge regarding products, and often influence each other's preferences.[18] Also, they appear to use many variables in addition to price to assess a product's cost and may frequently use price as a measure of product quality as well as cost.[19] Finally, consumers simply do not appear to be perfectly rational in all their purchase decisions. These unrealistic assumptions may not have hindered the usefulness of this model in explaining the behavior of an entire economic system, but they certainly are not useful in understanding how actual consumers behave in specific purchase situations of concern to marketers and others.

An additional shortcoming of the microeconomic scheme occurs as a result of its focus on the specific act of purchase. We have argued that much consumer behavior occurs before and after this act. Considerable decision making and search for information can precede it, and purchase evaluation as well as additional purchases can follow it. Since the model does not address these activities, we cannot accept it as a comprehensive representation of consumer behavior.

Even with its limitations, the microeconomic model has been useful. It provides a perspective from which to better appreciate contemporary models of consumer behavior. In addition, we should now be more sensitive to the critical way in which the usefulness of a consumer model depends on its assumptions, and we should be ready to evaluate other models in terms of their dependence on stated or implied assumptions. Finally, because economists have modernized certain aspects of the microeconomic model, it still influences contemporary thinking regarding consumer behavior.

Contemporary Consumer Models

As the study of consumer behavior evolved into a distinct discipline, newer approaches were offered to describe and explain what influenced consumers' purchase activity. These contemporary views are quite different from previous models because of their concentration on the *decision process* that consumers engage in for purchasing. Therefore, contrary to the economic models, emphasis is placed on the mental activity that occurs before and after the purchase.

A second distinguishing characteristic of contemporary models is their extensive borrowing from material developed in the behavioral sciences. In fact, most of the variables discussed were originally identified in the fields of psychology and sociology.[20] Explanations of how many of these variables influence consumer behavior have also been adapted from the behavioral sciences.

Another unique aspect of recent modeling efforts is their format, which generally portrays consumers' decision processes in flowchart fashion as well as verbally. This provides a concrete structure which graphically portrays the sequence of activities involved in purchase decisions.

A large number of contemporary consumer models have been developed, varying considerably in terms of their sophistication, precision, and scope. However, because space limits what can be presented here, only two will be discussed. These two models represent the most widely quoted comprehensive views of consumer behavior.

ENGEL-KOLLAT-BLACKWELL MODEL The Engel-Kollat-Blackwell model, graphically presented in Figure 2-4, is the latest refinement of one of the most respected views of consumer behavior of the last decade.[21] The scheme depicts consumer behavior as a decision process of five activities which occur over time: (1) problem recognition, (2) information search, (3) alternative evaluation, (4) choice, and (5) outcomes. Although these steps serve as its basic core, the model has been termed *multimediational,* since it focuses considerable attention on the numerous variables which mediate or influence this decision process. As shown in the model, the variables are grouped into five general categories: (1) information input, (2) information processing, (3) product-brand evaluations, (4) general motivating influences, and (5) internalized environmental influences. Arrows in the model depict the major directions of influence that specific variables exert. The following discussion of the decision process characterizes the role and nature of these variables.

Problem recognition occurs when the consumer becomes aware of a difference between his or her actual state of affairs and his or her concept of the ideal situation. As the model indicates, this can occur through internal activation of a motive (e.g., hunger) or through confronting external stimuli which have influenced the consumer's information and experience. In either case, however, action only occurs when the consumer perceives a sufficiently large discrepancy between the actual and ideal states.

Given that the consumer is aroused to action, the next step is to undertake an *information search.* The first stage of this activity involves a quick and largely unconscious review of stored information and experiences regarding the problem. This information is in the form of beliefs and attitudes which have influenced the consumer's preferences toward brands. Often such a review leads to recognizing a strong brand preference, and routine purchase action occurs. However, if an internal search does not provide sufficient information about products, or how to evaluate them, the consumer will engage in an external information search and more extensive problem-solving behavior. This results in exposure to a variety of informational inputs called *stimuli,* which can arise from personal sources (friends and salespeople) as well as from published or mass-media sources. In either case, these sources can be viewed as being dominated by firms interested in selling goods (e.g., advertisements) or as being general in nature and not controlled by the marketer (e.g., government-regulated information tags on products).

Any informational inputs are subjected to *information-processing* activities which the consumer uses to derive meaning from external stimuli. The first stage involves *exposure* to stimuli which must next capture his or her

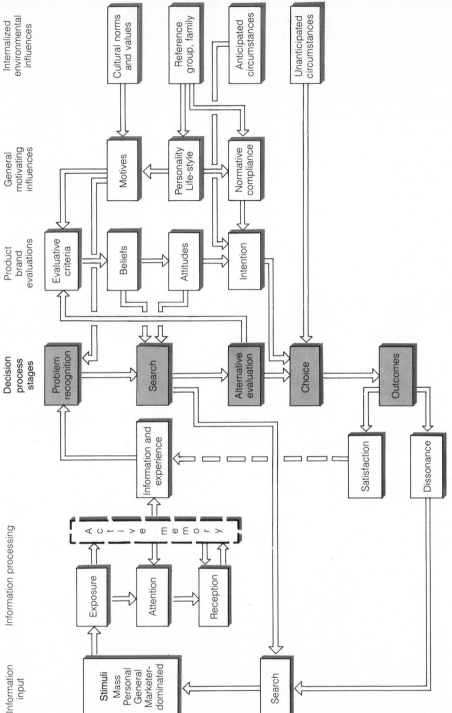

FIGURE 2-4
The Engel-Kollat-Blackwell model. (Source: James F. Engel, Roger D. Blackwell, and David T. Kollat, *Consumer Behavior*, 3d ed., copyright © 1978 by The Dryden Press, Hinsdale, Ill., A Division of Holt, Rinehart and Winston, p. 32. Reprinted by permission of Holt, Rinehart and Winston.)

conscious attention. The *attention* stage is highly selective, since it ignores most stimuli and only admits those which the individual believes are important. The *reception* stage then involves deriving meaning from stimuli and storing this information in *memory.* This can frequently lead to a distortion of stimuli and a change in their meaning to the consumer. Also, the process of storing information in memory can distort it or the meaning of closely related information. It should be clear from this description that the information processing stage is highly selective in nature and can significantly alter the meaning consumers derive from stimuli in their external environment.

As the model shows, a critical role of information is its use in evaluating alternatives through influencing evaluative criteria and beliefs. *Evaluative criteria* are the standards by which products are judged. They are derived from the consumer's underlying goals or motives and from information derived from the environment. *Beliefs* represent the consumer's estimation of the degree to which alternative brands possess the evaluative characteristics that the consumer has identified.

Given the consumer's beliefs regarding characteristics of a brand, his or her *attitude* represents a tendency to respond negatively or positively toward the brand. The attitude, then, is a negative or positive evaluation of the consequences of using a brand which has certain believed characteristics.

The consumer's attitudes will influence his or her *purchase intentions,* which are the subjective estimates of the chances that a particular purchase will be made. As the model shows, other influences on purchase intentions include normative compliance and anticipated circumstances. *Normative compliance* is the extent to which the consumer is influenced by others (friends and relatives). It is a function of their attempts to influence as well as the individual's susceptibility to such influence. *Anticipated circumstances* include a host of factors the consumer expects, the most important of which is usually the expected availability of funds for purchase.

The model shows that although choice usually follows intentions, *unanticipated circumstances,* such as a drop in income, can temporarily or permanently serve as a barrier to purchase. If no barrier is encountered, however, a purchase process is engaged in. This involves a series of selections including the type of retail outlet as well as the specific product or service.

The outcome of the decision process follows the consumer's choices. If the outcome is perceived as positive, the result is purchase *satisfaction.* An alternative outcome is *dissonance,* which is post-decision doubt about the relative satisfaction that a purchase provides when compared to unchosen alternatives. This can generate a heightened desire for information that supports the choice. As the model demonstrates, such information will be in the form of new inputs which will be processed as previously described.

Model Evaluation Advantages of the Engel-Kollat-Blackwell model include its consideration of the many variables influencing consumers and its emphasis on the conscious decision-making process. Also, the flow of the model is easy to follow and is quite flexible. For example, the authors recognize that in numerous purchase decisions many of the detailed steps are passed through very quickly or are bypassed, as in the case of habitual purchase behavior. Factors contributing to the model's clarity and flexibility, however, also generate some of its limitations. The primary drawback appears to be a vagueness regarding the role of some variables. For example, the influence of environmental variables is noted, but their role in affecting behavior is not well specified. The role of motives in influencing behavior is also quite vague. In addition, the model has been criticized as being somewhat mechanistic in its treatment of the decision process.

HOWARD-SHETH MODEL The Howard-Sheth model depicted in Figure 2-5 serves as an integrating framework for perhaps the most sophisticated comprehensive theory of consumer behavior.[22] It should be noted that the authors have used the term "buyer" in their theory to refer to industrial purchasers as well as ultimate consumers. Although we will adopt their terminology here, our interest will remain with ultimate consumers.

The model borrows from learning-theory concepts to explain brand choice behavior over time through four major components: (1) input variables, (2) output variables, (3) hypothetical constructs, and (4) exogenous variables.

Input Variables Input variables are depicted in the left portion of the model as stimuli in the environment. *Significative* stimuli are actual elements of brands that the buyer confronts, while *symbolic* stimuli are generated by producers representing their products in symbolic form, such as in advertisements. *Social* stimuli are generated by the social environment including family and groups.

Output Variables The five output variables in the right-hand portion of the model are the buyer's observable responses to stimulus inputs. They are arranged in order from attention to actual purchase and are defined as follows:

Attention—the magnitude of the buyer's information intake

Comprehension—the buyer's store of information about a brand

Attitude—the buyer's evaluation of a particular brand's potential to satisfy his or her motives

Intention—the buyer's forecast of which brand he or she will buy

Purchase behavior—the actual purchase act, which reflects the buyer's predisposition to buy as modified by any inhibitors

Hypothetical Constructs A number of intervening variables are proposed, represented by hypothetical constructs in the large central "black box." They are categorized into two major groups: (1) perceptual constructs dealing with information processing and (2) learning constructs dealing with the buyer's formation of concepts.

The three *perceptual constructs* of the model can be described as follows:

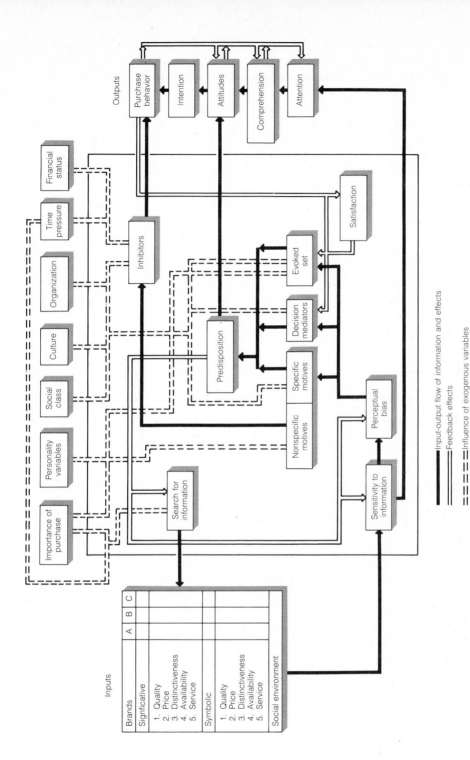

FIGURE 2-5
The Howard-Sheth
model. (*Source:*
John A. Howard
and Jagdish N.
Sheth, "A Theory of
Buyer Behavior" in
Harold H. Kassar-
jian and Thomas S.
Robertson (eds.),
*Perspectives in
Consumer Behav-
ior*, rev. ed., copy-
right © 1973, 1968
by Scott, Fores-
man, Glenview, Ill.,
1973, p. 523. Re-
printed by permis-
sion.)

Sensitivity to information—the degree to which the buyer regulates the stimulus information flow

Perceptual bias—distorting or altering information

Search for information—active seeking of information about brands or their characteristics

The buyer's six *learning constructs* are defined as:

Motive—general or specific goals impelling action

Brand potential of the evoked set—the buyer's perception of the ability of brands in his or her *evoked set* (those that are actively considered) to satisfy his or her goals

Decision mediators—the buyer's mental rules for matching and ranking purchase alternatives according to his or her motives

Predisposition—a preference toward brands in the evoked set expressed as an attitude toward them

Inhibitors—environmental forces such as price and time pressure which restrain purchase of a preferred brand

Satisfaction—the degree to which consequences of a purchase measure up to the buyer's expectations for it

Exogenous Variables At the top of the black box the model lists a number of external variables that can significantly influence buyer decisions. These variables are not as well defined as other aspects of the model because they are external to the buyer.

Model Dynamics Although there are various aspects of the model that are beyond the scope of this chapter, a brief review of its operation is appropriate. The process starts when the buyer confronts an input stimulus and it achieves attention. The stimulus is subjected to perceptual bias as a result of the influence of the buyer's predispositions as affected by his or her motives, decision mediators, and evoked set. The modified information will also influence these variables which, in turn, will influence his or her predisposition to purchase.

The actual purchase is influenced by the buyer's intentions and inhibitors which are confronted. A purchase leads the buyer to evaluate his or her satisfaction with it, and satisfaction increases the buyer's predisposition toward the brand. As the buyer acquires more information about brands, he or she engages in less external search for information and exhibits more routine purchase behavior.

Model Evaluation The Howard-Sheth model represents a significant contribution to understanding consumer behavior. It identifies many of the variables influencing consumers and details how they interact with each other. Also, the model, and the earlier work on which it is based, recognized explicitly for the first time different types of consumer problem solving and information-search behaviors.[23]

Of course, the model does have certain limitations. First, it does not make sharp distinctions between exogenous and other variables. Second, some variables are not well defined and have been difficult to measure. However, the third and perhaps greatest limitation of the model for our purpose is its complexity. The large number of interacting variables and their involved definitions are perhaps too complex for maximum usefulness to an introductory survey of consumer behavior.

A SIMPLIFIED FRAMEWORK

A number of insights regarding the behavior of consumers have been offered by the contemporary models just reviewed. These include the following:

1. Consumer behavior can best be understood as an ongoing decision process where the act of purchase represents only one stage.

2. This decision process can be extensive and time-consuming or very automatic and short in duration.

3. A large number of variables, both internal and external to the consumer, can influence the decision process.

4. Many of these variables also interact with each other to form new or modified influences.

5. Because many of the variables influencing consumers are unobservable, their existence must be inferred.

6. Since the study of consumer behavior is still in its infancy, it is to be expected that few concrete laws and considerable diversity of opinion would exist regarding why consumers behave as they do.

A further strength of contemporary decision-process models is the intricate view they allow of consumers. For those embarking on an initial study of consumer behavior, however, these models may represent overkill. That is, their intricate perspective may be too complex for such an early stage of study. A strategy for handling this problem is to concentrate on the major influences and show, at a very general level, how these variables might interact to affect consumers.

We have adopted such a simplified approach to guide our discussion, and a diagram of the result is presented in Figure 2-6. The first important point regarding this framework is that *it is not offered as a model of consumer behavior.* It is merely an organized schematic of the variables or processes that have been identified as the most important general influencers of consumer behavior. It also represents an outline for a major portion of this text. As the reader's study progresses, this framework may be outgrown because of its simplicity. When this occurs, the detail provided by one of the more comprehensive decision-process models just reviewed could serve as a useful framework for further analysis.

Reference to Figure 2-6 reveals that it is made up of three major sections: (1) external variables influencing behavior, (2) individual determinants of behavior, and (3) the consumer's decision process.

The external environment depicted in the outer circle is made up of five specific influences and one catch-all grouping for all other factors. The five specific influences are culture, subcultures, social class, social groups, the family, and personal influences. The opened partitions denote the influence of these variables on individual determinants and on each other. In addition, the large arrow depicts the more direct influence they have on consumers' decisions through the perceptual processing of information. These environmental variables are treated in Part Three of the text.

Major individual determinants of consumer behavior are portrayed in the inner circle of the figure. These variables determine how the consumer proceeds through the decision process. Relevant determinants are the consumer's perception, motives, learning, personality/self-concept, and attitudes. The opened circle between the decision process and these variables denotes the great influence they have on the decision process. The opened partitions between these determinants themselves represent their influence on each other. Part Four of the text focuses on these individual determinants.

The consumer's decision process is viewed as four major activities, ranging from problem recognition through postpurchase behavior, plus a

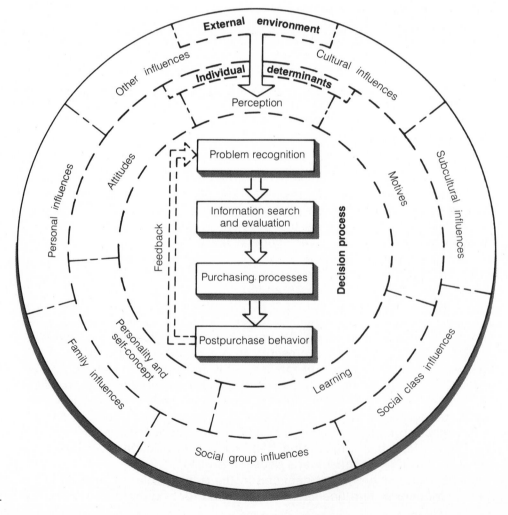

FIGURE 2-6
A simplified framework for studying consumer behavior.

feedback loop.[24] The feedback loop shows the influence of postpurchase evaluation on future purchases. Part Five of the text examines the decision process in detail.

SUMMARY

The purpose of this chapter was to establish a foundation for an organized study of consumer behavior. First, observable stimulus and response variables were discussed. Unobservable intervening variables were then introduced using the black-box approach to inference.

After addressing some of the major problems in studying consumers, the goals and methods of modeling their behavior were discussed. The organizing structure provided by these models was seen as a major benefit. Following this, the traditional macroeconomic and microeconomic views of consumer behavior were critically reviewed.

Two contemporary models developed by Engel, Kollat, and Blackwell and Howard and Sheth were then offered as representatives of contemporary, behavioral science-oriented models. An overview of these schemes provided many insights into consumer behavior, including the number of variables involved and their interactive effects. The flow of consumers' decision making over a period of time was also graphically portrayed.

The level of complexity provided by these contemporary views may result in an overload of information for the beginning student. For this reason a highly simplified schematic of the major variables influencing consumers was offered as a structure for this book.

DISCUSSION TOPICS

1. What is a model? How can our study of consumer behavior benefit from using models?

2. Characterize the process of inference and indicate its importance to understanding consumer behavior.

3. A hard-nosed marketing manager was heard to remark: "All of this talk about consumers' decision process still just boils down to the same old fact—it's what the consumer buys, and how much of it, that's really important to the practicing marketer." What is your response?

4. Discuss the microeconomic model, indicating its contributions and limitations for the marketer in understanding consumer behavior.

5. What are the major contributions of the contemporary models of consumer behavior?

6. How might producers of stereo equipment use the Engel-Kollat-Blackwell model to understand better the consumers of their products? How might producers of chewing gum do the same?

7. Relate one of your experiences where postpurchase outcomes significantly influenced your future purchase behavior.

NOTES

1. For a review of other approaches see Robert L. Karen, *An Introduction to Behavior Theory and Its Applications,* Harper & Row, New York, 1974, pp. 8–18.

2. Van Court Hare, Jr., *Systems Analysis: A Diagnostic Approach,* Harcourt, Brace & World, New York, 1967, p. 30.

3. Suggested by Kurt Lewin as presented in Calvin S. Hall and Gardner Lindzey, *Theories of Personality,* Wiley, New York, 1957, pp. 206–223.

4. George Katona, *The Powerful Consumer,* McGraw-Hill, New York, 1960.

5. See E. Aronson and B. Golden, "The Effect of Relevant and Irrelevant Aspects of Communicator Credibility on Opinion Change," *Journal of Personality,* **30**:135–146, for some factors affecting credibility.

6. Russell W. Belk, "Situational Variables and Consumer Behavior," *Journal of Consumer Research,* **2**:157–164, December 1975.

7. K. Grønhaug, "Buying Situation and Buyer's Information Behavior," *European Marketing Research Review,* **7**:33–48, September 1972.

8. Rom J. Markin, Jr., *Consumer Behavior: A Cognitive Orientation,* Macmillan, New York, 1974, p. 79.

9. Fred N. Kerlinger, *Foundations of Behavioral Research,* 2d ed., Holt, New York, 1973, p. 9.

10. Michael J. Brennan, *Theory of Economic Statics,* Prentice-Hall, Englewood Cliffs, N.J., 1965, p. 4.

11. Richard H. Leftwich, *The Price System and Resource Allocation,* 3d ed., Holt, New York, 1966, p. 8.

12. J. S. Duesenberry, *Income, Saving, and the Theory of Consumer Behavior,* Harvard, Cambridge, Mass., 1949.

13. Milton Friedman, *A Theory of the Consumption Function,* Princeton, Princeton, N.J., 1957.

14. George Katona, *Psychological Economics,* Elsevier, New York, 1975, p. 11.

15. Lee Smith, "The Economist Who Polls Consumers," *Dunn's Review,* **107**:68–69+, April 1976.

16. See John McNeil, "Federal Programs to Measure Consumer Purchase Expectations, 1946–1973: A Post-Mortem," *Journal of Consumer Research,* **1**:1–10, December 1974, and the following commentaries by F. Gerald Adams and F. Thomas Juster, pp. 11–15.

17. See James G. March and Herbert A. Simon, *Organizations,* Wiley, New York, 1958 for evidence of this in executive behavior.

18. Thomas S. Robertson, *Innovative Behavior and Communication,* Holt, New York, 1971.

19. Kent B. Monroe, "Buyers Subjective Perceptions of Price," *Journal of Marketing Research,* **10**:70–80, February 1973.

20. For a review of several behavioral science modeling contributions see Philip Kotler, "Behavioral Models for Analyzing Buyers," *Journal of Marketing,* **29**:37–45, October 1965, and Charles D. Schewe, "Selected Social Psychological Models for Analyzing Buyers," *Journal of Marketing,* **37**:31–39, July 1973.

21. This review is based on James F. Engel, Roger D. Blackwell, and David T. Kollat, *Consumer Behavior,* 3d ed., The Dryden Press, Hinsdale, Ill., 1978, pp. 21–33.

22. This review is based on John A. Howard and Jagdish N. Sheth, *The Theory of Buyer Behavior,* Wiley, New York, 1969, and John A. Howard and Jagdish N. Sheth, "A Theory of Buyer Behavior" in Harold H. Kassarjian and Thomas S. Robertson (eds.), *Perspectives in Consumer Behavior,* rev. ed., Scott, Foresman, Glenview, Ill., 1973, pp. 519–540.

23. See John A. Howard, *Marketing Management: Analysis and Planning,* rev. ed., Irwin, Homewood, Ill., 1963.

24. These steps are based on a more detailed series of activities proposed in Engel, Kollat, and Blackwell, *Consumer Behavior.*

CASES

CASE 1-1 A&P

In 1971, William J. Kane took over as chairman and chief executive officer of A&P at a time when sales had leveled off and profits were declining. In an attempt to overcome this slide, Kane ordered the conversion of thousands of regular A&P stores to WEO ("Where Economy Originates") supermarkets, which were described as superduper discount stores.

The average WEO store looked about the same as the old A&P and was about the same size (which was rather small by industry standards). The big difference between WEOs and the company's conventional units (aside from the new sign over the store entrance and a few banners inside) was lower prices on 90 percent of the merchandise and a reduction in the variety of products offered (from an average 11,000 products pared down to as few as 8,000 items in a WEO).

Chairman Kane summed up the company's philosophy in this move as follows: "This is a business based strictly on volume, with sales measured in tonnage . . . this is a tonnage recovery program . . . I want to get us back to good, sound, basic fundamentals. This company was built on quality foods sold at low prices."[1]

[1]"A&P's Ploy: Cutting Prices to Turn a Profit," *Business Week*, May 20, 1972, p. 76.

Questions

1. Which model of consumer behavior does A&P appear to be using?

2. Evaluate the relevance of consumer-behavior knowledge to developing a marketing plan for A&P.

3. Trace the development of A&P's operation since 1972, based on library research.

CASE 1-2 ELECTRIC POWER COMPANY

The Electric Power Company is faced with a problem in its service area—too much demand for the electricity it generates. The utility is, therefore, considering whether anything can be done about getting the users to cut back on their electrical consumption.

Executives are hopeful that reductions can be achieved through voluntary cutbacks especially during peak-load periods. Promotion is seen to be a key ingredient in gaining consumers' cooperation in this effort. If a voluntary program fails, the utility will be faced with employing automatic electronic devices on customers' electrical systems to control their electrical usage.

Questions

1. Suggest some strategies by which this utility could demarket electrical consumption through voluntary means.

2. What assumptions about consumer behavior are you making in these strategies?

CASE 1-3   COLLEGIATE UNIVERSITY

Dr. James, vice president of student affairs for a medium-size state university in the Northeast, was concerned over recent enrollment figures. The proportion of accepted in-state students who actually enrolled had decreased rather significantly during the last year. Since population data indicated that the size of graduating high school classes would soon begin a rapid slide, he was afraid the school might be in a position of attracting a declining portion of a declining market.

Dr. James noted these trends at a monthly staff meeting and suggested that it would be useful to study the university's image among in-state residents. This might uncover the reason for the decline and suggest appropriate action. Dr. Labell, dean of students, questioned the wisdom of this approach saying, "We're really not sure how decisions regarding college enrollment are made. Until we have a better understanding of this and what influences it, an image study would be premature."

Questions

1. Evaluate the arguments of Dr. James and Dr. Labell.

2. What guidance can you offer regarding different consumer roles and possible influences on the university enrollment decision process?

CASE 1-4   UNCLE SAM: THE SUPER SALESMAN[1]

When it comes to advertising, Uncle Sam isn't about to take a back seat to any corporate advertiser. In fact, the government's budget promoting various public agencies ranks it in the top ten among the country's largest national advertisers. The federal ad budget for 1975 totalled over $113 million up from $66 million in 1973, and it surpassed those of commercial giants such as Colgate-Palmolive, AT&T, General Mills, Chrysler, and Ford.

During 1975 the bill for selling American's defense forces approximated Procter & Gamble's $76-million outlay for its detergents, soaps, laundry, and household products alone. The U.S. Air Force spent the same amount of money promoting itself as did Head & Shoulders shampoo. The U.S. Army spent the largest amount, $33 million, which was only slightly more than Bristol-Myers used in promoting its Clairol hair-care products. Similarly the U.S. Marines spent somewhat less than the amount used in advertising Preparation H ($8 million).

Much of the growth in government publicity spending has occurred since 1973, when the draft ended and there was a concurrent need to recruit a volunteer armed service. During recession periods the services have generally had no difficulty filling their quota; but as recovery occurs more jobs are available to young people, and so the need for advertising reappears.

Although the government spends most of its budget on the armed forces, this is not its only area of advertising. It is promoting, among other things, railroad passenger travel; writing personal letters (to counteract ads by AT&T encouraging consumers to make long-distance telephone calls); and the free enterprise system (through economic education ads).

[1] Adapted from "Uncle Sam: A Super Salesman" *Providence Sunday Journal,* September 12, 1976, pp. F 14–15.

Questions

1. How can an understanding of consumer behavior be helpful in directing Uncle Sam's promotion plans?

2. Assume you are a U.S. senator and a member of the committee that approves funding requests for such campaigns as those cited above. What questions relating to consumer behavior might be asked to assess these campaigns' effectiveness?

UNDERSTANDING CONSUMERS AND MARKET SEGMENTS

3. **RESEARCHING CONSUMER BEHAVIOR** 4. **MARKET SEGMENTATION: BASIC APPROACHES** 5. **MARKET SEGMENTATION: ADDITIONAL DIMENSIONS** Cases for Part Two

RESEARCHING CONSUMER BEHAVIOR

THE NATURE AND SIGNIFICANCE OF CONSUMER BEHAVIOR   CONSUMER RESEARCH STRATEGIES   Goals of Consumer Research; Type of Data Used; Research Time Frame   METHODS OF GATHERING CONSUMER INFORMATION   Observation; Experiments; Surveys   MEASURING CONSUMERS   Demographic Measures; Cognitive Measures

The following chapters will present a significant amount of evidence about consumers that has been generated by research investigations. Thus, it is useful first to gain an appreciation of the nature of consumer research, its applicability to marketing decision making, and some of the problems and limitations confronting the researcher.

It is impossible to convey the breadth and depth of this subject in a single chapter. Consequently, no attempt is made to train the reader in research methods but merely to give exposure to a sample of important consumer-research concepts.

THE NATURE AND SIGNIFICANCE OF CONSUMER RESEARCH

Consumer research may be defined as the systematic gathering, recording, and analyzing of data about consumers. Such studies are very important to our economy, and particularly to certain companies. For example, Procter & Gamble spends millions of dollars each year on research and questions approximately 250,000 consumers annually.[1] Consumer research is also conducted by government to solve public-policy issues and by university researchers seeking to build better consumer-behavior theories. As mentioned in Chapter 1, the researcher might investigate several roles played by the consumer—user, buyer, initiator, or influencer. Therefore, the unit of analysis must be clearly specified when conducting consumer research.

CONSUMER RESEARCH STRATEGIES

Many strategies are available in the process of researching consumers. Studies may differ according to the goal of the research, the type of data used, and the time frame of the investigation. Each of these approaches is discussed in this section.

Goals of Consumer Research

Two major strategies of consumer research, classified according to their goals, are exploratory and conclusive studies.

EXPLORATORY RESEARCH Exploratory research is used to identify variables influencing consumers and discover how they may tend to react to these factors. This occurs in situations when there is not enough known about consumers to draw conclusions about what variables are influencing their behavior. Two significant methods used in exploratory research are consumer suggestions and focus groups.

Consumer Suggestions In the business world, many influences and problems encountered by consumers are discovered through the spontaneous suggestions of consumers themselves. For example, General Foods receives about 80,000 customer letters a year, some of which offer new product ideas. In addition, many retailers conduct an informal type of research similar to the familiar "suggestion box." Printed cards soliciting consumer feedback are placed for easy access, such as on tables in a restaurant or on sale counters in a retail store. Customers with complaints or compliments are able to express themselves instantly. For example, Wendy's restaurants place cards at each table with the headline "At Wendy's you are the chairman of the board." These cards solicit patrons' comments on the chain's food and service.

Focus Groups Another popular technique for exploratory research is the focus-group interview. Focus groups generally bring together in a casual setting six to eight people with similar backgrounds to apply the principles of group dynamics and free association to a marketing problem. A moderator guides the discussion but allows consumers to interact with each other. The sessions, which last about 2 hours, are usually recorded and frequently videotaped. In addition, the group may be observed by other researchers or client representatives through a one-way mirror.

This type of qualitative research gives the marketer a chance to "experience" a "flesh and blood" consumer. That is, the marketer can better understand the framework in which the product is being used by learning about all of the satisfactions, dissatisfactions, rewards, and frustrations experienced by the consumer when buying and using the product.[2]

The specific cases where focus groups can be helpful are when marketers:

—are unfamiliar with a product category and want to obtain broad ideas about it quickly

—need fresh and revitalized ideas

—need to check an advertisement or product concept to determine if anything about it is confusing, misleading, or negative

—need to learn the consumer's language and motivations

—need a feel for consumers' life-styles and personalities

—need information helpful in designing research projects[3]

It is important to appreciate that the objective of exploratory research such as focus-group interviewing is hypothesis formulation; that is, forming a conjectural statement about the relationship between two or more variables. For example, assume that the following focus-group interview occurred concerning paper towels. Mrs. Baker says she always buys ScotTowels because they are absorbent. Mrs. Smith claims that a store brand she has tried is not that absorbent, and she always buys Bounty now. She adds that Bounty also comes in a variety of colors. Mrs. Franklin says all paper towels are alike, and she buys whichever brand is on sale. Note that the focus group has revealed three attributes of paper towels: absorbency, color, and price. What does the researcher do with this type of information? He might begin to consider hypotheses regarding the role of these variables in influencing consumers' purchase decisions for the product.

Exploratory research is not designed to provide conclusive answers to the research questions it generates. Therefore, more extensive and rigorous studies are needed to determine how the variables that have been identified influence consumers. This is the role of conclusive research.

CONCLUSIVE RESEARCH The major goals of conclusive research are to describe fully consumers' behavior and to offer explanations for its causes. In addition, the prediction of consumers' behavior and methods of influencing it can be suggested by conclusive research. Of course, as we noted in Chapter 1, influencing consumer behavior is of interest to numerous groups, including marketers, the government, and consumer protectionists. We will examine some of the specific methods used for conclusive research later in this chapter.

Type of Data Used

Two basic sources of data may be used in consumer research: secondary and primary. *Primary data* are those the researcher gathers firsthand for the problem being investigated. However, there is a vast amount of information about consumers which is already compiled and readily accessible to the researcher who knows how to find and use it. Such data that have been collected for a purpose other than the research project at hand are termed *secondary data.* Before gathering primary data, the researcher should search through secondary sources to determine if any are applicable to the problem at hand. Because the types of secondary data are too numerous to describe here, an interested reader should refer to other sources for further information.[4] Our focus in this chapter will be on primary data and the methods used to gather them.

Research Time Frame

Generally speaking, in consumer research studies, primary data can be collected either at one time or over a period of time. We refer to these research designs as cross-sectional and longitudinal, respectively. These two approaches have different purposes.

CROSS-SECTIONAL RESEARCH Sometimes the researcher is interested in assessing the nature of some aspect of consumer behavior at one particular time instead of studying how it changes over time. As its name implies, the cross-sectional design is used to study such a situation by examining a cross section of behavior at any given time. For example, such a study may seek to determine the values and attitudes various consumers have about a particular product at one particular moment.

LONGITUDINAL RESEARCH Interest can also focus on how some aspect of consumer behavior changes over time, as in the case of consumers developing a loyalty for a particular brand of coffee. These situations are best studied by using a longitudinal design, which involves data gathering and analysis over a period of time. One popular type of longitudinal study is the continuous *consumer panel.* Consumers who are deemed representative of some particular group are chosen for inclusion in the panel, where the number of panel members may range from only a few people to several thousand households.

A continuous consumer panel provides the researcher with a fixed sample that can be repeatedly studied. By asking the same questions of panel members over a period of time, changes in their behavior, as well as reasons for these changes, can be determined.[5] Panel members generally maintain a continuous record or diary of their consumption activities, such as shopping, purchase, use, and product/brand decisions, as well as demographic and attitudinal characteristics. For example, in one major panel, sales are reported by brand for households classified according to such factors as total family income, age of housewife, number and ages of children, occupation and education of family head, and location by region and city size. Sales are also provided according to the types of stores from which purchases are made.

METHODS OF GATHERING CONSUMER INFORMATION

In both cross-sectional and longitudinal designs, there are two general ways of collecting consumer behavior data: observation and communication. These two basic approaches can be further categorized, however, into three information-gathering methods: observation, experiments, and surveys.

Observation

One way to study consumers is to observe their overt behavior. In some cases this alternative may be better than asking consumers how they act, because frequently discrepancies exist between how consumers say they behave and what they actually do. Many are not even consciously aware of all their activities or the influences of external purchase stimuli such as point-of-purchase store displays or window exhibits. For example, if a mother were asked why she purchased a particular brand of cereal she might respond, "Because of its nutritional value." Observation of actual shopping behavior, however, might reveal that her child grabbed the box off the shelf, claiming that he wanted the free toy inside. Another benefit of the observation method frequently is that it can be accomplished subtly, so that the consumers do not realize that they are subjects and thus change their behavior. Therefore, this method may be quite successful in obtaining certain types of behavioral information.

There are several illustrations of the observation technique being used in consumer research. Mechanical means of observation are sometimes used by researchers. For example, the A.C. Nielsen Company gathers television viewership data from a selected group of families by means of an electrome-chanical device that automatically records the times and channels of televi-sion viewing. This results in the famous Nielsen Television Ratings, which are issued every two weeks.

Another form of mechanical observation is "pupilometrics," or the obser-vation of eye pupil dilation, which accompanies the viewing of emotionally charged or interesting visual stimuli. In this technique a camera observes the pupils of the subjects' eyes when exposed to photographs of such stimuli as products, packages, or advertisements to determine their interest-arousing potential.[7]

Cameras (usually hidden) may also be used to observe accurately shop-pers' behavior in a store. This information could be very useful in many ways, such as planning or improving a store's layout. For example, the shopping patterns of a supermarket's customers might be observed and recorded. The data then could be used to determine which aisles are most heavily traveled, where "traffic jams" occur, and whether more people pick up meat and dairy items first or last. Because subjects are unaware of being observed, hidden cameras have the potential advantage of being more accurate than personal observation methods. It should be noted, however, that there are critics of this method who believe it is unethical to film shoppers without their permission. Unfortunately, if permission is first obtained, the consumer's behavior may become atypical. Therefore, if this technique is to be used, the consumer researcher should first determine his own view of the ethics involved.

Experiments

In experimental investigations the researcher selects consumers, stores, and so on (known as test units) and seeks to measure the effect of specific situations or conditions (known as experimental treatments) on a particular dependent variable such as consumers' attitudes or purchase behavior. In this process, an attempt is made to control or hold constant the effects of other so-called extraneous variables so that they will not influence the results. For example, if we wanted to determine whether the size of a magazine advertisement affects readers' attention, then the size of the ad might be varied, while such extraneous variables as the message or appeal used, and the color of the ads were held constant so that they would not influence the results and confuse the issue.

Consumer researchers may conduct experiments in the "field" (that is, the actual setting of the marketplace), or they may test hypotheses under "laboratory" conditions (which include any environment simulating real or actual conditions).

LABORATORY EXPERIMENTS These are useful because they typically allow greater control over extraneous variables than is possible in the real world. Also the investigator may be better able to manipulate experimental treatments in the controlled environment of the laboratory. However, a potential problem with such experiments is that they can sometimes become too artificial, thereby insufficiently representing the real world. An example of a laboratory experiment could be to discover consumer taste preferences regarding Pepsi, Coke, and Royal Crown Cola. Note how the laboratory situation allows control over extraneous variables such as containers, prices, and brand names. For example, rather than using the products' bottles or cans, drinks could be presented to subjects in glasses of the same size and color with no brand name or price information on them.

FIELD EXPERIMENTS These provide a natural setting for research in order to overcome the problems of artificiality sometimes found in the laboratory. However, gaining realism from the marketplace environment can come at the cost of losing some control over the experimental situation.

Market testing is one business equivalent of the scientist's field experiment. In a market test, different marketing variables (such as prices and advertisements) are tried in several market areas to determine which receives the most favorable consumer response. New-product introductions may be tested for about 6 months, during which the product is promoted and treated as if it were on the market in a full-scale way.

In the case of market testing, experimenters are faced with problems of control much different from those in the laboratory. For instance, competitors who are aware of a market test can interfere with the research by increasing their advertising, offering coupons, cutting prices, or other strategy changes. These changes reduce the experimenter's control over the test and can hide the true effect of the variable or variables under study.

Unfortunately, the expense of many field experiments can be prohibitive, and the length of time involved also makes this type of research inappropriate for some studies. The fact that the field experiment is conducted in the marketplace, however, can enhance the credibility of the results.[8]

Surveys

In the survey method of gathering data, consumers are not only aware of the fact that they are being studied, but actively participate. There are three survey data-collection techniques: personal interviews, telephone surveys, and mail surveys.

PERSONAL INTERVIEWS Direct face-to-face interaction between the interviewer and the respondent is perhaps the personal interview's greatest advantage over other types of surveys. A large amount of information can be obtained with a relatively high degree of accuracy by this approach. Flexibility is a further advantage, since questions can be modified to suit the situation or clarification can be provided if necessary. A major disadvantage of this approach, however, is its high cost.

TELEPHONE SURVEYS The telephone survey can be a useful alternative to the personal interview because it provides for interviewer-respondent interaction and is quicker and less expensive to conduct than personal interviews. Today, access to Wide Area Telephone Service (WATS) makes it easy for researchers to sample a vast geographic area for a comparatively low price. Telephone surveys work well when the objective is to measure certain behavior at the time of the interview or immediately prior to the interview, such as radio listening or television viewing. It is also easier to reach subjects by telephone, and many people who would not consent to a personal interview are willing to participate over the phone. These surveys generally achieve higher response rates than mail surveys or personal interviews.

Telephone surveys have three basic limitations, however. First, the amount of information that can be obtained is limited because of difficulty in keeping respondents on the phone and interested for any extended period. Second, the type of information obtainable is limited. For example, measuring the intensity of consumers' feelings is difficult, and questions containing numerous response options are cumbersome. Further, the method can produce distorted results because subjects without telephones or those with unlisted numbers often are not reached, and they can differ from other respondents in important ways.

MAIL SURVEYS Mail-questionnaire surveys have long been used by researchers because of their low potential cost per respondent, their ability to reach widely dispersed consumers, and their ability to obtain large amounts of data and allow more sophisticated questioning techniques, such as measuring scales.

In this approach consumers receive a questionnaire in the mail, complete it at their leisure, and return it in a postpaid envelope. Since respondents are seldom asked to identify themselves, a mail survey can reduce their reluctance to reveal sensitive information.

Of course, there are also disadvantages to this type of survey. Mail interviews can result in a small number of responses with many questionnaires ending up in wastebaskets. Another problem concerns the long time it may take for respondents to return the questionnaire. Follow-up letters to remind consumers of their delay can increase response rates, but also boost costs. Also, since there is no interviewer-respondent interaction, questions must be worded carefully to avoid ambiguity, and the questionnaire should be carefully pretested to detect any deficiencies.

MEASURING CONSUMERS

Consumer research may also be classified according to whether demographic or cognitive information is sought. The following discussion will focus primarily on cognitive research approaches.

Demographic Measures

Demographic research is concerned with gathering vital statistics about consumers—such characteristics as their age, income, sex, occupation, location, race, marital status, and education. Notice that since these characteristics are easily quantifiable they enable the marketer to describe accurately and specifically and to understand certain consumer characteristics.

Much of the demographic data on consumer markets is a product of federal, state, and local government sources. The next chapter will describe in some detail the demographic characteristics of the United States consumer market. Thus, little treatment of the topic is necessary at this point. However, it should be mentioned specifically that firms generally desire to obtain a demographic portrait of their customers. Through research such a profile may be constructed. As an example, consider the case of a retail store that offers charge accounts. Information supplied by consumers during their credit application can be useful in profiling such customers. With such a portrait the retailer may uncover the demographic strengths and weaknesses of his primary clientele.

Cognitive Measures

Consumer researchers who desire to know about their market more than just demographic characteristics may attempt to collect cognitive information; that is, information about consumers' knowledge, attitudes, motivations, and perceptions. Merely observing consumers cannot fully explain why they behave as they do, and questioning often does not provide reliable answers because of consumers' inability or reluctance to reveal true feelings to an interviewer. Thus, researchers attempt to explore intervening variables potentially useful in explaining consumer behavior by utilizing other techniques.

This section describes associative and projective techniques that are used in consumer research to help explain the *why* of consumer behavior. Also, the depth interview is discussed because of its primary use in uncovering motives. Finally, attitudinal research approaches incorporating rating scales are presented.

MOTIVATION RESEARCH During the 1950s companies became increasingly concerned with why consumers bought one product or brand instead of another. With the growth in income levels, particularly discretionary income, and as products became more alike, it grew even more important that marketers determine the attitudes, motives, values, perceptions, and images that might govern consumers' product/brand selections. To provide such answers a group of investigators termed "motivation researchers" came to the forefront of marketing studies.

A set of projective techniques that had originally been developed by clinical psychologists was adapted, and began to be used in consumer research along with various notions from the field of psychoanalysis. These techniques and notions became known by the general term of *motivation research,* or in its abbreviated form simply *MR.* It must be emphasized that these techniques are not used exclusively for studying consumers' motivations, nor do they include all the tools available for such study. Actually, motivation research shares many techniques with other areas of consumer research that are seeking to understand consumers. Several of these projective techniques are briefly characterized below.

Word-Association Tests Word association is a relatively old and simple technique used by researchers. Respondents are read a list of words, one at a time, and asked to answer quickly with the first thing that comes into their minds after hearing each one. By answering rapidly respondents presumably indicate what they associate most closely with the word offered and thereby reveal their true inner feelings.

The example in Figure 3-1 illustrates how a retailer might use word associations in determining consumer brand preferences in order to allocate advantageous shelf space and position to favorite brands.

Word-association tests can be used in numerous other ways in consumer research such as to generate brand names, check their meaning, determine the effectiveness of advertising, and compare brand or company images.

The *sentence-completion* test is an adaptation of the word-association test in which the interviewer begins a sentence and the respondent finishes it. In conducting a study for a radio station, the interviewer might use the following statements:

1. WHJY plays music that appeals to . . .

2. The commercials on WHJY are . . .

3. A person who listens to WHJY is . . .

Frequently consumers respond to sentence-completion tests without realizing it, such as in contests that say, "Complete the following sentence in ten words or less."

The *story-completion* test is yet another expanded word-association test in which the respondent is told part of a story and is instructed to complete it in his or her own words, as in the following example.

Mrs. Jones reads in the newspaper that Land O' Lakes butter is on sale at the local supermarket. She decides to take advantage of the sale and goes to the supermarket to buy it. When she gets there, the manager informs her that there is no Land O' Lakes butter left.
How would Mrs. Jones react?
Why?

The story technique can be useful in uncovering the images consumers have about stores and products, and this information can be applied in advertising and promotional themes.

The scoring for association tests consists of classifying the responses as either favorable or unfavorable. The numbers of each type of response can then be compared on a demographic basis. For instance, did women or men

---

For the following product category list I would like you to respond with the first brand name that comes to mind. For example, if I say "deodorant" you might respond by saying "Sure."

Product category	Brand
1. Hair spray	1. _____
2. Mouthwash	2. _____
3. Perfume	3. _____
4. Lipstick	4. _____
5. Eye makeup	5. _____

FIGURE 3-1
Word-association
questionnaire.

have more favorable responses, or, did those in upper-income brackets respond more unfavorably?

Projective Tests Projective tests call for the respondent to decide what another person would do in a certain situation. People may be reluctant to admit certain weaknesses or desires, but when they are asked to describe a neighbor or another person, they usually respond without hesitation. Thus projective techniques are based on the assumption that respondents express their own attitudes or motives as they infer the attitudes or motives of someone else.

A classic motivation research study based on this theory was conducted in 1950 by Mason Haire regarding consumer attitudes toward instant coffee.[9] Direct-question interviews revealed a dislike of instant coffee because of the taste; but this was believed to be a stereotyped response rather than the true reason. In an effort to discover other reasons for this negative attitude, an indirect approach was used. Respondents were shown one of two identical grocery shopping lists, varying only in the brand and type of coffee. One list contained "Nescafé Instant Coffee" and the other, "Maxwell House Coffee (drip ground)." They were then asked to characterize the woman who purchased the groceries. Descriptions indicated that compared to the drip-ground buyer, the instant-coffee purchaser was thought to be lazy, a spendthrift, not a good wife, and one who failed to plan household purchases and schedules well. Although these findings are probably not true today, they were initially useful in better understanding consumer motivations. They indicated that respondents were not really dissatisfied with the taste of instant coffee, but rather the idea of using it was unacceptable. Respondents were projecting their own feelings about instant coffee into the descriptions of the woman who purchased it.

Another form of projective test makes use of pictures as stimuli. One example is the *Thematic Apperception Test (TAT),* in which respondents are shown ambiguous pictures concerning the product or topic under study and asked to describe what is happening in the picture. Because the pictures are so vague, it is believed that the respondents will actually reveal their own personalities, motivations, and inner feelings about the situation.

A modern form of the TAT looks like a comic strip with two characters discussing the topic under study. One character has a statement printed in the "balloon" above him, but above the other character is an empty balloon. Respondents are asked to fill in the balloon as they think the character would reply. Once again, respondents are answering for someone else but are expressing their own ideas. Figure 3-2 illustrates the cartoon technique.

Depth Interviews As described in the focus-group approach, depth interviews are unstructured, informal interviews. General questions are usually asked, followed by more specific questions that probe for needs, desires, motives, and emotions of the consumer. Also, the questioning is sometimes indirect, such as, "Why do you think your friends smoke Marlboros?" as opposed to the direct question, "Why do you prefer Marlboro cigarettes?" Again, this method attempts to circumvent inhibitions the respondent may have about revealing inner feelings. By carefully following cues given by the respondent, an interviewer can ask a series of questions that probe for underlying motivations.

The key factor with depth interviewing (as well as focus-group interviewing) is the interviewer's skill, which calls for imagination and thoroughness in probing consumer leads while not influencing the respondent's answers. Because of their very nature, interview results are interpreted subjectively rather than quantitatively. Thus, there is a great possibility for bias. An additional source of error from depth and focus-group interviews may arise with the use of small samples, which may not be representative of the entire population.

ATTITUDE-MEASUREMENT SCALES Significant strides have been made in the area of measuring consumers' attitudes. This has resulted in the development of various self-reporting attitude-rating scales. The scales are termed self-reporting because consumers express their own evaluation of their attitudes by responding to the scale in the way they think most appropriate.

The many scales available differ mainly in their structure and in the degree to which they actually measure attitudes. This section presents two of the more widely used scales in consumer research—the Likert scale and the semantic differential.

Likert (Summated) Scales There are four stages involved in using a Likert scale:

1. A list of statements relevant to the attitudes under investigation is compiled, with each statement identifiable as either favorable or unfavorable.

2. Agreement-disagreement responses are selected. For example, five variations might be used, ranging from "strongly agree" to "strongly disagree."

3. After pretesting identifies the most relevant statements, the scales are

FIGURE 3-2
Cartoon projective technique.

administered to consumers who indicate which response most nearly expresses their attitude about the statement.

4. The score for each consumer is computed by summing the weights associated with each response checked.

The following is an example of an individual's response to a Likert scale:

	Strongly agree 5	Agree 4	Undecided 3	Disagree 2	Strongly disagree 1
Sears is generally a progressive store.	_____	X	_____	_____	_____
Sears' stores are generally well stocked.	X	_____	_____	_____	_____
Sears' merchandise is generally low-priced.	_____	X	_____	_____	_____

Often the responses are added based on the numerical value assigned to them. This consumer's score of 13 indicates a very favorable attitude toward Sears. A lower total score, such as 6, would be interpreted as an unfavorable attitude.

Semantic Differential The semantic differential consists of pairs of bipolar adjectives or antonym phrases as ends of a continuum with response options spaced in between. This technique can be used in marketing to rate the psychological meaning of concepts, products, companies, or people.[10]

Typically, a seven-position scale is utilized between the adjectives with the middle value being neutral. A consumer is asked to mark the position that most closely corresponds to his or her attitude toward the subject being studied. Responses can be tabulated and profiled, a procedure which dramatically illustrates consumer attitudes.

Below is a sample set of semantic differential scales (with only a few adjectives shown) which might be used to have consumers express their attitudes toward three brands of bread. A profile of consumers' responses is also drawn in.

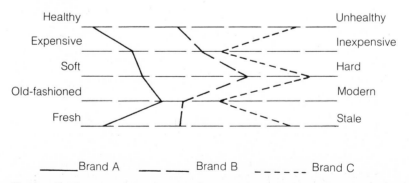

Healthy — Unhealthy
Expensive — Inexpensive
Soft — Hard
Old-fashioned — Modern
Fresh — Stale

_____Brand A   _ _ _ _ Brand B   _ _ _ _ _ _ Brand C

Notice that consumers have a favorable attitude toward Brand A while Brand B is viewed somewhat neutrally, and attitudes toward C are quite negative.

Such a finding would be of value to Brand C and could help guide the company in making strategy decisions to overcome this unfavorable image.

As in all of the approaches that have been discussed, the decision to use a specific method or scaling technique must depend on the type of information being sought by the researcher as well as the way in which the data are to be applied.[11]

SUMMARY

This chapter has examined the role of consumer research in studying consumer behavior. The goal of consumer research was seen to be either exploratory or conclusive in nature. Sources of consumer information were also discussed, including those already gathered for the marketer (secondary research) and those obtained by the marketer himself (primary research). Consumer information may be gathered at one time (cross-sectional study), or over an extended period (longitudinal research). In addition, data on consumers may be obtained via three basic approaches: observation, survey, or experiment. Finally, the nature of information gathered in consumer studies was discussed under the categories of demographic and cognitive research.

From the numerous techniques and their applications discussed in this chapter, it becomes clear that consumer research is essential in helping marketers make sound decisions. Yet research should not be used only retrospectively. Sometimes marketers spend so much money finding out what happened in the past that they cannot afford to find out what is about to happen. Therefore, the importance of looking ahead through research needs to be stressed.

In the remaining two chapters of this section, we will explore the use of consumer research in selecting target market segments. Chapter 4 will further discuss demographic research, and Chapter 5 will explain approaches to market selection that are primarily cognitive in orientation.

DISCUSSION TOPICS

1. Define consumer research.

2. Discuss the significance of consumer research to marketers, consumers, and the economy.

3. Discuss the role of focus-group interviewing. Find an example in the literature of its actual use by a company and briefly describe it to the class. Was the technique used properly?

4. Under what conditions should the marketer rely on secondary data? What potential limitations are there in their use?

5. Distinguish between cross-sectional and longitudinal research and illustrate each with an example.

6. Design and conduct a consumer panel for selected purchases among class members.

7. Design and conduct the following types of consumer research on subjects of your choosing:
a. observation

b. survey

c. experiment

8. With the objective of determining consumer attitudes toward instant coffee, design and conduct a cognitive research study using the following techniques:

a. word association

b. projective tests

c. semantic differential

What differences are found in the results using these approaches?

NOTES

1. Peter Vanderwicken, "P&G's Secret Ingredient," *Fortune,* July 1974, p. 77.

2. Myril D. Axelrod, "Marketers Get an Eyeful When Focus Groups Expose Products, Ideas, Images, Ad Copy, etc. to Consumers," *Marketing News,* February 28, 1975, p. 6.

3. Yolanda Brugaletta, "Gives Guidelines to Set Up, Use and Analyze Focus Groups," *Marketing News,* October 24, 1975, p. 1.

4. See Steuart H. Britt and Irwin Shapiro, "Where to Find Marketing Facts," *Harvard Business Review,* **40**:44–52, September–October 1962, and Harper W. Boyd, Jr., Ralph Westfall, and Stanley F. Stasch, *Marketing Research: Text and Cases,* 4th ed., Irwin, Homewood, Ill., 1977, for a partial list of guides to secondary data.

5. Harper W. Boyd, Jr., and Ralph L. Westfall, *An Evaluation of Continuous Consumer Panels As a Source of Marketing Information,* American Marketing Association, Chicago, 1960.

6. David A. Schwartz, "Research Can Help Solve Packaging, Functional and Design Problems That May Be Costing You Sales," *Marketing News,* January 16, 1976, p. 8.

7. Herbert E. Krugman, "Some Applications of Pupil Measurement," *Journal of Marketing Research,* **1**:15, November 1964.

8. For a more complete presentation of the experimental approach see Keith Cox and Ben M. Enis, *Experimentation for Marketing Decisions,* International Textbook, Scranton, 1969, and M. Venkatesan and Robert J. Holloway, *An Introduction to Marketing Experimentation,* Free Press, New York, 1971.

9. Mason Haire, "Projective Techniques in Marketing Research," *Journal of Marketing,* **14**:649–656, April 1950.

10. William A. Mindak, "Fitting the Semantic Differential to the Marketing Problem," *Journal of Marketing,* **25**:28–33, April 1961.

11. For a more complete presentation of cognitive research techniques see G. David Hughes, *Attitude Measurement for Marketing Strategies,* Scott, Foresman, Glenview, Ill., 1971.

MARKET SEGMENTATION: BASIC APPROACHES

CHAPTER 4

VIEWS OF THE MARKET AND ALTERNATIVE MARKETING STRATEGIES Market Aggregation; Market Segmentation **DEMOGRAPHIC CHARACTERISTICS AND MARKET SEGMENTATION** United States Population Growth; Changing Age Mix of the Population; Marketing Implications of Population Changes **GEOGRAPHIC CHARACTERISTICS AND MARKET SEGMENTATION** Regional Distribution of United States Population; Metropolitan Population in the United States; Nonmetropolitan Population in the United States; Geographic Mobility of the Population **SOCIOECONOMIC CHARACTERISTICS AND MARKET SEGMENTATION** Education; Occupation; Income; Expenditures; Willingness to Buy **LIMITATIONS OF DEMOGRAPHICS IN PREDICTING CONSUMER BEHAVIOR**

One of the most profound realizations to strike any marketer is that there is a great diversity among consumers. Upon closer inspection of the total market, however, it is found that smaller groups of consumers have more homogeneity in certain characteristics, especially their consumer behavior.

This chapter introduces the concept of selectively marketing to such homogeneous groups of consumers. The major alternatives in selecting market targets are discussed, stressing the value of market segmentation. Some of the most important bases for segmenting markets are also discussed. In Chapter 5, the topic of segmentation is continued with an examination of additional methods by which markets may be selected.

VIEWS OF THE MARKET AND ALTERNATIVE MARKETING STRATEGIES

Marketers may approach target markets in their aggregate and heterogeneous form or as smaller, more homogeneous segments. The following section will discuss these two alternatives.

Market Aggregation

A market-aggregation strategy means, in effect, that no subdivision of the market is applied. With this approach, a firm would produce a single product and offer it to all consumers with a single marketing program. Although the marketer recognizes that not everyone will buy his product, he expects to attract a sufficient number for profitable operations. This approach has also been described as *undifferentiated marketing* or *product differentiation.*

In the past, a number of firms have used market-aggregation strategies including soft drink companies, cigarette manufacturers, gasoline marketers, many packaged food producers, and home appliance manufacturers. For example, Coca Cola was for many years presented to consumers as a one-flavor soft drink available only in the familiar 6-ounce glass bottle and with the unchanging promotion theme "The Pause That Refreshes."

The reasoning behind market aggregation is that although consumers may differ, they are sufficiently alike to approach as a homogeneous grouping for the product under consideration. Market aggregation, therefore, presents a standard product that differs little if any from competition, makes heavy use of mass promotion, and attempts to distinguish the product as being superior. By so doing it seeks to have demand conform to what manufacturers are willing to supply.

The major advantage of pursuing such a strategy is lower costs of doing business. For example, efficiencies are gained from longer production runs with a single product. There may also be greater media discounts from a large-scale, undifferentiated advertising program.

There are dangers in this strategy, however. The marketer exposes himself to competitive attacks by other firms pursuing a strategy of serving unfulfilled consumer needs. Consequently, by attempting to satisfy all consumers *reasonably* well, he becomes vulnerable to other firms seeking to satisfy particular segments of the market *very* well. It is difficult for a product or brand to be all things to all people.[1]

Market Segmentation

In firms employing a strategy of segmentation the market is viewed as being made up of smaller segments, each more homogeneous than the total in important characteristics. Thus market segmentation is the process of partitioning the heterogeneous market into segments. The goal is to facilitate development of unique marketing programs which will be most effective for these specific segments.

There are ranges of market segmentation. A firm might pursue *concentrated* marketing, which means that it would seek to serve only one of several market segments. Examples of organizations that have at some point pursued this strategy are Volkswagen, Sony, U.S. Time (Timex), and Gerber. On the other hand, a company may pursue market *atomization* whereby each consumer is treated uniquely. Examples of firms that have adopted this approach abound in the specialty industrial goods field. In addition, those who custom-make cars, homes, and furniture are applying market atomization to consumer goods.

Most companies employing market segmentation, however, select several market segments to appeal to with different products, using different promotional efforts and prices, and perhaps selling through different distribution outlets. Many companies fit this description, such as General Motors with its various car divisions. Similarly, Proctor & Gamble produces not only Ivory Snow but Tide, Dash, Duz, Dreft and other detergents to meet different consumers' needs (at least as they are perceived by purchasers of these brands).

BENEFITS AND COSTS OF MARKET SEGMENTATION Clearly, market segmentation conforms supply to what consumers demand. In addition, because the segments contain fewer and more similar consumers, the marketer is able to obtain more detailed knowledge about their characteristics. As one author suggests, potential benefits of this approach lie in its ability to aid the marketing manager to:

—quickly detect trends in a rapidly changing market

—design products that truly meet the demands of the market

—determine the most effective advertising appeals

—direct the appropriate amounts of promotion in the right media to segments offering the greatest profit potential

—schedule promotional efforts during time periods when responsiveness is likely to be highest.[2]

Although market segmentation produces benefits for the firm, it also boosts costs. Typically, manufacturing costs are higher because of shorter production runs; research costs are higher because of the need to investigate more segments; promotion costs are higher when quantity media discounts are lost; and, in addition, overlapping market coverage may result in some "cannibalization" as one product steals sales from another in the same company's line. Ideally, a company would like to achieve what General Foods did when it introduced Cool Whip. Sales were taken away from competing aerosol toppings (which General Foods did not produce) rather than from its other brand of dessert topping, Dream Whip. Thus, market segmentation can result in greater sales for a company, but at higher costs. Of course, the goal is to increase sales more than costs, thus raising profits.

MARKET CRITERIA FOR EFFECTIVE SEGMENTATION A decision to use a market segmentation strategy should rest on consideration of four important criteria that affect its profitability. In order for segmentation to be viable, the market must be: (1) identifiable and measurable, (2) accessible, (3) substantial and (4) responsive.

Identifiable and Measurable Segments must be identifiable so that the marketer can determine which consumers belong to a segment and which do not. However, there may be a problem with the segment's measurability (i.e., the amount of information available on specific buyer characteristics) because numerous variables are difficult, if not impossible, to measure at the present time. For example, if it is discovered that consumers who perspire profusely favor a particular brand, what could the marketer do with this information? Probably very little since the size of this particular segment would be difficult to estimate through measurement. Consequently, such a variable does not appear to represent an effective means of segmenting the market.

Accessible This criterion refers to the ease of effectively and economically reaching chosen segments with marketing efforts. Some desired segments may be inaccessible because of legal reasons; for example, liquor manufacturers are unable to market directly to young teenagers. It is more likely, however, that segments may be inaccessible because the marketer is unable to reach them via existing promotional media and retail outlets at a reasonable cost and with minimum waste.

There are two ways to reach prospects: (1) controlled coverage of marketing effort and (2) customer self-selection.[3] A controlled-coverage approach involves trying to reach chosen target market segments while avoiding others not in the group. For example, assume a marketer desired to reach advanced skiers with a new product. Suppose that from media studies it can be determined that most of these prospects are regular readers of *Skiing.* With this information the marketer has the ability to largely control the coverage of her advertising so that it reaches mainly the target segment. She may further control her marketing coverage by offering the product only in exclusive ski shops where most advanced skiers might shop. Thus, such an approach is very efficient because it reaches mainly target segments with little "wasted" coverage of segments who are not prime prospects. Controlled coverage is also possible for some products by use of regional editions of such national magazines as *Time, Newsweek, Sports Illustrated,* and *Business Week.*

Customer self-selection, on the other hand, involves reaching a more general audience while relying on the product's and advertisement's special appeal to the intended target segments. For example, a product for skiers might be advertised in national editions of *Time, Newsweek, Sports Illustrated,* or *Business Week.* These general market media would cover many consumers who are not interested in the product, but those who are actually skiers (or perhaps those who might purchase the product as a gift) would be attracted to the ad. These consumers, in effect, select themselves by their attention to the ad. The product could also be sold through mass merchandisers shopped by a wide cross section of people. Yet only those who have an interest in this product category will tend to respond.

Although the approach of customer self-selection does result in some wasted effort, such widespread coverage can sometimes reach otherwise inaccessible prospects. A decision must be made on which of these strategies is best for gaining accessibility to the chosen target segment. However, it appears that when a controlled coverage approach can be applied it is economically advantageous.[4]

Substantial This criterion refers to the degree to which a chosen segment is large enough to support profitably a separate marketing program. As was cited previously, a strategy of market segmentation is costly. Thus, one must carefully consider not only the number of customers available in a segment but also the amount of their purchasing power.

Responsive There is little to justify the development of a separate and unique marketing program for a target segment unless it responds uniquely to these efforts. Therefore the problem is to define meaningfully market segments so that they favorably respond to marketing programs designed specifically for them.[5]

If the four criteria above are fulfilled, segmentation is an attractive marketing strategy. The question remaining, however, regards the variables or bases by which the market may be segmented. This is the issue to which we turn our attention in the following section.

BASES FOR SEGMENTATION There are a number of dimensions by which a company might segment its market. The most frequently used bases for segmentation are: (1) demographic, (2) socioeconomic, (3) geographic, (4) product usage, (5) perceived product benefits, and (6) life-style or psychographics. Each of these approaches offers advantages as well as disadvantages.

It is essential for us to review the general characteristics of the American consumer market and of some of its major segments. Only with a clear understanding of major consumer characteristics can we begin to appreciate the implications of environmental and individual determinants of their behavior. Hence, the remainder of this chapter will be devoted to isolating the most significant demographic, geographic, and socioeconomic characteristics of American consumers and discussing their relevance for developing segmentation strategies. The following chapter will expand on these approaches by incorporating more advanced segmentation concepts.

It is often said that a market consists of people with purchasing power and the willingness to buy. That is:

$$\text{market} = \text{people} \times \text{purchasing power} \times \text{willingness to buy.}$$

Consequently, if we examine these three elements of the consumer market we will obtain useful insights for segmentation decisions. We will begin by studying the first prerequisite in our definition of a market—people.

DEMOGRAPHIC CHARACTERISTICS
AND MARKET SEGMENTATION

The American consumer market may be segmented along a number of demographic dimensions. This section discusses the major demographic characteristics of which the reader should be cognizant.

United States Population Growth

It is helpful to first examine the overall size of the population in the United States even though it does not represent a "segment" of interest to most firms. At the beginning of 1978 the population stood at approximately 215 million. Tracing the history of our population growth during the last generation we find that two major distortions occurred. Between 1930 and 1945 births were unusually low because of the Depression and World War II. Between 1945 and 1960, however, the country experienced a period of unusually high births—popularly known as the "baby boom." Most demographers consider the postwar baby boom to be unusual, however, because the American birthrate has been generally declining almost since the Republic was founded. For example, in 1800 American women each had an average of seven children (although no more than five survived). Since the baby boom ended, the birthrate has fallen dramatically to only 1.9 children per woman in 1973.

DON'T LOOK FOR ZPG YET In spite of the decreasing number of children being born per family, zero population growth (ZPG) is not expected to occur soon, as shown in Figure 4-1.

More births than deaths will occur in any given year (e.g., 3.1 million births versus 2 million deaths in 1973). Thus, unless the number of deaths rises dramatically, the birthrate would have to stay down for about 50 years or so before a stationary population would be reached.

Although the birthrate may rise from time to time in the future, most demographers see such upturns simply as fluctuations around the major continuing downward trend. Thus, sooner or later ZPG is expected to arrive.

REASONS FOR THE DECLINE IN BIRTHS The main reasons pointed to for the decline in the United States birthrate include the following:

1. Modernization of our society such that it has become secular, industrialized, educated, and urban, and shifted from a high birth- and death rate to a low birth- and death rate

2. Contraception and the growing availability of abortion

3. The women's liberation movement, which has challenged the traditional roles of motherhood and homemaking among women

4. The growing environmental concern that a large population will use up too much of the world's limited natural resources

5. Economic causes such as inflation and the high cost of having and supporting children[6]

The shifts in birthrates can have very dramatic effects on the total population over a long period. For example, if young families decided to have two children, by 2030 the population would reach 264 million. However, if

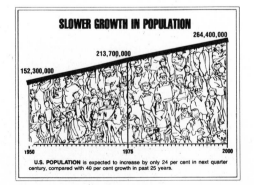

FIGURE 4-1
Slower growth in population. (*Source:* Reprinted from *U.S. News & World Report,* March 3, 1975, p. 35. Copyright 1975 U.S. News & World Report, Inc.)

each family had three children, the population would zoom to 444 million by that date.

Changing Age Mix of the Population

The mix of ages in the United States population can be an important factor to consider. *Business Week* describes the population age mix of 1985 as including more babies, fewer teen-agers, far more young adults, and many more oldsters than there are today.[7] The most important age-mix change will come about as post-World War II babies move toward middle age. Figure 4-2 reveals the shift in age composition of the population between 1975 and the year 2000.

IMPORTANT COHORT FACTORS[8] Demographers use the term cohort to mean the aggregate of persons born in any given year or specified period. Cohort factors, therefore, are the values and attitudes that a population group carries with it throughout life. It will become clear in later chapters (especially Chapters 6 and 8) that values and attitudes differ among age groups within the population. For example, when General Mills asked adults and teens in the same families what expenditures they thought of as luxuries, they found that youngsters were far less likely than their parents to cite a new

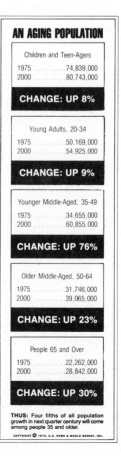

FIGURE 4-2
An aging population. (*Source:* Reprinted from *U.S. News & World Report*, March 3, 1975, p. 35. Copyright 1975 U.S. News & World Report, Inc.)

car each year or hired household help and were far more likely to classify having meat at most meals as a luxury.

Although cohort factors are difficult to predict, the following seem to be realistic trends. First, there will be more working wives in the decade ahead. In spite of the fact that the increase will amount to only a percent or two, the growth will be extremely meaningful because it will occur largely among women who have small children. Hence, some suggest there will be demands for more company-sponsored day care, and more paid maternity leave.

Secondly, there will be fewer children per family. However since a very large number of women are entering prime childbearing years total births could skyrocket, in spite of a low overall birthrate. Also, a large share of these births will be of first children—an estimated 40 percent of births in 1985 versus only 25 percent in 1960. This is significant since it has been estimated that an additional $700 is spent by parents "tooling up" for the first child.

A third cohort factor is the growth in households. Although the total population is important, for many companies it is not nearly so critical as the number of total households. One of the reasons for the rapid growth in households is the high rate of divorce. It is estimated that 970,000 couples were divorced in 1974 and a Census Bureau demographer estimates that among today's 30-year-old wives, one out of every three marriages has been or will be dissolved by divorce.[9]

A more important reason for the large growth in households, however, is the increasing tendency for young singles to establish their own accommodations apart from their parents. There is also a growing segment of oldsters who live apart from their children. Thus, the dramatic rise in number of households is occurring largely among single adults.

Marketing Implications of Population Changes[10]

There are a number of important marketing changes that have been wrought by shifts in the United States population. For example, companies that previously catered to babies are finding that it pays to diversify. Thus Gerber Products Co., the nation's largest producer of baby foods, has dropped the word "only" from its long-used slogan, "Babies are our only business." Gerber has gone also into life insurance, printing, and prepackaged meals for single diners. Johnson & Johnson is finding success by working both sides of the population street. On one hand, it still produces its line of baby products (although it has broadened its advertising appeal to stress how good these products are for adults too). On the other hand, Johnson & Johnson also owns Ortho Pharmaceutical Corporation, one of the country's largest manufacturers of contraceptives, aimed at those who want to avoid buying its baby products.

Magazines as well as products will find the need to adjust their marketing strategies. For example, *Playboy* magazine expects to reposition itself as the numbers of postadolescents that now represent its prime target decline. The editors will emphasize more sophisticated copy with less fantasy and more useful advice on vacations, investments, and clothes.

The changing age mix also brings about changes in consumer expenditures. For example, reports by the Bureau of Labor Statistics show that a family headed by someone between 35 and 44 years of age has an income near that of one headed by someone 45 to 54. However, the younger family spends 16 percent less on personal care services, 21 percent less on over-the-counter drugs, but 10 percent more on meat.

The increase in the number of working wives means that companies will make greater attempts to attract these busier, more monied women. For example, appliance manufacturers such as Whirlpool are designing their machines to take the burden of operation from the housewife and thus leave her more time for other chores. Convenience foods (particularly more expensive ones) should also grow in demand among this group. In addition, it is expected that working-wife families will make greater use of time-saving, convenience-shopping outlets. Working wives will also represent a positive factor in automobile demand, and offer greater opportunity to life insurance companies to sell two policies to a family.

The combination of two working parents and fewer children may also create a large potential market for selling what are now considered luxury goods. The future is expected to be a profitable one for airlines and hotels, developers of vacation homes, the automobile industry, and the manufacturers of such leisure goods as sports equipment, record players, and tape recorders.

The advent of smaller families will also affect the housing market, perhaps resulting in smaller units, more multiple-housing units, and locations closer to centers of population. Such a trend has obvious implications for furniture and appliance manufacturers. For example, General Electric is putting its new-product emphasis on compact appliances designed for smaller living quarters.

Market planners across the United States anticipate that the customer of the future will be much more self-confident, discriminating, and independent. This will have important implications for products to be offered this market as well as the nature of retail establishments to be patronized.

GEOGRAPHIC CHARACTERISTICS
AND MARKET SEGMENTATION

The American consumer market may also be grouped along geographic dimensions, which is one of the oldest forms of segmentation. It has long been evident that regional differences sometimes result in differences in buyer preferences or variations in product usage; for example, products primarily geared to warm-weather climates, such as swimming pools and air conditioners, having marketing programs built partially on a geographic-segmentation strategy. Other examples of geographic segmentation include gasolines that are "localized" for driving conditions in the area of their sale; magazines that publish regional editions allowing advertisers to tailor their messages and to pinpoint more accurately their audiences; and station wagons, which are primarily a suburban phenomenon and thus sold mainly by dealers in these areas.

This section discusses major geographic characteristics potentially useful in segmenting markets.

Regional Distribution of United States Population
Population is not distributed evenly across the United States, but instead is

concentrated in certain states and regions, with the states east of the Mississippi River accounting for the great bulk of our population.

Although current population data are important, one should not lose sight of the fact that population shifts are occurring that could dramatically alter the present picture. Examination of Figure 4-3 indicates that certain areas of the United States are expected to gain population rapidly, while others will gain slowly, and still other states will lose population over the period between 1973 and 1990.

One of the most important shifts in population occurring in the United

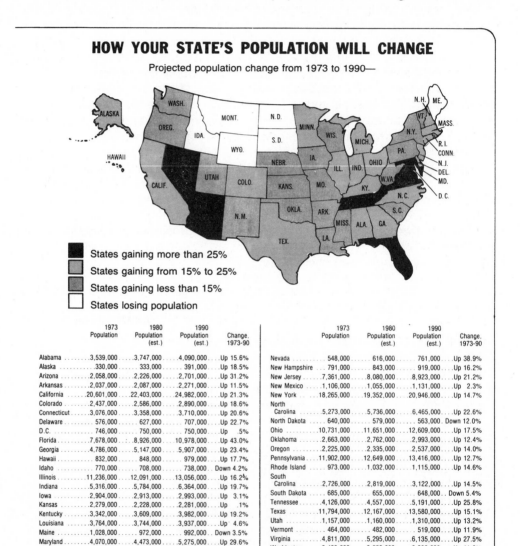

HOW YOUR STATE'S POPULATION WILL CHANGE

Projected population change from 1973 to 1990—

- ■ States gaining more than 25%
- ▨ States gaining from 15% to 25%
- ▩ States gaining less than 15%
- □ States losing population

	1973 Population	1980 Population (est.)	1990 Population (est.)	Change, 1973-90
Alabama	3,539,000	3,747,000	4,090,000	Up 15.6%
Alaska	330,000	333,000	391,000	Up 18.5%
Arizona	2,058,000	2,226,000	2,701,000	Up 31.2%
Arkansas	2,037,000	2,087,000	2,271,000	Up 11.5%
California	20,601,000	22,403,000	24,982,000	Up 21.3%
Colorado	2,437,000	2,586,000	2,890,000	Up 18.6%
Connecticut	3,076,000	3,358,000	3,710,000	Up 20.6%
Delaware	576,000	627,000	707,000	Up 22.7%
D.C.	746,000	750,000	750,000	Up .5%
Florida	7,678,000	8,926,000	10,978,000	Up 43.0%
Georgia	4,786,000	5,147,000	5,907,000	Up 23.4%
Hawaii	832,000	848,000	979,000	Up 17.7%
Idaho	770,000	708,000	738,000	Down 4.2%
Illinois	11,236,000	12,091,000	13,056,000	Up 16.2%
Indiana	5,316,000	5,784,000	6,364,000	Up 19.7%
Iowa	2,904,000	2,913,000	2,993,000	Up 3.1%
Kansas	2,279,000	2,228,000	2,281,000	Up .1%
Kentucky	3,342,000	3,609,000	3,982,000	Up 19.2%
Louisiana	3,764,000	3,744,000	3,937,000	Up 4.6%
Maine	1,028,000	972,000	992,000	Down 3.5%
Maryland	4,070,000	4,473,000	5,275,000	Up 29.6%
Massachusetts	5,818,000	6,267,000	6,876,000	Up 18.2%
Michigan	9,044,000	9,743,000	10,645,000	Up 17.7%
Minnesota	3,897,000	4,119,000	4,553,000	Up 16.8%
Mississippi	2,281,000	2,328,000	2,450,000	Up 7.4%
Missouri	4,757,000	5,071,000	5,439,000	Up 14.3%
Montana	721,000	670,000	665,000	Down 7.8%
Nebraska	1,542,000	1,499,000	1,557,000	Up 1.0%
Nevada	548,000	616,000	761,000	Up 38.9%
New Hampshire	791,000	843,000	919,000	Up 16.2%
New Jersey	7,361,000	8,080,000	8,923,000	Up 21.2%
New Mexico	1,106,000	1,055,000	1,131,000	Up 2.3%
New York	18,265,000	19,352,000	20,946,000	Up 14.7%
North Carolina	5,273,000	5,736,000	6,465,000	Up 22.6%
North Dakota	640,000	579,000	563,000	Down 12.0%
Ohio	10,731,000	11,651,000	12,609,000	Up 17.5%
Oklahoma	2,663,000	2,762,000	2,993,000	Up 12.4%
Oregon	2,225,000	2,335,000	2,537,000	Up 14.0%
Pennsylvania	11,902,000	12,649,000	13,416,000	Up 12.7%
Rhode Island	973,000	1,032,000	1,115,000	Up 14.6%
South Carolina	2,726,000	2,819,000	3,122,000	Up 14.5%
South Dakota	685,000	655,000	648,000	Down 5.4%
Tennessee	4,126,000	4,557,000	5,191,000	Up 25.8%
Texas	11,794,000	12,167,000	13,580,000	Up 15.1%
Utah	1,157,000	1,160,000	1,310,000	Up 13.2%
Vermont	464,000	482,000	519,000	Up 11.9%
Virginia	4,811,000	5,295,000	6,135,000	Up 27.5%
Washington	3,429,000	3,550,000	3,806,000	Up 11.0%
West Virginia	1,794,000	1,832,000	1,845,000	Up 2.8%
Wisconsin	4,569,000	4,737,000	5,013,000	Up 9.7%
Wyoming	353,000	331,000	334,000	Down 5.4%
UNITED STATES	**209,851,000**	**223,532,000**	**246,039,000**	**Up 17.2%**

Note: Population estimates by U.S. Census Bureau assume birth rates will remain near recent levels.

FIGURE 4-3
How your state's population will change. (*Source:* Reprinted from *U.S. News & World Report*, July 15, 1974, p. 57. Copyright 1974 U.S. News & World Report, Inc.)

States today is the movement toward the *Sunbelt,* the lower arc of warm states stretching from southern California to North Carolina. The growing popularity of the Sunbelt is a result of many people's search for a better quality of life. Escape from the colder weather, higher living expenses, and increasing crime and congestion in northern cities are the key motivations driving industry and individuals alike to relocate in this region.

It is important to understand regional trends in population, since this understanding may be helpful in segmentation and marketing strategy decisions. For example, it has been demonstrated that personality differences exist among geographic regions of the United States and these may be associated with differences in the demand for many products.[11] Many differences are also the result of climate, religion, social customs, and other factors. An example of regional patterns is the color, style, and weight of clothing. For instance, bright, warm colors are preferred in Florida and the Southwest, while grays and cooler colors predominate in New England and the Midwest. Westerners are less formal than Easterners, and they spend more time outdoors. As the population of the Sunbelt area, particularly of the Western states, grows, the demand for products such as patio furniture, backyard swimming pools, air conditioners for home and car, sports clothes, barbecue equipment, and other warm-weather products will also increase.[12]

A number of other studies have also found significant variations in consumer behavior among the different geographical regions. For example, Table 4-1 presents selected data on regional differences in consumption, appliance ownership, and media usage. In addition Table 4-2 illustrates other differences among consumers in the five regions of the United States (East, South, Midwest, West, and Southwest).

TABLE 4-1

REGIONAL DIFFERENCES IN CONSUMPTION, APPLIANCE OWNERSHIP, AND MEDIA USAGE

Product	Total	East	South	Mid-west	West	South-west
			Percentage Reporting Using Once a Week or More			
Regular chewing gum	26	17	40	30	24	26
Mouthwash	51	48	62	47	40	54
Men's cologne	61	58	72	61	55	71
Shaving cream in a can	55	55	54	55	45	54
Toothpaste	88	89	92	89	90	82
Regular coffee (nondecaffeinated)	62	59	63	58	72	66
Instant coffee (nondecaffeinated)	36	40	33	36	31	24
Hot tea	29	44	14	30	30	24
Iced tea (summer)	69	73	84	69	52	76
Regular soft drinks	53	46	67	53	35	63
Artificial sweetner	18	19	30	19	11	21
Nondairy powdered creamer (Coffee-mate, Cremora, etc.)	23	23	33	23	20	15
Potato chips	35	21	48	41	26	43

TABLE 4-1 (continued)

Product	Percentage Reporting Using Once a Week or More					
	Total	East	South	Mid-west	West	South-west
Fresh sausage	18	15	30	15	11	22
Bologna	33	30	23	36	31	28
Cottage cheese	32	27	17	41	40	30
Yogurt	5	9	2	4	11	3
Vitamin tablets	35	36	21	36	44	35
Domestic wine	14	15	5	16	28	8
Blended whiskey	11	16	4	13	13	7
Scotch	7	12	5	7	8	2

Product	Percentage Owning					
	Total	East	South	Mid-west	West	South-west
Automatic dishwasher	43	44	42	42	56	56
Garbage disposal	28	11	8	35	50	44
Freezer	58	48	68	62	58	60
Water softener	13	6	1	21	14	9
Room air conditioner	41	45	45	42	28	37
Color TV set	77	79	65	83	83	77

Category	Percentage Exposed					
	Total	East	South	Mid-west	West	South-west
Newspapers						
Sunday newspaper (read 4+ issues in past 4 weeks)	68	73	63	69	65	74
Daily morning (read 9+ issues in past 10 days)	31	34	31	30	30	37
Daily evening (read 9+ issues in past 10 days)	45	54	48	52	35	39
Radio station types						
Popular music—top 40	46	47	51	52	46	35
All talk—telephone discussion/ news	40	43	51	44	38	24
Country and western	53	38	70	56	42	54
Magazines						
TV Guide	37	41	47	28	49	38
National Geographic	33	37	30	31	42	44
Penthouse	17	19	7	15	24	14
*TV programs**						
"Hawaii Five-O"	35	36	41	31	26	35
"Sanford and Son"	40	37	48	38	32	41
"All in the Family"	46	55	47	34	40	40

*Rated "very good" to "one of my favorites."
Source: Needham, Harper & Steers Advertising, Inc., *Life Style Survey,* 1975. Adapted from F. D. Reynolds and W. D. Wells, *Consumer Behavior,* McGraw-Hill, New York, 1977, pp. 212–213.

TABLE 4-2

73

MARKET
SEGMENTATION:
BASIC
APPROACHES

REGIONAL CONSUMER PROFILE

Item	Percentage Agreeing					
	Total	East	South	Mid-west	West	South-west
Prefer a traditional marriage with the husband assuming the responsibility for providing for the family and the wife running the house and taking care of the children.	52	39	52	59	45	61
When making important family decisions, consideration of the children should come first.	52	49	62	51	48	50
Every vacation should be educational.	48	49	54	52	38	47
I am considering buying life insurance.	19	14	30	17	17	21
I nearly always have meat at breakfast.	29	14	52	22	26	34
Went out to breakfast instead of having it at home at least once last year.	57	57	42	61	71	61
Worked on a community project at least once during the past year.	35	39	50	34	31	34
Attended church 52 or more times last year.	28	23	37	31	20	30
I like to visit places that are totally different from my home.	72	79	63	72	75	65
I would like to spend a year in London or Paris.	33	40	36	27	38	24
Went on a trip outside the U.S. last year.	14	24	8	12	19	15
Rode a bus at least once last year.	32	49	26	28	40	24
It is hard to get a good job these days.	77	82	83	77	65	80
Used a bank charge card at least once last year.	43	52	43	41	52	50
Returned an unsatisfactory product at last once during the past year.	65	67	52	70	65	64
Used a "price off" coupon at a grocery store.	63	67	50	72	60	53
My days seem to follow a definite routine—eating meals at the same time each day, etc.	62	68	66	58	53	64
Cooked outdoors at least once last year.	81	86	82	84	80	84
Went on a picnic at least once during the past year.	75	78	65	79	79	73

TABLE 4-2 (continued)

Item	Percentage Agreeing					
	Total	East	South	Mid-west	West	South-west
Had wine with dinner at least once during the past year.	60	70	38	62	72	49
Had a cocktail or drink before dinner at least once last year.	70	78	59	75	77	53
I am interested in spice and seasoning.	43	46	44	41	54	35
Visited an art gallery or museum from one to four times in the past year.	30	29	27	32	40	34
Went bowling at least once last year.	36	42	20	44	34	24
Went hiking at least once during the past year.	46	49	47	43	59	45
Went backpacking at least once last year.	6	8	7	4	16	5
Went hunting at least once last year.	32	18	43	29	32	40

Source: Needham, Harper & Steers Advertising, Inc., *Life Style Survey,* 1975. Adapted from F. D. Reynolds and W. D. Wells, *Consumer Behavior,* McGraw-Hill, New York, 1977, p. 211.

Metropolitan Population in the United States

Population in the United States has migrated from rural to urban areas since 1800. In 1920, for example, approximately three out of ten persons lived on a farm, but by 1970 this had dropped to only about one out of twenty. Thus, rural population has been on a downtrend for a long while. Today, however, there is a resurgence of some rural areas, with in-migration occurring.

A movement of population has also occurred from city to suburb and is still very much a continuing process. Although the pace is slower than it was immediately after World War II, it is continuing at a steady rate. For example, between 1970 and 1975 the number of persons living in suburbs expanded by over 10 percent, accounting for 57 percent of the total metropolitan population, while the overall United States population grew by only about 4 percent. During this same period the population of the country's central cities actually declined by 2.5 percent. In spite of this general decline, downtown revivals in several major cities and social and cultural events have attracted young marrieds and older couples to move back to the city. Table 4-3 presents a list of major United States cities showing the population shifts which have occurred.

How do suburban consumers differ from those in the cities? According to Fabian Linden of the National Industrial Conference Board, the family that moves to the suburbs tends to be younger, to have more children, a higher level of educational accomplishments, and to be generally more affluent than the one that remains in the city. The typical city family, by contrast, tends to be older, less well educated, and less fortunate financially.[13] Thus, there are substantial differences in the demographic characteristics and hence in the consumer-behavior patterns of suburban versus urban consumers.

TABLE 4-3

75

MARKET
SEGMENTATION:
BASIC
APPROACHES

POPULATION CHANGES OF MAJOR CITIES

Rank 1974	Rank 1970	City	1974 Pop. (thous.)	Change in Population 1970–1974 (thous.)	Change in Population 1960–1970 (thous.)
1	1	New York	7572.9	−322.0	+112.9
2	2	Chicago	3266.2	−100.8	−183.4
3	3	Los Angeles	2735.6	− 80.5	+337.1
4	4	Philadelphia	1825.6	−123.0	− 53.9
5	5	Detroit	1383.3	−128.2	−158.6
6	6	Houston	1318.7	+ 85.9	+294.6
7	8	Dallas	870.4	+ 26.0	+164.7
8	7	Baltimore	845.2	− 60.6	− 33.2
9	14	San Diego	801.2	+104.4	+123.6
10	15	San Antonio	788.7	+134.5	+ 66.5
11	11	Indianapolis	749.5	+ 4.9	+268.3
12	20	Phoenix	730.1	+148.5	+142.4
13	9	Washington, D.C.	717.7	− 38.8	− 7.5
14	12	Milwaukee	682.3	− 34.8	− 24.2
15	17	Memphis	669.1	+ 45.6	+126.0
16	13	San Francisco	665.0	− 50.7	− 24.6
17	10	Cleveland	646.4	−104.5	+125.2
18	16	Boston	634.0	− 7.1	− 56.1
19	19	New Orleans	584.9	− 8.6	− 34.0
20	21	Columbus, Ohio	571.2	+ 31.5	+ 68.4
21	23	Jacksonville	568.4	+ 39.5	+327.9
22	18	St. Louis	542.2	− 80.0	−127.8
23	25	Denver	508.0	− 6.7	+ 20.8
24	27	Seattle	507.4	− 23.4	− 26.3
25	26	Kansas City	498.9	− 8.2	+ 31.6
26	27	Atlanta	488.2	− 8.8	+ 9.5
27	24	Pittsburgh	467.1	− 53.0	− 84.2
28	30	Nashville-Davidson	453.9	+ 5.9	+277.1
29	28	Buffalo	439.3	− 23.5	− 70.0
30	29	Cincinnati	425.3	− 27.2	− 50.1

Source: Sales Management's 1975 Survey of Buying Power, p. A–34. Reprinted by permission from *Sales & Marketing Management* magazine. Copyright 1975.

WHAT CONSTITUTES A METROPOLITAN AREA? With population migrating to the suburbs and spilling over the relevant political boundaries, old descriptions of market areas based on such political entities become obsolete. Consequently, the federal government established the concept of a *Standard Metropolitan Statistical Area (SMSA)* as a geographic unit for measuring market data. An SMSA is defined as a county or group of contiguous counties containing a central city of 50,000 (or two closely located cities of 50,000 combined population) and a total population of 100,000. SMSA boundaries may cross state lines but the counties must be socially and economically integrated. Nearly all employment in SMSAs is nonagricultural. Approximately 300 metropolitan areas have been identified by the United States government.

The federal government has recognized the inadequacy of even the term SMSA to describe major metropolitan areas where such mergers have occurred. Consequently, the government now reports data for thirteen *Standard Consolidated Statistical Areas (SCSA)* containing an SMSA of at least 1 million population and one or more adjoining SMSAs which are related by high-density population centers and intermetropolitan commuting of workers. These thirteen SCSAs account for one-third of the population of the United States.

All SMSA/SCSAs together account for over 70 percent of the nation's population. For the marketer, these areas represent geographically concentrated target segments which hold great market potential. Figure 4-4 presents the nation's SMSAs and SCSAs.

As urban sprawl causes metropolitan areas to extend their reach, these areas have begun to merge as suburbs of one spill over into suburbs of another. Such a development gives rise to the concept of a new type of supercity termed *megalopolis* or *interurbia*. Figure 4-5 indicates the projected growth through 1975 of such supercities. This process will continue in the years ahead.

Nonmetropolitan Population in the United States

An almost unnoticed population trend that has recently occurred in the United States is the growth of small towns and rural areas. Since 1970, rural America has grown much faster than metropolitan areas. For example, between 1970 and 1974, the population growth was 3.4 percent in metropolitan areas (including suburbs), 4.9 percent in rural counties not adjacent to metropolitan areas, and 6.2 percent in those nonurban areas just over the line from officially designated suburbs. Adding all of the noncity areas together, a growth rate of 5.6 percent has been achieved—almost 70 percent greater than metropolitan areas.

Why the trend back to small towns? Authorities include the following among major reasons: (1) a stabilizing farm population, (2) industrial migration to rural areas, and (3) a desire by some for a simpler, safer living environment.[14] Marketers should continue to be aware of this migration pattern and understand the implications it may have for marketing programs. For example, Kresge is opening "mini" K-marts in towns of 8000 to 15,000 population in order to reach consumers in less populated areas.[15]

Geographic Mobility of the Population

Another characteristic of our population and one that is a potentially useful segmentation dimension is geographic mobility. Vance Packard cites some impressive statistics to document our society's mobility:

The average American moves about fourteen times in his lifetime, compared with five times for the Japanese.

In many cities, over 35 percent of the population move every year. For example, a school in Great Falls, Montana, annually loses 70 percent of its pupils and 30 percent of its teachers.

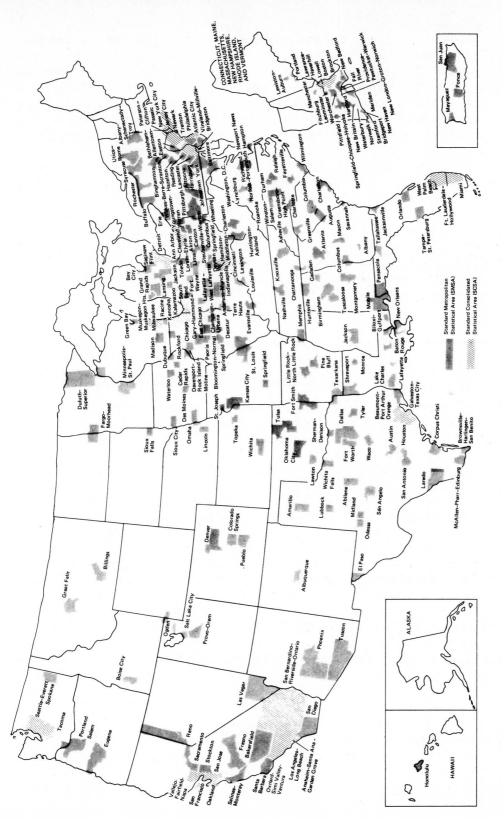

FIGURE 4-4
Metropolitan areas
in the United
States. (*Source:*
U.S. Office of Management and
Budget, Statistical
Policy Division,
*Standard Metropolitan Statistical
Areas, 1975*, rev.
ed., Washington,
D.C., 1975.)

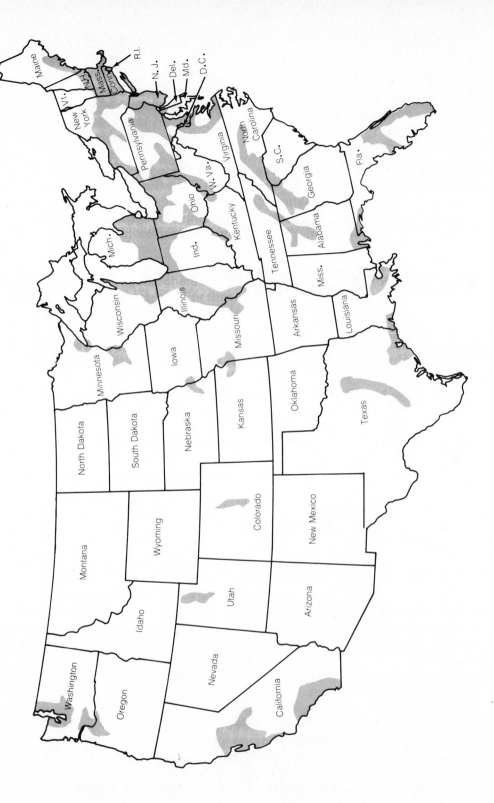

FIGURE 4-5
Interurbia in 1975. (*Source:* J. Walter Thompson Co., "Interurbia: The Changing Face of America," May 10, 1960. Courtesy of J. Walter Thompson Company.)

The families of many executives have had to move their households as many as twenty times.

Some 6 million Americans now live in mobile homes. Even though these homes are not often moved, their occupants feel little commitment to their home and community.

At any given time, half of the 18- to 22-year-olds in hundreds of towns are living away from home. Many of them come back only to visit.[16]

Over one-half of all moves are job-related. In fact, the average person entering the job market today can expect to move thirteen times and to change jobs seven times during his or her career.[17] Mobility also varies from region to region. For example, in the Northeast, only slightly over 13 percent of all families moved in 1970, while in the West the percentage was almost twice that.[18]

There are indications, however, that the game of musical houses is slowing down in the United States. The percentage of Americans who moved in 1970 was 19.1 percent while in 1977 it was 17.7 percent, the lowest rate in more than a generation. There are a number of reasons cited for such a trend:

More people are unwilling to give up the place, climate, and recreational facilities they like, just for more money.

Housewives and working wives are revolting against transfers for executive husbands.

Middle-class Americans are more inward-looking, concerned with the quality of life, and less interested in getting ahead by switching jobs and towns.

Corporate shifts to the Sunbelt have slowed migration to the North.

The trend to smaller families has reduced the need for moving to a larger house.[19]

In spite of the decreases in mobility in the United States, those who do continue to move are seen as a very attractive segment to be cultivated by many marketers.

A study of long-distance geographic mobiles found them to be relatively young (and in the early stages of the family-life cycle), well educated, in higher status occupations, and having above-average incomes. They also were in higher social classes, were socially active, and upwardly mobile.[20] This mobile segment has been found to be a potentially superior market for such products as furniture, clothing, drapes, slipcovers, other dry goods, and consumer durables such as automobiles and appliances.

Once relocated, mobiles must rebuild shopping patterns in their new community.[21] They learn about new suppliers primarily from word-of-mouth communication with friends, neighbors, and coworkers. However, mass-media sources such as newspapers and the yellow pages are also important, as is personal observation while driving around. Mobiles tend to rebuild shopping patterns rapidly, in part because of holding charge accounts with national retailers which allow them to transfer their store and brand loyalty to the new community.

Because of the value of this segment, retailers in particular should be cognizant of the efforts necessary to attract the geographically mobile market. For example, a retailer could benefit from setting up a newcomer program to identify new arrivals and make contact with these families before their shopping habits have been rebuilt. Such a program could include: (1) offering to extend check-cashing or credit privileges, (2) delivering a gift to the home, (3) providing coupons redeemable in the store, and (4) offering a price cut or refund on items purchased.[22]

Thus, geographic mobiles are often a worthwhile target segment because they can be identifiable, accessible, and substantial. Concentration of marketing effort on this segment, particularly by retailers, should pay great dividends.

SOCIOECONOMIC CHARACTERISTICS AND MARKET SEGMENTATION

A final dimension for market segmentation to be examined in this chapter involves socioeconomic characteristics. Included within this category are the variables of education, occupation, and income.

Education[23]

The future generation of adults is acquiring considerably more schooling than the present generation. This trend has been occurring as a result of affluence, changing social values, and the shifting employment needs of industry. Today approximately one out of four adults has had some college training and about 40 percent of young people go on to college, compared with only about 17 percent of those born around the turn of the century.

The relative importance of the educated segment of consumers will continue to expand rapidly during the 1970s. By 1980 the college-trained group that makes up about 25 percent of the population will account for 40 percent of all income and well over half of the total demand for an extensive repertoire of goods and services.

In addition to the aspects of income associated with increasingly educated consumers, there are also a number of unique characteristics that further differentiate them from the average consumer. They are more sophisticated in their product and store choices, for example. They are also more alert to quality, packaging, and advertising messages. Moreover, they have differing needs from those of the typical consumer, tending to spend somewhat more (after allowing for the income difference) on clothing, home furnishings, medical and personal care, entertainment, travel, and many other items. Thus, education does make a difference not only in what the consumer buys but often probably in the brand selected.

Occupation

Just after World War II the United States labor force contained more blue-collar than white-collar jobs. However, rising industrial productivity and the shifting needs of business have brought about a substantial rise in white-collar workers. This growth has been especially strong in the professional and technical category. Table 4-4 illustrates shifts in employment since 1950, and projected to 1985.

81

MARKET
SEGMENTATION:
BASIC
APPROACHES

Income

The marketer is highly interested in the second part of our formula concerning what constitutes a market: what people have available to spend. Before we examine income levels, however, we need to understand what is meant by "income" because there are several concepts of this term, not all of which are equally important in evaluating a market.

Personal income is the income from wages, salaries, dividends, rent, interest, business and professions, social security, and farming.

Disposable personal income is the amount available after deducting taxes for personal-consumption expenditures and saving.

Discretionary income is the income available for spending after deducting expenditures for essential or fixed items such as food, clothing, transportation, shelter, and utilities.

Supernumerary (or surplus) income refers to income that accrues to individual families in surplus of $20,000 (in 1976 prices). This represents a general measure of rising consumer affluence.[24]

Since these latter two concepts indicate the extent of the resources available for optional spending after all outlays have been made for the essentials of

TABLE 4-4

DISTRIBUTION OF EMPLOYMENT BY OCCUPATION

	Percent Distribution					
Occupation	1950	1960	1970	1975	1980	1985
Total employed	100.0	100.0	100.0	100.0	100.0	100.0
White-collar workers	37.5	43.1	48.3	49.8	51.5	52.9
Professional technical	7.5	11.2	14.2	15.0	15.7	16.8
Managers, administrators	10.8	10.6	10.5	10.5	10.5	10.3
Clerical workers	12.8	14.7	17.4	17.8	18.7	19.4
Sales workers	6.4	6.6	6.2	6.4	6.6	6.4
Blue-collar workers	39.1	36.3	35.3	33.0	33.1	32.3
Craft workers	12.9	12.8	12.9	12.9	12.8	12.8
Operatives	20.4	18.0	17.7	15.2	15.6	15.1
Nonfarm laborers	5.9	5.5	4.7	4.9	4.7	4.4
Service workers	11.0	12.5	12.4	13.7	13.3	13.2
Private household	3.2	3.3	2.0	1.4	1.3	1.1
Other services	7.8	9.2	10.4	12.4	12.0	12.9
Farm workers	12.4	8.1	4.0	3.5	2.1	1.6

Note: Data for 1950 and 1960 are for persons 14 years of age and over. Later years refer to population 16 years of age and over. All years refer to civilian employment only.
Source: U.S. Department of Labor.

everyday life, they are better measures of the market potential for luxury goods and services.

One of the most significant developments during the 1970s and beyond is the changing nature of income levels in the United States. Our nation is becoming a more affluent country, with the pattern of income distribution becoming an inverted pyramid. In other words, there will be relatively fewer poor and more wealthy families in future years than there are at present.

The number of families that have moved into the affluent income levels has increased dramatically in the 1970s.[25] It has been estimated that the top 5 percent of United States families hold over 40 percent of all wealth while the top 20 percent of families have three times the net worth of the lower 80 percent.[26] Figure 4-6 graphically presents the pattern of household income distribution in 1975. In addition, Table 4-5 presents information on income and family characteristics. In this table characteristics of the supernumerary families may be clearly seen.

For many business people this higher-income group is a market of considerable significance. This group is an important audience for a wide array of quality goods and services that appeal to the needs and fancies of the very well-heeled (sometimes referred to as the "carriage trade"). In fact many industries are heavily dependent on this market's patronage. Such items as boats, second homes, quality photographic and hi-fi equipment, gourmet foods, elegant cars, and top-of-the-line products in general are aimed at this income class.

As these upper-income brackets expand, changes will occur in the pattern of consumer demand and in marketing strategies. Certainly, industries producing for the income elite should find prosperity. Even for everyday merchandise the growing difference will cause consumers to demand more expensive items of better quality.

Expenditures

The spending patterns of the average American family and how they change over time are matters of great importance to the marketer. Unfortunately, little systematic and reliable information exists on how the typical family spends its money. Approximately every decade an expenditure survey is conducted by the federal government, the most recent of which was done in 1972–1973, updating a previous survey in 1960–1961.

During the interval between these two studies some major expenditure shifts have taken place. Two reasons account for many of these changes: (1) inflation (some items rose in price much more rapidly than others) and (2) changing demographics (births declined and the number of households increased greatly).

Generally, as can be seen in Table 4-6, expenditures increased markedly for housing, transportation, and recreation (i.e., home, car, and fun) and these three areas now account for a larger share of the budget. Food and clothing expenditures increased less dramatically and now account for a smaller share of the household budget.

It is also important to understand how expenditures vary with income level. Figure 4-7 provides data on the differences in spending patterns between lower- and middle-income households and between middle- and upper-income levels.

Willingness to Buy

The last portion of our equation regarding what constitutes a market is the consumer's willingness to buy. As George Katona states, "Consumers' discretionary demand is a function of both ability to buy—primarily

Consumer Buying Power's Upward Tilt

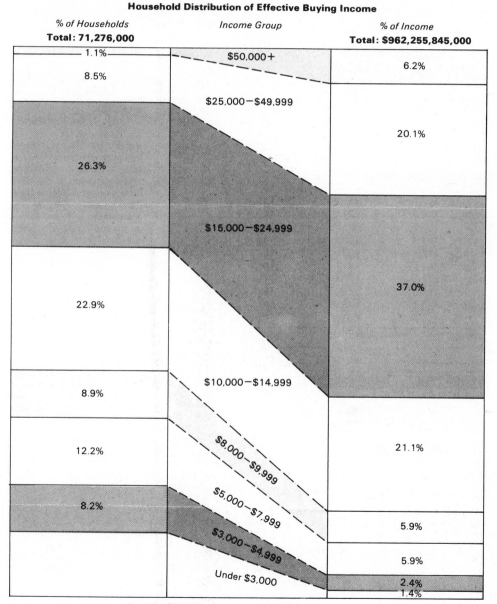

Household Distribution of Effective Buying Income

% of Households Total: 71,276,000	Income Group	% of Income Total: $962,255,845,000
1.1%	$50,000+	6.2%
8.5%	$25,000-$49,999	20.1%
26.3%	$15,000-$24,999	37.0%
22.9%	$10,000-$14,999	
8.9%	$8,000-$9,999	21.1%
12.2%	$5,000-$7,999	
8.2%	$3,000-$4,999	5.9%
	Under $3,000	5.9%
		2.4%
		1.4%

Note: The $962 billion figure is household EBI only and does not include military personnel or institutional population EBI.

Source: *Sales Management's 1975 Survey of Buying Power.* ©Sales Management.

FIGURE 4-6
Household distribution of effective buying income. (*Source: Sales Management's 1975 Survey of Buying Power,* p. A-29. Reprinted by permission from *Sales & Marketing Management* magazine. Copyright 1975.)

TABLE 4-5

FAMILY CHARACTERISTICS BY INCOME CLASS

	All Families	Under $3000	$3000–5000	$5001–7000	Annual Family Income $7001–10,000	$10,001–15,000	$15,001–25,000	$25,001 and over
Families								
Millions	50.5	4.7	5.4	6.2	10.9	13.5	7.9	1.9
Distribution	100.0%	9.3%	10.7%	12.3%	21.7%	26.7%	15.6%	3.7%
Average size (number)	3.6	3.0	3.3	3.5	3.7	3.9	4.0	4.0
Distribution all persons	100.0%	7.6%	9.6%	11.7%	21.8%	28.3%	17.0%	4.0%
Income								
Average income	$9670	$1754	$3957	$5963	$8385	$12,031	$18,129	$35,680
Distribution all income	100.0%	1.6%	4.0%	7.0%	17.3%	30.6%	27.0%	12.5%
Number of Earners								
None	8.2%	42.5%	19.3%	5.6%	1.6%	0.7%	0.7%	0.9%
One	38.2	39.4	48.7	51.2	43.4	29.0	20.8	37.7
Two	39.2	15.1	27.2	36.4	44.4	50.2	43.7	32.8
Three or more	14.4	3.0	4.8	6.8	10.6	20.1	34.8	28.6
Wife Working	38.0%	15.1%	23.8%	29.9%	37.0%	47.8%	53.4%	32.7%
Age of Family Head								
Under 25	6.6%	10.4%	10.6%	11.4%	8.5%	4.0%	0.9%	—%
25–34	20.3	12.1	15.6	22.0	26.1	24.4	15.7	6.6
35–44	21.7	10.0	12.8	18.0	21.7	27.3	27.6	23.9
45–54	21.1	10.7	13.4	15.6	18.0	24.1	32.3	37.0
55–64	16.3	15.4	15.2	16.1	16.2	14.6	18.5	24.6
65 & over	14.0	41.4	32.3	16.9	9.5	5.6	5.0	7.9
Type of Family								
Husband-wife	86.8%	61.5%	76.8%	84.4%	90.9%	94.1%	95.4%	96.8%
Other	13.2	38.5	23.2	15.6	9.1	5.9	4.6	3.2
Children: Families Having	58.0%	43.5%	48.0%	57.2%	63.6%	63.5%	59.6%	57.4%
One child	19.0	16.4	17.1	19.4	19.5	19.7	19.9	20.4
Two children	17.4	10.8	12.2	16.3	20.1	20.2	19.0	16.1
Three children	10.8	7.0	8.0	10.6	12.2	12.5	11.1	10.4
Four or more	10.8	9.3	10.7	10.9	11.8	11.1	9.6	10.5
Families with children	100.0%	7.7%	10.0%	14.3%	25.6%	27.4%	12.4%	2.6%
Distribution of children	100.0%	7.9%	10.8%	14.4%	25.7%	27.0%	11.7%	2.5%
Color								
White	90.0%	77.7%	81.8%	88.1%	92.3%	94.3%	95.9%	96.9%
Nonwhite	10.0	22.3	18.2	11.9	7.7	5.7	4.1	3.1

Source: Fabian Linden, "The Seven Stages of Income," The Conference Board Record, September 1970, p. 28.

TABLE 4-6

THE HOUSEHOLD BUDGET: ALLOCATION OF EXPENDITURES

	Early 1960s	Early 1970s	Increase*
Total Current Consumption	$5054	$8282	$3228
Percent distribution:	100.0	100.0	100.0
Food	24.4	20.1	13.3
Food at home	19.6	14.0	5.4
Food away from home	4.9	6.0	7.9
Alcoholic beverages	1.5	1.4	1.2
Tobacco	1.8	1.6	1.2
Clothing and upkeep	10.9	7.8	2.9
Men's and boys'	3.9	2.6	0.6
Women's, girls', infants	5.6	4.0	1.5
Materials, services	1.4	1.2	0.9
Housing	28.4	31.4	36.3
Shelter	13.1	16.4	21.6
Renter	5.3	6.9	9.4
Owner	6.9	8.7	11.5
Other	0.9	0.6	0.2
Utilities	4.9	4.9	5.0
Household operations	5.0	5.4	6.0
Housefurnishings, equipment	5.3	4.7	3.7
Transportation	15.2	21.4	30.9
Private	13.7	18.9	27.0
Public and other	1.5	2.4	3.8
Medical and personal care	9.6	8.4	6.4
Medical care	6.7	6.4	5.8
Personal care	2.9	2.0	0.6
Education and reading	1.9	1.8	1.6
Recreation	4.0	4.7	5.8
Miscellaneous	2.2	1.5	0.3

Note: Data are based on surveys conducted by Bureau of Labor Statistics in 1960–1961 and, more recently, in 1972–1973.
*The figures in this column denote the percent distribution of the total *dollar increase* in expenditures by category.
Sources: U.S. Department of Labor; The Conference Board. Adapted from Fabian Linden, "All in the Family Budget," *Across the Board*, August 1977, p. 42.

income—and of willingness to buy."[27] Katona maintains it is the combination of these two elements that holds the key to future buying. One indication of willingness to buy is the consumer's plans for future spending.

Probably the most important organization presently active in the quest to determine consumer spending plans is the University of Michigan's Survey Research Center, which polls consumers and attempts to blend psychology and economics to achieve an accurate estimate of consumers' willingness to buy.

Reports provided by such consumer surveys are closely watched by such major companies as General Motors, RCA, and General Electric, and by major banks. The surveys not only help businesses to anticipate trends in the economy, but also provide help in understanding the past. For example, during one year auto sales had an unexpected spurt in the third quarter despite the addition of a 10 percent income tax surcharge for that period. It was found that consumers expected new car prices to be higher and were trying to beat the increase.[28]

LIMITATIONS OF DEMOGRAPHICS IN PREDICTING CONSUMER BEHAVIOR[29]

There has been much discussion in recent years about the role of demographic factors as determinants or even correlates of consumption behavior of people. A number of researchers have expressed skepticism that such

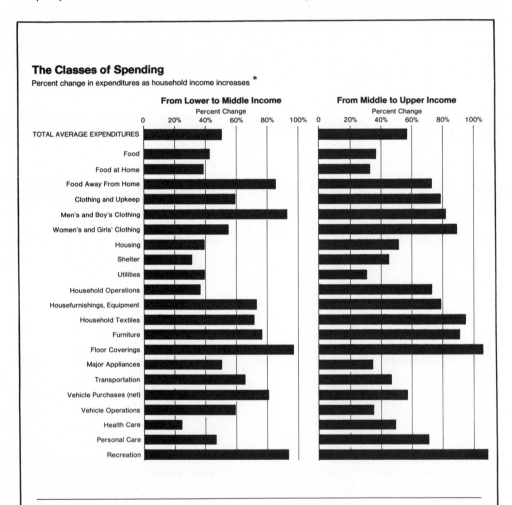

FIGURE 4-7
The classes of spending. (*Source:* U.S. Department of Labor, The Conference Board, in Fabian Linden, "Downstairs, Upstairs," *Across the Board,* October 1977, p. 59.)

*This chart shows the percent increase in spending for selected goods and services as household income increases. For example, as we move from the middle to the upper income brackets, total household expenditures for consumption rise by somewhat over 55%. Total spending for food, however, grows by about 35%, while outlays for recreation more than double. As defined in this presentation, "lower income" includes households in the $5,000–$10,000 earning bracket; "middle income," the $10,000–$20,000 bracket; and "upper income," the $20,000-and-over bracket. All data are based on a survey by the Bureau of Labor Statistics on consumer expenditures in the year 1973.

Sources: U.S. Department of Labor; The Conference Board

factors can be effectively used.[30] For example, there are some undeniable demographic patterns to purchase, such as that razor blades are purchased mainly for men. However, except for specific products aimed directly at specific demographic groups, evidence indicates that demographic measures, outside of education, are not an accurate predictor of consumer behavior.[31]

One limitation of demographics in explaining consumer behavior is based on the claim that while demographic factors may have been very relevant in the past (even up to World War II), they are now obsolete because of the narrowing differences in income, education, and occupational status. Nevertheless, there is much evidence showing that group differences among *categories* of income, education, and occupation are large and statistically significant in spite of a large number of within-group differences. It should also be noted that demographic factors include numerous other variables (such as age, sex, race, and religion) which are much less subject to influence from environmental change. For example, older people tend not to listen to rock music, per capita consumption of liquor is three times higher among blacks than whites, and Catholics still tend to use contraceptives much less than the rest of the population.

A second and more basic argument against demographics is that they have generally failed to explain and predict consumption behavior. However, although demographics have failed to explain brand-choice behavior, they seem to succeed in explaining buying behavior at the broad product class level of such items as durable appliances, automobiles, and housing. Thus, before demographics are abandoned because of their lackluster performance, it has been suggested that several past problems with demographic research be subjected to further study. These problems are mainly associated with techniques for measuring demographic variables, assumptions underlying their relationship to consumer behavior, inclusion of a small group of people in such studies who do not have a consistent pattern of behavior, and techniques of statistical analysis that are performed on the data.

Important reasons exist for the continued use of demographics in segmenting markets. First, they are easier to collect, easier to communicate to others, and often more reliable in measurement than many of the competing approaches to segmentation. Moreover, only through demographic factors is the researcher able to project results to the country's population, because the Bureau of the Census collects and updates only demographic profiles.

For these reasons, discarding demographics would seem to be premature. Instead, they should continue to be used as one element along with numerous other variables in the puzzle of explaining consumer behavior. In any event, demographics will continue to be used for projection, identification, and segmentation of markets as long as our census data are limited to a socioeconomic-demographic profile of citizens.

SUMMARY

In this chapter a large number of consumer characteristics have been presented. All of these consumer attributes were discussed within the framework of market segmentation; that is, an approach to selecting groups of homogeneous consumers as targets for marketing activity. Whereas market segmentation seeks to carve a large heterogeneous market into smaller, more uniform subsets, at the other end of the strategy spectrum—market aggregation—no subdivision of the market is applied. Most firms today follow a market segmentation approach. Furthermore, it was learned that in order for market segmentation to be effective the target group must be identifiable, measurable, accessible, substantial, and responsive.

With these criteria in mind, three alternative bases for segmentation were discussed: demographic, socioeconomic, and geographic. Major characteristics of American consumers were described within each of these categories. In addition, a number of marketing implications were suggested based upon these variables' influence on consumers' behavior.

Although socioeconomic-demographic variables are intuitively appealing and are widely available to marketers, their record as predictors of consumer behavior is not very strong. However, the problems in their use seem to be the result of a state-of-the-art limitation in analysis rather than a fundamental defect in their use. Consequently, they should continue to play an important role in segmentation efforts by marketers.

DISCUSSION TOPICS

1. Cite products (brands) in addition to those mentioned in the text that have followed a policy of market aggregation, concentrated marketing, and market atomization.

2. What are the benefits and costs of market segmentation?

3. Why are the following segmentation approaches or groups not very effective?
a. Segmenting a market on the basis of personality
b. Advertising to skeet shooters in *Time*
c. Developing an insurance plan for all quadruplets born in the United States

4. What are the major population changes taking place in the United States? What implications are there for the marketer of:
a. baby furniture
b. insurance
c. electronic products
d. sporting goods
e. food

5. Distinguish between SMSA and SCSA.

6. What are the directions of consumer movement? Discuss the implications of these trends to:
a. Allied Van Lines
b. Pizza Hut
c. J. C. Penney
d. General Electric

7. What products might effectively segment their market on the basis of education? occupation? income?

8. Find a recent article from *The Wall Street Journal, Business Week,* or *U.S. News & World Report,* and report on the current mood of consumers and their willingness to buy.

1. Burleigh Gardner and Sidney Levy, "The Product and the Brand," *Harvard Business Review,* **33**:37, March–April 1955.

2. Daniel Yankelovich, "New Criteria for Market Segmentation," *Harvard Business Review,* **42**:83–84, March–April 1964.

3. Ronald E. Frank, William F. Massy, and Yoram Wind, *Market Segmentation,* Prentice-Hall, Englewood Cliffs, N.J., 1972, pp. 7–11.

4. Frank, Massy, and Wind, *Market Segmentation,* p. 11.

5. James F. Engel, Henry F. Fiorillo, and Murray A. Cayley, *Market Segmentation: Concepts and Applications,* Holt, New York, 1972, p. 8.

6. "Those Missing Babies," *Time,* September 16, 1974, pp. 56, 61.

7. "How the Changing Age Mix Changes Markets," *Business Week,* January 12, 1976, p. 74.

8. This section is from "How the Changing Age Mix Changes Markets," pp. 74–75.

9. "Throwaway Marriages—Threat to the American Family," *U.S. News & World Report,* January 13, 1975, p. 43.

10. This section is drawn largely from "How the Changing Age Mix Changes Markets," pp. 74–78.

11. Samuel E. Krug and Raymond W. Kulhavy, "Personality Differences Across Regions of the United States," *The Journal of Social Psychology,* **91**:73–79, October 1973.

12. William J. Stanton, *Fundamentals of Marketing,* 4th ed., McGraw-Hill, New York, 1975, pp. 54, 56.

13. Fabian Linden, "A Decade of Suburban Growth," *The Conference Board Record,* September 1971, pp. 49–50.

14. "Out of the Cities, Back to the Country," *U.S. News & World Report,* March 31, 1976, p. 46.

15. "Keeping Up with Kresge," *Business Week,* October 19, 1974, pp. 72–73.

16. "The Nomadic American," *Time,* September 11, 1972, p. 39.

17. "Why Moving Day Comes Less Often Now for Executives," *U.S. News & World Report,* January 13, 1975, p. 53.

18. Linden, "A Decade of Suburban Growth," p. 52.

19. "The Immobile Society," *Time,* November 28, 1977, pp. 107–108.

20. Alan R. Andreasen, "Geographic Mobility and Market Segmentation," *Journal of Marketing Research,* **3**:345, November 1966.

21. See Andreasen, "Geographic Mobility," pp. 341–348, and James E. Bell, Jr., "Mobiles—A Neglected Market Segment," *Journal of Marketing,* **33**:37–44, April 1969.

22. James E. Bell, Jr., "Mobiles—A Possible Segment for Retailer Cultivation," *Journal of Retailing,* **46**:13–14, Fall 1970.

23. This section is from Fabian Linden, "The Degrees of Learning," *The Conference Board Record,* December 1973, pp. 42–46.

24. The terms "discretionary income" and "supernumerary income" were originated by the National Industrial Conference Board.

25. Fabian Linden, "Affluence and the Family," *The Conference Board Record,* October 1975, p. 49.

26. "Who Has the Wealth in America," *Business Week,* August 5, 1972, p. 54.

27. "How Good Are Consumer Pollsters?" *Business Week,* November 8, 1969, p. 108.

28. "How Good Are Consumer Pollsters?" p. 110.

29. Much of this section is based on Jagdish. N. Sheth, "Role of Demographics in Consumer Behavior," Faculty Working Papers, no. 218, College of Commerce and Business Administration, University of Illinois at Urbana-Champaign, November 20, 1974.

30. See, for example, Franklin B. Evans, "Psychological and Objective Factors in the Prediction of Brand Choice," *Journal of Business,* **33**:340–369, October 1959, and Arthur Koponen, "Personality Characteristics of Purchasers," *Journal of Advertising Research,* **1**:6–12, September 1960.

31. John C. Bieda and Harold W. Kassarjian, "An Overview of Market Segmentation," in Bernard A. Morin (ed.), *Marketing in a Changing World,* American Marketing Association, Chicago, 1969, p. 250.

MARKET SEGMENTATION: ADDITIONAL DIMENSIONS

PRODUCT-USAGE SEGMENTATION Technique of Product-Usage Segmentation; Applications of Product-Usage Segmentation **BENEFIT SEGMENTATION** Technique of Benefit Segmentation; Applications of Benefit Segmentation **LIFE-STYLE AND PSYCHOGRAPHIC SEGMENTATION** Technique of Life-Style Segmentation; Applications of Life-Style Segmentation; Benefits of Life-Style Segmentation **THE FUTURE OF MARKET SEGMENTATION**

This chapter enlarges on the discussion of the previous chapter by offering three additional dimensions by which markets may be segmented: (1) product usage, (2) perceived product benefits, and (3) life-style and psychographics. Each of these approaches offers the marketer a far richer understanding of market segments than was available with only a demographic, socioeconomic, or geographic understanding. However, these latter segmentation methods are still employed to obtain a more thorough portrait of potential target groups. The ultimate goal, certainly, is not just the definition of market segments but use of this information to develop marketing programs that appeal more strongly to chosen target groups.

PRODUCT-USAGE SEGMENTATION

Product-usage segmentation (also called *volume* segmentation) attempts to identify the "heavy users" of a product category. Marketers frequently advance the "20–80" thesis; that is, that 20 percent of the market account for 80 percent of sales of their product. Although the exact proportions may vary and the rule may not universally apply, it does indicate the importance of a relatively small group of consumers to the health of a firm's product or service.

Technique of Product-Usage Segmentation

Research has shown that purchase concentration is not always a simple function of obvious demographic factors such as income or household size. Thus, the marketer must measure consumption and identify the characteristics that are useful in distinguishing the various purchase intensities.

Frequently this is accomplished by dividing the market into heavy, light, and nonusers of the product and then examining their distinguishing characteristics. At one time this was an extremely difficult process for most companies, but today several marketing research organizations are able to provide such data. For example, Axiom Market Research Bureau, Inc., conducts periodic national studies of product usage, personal characteristics, and media habits of a sample of over 30,000 adults and 8000 teenagers. They regularly analyze 900 product categories and subcategories and publish Target Group Index (TGI) to assist the marketer in identifying potential audiences.

Figure 5-1 is based on analysis of household consumption data from a panel of *Chicago Tribune* newspaper subscribers and indicates the importance of the heavy user.

Notice in Figure 5-1 that relatively few households account for the bulk of sales in these products. For instance, 39 percent of the households purchase 90 percent of cola beverages, while an additional 39 percent of the households in the market account for only 10 percent of colas consumed. Also of importance is the finding that 22 percent of the market are nonusers of colas.

Applications of Product-Usage Segmentation

Target markets are often categorized in terms of their lucrativeness. This was the case with Quaker Oats Company when it segmented the market for its breakfast cereal Life, introduced in 1961. The firm determined that family size and age of the housewife were the two characteristics that distinguished intensity of product use. Consequently, Quaker ranked its target segments in the following hierarchy:

Families with above-average consumption ("extremely important" and "important" targets) were characterized by housewives under age 40, families of four or more members, in metropolitan areas of 50,000–500,000 population, with moderate incomes.

Families with average consumption ("average" targets) were characterized by housewives 40–49, living in cities of 2 million or more population.

Families with below-average consumption ("unimportant" and "very inferior" targets) were characterized by housewives 50 and over, less than four family members, low and high incomes, and small town or rural areas.[1]

It is probably for this reason that advertising for Life cereal (see Figure 5-2) often shows three children at the breakfast table, thus reflecting the large-family-size characteristics of their most important target segment.

Marketing efforts should not be exclusively aimed at heavy users until it has been determined that it is not feasible to convince nonusers and light users to increase their rate of purchase. Detailed analysis of these latter groups may also suggest effective marketing strategies. Of course, for many products, nonusers represent a significant marketing opportunity. Public goods and nonprofit-organization specialists are continually confronted with the reality of the need to convert nonusers to users. For example, consider the following marketing problems:

Convincing nonusing men and women to avail themselves of cancer checkups

Attracting nonriders to mass transportation

Attracting nonsubscribers to symphonies, lectures, and other cultural events

Each of these problems represents a marketing opportunity to convert nonusers to users. Obviously, the past rate of success for such projects has not been great; but with increased application of marketing research to understanding the motivations of various market segments, greater success should occur in the future.

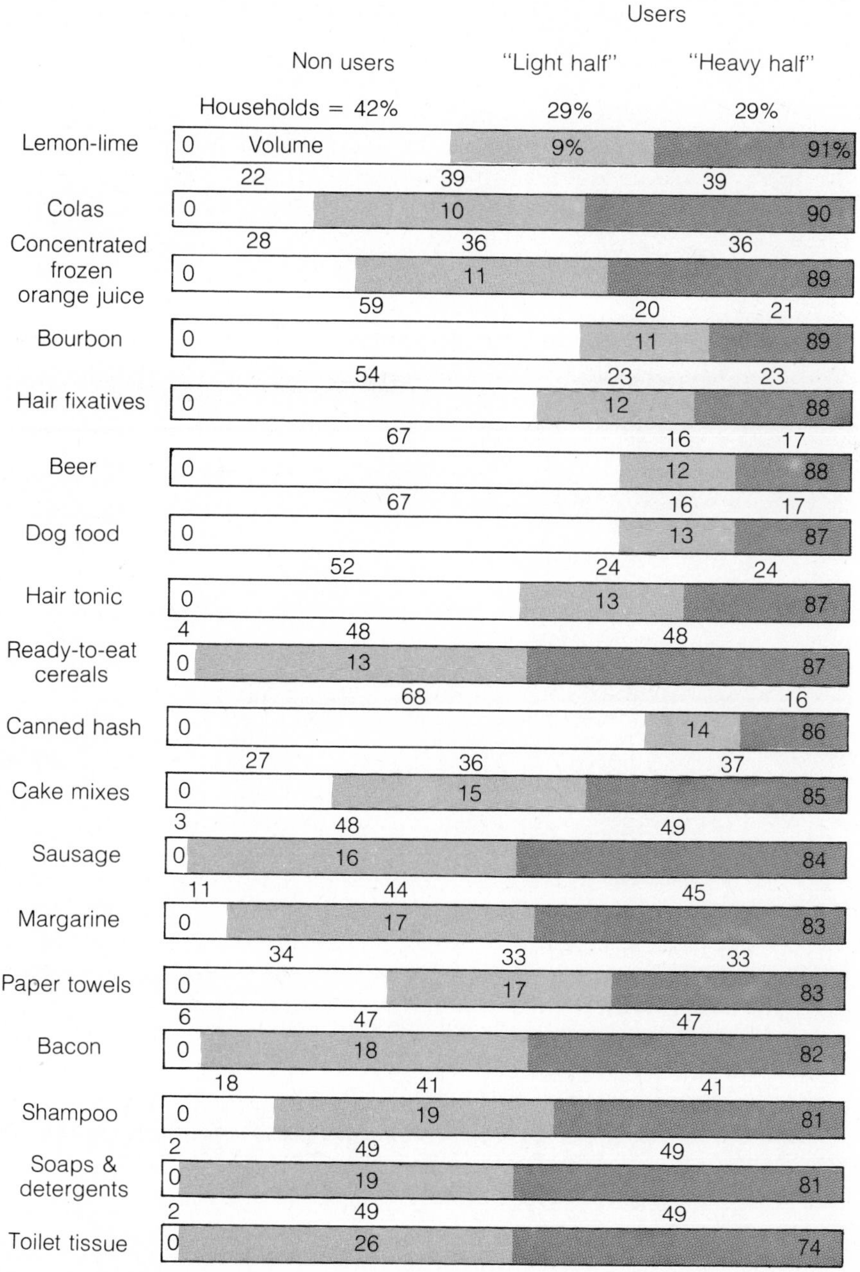

	Non users	Users "Light half"	"Heavy half"
Households =	42%	29%	29%
Lemon-lime	0 Volume	9%	91%
	22	39	39
Colas	0	10	90
	28	36	36
Concentrated frozen orange juice	0	11	89
	59	20	21
Bourbon	0	11	89
	54	23	23
Hair fixatives	0	12	88
	67	16	17
Beer	0	12	88
	67	16	17
Dog food	0	13	87
	52	24	24
Hair tonic	0	13	87
	4	48	48
Ready-to-eat cereals	0	13	87
	68		16
Canned hash	0	14	86
	27	36	37
Cake mixes	0	15	85
	3	48	49
Sausage	0	16	84
	11	44	45
Margarine	0	17	83
	34	33	33
Paper towels	0	17	83
	6	47	47
Bacon	0	18	82
	18	41	41
Shampoo	0	19	81
	2	49	49
Soaps & detergents	0	19	81
	2	49	49
Toilet tissue	0	26	74

FIGURE 5-1
The "heavy user": annual purchase concentration in eighteen product categories. (*Source:* Reprinted from Dik Warren Twedt, "How Important to Marketing Strategy is the 'Heavy User'?" *Journal of Marketing,* **28**:72, January 1964, published by the American Marketing Association.)

One of the real attractions of the usage approach to market segmentation is the ease with which the technique can be employed by so many firms. Most companies are able to segment consumers by usage rates because of access to marketing-research services and data processing systems that can quickly categorize and analyze consumers by purchase activity. Thus, department stores are able to analyze charge account customers' purchases with

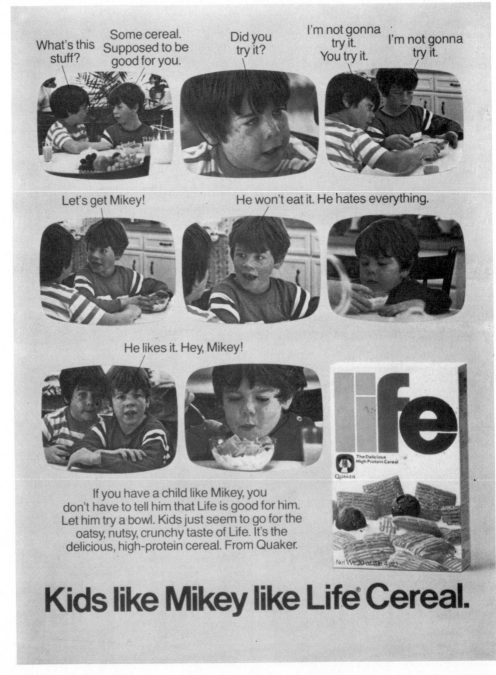

FIGURE 5-2
Example of advertisement for Life cereal aimed at heavy users. (Courtesy of The Quaker Oats Co.)

regularity; banks can assess their customers' banking usage; and as mentioned previously, many packaged-consumer-goods firms can subscribe to syndicated services to provide the same usage information.

BENEFIT SEGMENTATION

The approaches to market segmentation discussed so far are all helpful to the marketer. However, they suffer from an underlying disadvantage—all are based on an ex-post facto analysis of the kinds of people who make up specific segments of a market. That is, emphasis is on *describing* the characteristics of different segments rather than on learning what *causes* these segments to develop. However, proponents of benefit segmentation claim that the *benefits* that people are seeking are the basic reason for purchase and therefore the proper basis for market segmentation.[2]

Technique of Benefit Segmentation

The first step in benefit segmentation is to obtain detailed information on consumer value systems. This is typically accomplished by having a representative sample of consumers rate the importance of those benefits or values they seek in the product. Certainly most people would like as many benefits as possible. However, the *relative* importance they attach to individual benefits can differ significantly and thus be used as an effective technique in segmenting markets.

Although the concept appears simple, its implementation is very complex, requiring computers and sophisticated multivariate attitude-measurement techniques. The statistical methods employed relate the responses of each consumer to those of every other respondent and then develop clusters (typically three to seven segments) of consumers with similar rating patterns. Each of these segments represents a potentially profitable and different opportunity for marketing effort.

Applications of Benefit Segmentation

Three examples of benefit segmentation are presented below: cameras, toothpastes, and watches.

CAMERA BENEFITS First, consider a benefit segmentation of the under-$50 camera market resulting in the identification of consumer characteristics listed in Table 5-1.

This table shows that three segments exist, labeled "do-it-yourselfers," "black-box users," and "timid photographers." From an analysis of the benefits sought by these groups, the marketer is able to recognize product opportunities. For example, the do-it-yourself market for under-$50 cameras does not appear to be adequately satisfied, as evidenced by the lack of inexpensive cameras equipped with full settings and adjustments. This may represent a strong marketing opportunity for the innovative firm. The remaining segments, however, are presently being served with a variety of product alternatives, such as the inexpensive Kodak Instamatic and low-priced Polaroid and Kodak instant-picture cameras.

Segmentation along benefit lines can also be used to develop appropriate marketing strategies. For example, consider the use of benefits for develop-

TABLE 5-1

A BENEFIT SEGMENTATION OF THE UNDER-$50 CAMERA MARKET

The "Do-It-Yourselfer" (25 percent)
  Great pride in good pictures
  Gratification from making settings and adjustments
  Pride in a complex camera
The "Black-Box User" (40 percent)
  Taking pictures seen only as a necessary evil
  Little pride expressed if the picture is good
  Desire for camera to be as simple as possible
The "Timid Photographer" (35 percent)
  Great pride in good pictures
  High perceived risk that the picture will not be good
  No confidence in ability to manipulate camera and settings
  Desires camera to guarantee a good picture without his effort

Source: James F. Engel, Henry F. Fiorillo, and Murray A. Cayley (eds.), *Market Segmentation: Concepts and Applications.* Copyright © 1972 by Holt, Rinehart and Winston, New York, p. 18. Reprinted by permission of Holt, Rinehart and Winston.

ing advertising copy. Appeals to timid photographers could demonstrate that the user needs only to "aim and shoot."[3] In fact, this is precisely the copy approach that the Polaroid OneStep instant camera uses in its advertising.

TOOTHPASTE BENEFITS Table 5-2 presents information based on results of an actual benefit-segmentation study of the toothpaste market. The upper portion of the table describes four distinct benefit segments as discerned by market researchers. In addition, the table also presents supplementary information valuable to the marketer in understanding these consumer segments: demographic, behavioral, and personality characteristics.

Research has shown that the brands heavily favored by the *Sensory* segment are Colgate and Stripe while the *Sociables* prefer such brands as Ultra Brite and Close-up. The *Worriers* favor Crest, and *Independents* look for brands on sale. Sometimes a new brand attempts to straddle more than one segment, as in the case with Aim, which was introduced by Lever Brothers, apparently to attract both the sensory and the worrier segments.

From this type of information the marketer is able to develop a strategy tailored to each segment based on the benefits they seek. The lower portion of Table 5-2 indicates the promotional and packaging strategies that might be recommended for each group.

WATCHES A final illustration of value or benefit segmentation is drawn from the market for watches. Research identified three distinct groups, characterized as the *economy* segment, the *durability and quality* segment, and the *symbolic* segment, which were seeking different benefits as described below:[4]

Economy segment—This group wants to pay the lowest possible price for a watch that works reasonably well. If it fails within a year, they will replace it. (23 percent of buyers)

Durability and quality segment—This group wants a watch with a long life, good material, and styling. They are willing to pay a higher price for these qualities. (46 percent of buyers)

Symbolic segment—This group wants useful product features and meaningful emotional qualities. The watch should suitably symbolize an important occasion. Here, a well-known brand name, fine styling, a gold or diamond case, and a jeweler's recommendation are important. (31 percent of buyers)

In the late 1950s most watch companies were oriented almost exclusively

TABLE 5-2

TOOTHPASTE MARKET SEGMENT DESCRIPTION

		Segment name			
		The Sensory Segment	The Sociables	The Worriers	The Independent Segment
Segment characteristics	Principal benefit sought:	Flavor, product appearance	Brightness of Teeth	Decay prevention	Price
	Demographic strengths:	Children	Teens, young people	Large families	Men
	Special behavioral characteristics:	Users of spearmint flavored toothpaste	Smokers	Heavy users	Heavy users
	Personality characteristics:	High self-involvement	High sociability	High hypochondriasis	High autonomy
	Life-style characteristics:	Hedonistic	Active	Conservative	Value-oriented
Selected marketing recommendations	Copy tone:	Light	Light	Serious	Rational two-sided arguments. Stress price, product superiority.
	Copy depth-of-sell:	Superficial and mood oriented. Shorter commercial, higher frequency	Superficial and mood oriented. Shorter commercial, higher frequency	Intensive. Longer commercials, e.g., 60-second ads	Intensive. Longer commercials, e.g., 60 second ads
	Copy setting:	Focus on product.	Socially oriented situations		Demonstration and competitive comparison
	Media environment:	Youthful, modern, active; heavy use of TV	Youthful, modern, active; heavy use of TV	Serious; heavy use of print	Serious; heavy use of print
	Packaging:	Colorful	Gleaming white (to indicate white teeth)	Aqua (to indicate fluoride)	

Source: Adapted from Russell I. Haley, "Benefit Segmentation: A Decision-oriented Research Tool," *Journal of Marketing,* **32:**33, July 1968, published by the American Marketing Association.

on the third segment, thus leaving the major portion of the market open. Consequently, U.S. Time Company introduced a new low-priced watch, the Timex, and established a very strong position among buyers in the first two segments.

These three examples cite the advantage of benefit segmentation. The greatest difficulty in applying the approach exists in choosing the benefit to be emphasized. For example, the company must be certain that buyers' stated motives are their real motives for purchase, which is not an easy task because of the complexity of human motivation. Consequently, the number of consumers in each benefit segment is difficult to estimate; moreover, the proportions shift over time, presenting further complications. Thus, considerable research is needed to ascertain product benefits and the size of consumer segments for each.[5]

LIFE-STYLE AND PSYCHOGRAPHIC SEGMENTATION

An advertising executive recently stated: "I've never seen a time when there has been so great a difference between groups in the same demographic limits."[6] As this suggests, one of the major problems of demographic segmentation is its lack of "richness" in describing consumers for market segmentation and strategy development. It lacks color, texture, and dimensionality when describing consumers and often needs to be supplemented by something that fills in the bare statistical picture. Consequently, many firms are looking for a better way to define markets. One of the newest, most exciting, and promising approaches to selecting target markets is *life-style* and *psychographic segmentation.* Although the concepts of life-style and psychographics are often used interchangeably, they are not equivalent but are complementary.

The term "life-style" is not new, but its application to marketing has been rather recent. Alfred Adler coined the phrase "style of life" over 50 years ago to refer to the goal a person shapes for himself, and the ways he uses to reach it. From our perspective, life-style can be viewed as a unique pattern of living which influences and is reflected by one's consumption behavior.[7] Therefore, the way in which marketers facilitate the expression of an individual's life-style is by "providing customers with parts of a potential mosaic from which they, as artists of their own life-styles, can pick and choose to develop the composition that for the time seems best."[8]

Many products today are "life-style" products, that is, they portray a style of life sought by potential users. Revlon's Charlie perfume, for example, is a product women buy more to *live* like Charlie (a young, kicky, unmarried working girl who enjoys life—the ideal liberated woman) than to *look* or *smell* like her.[9] A Charlie advertisement is shown in Figure 5-3.

How does the concept of psychographics relate to life-style? Unfortunately, it is not an easy matter to define psychographics because there is no general agreement as to exactly what it is. One of the more precise statements about its nature is the following: *psychographics* is the systematic use of relevant activity, interest, and opinion constructs to quantitatively explore and explain the communicating, purchasing, and consuming behaviors of persons for brands, products, and clusters of products.[10]

Thus, psychographics may be viewed as the method of defining life-style in measurable terms. The basic premise underlying life-style research is that the more marketers understand their customers the more effectively they can communicate and market to them.[11] In many cases the primary targets of such marketing efforts are heavy users. Heavy users have traditionally been looked at demographically; but by incorporating life-style characteristics the marketer obtains a better, more true-to-life picture of such customers.

A most original fragrance.

Charlie

The gorgeous, sexy-young fragrance. By Revlon.

Concentrated Cologne • Concentrated Cologne Spray • Concentrated Perfume Spray
Fragranced Bath Soap • Body Silk • Perfumed Dusting Powder

FIGURE 5-3
Example of "life-style" advertising for Charlie perfume. (Courtesy of Revlon.)

Technique of Life-Style Segmentation

Life-style-segmentation research measures (1) how people spend their time engaging in activities, (2) what is of most interest or importance to them in their immediate surroundings, and (3) their opinions and views about themselves and the world around them. Together, these three areas are generally referred to as *Activities, Interests, and Opinions,* or simply *AIOs.* Table 5-3 indicates the life-style dimensions (particularly AIOs) that may be investigated among consumers.

In a typical large-scale, life-style research project, questionnaires are mailed to members of a nationwide consumer panel. The questionnaires solicit traditional demographic information, average usage rates for as many as 100 different products, media habits, and respondents' activities, interests, and opinions. Approximately 300 AIO statements may be included, to which respondents indicate the extent of their agreement or disagreement on six-point scales ranging from "definitely disagree" to "definitely agree." The following illustrates the nature of typical AIO statements employed:

I like gardening.

I do not get enough sleep.

I enjoy going to concerts.

A news magazine is more interesting than a fiction magazine.

There should be a gun in every home.

Instant coffee is more economical than ground coffee.

I stay home most evenings.

There is a lot of love in our family.[12]

Where do AIO items originate? They may come from intuition, hunches, conversations, research, reading, and group or individual in-depth interviews.[13]

Armed with these three sets of data (AIOs, demographics, and product

TABLE 5-3

LIFE-STYLE DIMENSIONS

Activities	Interests	Opinions	Demographics
Work	Family	Themselves	Age
Hobbies	Home	Social issues	Education
Social events	Job	Politics	Income
Vacation	Community	Business	Occupation
Entertainment	Recreation	Economics	Family size
Club membership	Fashion	Education	Dwelling
Community	Food	Products	Geography
Shopping	Media	Future	City size
Sports	Achievements	Culture	Stage in life cycle

Source: Reprinted from Joseph T. Plummer, "The Concept and Application of Life Style Segmentation," *Journal of Marketing,* **38**:34, January 1974, published by the American Marketing Association.

usage), the marketer constructs user profiles. The analysis involves relating levels of agreement on all AIO items with the levels of usage on a product and with demographic characteristics. Typically, a pattern emerges in which AIO statements cluster together; that is, similar respondents are grouped together from a life-style perspective.[14] For example, a major study by Needham, Harper & Steers advertising agency was able to categorize almost 3300 respondents into ten different life-style types—five female and five male.[15] To help clients understand the life-style data, the ten consumer composites were even given names as shown in Exhibit 5-1.

EXHIBIT 5-1

PSYCHOGRAPHIC PROFILES

The Female Segments

Thelma, the old-fashioned traditionalist (25%)
This lady has lived a "good" life—she has been a devoted wife, a doting mother, and a conscientious housewife. She has lived her life by these traditional values and she cherishes them to this day. She does not condone contemporary sexual activities or political liberalism, nor can she sympathize with the women's libbers. Even today, when most of her children have left home, her life is centered around the kitchen. Her one abiding interest outside the household is the church which she attends every week. She lacks higher education and hence has little appreciation for the arts or cultural activities. Her spare time is spent watching TV, which is her prime source of entertainment and information.

Mildred, the militant mother (20%)
Mildred married young and had children before she was quite ready to raise a family. Now she is unhappy. She is having trouble making ends meet on her blue-collar husband's income. She is frustrated and she vents her frustrations by rebelling against the system. She finds escape from her unhappy world in soap operas and movies. Television provides an ideal medium for her to live out her fantasies. She watches TV all through the day and into late night. She likes heavy rock and probably soul music, and she doesn't read much except escapist magazines such as True Story.

Candice, the chic suburbanite (20%)
Candice is an urbane woman. She is well educated and genteel. She is a prime mover in her community, active in club affairs and working on community projects. Socializing is an important part of her life. She is a doer, interested in sports and the outdoors, politics and current affairs. Her life is hectic and lived at a fast clip. She is a voracious reader, and there are few magazines she doesn't read. However, TV does relatively poorly in competing for her attention—it is too inane for her.

Cathy, the contented housewife (18%)
Cathy epitomizes simplicity. Her life is untangled. She is married to a worker in the middle of the socioeconomic scale, and they, along with their several preteen children, live in a small town. She is devoted to her family and faithfully serves them as mother, housewife, and cook. There is a certain tranquility in her life. She enjoys a relaxed pace and avoids anything that might disturb her equilibrium. She doesn't like news or news-type programs on TV but enjoys the wholesome family entertainment provided by Walt Disney, The Waltons, and Happy Days.

Eleanor, the elegant socialite (17%)
Eleanor is a woman with style. She lives in the city because that is where she wants to be. She likes the economic and social aspects of big city living and takes advantage of the

102

UNDERSTANDING
CONSUMERS
AND MARKET
SEGMENTS

EXHIBIT 5-1 (continued)

city in terms of her career and leisure time activities. She is a self-confident on-the-go woman, not a homebody. She is fashion-conscious and dresses well. She is a woman with panache. She is financially secure; as a result she is not a careful shopper. She shops for quality and style, not price. She is a cosmopolitan woman who has traveled abroad or wants to.

The Male Segments

Herman, the retiring homebody (26%)
Herman is past his prime and is not getting any younger. His attitudes and opinions on life, which are often in conflict with modern trends, have gelled. And he is resistant to change. He is old-fashioned and conservative. He was brought up on "motherhood and apple pie" and cherishes these values. Consequently he finds the attitudes of young people today disturbing. He realizes he cannot affect any change, and has withdrawn into a sheltered existence of his own within the confines of his home and its surroundings. Here he lives a measured life. He goes to church regularly, watches his diet, and lives frugally. He longs for the good old days and regrets that the world around him is changing.

Scott, the successful professional (21%)
Scott is a man who has everything going for him. He is well educated, cosmopolitan, the father of a young family, and is already established in his chosen profession. He lives a fast-paced active life and likes it. He is a man getting ahead in the world. He lives in or near an urban center and seems to like what a big city has to offer—culture, learning opportunities, and people. He also enjoys sports, the out-of-doors, and likes to keep physically fit. He is understandably happy with his life and comfortable in his life style.

Fred, the frustrated factory worker (19%)
Fred is young. He married young and had a family. It is unlikely that he had any plans to get a college degree; if he did, he had to shelve them to find work to support his family. He now is a blue-collar worker having trouble making ends meet. He is discontented, and tends to feel that "they"—big business, government, society—are somehow responsible for his state. He finds escape in movies and in fantasies of foreign lands and cabins by quiet lakes. He likes to appear attractive to women, has an active libido, and likes to think he is a bit of a swinger.

Dale, the devoted family man (17%)
Dale is a wholesome guy with a penchant for country living. He is a blue-collar worker, with a high school education. The father of a relatively large family, he prefers a traditional marriage, with his wife at home taking care of the kids. His home and neighborhood are central in his life. He is an easygoing guy who leads an uncomplicated life. Neither worry nor skepticism are a part of him. He is relaxed and has a casual approach to many things. He is a happy, trusting soul who takes things as they are.

Ben, the self-made businessman (17%)
Ben is the epitomy of a self-made man. He was probably not born wealthy, nor had he the benefit of higher education, but through hard work and shrewd risk-taking he has built himself a decent life. He has seen the system work. He believes if you work hard and play by the rules you will get your share (and perhaps some more). Therefore he cannot condone hippies and other fringe groups whom he sees as freeloaders. He embraces conservative ideology and is likely to be a champion of business interests. He is a traditionalist at home, and believes it is a woman's job to look after the home and to raise a family. He is gregarious and enjoys giving and attending parties. And he likes to drink.

Source: Reprinted from Sunil Mehrotra and William D. Wells, "Psychographics and Buyer Behavior: Theory and Recent Empirical Findings," in Arch G. Woodside, Jagdish N. Sheth, and Peter D. Bennett (eds.), *Consumer and Industrial Buying Behavior*, Elsevier North-Holland, New York; 1977, pp. 54–55.

Generally, then, the process of life-style segmentation involves two steps. First, a determination is made of which life-style segments will efficiently produce the greatest number of profitable customers. Often heavy users are sought; but as we have seen, other segments also have potential. The second step involves defining and describing the selected target customers in more depth to understand how they may be attracted and communicated with more efficiently and relevantly.[16]

Applications of Life-Style Segmentation

Three examples of life-style segmentation are described below. The situations range from fast-food retailing to product and promotional development for Irish Spring soap and Schlitz beer.

CARRY-OUT FRIED CHICKEN[17] Consider the case of the ready-to-eat, carry-out fried chicken consumer (RECFC), a market that is heavily dominated by the Kentucky Fried Chicken chain of drive-in restaurants.

An attempt was made to describe heavy users of this product, who were defined as women who purchased the chicken at least once a month. They were found to differ from nonusers in terms of their demographic profile and products they consumed. Demographically, heavy users were found to be young and working full-time; with slightly more children than the sample average but total family income significantly higher than the sample average; and not high on the scale educationally or occupationally.

Heavy users of RECFC were also found to be heavy users of eye makeup, nail polish, perfume and cologne, regular soft drinks, chewing gum and candy, gasoline, new shoes, and a wide range of convenience foods, a product set that fits the description of a young homemaker.

The life-style profile presented in Table 5-4 goes further to characterize the psychographic pattern of consumers of this product. This woman is very contemporary, active, impressed with doing and buying the right things and not willing to center her life around her family and home.

As an example of marketing strategy implications that may be drawn from such demographic and psychographic data, the following recommendations were suggested for fast-food retailers of fried chicken:

1. This product could be sold on credit through bank charge cards, American Express, gasoline cards, and others.

2. Outlets might consider adding such products as soft drinks, frozen foods, and party snack chips to their line, should display space permit it.

3. The concept of a friendly, informal atmosphere should be maintained.

4. Promotions for outlets could be tied in with bowling alleys, beauty parlors, dress shops, etc.

5. Promotions should not necessarily stress price-off coupons, since heavy users do not appear to be price-conscious.

6. Because the convenience factor is important, home-delivery service might be considered. It is not clear whether a move toward sit-in style restaurants and away from drive-ins would be appropriate.

TABLE 5-4

THE CARRY-OUT FRIED CHICKEN USER PROFILE: PERCENTAGE OF NON- AND HEAVY USERS WHO GENERALLY OR DEFINITELY AGREE WITH EACH AIO QUESTION

Life Style (AIO) Questions	Never use (N = 201)	Use once a month or more (N = 138)
The Swinging Party-Goer		
I like parties where there is lots of music and talk	31%*	49%
I like to think I am a bit of a swinger	17	37
I do more things socially than do most of my friends	16	31
I like to do things that are bright, gay, and exciting	38	48
Not a Homebody in a Rut		
I am a homebody	66	50
Our days seem to follow a definite routine such as eating meals at a regular time, etc.	72	55
I would like to have a maid to do the housework	25	42
Optimistic Mobiles		
My greatest achievements are still ahead of me	34	55
Five years from now, the family income will probably be a lot higher than it is now	37	69
I will probably have more money to spend next year than I have now	38	62
We will probably move once in the next five years	22	40
Fashion and Personal Appearance Conscious		
I often try the latest hairdo styles when they change	10	27
I would like to be a fashion model	15	30†
Women wear too much makeup these days	53	39
I like to feel attractive to men	36	55
I like the natural color of my hair	67	41
Credit, Borrowing, and Investment		
I buy many things with a credit card or charge card	30	45
In the past year, we have borrowed money from a bank or finance company	28	41†
I like to pay cash for everything I buy	65	48
Investing in the stock market is too risky for most families	56	44
I find myself checking the prices in the grocery store even for small items	75	57
Influential, New Brand Buyer, Information Seeker		
I often try new brands before my friends and neighbors do	46%	70%
I sometimes influence what my friends buy	23	33
My neighbors usually give me pretty good advice on what brands to buy in the grocery store	41	65
I like to be considered a leader	17	31
Convenience Foods, Casual Shopping		
I never go shopping in shorts or slacks	48	25‡

TABLE 5-4 (continued)

105

MARKET
SEGMENTATION:
ADDITIONAL
DIMENSIONS

Life Style (AIO) Questions	Never use (N = 201)	Use once a month or more (N = 138)
A good mother will not serve her family TV dinners	31	21
I depend on canned food at least one meal a day	41	58
I use Metrecal or other diet foods at least one meal a day	23	35
Signs of Middle-Class America		
I buy many things at Sears Roebuck or Montgomery Ward	47	67†
Every family should have a dog	39	57
I thoroughly enjoy conversations about sports	16	26
I like bowling	29	45
I would rather live in or near a big city than in or near a small town	31	52

*31 percent of those respondents who never purchase at carry-out fried chicken restaurants generally or definitely agreed they like parties where there is lots of music and talk.
†Percent who moderately, generally, and definitely agreed rather than just generally or definitely agreed.
‡Definitely agreed only.
Source: Douglas J. Tigert, Richard Lathrope, and Michael Bleeg, "The Fast Food Franchise: Psychographic and Demographic Segmentation Analysis," *Journal of Retailing,* **47:** 86–87, Spring 1971. Reproduced by permission of *Journal of Retailing,* New York University.

7. Advertising themes might stress the working mother, youth, families, parties, convenience, optimism, informality, and quality.[18]

The finding that these women were active, self-indulgent, inclined to be swingers, and interested in quality more than price fostered a creative strategy at Kentucky Fried Chicken aimed at convenience but stressing quality. Many of the company's advertisements have also focused on creating a cheerful, exciting store image which is consistent with the image many of these consumers appear to have of themselves.

SCHLITZ[19] Another case involves the use of life-style research to develop a national advertising campaign for Schlitz beer. Prior to 1969 Schlitz had been running a successful ad campaign formulated around the copy line of "When you're out of Schlitz, you're out of beer." There was a general feeling that a new, fresh approach was needed. The advertising director visited neighborhood taverns to observe and talk with target customers—heavy beer drinkers. In addition, one element emerged from past Schlitz advertising—the word "gusto." Research showed it to have strong connotations, conveying relevant meanings about beer, taste, and life, and it also turned out to be "owned" by Schlitz. Another element emerging from the review process was that Schlitz is sold almost everywhere in the world—in fact, the world was used as a symbol on the label.

The "tavern tour" of the advertising director yielded the following informal life-style portrait of the heavy beer drinker as:

. . . the man who belongs to the 20 percent of the population that drinks 80 percent of the beer. A man who drinks a case a weekend or even a case a day. . . . He is a guy who is not making it and probably never will. He is a dreamer, a wisher, a limited edition of Walter Mitty. He is a sports nut because he is a hero worshipper. . . . He goes to the tavern and has six or seven beers with the boys. . . . If we are to talk to this man where he lives, in terms he respects and can identify with, we must find for him a believable kind of hero he inwardly admires.[20]

Next, formal research on the life style of the heavy beer drinker was completed as shown in Table 5-5.

It was found that the heavy user:

—had a middle-class income level derived primarily from blue-collar occupations

—was young with at least a high school education

—was more hedonistic and pleasure-seeking toward life than the nondrinker

—had less regard toward family and job responsibilities than nondrinkers

—had a preference for a physical/male-oriented existence and was inclined to fantasize

—had a great enjoyment of drinking, particularly beer, which was seen as a real man's drink

Using the life-style portrait of the heavy beer drinker, it was decided that the "gusto man, and gusto life" approach would strongly appeal to the heavy user's sense of masculinity, hedonism, and fantasy. From this research Schlitz built an ad campaign around imagery of the sea to glamorize the adventure of seamen who lived their lives with gusto and enjoyed a "gusto brew." (See Figure 5-4.) The copy for the ads stated, "You only go around once in life. So grab for all the gusto you can."

IRISH SPRING[21] Between 1958 and 1970, Colgate introduced eleven bar soaps into test markets, but not one of them was successful enough to reach national distribution. Up to that time Colgate had been categorizing users into two basic functional segments—a complexion segment and a deodorant segment. There was no real understanding of why persons bought a particular brand of soap, that is, of how consumers perceived that a soap influences their roles in life and their expectations of physical benefits.

Colgate undertook a psychographic segmentation study and uncovered three clearly defined consumer groups—*independents, rejuvenators,* and *compensators*—with the following characteristics:

Independents—Forceful leaders concerned about getting ahead, confident, self-assured, calm and unflappable, practical, realistic, rugged, and self-reliant people who don't pamper themselves

Rejuvenators—Outward-directed, basically insecure people who need the social reassurance of those around them

Compensators—Inward-directed, passive, and withdrawn people

TABLE 5-5

107

MARKET
SEGMENTATION:
ADDITIONAL
DIMENSIONS

MALE BEER DRINKERS

	Percentage of Agreement		
	Nonusers	Light users	Heavy users
He is self-indulgent, enjoys himself, and likes risks			
I like to play poker	18	37	41
I like to take chances	27	32	44
I would rather spend a quiet evening at home than go out to a party	67	53	44
If I had my way, I would own a convertible	7	11	15
I smoke too much	29	40	42
If I had to choose I would rather have a color TV than a new refrigerator	25	33	38
He rejects responsibility and is a bit impulsive			
I like to work on community projects	24	18	14
I have helped collect money for the Red Cross or United Fund	41	32	24
I'm not very good at saving money	20	29	38
I find myself checking prices, even for small items	51	42	40
He likes sports and a physical orientation			
I would like to be a pro football player	10	15	21
I like bowling	32	36	42
I usually read the sports page	47	48	59
I would do better than average in a fist fight	17	26	32
I like war stories	33	37	45
He rejects old fashioned institutions and moral guidelines			
I go to church regularly	57	37	31
Movies should be censored	67	46	43
I have old-fashioned tastes and habits	69	56	48
There is too much emphasis on sex today	71	59	53
- - - - and has a very masculine view			
Beer is a real man's drink	9	16	44
Playboy is one of my favorite magazines	11	21	28
I am a girl watcher	33	47	54
Men should not do the dishes	18	26	38
Men are smarter than women	22	27	31

Source: Reprinted from Joseph T. Plummer, "Life Style and Advertising: Case Studies," in Fred C. Allvine (ed.), *Combined Proceedings 1971 Spring and Fall Conferences,* American Marketing Association, Chicago; 1971, p. 294, published by the American Marketing Association.

In terms of soap preferences, the Independents were on one end of the spectrum, oriented toward cleaning and refreshment in a toilet soap, while Compensators were on the other end, desiring luxury and comfort in the bath. Independents were found to have a disproportionate number of men and were shown to be a group ready for something new and fresh in bar-soap benefits. They wanted a long-lasting, hard soap that would keep them clean, fresh, and odor-free and could be used by the whole family.

To fulfill the needs of this vacant market niche, Colgate assessed many possibilities for product name, shape, color, and scent which best fulfilled the concept of a deodorant soap for men yet would be mild enough for the rest of the family. Emerging from this search was the product Irish Spring

FIGURE 5-4
Life-style advertisement for Schlitz beer. (Courtesy of Jos. Schlitz Brewing Co.)

with an advertising appeal aimed primarily at men. Sean, the ads' rugged-looking, self-assured spokesman, matched the Independents' characteristics (see Figure 5-5). However, in order to broaden the appeal to the household purchasing agent, women were also brought into the commercial with the selling phrase, "Manly, yes, but I like it too." In addition, the Irish setting for

IRISH SPRING

COLGATE-PALMOLIVE CO. CLIS 1100 "ARM WRESTLERS" (:30)

(SFX: GRUNTS, CROWD CHEERING)

SEAN: You're a strong man, John.
GAL: Aye!

JOHN: A mite stronger than I care to be.

SEAN: Then shower up with Irish Spring.

JOHN: Ah, the double deodorant soap.

SEAN: For long lastin' protection.

MUSIC UNDER) SEAN: (VO) Look. In hese green and white stripes...

(SFX: SHOWER) ...are 2 deodorants. That means long lastin' protection.

JOHN: What a fine fresh smell.

GAL: That's why I use it, too.

SEAN: Irish Spring with 2 deodorants.

(VO) For long lastin' deodorant protection.

FIGURE 5-5
Life-style advertisement for Irish Spring. (Courtesy of Colgate-Palmolive Co.)

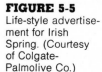

the advertisements created a sense of outdoors and freshness. Three years after national introduction Irish Spring was the third leading bar soap on the market.

Benefits of Life-Style Segmentation

Life-style segmentation has been the object of increasing research and application in marketing because of its potential benefits. The examples presented above are good testimony of the technique's ability to assist the development of marketing strategy. Thus, the marketing manager may be able to develop improved multidimensional views of key target segments, uncover new product opportunities, obtain better product position, develop improved advertising communications based on a richer, more lifelike portrait of the target consumer, and generally improve overall marketing strategies.[22]

There are additional benefits of psychographics that are being realized by consumer-behavior researchers who tend to have a more esoteric view than does the practicing marketer. For these researchers, psychographic methods are leading to enhanced general knowledge of consumer behavior in at least three ways. First, they have contributed to a better understanding of numerous consumer behavior facets such as opinion leadership, retail shopping, private-brands buying, consumerist activism, and other attributes. Second, with the repetition of studies, trend data may be accumulated to show how consumers may be changing. Third, general segmentations of consumer groups are creating new typologies for more efficiently describing and understanding consumer behavior.

Thus the result of psychographic research findings such as those presented here may lead marketers to think routinely in terms of segments marked off by common sets of activities, interests, needs, and values and to develop products, services, and media schedules specifically to meet them.[23]

THE FUTURE OF MARKET SEGMENTATION

The various bases for segmenting markets discussed in this and the previous chapter have underscored the need to understand consumers. Each segmentation approach has merit, and although not all have exhibited ability to predict consumers' purchasing habits, they do enable marketers to understand better their target markets. With enhanced understanding comes the ability to develop more tailored marketing programs.

The great deal of attention and interest generated by the concept of market segmentation is sure to become even more significant in the future. Three environmental factors are expected to lead to this growth. First, the advance of the consumerism movement will foster market segmentation, since critics have pointed to segments they believe are neglected in our present system. The result of pressures such as these is to cause managers to become more attentive to previously unrecognized consumer needs.

A second factor encouraging market segmentation is intensified competition. With the increasingly competitive markets (both domestic and worldwide) of the future, business people will seek untapped segments in order to gain an advantage over rivals.

The third factor stimulating market segmentation is the growing awareness of nonbusiness applications of the technique. It will be increasingly utilized for marketing in nontraditional areas such as politics, religion, and public issues.[24]

SUMMARY

In this chapter some newer approaches to market segmentation were presented. Traditional approaches, however, are still incorporated in these techniques because marketers must have demographic, geographic, and socioeconomic information about any segments chosen if they are to market effectively to them.

The thrust of this chapter has been to suggest techniques that may provide a richer portrait of potential customers, either through product usage, benefit, or life-style segmentation. This and the previous chapter should be viewed as a unit so that the reader does not form the impression that the approaches suggested are mutually exclusive. All of the techniques suggested overlap and are complementary. Therefore, choices have to be made regarding the best combination of methods to employ for each product or service.

Finally, from these two chapters on market segmentation a clearer understanding should have been gained about the *who* of consumer behavior—that consumers are people of widely varying characteristics. Appreciation of this fact and an understanding of the ways in which clusters of consumers with more homogeneous characteristics may be carved out of the heterogeneous marketplace should put the reader on a firmer foundation for further exploration into the factors that influence consumer behavior.

DISCUSSION TOPICS

1. What is the significance to the marketer of the heavy user?

2. Suggest a marketing strategy to convert nonusers of the following goods and services into users:

a. cancer detection checkups for women aged 40–50
b. bus mass transit and carpools for getting to work
c. unit price information in a supermarket
d. a symphony series
e. paper towels
f. home permanents

3. What are the primary benefits that might be sought by consumers of the following products?

a. hair coloring
b. mouthwash
c. barbecue grill
d. compact car
e. bread

4. How is life-style segmentation useful to developing promotion campaigns?

5. For the following goods and services suggest an appropriate segmentation strategy. How would you determine the size and behavioral attributes of the segments? What marketing strategy might be appropriate?

a. a dinner-theater in a medium-sized city
b. a church on campus
c. your university
d. sailboats
e. coffee
f. *Cosmopolitan* magazine

NOTES

1. "Quaker Oats Life Cereal (A)," Harvard Business School case M-220R, p. 26.
2. Russell I. Haley, "Benefit Segmentation: A Decision-oriented Research Tool," *Journal of Marketing,* **32**:31, July 1968.
3. James F. Engel, Henry Fiorillo, and Murrary A. Cayley (eds.), *Market Segmentation: Concepts and Applications,* Holt, New York, 1972, p. 18.
4. Daniel Yankelovich, "New Criteria for Market Segmentation," *Harvard Business Review,* **42**:83–90, March–April 1964.
5. Philip Kotler, *Marketing Management: Analysis, Planning, and Control,* 3d ed., Prentice-Hall, Englewood Cliffs, N.J., 1976, p. 149.
6. "Why Youth Needs a New Definition," *Business Week,* December 12, 1970, p. 35.
7. William Lazer, "Life Style Concepts and Marketing," in Stephen Greyser (ed.), *Toward Scientific Marketing,* American Marketing Association, Chicago, 1963, p. 130.
8. Harper W. Boyd, Jr., and Sidney J. Levy, *Promotion: A Behavioral View,* Prentice-Hall, Englewood Cliffs, N. J., 1967, p. 38.
9. "A Whiff of Immortality," *Forbes,* September 15, 1975, p. 36.
10. Fred D. Reynolds and William R. Darden, "An Operational Construction of Life Style," in M. Venkatesan (ed.), *Proceedings of the Third Annual Conference of the Association for Consumer Research,* 1972, p. 482.
11. Joseph T. Plummer, "The Concept and Application of Life Style Segmentation," *Journal of Marketing,* **38**:33, January 1974.
12. Reprinted from Joseph T. Plummer, "Life Style and Advertising: Case Studies," in Fred Allvine (ed.), *AMA Proceedings 1971 Conference,* American Marketing Association, Chicago, 1971, p. 291.
13. William D. Wells and Douglas J. Tigert, "Activities, Interests and Opinions," *Journal of Advertising Research,* **11**:31, August 1971.
14. Plummer, "Life Style and Advertising," p. 291.
15. Reprinted from "Film of Findings Shows Uses of Lifestyle Research," *Marketing News,* published by the American Marketing Association, June 17, 1977, p. 9. Also see Peter W. Bernstein, "Psychographics Is Still an Issue on Madison Avenue," *Fortune,* **97**:78–80, January 16, 1978.
16. Plummer, "The Concept and Application of Life Style," pp. 35–36.
17. Douglas J. Tigert, Richard Lathrope, and Michael Bleeg, "The Fast Food Franchise: Psychographic and Demographic Segmentation Analysis," *Journal of Retailing,* **47**: 81–90, Spring 1971.
18. Tigert, Lathrope, and Bleeg, "The Fast Food Franchise," pp. 89–90.
19. Plummer, "Life Style and Advertising," pp. 292, 294.
20. Reprinted from Plummer, "Life Style and Advertising," p. 292, published by the American Marketing Association.
21. "How Colgate Brand Manager Applied Psychos to Market and Media for Irish Spring," *Media Decisions,* December 1976, pp. 70–71, 104, 106.
22. Plummer, "The Concept and Application of Life Style," pp. 36–37.
23. William D. Wells, "Psychographics: A Critical Review," *Journal of Marketing Research,* **12**:209, May 1975.
24. Engel, Fiorillo, and Cayley, *Market Segmentation,* pp. 459–465.

CASES

CASE 2-1   THE JENN-AIR GRILL[1]

After years of successfully marketing commercial ventilation equipment, the Jenn-Air Corporation in 1967 developed its first consumer product. This product was an innovative grill for indoor countertop installation using electrically-heated permanent marble "rocks" which provided the same smoked flavor imparted by charcoal in outdoor grilling. The grill featured a highly efficient countertop exhaust system through which smoke and fumes were drawn by a fan and exhausted to the outdoors. The exhaust system was far more effective and much quieter than overhead hood fans commonly used with kitchen cooking equipment. With rotisserie, griddle, and shishkabob attachments, the grill retailed for approximately $270. The grill is pictured in Figure 1.

Several promotional strategy issues were especially troublesome, because of both the company's inexperience in consumer-goods marketing and the innovative nature of the product which prevented patterning its introductory promotion after that of existing successful products. A memo written by one member of the new product's marketing team summarized the issues and proposed an initial research effort as follows:

Several aspects of consumer attitudes and reactions to the recent new Jenn-Air grill need to be studied as a guide to future decisions on promotion. These decisions will affect the nature and content of consumer advertising undertaken directly by Jenn-Air, cooperative campaigns undertaken with dealers, advertising directed to builders and dealers, and the sales points emphasized by field men calling on dealers and builders and salespeople employed by dealers.

Although ideally a large-scale consumer-attitude survey might eventually be

FIGURE 1
Jenn-Air grill.

used to study these issues, I recommend the use first of intensive group-depth interviews to provide an initial feel for consumer responses.

Jenn-Air contracted with Walker Research to conduct a panel discussion during one afternoon with consumers invited to a model home in which there was a Jenn-Air installation. The group consisted of ten housewives, aged 35 to 45, representing ownership of homes in the $25,000 to $40,000 range. The session was tape-recorded, and the essence of it is captured in the following presentation.

Following a brief warm-up discussion in which each woman described her present cooking equipment, talk turned to the cooking of meat, especially in terms of outdoor grills and broiling.

GENERAL PATTERN OF OUTDOOR GRILLING

1. Every family represented cooked outdoors, several doing this year round.

2. It is common practice to bring the cooked meat back inside for eating.

Advantages of Outdoor Grilling

1. By far the strongest advantage is flavor.

2. Outdoor cooking also is seen as a way of reducing kitchen heat in the summer.

3. A less strongly held advantage is the fact that husbands sometimes do the cooking outside.

Disadvantages of Outdoor Grilling

1. A strong disadvantage (on which there was general agreement) is the problem of coordinating outdoor cooking with the balance of the meal preparation, which must take place in the kitchen.

2. The outdoor grill presents a cleaning problem.

3. Billowing smoke associated with outdoor cooking is disliked.

4. Outdoor cooking takes longer than conventional methods if fire preparation time is included.

Conclusion

A means of cooking that captures the flavor of outdoor cooking without the problem of coordination and clean-up would seem to be highly desirable. However, the suggestion of a family room location for the Jenn-Air unit would present the same coordination problem for food preparation as outdoor grilling.

DISCUSSION OF THE PRODUCT CONCEPT

Jenn-Air's home economist briefly explained the product concept after distributing a brochure. Her discussion included the ventilation concept; the removable grill feature; the availability of rotisserie, griddle, and shishkabob attachments;

the method of cooking meat by which the grill is preheated; the principle of grease vaporization which occurs as grease falls on to the heated rocks; and the system by which grease drains away and is captured beneath the grill. A number of questions and comments were offered by panel members. The most serious objections raised in these questions dealt with (1) heat generated during preheat cycle and (2) soil caused by splattering meat.

Conclusions

1. The product is considered far more attractive when the flexibility offered by the rotisserie and griddle are realized; most panel members initially thought of the product for broiling only, probably because of the nature of the information presented to them.

2. The low noise level of the unit is a strong product feature.

3. Women in this market group cannot compare the unit's price with that of other equipment because they don't have price information.

KITCHEN DEMONSTRATION

Simply seeing the physical product did not overcome the previously stated objections, nor did it significantly clarify any previous, poorly understood product characteristics. Therefore, an attempt was made to demonstrate the physical product itself. Round steak was placed on the already-preheated grill as soon as everyone reached the kitchen. From this point on, most comments were very favorable.

Conclusions

1. The most serious objections raised earlier were overcome by the kitchen demonstration. Panel members agreed that a kitchen location would be preferable, were convinced that the unit would not heat up the kitchen, and were agreeably surprised at the low level of splattering.

2. All were impressed with the flavor of the meat, but no one seemed overly *surprised;* they had been led to *expect* charcoal flavor. The flavor concept is more believable than other aspects of the unit's functioning and probably requires less promotional push in order to achieve believability.

3. The venting efficiency of the unit was rated very high.

---

[1]Adapted from the original case by Donald H. Granbois appearing in M. Wayne DeLozier (ed.), *Consumer Behavior Dynamics: A Casebook* Columbus, Ohio, Merrill, 1977. Used with permission of the author and Charles E. Merrill Publishing Company.

Questions

1. Evaluate and critique the use of the group depth interview in this situation.

2. Suggest additional research strategies that could lead to more conclusive findings.

3. How might research in cooking behavior create new product opportunities (or product modifications)? Explain.

4. Assuming the findings of later surveys substantiated the conclusion drawn from the reported group interviews, prepare detailed recommendations for promotional strategy for the new grill, including message content and media strategy.

CASE 2-2 THE FLAVORFEST COMPANY[1]

The Flavorfest Company manufactures and distributes a well-known bottled condiment product. The firm long has dominated the market for this product and its market share is approximately 85 percent. Its product line also includes spices and seasoning items.

Flavorfest could base a marketing program on the assumption that all potential consumers are equally valuable prospects, but such an assumption must be verified by research if it is to be followed. It is more likely that substantial differences exist, and research disclosed three distinct market segments, each of which offered very different prospects for successful demand stimulation. A summary of the research findings on the market for Flavorfest appears below:

I. Heavy users (39 percent of the market).
   A. Demographic attributes: housewives aged 20–45; well educated; higher-income categories; small families with most children under 5; concentration in Northeast and Midwest regions and in suburban and farm areas.
   B. Motivational attributes:
      1. Strong motivation not to be old-fashioned and a desire to express individuality through creative action and use of exciting new things.
      2. The traditional role as a housewife is viewed with displeasure, and experimentation with new foods is done to express her individuality—not to please her family.
      3. The image of Flavorfest suggests exciting and exotic taste, and the product is reacted to favorably in terms of taste, appearance, and food value. It is highly prized in experimental cooking. Hence, there is substantial compatibility between values of the user and product image.
II. Light to moderate users (20 percent of the market).
   A. Demographic attributes: housewives aged 35–54; large families with children under 12; middle-income groups; location mostly in Southeast, Pacific states, and Southwest.
   B. Motivational attributes:
      1. A strong desire to express individuality through creative cookery, but this desire is constrained somewhat by a conflicting desire to maintain tradition and subordinate herself to her family's desires.
      2. The desire to experiment with new foods is also constrained by a lack of confidence in the results of her experimental cooking.
      3. The image of Flavorfest is favorable. The product is liked in all respects, but is confined largely to use with one type of food. It is viewed as unacceptable in other uses. Hence, her vision is limited regarding new uses for Flavorfest.
III. Nonusers (41 percent of the market).
   A. Demographic attributes: older housewives; large families, lower-

income brackets; location mostly in the Eastern states and some parts of the South.

B. Motivational attributes:
1. A strong motive to maintain tradition and emotional ties with the past; identification with her mother and her role in the home.
2. A conservative nonventuresome personality.
3. Her role as a mother and housewife discourages experimental cookery, and Flavorfest is thus looked upon unfavorably. The image of Flavorfest connotes exotic flavors and a degree of modernity that is unacceptable.
4. No interest is expressed in new uses and experimentation with Flavorfest, for the product does not represent the values embraced by these housewives.

---

[1]Engel, J. F., Wales, H. G., and Warshaw, M. R., *Promotional Strategy,* Irwin, Homewood, Ill., 1967, pp. 90–92. Reprinted by permission of the publisher.

Question

1. Suggest a marketing program for Flavorfest.

CASE 2-3   DRUG-PRODUCT USERS[1]

In 1970 Benton & Bowles, Inc., conducted a study using a mail panel to discover whether psychographic profiles could be useful in identifying drug-product user segments. The research was intended to benefit the agency's clients and to provide information for development of promotional programs. A sample of 1600 housewives responded to the survey, representing a reasonable cross section of American homemakers in terms of territory, market size, age, and income.

To cover the dimensions considered important, 214 attitude statements were used. Housewives were asked to indicate the extent of their agreement with statements or the degree to which statements described them. Typical examples include the following:

When it comes to a choice between nutrition and taste in my family meal planning, I put nutrition first.

I wouldn't let animals come into the house because of the dirt.

I get upset when things are out of their place in my house.

If there's a flu bug going around, I'm sure to catch it.

Once you've got a cold, there is very little you can do about it.

In addition to securing responses to these attitudinal statements, the study obtained information on product and brand usage and demographic information.

The research was able to identify four distinct groups of drug-product users:

1. *Realists* are not health fatalists, nor excessively concerned with protection or germs. They view remedies positively, want something that is convenient and works, and do not feel the need of a doctor-recommended

TABLE 1

PRODUCT USAGE AMONG FOUR DRUG SEGMENTS

	Realists (%)	Authority Seekers (%)	Skeptics (%)	Hypo-chondriacs (%)
Upset stomach remedies	49	43	32	59
Acid indigestion, heartburn remedies	46	45	35	50
Hangover remedies	27	21	17	31
Cold or allergy tablets	74	57	41	72
Nasal sprays	33	27	21	38
Nasal inhalers	26	23	17	31
Liquid cold remedies	17	16	11	21
Cough drops	71	71	58	76
Sore throat lozenges	53	56	37	62
Cough syrup	59	54	31	65
Pain reliever tablets	90	88	77	95

medicine. Many are outgoing, innovative, community-oriented and have a positive attitude toward grooming. (35 percent)

2. *Authority seekers* are doctor- and prescription-oriented, are neither fatalists nor stoics concerning health, but they prefer the stamp of authority on what they do take. Many tend to be rigid and meticulous, have a careful shopping orientation, and tend not to be convenience-oriented. (31 percent)

3. *Skeptics* have a low health concern, are least likely to resort to medication, and are highly skeptical of cold remedies. Many also are relaxed and unworried, not innovative or outgoing. Also, they tend to have a strong economy orientation and tend not to be self-indulgent. (23 percent)

4. *Hypochondriacs* have high health concern, regard themselves as prone to any bug going around and tend to take medication at the first symptom. They do not look for strength in what they take, but need some mild authority reassurance. Many have a high cleanliness orientation, but are negative about grooming. They also tend to be self-indulgent, with a low economy and high convenience orientation. (11 percent)

Questions relating to product usage patterns revealed the information presented in Table 1.

[1]Adapted from Ruth Ziff, "Psychographics for Market Segmentation,"*Journal of Advertising Research,* **11**:3–9, April 1971, © Copyright 1971, by the Advertising Research Foundation.

Questions

1. What marketing-strategy implications does the research appear to present to the agency and its drug-product clients?

2. What additional information could you make use of in developing strategy decisions?

ENVIRONMENTAL INFLUENCES ON CONSUMER BEHAVIOR

**6. CULTURE   7. ETHNIC SUBCULTURES 8. AGE SUBCULTURES
9. SOCIAL CLASS 10. SOCIAL GROUPS   11. FAMILY
12. PERSONAL INFLUENCE AND DIFFUSION OF INNOVATIONS**
Cases for Part Three

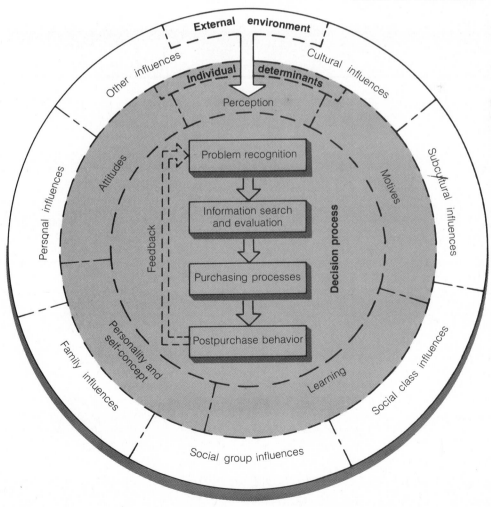

CULTURE

We begin our study of the environmental elements impinging upon consumers by first looking at a very broad, basic, and enduring factor—the pervasive influence of culture.

In this chapter we shall be investigating the role and usefulness of cultural analysis in developing marketing strategies. After defining and characterizing culture, the basic cultural values of American consumers are outlined. This will be followed by an examination of cultural change and its effect on consumer behavior. Finally, cross-cultural consumer behavior and its implications for international marketing are discussed.

CULTURE DEFINED

It is difficult to present only one definition of culture and expect it to portray the richness of the field and its relevance to understanding consumers. However, the following two are representative:

That complex whole that includes knowledge, belief, art, morals, law, custom, and any other capabilities and habits acquired by man as a member of society[1]

The distinctive way of life of a group of people, their complete design for living[2]

The influence of culture might be better understood by looking at Figure 6-1, which reveals the hierarchy of influence of environmental variables to be discussed in this section. Culture is seen to be the broadest determinant while personal influence is viewed as the most immediate influence on the individual.

The significance of culture in understanding human behavior (of which consumer behavior is a subpart) is that it extends our understanding of the extent to which people are more than just chemistry, physiology, or a set of biological drives and instincts.[3] The implication is that although all customers may be biologically similar, their views of the world, what they value, and how they act differ according to their cultural backgrounds.

CULTURAL RELEVANCE TO MARKETING DECISIONS

It has long been recognized that culture influences consumers. For example, Duesenberry observed in 1949 that all of the activities in which people engage are culturally determined, and that nearly all purchases of goods are made either to provide physical comfort or to implement the activities that make up the life of a culture.[4] Thus, an understanding of culture enables the marketer to interpret the reaction of consumers to alternative marketing strategies. Sometimes guidance from *cultural anthropologists* (those social scientists who study man and his culture) is sought in order to gain a better understanding of the market.

Anthropologists are able to assist the marketer in understanding a number of cultural facets of behavior, such as the following:

National character, or the differences that distinguish one national group from another. That is, the obvious as well as the more subtle cultural differences that distinguish Americans, Swedes, Germans, and Brazilians

Differences in *subcultures* such as blacks, Jews, and Puerto Ricans

FIGURE 6-1
The hierarchy of environmental influences on consumers.

The *silent language* of gesture, posture, food and drink preferences, and other nonverbal clues to behavior

The significance of *symbols* in a society

Rites of passage, or the central points in a person's life at which he may ritually be helped to go from one status to another, such as birth, puberty, or marriage

Taboos or prohibitions in a culture relating to various things such as the use of a given color, phrase, or symbol[5]

Two case histories in which anthropological knowledge was successfully used to solve marketing problems are presented in the following.

A beer manufacturer sought to extend his market share among blacks in a large, eastern United States city. An anthropologist familiar with the special subculture of blacks indicated the profound effect that membership in this group had on their purchasing behavior. Many blacks are especially aware of brands having status connotations and those symbolizing racial progress. Examination of the manufacturer's marketing program led to strategy changes aimed at improving the status connotation of the beer to blacks. The manufacturer began to support several major social events related to the arts in black communities and stressed that the beer was a national brand with quality-control procedures. Advertising was also redirected toward enhancing the brand's status and quality connotations.

A major manufacturer of women's products was uncertain about whether to continue using the *Fleur de Lis* emblem on its package. Anthropological analysis of this symbol indicated that its association with French kings and other cultural connotations made it more masculine than feminine. Hence, it was recommended that this symbol be replaced.

Although the definitions of culture presented earlier are excellent, they seek to characterize culture in only a few words. It is evident that such a concept is difficult to convey clearly in any definition. The following section, therefore, will expand on these definitions by discussing the significant characteristics or features of culture.

THE NATURE OF CULTURE
A large number of characteristics of culture may be cited to describe its nature, but most social scientists agree on the following features.

Culture Is Man-made
Culture does not simply "exist" somewhere waiting to be discovered. People invent their culture. This invention consists of three interdependent systems or elements: (1) an *ideological system* or mental component that consists of the ideas, beliefs, values, and ways of reasoning that human beings learn to accept in defining what is desirable and undesirable; (2) a *technological system* that consists of the skills, crafts, and arts that enable humans to produce material goods derived from the natural environment; and (3) an *organizational system* (such as the family system and social class) that makes

it possible for humans to coordinate effectively their behavior with the actions of others.[7]

Culture Is Learned

Culture is not innate or instinctive, but is learned early in life and charged with a good deal of emotion. The great strength of this cultural stamp is such that at an early age children are firmly imbued with their culture's ways of acting, thinking, and feeling. This obviously has important implications for the behavior of consumers since these preconditions are molded by our culture from birth.

Culture Is Prescriptive

Culture involves ideal standards or patterns of behavior so that members of society have a common understanding of the right and proper way to think, feel, and act in any given situation. Ideal patterns of behavior, thought, and feeling which groups share are termed *norms.* When actual behavior deviates from the ideal patterns or norms of society, *sanctions* are frequently taken. That is, certain types of pressures are brought to bear on deviant individuals so that they will conform their behavior to what society expects.

Culture Is Socially Shared

Culture is a group phenomenon, shared by human beings living in organized societies and kept relatively uniform by social pressure. The group that is involved in this sharing may range from a whole society to a smaller unit such as a family.

Cultures Are Similar but Different

All cultures exhibit certain similarities. For example, each of the following elements is found in all societies: athletic sports, bodily adornment, calendar, cooking, courtship, dancing, education, family, gestures, government, housing, language, law, music, religious ritual, and numerous other items. There is, however, great variation from society to society in the nature of each of these elements, which may result in important consumer behavior differences around the world.

Culture Is Gratifying and Persistent

Culture satisfies basic biological as well as learned needs. It consists of habits that will be strengthened and reinforced as long as they are gratified. Because of this gratification, cultural elements are handed down from generation to generation. Thus, people are comfortable doing things in the customary way.

Our thorough inculcation of culture causes it to persist even when we are exposed to new cultures. No matter where we go or what we do, we cannot escape our cultural heritage. Its persistence means that, although not impossible, change is often quite difficult because resistance to it may be strong.

Culture Is Adaptive

In spite of our resistance to change, cultures are gradually and continuously changing. Some societies are quite static with a very slow rate of change, while others are more dynamic with very rapid changes taking place.

125
CULTURE

Culture Is Organized and Integrated
A culture "hangs together," that is, its parts fit together. Although every culture has some inconsistent elements, it tends to form a consistent and integrated whole.

CULTURAL VALUES
Cultural values are important to the organized and integrated nature of culture. A *cultural value* can be defined as "a widely held belief or sentiment that some activities, relationships, feelings, or goals are important to the community's identity or well-being."[8] Values, therefore, produce inclinations to respond to specific stimuli in standard ways.

Since values are culturally determined, this means that they are learned from social interaction, largely from our families and friends in settings such as schools and churches. Values strongly influence consumer behavior; and even though the specific situation may dictate slightly different actions, overall there is much similarity in consumer behavior within a given culture, such as in tastes, methods of shopping, and so forth.

It is crucial for the marketer to understand society's basic value structure so that strategy decisions do not fly in the face of ingrained cultural patterns. It is much easier to harmonize with the culture than to attempt to change fundamental cultural values.

United States Cultural Values
Each culture has what may be termed *core values,* which are the dominant or basic cultural values that people accept with little question. In America, although values are not always obvious or easy to analyze, there are major patterns that can be identified. This is not to say that "American values" are exclusive to the United States, or that all Americans share them. However, the American value system is appreciably different from other cultures, and most Americans do subscribe to the cultural pattern described below.

The following discussion of our cultural values may seem obvious to the reader; but this simply underscores the fact that Americans accept these values as "givens." The values to be discussed represent abstracted dominant themes which are ideal types, and thus may be subject to some exceptions.

INDIVIDUALISM This value is complex and closely interrelated with a number of other facets such as freedom, democracy, nationalism, and patriotism. It is founded on a belief in the dignity, worth, and goodness of the individual. People have freedom; that is, they are independent from outside constraint. However, they are not freed from all social restraints, but are to act as responsible agents.

EQUALITY Americans believe in the intrinsic equality of man; that is, what the person is as an individual (e.g., all are equal before God). Everyone has an equal right to life, liberty, and the pursuit of happiness, and an equal opportunity for social and economic rewards.

During the 1960s and 1970s there has been an increasing push for social and economic equality in America. One of the most profound impacts during this period has been women's demand for equality, which has brought about changes in the marriage relationship and the American family. The women's liberation movement represents a value structure that has resulted in greater independence and equality of women. It has been expressed in numerous ways, such as more women with careers outside the home, changing sex roles within the home, and many women opting for life-styles other than marriage.

One manifestation of the movement toward equality in our culture is the general trend toward unisex clothing. Women have adopted "male styles," wearing pants, boots, and leather jackets, while men have begun wearing "female-styled" clothing in bright colors, of more delicate fabrics, shaped to the body, and with such accessories as necklaces.

ACTIVITY Our culture stresses activity, especially work, as a predominant value. This derives largely from the Puritan or Protestant ethic, which stressed that idleness is evil. An individual was expected to work hard, save money, and be thrifty. Thus, work was conceived as a means of religious discipline.

Today Americans believe not only in working hard but also in playing hard. Increased productivity and affluence have resulted in replacing long hours of hard work with longer vacation periods, shorter workweeks, and more paid holidays. This has generated increased leisure time in which activity is still stressed, but it is manifested in numerous leisure pursuits, as evidenced by the boom in participant sports such as tennis and golf.

PROGRESS AND ACHIEVEMENT Americans believe in progress for society and achievement and success for the individual. We are oriented toward the future rather than the past, and believe in change and forward movement. Personal achievement is stressed as evidenced by the "success story," and our desire to master the physical world. We also prize the characteristics of self-reliance and initiative.

One manifestation of our emphasis on progress in America is the sometimes wasteful use of material possessions and resources. Contemporary America stresses continuous style changes and discarding the still functionally useful product in order to buy what is new. Of course, the marketer benefits from an environment which is so conducive to innovation, in which consumers are eager to have the most up-to-date item.

An indication of our culture's orientation toward achievement from a marketing perspective is the importance of certain symbols in our society. Because achievement often has a materialistic aspect to it, Americans grant to owners of certain products the stamp of having "arrived." For example, a Cadillac or Mercedes tells something about the achievements of its owner, as does a large house in the "right neighborhood," and expensive clothing. These products are symbols to their owners as well as to others, and their meanings are usually unmistakable.[9]

EFFICIENCY AND PRACTICALITY Americans greatly appreciate technical values and constantly search for better ways of doing things. Our entire economic system is founded on this concept and emphasizes mass production and mass consumption.

Another example of our culture's value of practicality concerns the orientation toward informality. We have moved away from the formal traditions (long associated with the eastern United States) and have adopted more informal habits in manners, dress, speech, and social relationships. Moreover, the United States has never placed as much emphasis on formality, ceremony, and tradition as has Europe. Consequently, Americans tolerate, in fact welcome, less structure and rigidity and more comfort in the way they work and relax. Certain regions of the country are particularly high on this scale of informality. For example, the celebrated southern California life-style of casual dress, informal entertaining, and outdoor living is a prime example.

MASTERY OVER THE ENVIRONMENT Americans do not like to be controlled by their environment but rather seek to control it. This not only includes controlling the weather and harnessing the sun and tides as energy sources, but it also extends to areas like genetic engineering. Even the nature of products introduced in America is indicative of this underlying cultural value. For instance, there seems to be a product answer for every chore the consumer might face. During each Christmas season our television sets bring us news of products that knit our clothes; attach our buttons; and spin, chop, slice, and dice our vegetables. All of these items attest to our desire to provide an engineered answer for almost every situation we face.

Another aspect of this value is that we have long viewed the world and its resources as there to use as we saw fit. In so doing, however, we have encountered numerous environmental and diminishing resource problems. But on the positive side, a growing ecological orientation can be seen in the marketplace. Some manufacturers are using recycled materials to produce new items (such as glass and paper products); more biodegradable products are being marketed (such as laundry detergents); and alternatives to harmful aerosol spray products are now being offered (such as pump hair sprays and solid deodorants).

RELIGIOUS AND MORAL ORIENTATION According to a recent Gallup poll, 94 percent of Americans believe in God and 64 percent believe in life after death. Thus, we are a religious people, and our Judeo-Christian heritage has imbued us with a strong moral and ethical quality. Consequently, we tend to view the world in absolute terms and tolerate few gray areas—that is, we judge things in terms of good or bad, right or wrong, ethical or unethical. This value results in a strong evangelistic spirit among Americans. We are rather *ethnocentric,* believing that our culture and way of life is the best and feeling that it is our duty to bring others around to our way of thinking and acting.

One implication of the religious and moral orientation of Americans is our receptivity to the "marketing" of certain religious views and social causes. For example, some very effective marketers of Christianity include Billy Graham and Norman Vincent Peale.

HUMANITARIANISM Americans have a strong sense of personal concern for the rights and welfare of others. We provide aid in mass disasters, have a large philanthropic system, and feel that we should give our money and/or our time to such organizations as the United Fund, Red Cross, CARE, and the Peace Corps. For example, total contributions to charity in 1974 amounted to over $25 billion in the United States, of which religion received the largest share.[10] The operation of religious and other charitable institutions is a huge business and draws good support even in unfavorable economic times.

YOUTH AND ROMANCE Young people set much of the tone of our culture and have been a growing force in our society as their proportion has risen. Because Americans want to look and act young, we consume great quantities of those products that hold promise for achieving these ends. For instance, hair colorings for men and women are very much in demand, as are preparations to do away with wrinkles, flab, and spots caused by the aging process. The array of vitamins and other supplements (such as Geritol) is another indication of our youth orientation.

Marketers have played up the theme of youthfulness in numerous product and service promotions with slogans such as "you're as young as you feel" and "for those who think young." An effective twist on this approach, but accomplishing the same result, was Clairol's slogan for Loving Care hair coloring: "You're not getting older. You're getting better."

Underlying the youth theme pervading our culture is the implication of romance. The younger you look, presumably the more attractive you are, especially to the opposite sex. The weakening of sexual prohibitions in our society has led to more playful, thinly disguised appeals to romantic and sexual motives in product promotions. This *creative eroticism* is reflected in various products and promotional slogans. For instance, Love Cosmetics' choice of the product name "Love" suggests that the items are "love potions." Two other examples of creative eroticism in promotional campaigns are the English Leather cologne commercial in which a girl says "My men wear English Leather or they wear nothing at all," and a Noxema shave cream ad in which an attractive girl suggests that the user should "take it all off."

MATERIALISM AND HEDONISM The United States culture is materialistic, and Americans are the world's most voracious consumers, each year buying millions of color TV sets, washing machines, refrigerators, vacuum cleaners, lawn mowers, radios, and other items. Material progress has made America a land of abundance where more than half of all families own their homes, and two cars per family is the standard. Progress has also brought about urban renewal, universal education, and eradication of many diseases. Thus, there is a very positive aspect of materialism from which progress results.

There is also a negative side to materialism, however, seen in shoddy merchandise that falls apart soon after purchase, families that are drowning in debt because of their compulsive spending, resource depletion, and pollution.[11]

Related to the core cultural value of materialism is the growing trend toward *hedonism*, or devotion to pleasure. We desire maximum pleasurable sensation with minimum effort. Our culture's increasing devotion to hedonism is reflected in the sale of all sorts of products ranging from luxury cars and homes to many foods and such pastimes as electronic video games. In addition, we are more willing to admit the existence of this situation to ourselves and others. For example, L'Oréal hair color ads state, "It costs a little more, but I'm worth it." This and many other ads stress how good the feeling is that comes from using the product.

SOCIAL INTERACTION AND CONFORMITY These values seem in contrast to our emphasis on individualism, but some amount of conformity is necessary for a smoothly functioning society. Americans seem to be especially sensitive to group pressure. For example, David Riesman suggests that America can be characterized as a country of *inner-directed* and *other-directed* persons. Inner-directed individuals have their principles firmly instilled by their elders while other-directed persons receive their direction from contemporaries, directly or indirectly, personally or through the mass media. Although the majority of the population of this country would have to be categorized as inner-directed there is a trend in the metropolitan areas of America toward other-directedness.[12]

The trend of other-directedness suggests that people are seeking satisfaction of some need through greater social involvement with each other. Much of the advertising we are exposed to incorporates this theme. Promotions for products as diverse as motorcycles ("You meet the nicest people on a Honda"), clothing, recreation equipment, cigarettes, and beverages of all kinds incorporate the theme of how beneficial these products are in achieving pleasurable social interaction.

Do Values Influence Consumer Behavior?

Intuitively we can see that culture is a strong force in the consumer's milieu affecting his or her choice behavior. Unfortunately, little research has been conducted assessing the usefulness of cultural values in understanding or predicting consumer behavior.

Some recent studies, however, have found that commonly held cultural values do shape consumption choices to a certain extent.[13] One study examined the ownership of generic categories of automobiles (i.e., full-size, intermediate, compact, and subcompact-size cars) and concluded that culture is an underlying determinant of the type of car purchased.[14]

Another study also found that personal values have an important influence on consumers' automobile preferences.[15] Consumers classified as more liberal with more socially motivated values and attitudes had a higher preference for compact cars, while those having a more traditional or conservative outlook preferred larger, more prestigious standard-size cars. This study also cited other consumer products to which the groups were attracted, based on differences in their value structures.

Studies such as these indicate that understanding personal values of consumers can facilitate market-segmentation decisions as well as those relating to product and promotion planning. However, more research is needed to understand cultural value influences on consumer behavior, particularly across a broader range of products than has so far been investigated.

CULTURAL CHANGE AND COUNTERCULTURES

The core values just discussed are not fixed or static but instead are dynamic elements of our culture which may change over time. Cultural change may come about slowly in an evolutionary manner, or it may change rapidly, which tends to place more stress on the system. The marketer needs to understand that cultures do change and to appreciate the implications which this may have for consumer behavior.

Changing Cultural Values in the United States

American values are undergoing some major changes. The period during the 1960s and 1970s, for instance, saw one of the more substantial upheavals in value structures. The studies cited below suggest some of the attitudinal and behavioral changes of this period. They also suggest that attitudes prevailing during one period can change dramatically several years later. Thus, markets must be under continuous surveillance in order to detect the formation of new cultural values.

Philip Kotler suggests that, generally, the following changes are taking place in American core cultural values:[16]

FROM	TO
Self-reliance	Government reliance
"Hard work"	The "easy life"
Religious convictions	Secular convictions
Husband-dominated home	Wife-dominated home
Parent-centered household	Child-centered household
Respect for individual	Dislike of individual difference
Postponed gratification	Immediate gratification
Saving	Spending
Sexual chastity	Sexual freedom
Parental values	Peer-group values
Independence	Security

The values listed above may also be characteristic of intergenerational differences, since it is often the case that the youth of a culture adopt a different value set from their elders. In fact, research in the United States has determined that there is indeed a difference between older consumers' and younger consumers' attitudes.

Not only are there differences in values across age groups but differences can also be found between various groups of the same age. For example, noncollege youths appear to be about five years behind the college population in adoption of new social values and moral outlooks.[17]

Other evidence of significant cultural changes has been gathered by the Daniel Yankelovich organization. Their surveys have uncovered five major social trends in the United States today. These trends, presented in Table 6-1, represent an excellent means of summarizing our discussion of cultural change, and offer numerous implications for understanding consumers.

TABLE 6-1

131

CULTURE

FIVE MAJOR SOCIAL TRENDS AND THEIR IMPLICATIONS FOR CONSUMER BEHAVIOR

1. Psychology of affluence trends
The first group are traceable to the effects of "psychology of affluence." That is, they manifest themselves among consumers who feel sufficiently free from economic insecurity to seek the fulfillment of other needs.

Trend toward physical self-enhancement, spending more time, effort and money on improving one's physical appearance; the things people do to enhance their looks.

Trend toward personalization, expressing one's individuality through products, possessions and new life-styles. The need to be "a little bit different" from other people.

Trend toward physical health and well-being, the level of concern with one's health, diet and what people do to take better care of themselves.

Trend toward new forms of materialism, the new status symbols and extent of de-emphasis on money and material possessions.

Trend toward personal creativity, the growing conviction that being "creative" is not confined to the artist. Each man can be creative in his own way, as expressed through a wide variety of activities, hobbies and new uses of leisure time.

Trend toward meaningful work, the spread of the demand for work that is challenging and meaningful over and above how well it pays.

2. Antifunctionalism trends
A second group of trends underscores a major new force in American life—the quest for excitement, sensation, stimulation, and meaning to counteract the practical and mundane routines of everyday life. There is a reaction among certain groups in the population against the drabness of modern life, giving rise to a many-faceted hunger that reaches beyond the practical.

Trend toward the "new romanticism," the desire to restore romance, mystery and adventure to modern life.

Trend toward novelty and change, the search for constant change, novelty, new experience, reaction against sameness and habit.

Trend toward adding beauty to one's daily surroundings, the stress on beauty in the home and the things people do and buy to achieve it.

Trend toward sensuousness, placing greater emphasis on a total sensory experience—touching, feeling, smelling, and psychedelic phenomena. A moving away from the purely linear, logical and visual.

Trend toward mysticism, the search for new modes of spiritual experience and beliefs, as typified by the growing interest in astrology.

Trend toward introspection, an enhanced need for self-understanding and life experiences in contrast to automatic conformity to external pressures and expectations.

3. Reaction against complexity trends
A third and important group of trends cluster around the theme of reaction against the complexity of modern life. We find more and more people changing their habits and life styles in reaction to crowded conditions, complicated products, unresponsive institutions, restrictive regulations and information overloads.

Trend toward life simplification, the turning away from complicated products, services and ways of life.

Trend toward return to nature, rejection of the artificial, the "chemical," the man-made improvements on nature; the adoption of more "natural" ways of dressing, eating and living.

Trend toward increased ethnicity, finding new satisfactions and identifications in foods, dress, customs and life styles of various ethnic groups such as Black, Italian, Irish, Polish, Jewish, German.

Trend toward increased community involvement, increasing affiliation with local, community and neighborhood activities. Greater involvement in local groups.

Trend toward greater reliance on technology versus tradition, distrust of tradition and reputation that is based on age and experience, due to the swift tempo of change. Greater confidence in science and technology.

TABLE 6-1 (continued)

Trend away from bigness, the departure from the belief that "big" necessarily means "good," beginning to manifest itself with respect to "big" brands, "big" stores.

4. Trends that move away from puritan values

The fourth group of trends measure the penetration of certain new values at the expense of the traditional puritanical values.

Trend toward pleasure for its own sake, putting pleasure before duty; changing life styles and what that means for product usage and communication.

Trend toward blurring of the sexes, moving away from traditional distinctions between men and women and the role each should play in marriage, work and other walks of life.

Trend toward living in the present, straying from traditional beliefs in planning, saving, and living for the future.

Trend toward more liberal sexual attitudes, the relaxation of sexual prohibitions and the devaluation of "virtue" in the traditional sense, among women.

Trend toward acceptance of stimulants and drugs, greater acceptance of artificial agents (legal and illegal) for mood change, stimulation and relaxation as opposed to the view that these should be accomplished by strength of character alone.

Trend toward relaxation of self-improvement standards, the inclination to stop working as hard at self-improvement; letting yourself be whatever you are.

Trend toward individual religions, rejection of institutionalized religions and the substitution of more personalized forms of religious experience, characterized by the emergence of numerous small and more intimate religious sects and cults.

5. Trends related to child-centeredness

Children born into the child-centered homes of the 40s and 50s are now in their twenties and teens. Although the consequences of this orientation are difficult to isolate, research indicates that a few important personality characteristics and values associated with them can be identified. These provide the source for the final group of trends—trends which have a direct impact on marketing as well as on other facets of modern life.

Trend toward greater tolerance of chaos and disorder, less need for schedules, routines, plans, regular shopping and purchasing, tolerance of less order and cleanliness in the home, less regular eating and entertaining patterns.

Trend toward challenge to authority, less automatic acceptance of the authority and "correctness" of public figures, institutions, and established brands.

Trend toward rejection of hypocrisy, less acceptance of sham, exaggeration, indirection, and misleading language

Trend toward female careerism, belief that homemaking is not sufficient as the sole source of fulfillment and that more challenging and productive work for the woman is needed

Trend toward familism, renewed faith in the belief that the essential life satisfactions stem from activities centering on the immediate family unit rather than on "outside" sources such as work and community affairs

Source: Reprinted from *The Marketing News,* **4:**7, May 1971, and **4:** 8, first of June 1971, published by the American Marketing Association.

Implications for the Marketer

The general message that these trends have for the marketer is that fundamental moral, social, and cultural value-system changes are taking place among consumers today. These cultural changes are molding a new American consumer and have significant implications for marketing strategy—including segmentation decisions, new-product development, advertising, and distribution activities.[18]

MARKET SEGMENTATION The growing diversity of individual tastes, coupled with a hedonistic philosophy and increasing incomes are contributing to ever greater segmentation of the market. Thus, understanding such value shifts in American society could be useful in predicting changing consumption patterns for products. Also, the marketer may be able to identify large market segments on the basis of value profiles and then develop programs that would enhance those values important to each consumer segment. For example, where one group views a product in terms of status and another views it in a more functional way, then different promotional messages are likely to be needed for each group as well as, perhaps, tailored products.

PRODUCT PLANNING Assessing consumers' present and emerging value orientations can help the marketer identify new product opportunities and achieve better product positioning among consumer segments. For example, as values such as "pleasure," "an exciting life," "a comfortable life," and "self-respect" increase in importance, the marketer may find a need for having products with brand names, colors, and designs that enhance these important values. Consider a furniture manufacturer who might link these changing values with a growing demand for furniture style and design that incorporate bright colors, bold designs, unique materials of construction, and unusual comfort features.[19]

Therefore, contemporary marketing offerings require periodic audits of product and service lines to determine how well they satisfy the complex needs and wants of changing consumers.

DISTRIBUTION CHANNELS Changing consumer-value systems may lead to different shopping patterns and new outlets may be necessary to reach consumers. Examples of changing channels include the strong emphasis on in-home catalog buying and drive-in funeral parlors and churches.

PROMOTION New approaches in copy and artwork are called for in communicating memorably and persuasively with changing consumers. Weiss suggests a number of ways that advertising is moving to appeal to the values of this new society:

1. Defiance of social taboos. For example, Johnson & Johnson advertises condoms in women's magazines and urges that women suggest use of them to the male.

2. More informative copy. Some good examples here are ads for Sears furniture, Simmons studio beds, automobiles, and microwave ovens.

3. More true-to-life vignettes for television commercials. American Express travelers checks feature this approach.

4. Greater use of so-called damaging admissions such as calling the Volkswagen a "bug," or featuring Avis as "No. 2."

5. More advertising that names and debates competitors. For example, Tylenol and Datril have slugged it out, as well as Coke and Pepsi.

6. Increasingly genuine appeals to the young generation. Coke, Pepsi, and McDonald's are good illustrations of this.

7. More advertising segmented toward the higher-educated, higher-income

groups. No-fault insurance and advertisements for nutritious cereals are examples.

8. More advertising that frankly acknowledges mounting public cynicism about advertising. For example, a Whirlpool ad featuring its toll-free "Cool-Line" (a customer complaint system) admits that a number of those who read the ad will not believe it, so it challenges them to dial the number.

9. Greater stress on ecology. Exxon and Arm & Hammer are two diverse examples of this approach.

10. More advertising that realistically, not paternalistically, acknowledges women's changing role in our society. New York Life Insurance now aims some of its messages at working women.

11. Increasing recognition of the public's antiadvertising resentments, particularly among higher-income, higher-educated consumers. More sophisticated humor and a lighter touch are evident in such ads as those by Benson & Hedges, Alka-Seltzer, and New England Mutual Life Insurance Company.

12. More advertising that breaks with tradition. Charlie perfume is a classic example here.[20]

A number of problems are inherent in marketers' attempts at understanding, appreciating, and reflecting changing values, particularly among the young. First, these changes are elusive and hard to define and their practical effects are frequently indirect. Second, the marketer may tend to ascribe fundamental cultural changes simply to the "generation gap" and incorrectly assume that they are only fads which will quickly disappear. Finally, because change often generates complexity, marketers may resist changing cultural values rather than trying to take advantage of them.[21]

Countercultures and Their Meaning for Marketers

Not everyone in the United States embraces all the core cultural values that were described earlier in this chapter. In every society there exists what are termed *countercultures* in which certain values of a smaller group conflict with the values of the total society, that is, the dominant culture. According to Yankelovich, United States society has split into two vast blocs. Culturally conservative Americans who maintain a belief in self-denial, the work ethic, and upward mobility today represent about one-half of the population. The other half of the population is made up of "new value" Americans,[22] who are influencing changes in the dominant cultural pattern.

Within these two blocs of consumers, however, smaller segments emphasizing significantly different cultural values have evolved. For example, one important counterculture exists among some young people in America who have rebelled against the dominant value patterns. One author suggests that members of this group "seek to invent a cultural base for New Left politics, to discover new types of community, new family patterns, new sexual mores, new kinds of livelihood, new esthetic forms, new personal identities on the far side of the power politics, the bourgeois home, and the consumer society."[23]

If the values held by such people were to become widespread in America, the implications for marketing could be profound. The nature of marketing might be drastically altered to a system much different from the present one. Fortunately for the marketer, however, the size of this group has been rather small.

Another counterculture which, although unusual, offers the marketer opportunity because of its large size is a group described by Yankelovich as the "aimless" or "lost generation." They turned their backs on old values but could not measure up to new values, so they gave up and are said to live just from day to day. This group is comprised of 30 million people, a big chunk of whom are young. They are undereducated, live in cities, and are heavily weighted to the Northeast. Reaching this group with promotion can be difficult since they are not involved with print media. Yet they can be sold on products that provide a certain amount of sensation, such as movies, cosmetics, or travel. However, it is difficult to sell them products that involve a long-term investment, and they tend not to display any brand loyalty.[24]

Tracking Cultural Change

One should appreciate that countercultures, just as other consumer segments, evolve over time, and their values are also likely to change. Thus, groups once thought of as "radical" may over a period of time accept the main values of society. For instance, in the late 1960s and early 1970s United States youths were being described as rather unmaterialistic. Yet by the mid- and late 1970s this now older "radical" generation was being described as "good, unradical consumers" who are very materialistic and want to buy practically everything.[25] Thus, even countercultures may shift their values over time, requiring constant monitoring to make appropriate changes in marketing strategy. For example, the *Whole Earth Catalog*, a counterculture manual published in 1968, sold over 1 million copies, but required significant revision in 1975 to reflect changes in values and life-styles of its market. The marketer must maintain a surveillance not only on countercultures as these segments change but also on the dominant society as it comes to accept some of the counterculture's values.

CROSS-CULTURAL UNDERSTANDING OF CONSUMER BEHAVIOR

More and more companies have adopted a global outlook in which the world becomes their market. For example, numerous major corporations such as Coca-Cola, Hoover, IBM, Pfizer, and Gillette receive over half of their earnings from foreign operations, while many others also have significant international markets. Such situations require the marketer's appreciation of cultural differences that exist among international markets and their influence on consumer behavior. In this section some of the implications of these cultural subtleties will be discussed.

Unfortunately, there have been rather few published cross-cultural studies of consumer behavior that the marketer may use in making strategy decisions. There have been some important recent examples of research in this area, however.[21]

Need for Cross-cultural Understanding

When American managers venture abroad they experience what anthropologists call *culture shock,* that is, a series of jolts when encountering the wide variety of customs, value systems, attitudes, and work habits, thus reducing their effectiveness in foreign commercial environments.[27] Therefore, it is crucial to effective operations that the manager be well schooled in the host culture. A lack of understanding of the host culture will lead the manager to think and act as he would in his home culture. Such a *self-reference criterion,* that is, the unconscious reference to one's own cultural values—has been termed the root cause of most international business problems abroad. The goal should be to eliminate this cultural myopia.[28]

Decision Areas for the International Marketer

The outline presented in Table 6-2 has been suggested for use by the international marketer in conducting cultural analysis. It should also be noted that this outline is perhaps as helpful a framework to the domestic marketer as to the international marketer.

Gaining a better understanding of the host culture is made difficult, however, by problems confronting consumer research abroad. Researchers in underdeveloped foreign markets encounter numerous difficulties in ob-

---

TABLE 6-2

OUTLINE OF CROSS-CULTURAL ANALYSIS OF CONSUMER BEHAVIOR

1. *Determine relevant motivations in the culture:* What needs are fulfilled with this product in the minds of members of the culture? How are these needs presently fulfilled? Do members of this culture readily recognize these needs?

2. *Determine characteristic behavior patterns:* What patterns are characteristic of purchasing behavior? What forms of division of labor exist within the family structure? How frequently are products of this type purchased? What size packages are normally purchased? Do any of these characteristic behaviors conflict with behavior expected for this product? How strongly ingrained are the behavior patterns that conflict with those needed for distribution of this product?

3. *Determine what broad cultural values are relevant to this product:* Are there strong values about work, morality, religion, family relations, and so on, that relate to this product? Does this product connote attributes that are in conflict with these cultural values? Can conflicts with values be avoided by changing the product? Are there positive values in this culture with which the product might be identified?

4. *Determine characteristic forms of decision making:* Do members of the culture display a studied approach to decisions concerning innovations or an impulsive approach? What is the form of the decision process? Upon what information sources do members of the culture rely? Do members of the culture tend to be rigid or flexible in the acceptance of new ideas? What criteria do they use in evaluating alternatives?

5. *Evaluate promotion methods appropriate to the culture:* What role does advertising occupy in the culture? What themes, words, or illustrations are taboo? What language problems exist in present markets that cannot be translated into this culture? What types of salesmen are accepted by members of the culture? Are such salesmen available?

6. *Determine appropriate institutions for this product in the minds of consumers:* What types of retailers and intermediary institutions are available? What services do these institutions offer that are expected by the consumer? What alternatives are available for obtaining services needed for the product but not offered by existing institutions? How are various types of retailers regarded by consumers? Will changes in the distribution structure be readily accepted?

Source: James F. Engel, David T. Kollat, and Roger D. Blackwell, *Consumer Behavior,* 2d ed. Copyright © 1968, 1973 by Holt, Rinehart and Winston, New York, pp. 95–96. Reprinted by permission of Holt, Rinehart and Winston.

taining satisfactory consumer interviews because of a mistrust of strangers asking questions. Moreover, certain subjects may be taboo and thus are not to be discussed, especially with strangers. In a number of countries even the subject of consumption habits is considered inappropriate.[29] In such an environment, it is clear that the marketer will have a difficult time piecing together information on which to base the company's strategies. In the remaining pages several marketing-decision areas will be discussed to reveal some of the cultural barriers that may be present.

PRODUCT CONSIDERATIONS Each country has a different mix of consumption. Therefore, the types of products that are saleable in each culture varies. For example, household appliance ownership data for several neighboring Western European nations shows quite differing consumption patterns, even though these countries are at similar levels of economic development. Such a pattern of consumer behavior can be attributed more to cultural differences than to economic differences.

A product being considered for marketing in a foreign country should be assessed for its "fit" with that country's value system. There are numerous examples in the history of international business of products that succeeded here yet sputtered abroad because they failed to take account of differences between American and other countries' value systems. For example, General Mills experienced failure in the 1960s when it attempted to introduce its Betty Crocker brand of cake mixes to Great Britain. The success of the product in America was attributed to the fact that the mix was designed so that any woman could produce a "professional-looking" cake that would win her praise from her family, friends, and neighbors. Buying attitudes of the British housewife were incorrectly assumed to be the same as those in America. The product failed, however, largely because of traditionalism. Product names such as angel food cake and devil's food sounded too exotic for British housewives, who also felt that the expert-looking cakes pictured on the packages would be too hard to make. Basically, the market was accustomed to simple products such as tea cakes, jam surprise, fruit cakes, and cherry cakes.[30]

Even such seemingly simple elements as package and product color have played havoc with many international marketers. Consider the following cultural caveats regarding colors:

White is the color of mourning in the Far East and blue is the color of sorrow; but Greeks like white and blue.

People in Pakistan, Israel, China, and Venezuela dislike yellow, while in Africa it is a favorite.

Purple connotes death in Latin America.

Among Moslems in Egypt and Syria green would be frowned on for a package color. For many other African markets, however, it is preferred above all others; while in Malaysia it connotes jungle and illness to illiterate consumers.

PROMOTION CONSIDERATIONS Promotion represents another area of marketing strategy that must be culturally tempered. Promotion failures have occurred abroad because of lack of understanding of the foreign culture. Some marketers, for example, have committed fatal bloopers in their zeal simply to export intact their product's brand name or advertising themes to a foreign market or to attempt direct translation of such words, as the following examples illustrate:

"Body by Fisher" became "Corpse by Fisher" in Flemish.

Colgate-Palmolive's "Cue" toothpaste is a pornographic word in French.

A British cosmetics company was unable to use its brand name in the Middle East because the Arabic meaning was "prostitute"—hardly suitable for a cosmetics firm.

Enco means "stalled car" in Japanese—a good reason for changing to Exxon, which is meaningless in any language.

American Motors' "Matador" connotes virility and excitement to the United States consumer. It turned out to be an unfortunate choice in Puerto Rico, however, which has an unusually high traffic-fatality rate. In Spanish, matador means "killer."

Entire promotion campaigns may even fail due to cultural barriers encountered. The following examples illustrate what may happen when the marketer is unable to overcome the self-reference criterion.

Advertising of Listerine in Thailand was modeled after the well-known United States television commercials showing a boy and girl who obviously liked each other, with one telling the other to use Listerine to avoid bad breath. After sales failed to materialize, executives discovered a problem with the commercial. The public portrayal of boy-girl relationships appearing in the advertisement was objectionable to the Thai people. The commercial was quickly modified to show two girls discussing Listerine. The result was increased sales.[31]

A manufacturer of canned fish ran a series of advertisements in Quebec magazines and newspapers, showing a woman in shorts playing golf with her husband. The copy stated that the woman could be on the golf links all day and still prepare a delicious dinner that evening if she used the product. Every element in the advertisement represented a violation of some underlying theme of French-Canadian life. First, the wife would not be likely to be playing golf with her husband; second, she would not wear shorts; and third, she would not be serving that particular kind of fish as a main course.[32]

CHANNEL CONSIDERATIONS Failure to understand the foreign culture when making channel decisions often causes problems, as the following case indicates:

In Japan reciprocity is extremely strong; thus, a buyer will turn to a supplier to whom he owes a favor no matter what the competition offers. If a Japanese company broke away from these bonds, it would "lose face" and find it extremely difficult to conduct business in the future. Nevertheless, the Simmons Company tried to break the already strongly developed bonds between mattress manufacturers and their channel members by setting up its own distribution system.

Simmons soon discovered, however, that few retailers would handle the product. Thus their attempt to operate outside traditional distribution channels produced little success.[33]

SUMMARY

In this chapter we examined one of the most basic influencing factors in the behavior of consumers—their cultural heritage. We described the nature of culture, its functions, and its components. The core United States cultural values were presented and the changing orientation of these values was discussed. This shift in values may have great marketing significance, especially as it presents untapped market opportunities.

The chapter also presented examples of foreign cultural differences in order to warn the potential international marketer against an American self-reference criterion that could prove to be disastrous for decision making abroad.

It can be seen, therefore, that the concept of culture offers many general and specific insights into the behavior of consumers. This, then, is a starting point for the marketer who wishes to better understand his market. It is imperative for the marketer to appreciate cultural nuances governing the relevant marketplace whether it be in the United States or abroad.

DISCUSSION TOPICS

1. Define culture. What are the most important characteristics of culture that describe its nature?

2. Why is the study of culture important to the marketer?

3. What is the function of culture?

4. What are the core cultural values held by members of the American culture?

5. How have core cultural values changed in the United States over the past generation? What shifts do you expect in these core values over your own generation? What effects are likely on consumer behavior and marketing?

6. Cite examples of marketing practices that either conform to or actively take advantage of core cultural values.

7. Name three products that are presently culturally unacceptable. What marketing strategies would you use to overcome their cultural resistance?

8. Why is an understanding of the foreign cultural environment especially important to the international marketer?

9. Locate two articles on marketing failures by companies operating in a foreign market. Could an improved cultural understanding have prevented these failures? How?

10. Select a specific product and foreign market and perform the cross-cultural analysis outlined in Table 6-2.

NOTES

1. Edward B. Tylor, *Primitive Culture,* Murray, London, 1891, p. 1.

2. Clyde Kluckhohn, "The Study of Culture," in Daniel Lewer and Harold D. Lasswell (eds.), *The Policy Sciences,* Stanford, Stanford, 1951, p. 86.

3. R. P. Cuzzort, *Humanity and Modern Sociological Thought,* Holt, New York, 1969, p. 356.

4. James S. Duesenberry, *Income, Saving and the Theory of Consumer Behavior,* Harvard, Cambridge, 1949, p. 19.

5. Charles Winick, "Anthropology's Contributions to Marketing," *Journal of Marketing,* **25**:55–56, July 1961.

6. Winick, "Anthropology's Contributions," p. 57.

7. Richard T. LaPiere, *Sociology,* McGraw-Hill, New York, 1946.

8. Leonard Broom and Philip Selznick, *Sociology, A Text with Adapted Readings,* 4th ed., Harper & Row, New York, 1968, p. 54.

9. For examples of the symbols we buy, see Sidney J. Levy, "Symbols for Sale," *Harvard Business Review,* **37**:117–124, July-August 1959.

10. "A Record Year for Charity, but . . .," *U.S. News & World Report,* May 5, 1975, p. 29.

11. Myles Callum, "Materialism: A Threat to Family Life?" *Better Homes and Gardens,* November 1973, p. 4.

12. David Riesman, Nathan Glazer, and Reuel Denney, *The Lonely Crowd,* abr. ed., Yale, New Haven, 1961.

13. See for example, Walter A. Henry, "Cultural Values Do Correlate with Consumer Behavior," *Journal of Marketing Research,* **13**:121–127, May 1976; Joseph F. Hair, Jr., and Rolph E. Anderson, "Culture, Acculturation, and Consumer Behavior," in Helmut Becker and Boris Becker (eds.) *Combined Proceedings,* American Marketing Association, Chicago, 1972, pp. 423–428; and Roy A. Herberger and Dodds I. Buchanan, "The Impact of Concern for Ecological Factors on Consumer Attitudes and Buying Behavior," in Fred C. Allvine (ed.) *Combined Proceedings,* American Marketing Association, Chicago, 1971, pp. 644–646.

14. Henry, "Cultural Values," pp. 121–127.

15. Donald E. Vinson, Jerome E. Scott, and Lawrence M. Lamont, "The Role of Personal Values in Marketing and Consumer Behavior," *Journal of Marketing,* **41**:44–50, April 1977.

16. Philip Kotler, *Marketing Management: Analysis, Planning, and Control,* 3d ed., Prentice-Hall, Englewood Cliffs, N.J., 1976, p. 43.

17. "Changing Attitudes of Youth on Sex, Patriotism and Work," *U.S. News & World Report,* June 3, 1974, pp. 66–67.

18. Lee Adler, "Cashing-In on the Cop-out: Cultural Change and Marketing Potential," *Business Horizons,* February 1970, pp. 21–27.

19. Vinson, Scott, and Lamont, "The Role of Personal Values," p. 49.

20. E. B. Weiss, "Creative Advertising Moves toward the New Society," *Advertising Age,* **44**:27–28, July 2, 1973.

21. Adler, "Cashing-in on the Cop-Out," p. 20.

22. "There's a Market, Somewhere, for the New Lost Generation," *Providence Sunday Journal,* May 22, 1977, p. A-19.

23. Theodore Roszak, *The Making of a Counter Culture: Reflections on the Technocratic Society and Its Youthful Opposition,* Anchor Books, Doubleday, Garden City, N.Y., 1969, p. 66.

24. "There's a Market," p. A-19.

25. "Young Radicals Are Now Good Consumers," *Marketing News,* February 11, 1977, p. 8.

26. See for example, Hans B. Thorelli, Helmut Becker, and Jack Engledow, *The Information Seekers,* Ballinger, Cambridge, Mass., 1975; Jagdish N. Sheth and S. Prakash Sethi, "Theory of Cross-Cultural Buyer Behavior," *Faculty Working Papers,* University of Illinois, May 31, 1973; Robert T. Green and Eric Langeard, "A Cross-National Comparison of Consumer Habits and Innovation Characteristics," *Journal of Marketing,* **39**:34–41, July 1975; and Susan P. Douglas, "Cross-Cultural Comparisons: The Myth of the Stereotype," Marketing Science Institute, Cambridge, Mass., 1975.

27. Lawrence Stessin, "Incidents of Culture Shock Among American Businessmen Overseas," *Pittsburgh Business Review,* November-December 1971, p. 1.

28. James A. Lee, "Cultural Analysis in Overseas Operations," *Harvard Business Review,* **44**:106, March-April 1966.

29. Harper W. Boyd, Ronald Frank, William Massy, and Mostafa Zoheir, "On the Use of Marketing Research in the Emerging Economies," *Journal of Marketing Research,* **1**:23, November 1964.

30. Montrose Sommers and Jerome Kernan, "Why Products Flourish Here, Fizzle There," *Columbia Journal of World Business,* March-April 1967, p. 93.

31. R. S. Diamond, "Managers Away From Home," *Fortune,* August 15, 1969, p. 28.

32. Winick, "Anthropology's Contributions," p. 60.

33. "Simmons in Japan: No Bed of Roses," *Sales Management,* August 1, 1967, p. 28.

ETHNIC SUBCULTURES

DIMENSIONS FOR SEGMENTING ETHNIC SUBCULTURES   THE BLACK SUBCULTURE Demographic Characteristics; Consumer Behavior and Marketing Implications; Segmenting the Black Market   **THE SPANISH-AMERICAN SUBCULTURE** Demographic Characteristics; Consumer Behavior and Marketing Implications

We learned in the previous chapter that one's cultural heritage has a very basic and lasting influence on his or her consumer behavior. Culture was seen to consist of basic behavioral patterns which exist in a society. However, as we saw from the discussion of countercultures, not all segments of a society have the same cultural patterns. Perhaps, therefore, the marketer can distinguish certain more homogeneous subgroups within the heterogeneous American society.

We refer to these groups as *subcultures* because they have values, customs, traditions, and other ways of behaving that are peculiar to a particular group within a culture. This means that there are subcultures of students, professors, professional football players, prison inmates, rock musicians, marketers, and other groups. Moreover, individuals may be members of more than one subculture at the same time. Thus it is imperative that marketers understand who constitutes the most relevant subculture for their particular product or service. By knowing the characteristics and behavioral patterns of the segment they are in a better position to refine the marketing mix required to properly satisfy that target segment.

Although subcultures may be categorized along seemingly infinite dimensions, this chapter and the next will examine only a few of the less understood, but important, subcultures that exist in the United States. The fact that these groups are among the most easily identifiable subcultures in the United States makes their segmentation feasible.

We shall, first of all, define several dimensions along which subcultures are frequently segmented. Next, these dimensions will be illustrated by discussing four examples of important United States subcultures. In this chapter two ethnic subcultures will be examined, while the next chapter will discuss age subcultures.

DIMENSIONS FOR SEGMENTING ETHNIC SUBCULTURES

Ethnic is the generic term used to describe groups characterized by a distinctive origin. Generally, it refers to the minority groups of a society. Their members are identified as such at birth, and they have a shared tradition and social life. Ethnic identification is based on what a person *is* when he or she is born and is largely unchangeable after that.[1]

Consumers may be subdivided along the following three types of ethnic dimensions, only the first two of which will be examined further in this chapter:

1. *Race*—Racial subcultures are made up of people with a common biological heritage involving certain (usually permanent) physical distinctions. The two most significant minority races in the United States for the marketer are blacks and Orientals. We will examine only the black market, however.

2. *Nationality*—People with a common national origin constitute another ethnic subculture. The nationality grouping is usually characterized by a distinctive language or accent. The minority market segment to be discussed in this category will be the Spanish-Americans.

3. *Religion*—Religious subcultures are comprised of people with a common and unique system of worship. Two important minority religious segments are Jews and Catholics. However, useful knowledge about the consumer behavior of these groups is presently quite limited and will not be discussed in this chapter.

THE BLACK SUBCULTURE

There are four reasons why the black market exists and is important: (1) the people making up this market are identifiable, (2) they have definable purchase patterns, (3) the market is very large, and (4) the market is concentrated in certain locations within the United States.[2] This section will review some unique aspects of black consumer behavior and relevant marketing strategy implications.

Demographic Characteristics

Generally, blacks may be described as disadvantaged compared with whites in terms of educational and occupational attainment. They are also more likely than whites to live in the crowded, poorer neighborhoods of large cities.

SIZE In 1976 the black market amounted to 25 million people, or over 11 percent of the total United States market. This growth has been projected to 29 million, or approximately 12 percent of the nation's population by 1985.

LOCATION Although the percent of blacks in the total United States population has remained rather constant since 1900, their geographic distribution has changed significantly over the last few decades. The percent living in the South has decreased slowly yet still accounts for 52 percent of all blacks in the United States and for approximately 20 percent of the region's population (compared with a less than 10 percent share of the population in the North and West).

The movement of blacks has also been in the direction of metropolitan areas. While the white population in central cities dropped by 2.1 million between 1960 and 1969, the black population increased by 2.6 million persons. Fifty-five percent of all blacks now live in the central cities of metropolitan areas and only 5 percent live in the suburbs. In contrast, nearly 75 percent of all whites live in the suburbs or in rural areas.

INCOME AND EMPLOYMENT PATTERNS In 1976 blacks had an annual income of approximately $68 billion. The ratio of black family income to that of whites has increased but is still only 60 percent. Thus, in 1975 the median income for black families in the United States was almost $8800, while for white families it was $13,700.

The proportion of blacks in each occupational category is coming to approximate more closely their share of the total labor force. Thus, more members of this group have moved into skilled, better-paying jobs. However, in spite of this occupational upgrading, in 1969 about 40 percent of black workers remained in service, laborer, or farm occupations—more than double the proportion of whites in such jobs. Blacks, especially the young, have traditionally had high unemployment rates. In 1976 their official unemployment rate for those 16 to 19 years old was 40 percent.

EDUCATIONAL LEVELS On this factor blacks have steadily improved their position. Between 1970 and 1975 the enrollment of blacks in college increased about 80 percent, and the number of college graduates increased 65 percent. Nevertheless, approximately twice the proportion of whites in each age group have completed one or more years of college as compared to blacks.

FAMILY AND AGE PATTERNS One of the most striking patterns of the black family is its tendency toward matrilinealism. Almost 34 percent of all black families are headed by a female, compared to only about 10 percent of whites.

A final characteristic that distinguishes this group is its age distribution. It is considerably younger than the white population—with a median age of 21 compared to 29 for whites.

A RISING BLACK MIDDLE CLASS The rise of the black middle class is confirmed by a number of the statistics cited above. The yardsticks defining a growing black middle class include such factors as advancing income, improved housing and living conditions, greater college enrollment, and occupational advancement.[3] In addition, some view a prime component of the emerging black middle class as black consciousness and life-style.

Consumer Behavior and Marketing Implications
Now let us examine some of the consumer-behavior findings regarding this market. We shall look at the most important elements and see how they relate to marketing-strategy variables.

BLACK VERSUS WHITE LIFE-STYLE Recent life-style and psychographic segmentation research on the black market has led to some interesting and useful findings, some of which are presented in Table 7-1. The Leo Burnett advertising agency has concluded that black female life-style patterns, particularly in an urban setting, indicate a stronger interest in style and fashion than those of whites.[4] There is also less mobility and less involvement in traditional civic and community organizations, greater reliance on the

TABLE 7-1

BLACK AND WHITE LIFE-STYLE DIFFERENCES

	Percent agreed	
	White	Black
Strong Pride toward Home		
I take great pride in my home	73%	77%
I get satisfaction out of cleaning because that is what people notice	29	46
I am a very neat person	50	66
A house should be dusted and polished at least three times a week	23	41
A Desire to Improve It		
I would like to move to a larger house	33	47
I like ultra-modern style furniture	14	34
When buying appliances, it pays to get the best even though it's more expensive	61	73
I like to own the most expensive things	14	25
Attitudes toward Money Management		
Our income is satisfactory	48	27
Our family is too heavily in debt today	15	32
I wish we had more money	46	71
Five years from now our income will be a lot higher	39	48
Grocery shopping for my family means following a strict budget	34	43
I watch the advertisements for sales	66	70
I study the grocery store ads in the newspaper each week	66	74

Source: Leo Burnett Company.

electronic media, and a stronger sense of alienation than with the average white American. Black women also have a stronger commitment to the importance of work and a clearer career orientation than the white female. Their life-style patterns and attitudes generally reveal the importance of money and budgeting and the need to be conservative, smart shoppers.

There are important differences between middle-class black and white women in the area of the home. Blacks have stronger self-perception about neatness and traditional home pride. They work hard to keep their home neat and clean, and they have a strong desire to live even better and make improvements such as better fixtures and dependable appliances.

Although life-style research has found that there are really more similarities than differences between black and white women, there are still a number of implications from findings such as those cited above. First, since black families are larger than white ones, with more working mothers, this group could be an excellent target for many convenience foods and home appliances. Second, because of the unrealized aspirations among black women, advertisers should be careful not to "overpromise" them. Third, their shopping patterns suggest that advertising to black women could stress price and value. Finally, this group appears to be a promising market for home cleaning and personal hygiene products.

PRODUCT PURCHASE PATTERNS Research studies show that there are some important differences between black and white purchasing patterns.

General and Product-specific Patterns With regard to the general spending behavior of blacks versus whites the following three major findings have emerged:

1. Total consumption expenditures are less than for comparable income whites; that is, blacks save more out of a given income than do whites.

2. Black consumers spend more for clothing and nonautomobile transportation and less for food, housing, medical care, and automobile transportation than do comparable income whites.

3. There is no consistent racial difference in expenditures for either recreation and leisure or home furnishing and equipment at comparable income levels.[5]

Research presented in several studies indicates that there are also product-specific differences between blacks and whites. Data on the relative purchase patterns among the two racial groups is presented in Table 7-2.

There are some rather obvious reasons that account for these consumption differences as well as some causes that are more subtle. For example, with regard to major home appliances low ownership appears to be primarily a function of income, substandard housing, and lack of proper utility connections. Another reason behind the different black and white consumption pattern is the blacks' narrower spectrum of choice due to their history of discrimination. That is, blacks have had less selectivity in the purchase of a home, vacation, travel, dining, entertainment, and so on, which has resulted in a greater expenditure per unit on other things that were available to them.[7]

Another factor that may cause these different consumption patterns is thought to be the tendency by minority groups to engage in *compensatory consumption;* that is, an attempt to purchase the material goods that are reflective of their achievement of full status in American society. Results of product-usage research, in fact, support this general pattern and suggest that blacks spend more on socially visible products than do whites of the same income class.

Brand Loyalty Studies have consistently shown that blacks are prone to buy brands that are nationally advertised, those that have a prestige connotation, and those about which they can feel confident.[8] Apparently, they feel that with national brands they get their money's worth and are not shortchanged on quality. Some of this brand loyalty is also due to the simple reason that there have been fewer brand choices available to blacks in their local outlets. However, with growing economic and social mobility they are able to take more risks with unfamiliar products.

TABLE 7-2

PRODUCT PURCHASE PATTERNS OF BLACKS COMPARED TO WHITES

Blacks Purchase More Than Whites

Foods
Cooked cereals
Cornmeal
Cream
Rice and rice dinners
Spaghetti and sauce
Frozen vegetables
Vinegar
All-purpose flour
Shortenings
Salt
Peanut butter
Fruit juices
Canned chili
Packaged luncheon meat
Pork sausage
Butter
Salad and cooking oils
Strained baby food
Tomato paste
Catsup
Prepared gravy
Canned stew
Canned tuna
Cheese sauce
Refrigerated cookie mix
Ready-to-eat store-bought cookies
Refrigerated biscuit dough
Refrigerated dinner roll dough
Refrigerated turnovers
Refrigerated danish
Pancake/waffle mix
Frozen french toast
Weiner wrap

Beverages
Soft drinks
Tonic
Scotch whiskey
Liquor
Evaporated milk
Tea bags
Instant tea

Personal care items
Beauty soap
Facial tissues
Deodorant soap
Deodorants/anti-perspirants
Toothpaste
Mouthwash
Skin-care lotion

Household items
Waxes
Laundry soap
Insecticides
Household disinfectants
Black-and-white televisions
Paper towels
Aerosol rug shampoo
Oven cleaner
Air freshener

Medical
Vitamins
Laxatives

Blacks Purchase Less Than Whites

Foods
Prepared soups
Frozen prepared dinners
Table syrups
Cake mixes
Dry cereals
Prepared pudding
Salad dressing
Mayonnaise

Beverages
Regular coffee
Dietary soft drinks

Personal care items
Hair spray
Shampoos
Cosmetics

Household items
Washing machines
Clothes dryers
Dishwashers
Dishwashing detergents
Color televisions
Foil and plastic wrap

Source: Charles E. Van Tassel, "The Negro as a Consumer—What We Know and What We Need to Know," in M. S. Moyer and R. E. Vosburgh (eds.), *Marketing for Tomorrow—Today,* American Marketing Association, Chicago, 1967, pp. 166–168. Carl M. Larson, "Racial Brand Usage and Media Exposure Differentials," in Keith K. Cox and Ben M. Enis (eds.), *A New Measure of Responsibility for Marketing,* American Marketing Association, Chicago, 1968, pp. 208–215. James E. Stafford, Keith K. Cox, and James B. Higginbotham, "Some Consumption Pattern Differences between Urban Whites and Negroes," *Social Science Quarterly,* **49:** 619–630, December 1968. Leon Morse, "Black Radio Market Study," *Television/Radio Age,* February 28, 1977, pp. A-10, A-25.

Thus, although national brand loyalty has been strong in the past, there is some evidence that there is an erosion of brand preference among sophisticated, high-income blacks. One researcher has found a shift toward purchases on the basis of price, rather than by brand.[9]

New Product Adoption As blacks are moving toward greater experimentation with brands, new marketing opportunities are opened up. Nevertheless, the psychographic research conducted by one company indicates that almost twice as many blacks as whites are "non-risk takers."[10] Although this finding does not present a generally favorable environment for new product introduction, it does not automatically shut the door to innovations either. Black consumers are open to trying new products if they are appropriately presented as an item that can perhaps help them live better, save time, or achieve more status. For example, pop wines were positioned as a new, stylish drink to enjoy when having fun and immediately became popular with blacks.

One factor affecting new product adoption has been found to be the social visibility of the product. Blacks appear to be less innovative than whites with respect to appliances and food—two nonsocially visible items. They are more innovative than whites, however, with respect to socially visible fashion and clothing.[11]

Knowledge of such a pattern can help buyers for retail stores. For example, the merchandising manager of a large department store in Chicago states that the black shopper is his guide. He watches black clothing-purchase patterns to determine what will later become popular among white men.[12]

SHOPPING PATTERNS The black market has also been researched on the basis of its shopping patterns. Here, too, differences have been found between whites and blacks. While much of the research deals with food purchasing habits, other product shopping patterns have also been investigated.

Food Stores Table 7-3 presents results of a study by *Progressive Grocer* on factors influencing store choice. Notice that blacks' assessments of supermarkets generally match those of the population at large. There are several differences, however, that could prove useful to supermarket managers in planning marketing strategy. For example, the meat, dairy, frozen foods, and health and beauty aids departments are more crucial in black store choice than for all shoppers. These might be important departments for specialized black-oriented products (such as foods and cosmetics).

Although brand loyalty is generally high, store loyalty is not as strong. One study showed that only 59 percent of blacks are always or almost always satisfied with the food stores where they do most of their shopping, compared to 72 percent of whites.[13]

Discount Houses No firm conclusion can yet be drawn about black shopping patterns in nonfood stores. However, one study did find that blacks frequented discount stores (as opposed to department stores) more often than whites.[14] A probable reason for this patronage is the emphasis on price by black shoppers. Another reason could be related to the atmosphere of large department stores which has been found to cause some feelings of insecurity among black shoppers.[15] This early research finding indicated that blacks felt conspicuous in such department stores. However, this may be breaking down now due to greater self-confidence and pride among blacks.

TABLE 7-3

HOW 37 FACTORS AFFECT BLACK SHOPPERS' SUPERMARKET CHOICE

Importance to Black shoppers Rank	Index*	Factor	Importance to all shoppers** Rank
1	98.0	Cleanliness	1
2	97.8	Good meat department	7
3	97.0	All prices clearly labeled	2
4	96.6	Freshness date marked on products	6
5	95.6	Low prices	3
5	95.6	Good produce department	5
7	95.5	Accurate, pleasant checkout clerks	4
8	93.8	Good dairy department	11
9	93.3	Shelves usually well stocked	8
10	92.5	Helpful personnel in service departments	12
11	91.1	Convenient store location	10
12	90.5	Good layout for fast, easy shopping	13
13	89.6	Good parking facilities	9
14	89.1	Good frozen foods department	21
15	88.6	Good selection of nationally advertised brands	16
16	87.6	Short wait for checkout	15
17	87.5	Frequent "sales" or "specials"	14
17	87.5	Aisles clear of boxes	19
19	86.8	Good selection of low-priced store-brand items	18
20	86.0	Don't run short of items on "special"	17
20	86.0	Pleasant atmosphere/decor	24
22	85.8	Baggers on duty	20
23	85.1	New items that I see advertised are available	23
24	84.7	Unit pricing on shelves	22
25	83.8	Manager is friendly and helpful	25
26	83.0	Check-cashing service	26
27	73.8	Not usually over-crowded	27
28	73.6	Open late hours	30
29	69.3	Good drugs and toiletries section	33
30	67.0	Good assortment of nonfoods merchandise	29
31	65.8	Carry purchases to car	28
32	60.6	Eye-catching mass displays	34
33	59.6	Has in-store bakery	31
34	57.3	Has delicatessen department	32
35	52.0	Trading stamps or other extras	36
36	39.0	People know my name	35
37	37.5	Sell hot foods to take out or eat in store	37

*In filling out the questionnaire respondents rated each characteristic on a scale of 1-to-6. Their answers were converted into a 0-to-100% index. This means that the larger proportion of people who gave a top rating the closer the score is to the highest possible index figure: 100.0

**Based on a P.G.-H.T.I. survey of a national sample of housewives which included blacks in proportion to their incidence in the population.

Source: Robert F. Dietrich, "When Blacks Choose a Super, Some Departments Matter More," *Progressive Grocer,* August 1975, p. 34. Reprinted with permission.

Clothing Stores Fashion-conscious black and white women differ in their choice of stores for clothing purchases. Among black women, the fashion-conscious are more likely to shop at department stores, while white women are oriented more toward high-priced specialty stores.[16] Perhaps black women feel even more conspicuous in high-priced specialty shops than in department stores, and thus are less inclined to patronize the former.

PROMOTING TO BLACKS The lack of fuller understanding of black consumer behavior has probably perplexed marketers most in the area of promotion. For instance, marketers have wondered whether they should promote in a specialized way through specialized media to reach the black market or whether they should expect to reach it through their general appeal to the broad market of consumers. In addition, concern exists regarding whether advertisements should be all-black in content, mixed, or all-white. These questions are addressed in this section.

Choice of Medium The issue of specialized versus general advertising programs cannot be resolved easily, but one can obtain a better understanding of the problem by looking at the alternatives. There are three main avenues that may be taken in a specialized appeal to blacks—radio, magazines, and newspapers aimed specifically at the black market. Television, a fourth approach, has been tried, but only to a limited extent. The big advantage of black media is that blacks know the advertisement is meant for them while in other media they may not always be sure.

Black media have developed mainly since World War II and include dozens of magazines, several hundred newspapers and radio stations, and one TV channel. But only a very small amount of all advertising is placed in these media. For example, Sears' total advertising expenditures in 1975 amounted to $329 million; however only $8 to $10 million of this was allocated to black radio, newspapers, or magazines.[17]

The major black-oriented medium is *radio*, since research shows that blacks spend more time listening to radio than do whites. Moreover, approximately one-half of all listening done by blacks is to black radio stations.[18] There are several reasons for the influence and importance of radio in the black market:

1. Black radio is, for the most part, the only medium available on a day-to-day basis which specifically attempts to reach the black market.

2. Black radio supplies listeners with advertising which they can be sure is meant for them.

3. Blacks feel committed to listen to a medium which specifically gives them an identity and visibility.

Advertisers are becoming more and more convinced that black radio is the best route, both in terms of reach and in terms of black involvement with the medium. Attempting to reach the black community through general radio, as opposed to black radio, is likely to be a mistake for many products.

The black middle class probably identifies most closely with *black magazines. Ebony* is an example of a black magazine that has achieved national success. In addition, several new magazines have appeared—*Essence,* for black women; *Encore,* a *Time*-like news monthly; *Black Creation,* for the arts lover; *Relevant,* a wide-ranging discussion-type periodical; and *Black Sports,* for the athletic enthusiast. Blacks have a strong attachment to such media because they emphasize their achievements in government, business, sports, and the arts.

Ads in black magazines are run by most of the nation's largest advertisers, and could be mistaken for those in white-oriented magazines were it not for the color of the models. With such ads, blacks can identify more completely with the products. Advertising effectiveness in such media is also enhanced by using editorial material tailored to their self-image, interests, and life-style. A study by a black-oriented magazine, for example, found that ad copy in a magazine with black editorial content has a more positive effect on black readers than does the same advertising in general market magazines.[19]

Although there are numerous black-oriented radio and magazine vehicles, *black television* programming is less widespread. There have been a few network shows featuring blacks and their life-styles, with black situation comedies being the most popular. Daytime soap operas, news, and game shows also have high viewership among blacks. There is also an increase in the amount of syndicated television programming being developed for this audience. However, television is primarily a white-oriented medium, and as such many marketing experts doubt that sole reliance on television can effectively sell this ethnic market.

Outdoor advertising should also be mentioned as an attractive vehicle by which blacks can be reached because of their geographic concentration. Alka-Seltzer, for example, has used two versions of the same billboard ad. The words are the same on both, but black models are used in black areas and white models in other areas. Liquor, beer, soft drink and cigarette manufacturers are other heavy users of outdoor ethnic advertising.

Use of Integrated Advertising The use of black and white models in integrated ads for general coverage media is fairly recent. Since 1963 blacks have begun to appear in magazine and TV advertisements and most research on integrated advertising has shown that both races react favorably to such ads.[20] Thus, in most situations it appears that the marketer may use blacks and whites in advertising with favorable results. "Tokenism" in advertising, however, is not viewed favorably among blacks. Therefore, the marketer must take care to avoid such an impression.

Generalized versus Specialized Campaigns Some marketers advocate the use of specially prepared ads in black media as the surest way of reaching the black consumer. They claim that through black-oriented media prospects will more readily and strongly identify with the product. Others disagree, claiming that much of this type of advertising wins favor only with the lower economic group, while it alienates middle- and upper-class blacks by frustrating their aspirations to be fully integrated into American life. Noting that blacks are more sensitive to what whites buy than to what other blacks purchase, and that there are a number of similarities in each market, they feel that an integrated, all-inclusive campaign can catch everybody.[21]

Both of these arguments are reasonable. Besides, most advertisers don't have to make "either-or" decisions concerning this aspect. A campaign could be run on an integrated basis in the general media, for example, and at the same time special appeals could be made through black radio or magazines. It depends on the nature of the product being promoted and the particular socioeconomic class being approached as to which advertising path should be taken. However, it should never be assumed that any one medium reaches all blacks.

Even advertising themes or appeals may need tailoring to special market segments. For instance, while general market ads for General Foods' Maxwell House instant coffee were using Maxine the coffee lady, ads directed at the black market were taking a different approach. Print ads in black media were aimed at women now in their thirties and showed scenes recalling a little girl's first sip of Maxwell House coffee. Other folksy vignettes pictured the family serving Maxwell House to "The Reverend" who had come for one of his frequent visits.

Similarly, Kool-Aid ads in black magazines recently have appealed to the mother's dreams of her child growing up to be a successful pilot, lawyer, or ship navigator, with Kool-Aid being one of the good things the mother could provide for her children. This image-building approach appealed to upward mobility among blacks. In contrast, general market ads run at the same time sold mothers on Kool-Aid because children liked it, it was cheaper than soft drinks, and it contained vitamin C. Companies should test different appeals among market segments to find which one works best.

Blacks have a distinctive way of looking at ads. They tend to view advertising as doing two things—selling the product and contributing to the over-all process of building the image of black people in general. Thus the marketer should carefully attempt to accomplish both goals. The use of a black celebrity is one way companies can mount effective promotion programs. For example, Hank Aaron has appeared as a spokesman for Magnavox television and Pearl Bailey appears in White-Westinghouse appliance ads. Endorsements are also very important to sneaker manufacturers such as Converse and Keds in their battle to sell canvas basketball shoes to urban blacks who, it is claimed, set the national style in such shoes.[2]

Public relations and public service are also important promotional avenues in this market, because blacks are quite concerned with social improvements for their group. Companies such as Greyhound, Exxon, U.S. Steel, General Motors, *Reader's Digest,* Ford, and Pet Milk have sponsored many public service projects in this market.

PRICING AND THE BLACK MARKET There are also differences between whites and blacks regarding the influence of price in the marketplace.

General Price Behavior Price behavior of blacks can be described in two broad patterns. On one hand, low-income blacks appear to buy largely on a price basis; while on the other hand, higher income blacks seem interested in both price and status.

One study found that low-income black families are more concerned with prices for food than are either low-income whites or middle-class blacks.[23] Another study supports the contention of pricing's importance to black consumers with the finding that price is a dominant shopping attitude of blacks at every level. In contrast, it was found that among whites, price decreased in importance as income increased.[24]

Black response to couponing has traditionally been low. One study shows that considerably less than half as many black women as white redeem coupons from magazines, mail, or packages when shopping.[25] They aren't exposed to as many coupons because they have minimum readership of general magazines and newspapers which make up the major delivery mode. In addition, companies have had difficulty developing usable names and address lists for inner-city residents; consequently, there are virtually no coupon or sample mailings to these groups. There is some indication, however, that younger blacks are becoming more interested in coupons.[2]

With regard to the use of unit price information by blacks a study of inner-city (predominantly black) buyers found a lower incidence of its usage than among suburban buyers.[27]

Do Blacks Pay More? Much of the research on pricing in the black market relates to the *level* of prices; that is, whether blacks (used synonymously in most studies with the "poor") pay more than white (or "nonpoor") consumers.

Research indicates that blacks, in many instances, do not pay higher prices than whites for equivalent services. Most of the research has been oriented toward the question of price exploitation of blacks by merchants and the products researched have been primarily foods, with less attention given to other products such as durable goods. One review of fifteen studies of food prices charged blacks found that only five of the studies indicated higher prices paid by blacks or low-income area residents, while the other ten studies found no evidence of higher prices to blacks.[28]

One of the few investigations of durable goods purchases by low-income consumers found them to be active in the comsumption of major durables and strongly oriented toward buying new, rather than used, furniture and appliances. These families were found to rely on small neighborhood stores or buy from peddlers rather than shop in department stores or discount houses because of their pervasive need for less stringent credit.[29]

Even if the poor do not pay more for products because of exploitation, a Bureau of Labor Statistics study points out that they may pay more for what they get because of other reasons: (1) they buy smaller-size packages, which are more expensive per unit of measure; (2) stores in low-income areas are less orderly and clean; in addition meats and produce are not as fresh; (3) many of these stores experience much pilferage; and (4) independent stores are generally open more days per week and longer hours than are chains.[30]

Thus, these stores are unable to achieve the economies of scale that chains in higher-income areas do and consequently, managers may make up for these increased costs by charging higher prices or giving lower quality. While it may be true that consumers do pay higher prices in low-income areas and receive lower-quality food, the basis for this may not lie so much in exploitation as in the fact that this is a high-cost market to serve. It is clear that much more research needs to be done concerning this topic.

Segmenting the Black Market

Historically, the black market has been viewed as a single group, rather than as being made up of distinct market segments with different identifications, reference groups, life-styles, and buyer behavior. However, it has recently been suggested that four basic market segments with different buyer motivations exist in the black population, and are defined as follows:

1. *Negroes*—This segment is more closely identified with the white middle class than with other segments of the population. They strive to emulate the white middle class, purchase products with status and have high brand loyalty for some national brands.

2. *Blacks*—This segment has recently evolved and is in the process of developing its own set of cultural standards while minimizing the values of white society. Their reference group consists of other members of this movement, which makes the group transitory in nature. Because of this feature marketers may have a difficult time determining an appropriate strategy for this group.

3. *Afro-Americans*—This segment has not only discarded the white middle-class standards but may also be said to be rejecting the established standards of white supremacy. Reference groups and opinion leaders for this segment would be any strong antiestablishment individuals or groups. Marketing to this group could be difficult because of the degree of change occurring in the movement and the possibility of a backlash by appealing to them.

4. *Recent Black Immigrants*—This segment may still identify with the society from which it emigrated. Members may try to adapt their consumer behavior to the sophisticated American culture. Reference groups for this segment would be individuals and groups in their own culture. The small size of this market makes it insignificant to marketers.[31]

A large-scale survey conducted by National Black Opinions found that 62.1 percent of the black population want to be called "black," 18.3 percent think of themselves as "Negro," 11.2 percent want to be called "Afro-American," and 8.4 percent view themselves as "colored." It is primarily those 35 years old and younger who see themselves as black, those 36–55 as Negro, and those over 55 as colored, while Afro-Americans use that term to give themselves a greater sense of their identity.[32]

Unfortunately, much of the research on blacks has been conducted without accounting for the differences between these distinct black market segments referred to above. Therefore, the marketer should be aware of the potential for a more precise segmentation strategy and its implications for allocating marketing resources.

THE SPANISH-AMERICAN SUBCULTURE

Spanish-Americans make up the nation's second-largest minority market. In spite of their potential as a consumer goods market, however, they, too, are underresearched and underdeveloped. The Spanish-American segment is a very significant group with which the marketer should be familiar. Moreover, the future impact of this group on the United States and the marketer is expected to be even greater.

First, the important demographic characteristics of this market will be presented. This will be followed by a discussion of the most significant consumer behavior and marketing implications.

Demographic Characteristics

The Spanish-American market differs radically from other ethnic segments and mainstream America in that it is continually infused with new immigrants. The old country is never far away, either symbolically or geographically. This group also clings tenaciously to the Spanish language and generally defies the melting-pot concept.

SIZE In 1978 the size of this market was approximately 12 million people and was growing at a rate of about 1 million annually. At the present rate of growth this segment will become the country's largest ethnic group by the year 2030.[33] A large portion of this market's growth comes from immigration. The largest Spanish-American market segments are Mexican-Americans, Puerto Ricans, and Cubans in descending order.

LOCATION The Spanish subculture is largely an urban population segment. For example, in 1970 about 84 percent of all Spanish-Americans lived in metropolitan areas, compared to 68 percent of the total white population. Moreover, the Latin population is concentrated heavily in comparatively few metropolitan areas such as Los Angeles, New York, and Miami and in a few states—Texas, New Mexico, Arizona, California, Colorado, New York, Pennsylvania, New Jersey, and Florida.[34]

INCOME AND EMPLOYMENT PATTERNS The income level of Spanish-origin families lies between that of whites and blacks. Median income in 1971 totalled $7500, about $3100 below that of white families and $1100 above that of black families.

The occupations of Spanish-origin men are unlikely to be white-collar in nature. While 44 percent of white men hold white-collar jobs, only about 23 percent of Spanish-American men and 22 percent of black men are white-collar workers.

EDUCATION With regard to education, Spanish-Americans are generally at a lower level than blacks. Among persons 25 to 29 years of age, approximately 48 percent of the Spanish-Americans have graduated from high school, compared to 58 percent of blacks and 80 percent of whites. About one in five persons of Spanish origin over 25 has completed less than 5 years of school, compared to one in 25 whites. Younger members of the Spanish community are narrowing the education gap, however.

FAMILY PATTERNS Spanish families are larger than white families. In addition, a larger proportion of women of Spanish origin remain in the home than do whites or blacks. Finally, this market is a young one. Approximately

46 percent of Spanish-Americans are under age 18, compared with about 35 percent of the total population.

Consumer Behavior and Marketing Implications

More and more companies are recognizing the importance of the Spanish-American market. In this section each of the marketing-mix variables will be examined to understand the major implications of Spanish-American consumer behavior on these decision areas.

PRODUCT PURCHASES The marketer should be aware that the Spanish-American market is highly individualistic in its product and brand preferences, which are often reflective of cultural differences. For some products, particularly food purchases, this market is very significant. Partly because of their larger-than-average families they spend about 10 percent more per week on food purchases than non-Spanish. In addition, more Spanish households visit fast-food restaurants frequently than do non-Spanish consumers. For example, 20 percent of Spanish homes visit such outlets more than once per week, versus 9 percent of the non-Spanish homes.[35] They are also much heavier consumers of beverages such as soft drinks and beer. The Schaefer Brewing Company, for example, estimates Spanish beer consumption to be 1.5 times greater than the national average.

Latins are highly brand loyal, trusting well-known or familiar brands. Not only is brand loyalty high in this market, but related to this is the strong perceived risk among Spanish-Americans of trying a new or different product. Spanish-American women tend to be conservative shoppers. Of course, low incomes are a strong constraint, for with large families to feed, it is risky to veer away from tried-and-true products. There are other factors, however. Inability to read and understand English is a major inhibitor of new-product purchase among this group. Finally, because of value differences between this group and mainstream America, new product benefits often seem superficial or nonsensical to Latins.[36]

Thus, introducing a new brand to this market can be difficult. However, a marketing program carefully tailored to the Latin's self-image and interests can be effective in gaining successful entry into this market. In developing new-product plans the marketer should investigate this group carefully to determine its receptivity to the innovation being considered. Packaging of products sold to the Spanish-American market must also be carefully tailored to meet their needs. For example, Campbell soups once had little success in the Spanish-American market because many consumers weren't aware of what the product was. For one thing there was no familiarity with the concept of condensed soup, and no picture appeared on the label illustrating the use of the soup. In addition, some Spanish people misread soup labels, purchasing celery soup, thinking it was cereal.[37]

PROMOTING TO SPANISH-AMERICANS The Spanish-American market, although concentrated geographically and in urban areas, is sometimes difficult to reach because of the language barrier. A 1969 survey found that approximately 72 percent of the Puerto Ricans, 87 percent of the Cubans, and 47 percent of the Mexicans living in the United States speak mostly Spanish at home. Therefore, in order to effectively reach this market Spanish-language media frequently must be used.[38]

Spanish Media *Television* has developed into an important medium for Spanish advertising with ten stations in the United States and four more just across the Mexican border. One 1973 study found that 64 percent of Spanish households in the New York City area were tuned in to a Spanish television station during one weekday evening at prime-time.[39] With Spanish television ownership at approximately the same level as the general population, and the increase in UHF television penetration, the marketer is increasingly able to reach the Spanish-American segment by using this medium.

Radio is also an important medium for the Spanish-American market. There are at least 185 United States radio stations that present Spanish language programming on a full- or part-time basis. Radio ownership in this market is comparable to that for all United States households. Moreover, Spanish-Americans are heavy listeners. A survey of New York Spanish-speaking radio households showed median daily listening of more than four hours per day, compared to average adult listening of 2.5 hours per day for all United States radio households. In addition to being heavy listeners, about 60 to 80 percent of their listening is to Spanish-language programming.[40] Spanish teens, however, devote 61 percent of their listening time to contemporary music stations versus only 14 percent for Spanish stations, and almost as much time listening to black radio.[41]

Print media, including magazines and newspapers, are also used to reach the Spanish-American market. These, however, tend to have much less impact than other media because of lower literacy rates.

Effective Promotional Messages In order for advertising to the Spanish-American market to be successful, the communication must fit the people's subculture. Ads that are authentically Latin in setting and language, and highly personal in approach are perceived as meaningful. Even mass-appeal commercials can be used by substituting a Spanish voice-over, but the marketer should be sure that the video is appropriate. Some well-known advertising personalities are effectively used in this market. For instance Colonel Sanders and Frank Perdue appear in commercials for their chicken products speaking Spanish.

Companies are turning away from mere translations toward complete ad campaigns tailored to Latin consumers, particularly when direct translations may be an embarrassment. Coca-Cola learned this when its slogan "It's the Real Thing" had an off-color meaning in Spanish. As tailored promotions appear, advertising agencies must try to keep cultural differences in mind to attain credibility with their Latin audiences.[42] For example, a television commercial for General Foods' Tang breakfast drink had to be changed to enhance its believability. The English-language version of the commercial featured a woman Ph.D. saying she serves Tang to her family; but the Spanish community would have had great difficulty relating to that situation. Therefore, the company's ad agency researched the subject and found that both teachers and grandmothers are authority figures that command Latins' respect. The result was that in Tang's Spanish ads the drink was served by a teacher and a grandmother.[43]

A family tie-in can often be appealing because of this group's large family size and their high regard for strong family bonds. Colgate made effective use of this appeal in one commercial in which a child's birthday party was shown being attended by the whole family. Borden has also been successful in this market with the slogan "We'd like your family to meet our family at La Casa Borden."

The marketer should conduct research to find out what appeals are best for this segment. It may be found that appeals used in the general market are not as successful. For example, while Colgate stresses a cavity-fighting theme in the general market, it promotes "Happy Smiles" in the Spanish segment. Kent cigarettes advertises taste rather than low tar content, and Mazola ads don't even mention cholesterol.

SHOPPING PATTERNS Research has shown that many Spanish-speaking housewives feel lost in giant supermarkets where they are surrounded by many unfamiliar products and are inhibited about asking questions. Although such uneasiness exists with regard to large stores, Latins, nevertheless, do most of their shopping in them. For example, in New York, bodegas (small shops) account for only 30 percent of grocery volume among Spanish-speaking residents.

PRICING IMPLICATIONS The language barrier also affects pricing policies. For example, one of the most frequent complaints of Spanish-speaking supermarket customers is over such pricing techniques as multiple pricing, the presence of both preprinted and stamped prices, and cents-off labels.

Thus, it is clear that effective marketing to the Spanish-American segment requires a tailored marketing program. Moreover, the need for such a special marketing program (particularly with regard to advertising) to reach this group is likely to continue to exist for some time in the United States.

SUMMARY

This chapter has introduced the concept of ethnic subcultures and ethnic segments in the United States. Ethnic groups were classified according to racial, nationality, or religious bases. Only race and national origin were discussed in this chapter, however.

The black and Spanish markets were described as being very large, as being identifiable, and as having important differences in their consumer-behavior patterns from the rest of society. Even within these ethnic subcultures are heterogeneous subgroups which the marketer needs to understand.

Each major marketing element was discussed, and consumer-behavior implications were cited. For the marketer, it is important that these significant ethnic groups be approached with carefully planned and executed strategies based on a knowledge of their similarities with and differences from the broader American market.

DISCUSSION TOPICS

1. What is a subculture?

2. Describe some important subcultures that exist in the United States. Why are these important? Are all subcultures equally important to or usable by the marketer?

3. Prepare a report on the current demographic picture of the black market.

4. Suggest some marketing implications of the following market segments: (1) blacks, (2) Afro-Americans, and (3) recent black immigrants.

5. Look through some black-oriented magazines (e.g., *Ebony*) and select three advertisements that are similar to those appearing in predominantly white-oriented media except for the models (bring in white ads too). Are there any other differences between the ads, such as language or situation? Explain why or why not.

6. Assume that you are the product manager in charge of marketing for Tide detergent and you are developing an advertising campaign. Use the knowledge you gained in this chapter to put together an effective campaign for the black and Spanish subcultures.

7. Prepare a report on the current demographic picture of the Spanish-American subculture.

8. What are the most important considerations in marketing to the Spanish-American market?

NOTES

1. Bernard Berelson and Gary Steiner, *Human Behavior: An Inventory of Scientific Findings,* Harcourt, Brace & World, New York, 1964, p. 494.

2. D. Parke Gibson, *The $30 Billion Negro,* Macmillan, New York, 1969, p. 9.

3. "America's Rising Black Middle Class," *Time,* June 17, 1974, pp. 19–20.

4. Leon Morse, "Black Radio Market Study," *Television/Radio Age,* February 28, 1977, pp. A-1–A-31.

5. Marcus Alexis, "Some Negro-White Differences in Consumption," *American Journal of Economics and Sociology,* **21**:11–28, January 1962.

6. James E. Stafford, Keith K. Cox, and James B. Higginbotham, "Some Consumption Pattern Differences between Urban Whites and Negroes," *Social Science Quarterly,* **49**:629, December 1968.

7. "Is There Really a Negro Market?" *Marketing Insights,* January 29, 1968, p. 14.

8. "The Negro Market: 23 Million Consumers Make a $30 Billion Market Segment," *Marketing Insights,* January 29, 1968, p. 11.

9. W. Leonard Evans, Jr., "Ghetto Marketing: What Now?" in Robert L. King (ed.), *Marketing and the New Science of Planning,* American Marketing Association, Chicago, 1968, p. 530.

10. Robert F. Dietrich, "Know Your Black Shopper," *Progressive Grocer,* June 1975, p. 46.

11. Donald E. Sexton, Jr., "Black Buyer Behavior," *Journal of Marketing,* **36**:38, October 1972; and "Consumer Dynamics in the Supermarket," *Progressive Grocer,* New York, 1969.

12. *Men's Wear,* January 5, 1968, p. 3.

13. Dietrich, "Know Your Black Shopper."

14. Lawrence P. Feldman and Alvin D. Star, "Racial Factors in Shopping Behavior," in Keith K. Cox and Ben M. Enis (eds.), *A New Measure of Responsibility for Marketing,* American Marketing Association, Chicago, 1968, pp. 216–226.

15. Henry Allen Bullock, "Consumer Motivations in Black and White—Part I," *Harvard Business Review,* May-June 1961, pp. 99–100.

16. Bernard Portis, "Negroes and Fashion Interest," *Journal of Business,* **39**:314–323, April 1966.

17. Morse, "Black Radio," p. A-20.
18. Morse, "Black Radio," p. A-24.
19. Jessica Sinha, "Ethnic Marketing," *Product Marketing,* June 1977, p. 32.
20. See Arnold M. Barban and Edward W. Cundiff, "Negro and White Response to Advertising Stimuli," *Journal of Marketing Research,* **1**:53–56, November 1964; Arnold M. Barban, "The Dilemma of Integrated Advertising," *Journal of Business,* **42**:477–496, October 1969; B. Stuart Tolley and John J. Goett, "Reactions to Blacks in Newspaper Ads," *Journal of Advertising Research,* **11**:11–17, April 1971; Lester Guest, "How Negro Models Affect Company Image," *Journal of Advertising Research,* **10**:29–34, April 1970; Mary Jane Schlinger and Joseph T. Plummer, "Advertising in Black and White," *Journal of Marketing Research,* **9**:149–153, May 1972; William V. Muse, "Product-Related Response to Use of Black Models in Advertising," *Journal of Marketing Research,* **8**:107–109, February 1971; and James W. Cagley and Richard N. Cardozo, "White Response to Integrated Advertising," *Journal of Marketing Research,* **10**:35–40, April 1970.
21. Henry Allen Bullock, "Consumer Motivations in Black and White—Part II," *Harvard Business Review,* July-August 1961, pp. 110–124.
22. Frederick C. Klein, "Foot Race: Sneaker Makers are Set to Pursue the Athletes at Summer Olympics," *The Wall Street Journal,* April 23, 1976, p. 20.
23. Robert L. King and Earl R. DeManche, "Comparative Acceptance of Selected Private-Branded Food Products in Low-income Negro and White Families," in Philip R. McDonald (ed.), *Marketing Involvement in Society and the Economy,* American Marketing Association, Chicago, 1969, pp. 63–69.
24. Feldman and Star, "Racial Factors," pp. 216–226.
25. Dietrich, "Know Your Black Shopper."
26. Sinha, "Ethnic Marketing," pp. 32–33.
27. Monroe Friedman, *Dual-Price Labels: Usage Patterns and Potential Benefits for Shoppers in Inner-city and Suburban Supermarkets,* Center for the Study of Contemporary Issues, Eastern Michigan University, Ypsilanti, Mich., 1971.
28. Donald E. Sexton, Jr. "Comparing the Cost of Food to Blacks and to Whites—a Survey," *Journal of Marketing,* **35**:40–46, July 1971.
29. David Caplovitz, *The Poor Pay More,* Free Press, New York, 1963.
30. Phyllis Groom, "Prices in Poor Neighborhoods," *Monthly Labor Review,* **89**:1085–1090, October 1966.
31. Thomas E. Barry and Michael G. Harvey, "Marketing to Heterogeneous Black Consumers," *California Management Review,* **17**:53, Winter 1974.
32. Morse, "Black Radio," p. A-3.
33. "The Newest Americans: A Second 'Spanish Invasion,' " *U.S. News & World Report,* July 8, 1974, p. 34.
34. Paul M. Ryscavage and Earl F. Mellor, "The Economic Situation of Spanish Americans," *Monthly Labor Review,* **96**:3, April 1973.
35. Joseph M. Aguayo, "Latinos: Los Que Importan Son Ustedes," *Sales and Marketing Magazine,* July 11, 1977, p. 29.
36. "Habla Usted Espanol?" *Marketing Insights,* January 12, 1970, p. 12.
37. Karen Rothmyer, "A Spanish Accent is Very 'In' These Days on Madison Avenue," *The Wall Street Journal,* January 24, 1975, p. 1.
38. Rothmyer, "A Spanish Accent," p. 1.
39. Rothmyer, "A Spanish Accent," p. 1.
40. Richard P. Jones, "Spanish Ethnic Market Second Largest in U.S.," *Marketing Insights,* November 27, 1967, p. 11.
41. "Latino Media: Available in Any Mood from Conservative to Salsa," *Sales and Marketing Magazine,* July 11, 1977, p. 25.
42. Aguayo, "Latinos," p. 28.
43. Rothmyer, "A Spanish Accent," p. 25.

AGE SUBCULTURES

CHAPTER 8

THE YOUTH MARKET Demographic Characteristics;
Psychographic Characteristics; Consumer Behavior and Marketing
Implications; The Child Market **THE SENIOR MARKET**
Demographic Characteristics; Psychographic Characteristics;
Consumer Behavior and Marketing Implications

In addition to consumer-behavior differences based on ethnic factors, marketers also recognize distinct patterns based on age categories. There are two significant age subcultures that many marketers should be vitally interested in yet which they may fail to understand and appreciate. These two groups are the *youth* market and the *senior-citizen* market. The characteristics and marketing significance of each of these subcultures will be discussed in this chapter.

THE YOUTH MARKET

The youth market is a significant subculture for the marketer. By youth, we are speaking of those between the ages of 14 and 24. However, in this section we shall also briefly examine some consumer-behavior aspects of children under 14 because of the public policy implications of marketing to this group.

Demographic Characteristics

There are a number of important characteristics of the youth market with which marketers should be familiar. Figure 8-1 presents a summary of these factors.

INCOME AND SPENDING There is no market without income, and the youth market is also important in this regard. Ninety-four percent of all young men 20 to 24 years old received income in 1971, as did 76 percent of the women. The most important facet of these incomes is that for some groups, such as most teens, they are almost entirely discretionary; that is, there are few if any fixed obligations such as taxes, rent, insurance, or utilities that these youths must meet. Consequently, they are able to spend their dollars on luxuries of all sorts.

Total spending by the 30 million teenagers in the United States in 1975 was estimated at $25.3 billion, a $600,000 growth over 1974. According to the president of a youth research company, "Products which were considered luxuries a few years ago are deemed necessities by youths and parents alike."[1]

SPENDING MOTIVATIONS OF YOUTH Why do youth have such a strong consumption orientation? According to one researcher, three significant forces have molded their attitudes and consumer behavior. First, the experience of growing up in a period of almost unbroken prosperity has produced a widely shared feeling of economic optimism. A second factor is permissive child rearing which has been linked by researchers to a reduced capacity for initiative and independence. Third, the new generation has a higher education level and heavier exposure to the mass media. These environmental

Mobility

47% of the 14–24 age group moved between 1970 and 1975.

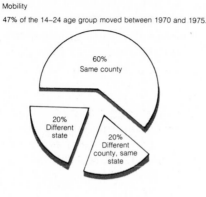

Marital Status

The 18–24-year-olds are slower to marry.

Youth population by regions

Education

53% of all 14–24-year-olds are enrolled in school.

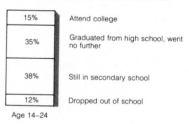

Income

Median amount

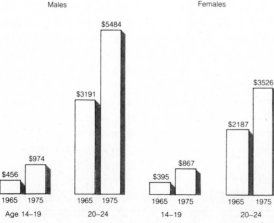

Percent receiving income

FIGURE 8-1
Characteristics of the youth market. In 1976, 45,063,000 people, or 20.9 percent of the total U.S. population, were between 14 and 24 years old. (*Source:* U.S. Bureau of the Census.)

forces have had a significant influence on their consumer-behavior orientations. The result has been that youth tend to be rather optimistic about their future financial situations and level of living. For example, almost all young people look forward to what has been labeled the "standard package," the set of durable goods, clothing, food products, and services enjoyed by the majority of Americans.[2]

TABLE 8-1

FEMALE INTERESTS AND OPINIONS (PERCENT AGREEING BY AGE GROUP)

Statement	Sample total	Age group				
		Under 25	25–34	35–44	45–54	55 and older
Optimism and Happiness						
My greatest achievements are still ahead of me	64%	92%	84%	73%	52%	28%
I dread the future	23	20	18	17	24	30
I am much happier now than I ever was before	79	85	82	80	74	74
Modern—Traditional Ideas						
I have somewhat old-fashioned tastes and habits	86	78	84	87	88	89
There is too much emphasis on sex today	87	70	74	90	89	93
I like to think I am a bit of a swinger	26	43	34	26	19	15
A woman's place is in the home	46	39	39	44	49	60
The working world is no place for a woman	17	15	11	14	19	28
Young people have too many privileges	76	57	74	77	76	83
The U.S. would be better off if there were no hippies	55	32	37	46	54	82
My days seem to follow a definite routine —eating meals at the same time each day, etc.	67	59	62	61	67	75
Travel						
I would like to take a trip around the world	67	78	83	73	65	51
I would like to spend a year in London or Paris	34	38	40	34	34	25
I would feel lost if I were alone in a foreign country	68	66	66	64	68	76
I like to visit places that are totally different from my home	85	85	83	86	82	88
Mobile						
We will probably move at least once in the next five years	38	71	53	27	28	23
Our family has moved more often than most of our neighbors have	24	36	32	26	18	17
Anxious						
I have trouble getting to sleep	33	29	24	26	33	49
I wish I knew how to relax	52	51	49	49	51	59

TABLE 8-1 (Continued)

Statement	Sample total	Age group Under 25	25–34	35–44	45–54	55 and older
Personal Adornment and Self						
Dressing well is an important part of my life	81	84	80	78	79	83
I like to feel attractive to members of the opposite sex	85	93	91	77	82	72
I want to look a little different from others	69	71	78	70	63	72
I often wear expensive cologne	28	19	24	28	27	33
I have more stylish clothes than most of my friends	30	31	34	27	29	27
View toward Income, Personal Equity, and Spending						
I will probably have more money to spend next year than I have now	45%	71%	70%	58%	53%	30%
Five years from now our family income will probably be a lot higher than it is now	65	87	85	75	61	26
Our family income is high enough to satisfy nearly all our important desires	74	59	66	78	78	80
No matter how fast our income goes up we never seem to get ahead	53	62	65	61	47	32
Investing in the stock market is too risky for most families	86	79	83	82	85	87
Our family is too heavily in debt today	27	36	33	37	23	11
I like to pay cash for everything I buy	77	83	79	74	71	77
I pretty much spend for today and let tomorrow bring what it will	22	33	21	22	25	18
Staying at Home						
I would rather spend a quiet evening at home than go out to a party	65	50	66	64	68	78
I am a homebody	69	59	65	64	72	79
I stay home most evenings	83	81	95	80	83	83
Husband and Children						
A wife's first obligation is to her husband, not her children	69	53	65	74	74	76
When children are ill in bed, parents should drop everything else to see to their comfort	74	61	71	73	80	83
Children are the most important thing in a marriage	52	42	44	49	56	64
When making important family decisions, consideration of the children should come first	54	69	58	44	48	56
A wife should have a great deal of information about her husband's work	82	83	84	75	88	85
View toward Durable Goods						
Our home is furnished for comfort, not for style	90	83	88	88	94	94
If I must choose, I buy stylish rather than practical furniture	17	19	31	13	15	15
When buying appliances, I am more concerned with dependability than price	90	85	89	89	89	94
A subcompact car can meet my transportation needs	66	85	74	60	61	57

TABLE 8-1 (Continued)

Statement	Sample total	Age group				
		Under 25	25–34	35–44	45–54	55 and older
Housekeeping and Cooking						
When I see a full ashtray or wastebasket, I want it emptied immediately	71%	77%	70%	72%	64%	64%
I am uncomfortable when the house is not completely clean	67	76	67	70	61	68
The kind of dirt you can't see is worse than the kind you can see	77	77	72	73	79	85
I am a good cook	91	93	92	88	90	91
I like to cook	87	91	88	84	85	87
I like to bake	40	43	43	42	39	38
Meal preparation should take as little time as possible	42	42	41	40	41	44
Grocery Shopping						
Shopping is no fun anymore	54	49	43	58	55	51
Before going shopping, I sit down and prepare a complete shopping list	72	68	73	71	69	74
I try to stick to well-known brands	74	58	67	71	82	86
I find myself checking prices even on small items	90	89	93	92	89	86
I like to save and redeem savings stamps	75	72	70	70	75	83
I pay a lot more attention to food prices now than I ever did before	90	92	91	88	88	87
I am an impulse buyer	38	39	40	37	42	27
I shop a lot for specials	84	85	86	83	84	81
Health and Nutrition						
I am very concerned about nutrition	87	87	89	87	82	89
I am concerned about how much salt I eat	56	52	55	56	50	66
I am careful what I eat in order to keep my weight under control	57	63	57	58	62	68
I try to avoid foods that are high in cholesterol	62	37	53	60	65	79
I try to avoid foods that have additives in them	56	45	52	57	53	62
I get more headaches than most people	28	30	31	28	27	22
I eat more than I should	70	68	70	75	73	69

Source: Needham, Harper & Steers Advertising, Inc., *Life Style Survey,* 1975.

Psychographic Characteristics

The gap between young people and the rest of the population is closing in some areas of attitude and behavior, such as appearance, according to a recent advertising agency report. It finds that today's youth want to look young, healthy, and refreshing, but, unlike their counterparts of a decade ago, are willing to use artificial means (such as cosmetics, hair coloring, and beauty treatments) to obtain that look.[3]

Nevertheless, Tables 8-1 and 8-2 indicate a number of other areas in which substantial differences may be found between youths and older age segments.

TABLE 8-2

MALE INTERESTS AND OPINIONS (PERCENT AGREEING BY AGE GROUP)

Statement	Sample total	Age group				
		Under 25	25–34	35–44	45–54	55 and older
Optimism and Happiness						
My greatest achievements are still ahead of me	64%	98%	93%	76%	55%	25%
I dread the future	20	21	19	19	23	23
I am much happier now than I ever was before	78	87	92	97	76	74
Modern—Traditional Ideas						
I have somewhat old-fashioned tastes and habits	85	73	78	84	92	89
There is too much emphasis on sex today	66	56	65	74	81	93
I like to think I am a bit of a swinger	31	51	43	29	26	15
A woman's place is in the home	54	45	52	53	52	62
The working world is no place for a woman	27	24	20	25	26	37
Young people have too many privileges	75	60	63	77	74	88
The U.S. would be better off it there were no hippies	59	33	38	57	67	81
My days seem to follow a definite routine —eating meals at the same time each day, etc.	63	50	53	59	67	76
All men should be clean shaven every day	67	47	55	66	75	85
Travel						
I would like to take a trip around the world	67	74	73	77	68	53
I would like to spend a year in London or Paris	34	38	39	40	32	23
I would feel lost if I were alone in a foreign country	52	59	46	47	44	67
I like to visit places that are totally different from my home	72	80	73	75	73	67
Mobile						
We will probably move at least once in the next five years	37	75	52	28	23	20
Our family has moved more often than most of our neighbors have	22	27	30	23	18	17
Anxious						
I have trouble getting to sleep	24	20	20	23	25	30
I wish I knew how to relax	47	40	48	51	44	50
Personal Adornment and Self						
Dressing well is an important part of my life	72	70	73	72	72	67
I like to feel attractive to members of the opposite sex	81	87	87	87	66	74
I want to look a little different from others	55	74	62	55	49	42

TABLE 8-2 (Continued)

Statement	Sample total	Age group				
		Under 25	25–34	35–44	45–54	55 and older
I often wear expensive cologne	14%	16%	14%	12%	15%	13%
I have more stylish clothes than most of my friends	25	24	26	28	24	22
View toward Income, Personal Equity, and Spending						
I will probably have more money to spend next year than I have now	56	74	65	64	58	29
Five years from now our family income will probably be a lot higher than it is now	68	87	85	79	69	28
Our family income is high enough to satisfy nearly all our important desires	75	63	72	78	78	79
No matter how fast our income goes up we never seem to get ahead	58	60	68	56	52	39
Investing in the stock market is too risky for most families	83	86	82	81	87	86
Our family is too heavily in debt today	28	41	42	28	25	11
I like to pay cash for everything I buy	75	79	74	70	69	81
I pretty much spend for today and let tomorrow bring what it will	26	31	29	23	23	26
Staying at Home						
I would rather spend a quiet evening at home than go out to a party	73	65	67	73	75	79
I am a homebody	72	55	67	73	79	82
I stay home most evenings	80	70	77	79	78	89
Husband and Children						
A wife's first obligation is to her husband, not her children	57	43	52	54	64	66
When children are ill in bed, parents should drop everything else to see to their comfort	70	66	68	66	73	78
Children are the most important thing in a marriage	53	37	44	50	57	78
When making important family decisions, consideration of the children should come first	53	63	54	48	49	53
A wife should have a great deal of information about her husband's work	77	74	75	73	80	82
Our family is a close-knit group	87	86	94	89	83	88
View toward Durable Goods						
Our home is furnished for comfort, not for style	93	89	92	94	95	94
If I must choose, I buy stylish rather than practical furniture	15	18	20	14	15	9
When buying appliances, I am more concerned with dependability than price	93	91	93	90	94	95
When buying appliances, the brand name is more important than the reputation of the store	56%	56%	53%	49%	55%	64%
A subcompact car can meet my transportation needs	59	71	57	56	58	57

TABLE 8-2 (Continued)

Statement	Sample total	Age group				
		Under 25	25–34	35–44	45–54	55 and older
Housekeeping and Cooking						
When I see a full ashtray or wastebasket, I want it emptied immediately	56	56	46	54	60	63
I am uncomfortable when the house is not completely clean	51	57	48	53	49	52
The kind of dirt you can't see is worse than the kind you can see	77	68	74	73	79	86
I am a good cook	51	63	57	50	48	41
I like to cook	50	60	58	48	48	41
I like to bake	30	34	35	27	26	30
Meal preparation should take as little time as possible	42	42	41	38	40	46
Grocery Shopping						
Shopping is no fun anymore	59	54	55	55	63	64
Before going shopping, I sit down and prepare a complete shopping list	44	35	42	38	38	56
I try to stick to well-known brands	79	71	79	76	71	86
I find myself checking prices even on small items	79	78	74	75	78	84
I like to save and redeem savings stamps	43	43	31	35	42	58
I pay a lot more attention to food prices now than I ever did before	81	81	79	81	81	84
I am an impulse buyer	38	46	47	40	33	30
I shop a lot for specials	60	61	59	63	56	61
Health and Nutrition						
I am very concerned about nutrition	61	66	65	60	57	63
I am concerned about how much salt I eat	40	28	32	32	46	54
I am careful what I eat in order to keep my weight under control	51	38	43	44	55	64
I try to avoid foods that are high in cholestrol	49	31	42	41	60	63
I try to avoid foods that have additives in them	44	36	35	39	49	56
I get more headaches than most people	17	18	17	19	21	12
I eat more than I should	66	57	67	68	70	64

Source: Needham, Harper & Steers Advertising, Inc., *Life Style Survey*, 1975.

Consumer Behavior and Marketing Implications

This section explores the nature of consumer behavior within the youth market of the United States. However, it should be emphasized that many of the findings presented below are for teens. Thus, there may be substantial differences between this group and older youths. The three marketing variables to be discussed are product decisions, shopping patterns, and promotion.

PRODUCT DECISIONS Marketers are quite interested in understanding what products will sell well in the youth market. Moreover, it is important to appreciate the influence which youths exert on purchases by others, such as parents. This secondary influence may be more significant to most marketers than is youth's role as primary purchasers of certain items.

Product Purchase Patterns It is estimated that youths under 25 spend about $25 billion a year. How do they spend their incomes? The following purchase patterns give an indication of the importance of certain products:

Teens are said to account for 55 percent of all soft drink sales and 20 percent of all potato chip consumption.

Teenage girls (representing about 12 percent of the total female population) account for 23 percent of all cosmetic expenditures and 22 percent of all women's apparel sales. Teenage boys account for 40 percent of all men's slacks and 33 percent of all men's sweater sales.[4]

31 percent of people surveyed in the 18 to 29 age bracket took air trips in 1971, 33 percent bought cameras, 36 percent bought ski equipment.

90 percent own radios, 86 percent have record players or tape-playback equipment, 86 percent own cameras, and 22 percent own automobiles.

Consumers between the ages of 21 and 30 drink an average of 5 gallons of wine a year, compared with 2 gallons for older buyers.

About half of the movie audiences are people between 16 and 24 while three out of every four movie tickets are purchased by customers under 30.

About 60 percent of the buyers of phonograph records and tapes in 1971 were under 25.[5]

Secondary Purchase Influence In addition to their direct impact on the marketplace, youths are estimated to influence expenditures of at least another $135 billion. This secondary influence on their parents' product and brand choices is important for a number of items. For example, research by *Scholastic Magazine* reveals the following pattern:

Among teens who own TV sets, 34 percent took part in its selection; for cameras, 43 percent; tape recorders, 42 percent; record players, 29 percent; and typewriters, 42 percent.

Teens also influence brands chosen by buying the product themselves or specifying the brand. For selected products the percentages are as follows: mouthwash, 58 percent of girls, 47 percent of boys; toothpaste, 51 percent of girls, 42 percent of boys; shampoo, 75 percent of girls, 72 percent of boys; deodorants, 83 percent of girls, 73 percent of boys; safety razors, 66 percent of girls, 52 percent of boys.[6]

A study of university students' influence on their families' purchases of television sets and automobiles found that many students not only provided opinions and information about both products, but also participated in shopping.[7]

With the large growth in the number of working wives, youth are doing more of the food and other shopping for parents. For example, a *Seventeen* study of teenage girls found that 78 percent shop for family food, 40 percent "help mother" with product and brand selection, and over half make specific brand recommendations when asking their mothers to buy snack food.[8] Thus, it is clear that this market also occupies an important position in terms of its secondary influence on parents' buying decisions.

Brand Decisions Another factor emphasizing the market importance of the youth group is that this is the time when brand loyalties may be formed that could last well into adulthood. For example, one research study showed that, after 20 years, about 30 percent of the women interviewed still used the same brands of cosmetics, nail polish, soap and cologne they used in high school.[9]

Influences on Product Decisions In the process of making their buying decisions, to what extent are teens influenced by parents, friends, sales clerks, media, or other sources? For many product decisions friends are the most significant influence. For example, one study comparing data from 1961 and 1971 found that significant changes had occurred in the buying frames of reference of teenagers. Parents were found to have declined in importance as a source of influence of teens' buying decisions in most of the product lines researched, while friends of the teenagers had increased in influence.[10] The role of influencing agents appears to shift over time, however, as shown by another study that found a trend of teens doing more shopping with members of their immediate family such as parents or brothers and sisters. This represented a shift from several years ago when teens tended to shop alone or with friends.[11] The important point for the marketer is that peer pressure is quite strong, but family influences are also significant. The marketer should attempt to keep up with which group predominates at any period in order to properly orient merchandising strategies.

SHOPPING BEHAVIOR Teenagers spend more time shopping today than they did 10 years ago. One study learned that over one-fourth of the teenagers questioned spent more than two hours shopping on weekends, while another one-fifth spent between one and two hours.[12] The fact that teens are doing more shopping may result in their spending more money in stores they patronize.

While the popular belief is that young people buy products impulsively and are less rational than the market as a whole, surveys indicate a different pattern. One 1974 study of persons aged 14 to 25 showed that 74 percent of the respondents do compare prices and brands before buying.[13]

Store Selection and Loyalty Youth often have a great deal of authority in store selection decisions. For example, one study found that 89 percent of the girls and 80 percent of the boys claimed to have all or most of the say in the choice of a clothing store.[14] The manner of store selection often involves window-shopping and talking with parents and friends about where to purchase.

The evidence is mixed with regard to store loyalty of teens. For example, one study of teenagers found that three-fourths of the respondents bought clothing at a number of different stores.[15] Another study, however, discovered a pattern of store loyalty among younger teens in clothes purchasing.[16] Thus, the extent of youth store loyalty is unclear, but it may be age-related, with younger teens being more loyal than older teens. Store loyalty may also be product-related.

Attracting the Teenage Buyer What makes for a successful retailing approach to attract teens? One writer has the following suggestions for retailers in their appeal to youth:

1. Do not use the word "teens," in naming the shop.

2. Locate the junior or high school departments separate from the girls' or boys' departments; but keep the junior departments together so there can be inter-selling and merchandise selection.

3. Take customer surveys to check on strategy acceptance.

4. Departmental decor should reflect the customer and merchandise.

5. Set up a definite promotion and advertising program to be aimed exclusively at teens. Promotions involving school leaders are very important. These could include fashion boards, fashion shows, and cooperation with local school events.

6. Personal selling is important. Try to hire people representative of the teens in your area, and train them in methods of selling to young adults.[17]

Another feature that increases store appeal to youths is credit. Many stores find it wise to make special efforts to open charge accounts for teenagers, and engage in direct-mail campaigns with these customers. In many areas the ratio of retail credit-card holders is quite high. For example, 32 percent of the teenagers in a typical New York City suburb have charge accounts in their names at local stores.[18]

PROMOTION IMPLICATIONS A final marketing element that is very important in the mix designed to appeal to youth is promotion. There are a number of effective media available to reach the youth market—radio, television, direct mail, magazines, and newspapers. Let's examine the media habits of youth and potential promotional strategies that might be successful in appealing to this group.

Radio Advertising[19] Nearly all teenagers own radios, and they spend considerable time listening to them. Surveys show that 75 percent of teens listen on a daily basis and average almost three hours per day—about one-fifth of their waking hours. In addition, radio reaches over 90 percent of all teenagers in the course of a week. These listening patterns vary significantly by time of day, exhibiting heavy nighttime listening, particularly during winter months when apparently the radio is used while studying.

Teen radio listening preferences are clearly toward contempoary or rock music stations. They tend to select one or two favorite stations and listen to them repeatedly day after day. Consequently, massive teen audiences are available with relatively concentrated station schedules. A large advertising agency has calculated that typically the three leading teen stations in a market combine to reach over 80 percent of the teen audience in each time period. In addition, data for the top twenty-five to thirty markets across the country indicate that in each one the first and second highest rated teen stations cover about 90 percent of the entire teenage market. It would take four to six adult-oriented stations to capture similar market shares of adult listeners. Hence, radio is probably the fastest, easiest, and most effective way to reach teens.

Television Advertising[20] In contrast to adults, who spend much of their leisure time watching television, teens are relatively light viewers, although virtually all have access to sets. Teens appear to be too busy to spend a lot of time watching television; however, they do have preferred programs and may watch these quite regularly. Young teens are significantly heavier viewers than older teens.

Television programming that has proved popular with teens includes music-dance shows, movies, sports, situation comedies, and suspense-mystery shows. In 1976 the top network shows among teens were "Happy Days," "Laverne and Shirley," "Six Million Dollar Man," "Bionic Woman," and "Welcome Back, Kotter."

Print Advertising Print media also have a place in promoting to the youth market. Magazines for example, are viewed by young people as being a prime source of information on a number of different subjects. Eighty-one percent of girls questioned in one study stated that they received most of their knowledge about beauty and grooming from magazines, while 63 percent got most of their information about health from this source. Sixty-one percent responded that magazines were "informative" whereas only 35 percent described television in this way.[21] This has implications for the marketer advertising to youth because it appears that magazines may be especially effective in contributing to brand preference by providing informative sales messages to young people in search of such information.

Newspapers also have heavy youth readership. An Opinion Research Corporation study found that 59 percent of 12- to 14-year-olds and 81 percent of 15- to 17-year-olds read a daily newspaper "yesterday."[22]

Other Types of Promotion Direct mail may also be effective in reaching the youth market. This is one medium that probably will attract more attention than some other alternatives, because youths receive little mail and they are likely to be quite receptive to advertising in this form. "Mailbag" is an example of a company offering a cooperative direct-mail effort aimed at the youth market. Such mailings, which are sponsored by a number of firms, contain offers for sample packages, ads, and discount coupons for noncompeting products and services.

Other effective promotional efforts are utilized by marketers. For example, a number of companies hire student representatives on many college campuses whose job may include selling or renting merchandise, putting up posters, or distributing advertisements and product samples. Ford provides *Insider,* a continuing series of college newspaper supplements that offers interesting reading material and car ads aimed at students.

Developing Promotional Messages Promotional messages must be carefully designed for today's youth because they are becoming increasingly skeptical about such communications. For example, a recent youth poll found that 24 percent of the respondents said ads directed at them are not believable; 19 percent find them uninformative; 28 percent think they are silly; and only 7 percent view them as sincere. Nevertheless, 87 percent of youth 14 to 25 years old would rather buy advertised than nonadvertised products.[23]

In developing effective sales appeals to the youth market the advertiser should keep in mind the following rules:

1. Never talk down to a teenager.

2. Be totally, absolutely, and unswervingly straightforward.

3. Give the teenager credit for being motivated by rational values.

4. Be as personal as possible.[24]

Understanding the Youth Market There are two additional factors that should be cited in order to ensure greater success in the youth market. The first is that the youth group is a *perpetually* new market. As consumers move into this market, the advertiser needs to attract them, since every brand is a new brand to someone who has never used it before. This stream of young consumers moves along in age and finally drifts into an older pool of householders. Thus, a marketer must not neglect young consumers who come "on stream" if the company's brand is to have continued success in the older age market.

Two companies utilizing this approach to successfully attract youth are presented below:

Tampax originally had a minimal share of the feminine sanitary protection market dominated by Kotex and Modess. Outspending these brands to sell its new internal concept of sanitary protection was out of the question. Thus, the company went after newer, younger users who were more open-minded and could become a highly brand-loyal group; and it has since become the overwhelming leader in tampon sales, which account for over 35 percent of the total sanitary protection market.

Shick has been able to outflank Gillette, the dominant company in the razor blade market, by consistent and specific efforts to win young shavers. Through various means it offers young men the opportunity to receive Shick razors, either free or at nominal expense. The result has been that Shick has gained a significant presence in this market.[25]

A second point to remember is that companies may be able to utilize youth appeals to a market broader than the traditional age boundary would indicate. Marketers today are defining "youth" more in terms of a state of mind than of a specific age. The result of this is that many companies, ranging from retailers to manufacturers, are broadening their emphasis to include the mature and more affluent customer who "thinks young."[26] For example, a recent promotion by California Ford dealers was geared to the youth market with radio rock music, a logo that conveyed the mood of "Fun Trucking," and TV commercials showcasing youth-market cars and trucks. The promotion, however, was designed to appeal not only to the 20 to 29 age market but also to buyers from 30 to 40 years of age "who have the same mode of living as their younger-in-age counterparts.[27]

The Child Market

There is another youth segment of interest to some marketers—the child market. This group is considered to be those children between the ages of 5 and 13.

SIGNIFICANCE OF THE MARKET Is this group actually a "market"? Well, it does have size—an estimated 36,732,000 children aged 5 to 13 in 1967; and perhaps as many as 52,719,000 may be in this group by 1985. A large part of this market also has incomes available to spend, and although they are small individually, in total they are conservatively estimated at $2 billion annually.[28] And spend they do, as one writer describes:

In a year, children in the United States consume enough peanut butter to coat the Empire State Building with a layer three feet thick, enough soft drinks to fill the Queen Mary ten and one-half times, and enough bubble gum to blow a bubble the size of the Rock of Gibraltar.[29]

These facts are clear reasons why many marketers are interested in the child consumer. However, just as with older youth, this group is also important to the marketer for the influence they may exert on their parents' buying decisions as well.

DEVELOPMENT OF CONSUMER-BEHAVIOR PATTERNS BY CHILDREN

McNeal describes the development of consumer-behavior patterns in children as an evolutionary process. Americans tend to give their children consumer training at an early age, with the youngsters making their first independent purchases around 5 years of age.

By age 7 the child begins to perfect consuming skills. He largely copies the consumer-behavior patterns of his parents, asks to make trips to the store, and when shopping with his parents, attempts to help them. Peer influence is also strong at this age; thus, children often copy their friends' patterns and seek their advice about consumption, typically with regard to flavors and brands of sweets.

By the child's ninth or tenth birthday, he has a rudimentary understanding of the marketing process and by this age becomes enamored with the shopping process and may exhibit discrimination in making shopping trips. He has by now developed such competence that shopping activities have become ritualized, giving him freedom to meet new kinds of experience.

By the last year of elementary school, the child's consumer-behavior patterns are similar to those of an adult. He is able to assign social value to many products and to participate in family discussions about large purchases.[30]

THE GREAT ADVERTISING DEBATE A number of critics feel that any advertising to children is harmful and should be banned. One group, Action for Children's Television (ACT), feels so strongly about this that in 1970 it filed a petition with the Federal Communications Commission to do away with commercial children's programming. In its place ACT wants "to substitute a new system of financial support of children's programming by commercial underwriting and public-service funding in the belief that this system would look to the benefits of children rather than the profits of advertisers."[31]

The charges levied at children's television commercials could be described as follows:

1. Commercials sometimes contain the assertion that a product costs "only" a given amount.

2. Commercials sometimes seem to magnify the benefits of particular toys or the size of snack foods.

3. Commercials sometimes portray fantasy situations in which the child using a particular toy or food product is endowed with marvelous powers.

4. Commercials are designed to arouse desires that would not otherwise be salient.

5. Commercials exploit children's suggestibility.

6. Commercials often depict vanity as a reason for choosing one product or another.

7. Commercials often contain misrepresentation, exaggeration, fantasy, and deceit.

8. Commercials often suggest that food products are to be bought for their sugar content or for the prizes and bonuses offered in conjunction with their purchase.[32]

Along with the charges made against children's advertising have come a number of rebuttals, however. For example, a study by the National Association of Broadcasters (NAB) Code Authority found that many of the attacks on children's advertising are not supported by fact. Among its findings from a study of over 236 commercials are the following:

"Charismatic superpersonalities" are not being heavily used to sell products.

Children generally are not being urged to ask parents to buy advertised products.

There are few exaggerated claims.

Information regarding nutrition of food products is being provided.[33]

Some data indicate that most people do not even perceive a significant problem with regard to children's television advertising. For example, of

55,000 letters received by the Federal Communication Commission in 1973 relating to television only 34 complained about advertising to children.[34]

In addition, children's television advertising is not without regulation. For example, advertisers and their agencies must comply with broadcaster regulations for children's commercials, or the ads will not be aired. Moreover the NAB TV Code Authority, which covers the three networks and signatory stations, requires mandatory clearance by its unit for all toy commercials and ads that offer premiums to children. In fact, between 1970 and 1973 the TV code rejected 13 percent of the 2850 commercials submitted to them.[35]

However, the censorship "cure" can sometimes be worse than the "disease" and has produced some ludicrous situations. For instance, a large agency for a toy company once turned out a commercial that pictured a kid with a little machine gun on top of a mound of dirt blasting away at the enemy. The code censor rejected the commercial by claiming that children would obviously think that the dirt was part of the game "since it's on the screen for the entire commercial and the kid spends his time on the top of this mound of dirt." The censor argued that children—especially the 1- and 2-year-olds who it was thought would be most swayed—would, therefore, be expecting a mound of dirt to come with every machine gun. Consequently, to gain the commercial's acceptance a visual was run on the screen saying, "The mound of dirt does not come with the gun." This action was primarily for the benefit of 1- to 2-year-olds, who, incidentally, could not read.[31]

CHILDREN'S RESPONSES TO ADVERTISING It is true that children's television advertising can be extremely effective. For example, a recent study showed that children between the ages of 6 and 9 can discriminate between brands, and are highly brand-conscious. In addition, their receptivity to some advertisements appears unmatched among adults. For example, the Wrigley Company tested a new chewing gum commercial in three cities and found a phenomenal 89 percent total recall among children. Another firm found through research that the impressions its candy commercial made were also staggering. As the company's marketing manager stated, "These kids would play back the commercial exactly, even to reenacting parts of it and singing about product benefits to the tune we use in the commercial."[37] Such singing jingles seem particularly effective among children, even for products they don't use. For example, two of the most popular songs among youngsters recently were the "short shorts" jingle for Nair and Miles Laboratory's Alka-Seltzer jingle, "Plop, plop, fizz, fizz."

Children's promotions, however, are not as all-powerful as these cases might lead one to believe. A series of studies on children and television advertising found, among other things, that by age 7, children already have a "concrete distrust" of commercials, often based on experience with advertised products. Some additional insights from the research on this subject are the following:

Preschool children find it difficult to determine when a television program ends and a commercial begins.

Highest attention is paid to programs and commercials by 5- to 7-year-olds while 11- to 12-year-olds pay the least attention.

For all age groups the greatest attention is paid to commercials at the beginning of a program. Attention to commercials in clusters drops off rapidly.

All children pay attention to relevant commercials (e.g., food, toys), but older children pay less attention to irrelevant ones (e.g., cleansers, cosmetics).

Best-liked commercials are those that are "funny" or "straightforward."

Commercials are disliked when they are seen as "stupid," "false and hypocritical," or "insulting the intelligence."

Children do learn relevant consumer skills and attitudes from television advertising.[38]

In summary, marketing to youths involves an understanding of the nuances of this subculture. The marketer should keep in mind the following guidelines to reach this segment effectively:

1. Never appeal to the youth market as a single group. Recognize that there are several distinct segments to the market, each with its own media, characteristics, motivations, and appeals.

2. Determine which group you wish to reach and talk specifically to them.

3. Research and use the appeals best suited to this group for your own product or service.

4. Select the best media to deliver your message to the age group you have chosen.[39]

THE SENIOR MARKET

Although business people have painted a glowing picture of the opportunities in the youth market, the opposite end of the age spectrum has been largely neglected by marketers and frequently by society itself. Many feel that American marketers have gone overboard in courting the youth market. As one advertising executive explained in *Business Week,* "As I watch television and read magazines and attend movies these days, I sometimes wonder if anybody besides myself is over 30. There seems to be a conscious denial of middle age—and certainly of old age."[40]

Why the neglect? One writer explains, "Youth suggests excitement and glamour; the no-longer-young are considered dowdy and uninspiring."[4] But while this situation may be understandable psychologically, it may make poor economic sense, because the middle-aged hold considerably more promise for a wide range of consumer goods and services than do the young. The over-65 market has been described as worth $60 billion in 1971. Thus, the senior market represents a very sizable consumer segment and a significant opportunity for many business people.

Demographic Characteristics

Table 8-3 summarizes important characteristics of older families, which are also described below.

SIZE AND GROWTH RATE The 1970 census counted 20 million people 65 years of age or older, or almost 10 percent of our total population. Each

TABLE 8-3

THE OLDER FAMILY IN PROFILE

	All families	Family head age 65 and Over
Families:		
Millions	51.9	7.2
Distribution	100.0%	13.8%
Average size of family	3.5	2.3
Family income:	100.0%	100.0%
Under $3000	8.9	25.0
$3000-$4999	10.4	26.4
$5000-$6999	11.8	15.3
$7000-$9999	19.8	13.9
$10,000-$14,999	26.7	11.1
$15,000 & over	22.4	8.3
Distribution by income class		
Under $5,000	100.0%	36.6%
$5,000-$9999	100.0	12.7
$10,000-$14,999	100.0	7.4
$15,000 & over	100.0	5.3
Average income	$11,106	$7140
Median income	$ 9867	$5053
Distribution of all income	100.0%	8.9%
Distribution of discretionary income	100.0%	6.5%
Wife working*	40.8%	7.4%
Residence†		
Metropolitan area	68.6%	62.5%
Central city	31.7	32.4
Outside central city	36.9	30.1
Nonmetropolitan area	31.4	37.5
Ownership		
Own home	64.2%	70.5%
Own auto	80.0	54.1
Two or more	29.8	9.0
Educational attainment	100.0%	100.0%
Elementary school	28.0	61.1
Some high school	15.8	12.6
High school graduate	30.5	13.0
Some college	11.1	5.4
College graduate	14.6	7.9
Projections:		
1980 Family income	100.0%	100.0%
Under $3000	6.0	17.0
$3000-$4999	7.0	20.5
$5000-$6999	8.5	16.5
$7000-$9999	14.5	15.5
$10,000-$14,999	26.0	15.5
$15,000 & over	38.0	15.0

*Based on age of wife
†Based on 1970 male population 20 years and over
Source: Fabian Linden, "The $200 Billion Middle-aged Market," *Conference Board Record,* December 1972, p. 18.

census during this century has found the elderly to make up a larger share of the total population. In fact, this growth has far outpaced the percentage increase of the population generally, and if present trends continue the elderly could account for 20 percent of the population by the year 2000. Thus, statistics negate a long-held concept that the United States is a nation of young people and is getting younger.

LOCATION OF MARKET The largest group of elderly consumers lives in the central cities of our metropolitan areas. This characteristic differs from the population as a whole, in which suburbanites outnumber residents of central cities.

States with the largest populations also have the largest numbers of senior citizens. For example, New York, California, Pennsylvania, and Illinois account for nearly one-third of the elderly. However, states with the highest proportions of older people are those which have had heavy out-migration by younger people. This is especially true of much of the midwestern farm belt—Iowa, Kansas, Missouri, Nebraska, Oklahoma, and South Dakota.

Many older people who have the means move toward the "gerontopolises" of the Sunbelt when they retire. Florida's elderly, for example, make up 14.6 percent of its population—the highest proportion of any state.

MARITAL AND FAMILY STATUS A large majority of the elderly are women, most of whom are widowed, and many of whom live by themselves. However, most elderly men are married and live with their wives. Contrary to the general impression, very few American elderly live in homes for the aged. Only 3 percent of men and 5 percent of women are in such arrangements. The percentage of men and women living as dependent "other relatives" in family groups may also be lower than commonly believed (7 percent and 17 percent, respectively).

SPENDING CAPACITY The median income for all families in the United States in 1973 was $12,051; but the median family income of persons age 65 and over was only $6426 for the year. Nearly one in six people 65 and over lives in poverty, compared with one in ten people under age 65. While it is true that a sizeable segment of the market is at the poverty-income level, it is also true that a much more significant number of elderly persons live at "comfortable" levels of income. Data from the Bureau of Labor Statistics indicate that a retired couple needed $3763 to live at a lower-budget level, $5414 for a medium level, and $8043 at a higher-budget level in urban United States areas during 1973. Considering the median family-income level of $6426 in 1973 for persons 65 and over, many families are able to live at least within a medium budget figure. Thus, this group forms a substantial market. Moreover, even though the incomes of many elderly may be low, these incomes are often able to go farther than those of younger customers because of fewer obligations such as mortgages, education expenses, and so on.[42]

Psychographic Characteristics

As seen in Tables 8-1 and 8-2, the segment age 55 and over has in many cases a different set of activities, interests, and opinions from those of younger segments.

One research study has isolated six useful buying style and psychographic segments based on analysis of a national consumer data base. As can be seen from this information, which is presented in Table 8-4, the elderly market consists of not one, but several segments.

Consumer Behavior and Marketing Implications

The lack of attention by marketers to the senior market shows up in the dearth of research findings on this group's behavior as consumers. This section distills some of the most important findings and presents some useful insights for the marketer.

PRODUCT DECISIONS It appears that there is significant marketing potential available to those who provide the proper kinds of products to meet the needs of the senior market.[43] The biggest opportunities are thought to be in travel, housing, appliances, foods, clothing, personal care, hobbies, and medicines and drugs.[44]

Some have ventured into this market to sell specially designed products

TABLE 8-4

BUYING STYLE SEGMENTS—PSYCHOGRAPHIC DESCRIPTIONS

Segment	Psychographic Description	Share of Elderly Market (Percentage)
Saver/planner (buys unknown brands)	Frank, candid, self-assured, confident	25.1
Brand loyalist (Does not buy for approval of friends)	Brave, courageous, reserved, conventional Insecure Not stubborn	8.4
Information seeker (persuasible)	Kind, sincere	10.1
Economy shopper (not brand loyal)	Not brave, not dominating, not egocentric, not frank, candid, funny, witty	10.6
Laggard (not persuasible)	Not witty, not kind, not reservitive, liberal	11.2
Conspicious consumer	Stubborn Egotistical Dominating	34.6

Source: Jeffrey G. Towle and Claude R. Martin, Jr. "The Elderly Consumer: One Segment or Many?" in Beverlee B. Anderson (ed.), *Advances in Consumer Research* **3:**467, Association for Consumer Research, Cincinnati, 1976.

more attuned to elderly needs. Not all, however, have succeeded. H. J. Heinz developed a line of new products called "Senior Foods" because many oldsters seemed to be eating the company's baby food, but claiming they were buying it for their grandchildren. However, the new food product failed for reasons which apparently included lack of taste, a patronizing attitude by the company's advertising campaign, and a high retail price.[45]

A number of other manufacturers, however, have successfully launched products in this market. For instance, Bulova made a deliberate attempt to cater to older people with watches having large, easy-to-read dials and numerals. Older customers now contribute about 5 percent of Bulova's total sales. In addition, Winchester has designed a lighter shotgun for this market; MacGregor and Spaulding produce specially designed golf clubs; and there are many retirement communities, such as Del Webb's Sun City, that are geared to the elderly.[46]

There is an impression generally that senior citizens are less inclined to try new products. One writer points out, "It is the younger people who are most willing to try the new product, or switch to the new brand. Older people appear to be more suspicious and distrustful of the new or different, more set in their ways, harder to sell . . . more addicted to loyalty."[47] This impression is not confirmed by Table 8-4, however. Interestingly, another study even found that the group aged 65 and over was more inclined than the middle-aged, 55- to 64-year-olds, to say they buy products for the fun of it or just to try them once. But it was also found that there is little self-initiated experimenting; instead, trial comes as a response to recommendations by peers.[48] The important implication of this is that promotional messages must be well planned to take advantage of this word-of-mouth communication.

SHOPPING PATTERNS Most of the research on senior citizens' shopping patterns has been conducted in an exploratory manner with limited samples; therefore, the findings must be interpreted with caution. Nevertheless, there are a number of helpful insights.

Business Week provides perspective regarding the shopping patterns of senior citizens by observing that they "tend to be more cautious than younger consumers, more set in their preferences, and shrewder comparison shoppers. They favor larger chain stores and shun small specialty outlets, especially those that gain a name for catering just to the elderly."[49] Another study found that the primary sources of product information were newspapers and personal observation while shopping. Also, shopping appears to be a major part of their life-style and provides more of a pleasure than a burden.[50]

Other studies have shown that senior citizens shop near their residences since many lack personal transportation. In addition, substantial store loyalty has been exhibited by this group for low-cost items or for products about which the store owner may give advice (e.g., drugs and medicines). Store loyalty disappears as unit value of an item increases and frequency of purchase decreases (e.g., appliances). Greater store loyalty is also exhibited by those at higher incomes and older ages.[51]

Some of this country's important retail institutions such as shopping centers and supermarkets have features that make them quite attractive to senior shoppers. The generally favorable prices and the safe, comfortable atmosphere of these stores contribute to their appeal. At the same time, however, certain other features of these institutions inhibit older consumers from taking advantage of them. First, they are generally located away from older neighborhoods where many aged and most poor live. Moreover, there are problems of the right merchandise assortment to satisfy the needs of older consumers. For these and other reasons, such retail institutions have not adequately met the needs of senior citizens.[52]

One writer has suggested several ways in which larger retailers or retail associations can expand their business among senior citizens: (1) sponsor low-cost or free bus transportation from senior centers to shopping centers, (2) expand and promote telephone shopping, (3) provide free or lost-cost bus tokens for patrons, (4) provide lounges or rest areas, (5) provide larger print on labels and price tags, and (6) experiment with senior clothing departments.[53]

Supermarkets could also make their operations more attractive and profitable among senior citizens by offering the following: (1) special checkout counters equipped with comfortable seating, (2) provision of smaller-sized and prepackaged foods, (3) better access to public transit and assistance in carrying packages to buses or private vehicles, and (4) optional, fee-supported home delivery programs.[54]

PROMOTING TO THE SENIOR MARKET Many business people have been reluctant to solicit the trade of senior citizens. A 1967 study by the National Council on the Aging found that local store managers, even when convinced that elderly consumers represented a sizeable market, refused to direct any advertising or promotion efforts toward the aged for fear it would "hurt their public image" and tend to keep away their most desirable age group—the youth.[55]

On the other hand, promotion should generally not blatantly single out senior citizens as the target. As Howard explains, "Many older people don't want to be reminded that they are old, and they often tend to react against advertising and marketing programs that separate them from the masses."[56] An approach that works for many companies is the "transgenerational" strategy or "fence-straddling." In this case ads feature both youngsters and oldsters using and enjoying the product. Advertising for Greyhoud, McDonald's, Polaroid, and Kentucky Fried Chicken are examples of this strategy. Thus, the marketer is careful not to alienate any age group.

Others catering to the senior market have found success by using well-known senior citizens as spokespeople for their products. For example, Fred MacMurray and Lawrence Welk have been very effective in this role. Such representatives can act as authority figures who attest to the time-proven reliability of the product.[57]

Also of concern is the selection of media to be used in promoting to the senior market. Unfortunately, there is difficulty segmenting the senior market by medium. Television programming, except for such fare as the Lawrence Welk show, is largely youth-oriented. There are certain general television offerings, however, that attract a large audience of senior viewers. Early evening newscasts, for example, are prime vehicles for such products as hair darkeners, laxatives, denture adhesives, and Geritol—all of which are designed to minimize the effects of aging. With regard to print media aimed at this market, the choices are also rather limited.

PRICING AND THE SENIOR MARKET Little is known about this facet of the marketing mix as it pertains to the senior market. There may be two general patterns, however—a price-quality market and a lower-to-moderate price appeal group. One study found, "Products in the low or moderate price ranges are more likely to be sought by the 'retired' customers who are necessarily price conscious because of lower incomes due to retirement."[58] *Forbes* magazine, on the other hand, notes that many of the elderly want to buy the best. Bulova is said to have discovered this when its market research discouraged putting a low price on a watch designed to sell to the elderly.[59]

Another aspect of price concerns the credit practices of this market. A recent nationwide mail survey of the consumer credit usage patterns of the over-65 age group found that it is a growing market that is generally being ignored by credit grantors.[60]

In summary, the senior market represents a powerful economic force that is certain to grow even stronger. Although the youth market has become almost a "religion" to many companies, some are beginning to feel that the senior market is really the "now" generation, because older consumers don't know how long the "now" will last. Thus, there is a substantial opportunity in this subculture for the marketer not only to satisfy the goals of his firm but at the same time to help accomplish some of society's aims as well. However, in order for these goals to be effectively realized, marketers will need to know much more about this neglected segment.

SUMMARY

This chapter has presented two additional subcultures with which marketers need to be more familiar—youth and older citizens. Groups classified by age represent a viable approach to market segmentation, and therefore two of the more important age categories were discussed. Many of the consumer-behavior insights which have been gained through numerous studies of these markets were presented. At the same time, however, it is clear from this chapter as well as the previous one that much more needs to be learned by marketers in order to really understand these subcultures. Nevertheless, a foundation has been laid for more effective marketing.

DISCUSSION TOPICS

1. Why are the youth and senior-citizen markets characterized as "subcultures"?

2. Prepare a report on the demographic changes occurring in the youth market or the senior market.

3. How do the activities, interests, and opinions of youth differ from other age groups? How do those of senior citizens differ?

4. Illustrate with food products and automobiles how the marketer might promote to youth in order to take advantage of their secondary influence in family-purchase decisions.

5. Select two product areas that appear to have good potential in the senior market but are at present being poorly marketed. Present a plan for more effective marketing in order to take advantage of this opportunity.

6. What additional improvements can you suggest for the retail environment in order to better meet the needs of today's senior citizens?

NOTES

1. "Special Interest Group: Teenagers Continue to Set Spending Records," *The Wall Street Journal,* November 6, 1975, p. 1.

2. Robert O. Herrmann, "Today's Young Adults as Consumers," *Journal of Consumer Affairs,* **4**:23, Summer 1970.

3. "Youth Market Growing More Conventional," *Advertising Age,* May 16, 1977, p. 84.

4. "The U.S. Teen Market," *Sponsor,* **22**:25, January 1968.

5. "44 Million Adults—a New Wave of Buyers," *U.S. News & World Report,* **72**:16–19, January 17, 1972.

6. "The U.S. Teen Market," p. 25.

7. William P. Perreault, Jr., and Frederick A. Russ, "Student Influence on Family Purchase Decisions," in Fred. C. Allvine (ed.), *Combined Proceedings,* American Marketing Association, Chicago, 1971, pp. 386–390.

8. "The U.S. Teen Market," pp. 25–26.

9. "Look out! Teenagers Are Here," *Sponsor,* **19**:49, March 29, 1965.

10. Paul Gilkison, "Teen-Agers' Perceptions of Buying Frames of Reference: A Decade in Retrospect," *Journal of Retailing,* **49**:25–37, Summer 1973.

11. Dennis H. Tootelian and H. Nicholas Windeshausen, "The Teen-Age Market: A Comparative Analysis, 1964–1974," *Journal of Retailing,* **52**:56–58, Summer 1976.

12. Tootelian and Windeshausen, "The Teen-Age Market," pp. 55–58.

13. "Youth Market Growing More Conventional."

14. Paul E. Smith, "Merchandising for the Teenage Market," *Journal of Retailing,* **37**:12, Summer 1960.

15. A. Coskun Samli and H. N. Windeshausen, *Sacramento Teenage Market Study,* Advertising Club of Sacramento, Sacramento, Calif., 1965, pp. 37–39.

16. Josephine R. Saunders, A. Coskun Samli, and Enid F. Tozier, "Congruence and Conflict in Buying Decisions of Mothers and Daughters," *Journal of Retailing,* **49**:3–18, Fall 1973.

17. Adapted from Smith, "Merchandising," p. 14.

18. Los Angeles Chamber of Commerce Research Committee, *The Dynamics of the Youth Explosion—A Look Ahead,* 1967, p. 34.

19. Much of this section is drawn from Edward Papazian, "Teenagers . . . and Broadcast Media," *Media/Scope,* **11**:111–115, December 1967.

20. This section is drawn from Papazian, "Teenagers," pp. 110–111.

21. "Young People Read Magazines for Information," *American Druggist,* **160**:60, December 1, 1969.

22. Ellis I. Folke, "Teenagers . . . and Print Media," *Media/Scope,* **11**:118, December 1967.

23. Frank Reysen, "Youth Markets: A Psychedelic Maze," *Media/Scope,* **14**:40, February 1970.

24. George W. Schiele, "How to Reach the Young Consumer," *Harvard Business Review,* **52**:85–86, March 1974.

25. Schiele, "How to Reach," pp. 83–84.

26. "Why Youth Needs a New Definition," *Business Week,* December 12, 1970, pp. 34–35.

27. *Marketing News,* February 25, 1977, p. 2.
28. James U. McNeal, "The Child Consumer: A New Market," *Journal of Retailing,* **45**:17–18, Summer 1969.
29. William D. Wells, "Communicating with Children," *Journal of Advertising Research,* **5**:2, May 1965.
30. McNeal, "The Child Consumer," pp. 20–21.
31. William H. Melody and Wendy Ehrlich, "Children's TV Commercials: The Vanishing Policy Options," *Journal of Communication,* **24**:113, Autumn 1974.
32. Shel Feldman and Abraham Wolf, "What's Wrong with Children's Commercials?" *Journal of Advertising Research,* **14**:39–40, February 1974.
33. "A Kind Word for Kidvid," *Sales Management,* June 25, 1973, p. 3.
34. Seymour Banks, "Public Policy on Ads to Children," *Journal of Advertising Research,* **15**:7, August 1975.
35. Banks, "Public Policy," pp. 11–12.
36. Jerry Della Femina, in Charles Sopkin (ed.), *From Those Wonderful Folks Who Gave You Pearl Harbor,* Pocket Books, New York, 1970, pp. 188–189.
37. "The Changing Face of the Children's Market," *Sales Management,* December 18, 1964, p. 36.
38. For a summary of this research, see Anees A. Sheikh, V. Kanti Prasad, and Tanniru R. Rao, "Children's TV Commercials: A Review of Research," *Journal of Communication,* **24**:126–136, Autumn 1974.
39. Penelope Orth, "Teenager: What Kind of Consumer?" *Printer's Ink,* September 20, 1963, p. 70; and "Youth: The Frontier Market," p. 82.
40. "The Power of the Aging in the Marketplace," *Business Week,* November 20, 1971, p. 52.
41. Fabian Linden, "The $200 Billion Middle-aged Market," *Conference Board Record,* December 1972, p. 17.
42. Leon Morse, "Old Folks: An Overlooked Market?" *Duns Review and Modern Industry,* April 1964, p. 46; and "The Over-65 Set: A Bonanza for Business?" *Nation's Business,* November 1971, p. 36.
43. For an example of this in the fashion area see Claude R. Martin, Jr. "A Transgenerational Comparison—the Elderly Fashion Consumer," in Beverlee B. Anderson (ed.), *Advances in Consumer Research,* **3**:453–456, Association for Consumer Research, Cincinnati, 1976.
44. Richard Seclow, "Coming Boom in Early Retirement Offers Big Market for Travel, Apparel, Housing," *Advertising Age,* May 15, 1972, p. 69.
45. Joyanne E. Block, "The Aged Consumer and the Market Place: A Critical Review," *Marquette Business Review,* **18**:78, Summer 1974; James MacDonald, "Rising Market," *The Wall Street Journal,* June 24, 1960, p. 14; and Morse "Old Folks," p. 46.
46. MacDonald, "Rising Market."
47. Donald L. Miller, "The Life Cycle and the Impact of Advertising," in Lincoln Clark (ed.), *Consumer Behavior,* **2**, New York University Press, New York, 1955.
48. *Consumer Interests of the Elderly* (Remarks by Professor John A. Howard), hearings before the Subcommittee on Consumer Interests of the Elderly of the Special Committee on Aging, United States Senate 90th Cong., lst Sess., January 17 and 18, 1967, U.S. Government Printing Office, 1967, p. 128.
49. "The Power of the Aging in the Marketplace," p. 56.
50. Joseph Barry Mason and Brooks E. Smith, "An Exploratory Note on the Shopping Behavior of the Low Income Senior Citizen," *The Journal of Consumer Affairs,* **8**:204–210, Winter 1974.
51. A. Coskun Samli, "The Elusive Senior Citizen Market," *Business & Economic Dimensions,* **3**:7–16, November 1967; and A. Coskun Samli and Feliksas Palubinskas, "Some Lesser Known Aspects of the Senior Citizen Market—A California Study," *Akron Business and Economic Review,* Winter 1972, pp. 47–55.
52. John A. Reinecke, "Supermarkets, Shopping Centers and the Senior Shopper," *Marquette Business Review,* **19**:106, 1975.

SOCIAL CLASS

THE PROCESS OF SOCIAL STRATIFICATION   THE NATURE OF SOCIAL CLASS   No Value Judgments; Social Class Indicators; Social Class Categories; Class versus Status   THE SIGNIFICANCE OF SOCIAL STRATIFICATION   SOCIAL CLASS LIFE-STYLES   Upper-Upper Class; Lower-Upper Class; Upper-Middle Class; Lower-Middle Class; Upper-Lower Class; Lower-Lower Class   THE ROLE OF SOCIAL CLASS IN SEGMENTING MARKETS   SOCIAL CLASS AND CONSUMER BEHAVIOR   Products and Services Consumed; Shopping Behavior; Promotional Response Patterns; Price-Related Behavior

I n this chapter we shall examine the influence of social class on consumer behavior. In a sense we may think of social classes or strata as being subcultures, for each class has its distinguishing mode of behavior, or life-style. We shall first discuss what is meant by social stratification and how social class divisions are determined. This will be followed by a discussion of differences in the values of each class and their life-style differences. Finally, the nature of consumer behavior within each class will be described as it is determined by these values and life-style differences.

THE PROCESS OF SOCIAL STRATIFICATION

As much as we Americans like to think that all people are created equal, we are aware that some are "more equal" than others; that is, there are some people who stand high in the community, while others rank low on the totem pole. We refer to these levels as social strata, or classes. "Social stratification," then, is the general term whereby people in a society are ranked by other members of the society into higher and lower social positions which produces a hierarchy of respect or prestige.[1]

Each society subjectively establishes its set of values. These values are reflected in the ideal types of people in that society. That is, those who more nearly conform to the ideal are accorded more respect and prestige, while those who conform less nearly are ranked lower by the society. In one country members of the armed services may be accorded the greatest prestige; in another politicians, educators, or business people may be selected. The particular criteria used, as well as their relative weights, are determined by the values which that society stresses. The concept of social class can be useful to the marketer in understanding consumer behavior and plotting a marketing strategy. In order to use it wisely, however, one must first understand its meaning. The following section elaborates on the nature of social class.

THE NATURE OF SOCIAL CLASS

The term "social class" has been defined as a group consisting of a number of people who have approximately equal positions in a society. These positions may be achieved rather than ascribed, with some opportunity for upward or downward movement to other classes.[2] The following are some basic premises in our study of class and consumer behavior.

No Value Judgments

The term social class is used here in the descriptive, not normative, sense. That is, we are not implying that one class is better than another. We are simply describing the class structure as we know it to be. Some may resent such a discussion or be uncomfortable about it, feeling that it is undemocratic. However, social classes exist and if the marketer is to be successful, their patterns must be understood.

Social Class Indicators

Social class is not equivalent to occupation, or income, or any one criterion; however, it may be indicated by or be related to one or more of these measures. It is important for the marketer to realize that some of these variables are more reliable "proxies" (substitutes) than others. As we shall discuss later, income is often misleading as an indicator of social class position. On the other hand, occupation generally provides a fairly good clue to one's social class; in fact, it is probably the best single indicator available. This appears to be so because certain occupations are held in higher esteem than others by Americans. Table 9-1 illustrates the hierarchy of prestige accorded to many occupations in the United States.

TABLE 9-1

THE RATINGS OF OCCUPATIONS

Occupation	Rank
U.S. Supreme Court Justice	1
Physician	2
Nuclear physicist	3.5
Scientist	3.5
Government scientist	5.5
State governor	5.5
Cabinet member in the federal government	8
College professor	8
U.S. Representative in Congress	8
Chemist	11
Lawyer	11
Diplomat in the U.S. Foreign Service	11
Dentist	14
Architect	14
County judge	14
Psychologist	17.5
Minister	17.5

TABLE 9-1 (continued)

191

SOCIAL
CLASS

Occupation	Rank
Member of the board of directors of a large corporation	17.5
Mayor of a large city	17.5
Priest	21.5
Head of a department in a state government	21.5
Civil engineer	21.5
Airline pilot	21.5
Banker	24.5
Biologist	24.5
Sociologist	26
Instructor in public schools	27.5
Captain in the regular army	27.5
Accountant for a large business	29.5
Public school teacher	29.5
Owner of a factory that employs about 100 people	31.5
Building contractor	31.5
Artist who paints pictures that are exhibited in galleries	34.5
Musician in a symphony orchestra	34.5
Author of novels	34.5
Economist	34.5
Official of an international labor union	37
Railroad engineer	39
Electrician	39
County agricultural agent	39
Owner-operator of a printing shop	41.5
Trained machinist	41.5
Farm owner and operator	44
Undertaker	44
Welfare worker for a city government	44
Newspaper columnist	46
Policeman	47
Reporter on a daily newspaper	48
Radio announcer	49.5
Bookkeeper	49.5
Tenant farmer—one who owns livestock and machinery and manages the farm	51.5
Insurance agent	51.5
Carpenter	53
Manager of a small store in a city	54.5
A local offical of a labor union	54.5
Mail carrier	57
Railroad conductor	57
Traveling salesman for a wholesale concern	57
Plumber	59
Automobile repairman	60

TABLE 9-1 (continued)

Occupation	Rank
Playground director	62.5
Barber	62.5
Machine operator in a factory	62.5
Owner-operator of a lunch stand	62.5
Corporal in the regular army	65.5
Garage mechanic	65.5
Truck driver	67
Fisherman who owns his own boat	68
Clerk in a store	70
Milk route man	70
Streetcar motorman	70
Lumberjack	72.5
Restaurant cook	72.5
Singer in a nightclub	74
Filling station attendant	75
Dockworker	77.5
Railroad section hand	77.5
Night watchman	77.5
Coal miner	77.5
Restaurant waiter	80.5
Taxi driver	80.5
Farm hand	83
Janitor	83
Bartender	83
Clothes presser in a laundry	85
Soda fountain clerk	86
Share-cropper—one who owns no livestock or equipment and does not manage farm	87
Garbage collector	88
Street sweeper	89
Shoe shiner	90

Source: Robert W. Hodge, Paul M. Seigel, and Peter H. Rossi, "Occupational Prestige in the United States, 1925–1963," American Journal of Sociology, **70**:286–302, Nov. 1964. Published by the University of Chicago.

Social Class Categories

Various research studies have attempted to stratify social classes in the United States. Probably the best-known study has been that done by W. Lloyd Warner and his associates.[3] Warner discerned a six-class system of stratification based upon research conducted in several small communities. He categorized the six classes as follows: upper-upper, lower-upper, upper-middle, lower-middle, upper-lower, and lower-lower.

Using another approach, Richard Centers developed similar groupings. In a representative survey of the United States, respondents categorized themselves into one of the following classes: upper, middle, working, and lower.[4] In a larger and more recent sample from the United States Census of Population, Carman isolated five social class categories.[5] Table 9-2 presents the approximate percentage of responses for each class determined by these three research studies, using different methods.

TABLE 9-2

193
SOCIAL
CLASS

SOCIAL CLASS PLACEMENT

	Percentage Distribution		
	Warner	Centers	Carman
Upper-upper class	1.44%		
Upper class		4.0%	0.38%
Lower-upper class	1.56		
Upper-middle class	10.22		10.82
Middle class		36.0	
Lower-middle class	28.12		30.82
Working class		52.0	
Upper-lower class	32.60		49.96
Lower class		5.0	
Lower-lower class	25.22		8.02
Other responses	0.84	3.0	
	100.00	100.0	100.00

Source: W. L. Warner, Marchia Meeker, and Kenneth Eells, *Social Class in America,* Science Research Associates, Chicago, 1949, p. 14; Richard Centers, *The Psychology of Social Classes,* Princeton University Press, Princeton, N.J., 1949, p. 77; James M. Carman, *The Application of Social Class in Market Segmentation,* University of California Graduate School of Business Administration, Institute of Business and Economic Research, Berkeley, Calif., 1965, p. 53.

Although the size of various classes may vary depending on the classification method used and may shift over time, it is nevertheless quite important to realize that the bulk of the market for most products exists in the broad middle- and lower-class groups. The upper class is made up of only about 3 percent of the population; because of its wealth it is of the utmost importance for the marketing of certain luxury items. However, this group is too small in number to provide the focal point for most marketers. On the other hand, at the lower end of the class spectrum—the lower-lower class—one generally finds a market that, even though sizable, does not have sufficient income for many products. Therefore, most consumer-goods marketers concentrate their major attention on the remaining groups of middle and upper-lower classes.

Class versus Status

Social class and status are not equivalent concepts although they do have an important relationship. *Status* generally refers to one's rank in the social system as perceived by other members of society. An individual's status, therefore, is a function not only of the social class to which he belongs but also of his personal characteristics. For example, the fact that an individual is a scientist means that he has a high rank in the total social system (as seen in Table 9-1). However, a scientist employed by a prestigious research institute earning $50,000 a year will have higher status or rank than a scientist employed by a small firm and earning $25,000, even though both may be members of the same social class. Moreover, an individual's personal contributions to society will help determine his or her status. A scientist who discovers a breakthrough in laser technology, for example, will have higher status than another who has made no such significant contribution.

Although social status and social class are often used interchangeably, it should be realized that they are not equivalent concepts. However, since we are discussing groups of consumers, not individuals, there is little problem in doing so.

SYMBOLS OF STATUS People buy products for what they mean as well as what they can do. That is, products and services are seen to have personal and social meanings in addition to their purely functional purpose. The things consumers buy become "symbols," telling others who they are and what their social class or status is.

This idea was expressed long ago by Thorstein Veblen who suggested that there is a tendency by some members of each social class to engage in *conspicuous consumption* while others spend more conservatively.[6] By conspicuous consumption Veblen referred to consumers purchasing things that they do not really need so that others can see what they have done. In a complex society in which financial wealth dictates status, one's possessions become a substitute indicator of the individual's worth, value, wealth, and so forth. Possessions, therefore, take the place of income as an indicator of status, since we aren't likely to know how much others are paid. Consequently, there may be members of a society at each social class level who seek to achieve a certain higher status by virtue of their possessions. It should be noted, however, that others at that same level may be content to save more and spend much less extravagantly.

Marketers have always catered to consumers who were looking for something to give them an edge, whether real or imagined, over their peers. The key to status symbols is their scarcity and social desirability. As such, they are marks of distinction, setting their owners apart from others.

At one time, class differences in status and its symbols were an accepted fact of life in clothing, housing and furnishings, food, drink, speech, and even religious affiliation. Today, however, views of status symbols are changing.[7] Rapid advances in technology and communications have spread the desire for these material pleasures among all social classes. And as Americans have become more affluent, even those with moderate incomes are able to own their own homes, color televisions, boats, all sorts of home appliances, and take exotic vacations. Consequently, if "perfectly ordinary" people can display big cars and fancy appliances, then these things obviously have lost much of their effectiveness as status symbols.

The status symbols of today have changed somewhat from the conventional to the unconventional. The Volkswagen, for instance, became an unconventional status symbol—one that consumers supposedly purchased for function rather than show. It conveyed a reverse kind of low-key status. Bicycle makers have also capitalized on this. Thus, the acquiring of expensive items is no longer the simple key to success in status seeking it once was.

In addition many of the status symbols of today have not filtered down from the upper class to the middle and working classes but instead have percolated up from the bottom. Recent styles such as blue jeans, beads, and long hair are indicative of this. Another confusing element is that traditional status symbols are available today even to those who are not wealthy. For instance, art and sculpture can be rented; inexpensive opera and ballet offerings are available; and tennis, skiing, and sailing can be pursued on a low budget.

Thus, traditional status symbols are no longer the clear indicator of social class they once were and marketers must understand these trends in order to take advantage of consumers' changing values. It should also be noted that what is "in" in one region of the United States may be "out" in another. Consequently, status symbols can vary geographically, as Exhibit 9-1 illustrates.

THE SIGNIFICANCE OF SOCIAL STRATIFICATION

The significance of social stratification for the marketer is that there are differences in values, attitudes, and behavior of each of the classes. These differences provide a basis on which to segment markets and obtain an enhanced understanding of the behavior of consumers. Some of the major findings from research on general social class differences are summarized in Table 9-3.

It is clear from the findings in Table 9-3 that the classes exhibit many differences. Pierre Martineau has conducted research to determine what these differences are and how they relate to the marketer's strategies. He found that the prime general targets for the marketer—the middle and lower classes—had numerous contrasting psychological orientations as described below:[8]

Middle Class	Lower Class
1. Pointed to the future	1. Pointed to the present and past
2. Viewpoint embraces a long expanse of time	2. Lives and thinks in a short expanse of time
3. More urban identification	3. More rural identification
4. Stresses rationality	4. Nonrational essentially
5. Has a well-structured sense of the universe	5. Vague and unclear structuring of the world
6. Horizons vastly extended or not limited	6. Horizons sharply defined and limited
7. Greater sense of choice making	7. Limited sense of choice making
8. Self-confident, willing to take risks	8. Very much concerned with security and insecurity
9. Immaterial and abstract in thinking	9. Concrete and perceptive in thinking
10. Sees himself or herself tied to national happenings	10. World revolves around his or her family and body

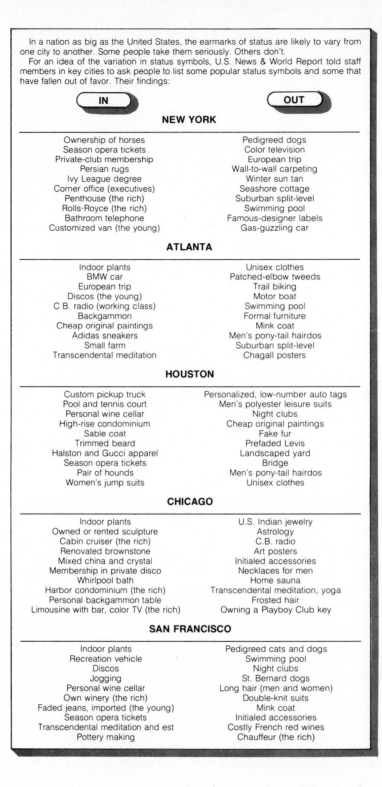

In a nation as big as the United States, the earmarks of status are likely to vary from one city to another. Some people take them seriously. Others don't.

For an idea of the variation in status symbols, U.S. News & World Report told staff members in key cities to ask people to list some popular status symbols and some that have fallen out of favor. Their findings:

IN	OUT

NEW YORK

IN	OUT
Ownership of horses	Pedigreed dogs
Season opera tickets	Color television
Private-club membership	European trip
Persian rugs	Wall-to-wall carpeting
Ivy League degree	Winter sun tan
Corner office (executives)	Seashore cottage
Penthouse (the rich)	Suburban split-level
Rolls-Royce (the rich)	Swimming pool
Bathroom telephone	Famous-designer labels
Customized van (the young)	Gas-guzzling car

ATLANTA

IN	OUT
Indoor plants	Unisex clothes
BMW car	Patched-elbow tweeds
European trip	Trail biking
Discos (the young)	Motor boat
C.B. radio (working class)	Swimming pool
Backgammon	Formal furniture
Cheap original paintings	Mink coat
Adidas sneakers	Men's pony-tail hairdos
Small farm	Suburban split-level
Transcendental meditation	Chagall posters

HOUSTON

IN	OUT
Custom pickup truck	Personalized, low-number auto tags
Pool and tennis court	Men's polyester leisure suits
Personal wine cellar	Night clubs
High-rise condominium	Cheap original paintings
Sable coat	Fake fur
Trimmed beard	Prefaded Levis
Halston and Gucci apparel	Landscaped yard
Season opera tickets	Bridge
Pair of hounds	Men's pony-tail hairdos
Women's jump suits	Unisex clothes

CHICAGO

IN	OUT
Indoor plants	U.S. Indian jewelry
Owned or rented sculpture	Astrology
Cabin cruiser (the rich)	C.B. radio
Renovated brownstone	Art posters
Mixed china and crystal	Initialed accessories
Membership in private disco	Necklaces for men
Whirlpool bath	Home sauna
Harbor condominium (the rich)	Transcendental meditation, yoga
Personal backgammon table	Frosted hair
Limousine with bar, color TV (the rich)	Owning a Playboy Club key

SAN FRANCISCO

IN	OUT
Indoor plants	Pedigreed cats and dogs
Recreation vehicle	Swimming pool
Discos	Night clubs
Jogging	St. Bernard dogs
Personal wine cellar	Long hair (men and women)
Own winery (the rich)	Double-knit suits
Faded jeans, imported (the young)	Mink coat
Season opera tickets	Initialed accessories
Transcendental meditation and est	Costly French red wines
Pottery making	Chauffeur (the rich)

EXHIBIT 9-1
Across the nation—thumbnail guide to Americans' tastes. (*Source:* Reprinted from *U.S. News & World Report*, February 14, 1977, p. 39. Copyright 1977 U.S. News & World Report, Inc.)

TABLE 9-3

197
SOCIAL
CLASS

SOCIAL CLASS DIFFERENCES

Childbearing and Rearing
The higher the class, the lower the fertility rate. Compared with their middle-class counterparts, lower-class infants and children are subject to less . . .
control of sexual and other impulses
development of conscience
stress on achievement
equalitarian treatment vis-à-vis parents
permissive upbringing
but more . . .
parental authority
physical punishment
freedom to be aggressive

Marital and Family Relations
Husbands and wives generally come from the same class
The higher the class, the more companionable are the husband's and wife's relations
The lower class has the greatest family instability, followed by the upper class, and middle class.

Education, Learning, Intelligence
The higher the class, the greater the value and extent of education
Upper classes are oriented more toward private institutions and are educated not only in academic subjects, but also dancing, tennis, golf, and music.
The higher the class, the higher the I.Q. and the tendency to learn rapidly.

Values
Class consciousness decreases with class level, with upper-middles the most class-sensitive.
The middle classes (especially the upper-middle) value achievement more than do the lower classes
Upper classes value self-expression in their occupations and lives, whereas the lower classes desire security.
Middle-class people tend to be more "other-directed" while the lower class tends to be more "inner-directed."

Social Relations
The higher classes have more organizational memberships.
Upper-class women join upper-class philanthropic organizations, supporting them with their time and money; upper-middle women spend much time but less money on such activities; while women in other classes are oriented toward home or job.

Other Patterns
Religious affiliation varies with class. Upper-class Christians are likely to belong to Episcopal or Unitarian churches, while middle classes belong to Methodist, Presbyterian, or Baptists; and lower classes belong to Baptist, Catholic, or smaller Protestant groups.
Language patterns differ among the classes. Whereas lower classes use slang, trite phrases, double negatives, and mispronounce words, the upper classes are marked by their pitch and tone, avoidance of popular phrases, using fewer words to express the same thought, and correct enunciation and pronunciation.

Source: James F. Engel, David T. Kollat, and Roger D. Blackwell, *Consumer Behavior,* Holt, New York, 1968, pp. 299–303; Bernard Berelson and Gary Steiner, *Human Behavior: An Inventory of Scientific Findings,* Harcourt, Brace & World, New York, 1964, pp. 477–488; and James M. Carman, *The Application of Social Class in Market Segmentation,* University of California Graduate School of Business Administration, Institute of Business and Economic Research, Berkeley, Calif., 1965, pp. 25–29.

In the next section we shall examine these class differences in greater detail. The concluding section of this chapter will report on the major consumer-behavior differences between the classes and point out significant implications for the marketer.

SOCIAL CLASS LIFE-STYLES

This section discusses findings regarding class variations and life-style differences. As we describe the life-styles of each of the major social class groups the terminology adopted by most marketers will be used, which includes the categories of upper-upper, lower-upper, upper-middle, lower-middle, upper-lower, and lower-lower class. At times the term "working class" will be used, which is roughly synonymous with the upper-lower class.

As the following classes are discussed it should be kept in mind that we are not implying that all members of the same class have homogeneous behavior. As Coleman observes, "there is a considerable variation in the way individual members of a class realize these class goals and express these values."[9] Moreover, it is impossible to point to a clear line of demarcation where one class changes to another. There is a great deal of blurring and overlapping of the social strata. Nevertheless, we will attempt to make some major distinctions between the six-class system as developed by Warner.[10]

Upper-Upper Class

This is the "Social Register" class composed of old, locally prominent families—the aristocracy of birth and wealth with at least three generations in the community and class. It is the smallest class group, international in residence, friendships, and relationships. Its members have occupations as large merchants, financiers, and in the higher professions. Their reference group is the British upper class. They are oriented toward living graciously, upholding the family reputation, reflecting the excellence of one's breeding, and displaying a sense of community responsibility.

Lower-Upper Class

This is the nouveau riche, or "newly rich" class, composed of those who have recently arrived at their wealth and are not quite accepted by the upper-uppers. They are the "executive elite," founders of large businesses, and wealthy doctors and lawyers. They have the highest incomes of all the classes and their goals are a blend of the upper-uppers' pursuit of gracious living and the upper-middle success drive.

Upper-Middle Class

This class consists of moderately successful professional men and women, such as doctors, lawyers, and professors; owners of medium-sized businesses; and "organization men" at the managerial level. It also includes younger men and women who are expected to reach those occupational-status levels within a few years. Most members are college-educated, hence, this group is sometimes referred to as "the brains and eyes" of our society.

The motivations of this group are toward achieving success in their careers, reaching a higher income level and achieving social advancement for themselves and their children. They strive to cultivate charm and polish, and handle a broad range of civic and/or cultural interests. They play bridge, and Scrabble; go to plays, museums, symphonies, and art galleries; and are members of golf clubs, yacht clubs, and college clubs. Their possessions are usually new and their reference group is the upper class.

Lower-Middle Class

This class is at the top of the "common man" or "average man" level. It is composed of nonmanagerial workers, small business owners, and highly paid blue-collars. These lower echelon white-collar workers and small businessmen are at the bottom of the white-collar status ladder while their blue-collar counterparts are at the top of theirs.

The key motivations for this group are "respectability" and "striving." Men and women want to be judged respectable in their personal behavior by their fellow citizens; that is, they desire to live in well-maintained homes which are neatly furnished and located in neighborhoods that are on the right side of the tracks. They strive to do a good job at their work. Home is their focus and much time and effort is spent in it, especially keeping it clean and tidy.

Upper-Lower Class

These are "poor but honest" folks who are also referred to as the "ordinary working class." The largest of all classes, it is composed of skilled and semiskilled workers and small tradesmen. Contrary to what may be expected, many of these class members make very good money; they simply don't use it to become "respectable" the way the lower-middle class does. Upper-lowers are oriented toward living well and enjoying life from day to day rather than saving for the future or being concerned about what the middle classes think of them. They want to be modern, to keep up with the times rather than the Joneses.

The working-class family's world view is one of great anxiety. They value the present, the known, and the personal, while avoiding the competitive, the impersonal, and the uncertain. They indulge rather than invest. They are preoccupied with stable human relationships in their everyday lives. Moreover, because they see themselves as being quite restricted in their ability to rise in social status, those with whom they identify are largely chosen from their own class. Thus, more than in any other class, the working-class family generally looks horizontally for its norms and standards rather than up to the next class.

In lumping people of this class together with lower-middles, the resulting group has been termed "the muscles and hands" of our society, and is characterized as enjoying canasta, rummy, poker, TV, movies, and bowling. The men belong to unions, lodges, and fraternal orders.

Lower-Lower Class

This group consists mostly of unskilled workers, unassimilated ethnics, and those who are sporadically employed. Many are on welfare, and they live in the deteriorated sections of town. Many are categorized as the "American underclass" whose environment is often a "junk heap of rotting housing, broken furniture, crummy food, alcohol and drugs."[11] Their outlook is apathetic and fatalistic and their behavior generally and as consumers is toward "getting their kicks wherever they can." They have a bad reputation among higher classes who view them as lazy, shiftless, against work, and immoral.

THE ROLE OF SOCIAL CLASS IN SEGMENTING MARKETS

It is evident that the concept of social class should help us to understand better the behavior of the various market segments. However, the marketing practitioner wants to know if segmentation on the basis of social class is an advantageous approach.

Social class segmentation involves two basic issues.[12] First, opinions differ concerning which procedures are best for identifying social classes. This issue is beyond the scope of our discussion. However, it should simply be noted here that there are various approaches to social class measurement, with each one offering certain advantages and disadvantages. A second and more fundamental problem is whether even to use social class (which is, in effect, a composite index consisting of several variables) in segmenting markets, or to use a single proxy variable such as income (for which data more readily exist). Thus, the basic question here is, Which approach better explains consumer behavior?

Those who believe that social class is much better than income for market segmentation claim that income categories are quite often irrelevant in analyzing markets and explaining consumers' shopping habits, store preferences, and media usage. An example of the superiority of social class to income is the following case of three families, all earning approximately $18,000 per year, but belonging to different social classes with radical differences in their spending patterns.[13]

An *upper-middle class* family headed, perhaps, by a young lawyer or a college professor is likely to spend a relatively large share of its income on housing in a prestige neighborhood, on expensive furniture, clothing from quality stores, and on cultural amusements or club memberships.

A *lower-middle class* family headed, let's say, by an insurance salesman or a successful grocery store owner probably has a better house, but in not as fancy a neighborhood; as full a wardrobe, although not as expensive; more furniture, but none by name designers; and a much bigger savings account.

A *working-class* family headed, perhaps, by a welder or cross-country truck driver, is likely to have less house and less neighborhood than the others; however it will have a larger, newer car, more expensive kitchen appliances, and a larger TV set in the living room. This family will spend less on clothing and furniture, but more on food and sports.

Nevertheless, most of the research that has been conducted has found income to be more useful than social class for segmenting markets. One study showed that for a number of low-priced consumer packaged goods, both income and social class were found to correlate with buying behavior. However, product usage generally proved to be more closely related to income than to social class.[14] A follow-up study included certain durable-goods items plus a few services and confirmed the earlier one by showing income to be superior to social class in segmenting the market for nearly all items.[15] Thus, some products appear to be classless in their appeal. For example, in the hot Southwest, income, not social class, largely determines whether a family buys air conditioning. If the family can afford it, it purchases it. Based upon such findings, it would appear that social class, although useful as a concept, has often not been as successful as other approaches in segmenting markets.

Much of the earlier research, however, based its findings on *use* or *nonuse* of a product or service rather than on *how often* that product or service was used. Since there are many products or services that a broad spectrum of consumers would buy or use at least once, one research study examined the role of *frequency of use* in selecting the superior segmentation bases among income, social class, age, and stage in family life cycle for various entertainment activities. This research showed that income and stage in the life cycle were more highly related to *use* of all the entertainment activities than were age and social class. However, all four variables—especially social class— showed strong associations with the *frequency of use* of these entertainment activities.[1] More research is needed on a broad variety of products before a generalization of this finding is made.

Several explanations have been suggested for the apparent lackluster performance of social class as a basis for market segmentation.[17] One factor is the recent and dramatic changes which have taken place in our society's economic, social, and cultural climate and which have diminished the differences in consumer behavior between the classes.

Another explanation for the poor showing of social class is that researchers have failed to account for the diversity within classes. That is, individuals, although in the same social class, may show considerable discrepancy in their ratings on the variables comprising it. For example, some may have high education with low income or vice versa, yet be members of the same social class. This inconsistency in strata variables known as *status incongruency* or *low status crystallization,* presents difficulties not only in ranking individuals but also in understanding their behavior.

The diversity within social classes is particularly evident with income level variations. For example, it has been suggested that there are *overprivileged* and *underprivileged* members within each class; that is, those whose incomes are above average for their class, and those with incomes below the average for that class.[18] This concept is believed to explain the purchase of certain consumer durables. For example, compact cars were bought initially by the underprivileged segments of each class. Thus, a struggling young lawyer, as an underprivileged member of the upper-middle class, may purchase a Volkswagen as a temporary transportation solution until her income rises, then buy a Buick when she gets to be overprivileged. Similarly, costly household appliances and recreational activities tend to have been consumed by the overprivileged members of each class. Color television sets, for instance, were first bought primarily by this segment.

In attempting to use social class to segment markets, Robertson suggests that the marketer remember three guidelines:

1. Social class may not always be a relevant consideration; i.e., segmentation by other criteria, such as age and sex, are frequently more appropriate.

2. Benefits from social class segmentation for undifferentiated products may be less than the costs incurred to achieve such segmentation.

3. Social class segmentation is frequently most effective when used in conjunction with such additional variables as life-cycle stage and ethnic group.[19]

In spite of the limitations discussed with regard to the use of social class for segmentation, it does provide the marketer with helpful insights—some of which may be specifically used in developing marketing strategies, and others of which at least offer an improved general understanding of consumer behavior.

In the remaining section of this chapter, we will present some of the research findings on the relationship of social class, consumer behavior, and the development of marketing mixes.

SOCIAL CLASS AND CONSUMER BEHAVIOR

This section examines the most significant findings concerning various classes' behavior with regard to the products they buy, the places they shop, and the promotions and prices they respond to.

For many products the groups of interest to the marketer are the middle and working classes—by far the largest segment of the market. Because of this, the bulk of our attention in this section will be focused on these two categories in order to provide a more complete understanding of these groups. Where possible, special emphasis will be given to the working class because of the marketer's inherent difficulty in understanding this market, which springs from the fact that most marketing managers are members of the middle or upper classes. These are the groups that form the basis of their *self-reference criterion;* that is, they tend to assume that everyone else is like themselves in values, attitudes, tastes, life-style, and so forth. Such a premise is very likely to result in marketing strategy failure.

Products and Services Consumed

Product choice and usage differ among the social classes. There are items that are bought mainly by the upper classes, such as bonds and exotic vacations, and others that are purchased mainly by lower classes, such as roller derby tickets and cheap wine. Not only are there between-class purchasing differences but also within-class variations. As mentioned previously, each class level has its conspicuous consumers and its more conservative buyers—i.e., its overprivileged and its underprivileged members. However, most products are purchased by all consumers so it becomes difficult to distinguish class differences in purchasing patterns. For example, all people purchase food, clothing, and shelter items. The differences come into view when we examine not just generic categories, but types of products and particular brands, and frequency of purchase. Before discussing each class specifically, some general product/service differences among the classes will be noted.

Modes of travel have differential appeal to the classes. Airlines are basically a form of travel for middle-class people. Waiting rooms, plane interiors, food, drinks, and even stewardess behavior are directly aimed at the upper-middle class. Lower-class people perceive that air travel is not for them and as a consequence, only a very small proportion of air travelers are from these lower classes. Instead, they are more likely to go by bus, train, or car. Even though the airlines have attempted "no frills" service, lower middles have probably been the major beneficiaries of this strategy.

Home furnishings and appliances are another area where orientations differ because of social class. Furniture style has greater symbolic value to the upper-middle and upper classes. They will seek furniture that is stylish and in keeping with some specific personal or family esthetic. They are also likely to depart from the norm because they have great confidence in their taste and because their desire to set themselves apart from lower-class symbols outweighs any fear they may have of being criticized for their taste. This group would have a greater affinity for modern furniture and sterling silver, for example. Lower-middles have some anxiety over selecting furniture that is "right," (i.e., respectable, neat, or pretty). They would probably refuse to hang an original Picasso on their walls even if it were received as a gift. Not only would they dislike the painting, but would also fear the reaction of their friends. This group tends toward formica-covered dinette sets, silverplated tableware in a fancy design, and highly conventional furniture. Lower classes are likely to emphasize sturdiness, comfort, and maintenance in their furniture.[20]

Recreational activities also have class patterns. Major league baseball, for example, is patronized mostly by upper-lower class fans, while college football attendance is practically all middle class, and predominantly upper-middle. Similarly, bridge, tennis, and opera have traditionally been upper-class while bingo, boxing, and bowling are lower-class activities.

Working-class men are also much more likely to pursue outdoor "masculine" activities such as hunting, camping, and fishing than are middle-class men. Guns and fishing equipment are aimed primarily at this market by manufacturers. Similarly, upper-lower class men have been the primary target for camping vans. Members of this group also tend to combine their vacations with their sporting interests and are likely to go on hunting or fishing trips as vacations without their wives, and often spend an evening "out with the boys." Such separate vacations and nights out are rare for the middle-class man, whose wife would quickly become suspicious of his strange behavior.[21]

Magazines are also segmented by social class. For example, readers of *National Geographic* and *The New Yorker* are typically of a higher class than the readers of *Police Gazette, True Confessions,* and *The Star.* Even magazines in the same topic area may be aimed at different social classes as target audiences. An example of this is the kind of readers of *Hustler* and *Playboy,* as reflected by the men often pictured in ads for the two magazines. Figure 9-1 presents a somewhat tongue-in-cheek "profile" of the *Hustler* reader segment. In contrast to this is the well-known picture of the sophisticated "*Playboy* man." Obviously, these magazines appeal to different class segments.

Finally, there are important differences between the classes regarding their *savings/spending* habits and *financial services* orientation. It has been found that the higher the individual's class position, the more likely he is to express some saving aspiration, particularly investment savings. Spending orientations also differ. For example, lower-class people tend to mention only material artifacts that they would like to purchase while higher-class people tend to mention spending on experiences, such as vacations, recreation, self-education, and hobbies.[22] A last example of money-handling differences shows up in their orientations toward sources for borrowing money. While middle-class people tend to mention banks or insurance policies, lower-class people cite personal loan companies, credit unions, and friends.[23]

WHAT SORT OF MAN <u>REALLY</u> READS HUSTLER?

When Larry Flynt started HUSTLER three years ago, he said it would be a mass-appeal vehicle—a magazine that would mock the myth of pseudosophisticated values glorified by other men's magazines and capture the realism that is the true spirit of Middle America today. Now the figures are in. Our first TGI Survey (Spring '77) proves Larry was right on target! Pick any category and compare HUSTLER with the other two leading men's magazines: You'll see a profile of the typical Middle American male . . . some college men, but *more* high-school men; some managers, but *more* salesmen, craftsmen and foremen. More than 64% of them are married, almost 60% of them make over $15,000 a year, and <u>more</u> of them own homes worth over $25,000! It's a valuable market, with families and money to spend. And HUSTLER delivers it at a lower CPM! We've given you the vehicle—do you have the courage to give us a contract?

HUSTLER Magazine • 40 West Gay Street • Columbus, Ohio 43215 • (614) 464-2070

FIGURE 9-1
Advertisement reflecting social class. (Courtesy of *Hustler* Magazine, Inc.)

Although our understanding and appreciation of social class differences and similarities in product choice and usage is limited, we can make some rather general statements regarding the product and service orientations of the classes.

UPPER-UPPER CLASS The consumption patterns of upper-uppers are quite different from those of other classes. Although expense is frequently no object, they do not purchase in order to impress others. Therefore, they may be content to wear 20-year-old sportcoats and drive 10-year-old cars. They tend to be conservative in their consumption, buying relatively few goods, and use more services than goods. One reason for their low consumption of goods is that many of their belongings are passed on from generation to generation.

LOWER-UPPER CLASS The consumer behavior of lower-uppers may be characterized as oriented strongly toward conspicuous consumption. Their purchase decisions are geared toward demonstrating wealth and status through such items as expensive cars, large estates, expensive jewelry, and so forth. This is the market for Mercedes autos, $250,000 homes with heart-shaped swimming pools, $1500 18-carat gold-framed eyeglasses, diamond brooches from Tiffany's, and Gucci apparel.

While the upper class may be a significant market for many high-priced luxuries, for most new-product introductions this group can be largely ignored. However, to some extent they do act as reference groups to those below them and sometimes their use of certain products will "trickle down" to the other social class groups.

UPPER-MIDDLE CLASS This group purchases a far greater number of products than any other class. Because they are successful, their purchase decisions reflect strong social implications. Through their consumption they want to project an image of success and achievement. Their purchases emulate higher strata and are a display of their success, not only for their peers but for others lower on the social scale. Because they purchase higher-quality products and attempt to display good taste they are frequently termed the "quality market."

Because this group is so important as a market, many businesses are broadening their appeal to include upper-middles. Country clubs, for example, long considered to be plush, snobby, and oriented mainly to the upper class, have changed their image. Today many of them appear to have a more democratic image and a growing middle-class orientation where members tend to be younger, more informal, and where women and minorities are increasingly included.

The high education level of this group strongly influences the kinds of expenditures they make. As cited earlier their desired consumption pattern is heavily "experience" centered, that is, spending where one is left typically with memories rather than tangible assets.

LOWER-MIDDLE CLASS Social acceptability is an important guideline in the consumption activity of this group also. They are more interested in a product's giving them social acceptance than the luxuriousness or functionality of the item. Products, especially home furnishings, are bought on the basis of what is "pretty" and stylish and will suit the housewife and win praise from her friends and neighbors. Product choices are made along safe and conservative lines rather than on the basis of original and imaginative thoughts.

UPPER-LOWER CLASS Rainwater reports that there are five basic goals that activate the consumer behavior of the working-class housewife:

1. The search for social, economic, and physical security

2. The drive for a "common man" level of recognition and respectability

3. The desire for support and affection from the people important to her

4. The effort to escape a heavy burden of household labors

5. The urge to decorate, to "pretty up," her world[24]

Their world tends to be more limited in both direct and vicarious experiences, which is reflected in their consumption patterns. Expenditures are concentrated into fewer categories of goods and services. They are more concerned with immediate gratification than are middle-class families, but avoid spending their money in ways that are considered "out-of-place." Their spending is centered more on the interior-exterior interest of their house than on the size and location of the house itself. Since their upward social mobility is quite limited, they are not concerned about socially elite addresses. Instead, their housing tastes are very practical and utilarian with "decent," "clean," "new," and "safe" characterizing their outlook. An example of this orientation, in spite of an income that would allow other alternatives, is illustrated by Michigan's first million-dollar lottery winner, who collects $50,000 a year for the next 20 years. Although he retired from his manual labor job, he did not move his family from their one-bedroom bungalow. Instead he installed aluminum siding, central air conditioning, storm windows, a sun porch, double-oven gas stove, color television, and finished his basement recreation room with dark green paneling and indirect lighting.[25]

Although working-class consumer behavior resembles middle-class behavior in hard goods spending, the expenditures by upper-lowers for services lags behind. It is also lower than their own expenditures for durables. Some of the reasons suggested for the lack of service-oriented consumption among the working class in comparison with the middle class are: (1) they tend to be do-it-yourselfers; (2) their expenditures for children's education are much smaller; (3) they are more likely to spend their vacation at home or visiting relatives, saving on motel and transportation costs; (4) they do not frequent expensive restaurants, but tend to consume their meals away from home with relatives, or at a franchised drive-in.[26] Thus, the tremendous boom in the service sector of our economy is largely a middle-class phenomenon.

LOWER-LOWER CLASS Contrary to what might be expected, some members of this group may represent an attractive segment for manufacturers of food products or other frequently purchased items, and certain durables. For example, one study found that such families are consumers of many major consumer durables, frequently the new, more expensive models.[27] Another researcher found that the prevailing market value of the lower-class family's car, television set, and basic appliances average almost 20 percent higher than the average value of similar possessions for upper-lowers, despite a median income which was one-third lower than the working class group.[28] Their behavior can be described as "compensatory consumption." The lower-lower class family's pessimistic outlook on life causes them to spend for immediate gratification. Thus, through their purchasing they try to emulate the "good life."

This group's purchasing patterns also reveal a tendency to buy on impulse with little planning. Low educational level appears to be a primary cause of this.

Shopping Behavior

Shopping behavior also varies by social class. For example, a very close relation between store choice and social class membership has been found, indicating that it is wrong to assume that all consumers want to shop at glamorous, high-status stores. Instead, people realistically match their values and expectations with a store's status and don't shop in stores where they feel out of place.

Thus, no matter what the store, each shopper generally has some idea of the social-status ranking of that store and will tend not to patronize those where they feel they do not "fit," in a social class sense.[29] The result is that the same products and brands may be purchased in different outlets by members of different social classes.[30] Therefore, an important function of retail advertising is to allow the shopper to make social class identification of stores. This is done from the tone and physical character of the advertising.

One research study of the shopping behavior of a group of urban women has provided a number of valuable insights into the influence of social class on the shopping process:

Most women enjoy shopping regardless of their social class; however, reasons for enjoyment differ. All classes enjoy the recreational and social aspects of shopping, as well as being exposed to new things, bargain hunting, and comparing merchandise. However, lower classes found acquiring new clothes or household items more enjoyable, while upper-middles and above specified a pleasant store atmosphere, display, and excitement more frequently.

Middle- and upper-class women shopped more frequently than those in the lower class.

The higher a woman's social class the more she considered it important to shop quickly.

Middle and working classes had a greater tendency to browse without buying anything.

The lower the social status, the greater the proportion of downtown shopping.

A greater percentage of lower-class women favored discount stores than did women in the middle or upper classes. The attraction to high-fashion stores was directly related to social class. Broad-appeal stores were more attractive to the middle class.[31]

Let us examine more closely the nature of social class variations in shopping patterns in order to better understand marketing-strategy decisions.

UPPER AND UPPER-MIDDLE CLASSES Women of this group organize shopping more purposefully and efficiently than those of lower status. They tend to be more knowledgeable about what they want, where and when to shop for it; their shopping is both selective and wide-ranging.

There is also an emphasis by this group on the store environment. Stores must be clean, orderly, and reflect good taste. Moreover, they must be staffed with clerks who are not only well-versed in their particular product line, but also well aware of their customers' status. This attitude indicates a leaning toward urban and suburban specialty stores and away from larger, more general outlets. For example, the upper-middle-class wife has been characterized as usually buying all her public appearance clothes at specialty shops or in specialty departments of the town's best department stores.[32]

Is there a paradox between consumer status and discount-house patronage among this group? Actually, the extent of patronage depends on the nature of the product sought. This group apparently has few qualms about buying appliances in discount houses because they feel they cannot "go wrong" with nationally advertised brand names. A furniture purchase, however, is another matter, and the same consumer is likely to go to a status store which can act as an "authority" on tasteful home furnishings.

LOWER-MIDDLE CLASS Women of this class "work" more at their shopping. They exhibit more anxiety, particularly when purchasing nonfoods, which they feel can be a demanding and tedious process filled with uncertainty. They are value-conscious and try to seek out the best buy for the money. Such an orientation would indicate a strong tendency to patronize discount houses.

UPPER-LOWER CLASS Because of this group's strong concern with personal relationships there is a tendency to shop along known, local friendship lines. This attitude also explains their loyalty to certain stores in which they feel at home. Martineau describes situations in which lower-status women who shop in high-status department stores felt clerks and higher-class customers in the store "punished" them in various subtle ways. One woman expressed her feeling that in a higher-status store "the clerks treat you like a crumb." Another related how she had vainly tried to be waited on, finally to be told, "We thought you were a clerk."[33]

The shopping behavior of this group has been described as a pattern of routine standardized purchasing, usually of national brands, having infrequent impulsive or unplanned purchases. The factors contributing to this behavior are thought to be their limited perspective, short time horizons, and frustrations.[34] The routinized nature of their shopping suggests for the marketer an emphasis on enticing point-of-purchase displays and easy availability of items. It is clear that this group is a prime target for discount houses, and in fact it has been a potent force in the development of suburban discount retailing.[35]

SOCIAL
CLASS

LOWER-LOWER CLASS This group is one that buys largely on impulse. This tendency results in the necessity to rely heavily on credit, since money that might have been spent for big-ticket items has been drained off in impulse buying of small things. At the same time, however, these people can be poor credit risks because of their low-income status. This often forces them into a pattern of dealing with local merchants who offer tailor-made (yet sometimes quite exorbitant) credit terms.

Promotional Response Patterns

Important class differences exist with regard to promotional response. The social classes have differing media choice and usage patterns. They also have different perceptions and responses to advertising and other promotional messages which are significant in the development of proper marketing strategies. The basis of advertising differences directed at the various classes should be founded on the differing communication skills and interests of these groups. For example, sophisticated and clever advertising such as that appearing in *The New Yorker* and *Esquire* is almost meaningless to lower-class people who don't understand the subtle humor, and are baffled by the bizarre art. This certainly does not imply that they lack intelligence or wit, but merely that their communication skills or experiences have been oriented in a different way. Thus, their symbol systems are different, and they have a quite different approach to humor.[3]

Some marketers fail to learn the appropriate style of communication because they do not understand their consumers' social class level. A brand of beer once had an advertising campaign built around a fox hunter who appeared in every ad clad in a red coat, tiny black patent leather boots, and a velvet cap. But the audience representing the primary market for this product had no idea what this symbol meant and reacted unfavorably to him. Similarly, testimonials by intellectuals and Broadway stage stars will have less meaning to social classes having no acquaintance with the legitimate theater or the fine arts.[37]

Cologne and perfume manufacturers develop their advertising with a view toward social class considerations. For instance, because French associations for perfume are not very meaningful for the mass-market housewife, the newer women's perfumes (such as Charlie, Maxi, Babe, and Smitty) have adopted an American life-style portrayal to appeal to this group. Similarly some new cologne brands appeal to higher classes with exclusive-sounding names (for example, Aramis, British Sterling, Royal Copenhagen) while other brands (such as Aqua Velva and Old Spice) prominently feature blue-collar workers in some of their ads and aim at the mass male audience.

The marketer must also cautiously select key advertising words because of their different perceptions among the classes which could cause problems. Consider, for example, potential class reactions to an advertisement for a soap product used to wash baby clothes. In a motivation study of soaps and detergents it was learned that middle-class women associated the words "darling," "sweet," or "mother" with the word "baby," while lower-class women, reacted with such terms as "pain in the neck," "more work," or "a darling but a bother."[38]

Consequently, marketers must understand their market thoroughly and communicate meaningfully to it within the range of their skills. The media patterns of each class are described below as well as some possible promotional appeals.

UPPER CLASS The upper class tends to buy more newspapers, read more of the newspaper, see more magazines, and watch less television than other classes. They also listen to FM radio.

UPPER-MIDDLE CLASS The media choices of this group tend toward FM radio, particularly classical music stations, magazines such as *Time, Fortune, Vogue, The New Yorker, Consumer Reports*, and *House & Garden*, and newspapers. The upper-middle class does not fully embrace television, worrying about its effect on their children. Nevertheless, they do watch significant amounts, with their programming tastes tending toward current events and drama. Because of later dinner hours and bedtimes, they have a high exposure to late-night television shows, such as the "Tonight Show."

This group and the upper class represent challenging targets to the marketer in developing promotion appeals. They tend to be more critical of advertising, are suspicious of its emotional appeals, and question its claims. They usually display an attitude of sophisticated superiority to it. This is not to say, however, that they are unresponsive to advertising. They can be attracted by approaches that are different, individualistic, witty, sophisticated, stylish, that appeal to good judgment, discriminating taste, and offer the kinds of objects and symbols that are significant to their status and self-expression goals.

LOWER-MIDDLE CLASS This group tends to read morning newspapers, and middle-class magazines such as *Reader's Digest, Sports Illustrated, Esquire, Good Housekeeping*, and *Ladies' Home Journal* and watches a good deal of television. This group, as well as the upper-lower class, takes a rather straightforward, literal-minded, and pragmatic approach to advertising. Effective promotion appeals are those portraying the home and relating use of the product to success as a housewife and mother. Labor-saving products such as instant foods, for example, are best promoted in a way that also satisfies her conscientiousness.

Although attracted by discount coupons, they are careful in their use of them. They want to be sure that the incentive is worth the effort, that they are being sensible in their use of them.

UPPER-LOWER CLASS The media choices of this group tend toward afternoon newspapers, if any, AM radio, heavy television viewing, especially soap operas, game shows, situation comedies, variety shows, and late movies, and magazines such as *True Story.*

A recent study made by Social Research, Inc. of the women in this group found that some interesting changes are taking place, which could have relevance to the marketer's promotional strategy:

Although they are no longer captives of husband, children, and home and have a new desire for independence, they resent efforts to "put down" the role of wife, mother, and homemaker.

Most have new interests in their communities and jobs.

They want products that will free them from housework or contribute to their comfort or gratification.

They are critical of big business as an institution and believe that it does not charge fair prices and forgets about the public welfare. But they find no great emotional appeal in the consumerism movement and are interested in accumulating all the products they never had.[39]

Housewives in this group are also uncertain and suspicious of the world around them.

Given these attitudes, the following conclusions have been advanced for advertising strategy directed at this market:

They are quite receptive to advertising that has a strong visual character, showing activity, energy, on-going work and life, and solutions to practical problems in everyday situations and social relationships.

Advertising should convey an image of the gratifying world in which products fit functionally into the drive for a stable and secure life.

It should communicate a feeling of confidence and safety about the product and its operation.

Advertising should counteract the suspicion and distrust they have of business people.

The advertising setting is important. It should make the item seem desirable—that is, the item should be portrayed as part of the average woman's living and consuming, an expected item in the good life. It could also serve to educate the woman as to how she might use the product and how she might relate it to her own situation.

Advertising should reassure the woman that the product is within her reach socially, psychologically, and economically.

Advertising that emphasizes easing the housewife's burdens should at the same time communicate a sense of her continuing importance to the family and offer fruitful ways to use her idle time to gain more love from them.

Advertising (especially in color) that communicates a "prettied-up" atmosphere gains a good reception.[40]

This class is also the most receptive group to sales promotion offers. They are eager to take advantage of many of the offers that come their way, to cut costs or get something extra.

LOWER-LOWER CLASS The media habits of this group are similar to those of the upper-lowers except that they have even lower readership of magazines and newspapers. They are more audio (AM radio)- and video (television)-oriented. Both groups have early dinner hours and thus have heavier exposure to early-evening television than higher social classes.

Promotion directed to this class is constrained by their lower education and intelligence levels and the difficulty they have in thinking abstractly. For these reasons it is suggested that simple, concrete appeals be used, with greater visual stimulation, such as the use of color and heavy reliance on symbols.

Price-related Behavior

Research on these variables is extremely limited and most of what exists relates to the poor. Regarding price perceptions among the middle and working classes, a shopping simulation showed that working-class housewives have a greater reliance on the general belief that there is a price/quality association; that is, the higher the price of a product the higher the quality. They perceive that they have an inability to discriminate between products and are therefore forced to fall back on a general belief in order to handle this problem of which product to buy. Although the better-educated housewives in both classes had stronger beliefs that price and quality are related, they preferred lower-priced product alternatives. They apparently felt capable of judging the product alternatives on their own merits rather than having to rely on general beliefs in price/quality to make a decision.[41]

A study on commercial-bank credit card holders has uncovered social class variations in card use patterns. For example, members of the lower class tend to use their cards for installment purchases and seek out stores that honor their cards, while upper classes use them for convenience and do not seek stores accepting the card.[42]

SUMMARY

This chapter has discussed the major implications of social class for consumer behavior. We defined the concept of social class, and discussed the process of stratification, including the bases on which it may be carried out and the ways it may be studied, emphasizing Warner's pioneering and enduring work. It was pointed out that different social classes have different values, attitudes, and behavior. Numerous examples of these differences were cited, especially with regard to the characteristic life-styles of each class.

We learned that social class segmentation, while offering potential, is fraught with difficulties, and limitations in its current stage of evolution. Nevertheless we described much of what is presently known about reactions to products, promotions, shopping, and prices among the different social classes. From this we should now have a better understanding of how and why consumer behavior differs among social classes.

DISCUSSION TOPICS

1. What is meant by the term social stratification?

2. Discuss the use of social class as a market-segmentation approach.

3. Select one of the social class categories and prepare a report on its life-style.

4. How might a marketer have a problem with his "self-reference criterion" when making marketing decisions involving social class ramifications?

5. Find at least two manufacturer's ads for the same generic product (e.g., clothing) that you think are aimed at different social classes. Explain the differences in the ads.

6. Find three newspaper advertisements by local retailers that you think reach the different social classes. Explain the differences in the ads.

7. Classify the major department stores in your area according to your estimation of the social class of their customers. How do the marketing features of these stores differ?

8. What social class would you choose for initial marketing efforts if you were to introduce color video-recording machines for television owners? Suggest a marketing strategy.

9. Discuss the relationship of social class and consumption.

NOTES

1. Bernard Berelson and Gary Steiner, *Human Behavior: An Inventory of Scientific Findings,* Harcourt, Brace & World, New York, 1964, p. 453.

2. David Dressler and Donald Carns, *Sociology: The Study of Human Interaction,* 2d ed., Knopf, New York, 1973, p. 370.

3. W. Lloyd Warner, Marchia Meeker, and Kenneth Eells, *Social Class in America,* Science Research Associates, Chicago, 1949, pp. 11–15.

4. Richard Centers, *The Psychology of Social Classes,* Russell & Russell, New York, 1961.

5. James M. Carman, *The Application of Social Class in Market Segmentation,* University of California Graduate School of Business Administration, Institute of Business and Economic Research, Berkeley, Calif., 1965.

6. Thorstein Veblen, *The Theory of the Leisure Class,* Macmillan, New York, 1899.

7. "What's In, What's Out, the Search for Status," *U.S. News & World Report,* February 14, 1977, pp. 38–40; and "An Authority Tells Why Status Symbols Keep Changing," *U.S. News & World Report,* February 14, 1977, pp. 41–42.

8. Pierre Martineau, "Social Classes and Spending Behavior," *Journal of Marketing,* **23**:129, October 1958, published by the American Marketing Association.

9. Richard P. Coleman, "The Significance of Social Stratification in Selling," in Martin L. Bell (ed.), *Marketing: A Maturing Discipline,* American Marketing Association, Chicago, Winter 1960, p. 175.

10. This section is drawn from Colemen, "The Significance of Social Stratification," pp.

171–184; Warner, Meeker, and Eells, *Social Class,* pp. 11–21; Margaret C. Pirie, "Marketing and Social Classes: An Anthropologist's View," *Management Review,* **49**:45–48, September 1960; Kim B. Rotzoll, "The Effect of Social Stratification on Market Behavior," *Journal of Advertising Research,* **7**:22–27, March 1967; Ronald E. Frank, William F. Massy, and Yorman Wind, *Market Segmentation,* Prentice-Hall, Englewood Cliffs, N.J., 1972, pp. 44–48; and James M. Patterson, "Marketing and the Working-Class Family," in Arthur B. Shostak and William Gomberg (eds.), *Blue-Collar World,* Prentice-Hall, Englewood Cliffs, N.J., 1964, p. 78.

11. "The American Underclass," *Time,* August 29, 1977, p. 14.

12. Frank, Massy, and Wind, *Market Segmentation,* p. 45.

13. Coleman, "The Significance of Social Stratification," pp. 176–177.

14. James H. Myers, Roger R. Stanton, and Arne F. Haug, "Correlates of Buying Behavior: Social Class vs. Income," *Journal of Marketing,* **35**:8–15, October 1971.

15. James H. Myers and John F. Mount, "More on Social Class vs. Income as Correlates of Buying Behavior," *Journal of Marketing,* **37**:71–73, April 1973.

16. Robert D. Hisrich and Michael P. Peters, "Selecting the Superior Segmentation Correlate," *Journal of Marketing,* **38**:60–63, July 1974.

17. Frank, Massy, and Wind, *Market Segmentation,* p. 49.

18. Coleman, "The Significance of Social Stratification," pp. 179–182.

19. Thomas S. Robertson, *Consumer Behavior,* Scott, Foresman, Glenview, Ill., 1970, p. 129.

20. William T. Tucker, *The Social Context of Economic Behavior,* Holt, New York, 1964, pp. 42–43.

21. James H. Myers and William H. Reynolds, *Consumer Behavior and Marketing Management,* Houghton Mifflin, Boston, 1967, p. 214.

22. Martineau, "Social Classes," pp. 128–129.

23. Pierre D. Martineau, "Social Class and Its Very Close Relationship to the Individual's Buying Behavior," in Martin L. Bell (ed.), *Marketing: A Maturing Discipline,* p. 191.

24. Lee Rainwater, Richard P. Coleman, and Gerald Handel, *Workingman's Wife,* Oceana Publications, Inc., New York, 1959, p. 205.

25. William Mitchell, "First Lottery Millionaire Settles into Easy Living," *Detroit Free Press,* July 8, 1973, p. 3a.

26. Gerald Handel and Lee Rainwater, "Persistence and Change in Working-Class Life Style," in Shostak and Gomberg (eds.), *Blue-Collar World,* p. 41.

27. David Caplovitz, *The Poor Pay More,* Free Press, New York, 1963.

28. Patterson, "Marketing and the Working-class," p. 79.

29. Martineau, "Social Class and Spending Behavior," pp. 126–127.

30. Sidney J. Levy, "Social Class and Consumer Behavior," in Joseph W. Newman (ed.), *On Knowing the Consumer,* Wiley, New York, 1966, p. 153.

31. Stuart U. Rich and Subhash C. Jain, "Social Class and Life Cycle as Predictors of Shopping Behavior," *Journal of Marketing Research,* **5**:41–49, February 1968.

32. Coleman, "The Significance of Social Stratification," p. 177.

33. Martineau, "Social Classes," p. 121.

34. Frank, Massy, and Wind, *Market Segmentation,* p. 47.

35. David J. Rachman and Marion Levine, "Blue Collar Workers Shape Suburban Markets," *Journal of Retailing,* **42**:5–13, Winter 1966–1967.

36. Martineau, "Social Classes," p. 127.

37. Pierre Martineau, *Motivation in Advertising,* McGraw-Hill, New York, 1957, p. 165.

38. Martineau, *Motivation in Advertising,* p. 166.

39. "Blue Collar Wives Seek Convenience: MacFadden," *Advertising Age,* October 8, 1973.

40. Rainwater, Coleman, and Handel, *Workingman's Wife,* pp. 207–216.

41. Joseph N. Fry and Frederick H. Siller, "A Comparison of Housewife Decision Making in Two Social Classes," *Journal of Marketing Research,* **7**:333–337, August 1970.

42. H. Lee Mathews and John W. Slocum, Jr., "Social Class and Commercial Bank Credit Card Usage," *Journal of Marketing,* **33**:71–78, January 1969.

SOCIAL GROUPS

WHAT IS A GROUP? CLASSIFICATION OF GROUPS Content or Function; Degree of Personal Involvement; Degree of Organization **GROUP PROPERTIES** Status; Role; Power **REFERENCE GROUPS** Types of Reference Groups; Reasons for Accepting Reference-Group Influence; Research on Reference-Group Influence; Marketing and Reference-Group Relevance; Identifying Reference Groups

We are continuing to narrow our discussion of the environmental variables that influence consumer behavior. In this chapter we discuss ways in which groups impinge on consumer decision making. This is an important ingredient in the marketer's understanding of consumer behavior.

Our first task will be to define several group concepts essential to our discussion. Next, the major characteristics of groups and group types will be examined. Finally, we shall discuss reference groups and their special relevance for the marketer in understanding consumer behavior.

WHAT IS A GROUP?

Not every collection of individuals is a group, as the term is used by sociologists. Actually, we can distinguish three different collections of people: aggregations, categories, and groups. An *aggregation* is any number of people who are in close proximity to one another at a given time. A *category* is any number of people who have some particular attributes in common. A *group* consists of people who have a sense of relatedness as a result of interaction with each other.[1]

To illustrate these concepts consider four people sitting on a bench at a university. They are an "aggregation" since they are in close proximity. They may be a "category" if they share some attribute such as being majors in the College of Business Administration. They may also be a "group" if they have a shared sense of relatedness through interaction, that is, if they are all friends, or classmates in a consumer behavior course, for example.

While our emphasis in this chapter is on groups, this does not mean that the marketer is not interested in aggregations and categories. These collections are frequently the focus for developing marketing strategies. For example, market segmentation typically does not involve social groups but instead uses categories, since the people are not all interacting with one another.

CLASSIFICATION OF GROUPS

Groups may be classified according to a number of dimensions including function, degree of personal involvement, and degree of organization.

Content or Function

Most of us view the content of groups in terms of their function. For example, we categorize them along such lines as students, factory workers, church members, and so on. Actually, these are subtypes of the major kinds of groups that we encounter in a complex society which could generally be categorized along such lines as family, ethnic, age, sex, political, religious, residential, occupational, educational, and so forth.[2]

Degree of Personal Involvement

Using this criterion we can identify two different types of groups: primary and secondary. The hallmark of a *primary group* is that interpersonal relationships take place usually on a face-to-face basis with great frequency, and on an intimate level.[3] These groups have shared norms and interlocking roles. Families, work groups, and even recreational groups (if individuals have some depth of personal involvement) are examples of such groups.

Secondary groups are those in which the relationship among members is relatively impersonal and formalized. This amounts to a residual category that includes every group that is not primary, such as political parties, unions, and the American Marketing Association. Although such groups are secondary, the interpersonal relationships that occur may nevertheless be face-to-face. The distinction lies in the lack of intimacy of personal involvement.

Degree of Organization

Groups range from those that are relatively unorganized to highly structured forms. We usually simplify this continuum, however, into two types: formal and informal. *Formal* groups are those with a definite structure. They are likely to be secondary groups designed to accomplish specific goals, whether economic, social, political, or altruistic. *Informal* groups are typically primary groups, characterized by a relatively loose structure, a lack of clearly defined goals or objectives, unstructured interaction, and unwritten rules. Because of the extent of their influence on individuals' values and activities, informal groups are probably of greater importance to us in seeking to understand consumer behavior.

It should be evident from this discussion that the term "group" is multifaceted and that groups have important influences on individuals, including their activities as consumers.

GROUP PROPERTIES

In order to better understand the nature of groups we need to examine several other important concepts, including status, role, and power, and their significance for consumer behavior.

Status

Status refers to the achieved or ascribed position of an individual in a group or in society, and it consists of the rights and duties associated with that position. In the last chapter we referred to status in a prestige sense; however, this is only one of several different ways in which statuses may be classified. Status also may refer to some grouping on the basis of age or sex, family, occupation, and friendship or common interest.[4]

Role

This term is used to designate all of the behavior patterns associated with a particular status. Role is the dynamic aspect of status and includes the attitudes, values, and behavior ascribed by the society to persons occupying this status. Essentially, role theory recognizes that an individual carries out life by playing different roles. This concept was expressed in a poetic way by Shakespeare in the following well-known passage:

All the world's a stage,
And all the men and women merely players.
They have their exits and their entrances;
And one man in his time plays many parts,
His acts being seven ages.[5]

This means that each consumer enacts many roles, which may change over time. For example, a woman may have the role of wife, mother, employee, family financial officer, lover, Sunday School teacher, and many others. Her behavior in each of these roles will differ as she keeps "switching hats," depending on her role at each moment.

Carrying the concept of playing a role further, Goffman suggests that the individual must not only learn his lines (the group's special language) but he needs a costume (the group's accepted dress), props (the group's equipment or accoutrements), a set (where the group interacts), and a team or cast of players (the group members).[6]

Many social and work situations can be viewed in this way as the following tennis situation illustrates:

Dialogue: "Volley for serve"; "Score: love, thirty"; "double fault"; "Hold your racket up, partner."

Costume: Multicolored outfits; see-through dresses; maternity tennis wear; court togs for babies; $60 tennis shoes.

Props: Rackets, balls, even extraneous equipment such as mechanical partners to lob tennis balls.

Set: Outdoor and indoor courts and clubs—some for swinging singles, others for suburban housewives; tennis ranches; even backyard courts costing $11,000 or more.

Team: Singles, doubles, or mixed doubles.

Roles in groups (just as those in a play) are learned, but not every individual learns a given role in the same way.[7] Society allows some variation in role performance; but if too much latitude is taken, sanctions of some sort will be imposed. Thus other people expect us to behave in a certain way, and will reward conformity and punish nonconformity to those expectations.

Roles have a strong, pervasive influence on our activities as consumers. For example, other people have expectations regarding the products we buy to meet the needs of our roles. Just a few of the many consumption decisions directly affected include the places we shop, the clothes we wear, the cars we drive, the houses in which we live, and the recreational activities we engage in. Marketers, therefore, help individuals play their roles by providing the right costumes and props to be used in gaining acceptance by some group. Again, it's the symbols of products that provide so much of the satisfaction that accrues from a product.

Because of the many roles we try to fulfill, whether at different times or simultaneously, we may develop *role conflict* which means that two or more of our roles are incompatible with each other. The strain may often be evidenced in the behavior of consumers. For example, a working wife may feel that the demands on her time may be more easily met by fixing her family quick and easy meals, particularly by using frozen TV dinners. However, in her role as a loving wife and the family's gourmet cook, such product usage may be abhorrent. Thus, some resolution of this conflict will be necessary. A creative advertiser may suggest a solution through purchasing the company's TV dinners because, although easily prepared, when served on her regular china, seasoned to taste, and garnished attractively, they resemble a gourmet meal.

Power

Groups have power to influence their members' behavior. Various sources of social power may be operative in different social group situations, however: reward power, coercive power, legitimate power, referent power and expert power.[8] Marketers also seek to use these forms of power to influence consumers.

REWARD POWER This is based on the perception one has of another's ability to reward him. The strength of reward power increases with the size of the rewards which an individual perceives another can administer. Rewards might include either tangible items such as money or gifts, or intangible things like recognition, praise, or other nonmaterial satisfaction.

Social groups often have a great deal of reward power which they may dispense to their members. This "carrot" approach can often result in the desired behavior being exhibited by members. For example, Amway Products, which uses direct-selling methods for its 150-item line of household products, makes effective use of reward power in motivating its sales force, as the following indicates:

Sales rallies are often held in large auditoriums where young salespeople, usually middle-class couples, watch a 20-minute color film that features family scenes of successful Amway couples enjoying the fruits of their labors—swimming pools and motor homes. The next day local sales rise sharply. The company's two owners also rely on a gold Rolls-Royce and Twin Lockheed Jetstars to whisk them to sales meetings out in the field. In addition, the top performers among Amway's distributors are occasionally entertained on the company's 116-foot yacht. The motivation behind such luxuries is that they have a way of making Amway's distributors lust after—and therefore work harder for—a similar life-style.[9]

Marketers also use reward power in order to influence consumers. Of course, they are able to reward consumers directly by providing high-quality products and services. By making such things available, consumers in turn, express their satisfaction by repurchasing from the company. Reward power is operating directly in this case.

In other situations marketers promise (implicitly, at least) the rewards of group acceptance, such as love, through use of a product. For example, some brands of beer (such as Lowenbrau and Old Milwaukee) show how group acceptance takes place through purchase and consumption of their product. Similarly, Prell Shampoo ads show the rewards of product use as friends and coworkers notice how nice your hair smells.

In other instances retailers employ cliques and clubs to make use of reward power. Clothing shops attempt to influence dress styles by telling customers what is "in"—that is, what their group or friends will accept in terms of dress. Also, photography retailers frequently sponsor camera clubs partly to be able to employ group power to influence product purchases.

COERCIVE POWER This is the power to influence behavior through the use of punishment or the withholding of rewards. Punishment, for our purpose, does not refer to the physical kind, but the more subtle, psychological sanctions. For example, students may readily conform to the dress code of some group on campus such as a sorority or fraternity and purchase the accepted clothing of this group in order not to be ridiculed by it.

Marketers are also able to use coercive power effectively in certain situations. Inducing fear is one approach that may be taken by advertisers of some items such as life insurance and deodorants. Coercion occurs through showing the unfortunate consequences that could befall a consumer who fails to own or use such products. For example, the embarrassment of having loose dentures is brought to our attention by Poligrip and other denture adhesive manufacturers. Similarly, the group ridicule which comes from having "b.o." is humorously but effectively illustrated in a Dial soap ad in which several car-pool members all ride in the rear seat of a car while the driver, alone in the front seat, gets the message that she needs to use Dial.

Salespeople also use coercion in some situations. For example, they may imply that if the consumer does not buy soon the supply of the item will be exhausted and he will be left out in the cold.

Tupperware and other products sold in social group situations also make effective use of group coercive power. For example, in the case of Tupperware a dealer holds an informal party in a friend's or acquaintance's home to which a group of her friends or neighbors are invited. After a few ice-breaking games are run by the dealer, the group is served coffee and dessert while the dealer demonstrates various Tupperware items and takes orders. The hostess has an opportunity to win a significant prize if enough orders are placed and if two guests agree to host parties in their homes. Thus, group pressure is strong because attendees at these sales parties tend to feel that if others are buying something they do not want to be embarrassed by not also making a purchase. They may feel that such an action would let the hostess and her friends down.[10]

LEGITIMATE POWER This power stems from members' perception that the group has a legitimate right to influence them. We speak of such behaviors with expressions like "should," "ought to," etc. Many of these feelings have been internalized from parents, teachers, and religious institutions. Thus, there is some sort of code or standard that the individual accepts, and by virtue of which the group can assert its power.

One small group in which legitimate power can be seen to operate is the family. Each member has a set of roles to carry out which are legitimized by the other members. Thus, the father is expected to perform certain functions while the mother is expected to perform others. There are also functions that are performed jointly by the spouses. Much of the purchasing responsibilities which fall to each of the family members are those that society has inculcated into its members, based on these role patterns.

Marketers are also able to utilize legitimate power in many situations by appealing to consumers' internalized values. That is, appeals are often made on the basis of what one "ought to" or "should do." Appeals from charitable organizations (such as the United Way, Red Cross, etc.) exert legitimate power, as do those for patriotic and nationalistic causes such as "Buy American" or "See America First."

REFERENT POWER This influence flows from the feeling of identification an individual has with the group. As a consequence of this feeling of oneness or desire for such an identity, the individual will have a desire to become a member or gain a closer association with the group. The individual's identification with the group can be established or maintained if he or she behaves, believes, or perceives as the group does. The stronger this identification with the group, the greater its referent power. In this chapter and Chapter 12 we will look more closely at the use of referent power.

EXPERT POWER This influence results from the expertise of the individual or group. Consumers regularly accept influence from those they perceive to have superior knowledge. For instance, we may accept the recommendation of another person for a purchase we are about to make if we view that person as more knowledgeable than ourselves. Salespeople make effective use of this approach with their own product expertise. Advertisers also employ it by having celebrities recommend certain products such as sports equipment. Manufacturers may even "create" experts when no one else seems suitable. For example, General Motors' Mr. Goodwrench, General Mills' Betty Crocker, and A&P's Ann Page are all fictitious, but effective endorsers.

REFERENCE GROUPS

Having discussed some important group concepts necessary for our interests, let us further examine the topic of reference-group influence.

Types of Reference Groups

Reference groups are those an individual uses (that is, refers to) in determining his judgments, beliefs, and behavior. These may be of a number of types, as explained by the following classification system.[11]

NORMATIVE VERSUS COMPARATIVE In a *normative* reference group the group's norms of behavior and values are assumed by the individual. A *comparative* reference group is one that serves as the standard or checkpoint for the individual in making comparisons or contrasts, particularly about his or her status in the group.

MEMBERSHIP VERSUS NONMEMBERSHIP *Membership* groups are those to which the individual belongs. Membership in some groups is automatic by virtue of the consumer's age, sex, education, and marital status. Before acting, a consumer might consider whether purchase or use of a product would be consistent with one's role as a member of one of these groups. For example, an elderly woman would probably have serious reservations about purchasing extremely wild-looking clothing designed for the young because such a product would not fit her expected role as a senior citizen.

Nonmembership groups are those to which the individual does not presently belong. Many of these groups are likely to be *anticipatory* or *aspirational* in nature, that is, those to which the individual aspires to belong. Such aspirational groups can have a profound influence on nonmembers because of their strong desire to join the group. This pattern of behavior is evident among upwardly mobile consumers who aspire to join higher-status clubs and social groups.

POSITIVE VERSUS NEGATIVE Reference groups can also be classified as to whether they attract or repel the individual. For instance, a *positive* reference group for the upwardly mobile consumer may be the "country club crowd" in that city. There are *negative* groups, however, that a person attempts to avoid being identified with. For example, an individual who is trying to succeed as a new management trainee may attempt through her speech, dress, and mannerisms to disassociate herself from her lower-social-class background in order to have a greater chance of success in her job.

Thus, reference groups can function in important ways for the consumer. They may affect aspiration levels and may also influence the kinds of behavior consumers enact. That is, they may strongly affect store and product choices as well as basic value systems. Reference groups, therefore, are powerful forces influencing members to conform to the group's beliefs, values, norms, and behavior patterns.

Reasons for Accepting Reference-Group Influence

Earlier we examined the sources of power that groups, including reference groups, may appeal to in affecting consumers. In this section the reasons why reference-group influence is accepted are discussed. Generally consumers accept reference-group influence because of the perceived benefits in doing so. Homans has suggested that the nature of social interactions between individuals will be determined by the individual's perception of the *profit of the interaction.* In effect, Homans says that an interaction situation may result in *rewards* (such as friendship, information, satisfaction, and so on) but will also exact *costs* (lost time, money expended, alternative people and activities sacrificed). The difference between these rewards and costs, that is, the net profit from the social exchange, will attempt to be maximized by individuals. Thus individuals will choose their groups and interact with members based upon their perception of the net profit of that exchange, rather than rewards or costs alone.[12]

At a more specific level, consumers may be seen to accept reference-group influence because of their role in providing informational, utilitarian, and value-expressive benefits.[13]

INFORMATIONAL BENEFITS One reason reference-group influence is accepted (or internalized) is that the consumer perceives that his knowledge of his environment and/or his ability to cope with some aspect of it (such as buying a product) is enhanced. Consumers most readily accept those information sources that are thought to be most credible. A consumer using an informational reference group may (1) actively search for information from opinion leaders or some group with the appropriate expertise or (2) come to some conclusion through observing the behavior of other people. Therefore, actual physical interaction with the group is not necessary in this type of information search.

UTILITARIAN BENEFIT This reason refers to pressure on the individual to conform to the preferences or expectations of another individual or group. In a product-purchasing situation the consumer would comply if (1) she believes that her behavior is visible or known to others, (2) she perceives that the others control significant sanctions (rewards or punishments), and (3) she is motivated to realize the reward or avoid the punishment.

Thus an individual accepts influence from the group because she hopes to attain certain specific rewards or avoid certain punishments controlled by the group. In effect, the individual learns to say or do the expected thing in certain situations, not because she necessarily likes it, but because it is instrumental in producing a satisfying social effect.

VALUE-EXPRESSIVE BENEFITS This relates to an individual's motive to enhance or support his self-concept by associating himself with positive reference groups and/or disassociating himself from negative referents.

This value-expressive reference-group influence is characterized by two different processes. First, an individual may utilize reference groups to express himself or bolster his ego. Second, an individual may simply like the group, and thus accept influence. Thus, an individual adopts behavior derived from the group as a way of establishing or maintaining the desired relationship to the group and the self-image provided by this relationship. The individual may say what the group members say, do what they do, and believe what they believe in order to foster the relationship and the satisfying self-image it provides.

Table 10-1 presents a series of statements that typify these three types of reference-group influence situations.

RESEARCH ON REFERENCE-GROUP INFLUENCE

So far we have merely hinted that reference-group influence can be quite strong. What research support do we have for this judgment? Several studies confirming this fact are described in this section.

One experiment showing that a group may induce strong pressure on an

TABLE 10-1

223

SOCIAL
GROUPS

TYPICAL REFERENCE-GROUP INFLUENCES ON BRAND DECISIONS

Informational Influence
1. The individual seeks information about various brands of the product from an association of professionals or independent group of experts.
2. The individual seeks information from those who work with the product as a profession.
3. The individual seeks brand-related knowledge and experience (such as how Brand A's performance compares to Brand B's) from those friends, neighbors, relatives, or work associates who have reliable information about the brands.
4. The brand which the individual selects is influenced by observing a seal of approval of an independent testing agency (such as Good Housekeeping).
5. The individual's observation of what experts do influences his choice of a brand (such as observing the type of car which police drive or the brand of TV which repairmen buy).

Utilitarian Influence
1. To satisfy the expectations of fellow work associates, the individual's decision to purchase a particular brand is influenced by their preferences.
2. The individual's decision to purchase a particular brand is influenced by the preferences of people with whom he has social interaction.
3. The individual's decision to purchase a particular brand is influenced by the preferences of family members.
4. The desire to satisfy the expectations which others have of him has an impact on the individual's brand choice.

Value-expressive Influence
1. The individual feels that the purchase or use of a particular brand will enhance the image which others have of him.
2. The individual feels that those who purchase or use a particular brand possess the characteristics which he would like to have.
3. The individual sometimes feels that it would be nice to be like the type of person which advertisements show using a particular brand.
4. The individual feels that the people who purchase a particular brand are admired or respected by others.
5. The individual feels that the purchase of a particular brand helps him show others what he is, or would like to be (such as an athlete, successful businessman, good mother, etc.).

Source: C. Whan Park and V. Parker Lessig, "Students and Housewives: Differences in Susceptibility to Reference Group Influence," *Journal of Consumer Research,* **4:**105, September 1977.

individual to conform involved groups of seven to nine college students brought together and instructed to judge the lengths of lines drawn on cards. All groups members but one—the naive subject—were instructed to give an incorrect response. The naive subject gave his answer after most of the group had answered. He thus found his judgment in opposition to that of the rest of the group. The result of the experiments with 123 naive subjects tested on 12 critical judgments was that 37 percent of the total number of judgments conformed to the incorrect answers of the remainder of the group acting in unison.[14]

Other experiments have been conducted with similar goals but with a different technique. Rather than allowing group members to have face-to-face oral communication with the group as in the situation above, individuals in these experiments were somewhat removed from each other, communicated only indirectly, and were to some degree anonymous. The kind of yielding that occurred and its psychological significance were determined to be the same under both experimental approaches. However, the former situation imposed more powerful group pressure on the individual, resulting in a greater average amount of conformity.[15]

Another experiment provided an indication of the strength of the group norms in forcing conformity. Subjects were brought into a dark room and asked to judge the distance and direction of movement of a small point of light. Although the light was actually stationary, it appeared to move because of the autokinetic effect, that is, an illusion of movement due to small tremors in the eye. Group members arrived at a consensus that tended to be maintained when individual members were asked to give their judgments after the group had dispersed.[16]

Another researcher studied the influence of group pressure on consumer decision making and the effects of choice restriction by group pressure in the consumer decision making process. Student subjects were instructed to evaluate and choose the best suit among three identical men's suits. Three group members (all confederates of the researcher) were instructed to select suit "B" which then put pressure on the naive subject, who was questioned last to agree with the group or to differ in his judgment and thus resist the group influence. It was found that individuals tended to conform to the group norm. The implication is that consumers accept information provided by their peer groups on the quality of a product, of a style, and so forth, which is difficult to evaluate objectively.

In addition, the study sought to determine the extent to which individuals might conform in a buying situation. The study's confederate subjects were instructed to give responses which indicated that they were "good guys" merely going along with the group consensus. The implication was that the naive subjects should also go along with the group. They were thus in a position of having to respond to an obvious effort at group pressure. It was found that any attempt to restrict independent choice behavior in the consumer decision-making process may be resisted under certain conditions. We see the occurrence of this in the marketplace when an individual conforms to the group norm by keeping a new product or adopting a new style, but maintains his or her independence by purchasing a different color or brand. This situation is known as "reactance," whereby the individual is motivated to resist further reduction in his or her set of free behaviors and to avoid compliance with the inducing agent, in this case his or her reference group. It is possible, therefore, that too obvious an attempt to force compliance with a group may have the opposite effect on consumers and thus they may strike out in an independent direction to avoid going along with the group.[17]

Another experiment was conducted to determine whether small, informal groups influence the formation of brand loyalty. In this study consumers from preexisting reference groups selected a loaf of bread from four identical loaves marked with different letters representing fictitious brands. Based on the individual's choices, it was concluded that informal groups had definite influence on their members toward conformity behavior with respect to brands of bread preferred. Moreover, the extent and degree of brand loyalty within a group was closely related to the behavior of the informal leader.[18]

The research approaches described above suggest that the responses of others establish a norm to which subjects comply. A recent study, however, suggests that such normative effects may have been too readily inferred from observations of unanimous or consensus behavior among group members. In effect, people may use the product evaluation of others as a source of information about products; that is, they infer from such evaluations that the product is, indeed, a better product. Such a situation probably occurs regularly in shopping activities and in social groups.[19] Thus rather than a situation whereby the basis for group agreement is normative, it may be that members go along with the group because, as a result of observing the group's reaction, they perceive the product differently.

A final research area has been the influence of group discussion versus lecture or one-way communication in changing consumer attitudes and behavior. In one experiment, an attempt was made to change housewives' meat consumption habits; half of the groups involved heard a lecture on the subject, while the other groups engaged in discussions. Although each group received the same information, results indicated that more women in the discussion groups used the recommended meats than did individuals in the lecture groups. The implications from this and other research are that group discussion is often a more effective means of imparting information than either lecture or individual instruction. Thus, group interaction was found to be a strong influence in promoting changed attitudes and behavior in various types of groups, even among those whose members were initially strangers.[20]

The types of groups involved in most of these experiments were made up of subjects who either did not know each other initially or were only slightly acquainted. Imagine how much more significant and strong the potential influence, then, from a group with which the individual strongly identifies or uses as a referent, such as family, close friends, or colleagues.

Generally, as these experiments illustrate, the conformity of the individual influenced by group pressure depends on the nature of the situation and the characteristics of the individual.[21] For example, conformity has been shown to depend on *group cohesiveness,* as some of the previous experiments indicate. Another study of brand-choice behavior found group cohesiveness and brand similarities to be positively related.[22] It has also been found to depend on *group size.* One set of experiments showed that increasing the number of confederates up to three increased the pressure toward conformity on the naive subject, but beyond this number, the influence was found to be no greater.

Conformity also varies by *personality type,* and has been found to be positively related to the following personality traits: low intelligence, extroversion, ethnocentrism, weak ego, poor leadership, authoritarianism, need for affiliation, being a firstborn or only child, and feelings of personal inferiority or inadequacy.[23]

The *individual's relationship* to the group is another factor that determines its influence on conformity. His or her social integration (i.e., level of acceptance by other group members) and his or her group role are factors that generally are positively related to the degree of group influence on the individual.[24] Similarity to the group's outlooks and values is also important.' For example, consumers are more likely to seek product information from friends who are similar on various attributes, to trust this information, and to choose the same products as these friends.[25]

Marketing and Reference-Group Relevance

Although a few of the previous studies concerned reference-group influence on the behavior of consumers, this section will pertain strictly to such behavior. We have seen that reference groups can be very potent influences on behavior generally. They should also be very influential on consumer behavior. For example, before making a decision about purchasing a product, consumers often consider what a particular group would do in this situation, or what they would think of the consumer for purchasing the product. This commonsense notion, however, has been difficult to apply meaningfully in specific marketing situations. The basic problem is one of determining which kinds of groups are likely to be referred to by which kinds of individuals under which kinds of situations in making which decision, and of measuring the extent of this influence.[26] Nevertheless, a start has been made in understanding this process.

Bourne studied the influence of reference groups on the purchase of a number of consumer goods and found that the conspicuousness of a product is a strong determinant of its susceptibility to reference-group influence. By conspicuousness we mean that the product can be seen and identified by others. It must also be conspicuous in the sense of standing out and being noticed. Reference groups may influence either the purchase of a product, the choice of a particular brand, or both.

Figure 10-1 suggests the possible susceptibility of various products and brands to reference-group influence. As diagramed in the figure, reference groups may exert strong influence with regard to purchase of the brand or type as well as the product (upper right cell), or there may not be any

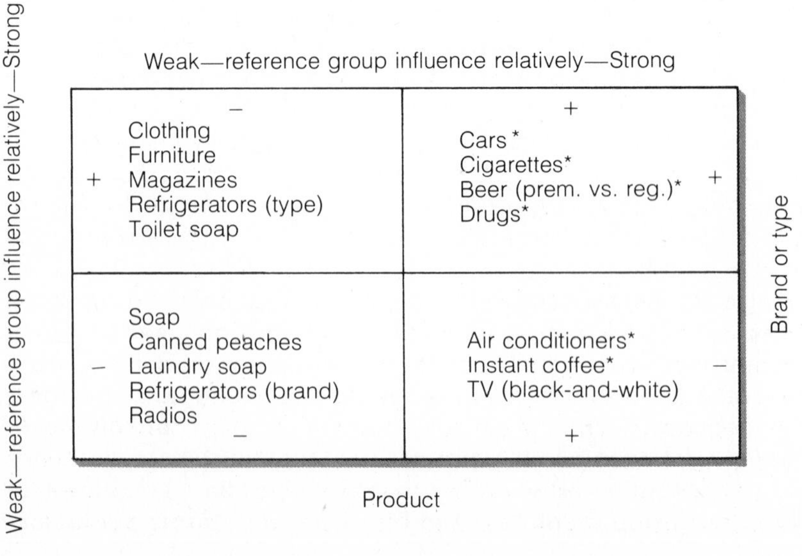

FIGURE 10-1
Products and brands of consumer goods may be classified by extent to which reference groups influence their purchase. *Note:* The classification of all products marked with an asterisk is based on actual experimental evidence. Other products in this table are classified speculatively on the basis of generalizations derived from the sum of research in this area and confirmed by the judgment of seminar participants. [*Source:* Francis S. Bourne, "Group Influences in Marketing and Public Relations," in Rensis Likert and Samuel P. Hayes, Jr., (eds.), *Some Applications of Behavioural Research*, UNESCO, Paris, 1957. Reprinted by permission of Charles Y. Glock, University of California Survey Research Center, and UNESCO.]

Weak—reference group influence relatively—Strong

	Product	
	−	+
+	Clothing Furniture Magazines Refrigerators (type) Toilet soap	Cars * Cigarettes* Beer (prem. vs. reg.)* Drugs*	+
−	Soap Canned peaches Laundry soap Refrigerators (brand) Radios	Air conditioners* Instant coffee* TV (black-and-white)	−

Weak—reference group influence relatively—Strong (vertical axis)

Brand or type

significant reference-group influence (lower left cell). In between these extremes, the influence of a reference group on the product may be strong, but on the brand or type it is weak (lower right cell), or the brand or type purchased may be strongly influenced, but not the product itself (upper left cell).

Let us examine in further detail each of these categories and the kinds of products contained in each one.

1. *Product plus, brand plus.* All products in this category are items that are socially conspicious; hence, both product and type or brand are strongly influenced by what others say or do. As the table indicates, cars, cigarettes, drugs, and types of beer are products of this type. For example, among teens having a car is an important status symbol which may put the individual high above others. At the same time, however, having a new Corvette enhances one's status more than an old handed-down family sedan.

2. *Product plus, brand minus.* Whether these products are used is strongly influenced by the consumer's reference group and image of its attitudes toward these products. However, the brand or type is not socially conspicious and is only weakly influenced by one's reference group, being largely a matter of individual choice. Examples would include air conditioners, instant coffee, and black-and-white television. In other words, reference groups influence the consumer's decision to buy an air conditioner, but have little effect on his decision to buy a Fedders rather than a Sears brand.

3. *Product minus, brand plus.* Products in this group are those that nearly everyone uses, although not the same type or brand. Clothing, furniture, magazines, type of refrigerator, and toilet soap are products that fit this category. These products are all socially visible, and because they are so highly visible the use of these products is not influenced by reference groups. However, the type or brand of product used is strongly influenced by reference groups. In other words, in buying a dress it is not the dress decision *per se* that is influenced by reference groups but its style and the label that are the key.

4. *Product minus, brand minus.* Purchasing behavior for these items is influenced by product attributes rather than by one's reference group. Products and brands in this category tend not to be socially conspicuous. Examples include bath soap, canned peaches, laundry soap, brands of refrigerators and radios. Thus, when buying peaches, for instance, reference groups exert little influence on the consumer.[27]

Some shifting of product perceptions may have occurred since the mid-1950s when Bourne reported his results. For example, products may shift over a period of time from a category in which reference-group influence is weak to another in which it is strong, especially through the use of heavy promotional efforts designed to create a favorable image and make a product or brand socially conspicuous. Instant coffee has probably moved to the product plus, brand plus quadrant. Of course, products may also slip in their degree of reference-group influence as they near saturation levels of ownership. The black-and-white television, for instance, has probably moved into a product minus, brand minus position.

How may the kind of information presented in Figure 10-1 be used in making marketing decisions? Bourne suggests that the following advertising strategies be adopted depending on the degree of reference-group influence found for the product or brand:

1. Where neither product nor brand appear to be associated strongly with reference-group influence, advertising should emphasize the product's attributes, intrinsic qualities, price, and advantage over competing products.

2. Where reference-group influence is operative, the advertiser should stress the kinds of people who buy the product, reinforcing and broadening where possible the existing stereotypes of users. The strategy of the advertiser should involve learning what the stereotypes are and what specific reference groups enter into the picture, so that appeals can be "tailored" to each main group reached by the different media employed.[28]

A recent study of reference-group influence on brand decisions of students and housewives has provided insight into the susceptibility to influence of each group for twenty products. This investigation examined the relevance of three types of reference-group influence (informational, utilitarian, and value-expressive) to a consumer's selection of a brand or model. Thus, the consumer was assumed to have already decided to buy the product but was undecided on the brand or model.

A comparison of reference-group influence scores for the two groups and twenty products showed that there are significant differences between students and housewives in terms of the influence of reference groups on brand selection and that students are generally more susceptible to reference-group influence. Why? Perhaps differences in needs or motivations among the groups result in different responses to reference-group influence. First, the lower age of students probably results in their having less familiarity with products and less product information and in their facing greater purchase risk than housewives. Second, social surroundings and daily activity differences exist between the groups. Students have more frequent social contacts, interact within groups (e.g., sororities, fraternities, and dormitories) which impose more rules and norms, and have more visible behavior subject to group pressure than do housewives. Third, hedonism may be stronger among students than housewives so that they are more highly ego-involved in their purchases.[29]

Identifying Reference Groups

We see, then, that reference groups are highly relevant and potent influences in consumer decision making. But how do we identify the specific individual, group, or groups who are most relevant to the consumer's behavior? Unfortunately, at this stage we are unable to answer this question definitively; we simply are not sure which reference groups will be most important in a given buying decision. Thus, when a young woman goes to the store to buy a new outfit, the ultimate choice may reflect her sorority, her family, her church group, her boyfriend and his friends, or any other group. It is very difficult for the marketer to know which reference group generally dominates.

We can attempt to get some idea of those whom a consumer uses as referents in decision making by using one or more of the following approaches.[30]

1. Asking respondents directly about the groups that may be influencing their opinions or actions in a given situation.

2. Using associative-projective techniques (see Chapter 3) designed to elicit responses from people in such a way that they are not aware that they are committing themselves personally to any specific point of view or attitude. In this technique the respondent would be asked to react to a reference-group situation indirectly through being asked her opinion of *someone else* behaving in a certain way.

3. Using the sociometric technique which traces personal relationships by detailed questioning of an entire group of people who are in significant association with each other. Such questions as the following are asked of these people: With whom do they associate? Whom do they like and respect? To whom do they look for advice on specific subjects? To what extent do people turn to them for advice on given subjects?

4. Seeking to identify reference-group influence through observation of the act of buying and social interaction which takes place.

SUMMARY
This chapter has described social group influences which impinge on the consumer. We first defined the term "group" and distinguished small groups from other collections of individuals. We next described various types of groups classified along a number of dimensions. This was followed by a discussion of group properties including role and status, and the nature of social interaction which is the way in which consumers are influenced by their groups.

Reference groups were examined in detail because these are of great significance for the marketer. We defined various types of reference groups, discussed their functions, and described the nature of their influence on individuals. Finally, we elaborated on the marketing implications of reference groups by citing their relevance in consumer decision making and discussed ways the marketer may go about identifying the consumer's relevant reference groups.

DISCUSSION TOPICS
1. What is meant by the term "group"? What are some types of groups?

2. On what bases may groups be classified?

3. Distinguish between the following types of groups:
a. primary versus secondary
b. formal versus informal
c. social group versus aggregation

4. Discuss the basic properties of a group. How do these properties relate to consumer behavior?

5. What is a reference group? Name two reference groups that are important to you. In what way do they influence your consumer behavior?

6. What groups do you belong to that you feel are not influential on you and your behavior as a consumer?

7. What techniques are used by the marketer in identifying reference groups?

8. Suggest a product not listed in Figure 10-1 over which reference groups would exert a strong or weak influence with regard to the purchase of the product and brand or type. Explain.

9. For the following purchase decisions, which of the consumer's reference groups would appear to be most important?
a. formal evening gown
b. selection of a physician
c. a new home
d. a basketball and warm-up suit

NOTES

1. David Dressler and Donald Carns, *Sociology: The Study of Human Interaction,* Knopf, New York, 1973, p. 259.

2. Robert Bierstedt, *The Social Order,* 2d ed., McGraw-Hill, New York, 1963, p. 302.

3. Charles H. Cooley, *Social Organization,* Scribners, New York, 1909, p. 23.

4. Ralph Linton, *The Cultural Background of Personality,* Appleton Century Crofts, New York, 1945.

5. William Shakespeare, *As You Like It,* act 2, scene 7, lines 140–143.

6. Erving Goffman, *The Presentation of Self in Everyday Life,* University of Edinburgh Social Sciences Research Centre, London, 1958.

7. David Krech, Richard S. Crutchfield and Egerton L. Ballachey, *Individual in Society,* McGraw-Hill, New York, 1962, p. 313.

8. John R. P. French and Bertram Raven, "The Bases of Social Power," in D. Cartwright (ed.), *Studies in Social Power,* Institute of Social Research, Ann Arbor, Mich., 1959, pp. 150–167.

9. "Soft Soap and Hard Sell," *Forbes,* September 15, 1975, pp. 72, 78.

10. Ellen Graham, " 'Tupperware Parties' Create a New Breed of Super-Saleswoman," *The Wall Street Journal,* May 21, 1971, pp. 1, 18.

11. Francis S. Bourne, "Group Influence in Marketing and Public Relations," in Rensis Likert and Samuel Hayes, Jr., (eds.), *Some Applications of Behavioural Research,* UNESCO, Paris, 1957, pp. 208–209; and Tamotsu Shibutani, "Reference Groups as Perspectives," *American Journal of Sociology,* **60**:562–569, May 1955.

12. George Homans, *Social Behavior: Its Elementary Forms,* Harcourt, Brace & World, New York, 1961.

13. C. Whan Park and V. Parker Lessig, "Students and Housewives: Differences in Susceptibility to Reference Group Influence," *Journal of Consumer Research,* **4**:102–110, September 1977; Herbert C. Kelman, "Processes of Opinion Change," *Public Opinion Quarterly,* **25**:57–78, 1961; and M. Deutsch and H. B. Gerard, "A Study of Normative and Informational Social Influences upon Individual Judgment," *Journal of Abnormal and Social Psychology,* **51**:624–636, 1955.

14. Soloman E. Asch, "Studies of Independence and Submission to Group Pressure; A Minority of One against a Unanimous Majority," *Psychological Monographs,* **70**, 1956.

15. Krech, Crutchfield, and Ballachey, *Individual in Society,* p. 511.

16. Muzafer Sherif, *The Psychology of Social Norms,* Harper, New York, 1936, pp. 89–107.

17. M. Venkatesan, "Experimental Study of Consumer Behavior, Conformity and Independence," *Journal of Marketing Research,* **3**:384–387, November 1966.

18. James E. Stafford, "Effects of Group Influence on Consumer Behavior," *Journal of Marketing Research,* **3**:68–75, February 1966.

19. Robert E. Burnkrant and Alain Cousineau, "Informational and Normative Social Influence in Buyer Behavior," *Journal of Consumer Research,* **2**:206–215, December 1975.

20. Kurt Lewin, "Group Decision and Social Change," in Harold Proshansky and Bernard Seidenberg (eds.), *Basic Studies in Social Psychology*, Holt, New York, 1965, pp. 423–436.

21. Krech, Crutchfield, and Ballachey, *Individual in Society,* p. 504.

22. Robert E. Witt, "Informal Social Group Influence on Consumer Behavior," *Journal of Marketing Research,* **6**:473–476, November 1969.

23. Lyman E. Ostlund, "Role Theory and Group Dynamics," in Scott Ward and Thomas S. Robertson (eds.), *Consumer Behavior: Theoretical Sources,* Prentice-Hall, Englewood Cliffs, N.J., 1973, p. 245.

24. Thomas S. Robertson, *Consumer Behavior,* Scott, Foresman, Glenview, Ill., 1970, p. 74.

25. George Moschis, "Social Comparison and Informal Group Influence," *Journal of Marketing Research,* **13**:237–244, August 1976.

26. Bourne, "Group Influence," p. 208.

27. Bourne, "Group Influence," pp. 219–221.

28. Bourne, "Group Influence," pp. 221–222.

29. Park and Lessig, "Students and Housewives," pp. 103–104.

30. Bourne, "Group Influence," pp. 230–233.

FAMILY

This chapter examines the family as one of the strongest, most immediate, and most pervasive environmental influences on our behavior as buyers. Consumers' attitudes toward spending and saving and even the brands and products purchased have been molded, often quite indelibly, by their families. Thus, marketers need to understand the nature of the family's influence on its members and the way in which purchase decisions are made by members so that they may effectively program their marketing mix.

The thrust of this chapter will be first to familiarize ourselves with several terms important in understanding this subject. Second, we shall describe the basic functions of the family. Next, we shall examine the family life-cycle concept and assess its meaning for the marketer. Family organization and decision-making roles will then be discussed, also incorporating marketing implications and examples. Finally, the changing nature of the family, especially here in America, will be discussed along with implications for the marketer who faces this changing scene.

FAMILIES AND HOUSEHOLDS

It is important to understand the difference between various terms that are frequently encountered when discussing the concept of family. First, we should distinguish between the terms "family" and "household," since market statistics may be gathered on either of these bases. A *household* includes the related family members and all the unrelated persons who occupy a housing unit (whether house, apartment, group of rooms, or other). The term "family," however, is more limited and refers to a group of two or more persons related by blood, marriage, or adoption and residing together in a household. In 1977 there were approximately 74.1 million households and 56.7 million families.

It should be noted that marketers are interested not only in the concept of families but also of households since both may form the basis or framework of much consumer decision making and buying behavior. The marketer will use the concept that seems most relevant for segmenting markets. For instance, manufacturers of refrigerators, dishwashers, ranges, and other kitchen appliances would probably find households to be the most relevant dimension in estimating market size since purchase and replacement of these appliances would depend more on household formation than family formation. On the other hand, sellers of children's clothing and toys would probably be more interested in data on families.

SIGNIFICANCE OF THE FAMILY IN CONSUMER BEHAVIOR

In Chapter 10 we examined the topic of social groups in order to understand their relevance to individuals and how marketers could use this knowledge. Now we turn to the family not just as a type of small group, but one that is often predominant in its influence over consumer behavior. The family is both a *primary* group (characterized by intimate, face-to-face interaction) and a *reference* group (with members referring to certain family values, norms, and standards in their behavior). These two factors, however, are not the sole reasons accounting for the strength of the family's influence. Rather it is, first, the fact that the bonds within the family are likely to be much more powerful than those in other small groups. Second, contrary to most other groups to which the consumer belongs, the family functions directly in the role of ultimate consumption. Thus, the family functions as an economic unit earning and spending money. In doing this, family members must establish individual and collective consumption priorities, decide on products and brands that fulfill their needs, and also decide where these items are to be bought, and how they are to be used in furthering family members' goals.

FAMILY LIFE CYCLE

The concept of family life cycle has proven very valuable for the marketer, especially for segmentation activities. This section will describe the concept and discuss its application to consumer behavior and marketing strategy.

Life-Cycle Stages

The term "life cycle" refers to the progression of stages through which individuals and families proceed over time. In the United States the following stages are typical of the life-cycle progression:

1. The Bachelor Stage: young, single people

2. Newly Married Couples: young, no children

3. Full Nest I: young married couples with youngest child under 6

4. Full Nest II: young married couples with youngest child 6 or over

5. Full Nest III: older married couples with dependent children

6. Empty Nest I: older married couples with no children living with them and household head in labor force

7. Empty Nest II: older married couples with no children living with them and household head retired

8. Solitary Survivor I: older single people in labor force

9. Solitary Survivor II: older retired single people

With the life-cycle concept the marketer is able to better appreciate how the family's needs, outlooks, product purchases, and financial resources vary over time. The major life-cycle stages are further described below.[1]

BACHELOR STAGE At this stage of the life cycle earnings are relatively low because the individual is often just beginning a career. In spite of a low income, there are also few financial burdens which must be assumed; consequently, discretionary income is quite high. This group is generally recreation-oriented and high on fashion-opinion leadership. As a result, purchase patterns consist of vacations, cars, clothing, and various other products and services needed for the mating game. In addition, the establishment of their own residences away from their family usually requires the purchase of some basic furniture and kitchen equipment.

NEWLY MARRIED COUPLES This group is generally better off financially than when they were single because both spouses are likely to be working. They are also healthier financially than they will be in the next stage, which brings added demands on their resources. But for now this family has the highest purchase rate and the highest average purchase of durable goods, especially furniture and appliances. They also spend heavily on cars, clothing, and vacations.

FULL NEST I When the first child is born most wives stop working, which causes a reduction in family income. At the same time new demands are added to the family's purchasing requirements. For example, the increased family size may necessitate more space, so the family moves into a new home and purchases items necessary to fill their new environment. Furniture for the baby's room and other furnishings are bought, as well as such appliances as a washer, dryer, and television set. In addition, numerous child-related expenses are now added, including baby food, baby medicines, doctor's visits, and toys of all sorts. The parents are quite interested in new products and are susceptible to things they see advertised; however, they also grow more dissatisfied with their financial position and the amount of money capable of being saved.

FULL NEST II In this stage the family's financial position has improved with the husband's advancement and perhaps, too, the wife's return to work. Families in this stage are still new-product-oriented, but tend to be less influenced by advertising because they have more buying experience. Products heavily purchased during this time include many foods (especially in larger packages and multiple-unit deals), cleaning materials, bicycles, and musical instruments and lessons.

FULL NEST III During this stage the family's income continues to advance, more wives return to work, and even the children may be employed. Although they are more resistant to advertising, this family has a high average expenditure for durable goods, primarily because of their need to replace older items. They purchase new, more tasteful furniture, luxury appliances, boats, and automobiles. They also do more traveling, and spend more on dental bills and magazines.

EMPTY NEST I At this stage the family is most satisfied with its financial position and savings accumulation. Home ownership is at a peak, and major expenditures are necessary for home improvement. Although the couple is not interested in new products, they do show an interest in travel, recreation, and self-education. This spending pattern emphasizes gifts and contributions, vacations, and luxuries.

EMPTY NEST II During this stage the couple's income is drastically cut. They stay at home more and spend more for medical appliances, medical care, and products that aid their health, sleep, and digestion.

SOLITARY SURVIVORS If these individuals are still active in the labor force, their income is likely to continue to be good. However, the home is likely to be sold, and more money will be spent for vacations, recreation, and health-oriented items.

Those who are retired will suffer a drastic cut in income, but will continue to have the same medical and product needs as other retired groups. During this stage individuals also have a special need for attention, affection, and security.

Relationship between Life Cycle and Consumer Behavior

Although nine distinct stages were suggested above, there is no unanimity among research studies as to the most appropriate categorization of life cycle. For example, the dividing line for terms such as "young" and "older" might be 40 years of age in one study and 45 in another, which makes it difficult to compare results among various research studies. In spite of these definitional difficulties there is, nevertheless, widespread agreement on the relationship between life cycle and consumer behavior. For example, a study conducted for the Kroehler Manufacturing Company points out that family furniture purchase orientations vary according to life-cycle stage in the following way:

1. The young family places relatively greater emphasis on sensibility and practicality than style and beauty in the majority of its furniture purchases.

2. At later periods of furniture purchase, attractiveness and reflection of good taste become relatively more important.

3. Individual pieces of furniture are typically seen as appropriate to some particular age or stage in the life cycle.[2]

Several other studies relate shopping behavior to life-cycle stage.[3] For example, one investigation found that the frequency of shopping trips varied over the life cycle, with younger women shopping more often than older women. It was also found that younger women had a greater tendency than older women to patronize shopping centers, to do more browsing, and to prefer discount stores.[4]

The reader may wonder whether the life-cycle concept offers a richer explanation of consumer behavior than a single variable such as age. You will recall that we raised a similar question earlier when considering the merits of social class versus income in segmenting markets.

The evidence heavily favors the use of life cycle as a way of segmenting markets. As one source states, "Whether the item in question is a product or a service, a durable or a nondurable, life cycle is likely to be a more meaningful way of classifying consumers."[5]

One in-depth study on this subject found that for most items investigated life cycle was more sensitive to product consumption than was age. It should be noted, however, that for several categories of products and services the reverse was true. One category for which this was the case was products tied to age-related physical difficulties (for example, medical appliances and other medical-care items). Age was also more sensitive for products and services classified mainly as luxuries, and for a diverse catchall category.

For most products, however, life-cycle analysis allows the marketer to achieve a richer understanding of the market. A summary overview of life-cycle stages for all family members and their consumer behavior is presented in Table 11-1.

FAMILY PURCHASING DECISIONS

This section probes more deeply into the nature of the decision-making process within the family and its implications for consumer behavior and marketing. Family purchasing decisions will be examined from four perspectives: (1) role structure, (2) power structure, (3) stages in the decision-making process, and (4) family-specific characteristics. It is very important that the marketer understand who influences whom and how in the family buying process so that the proper marketing strategy may be developed.

Role Structure

In our earlier discussion of the concept of roles we described how society is structured of roles that are occupied (or played) by its members. So, too, does the family have its own structure, with each member playing his or her role.[7] Although several theories have been used to describe the structure of marital roles in decision making, from the standpoint of those interested in consumer behavior, the following role categorizations appear to be perhaps the most helpful.

INSTRUMENTAL AND EXPRESSIVE ROLES Generally among societies throughout the world the husband is more likely to provide material support and primary leadership authority within the family, and the wife is more likely to provide affection and moral support. This distinction relates to what are known as instrumental and expressive needs of all small groups (including the family); that is, the need for leadership and fulfillment of the task on the one hand, and the need for morale and cohesion on the other.[8]

This differentiation of roles is known to result from small group interaction. Leaders are produced who specialize in either *instrumental* functions

TABLE 11-1

CHARACTERISTICS OF VARIOUS STAGES IN THE FAMILY LIFE CYCLE

Age group name	Age group subname	Age	Behavioral characteristics	Products of interest	Major roles in the buying process	Amount and source of income	Major sources of information
Early Years	Early childhood	Birth–5	Total dependency on parents; development of bones and muscles and use of locomotion; accident- and illness-prone; ego centered; naps; accompanies guardian shopping	Baby foods; cribs; clothes; toys; pediatric services; room vaporizers; breakfast cereals; candy; books	Limited influencer; consumer or user	None	Parents; television; friends
	Late childhood	6–12	Declining dependency on parents; slower and more uniform growth; vast development of thinking ability; peer competition; conscious of being evaluated by others; attends school	Food; toys; clothes; lessons; medical and dental care; movies; candy; uniforms; comic books	Influencer; limited decision maker; consumer or user	Very small quantity Allowance; gifts	Parents; friends; school; television; comic books
Young Consumers	Early adolescence	13–15	Onset of puberty; shifting of reference group from family to peers; concern with personal appearance begins; desire for more independence; transition to adulthood begins	Junk food; comic books and magazines; movies; records; clothing; hobbies; grooming aids	Influencer; limited financer; decision maker; limited buyer; consumer or user	$5 weekly average Allowance; earnings	Family; peer group; school; television; radio; magazines
	Late adolescence	16–18	Transition to adulthood continues; obtains working papers; obtains driver's license; concern with personal appearance increases; active in sports; dating; less reading for fun	Gasoline; auto parts; typewriters; cameras; jewelry and trinkets; cigarettes; books and magazines	Influencer; limited financer; decision maker; buyer; consumer or user	$17.50 weekly average Allowance; earnings	Family; peer group; school; television; radio; magazines
	Pre-marrieds		Enter labor market on a full time basis; enter college; interest in personal appearance remains high; increased dating; varying degrees of independence; activity in sports decreases	Auto; clothing; dances; travel; toiletries; quick and easy-to-prepare foods	Influencer; less limited financer; decision maker; buyer; consumer or user	$500–$10,000 per year. Earnings; parents; credit	Family; peer group; college; job; television; radio; newspaper; magazines

Group	Stage	Age	Life description	Products	Roles	Income	Information sources
Adults	Marrieds	19–24	First marriage; transition to pair-centered behavior; financially optimistic; interest in personal appearance still high; homemakers; working wives and husbands	Home renting; furniture; major appliances; second auto; food; entertainment; small household items	Influencer; financer; decision maker; buyer; consumer or user	$3000–$15,000 per year. Earnings; credit	Spouse; close friends; job; television; radio; newspaper; magazines
	Young parents	25–34	Transition to family-centered behavior; decline in social interests; companionship with spouse drops; leisure activities centered more at home	Houses; home repair goods; health and nutrition foods; family games; health-care services	Influencer; financer; decision maker; buyer; consumer or user	$5000–$25,000 per year. Earnings; credit; investments	Spouse; children; job; close friends; parents; television; newspaper; magazines
Middle Years	Middle adulthood	35–44	Family size at its peak; children in school; security conscious; home-maker's time is impinged upon; husband's career advances; picnics; pleasure drives	Durables are replaced; insurance; books; sporting equipment; yard furniture; gifts	Influencer; financer; decision maker; buyer; consumer or user	$5000 and over per year Earnings; credit; investments	Spouse; children; job; extended family; television; newspaper; magazines
	Later adulthood	45–54	Children have left home; physical appearance changes; increased interest in appearance; community service; strenuous activity decline; pair-centered	Clothing; vacations; leisure time services; food; gifts; personal health-care services	Influencer; financer; decision maker; buyer; consumer or user	$5000 and over per year Earnings; credit; investments	Spouse; close friends; television; job; family; newspaper; radio; magazines
Older Consumers	Soon-to-be-retired	55–64	Physical appearance continues to decline; interest and activities continue to decline; pair-centered	Gifts; slenderizing treatments; manicures and massages; luxuries	Influencer; financer; decision maker; buyer; consumer or user	$500 and over per year. Earnings; transfer payments; credit; investments	Spouse; close friends; television; job; family; newspaper; radio; magazines
	Already retired	65 and older	Physical appearance continues its decline; mental abilities decline in sharpness; homebody behavior; ego-centered behavior; insomnia	Drugs; dietetic canned foods; laxatives; nursing home care; denture products	Influencer; financer; decision maker; limited buyer; consumer or user	$500–$25,000 per year. Retirement; transfer payments; investments	Extended family; television; surviving friends; radio; children

Adapted from Fred D. Reynolds and William D. Wells, *Consumer Behavior*, McGraw-Hill, New York, 1977.

(known as functional or task leaders) or *expressive* functions (social leaders). The former concern themselves with the basic purpose or goal of the group, while the latter attempt to reduce tension and give emotional support to members in order to maintain intragroup cohesion.[9] Within the family, the instrumental role has typically been played by the father and the expressive role by the mother. That is, men tend to be task-oriented leaders, while women lead in social-emotional behavior. The result of this is that in purchasing decisions husbands tend to concern themselves with functional product attributes and to exert more influence in deciding whether to buy and in closing the sale. The wife concerns herself more with aesthetic product attributes and with suggesting the purchase.[10]

INTERNAL AND EXTERNAL ROLES Another differentiation of roles occurs in the family with regard to the husband's primary concern with matters *external* to the family and the wife's concern largely with *internal* matters.

Myers and Reynolds have concisely diagramed the interaction of the two basic types of roles discussed above, and this is presented in Figure 11-1. This matrix indicates that where expressive-external and instrumental-internal roles are involved in a purchase decision, both husband and wife will be involved; that is, joint decision making will be the case. For product decisions involving expressive-internal and instrumental-external roles, wives and husbands, respectively, will be more heavily involved. We shall elaborate on the nature of each spouse's decision-making input to purchasing processes for various products in a later section of this chapter.

GATEKEEPERS AND OPINION LEADERS These are two additional roles that may be played by family members. The *gatekeeper* is a family member who is able to control the flow of products into the family. That is, the purchase may be consummated or blocked by this individual. An *opinion leader* within the family is one who is able to exert personal influence with regard to a particular purchase situation.

The roles of gatekeeper and opinion leader were well-illustrated in a study of children's purchase influence on parents. In this research, children were found to be opinion leaders with regard to cereal purchases. That is, they suggested which brands their mothers should purchase when shopping. The mothers, however, were in the gatekeeper position, frequently disagreeing with their children as to what cereal should be purchased, and hence controlling the flow of this product into the family.

The gatekeeper role, as illustrated by this situation, has implications for many manufacturers, especially those selling products to children. The

FIGURE 11-1
Role interaction.
(*Source:* Adapted from James H. Myers and William H. Reynolds, *Consumer Behavior and Marketing Management,* Houghton Mifflin Co., Boston, 1967, p. 245.)

	External	Internal
Expressive	Both	Wife
Instrumental	Husband	Both

following strategy was suggested for such marketers: "Given that the mother is not only a purchasing agent for the child but also an agent who superimposes her preferences over those of the child, it is clear that a lot of advertising would be well directed at the mother, even if the mother is not a 'consumer' of the product."[11] Some toy companies such as Fisher-Price have followed this suggestion and advertise heavily in women's magazines.

Power Structure

This factor has to do with which family member is dominant or considered to be the family's head. A family may be *patriarchal,* in which case the father is considered to be the dominant member. In a *matriarchal* family, the woman plays the dominant role and makes most of the decisions, while in the *equalitarian* family, the husband and wife share in decision making somewhat equally. Although the American family is still generally patriarchal and our society is male-dominated, egalitarianism is a continuously emerging pattern. At the same time, however, within many middle-class suburban American families today the father's extended absence and preoccupation with his career has given rise to a more matriarchal family in which the mother takes on most of the everyday functions of the family. Because of this the children identify more with her than with the father, and she enjoys a degree of power accordingly.[12]

The United States is also moving increasingly toward a child-centered family in which children have a strong influence on their parents' consumption decisions. For example, parents often yield to their children's television-viewing preferences (such as watching "Sesame Street" rather than an afternoon movie), recreation or entertainment requests (a vacation to Disney World rather than Europe), and product choices (Frosted Flakes rather than Special K).

PURCHASE INFLUENCE PATTERN Research on power relationships in the family has taken several directions. One approach to understanding the marital power structure in consumer decision making categorizes the possibilities for dominance in the following way: (1) *autonomic,* in which an equal number of decisions is made by each spouse, (2) *husband dominant,* (3) *wife dominant,* and (4) *syncratic,* in which most decisions are made by both husband and wife.[13]

A study using this concept measured the relative influence of Belgian husbands and wives in purchase decisions for twenty-five representative products.[14] Figure 11-2 positions these decisions according to the four marital decision-making categories of autonomic, husband dominant, wife dominant, and syncratic. Each decision is positioned in this figure according to two axes. The vertical axis is a scale of the relative influence between husband and wife. Decisions can range along a continuum from 1 (if respondents report husband dominance) to 3 (if respondents report wife dominance). The horizontal axis is a scale of the extent of role specialization as measured by the percentage of families reporting that a decision is made jointly. In reading the figure, it may be seen that the relative influence score for household cleaning products is approximately 2.9, with only 6 percent of the families deciding jointly on this item's purchase. Thus, the wife dominates this purchase decision. Similarly, the relative influence score for vacations is approximately 2.0, with 78 percent of families deciding jointly (a syncratic role structure).

Other studies of family purchasing have also found that dominance in the marital decision-making process varies significantly across product categories.[15] Results of these studies lead to the conclusion that joint decision making is most likely to occur for purchases that represent significant economic outlays; whereas routine expenditures for items viewed as necessities will probably be delegated to one of the spouses.

Table 11-2 presents selected data from a thorough analysis of husband-wife relative purchase influence sponsored by five national magazines. The research was conducted among over 4000 respondents in nearly 2500 United

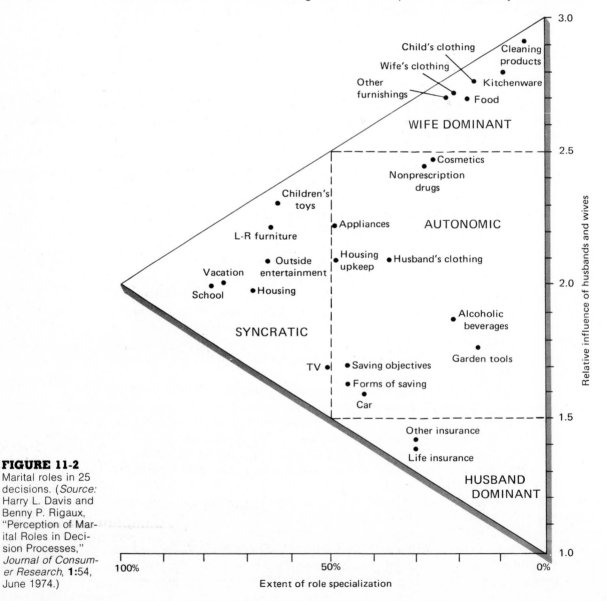

FIGURE 11-2
Marital roles in 25 decisions. (*Source:* Harry L. Davis and Benny P. Rigaux, "Perception of Marital Roles in Decision Processes," *Journal of Consumer Research*, **1**:54, June 1974.)

TABLE 11-2

WHO MAKES THE BUYING DECISIONS?*

Relative Purchase Influence: Husbands and Wives

Percentage of Influence

	Purchased by		Direct influence				Indirect influence			
			Product		Brand		Product		Brand	
	W	H	W	H	W	H	W	H	W	H
Cereals:										
Cold (unsweetened)	84	16	74	26	71	29	65	35	67	33
Hot	84	16	67	33	67	33	63	37	59	41
Packaged lunch meat	73	27	60	40	64	36	56	44	57	43
Peanut butter	81	19	70	30	74	26	65	35	68	32
Scotch whiskey	35	65	18	82	18	82	22	78	23	77
Bar soap	85	15	65	35	64	36	60	40	61	39
Headache remedies	67	33	67	33	67	33	64	36	65	35
Cat food (dry)	66	34	75	25	81	19	80	20	80	20
Dog food (dry)	76	24	60	40	59	41	60	40	61	39
Fast-food chain hamburgers	68	32	55	45	55	45	53	47	52	48
Catsup	75	25	68	32	68	32	60	40	62	38
Coffee:										
Freeze-dried	68	32	57	43	62	38	56	44	59	41
Regular ground	74	26	65	35	65	35	58	42	60	40
Mouthwash	72	28	56	44	56	44	52	48	53	47

Share of influence

	Purchase Decision Influence				Initiation				Information Gathering			
	Product		Brand		Product		Brand		Product		Brand	
	W	H	W	H	W	H	W	H	W	H	W	H
Vacuum cleaner	60	40	60	40	80	20	69	31	66	34	65	35
Electric blender	59	41	53	47	67	33	50	50	53	47	52	48
Broadloom carpet	60	40	59	41	82	18	74	26	72	28	69	31
Automobiles	38	62	33	67	22	78	21	79	18	82	18	82

*Source: "Purchase Influence Measures of Husband/Wife Influence on Buying Decisions," Haley, Overholser & Associates, Inc., New Canaan, Conn., January 1975 "Buying Study Called Good Support Data," *Advertising Age,* March 17, 1975, p. 52. Percentages reflect relative purchase activity, direct and indirect influence of husbands and wives in the sample. For durables and services, percentages reflect relative activity in purchase decision, initiation of idea to purchase and the gathering of information.

States households and covered 108 different products and services ranging from packaged products to durable goods and services.[16] The study was conducted among both husbands and wives and measured purchase patterns and direct and indirect influences. For all products, measures were made of influence on both the decision to buy the product, and on the decision to select the particular brand purchased. Spousal influence was defined as "a state of mind recalled by the purchaser which affected a specific recent purchase," and was categorized for packaged products as direct (that is, consciously recalled) and indirect (that is, consideration given to satisfaction of the wants and preferences of each spouse by the purchaser). For durables, however, no important distinction was made between direct and indirect influence, since the purchase is discussed and deliberately decided on, thus satisfying both spouse's wants and preferences. Information was also gathered on relative influence on two aspects of prepurchase activity: initiation of the purchase and information gathering prior to the purchase decision.

Although the previous studies describe *what* the patterns of spousal influence are for various products, perhaps the best explanation of *why* husband or wife dominance arises is provided by the model presented in Figure 11-3. In order for dominance to occur at any given point in a complex decision process there must be (1) a desire and ability on the part of one marriage partner to dominate the other and (2) a willingness on the part of the other partner to accept that attempt at dominance. Both are necessary conditions for dominance to exist; neither alone is a sufficient condition.[17]

Stages in the Family Decision Process

The marketer is interested not only in the physical act of purchasing a product or brand but also in the stages leading up to that decision. The research study on family participation and influence in purchasing behavior described above and presented in Table 11-2 also found that roles and influence vary throughout the buyer decision-making process. Such knowledge can be of great help in formulating product, promotion, channel, and pricing strategies. As shown in Table 11-2, for most of the products wives are involved more heavily in the initiation, information seeking, and purchasing stages than are husbands. At all stages, however, there is a greater tendency for husbands to participate in the decision process when the product is high-priced and technically or mechanically complex.

Other studies have examined products not included in the study cited above, with similar findings. Their data support the contention that the extent of husband-wife involvement varies considerably from product to product throughout the decision-making process.[18]

Family-specific Characteristics

There are a number of additional variables that have been found to influence the nature of purchasing decisions made within the family. The influencing factors to be discussed below include culture, subculture, social class, reference groups and social interaction, stage in life cycle, mobility, geographical location, working wives, and children.

CULTURE The roles of husbands and wives may differ dramatically from culture to culture, which may result in numerous differences in consumer decision making. The basic family systems encountered by the marketer around the world fall into three general patterns illustrated as follows: (1) in Moslem areas the wife is generally in a subordinate and secluded role, with few rights and little control over the affairs of the family; (2) in Latin America the wife is freer but is still definitely a junior member of the partnership, with the husband having the final authority in all but minor matters; and (3) in Europe and the Anglo-Saxon countries the basic pattern is equality.[19]

SUBCULTURE In addition to cultural variations from one country to another, there are also subcultural or ethnic variations in consumer behavior within a country's heterogeneous population. For example, in the United States joint decision making is most pronounced among white families, with husband dominance strongest among Japanese-Americans, and wife dominance strongest among black families.[20]

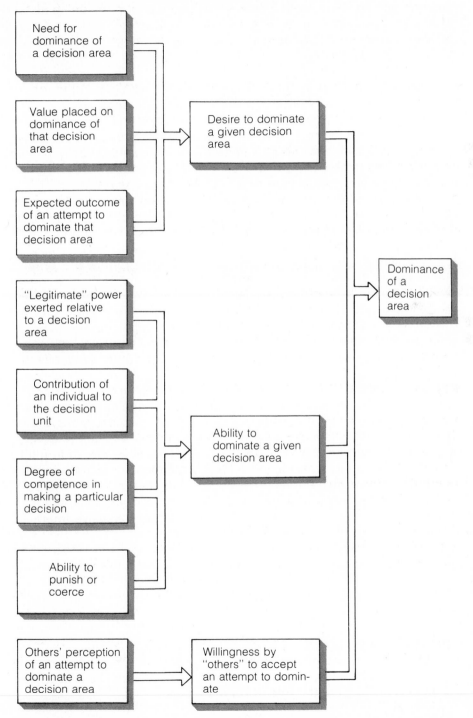

FIGURE 11-3
Factors contributing to dominance in husband-wife interactions. [*Source:* Robert F. Kelly and Michael B. Egan, "Husband and Wife Interaction in a Consumer Decision Process," in Philip R. McDonald (ed.), *Marketing Involvement in Society and the Economy*, American Marketing Association, Chicago, 1969, pp. 251–252.]

SOCIAL CLASS Several studies on the relationship of socioeconomic class and joint participation in purchase decision making have indicated that a curvilinear relationship exists. That is, autonomy in decision making is most likely at upper and lower social classes, while joint decision making is most common among the middle class. Spousal power in purchasing also varies by social class with husbands having a greater tendency to dominate decisions in upper-class families and wives tending to dominate among lower-social class levels.[21]

REFERENCE GROUPS AND SOCIAL INTERACTION Although no research has been conducted on the role of reference groups in family purchase decisions, it is thought that such relationships are influential. Some authors indicate that the greater the extent to which spouses have social ties or connections with relatives or friends, the less the amount of joint or shared decisions. This is because some decisions may be made in consultation with friends or relatives rather than only with one's spouse.[22]

Another area that has been relatively unconsidered is the reference influence between generations. Many questions regarding intergenerational patterns of consumption are presently unanswered. For example, we don't know to what extent general patterns of spending, saving, and money management observed by children in the parental home are reflected in similar behavior when these children become adults. Nor do we know the extent to which specific consumer choices are made from generation to generation within family lines; or whether there are certain products or classes of products with high brand loyalty between generations.[23] It seems quite plausible, however, that there is an intergenerational influence; and future research may confirm its existence and the nature of its effect.

STAGE IN LIFE CYCLE The nature of family decision making changes over the life cycle. For example, wives with pre-school-age children have considerably less independent responsibility for economic decisions than other wives. In addition, families in the under-24 age group show a very high frequency of joint decisions.[24] However, evidence indicates that joint decision making declines over the life cycle. This tendency has been explained in terms of an increased efficiency or competence that people develop over a period of time in making purchasing decisions that are acceptable to their spouses. Such competence eliminates the need for extensive interaction.[25]

MOBILITY Mobility, both social as well as geographic, tends to increase the extent of intrafamily communication and the degree of joint decision making. One researcher attributes this to the fact that movement away from stable primary groups such as family and close friends "throws spouses upon each other."[26]

GEOGRAPHICAL LOCATION Limited research on the influence of place of residence on family decision making indicates that rural families have a higher frequency of joint decisions than urban families. Also, the wife occupies a less influential role in rural families.[27]

WORKING WIFE The evidence on this facet of family purchasing decisions is unclear. It has been suggested that the employment status of the wife affects her role in decision making. The wife's relative influence increases as her financial and intellectual contribution to the family increases.[28] It is also claimed that wives regularly in the labor force would be less likely to play the expressive role in family decision making.[29] However, other research has found that the working status of the wife had no effect on her decision-making function.[30]

CHILDREN As children are added to the family structure there may be a reorganization and redefinition of the roles of the husband and wife. It is suggested by Kenkel that husband and wife roles would shift in the direction of more clearly defined distinctions, typically along traditional lines. Wives would also be more likely to play the expressive role, and husbands the instrumental role in family decisions as compared with childless couples.[31]

Table 11-3 presents a summary diagram of the most important variables influencing participation in family purchase decisions.

TABLE 11-3

SUMMARY OF MAJOR DETERMINANTS OF JOINT VERSUS INDIVIDUAL INVOLVEMENT IN FAMILY DECISION-MAKING ROLE STRUCTURE

	Joint	Individual		
		Husband Dominant	Wife Dominant	Autonomic
Family characteristics	Middle class Husband education = wife education Middle income Small family size Wife not employed	Upper class Husband education > wife education High income Large family size	Lower class Wife education > husband education Lower income	Wife employed.
Decision type	High unit price			Husband: Male use, technical. Wife: female use, aesthetic; product form not visible in use.
	High social visibility			
	Joint use			
Life cycle	Newlywed; empty nest	Small children		Older children at home.

Source: Donald H. Granbois, "A Multi-Level Approach to Family Role Structure Research," in David M. Gardner (ed.), *Proceedings of the 2nd Annual Conference, Association for Consumer Research,* College Park, Md., 1971, p. 102.

THE CHANGING AMERICAN FAMILY

It should come as no surprise to the reader that families in America and other parts of the world are changing. One of the most important changes relates to the woman's role in that group. But in addition to this there are other perceptible shifts which have occurred in family members' roles and relationships.

What are the major family changes and what do these shifting patterns mean for the marketer of the 1980s? This section provides insight into these questions. Figure 11-4 summarizes several of the more important trends taking place among American families.

Changing Family Life-Styles and Life Cycles

The data available on marriage and families indicate that important changes in American family life-styles and life cycles are occurring. One writer describes the direction of these basic changes for the middle-class family in the following way:

A middle-class family's cycle has typically involved early marriage, three or four children, a house in the suburbs and two cars, commuting, the wife working

Divorces on the rise

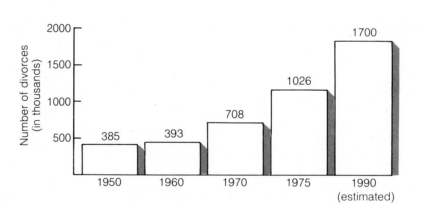

Shift to smaller families

Number of children expected by wives 18-24 years old

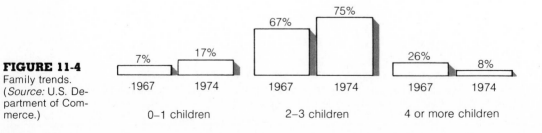

FIGURE 11-4
Family trends.
(*Source:* U.S. Department of Commerce.)

Births heading upward again

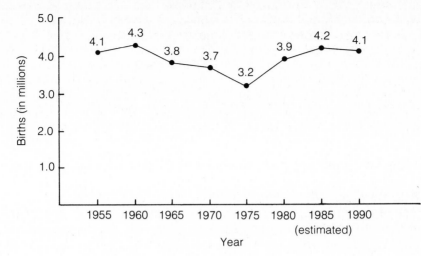

Number of marriages rising to new plateau

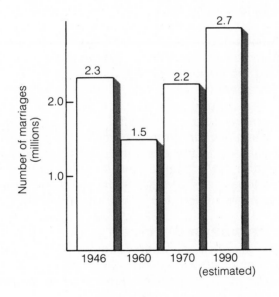

Older age at marriage

Percent of males not yet married			Percent of females not yet married		
	Age 20–24	Age 25–29		Age 20–24	Age 25–29
1960	53%	21%	1960	28%	11%
1970	55	19	1970	36	11
1980 (estimate)	58	22	1980 (estimate)	43	14
1990 (estimate)	60	21	1990 (estimate)	49	16

part-time when the children are in their teens, trying to squeeze in some travel and savings and perhaps college for the children, and then coming to terms with—or feeling relieved about—a childless home.

Now consider the emerging variation on this theme. The couple marry later and the wife works longer before the first child. She is apt to have only two children and go back to work while they're still quite young—all of which tends to improve the family's financial situation considerably. Largely because wives as well as husbands expect to be employed most of the time, couples may increasingly want to live in homes near their jobs. All along they will have wide options—e.g., whether to save more, to increase their stocks of consumer durables and clothing, or to spend freely on recreation and travel.[32]

Thus, family life-cycle and life-style patterns are being redefined.

Role Changes within the Family

One of the important changes occurring among families today is the shifting view of the roles of marriage partners. Over the last several years the number favoring shared roles in marriage (in which both work, share homemaking, and child raising) has surpassed those favoring a traditional marriage (in which the husband is the breadwinner and the wife is homemaker) by a ratio of 48 percent to 43 percent. However, the small remaining number favoring other living alternatives (such as unmarried couples) reinforces the basic and continuing strength of Americans' belief in the nuclear family system.[33]

Another recent survey found that at least 94 percent of women are still in favor of having at least one child. The real shift has come, however, in attitudes toward the ideal number of children to have, which has decreased over the past 20 years.[34]

One of the most significant areas of change to occur in the American family concerns the role of the wife. More than either the husband or children, the wife has undergone the greatest transformation in the past few decades. As reflected in the changing views of marriage, more and more women are opting for a shared role situation rather than the traditional approach. To a large extent what this means is that the wife has accepted a job outside the home in addition to her job within the home.

INFLUENCE OF WORKING WIVES The predictions are that women will continue to go to work at an unprecedented rate, increasing from approximately 48 percent of all women by 1980 to 51 percent by 1990.[35] In 1977 working wives existed in about 44 percent of all married households and amounted to over 37 million individuals working either full-time or part-time. Moreover, the greatest increase in the participation rates of wives has generally been among mothers of children under 3. Figure 11-5 presents a summary of working wife characteristics.

A woman works outside the home for one or more of the following reasons: (1) to add to the family's economic security, (2) to join the mainstream of worldly endeavor, (3) to get acquainted with achieving people and sharpen her own talents and skills, (4) to escape the dullness of housework, and (5) to prepare for the time when she might again be single or the children may be grown.[36]

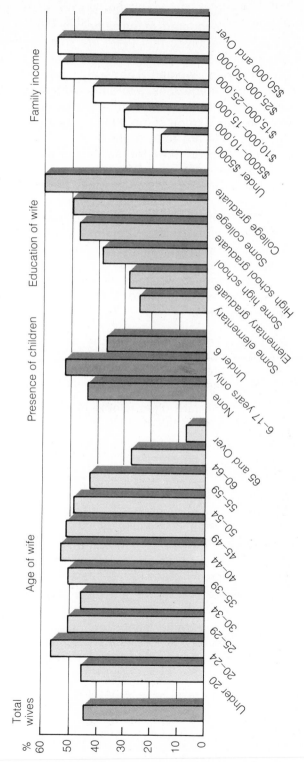

FIGURE 11-5
The working wife:
proportion of wives
working by select-
ed characteristics,
1975. (*Source:* U.S.
Department of
Labor and Com-
merce, The Confer-
ence Board, in Fa-
bian Linden,
"Woman, Worker,"
Across the Board,
March 1977, p. 26.)

An important consideration for the marketer is whether working women behave as consumers in the same way their nonworking counterparts do. The answer generally is that there are some important distinctions between the two groups. For example, working women's media behavior differs from that of nonworking women. They watch less television (particularly daytime) and read more magazines. Working women also spend somewhat more time listening to radio and reading newspapers.[37] Working versus nonworking women also exhibit some differences in usage patterns. The data presented in Table 11-4 are representative of some of these differences. It should be noted, however, that for some durable goods and other products and services the existence of a working wife does not appear to be a determinant of whether the goods and services are purchased or of how much is spent, according to one recent study. Thus, once the fact that the wife's earnings raise family income is taken into account, families with working wives do not spend any more or less frequently or heavily on some items than do families without working wives.[38]

Mountains of statistical data could be cited regarding the changing role of women. However, what are some of the fundamental marketing implications suggested by these trends? The following list includes some of the more important ones:

Working women can justify economic expenditures for, and psychologically accept, expensive appliances and household equipment, such as microwave ovens and prepared foods, which may even reduce the wives' roles in important household tasks.

Working wives are often unable to shop during regular retailing hours. They might prefer that sales be held in the evening.

Some shopping may be done by wives' surrogates—daughters and sons. Shopping also becomes more of a shared husband and wife activity, or even a family venture. Saturdays, Sundays, and evenings become very important shopping times.

The distinction between men's and women's work in the home has blurred and a sense of shared household duties prevails. Appliances that formerly had an image of being a female appliance, such as a vacuum cleaner, tend to take on a unisex image.

Working women place a premium on a youthful appearance and on the "maintenance of self." Advancement in business is often associated with being young.

The family-dominated meal scene and the wife's role have changed. Prepared foods, convenience foods, fast-food and family-style restaurants occupy a significant position in the family feeding function.

Working women are more education-oriented and interested in self-improvement, travel, leisure and their own individualism. They tend to be more independent and confident.

Working wives tend more to become equal decision makers in the home. This change is particularly noticeable among lower social classes where wives were very subordinated.

TABLE 11-4

253
FAMILY

PRODUCT USAGE INDEX: WORKING VERSUS NONWORKING WOMEN

Here's a handy extract for marketers and others from Simmons 1975 study indexing products and services used by working women compared to nonemployed homemakers.

As might be expected, working housewives are not the best market for baby foods or hot cereals, but they do have greater clout as consumers of prepared foods, pet foods, diet sodas, panty hose, cigarettes, gasoline.

Employed women also spend more for bed linens and the like and attend more Tupperware parties (where they buy the brand), probably because it gives them an opportunity to mix with their neighbors at times when they are not away at work.

This cross section also reveals a greater tendency of employed women to buy/use discretionary goods and services, but they also have higher indices in some areas that are not discretionary (cold/allergy remedies, for example).

Product Category	All Women	Employed	Not Employed
Drank beer in the past month	100	115	89
Drank any alcoholic beverages in past month	100	116	89
Drank any wine in past month	100	123	83
Bought panty hose in past month	100	120	86
Own electric hair dryer	100	117	88
Bought gasoline in past three months	100	122	85
Took color snapshots in past year	100	116	89
Bought 33 rpm records in past six months	100	125	82
Bought sterling silver flatware past year	100	124	83
Used analgesic in past month	100	104	97
Used cold/allergy remedy past month	100	116	88
Used indigestion remedy in past month	100	97	103
Used laxatives in past month	100	85	110
Bought securities in past two years	100	126	82
Regularly smoke cigarettes	100	114	90
Went bowling in past year	100	125	82
Played tennis in past year	100	134	77
Used any eye makeup in past month	100	123	84
Used any face powder in past month	100	102	99
Took domestic air trip in past year	100	120	85
Bought travelers checks in past year	100	126	81
Baby food	100	79	116
Instant powdered breakfast	100	113	91
Hot cereal	100	90	107
Barbecue sauce	100	112	92
Snack or dip cheese	100	118	89
Corn snacks	100	114	90
Frozen main courses	100	115	92
Pizza mix or prepared pizza	100	113	91
Diet cola drinks	100	114	91
Canned dog food	100	112	91
Canned cat food	100	123	84
Avg. wkly. food market expenditures $41+	100	104	97
Spent $15+ for bed sheets past year	100	112	91
Attended Tupperware party in past year	100	115	90

Source: Simmons 1975, in "Buying Habits of the Working Woman," *Media Decisions,* March 1976, p. 69.

The availability of household services beyond the usual morning and afternoon household hours, e.g., repair services during weekends, will become increasingly important.

Women dislike the way they are depicted in some advertisements, which is often at considerable variance with both their desired and actual roles.

Price for some products may become less important than convenience, availability, service, and time savings.

Women are becoming more cosmopolitan in their tastes and expectations as they become more involved with, and exposed to, the world external to the home.[39]

INFLUENCE OF CHANGING ROLES ON FAMILY DECISION MAKING

These changing role patterns are having numerous effects.[40] Previous marriage patterns meant that there were generally no decisions to be made regarding the wife's chief life interest and sphere, nor the husband's. She concentrated on domestic activities, and he concentrated on occupational efforts. Today, however, sex-role shifts toward egalitarianism mean that there is less inevitability of such a pattern and many new and critical decisions must be made. Increasing numbers of younger and better-educated men and women are bargaining with each other about their chief life interests. And this is occurring not only among those soon-to-be or newly married but also among couples married for some time. There are virtually no nonnegotiable issues among such modern marriages. For example, where to live (near his work or hers), how many children to have and when, who will perform child care and domestic chores, how to spend *their* incomes, and so forth.

In addition to the number of issues to be decided, there is also the matter of how this is negotiated. Women who have more traditional roles in marriage tend to negotiate with their husbands and try to persuade him to compromise on the basis of *collective* interest—what is best for the family group, for their marital relationship, for the children. Women who have adopted modern roles tend to negotiate more in terms of their own *individualistic* interests— what is best for her. Such a strategy seems to result in achieving more equitable compromises in terms of reaching her goals.

Another dimension of negotiation that may differ between modern and traditional women regards their toughness in bargaining. It has been hypothesized that modern women are much tougher (that is, make high demands and grant few concessions) than their traditional counterparts in negotiating family-decision issues.

There are other dimensions of decision-making behavior which need to be investigated. Nevertheless, it is clear that as women shift their interests solely from domestic goals and interests to include extra-familial areas as well, they are also likely to change their processes of decision making.

Although purchase influence may shift over a period of time as the American family structure changes, evidence of such a shift in family purchase-decision roles is not yet conclusive. For example, a survey conducted in 1955 among 727 Detroit housewives to determine whether purchase decisions for several products and services were made by the husband, the wife, or jointly was compared with a similar study conducted in

1973 among a small sample of Houston housewives. Several shifts in decision-making influence were noted from a comparison of the results of the two surveys, which are presented in Table 11-5. This evidence led the authors of the 1973 study to conclude that

. . . it is impossible to generalize the effects of environmental change on purchasing decision roles. Family decision-making with regard to some products has apparently become more specialized (e.g., groceries and life insurance), possibly due to the increasing complexities of modern life. Conversely, the tendency toward more joint decision making in the selection of housing and vacation spots may result from the trend toward egalitarianism between spouses.[41]

Two more recent studies, however, do not confirm the shift in influence

---

TABLE 11-5

HUSBAND-WIFE DECISION-MAKING ROLES IN 1955 AND 1973

Decision Area	1955* (%)	1973† (%)
Food and groceries		
Husband usually	13	10
Both husband and wife	33	15
Wife usually	54	75
Life insurance		
Husband usually	43	66
Both husband and wife	42	30
Wife usually	15	4
Automobile		
Husband usually	70	52
Both husband and wife	25	45
Wife usually	5	3
Vacation		
Husband usually	18	7
Both husband and wife	70	84
Wife usually	12	9
House or apartments		
Husband usually	18	12
Both husband and wife	58	77
Wife usually	24	11
Money and bills		
Husband usually	26	27
Both husband and wife	34	24
Wife usually	40	49

*Harry Sharp and Paul Mott, "Consumer Decisions in the Metropolitan Family," *Journal of Marketing,* **22:**149–156, October 1956.
†Isabella C. M. Cunningham and Robert T. Green, "Purchasing Roles in the U.S. Family, 1955 and 1973," *Journal of Marketing,* **38:**61–64, October 1974
Source: Reprinted from Isabella C. M. Cunningham and Robert T. Green, "Purchasing Roles in the U.S. Family, 1955 and 1973," *Journal of Marketing,* **38:**63, October 1974, published by the American Marketing Association.

claimed above.[42] Consequently, it is difficult to judge whether, and if so, how far purchase-influence roles have shifted. Clearly, more uniformly comparable research must be conducted. Most importantly, however, the marketer who desires to segment markets on the basis of purchase influence within the family must obtain product-specific measures of this influence to be successful.

ADVERTISING AND THE CHANGING WOMAN One area of marketing that is likely to be strongly influenced by women's changing roles is advertising. As one writer observes, "If advertising to the new woman is to persuade, it must treat women as intelligent adults who will respond to a reasonable and believable presentation of the product's case."[43] Many have been critical about the treatment of women in advertisements, particularly their limited role portrayal.[44]

Research on women's role portrayal preferences in advertisements indicates that liberationists and nonliberationists alike agree on the following:

Advertisements showing women may portray them in household roles if these roles provide an appropriate usage environment for the product and reinforce and support the product's end benefits.

If the product is one that women use personally, which enhances their concept of themselves as women, then nontraditional roles are preferred.[45]

As advertisers seek to appeal to the changing woman, particularly women who work, some are breaking away from the stereotypes by showing dual roles, role switching, and role blending.[4] The use of *dual roles* portrays women in roles that are in addition to a more traditional role in the house, such as a wife/manager or mother/professional. For example, in a campaign aimed at getting female passengers to fly on Boeing aircraft, Boeing shows a businesswoman poring over paper work on a night flight with the caption, "A woman's work is never done."[47]

With *role switching,* purchase or use of the product is portrayed by persons of the sex opposite that of the traditional stereotype. For example, a recent "give-me-the-Campbell's-life" commercial showed a husband home from work dancing around the kitchen fixing soup and sandwiches just in time for his working wife to arrive home from the office. Similarly, Dunlop Tire & Rubber Co. pictured a well-known woman race-care driver with the copy, "Dunlop makes tires for little ladies who drive on Sunday. Sunday at Watkins Glen. Sunday at Daytona. Sunday at Riverside."

Role blending obscures the role stereotype of purchaser or user by showing scenes in which no sex dominates. For example, car manufacturers often show a man and woman (or even the entire family) engaged in decision-making activity. In addition, food manufacturers sometimes show a man and woman shopping in the supermarket.

Strength in the Traditional Homemaker Market

The marketer should remember, however, that there is also a sizable segment of American men and women who prefer traditional roles in marriage (43 percent according to a 1977 survey). Consequently, appealing to this group on the basis of its own value system may be very rewarding to many companies. As success of the book *The Total Woman* and attendance at its seminars across the country showed, there are millions of American home-makers who seek to find ways in which the traditional marriage can be made more fulfilling.[48] These women prefer the role of homemaker to competing in the world of factories and offices.

This is indeed a large segment, and it can be effectively appealed to by positively reflecting the traditional female family role in product concepts, and particularly in advertising messages, rather than by using a negative stereotype. As has been mentioned before, some advertisers have moved away from the idea of the dizzy housewife who can't think for herself to the concept of a more "together" woman who can cope with the situation effectively and thereby win her family's affection. Household product adver-tisers are also showing how use of a product will free the homemaker from the drudgery of housework and enable her to have more time to become fulfilled and also to help fulfill the needs of others in the family, whether husband or children.

Growth of the Singles Market

One of the important market developments to occur in the last decade has been the tremendous rise of *singles,* especially among the young, which is a segment growing over five times as fast as the nation as a whole, according to the U.S. Census Bureau. Several interesting facts on this market indicate that among those 18 and over almost 40 million, or about 30 percent, of the adult population are singles. This market includes nearly 23 million who never married, almost 12 million widows and widowers, and over 5 million divorced people. Nearly 60 percent of the singles group consists of females, and almost half of this segment are under age 30.[49]

This growing segment of the American market has not been ignored by marketers. New product and service opportunities have opened up in a wide range of categories geared to this market. For example, consider the following:

Building and home furnishing: The smaller household of the future—both families and singles—means more apartments and condominiums and fewer homes. More furniture will be suitable for apartments. Practicality rather than status and prestige will be stressed. Mobility of furniture will be important, giving added emphasis to new design and styles, such as modular arrangements.

Autos: Smaller cars are the big seller here, but with emphasis on sporty syling and plenty of pleasure-oriented options, such as stereo. For example, Porsche estimated that in 1974 about half of their autos were bought by singles. Sim-ilarly, AMC reported that singles purchased 40 percent of its 1974 Gremlins.

Foods: More single and dual-serving packages, cans, plastic bags, and so on will be marketed, with convenience and disposability rather than economy the prime benefits. Gerber, for instance, is offering single serving jars of adult food. Campbell is also selling soup for one. Since more single men will be pushing supermarket carts, foodmarkets will have to find new ways to reach them through advertising.

Appliances: Portability and practicality are the selling appeals being used here.

Multifunctionalism is another benefit—such as with tabletop toaster-ovens. Small size also becomes a factor, keyed to smaller housing units.

Toiletries and cosmetics: These will appeal to the narcissistic concerns of many singles with time, money, and interest in self-enhancement.

Financial services: Traditionally prejudiced against singles as high-risk, these will be taking a new look at this group and their needs. For example, BankAmericard estimates that as many as 50 percent of its new customers in many metropolitan areas are singles.

SUMMARY

This chapter has described the influence of the family on consumer behavior. First, the terms "family" and "household" were defined. Next, we described several types of families and the purposes of the family. The concept of family life cycle was examined in some detail. This progression of stages through which individuals and families proceed over time was found to be a primary determinant of the family's purchasing behavior. In addition, it was suggested that life cycle offers a richer explanation of consumer behavior than single variables such as age.

The nature of family purchasing decisions was discussed next from four vantage points: (1) role structure and the influence of each family member based on his or her role in the family, (2) power relationships within the family and their ability to explain the dominance of particular family members in various purchase decisions, (3) the purchase decision and the varying roles and influences of particular family members at each stage in the process, and (4) additional variables that are family-specific and have an influence on purchase decisions.

The final section of this chapter discussed the changing family system especially with regard to the role of women and suggested some of the effects on marketing activities likely to result.

DISCUSSION TOPICS

1. Distinguish between families and households. In what ways is each important to the marketer in analyzing consumer behavior?

2. Discuss the significance of the family in consumer behavior.

3. Describe the family life-cycle stages. What influence does life cycle have on consumer behavior?

4. How would marketers of the following items use the life-cycle concept in their strategies?

a. mutual funds
b. pianos
c. motor homes
d. camping equipment

5. Describe the meaning of the following family roles. What is their significance in terms of consumer behavior and marketing strategy?

a. instrumental and expressive
b. internal and external
c. gatekeeper and opinion leaders

6. Assuming Figure 11-2 represented United States family decision-making power structures, how could a marketer use this information in developing marketing strategies (especially advertising and personal selling activities) for the following products?

a. living room furniture
b. life insurance
c. kitchenware
d. automobile

7. Describe how family-specific characteristics influence the nature of purchasing decisions within the family.

8. Who is the gatekeeper in your family or household for the following product/brand decisions? The opinion leader?

a. furniture
b. foods
c. clothing
d. financial services
e. toys

9. Write a report on one of the following subjects indicating specifically what some of the effects on consumer behavior and marketing might be:

a. changing family values
b. the changing role of women
c. women in advertisements
d. divorce and alternative "family" arrangements

10. Discuss the role of children in family decision making.

NOTES

1. This summary of life-cycle stages has been adapted from the following sources: William D. Wells and George Gubar, "Life Cycle Concept in Marketing Research," *Journal of Marketing Research,* **3**:355–363, November 1966; S. G. Barton, "The Life Cycle and Buying Patterns," in Lincoln H. Clark (ed.), *Consumer Behavior,* **2**:53–57, New York University Press, New York, 1955; John B. Lansing and James N. Morgan, "Consumer Finances over the Life Cycle," in Clark (ed.), *Consumer Behavior,* pp. 36–51; and John B. Lansing and Leslie Kish, "Family Life Cycle as an Independent Variable," *American Sociological Review,* **22**:512–519, October 1957.

2. Social Research, Inc., "Furniture Buying and Life Stages," in Martin H. Grossack (ed.), *Understanding Consumer Behavior,* Christopher Publishing House, Boston, 1964, pp. 288–290.

3. Stuart U. Rich and Subhash C. Jain, "Social Class and Life Cycle as Predictors of Shopping Behavior," *Journal of Marketing Research,* **5**:41–49, February 1968; Ben M. Enis and Keith K. Cox, "Demographic Analysis of Store Patronage Patterns: Uses and Pitfalls," in Robert L. King (ed.), *Marketing and the New Science of Planning,* American Marketing Association, Chicago, 1968, pp. 366–370; and Barton, "The Life Cycle."

4. Rich and Jain, "Social Class."

5. Wells and Gubar, "Life Cycle," p. 360.

6. National Industrial Conference Board, *Expenditure Patterns of the American Family,* Life, New York, 1965.

7. P. G. Herbst, "The Measurement of Family Relationships," *Human Relations,* **5**:3–35, February 1952.

8. Bernard Berelson and Gary Steiner, *Human Behavior: An Inventory of Scientific Findings,* Harcourt, Brace & World, New York, 1964, p. 314.

9. R. F. Bales, "In Conference," *Harvard Business Review,* **32**:44–50, March-April 1954.

10. William F. Kenkel, "Husband-Wife Interaction in Decision-Making and Decision Choices," *The Journal of Social Psychology,* **54**:260, 1961.

11. Lewis A. Berey and Richard Pollay, "The Influencing Role of the Child in Family Decision-Making," *Journal of Marketing Research,* **5**:72, February 1968.

12. David Dressler and Donald Carns, *Sociology: The Study of Human Interaction,* 2d ed., Knopf, New York, 1973, p. 483.

13. P. G. Herbst, "Conceptual Framework for Studying the Family," in O. A. Oeser and S. B. Hammond (eds.), *Social Structure and Personality in a City,* Routledge, London, 1954.

14. Harry L. Davis and Benny P. Rigaux, "Perceptions of Marital Roles in Decision Processes," *The Journal of Consumer Research,* **1**:51–62, June 1974.

15. See for example, Arch G. Woodside, "Dominance and Conflict in Family Purchasing Decisions," in M. Venkatesan (ed.), *Proceedings of the Third Annual Conference,* Association for Consumer Research, Chicago, 1972, pp. 650–659; Elizabeth H. Wolgast, "Do Husbands or Wives Make the Purchasing Decisions?" *Journal of Marketing,"* **22**:151–158, October 1958.

16. Haley, Overholser & Associates, Inc., *Purchase Influence,* New Canaan, Conn., January 1975.

17. Robert F. Kelly and Michael B. Egan, "Husband and Wife Interaction in a Consumer Decision Process," in Philip R. McDonald (ed.), *Marketing Involvement in Society and the Economy,* American Marketing Association, Chicago, 1969, p. 251.

18. See for example, Arch G. Woodside and John F. Willenborg, "Husband and Wife Interactions and Marketing Decisions," *Southern Journal of Business,* **7**:55, May 1972; and "A Pilot Study of the Roles of Husbands and Wives in Purchasing Decisions," conducted for *Life* magazine by L. Jaffe Associates, Inc., 1965.

19. John Fayerweather, *International Marketing,* 2d ed., Prentice-Hall, Englewood Cliffs, N.J., 1970, p. 25.

20. Douglas J. Dalrymple, Thomas S. Robertson, and Michael Y. Yoshino, "Consumption Behavior across Ethnic Categories," *California Management Review,* **14**:65–70, Fall 1971.

21. Mira Komarovsky, "Class Differences in Family Decision-Making on Expenditures," in Nelson Foote (ed.), *Household Decision-Making,* New York University Press, New York, 1961, pp. 255–265.

22. James F. Engel, David T. Kollat, and Roger D. Blackwell, *Consumer Behavior,* 2d ed., Holt, New York, 1973, pp. 199–200; and Komarovsky, "Class Differences," p. 258.

23. Brent C. Miller, "Intergenerational Patterns of Consumer Behavior," in Mary Jane Schlinger (ed.), *Advances in Consumer Research,* **2**:92–101, Association for Consumer Research, Chicago, 1975.

24. Wolgast, "Do Husbands or Wives," p. 154.

25. Donald H. Granbois, "The Role of Communication in the Family Decision-Making Process," in Stephen A. Greyser (ed.), *Toward Scientific Marketing,* American Marketing Association, Chicago, 1963, pp. 44–57.

26. Komarovsky, "Class Differences," p. 258.

27. Wolgast, "Do Husbands or Wives," p. 154.

28. Donald M. Wolfe, "Power and Authority in the Family," in D. Cartwright (ed.), *Studies in Social Power,* Research Center for Group Dynamics, Ann Arbor, Mich., 1958, p. 109.

29. William F. Kenkel, "Family Interaction in Decision-Making on Spending," in Foote (ed.), *Household Decision Making,* p. 152.

30. Wolgast, "Do Husbands or Wives," p. 154.

31. Kenkel, "Family Interaction," p. 151.

32. Lawrence A. Mayer, "New Questions about the U.S. Population," *Fortune,* February 1971, pp. 122, 124.

33. "Poll Shows Shared Roles in Marriage Are Gaining," *Providence Sunday Journal,* November 27, 1977, p. A-20.

34. "Sex . . . Marriage . . . Divorce—What Women Think Today," *U.S. News & World Report,* October 21, 1974, p. 107.

35. Rena Bartos, "The Moving Target: The Impact of Women's Employment on Consumer Behavior," *Journal of Marketing,* **41**:31, July 1977.

36. "The Working Woman," *Media Decisions,* February 1976, pp. 53–54.

37. "The Working Woman," p. 54.

38. Myra H. Strober and Charles B. Weinberg, "Working Wives and Major Family Expenditures," *Journal of Consumer Research,* **4**:141–147, December 1977.

39. Reprinted from William Lazer and John E. Smallwood, "The Changing Demographics of Women," *Journal of Marketing,* **41**:21–22, July 1977, published by the American Marketing Association.

40. John Scanzoni, "Changing Sex Roles and Emerging Directions in Family Decision Making," *Journal of Consumer Research,* **4**:185–188, December 1977.

41. Isabella C. M. Cunningham and Robert T. Green, "Purchasing Roles in the U.S. Family, 1955 and 1973," *Journal of Marketing,* **38**:64, October 1974.

42. "Marketing Observer," *Business Week,* September 28, 1974, p. 18; and Haley, Overholser & Associates, Inc., *Purchase Influence.*

43. E. B. Weiss, "New Life Styles of 1975–1980 Will Throw Switch on Admen," *Advertising Age,* September 18, 1972, p. 62.

44. See for example Michael B. Mazis and Marilyn Beuttenmuller, "Attitudes toward Women's Liberation and Perception of Advertisements," in M. Venkatesan (ed.), *Proceedings of the Third Annual Conference,* Association for Consumer Research, Chicago, 1972, p. 428; Alice E. Courtney and Sarah W. Lockeretz, "A Woman's Place: An Analysis of the Roles Portrayed by Women in Magazine Advertisements," *Journal of Marketing Research,* **8**:95, February 1971; and Louis C. Wagner and Janis B. Banos, "A Woman's Place: A Follow-up Analysis of the Roles Portrayed by Women in Magazine Advertisements," *Journal of Marketing Research,* **10**:213–214, May 1973.

45. Lawrence H. Wortzel and John M. Frisbie, "Women's Role Portrayal Preferences in Advertisements: An Empirical Study," *Journal of Marketing,* **38**:46, October 1974.

46. William J. Lundstrom and Donald Sciglimpaglia, "Sex Role Portrayals in Advertising," *Journal of Marketing,* **41**:78, July 1977.

47. Ellen Graham, "Advertisers Take Aim at a Neglected Market: The Working Woman," *The Wall Street Journal,* July 5, 1977, pp. 1, 5.

48. "The New Housewife Blues," *Time,* March 14, 1977, pp. 62–70.

49. "Rise of the 'Singles'—40 Million Free Spenders," *U.S. News & World Report,* October 7, 1974, pp. 54–56.

PERSONAL INFLUENCE AND DIFFUSION OF INNOVATIONS

NATURE AND SIGNIFICANCE OF PERSONAL INFLUENCE MODELS OF COMMUNICATION AND INFLUENCE FLOW One-Step Model; Two-Step Flow Model; Multistep Models OPINION LEADERSHIP IN MARKETING Who Are Opinion Leaders?; Why Opinion Leaders Attempt to Influence Others; Why Followers Accept Personal Influence ADOPTION AND DIFFUSION OF INNOVATIONS What Is an Innovation? The Adoption Process; The Diffusion Process MARKETING IMPLICATIONS OF PERSONAL INFLUENCE Identifying and Using Opinion Leaders Directly; Creating Opinion Leaders; Simulating Opinion Leadership; Stimulating Opinion Leadership; Stifling Opinion Leadership

This chapter further investigates the way in which individuals influence each other's behavior as consumers. We shall first describe the nature of influence, and then discuss its significance as evidenced by word-of-mouth communication among individuals. Next, models of the flow of communication will be examined to better understand how personal influence occurs. Then we shall discuss the nature and significance of opinion leadership in marketing, and the characteristics of leaders as well as followers. The concept of personal influence is strongly embodied in the process of adoption and diffusion of innovations; thus this topic will also be examined to understand better its significance to the marketer. Finally, we shall see how the marketer can use the concept of influence to his or her advantage by incorporating opinion leadership as a cornerstone of promotional programs.

NATURE AND SIGNIFICANCE OF PERSONAL INFLUENCE

Personal influence is best described as the effect or change in a person's attitudes or behavior as a result of communication with others. It can occur in a number of ways. The following distinctions can be made to indicate the multidimensional nature of this communication phenomenon:

1. Communication leading to influence may be *source initiated* (by the influencer) or *recipient initiated* (by the influencee).

2. Communication may result in *one-way* or *two-way* influence. That is, the individual may influence while being influenced.

3. Communication resulting in influence may be *verbal* or *visual.*[1]

Personal influence is frequently used synonymously with the term "word-of-mouth" advertising or communication, even though the above classification indicates that they are not the same. Since word-of-mouth is oral communication, it is actually a subset of personal influence; however, we shall use the terms synonymously in this chapter.

Promotional activities conducted by the marketer are not the only or necessarily the most important influences on purchasing behavior. There is evidence that favorable word-of-mouth communication can actually have more influence than the huge sums spent on advertising. Consequently, many companies advertise little and depend, instead, on word-of-mouth promotion. As the president of Loehmann's, one of the country's most successful retailers of women's clothing, explains, "There's nothing like a woman's mouth."[2] Of course, this dictum should be broadened to include men as well. Here are some examples of word-of-mouth advertising's impact:

In-depth interviews on buyer motivations by Ernest Dichter's organization frequently found that friends, experts, or relatives told the individual about the product—and that is why the product was purchased. At times, the influence of "recommenders" ran as high as 80 percent.[3]

A study of durable goods purchases found that word-of-mouth was the major information source, with over 50 percent of the sample turning to friends for advice.[4]

Among male and female students at a large southern university, nearly 50 percent discussed clothing brands, styles, retail outlets, and prices with their friends.[5]

Word-of-mouth advertising is very important in the motion-picture industry. For example, much of the success of *Star Wars,* the biggest grossing movie in history, has been attributed to the fact that word-of-mouth advertising "hit like lightning."

The marketer frequently tries to create a "synthetic" word-of-mouth program by using celebrities in advertising campaigns. These spokespeople enter our homes via the media and speak to us as if it were a one-to-one conversation. This simulated personal influence may nevertheless be very effective. There are two excellent illustrations of the way in which celebrities may affect our behavior as consumers:

When Clark Gable took off his shirt in a 1934 movie *It Happened One Night,* he revealed a bare chest. As a result, undershirt sales are said to have dropped 75 percent that year.[7]

On December 19, 1973, Johnny Carson suggested in his "Tonight Show" monologue that there was an acute shortage of toilet paper in the United States. (His source was a Wisconsin congressman who had actually been referring only to the cheaper federal government issue of toilet paper.) As a result, people dashed to their supermarkets to stock up; and by December 23, there actually was a shortage of the better toilet paper![8]

265

PERSONAL
INFLUENCE
AND
DIFFUSION OF
INNOVATIONS

It is clear that personal influence—whether actual or synthetic—can be quite convincing. The marketer is vitally interested in this process because a product's success appears dependent on it. It is very important, therefore, that mostly favorable, not unfavorable, communications take place. As one study of the spread of a new food product in a married students' housing complex showed, exposure to favorable word-of-mouth communication increased the probability of purchase, while exposure to unfavorable comments decreased the probability.[9]

Why is word-of-mouth communication so strong? There seem to be three main reasons for its dominant position in relation to impersonal media:

1. Consumers view word-of-mouth as reliable and trustworthy information which can help people to make better buying decisions.

2. In contrast to the mass media, personal contacts can provide social support and give a stamp of approval to a purchase.

3. The information provided is often backed up by social group pressure to force compliance with recommendations.[10]

In order to understand better the way in which personal influence and word-of-mouth advertising occur, several models of the communication process will be presented.

MODELS OF COMMUNICATION AND INFLUENCE FLOW
Personal influence is necessarily dependent upon the process of communication. The marketer may view the situation in several ways: as a one-step process; as a two-step flow of communication; or as a multiple-step model of interaction. Let's examine these various interpretations of the way in which influence results from communication.

One-Step Model
For years marketers operated under the assumptions contained in the one-step or one-way model of communication. In this model, which is portrayed in Figure 12-1, communication is represented as a one-way process flowing from the marketer to consumers. Notice that this model of communication assumes the marketer is directing the appeal to *each* consumer expecting that the consumer will: (1) notice the advertisement, (2) be informed, persuaded, or reminded by it, and (3) buy the product or service.[11]

This model has been criticized, however, for its oversimplification. First of all, few messages actually reach consumers, and those that do are not likely to elicit a response directly. Product sales are influenced by many other marketing and extraneous variables in addition to the promotional communication.

Because of these drawbacks, communications researchers turned to a more sophisticated explanation of the influence process—one that recognized the influence not only of impersonal channels (such as radio, television, and magazines), but also personal channels of communication and influence. This was the development of the two-step flow theory of communication.

Two-Step Flow Model

The process of communication and influence has been found not to be an exclusively direct flow as had been originally supposed. Instead it appears that influence occurs in a two-step flow, moving first from the mass media directly to influentials or *opinion leaders* who then through interpersonal networks pass on what they have seen or heard to their associates. The two-step model is illustrated in Figure 12-2.

The two-step model represents an improvement over the one-step scheme because it recognizes the influence of interpersonal contact. However, it also has certain limitations. Among the biggest problems are: (1) it suggests that an absolute leader exists for each informal group, when actually all group members have some amount of opinion leadership; (2) information is assumed to flow only from the mass media to opinion leaders who disseminate it to followers—actually followers are also in touch with mass media, but perhaps not to the same degree as leaders; and (3) it is not always *influence* that is transmitted interpersonally, but in some cases simply information, which may be relatively free of influence.[12]

Thus, the two-step communication model has some merit, but it implies a passive audience and active, information-seeking opinion leaders. Because of these limitations, many communications researchers now suggest a multistep interaction model as a more accurate representation of personal influence.

Multistep Models

Researchers have shown that audiences are not simply passive receivers of communication. Instead they have been found in several studies to be active

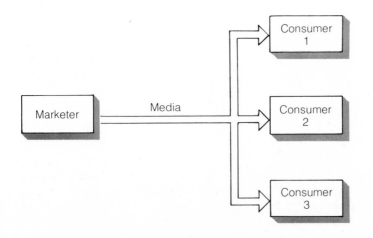

FIGURE 12-1
One-step model of communication.

seekers of information. Many audience members act as transmitters and receivers of information. It has, furthermore, been suggested that the flow of communication may take place through three or more stages.

267

PERSONAL
INFLUENCE
AND
DIFFUSION OF
INNOVATIONS

Consider the following examples of the different directions that a verbal flow of communication and personal influence may take between a source and a receiver:

1. Source-initiated, one-way influence (this is most typical of the two-step flow model): "Jim told me how good his B.F. Goodrich radials are, so I decided to buy a set."

2. Receiver-initiated, one-way influence: "I asked Jim what kind of tire he recommends."

3. Source-initiated, two-way influence: "I showed Susan our new Jenn-Air range. She really wants to buy one when her old stove gives out. Her interest made me feel better about our range's higher price."

4. Receiver-initiated, two-way influence: "I asked Carol what she knew about electric ranges. We had an interesting discussion of the features of different brands."

Of course, we could add additional levels to the flow and a visual mode of communication as well. The point is that obviously the communication process and flow of influence is much more involved than previously imagined. In the next section we will more closely examine the nature of personal influence as effected through opinion leadership.

OPINION LEADERSHIP IN MARKETING

Opinion leaders were defined in Chapter 11 as those people who are able, in a given situation, to exert personal influence. They are the ones to whom others look for advice and information. Now let us describe these people more specifically.

The term opinion leader is perhaps unfortunate because it tends to connote people of high status who make major decisions for the rest of us. In the marketing context, such a designation is unfortunate because it errone-

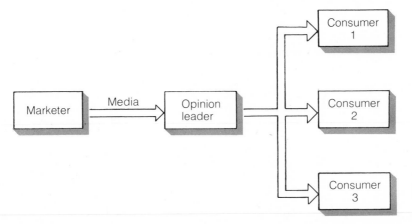

FIGURE 12-2
Two-step model of communication.

ously suggests an absolute leader whom others seek to follow. In effect, opinion leadership is a relative concept, and the opinion leader may not be much more influential than his followers.[13]

Nevertheless, opinion leaders can informally and subtly affect the behavior of others toward products, either positively or negatively. If they like a product or service they can help to assure its success; and if they do not like it, they can contribute to its failure. It all depends on the verbal and/or visual communication that flows between them and others whom they influence.

For communication of marketing information through two- or multistep flow models, opinion leadership is important and is found at all levels in society. That is, consumers tend to be influenced by those who are members of the same groups, people very much like themselves. Thus, every status level and every group will have opinion leaders, with the flow of influence being generally horizontal within them. However, the fact that opinion leaders are found in all strata of society does not necessarily mean that they are equally effective or important to the marketer at each social level. In fact, personal influence appears to be more operative and to have greater importance and effectiveness at higher-income and status levels.[14] These, then, are the levels which the marketer is often more concerned about reaching.

Who Are Opinion Leaders?

Because personal influence of opinion leaders is quite significant, marketers are obviously interested in trying to reach such influentials. To do so, however, requires that they first be identified and segmented. Perhaps they may then be reached with promotional messages, and participate in additional communication and influence with their fellow group members.

CHARACTERISTICS Numerous studies have been conducted attempting to identify opinion leader characteristics. The research is not conclusive, but we have some understanding of the opinion leader's profile:

1. Opinion leaders have approximately the same social class position as nonleaders, although they may have higher social status within the class.[15] This does not mean that personal influence does not flow across different class lines, but it is likely to be infrequent and of a visual nature rather than verbal.

2. Opinion leaders have greater exposure to mass media that are relevant to their area of interest.[16] For example, opinion leaders for women's fashions could be expected to have higher exposure to such magazines as *Vogue* and *Glamour.* Similarly, automobile opinion leaders might be expected to read *Motor Trend* or *Hot Rod.* Exposure to relevant mass media provides them with information useful in enhancing their leadership potential.

3. Opinion leaders have greater interest and knowledge of the area of influence than do nonleaders. This finding is closely related to their greater media exposure. Of course, knowledge is not a prerequisite for opinion leader influence. Undoubtedly much influence takes place by those who are ignorant of the topic of conversation.

4. Opinion leaders are more gregarious than nonleaders. This finding is logical

given that they must interact with those whom they influence. Thus, opinion leaders are generally more sociable or companionable.

269

PERSONAL
INFLUENCE
AND
DIFFUSION OF
INNOVATIONS

5. Opinion leaders are higher on innovativeness than are nonleaders. This does not mean, however, that they are *innovators* (the first people to purchase a new item). In fact, innovators and opinion leaders have been found to have differing characteristics and life styles in several studies. In the fashion market, for instance, the innovator is seen as an adventurer who is the earliest visual communicator of the newest styles aimed at the mass of fashion consumers.[17] The opinion leader, however, may be characterized more as an "editor" of fashions, who defines and endorses appropriate standards.

6. Opinion leaders are also more familiar with and loyal to group standards and values than are nonleaders. This refers to the fact that opinion leaders are vested with leadership authority by group members, and in order to maintain this position, the individual has to reflect underlying norms and values for that area of consumption leadership. The clothing influential, for instance, cannot be too far ahead of or behind fashion, but must reflect the current norms in clothing.

ARE THERE "GENERAL" OPINION LEADERS? The question of whether generalized opinion leaders exist for a wide variety of products as opposed to specialized opinion leaders for each product has been the subject of much debate. Although research is often conflicting, it appears that there is *moderate* opinion leadership overlap across product categories; that is, general opinion leaders do appear to exist to some extent. One of the keys to this question seems to be the interest patterns of opinion leaders, with highest overlap existing among product categories involving similar interests.[18]

The existence of generalized opinion leaders, or more precisely, opinion leadership overlap, does not mean, however, that such individuals are opinion leaders for *all* product categories. One study of seven product-interest areas, for example, found that only about 3 percent of the respondents were opinion leaders for at least five of the items.[19]

OPINION LEADERSHIP IS SITUATIONAL In the absence of a standardized, clear-cut opinion leader profile applying across all products, and where influencers and influencees seem to be so much alike, how is the opinion leader distinguished from those who follow? It has been suggested that influence is related to the following factors:

1. *The personification of certain values* (who one is). Thus, individuals who closely represent or personify group values are likely to be opinion leaders. For example, if some particular clothing style is valued by the group, the individual most closely representing this is likely to be influential.

2. *Competence* (what one knows). An individual who is very knowledgeable about some topic valued by the group will probably be influential.

3. *Strategic social location* (whom one knows inside and outside the group). For example, an individual who is available and active in the interpersonal communication process in her sorority will have a better chance for a leadership position.[20]

Thus, influence takes place because opinion leaders personify group norms, exhibit competence, and are accessible with active communication among others.

Because such leadership is situational and does not have a consistent pattern of characteristics across products, marketers might investigate the three characteristics cited above with regard to those who consume particular goods or services. In this way they may uncover specific patterns which could then guide marketing strategies.

Why Opinion Leaders Attempt to Influence Others

Consumers, generally, do not speak about products or services unless they expect to derive some kind of satisfaction from the activity. We can categorize four reasons why opinion leaders engage in word-of-mouth communication about products or services:

1. *Product-involvement*—Use of a product or service may create a tension that may need to be reduced by way of talk, recommendation, and enthusiasm to provide relief. For example, consumers often are fascinated by new items and feel they must tell someone about how good a product they've found.

2. *Self-involvement*—In this case the emphasis is more on ways the influencer can gratify certain emotional needs. Product talk can achieve such goals as the following:

Gaining attention—people can have something to say in a conversation by talking about products rather than people or ideas.

Showing connoisseurship—talk about certain products can show one is "in the know," and has good judgment.

Feeling like a pioneer—the speaker likes to identify with the newness and uniqueness of products and their pioneering manufacturers.

Having inside information—the speaker is able to show how much more he or she knows about the product and its manufacturer than the listener (and thus how clever the speaker is).

Suggesting status—talking about products with social status may elevate the speaker to the level of its users.

Spreading the gospel—the speaker may be able to convert the listener to using the product.

Seeking confirmation—the more followers accept his or her advice about the product, the more assured the speaker feels about his or her own decision.

Asserting superiority—recommending products to listeners can help the speaker gain leadership and test the extent to which others will follow.

3. *Other-involvement*—In this case product talk fills the need to "give" something to the listener, to share one's happiness with the influencee, or to express care, love, or friendship.

4. *Message-involvement*—Talking may also be stimulated by great interest in the messages used to present the product. For example, advertising that is highly original and entertaining may be the topic of conversation, especially

since most of us feel we are experts on effective advertising and can thus speak as critics.[21]

271

PERSONAL
INFLUENCE
AND
DIFFUSION OF
INNOVATIONS

Why Followers Accept Personal Influence

The marketer would certainly want to know the situational attributes under which opinion leadership will most likely occur so that he or she could actively cultivate the process. There are numerous product, individual, and group characteristics that can be expected to influence the acceptance of opinion leadership by followers. Only a few of these will be cited here. [2]

Product characteristics are important in judging the significance of personal influence. For example, when products are highly visible or conspicuous (such as clothing as opposed to laundry detergents) they are more susceptible to personal influence. Products that can be tried or tested and compared against objective criteria are less suceptible to personal influence than those that cannot be tried. Product complexity may also give rise to the occurrence of personal influence, as would a product that is high on the amount of risk which consumers perceive to be associated with its purchase.

Use of these four factors to evaluate products helps the marketer to determine when opinion leadership is apt to be strong. For example, most food products would be subject to rather little opinion leadership while small appliances would be subject to much more personal influence. More will be said about these product characteristics under the topic of diffusion.

Individual consumer characteristics and group influences are also important in determining the extent to which opinion leadership will be operative. For example, individuals who are other-directed look to other people for behavioral guidance, in contrast to those who are inner-directed and rely on their own value systems for direction. Also, individuals who face new life experiences (such as newlyweds or retirees) may be very receptive to information and consequently be quite susceptible to personal influence. In addition, those who aspire to membership in particular groups are receptive to personal influence and may emulate the behavior of group members. A final factor to be mentioned that affects acceptance of opinion leadership is the individual's personality. For example, some individuals are more persuasible than others.

ADOPTION AND DIFFUSION OF INNOVATIONS

The adoption and innovation diffusion processes will be discussed in this section to illustrate the way in which communication and interpersonal influence work with new products.

What Is an Innovation?

New-product innovation is an essential element of the dynamic American economy. As new and better products are discovered, they are launched in the marketplace and their fate is determined by votes of consumers through their purchase or rejection.

The term "new" however, is not at all clear in its relation to products and services. Several criteria may be used to assess the newness of products. One concerns the *extent of difference from existing products.* For example, some feel that a new product must be quite different from existing products (although this definition is obviously difficult to measure). The Federal Trade Commission (FTC) is representative of this view as it suggests that a product may properly be called new only if it is either entirely new or has been changed in a functionally significant and substantial respect.[23] Package changes or other modifications that are functionally insignificant or insubstantial do not qualify.

A second way new products may be classified is by the *length of time on the market.* The FTC, for example, advises that the word "new" be limited to 6 months from when the product enters regular distribution after test marketing.[24]

A third way in which new products may be categorized is according to the *sales penetration level.* Marketers frequently refer to products as innovations if they have achieved less than 10 percent of the market potential in a given geographic location.[25]

Fourth, products may be categorized as new depending on *consumer perception of the items.* For example, one source defines an innovation as "any idea, practice, or material artifact perceived to be new by the relevant adopting unit."[26] Although this approach is typical of that taken by many researchers, it too, presents a number of operational difficulties.

In an attempt to overcome the weaknesses in the above approaches, (especially the dichotomy of products being either new, or not new), a continuum or range of newness has been suggested based on the product's effect on established consumption patterns. Under this conception three categories of innovation are classified as described below:

1. *Continuous innovations* have the least disrupting influence on established consumption patterns. Product alteration is involved, rather than the establishment of a totally new product. Examples of products that are representative of this situation are fluoride toothpaste, new-model automobile changeovers, and menthol cigarettes.

2. *Dynamically continuous innovations* have more disrupting effects than continuous innovations, although they do not generally alter established patterns. It may involve the creation of new products or the alteration of existing items. Examples of this would include electric toothbrushes, electric autos, wall-size television screens, and videotelephones.

3. *Discontinuous innovations* involve the establishment of a new product with new behavior patterns. Examples of this situation would include television, computers, and automobiles.[27]

The Adoption Process

Before we examine how products spread among population groups, we need to look at the process as it relates to individuals. The acceptance and continued use of a product or brand by an individual is referred to as "adoption." Figure 12-3 presents a simplified diagram of the adoption process. This model consists of the following stages:

1. *Awareness* At this stage the potential adopter finds out about the existence of a product, but has very little information and no well-formed attitudes about it.

2. *Comprehension* This stage represents the consumer's knowledge and understanding of what the product is and can do.

3. *Attitude* Here the consumer develops favorable or unfavorable behavioral predispositions toward the product. Termination of the adoption process is likely at this stage if attitudes are not favorable toward the product.

4. *Legitimation* Here the consumer becomes convinced that the product should be adopted. This stage is predicated upon favorable attitudes toward the innovation, and the consumer may use information already gathered as well as additional information in order to reach a decision.

5. *Trial* If possible, the consumer tests or tries the product to determine its utility. Trial may take place cognitively, that is, whereby the individual vicariously uses the product in a hypothetical situation; or it may be actually used in a limited or total way, depending on the innovation's nature.

6. *Adoption* At this stage the consumer determines whether or not to use the product in a full-scale way. Continued purchase and/or use of the item fulfills the adoption process.[28]

Thus, adoption is seen to be a sequence of events through which

273

PERSONAL
INFLUENCE
AND
DIFFUSION OF
INNOVATIONS

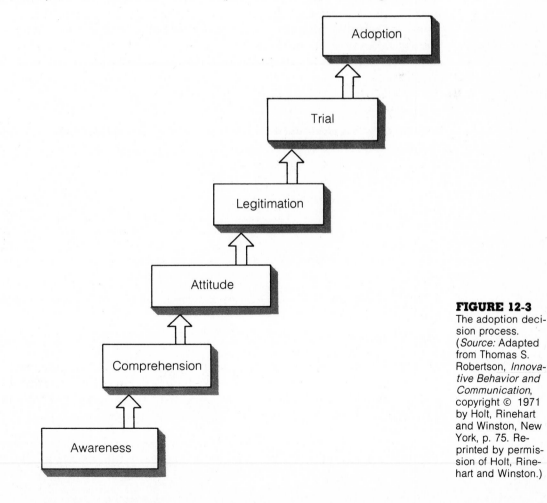

FIGURE 12-3
The adoption decision process. (*Source:* Adapted from Thomas S. Robertson, *Innovative Behavior and Communication*, copyright © 1971 by Holt, Rinehart and Winston, New York, p. 75. Reprinted by permission of Holt, Rinehart and Winston.)

individual consumers pass over a period of time. Some consumers pass through these stages early in a product's life while others may be much later.

The significance of the adoption process to the marketer is two-fold. First, not all consumers pass through the adoption process with the same speed—some move swiftly while others proceed more slowly. Second, the marketer's communication forms vary in their effectiveness over the different stages in the adoption process. These points can be important in assisting the marketer to develop an effective promotional program. It has been found, for example, that for early stages of the adoption process, the mass media appear to be most effective in creating awareness; thus, the marketer would design awareness- and interest-generating messages to be transmitted by such impersonal sources. At later stages in the adoption process, however, personal sources of information appear to become more important; so the marketer would desire to have effective personal selling and word-of-mouth communications at these points. This indicates then, that as consumers move through the adoption process, the amount of mass-media advertising might be decreased while the amount of personal selling is increased.

The adoption process may not be completed by the individual, which means that the innovation will not be adopted. Several factors that may lead to an incomplete adoption process are listed in Table 12-1. The marketer should take care to see that the marketing problems leading to consumer failure to complete the adoption process are minimized.

TABLE 12-1

POTENTIAL CAUSES OF INCOMPLETED ADOPTION PROCESS

Acceptance Process Stage	Marketing Organization Causes of Incompleted Processes	Consumer Causes of Incompleted Processes
Adoption	Failure to develop new products and improve old products	Replaced by another innovation
Trial	Behavioral response not specified in communications	Alternative equally as good
	Poor distribution system	Innovation not available
Legitimation	Poor source effect of communications	Peer-group pressure against adoption
		Laws regulating use of innovation
Attitude	Communication not persuasive	Complacency
		Suspended judgment
Comprehension	Communication difficult to understand	Selective retention
Awareness	Poorly used or too little communication	Selective exposure
		Selective perception

Source: Gerald Zaltman and Ronald Stiff, ''Theories of Diffusion'' in Scott Ward and Thomas S. Robertson, *Consumer Behavior: Theoretical Sources,* © 1973, p. 451. Reprinted by permission of Prentice-Hall, Inc., Englewood Cliffs, N.J.

275

PERSONAL
INFLUENCE
AND
DIFFUSION OF
INNOVATIONS

The Diffusion Process

In this section we shall discuss the nature of the process by which innovations spread. The marketer is vitally interested in this because it determines the success or failure of any new product brought to market. The marketer usually desires to secure the largest amount of adoption within the shortest period of time. Whether such an accelerated strategy is chosen (as is the case for most continuous innovations), or one that moves more slowly (as might be taken with discontinuous innovations), the marketer needs to understand the diffusion process so that he can properly manage the spread of the new product or service. While there are many limitations and weaknesses in much of the diffusion research that has been conducted by scholars, it has helped us understand the communication process for innovations and the social structure within which this occurs.[29]

We should first distinguish the concept of diffusion from that of adoption. As we saw earlier the adoption process is an *individual* phenomenon relating to the sequence of stages through which an individual passes from first hearing about a product to finally adopting it. The diffusion process, however, refers to a *group* phenomenon, indicating how an innovation spreads among consumers. The diffusion process, of course, necessarily involves the adoption process of many individuals over time.

Perhaps the best marketing-oriented definition of the diffusion process is "the adoption of new products and services over time by consumers within social systems as encouraged by marketing activities."[30] This definition recognizes the various components of the process which are important in the spread of an innovation. Now let's look more closely at diffusion and what it means for the marketer.

CATEGORIES OF ADOPTERS Since we know that people will not all adopt an innovation at the same time, we might classify consumers on the basis of time of adoption. In so doing we will also discover that those who adopt new products at approximately the same point in time have similar characteristics. Armed with such knowledge, the marketer may thus be able to segment a market by adopter type, and aim strategies, in turn, at each group over a period of time. Five adopter categories have been identified: innovator, early adopter, early majority, late majority, and laggard. Each of these groups' characteristics is summarized below.[31] The percentages that follow represent the proportion of all who adopt an innovation, which may be only a small proportion of the total market.

Innovators (2.5 percent of a market) are the first to adopt new products. They are quite venturesome and are eager to try new ideas. They have more risk capital (both material and social) and can afford to take calculated risks. Innovators are well educated, come from well-established families, and are cosmopolitan, having friends outside the community. Their sources of information also transcend the local community, incorporating other innovators and impersonal and scientific sources. They may belong to state, regional, or national organizations, and are respected for their success by local community members.

Robertson has distilled twenty-one studies of new product diffusion and developed a profile of the innovative consumer. Because the studies span various product categories, sampling populations, research methodologies, and definitions of innovation, the picture they provide of the consumer innovator must be viewed with caution. Nevertheless, Table 12-2 summarizes these characteristics.

Early adopters (13.5 percent of a market) are the second group to adopt an innovation. This group is more socially integrated locally than are innovators and has the greatest degree of opinion leadership in most social systems. They are likely to hold positions of leadership within the community and are respected as good sources of information and advice about the innovation. For this reason, they are very important in speeding the diffusion process. They watch the innovators and adopt when the innovation appears success-ful. They are just ahead of the average individual in innovativeness, so they are able to serve as role-models for others in the market.

Early adopters have less risk capital than do innovators. They are younger than later adopters, higher in social status, and above average in education. Early adopters subscribe to more magazines than later adopters (yet not as many as innovators). They also have been found to have the greatest contact with salespeople.

How important are innovators and early adopters in the success of new products? Quite significant, as General Electric has found in studies of its appliances. One study of a new cordless electric clothes brush, for example,

TABLE 12-2

A PROFILE OF THE CONSUMER INNOVATOR

Findings for the Innovator vs. Noninnovator

Demographic factors
  Higher income levels
  Often younger
  Better educated
  Higher occupational status

Social interaction factors
  Greater participation in friendship and organizational groups
  An opinion leader
  Socially mobile
  Favorably disposed to innovation

Attitudinal and perceptual factors
  More venturesome and perceives less risk in buying new products
  Perceives himself as an innovator
  Has favorable attitudes toward new products

Communication behavior
  Reads more print media

Consumption patterns
  Higher usage rate for the innovative product category
  Marked willingness to buy new products

Source: Thomas Robertson, *Innovative Behavior and Communications*, Holt, New York, 1971, pp. 100–110.

obtained data from warranty cards for the new product and through personal interviews with early buyers. GE found that these early buyers directly influenced other consumers by talking about the product and by having it in their homes.[32]

Moreover when the early adopters begin buying something new, retailers see the product moving and are likely to advertise it more heavily and feature it prominently in stores. This can enhance the retailer's image as an innovative store by handling "hot" new products.

The *early majority* (34 percent of a market) are the next group to adopt an innovation, and are the most deliberate of all adopter categories. They may consider an innovation for some time before adopting; thus their adoption period is longer than that of the two previous groups. They adopt an innovation just before the average member of a social system, which puts them in a crucial position to legitimize the new idea for others.

The early majority are slightly above average in age and education, and social and economic status. Although they belong to formal organizations, they are likely to be active members rather than leaders. They rely more heavily on informal sources of information than do earlier adopters. The early majority subscribe to fewer magazines and journals than do previous adopters but have considerable contact with salespeople. They are frequently the neighbors and friends of early adopters.

The *late majority* (34 percent of a market) adopt an innovation just after the average consumer in the market place. This group can be described as "skeptical" about new ideas, and may yield only because of economic necessity or increasing social pressures. The late majority are above average in age and below average in education, social status, and income. They belong to few formal organizations and exhibit little opinion leadership with communication patterns oriented primarily toward other late majority members in their neighborhood. There is little use of the mass media (e.g., fewer magazines are taken) but heavy reliance on informal sources of information and influence.

Laggards (16 percent of a market) are the last group to adopt an innovation. They are tradition-bound, with decisions based on what has been done in the past. Laggards are suspicious of innovations and perhaps of those who offer them. The length of the adoption process for this group is quite long; and when adoption finally comes, a new innovation has likely superseded the previous innovation.

Laggards have the least education, the lowest social status and income, and are the oldest of any adopter category. They are the most local in orientation, which tends to be their immediate neighborhood, and they communicate mostly with other laggards, who are their main sources of information. Laggards possess almost no opinion leadership, have little participation in formal organizations, and subscribe to few magazines.

Although these categories and descriptions may vary for different products, they do provide the marketer with a helpful framework for managing an innovation's diffusion. One of the most important facets of the work in this regard will be to develop a sound promotional strategy. Clearly, adopter characteristics differ greatly among categories, and this requires that the

277

PERSONAL
INFLUENCE
AND
DIFFUSION OF
INNOVATIONS

marketer tailor promotions to appeal to each group over time. Table 12-3 illustrates the kinds of promotional approaches that appear to be most effective for each adopter category.

FACTORS INFLUENCING THE RATE OF DIFFUSION The rate of an innovation's diffusion could range from several weeks to several decades, depending upon consumers' acceptance of the item which, in turn, is determined by how the innovation is perceived by consumers. There are five product characteristics that seem to influence the rate and extent of adoption of an innovation: (1) relative advantage, (2) compatibility, (3) complexity, (4) trialability, and (5) observability. These five characteristics are described below.[33]

Relative advantage is the degree to which an innovation is perceived as superior to preceding products or those with which it will compete. This might be reflected in lower cost, longer life, easier maintenance, or other measures. Products that have a strong relative advantage will be adopted more rapidly.

Compatibility is the degree to which an innovation is consistent with existing

TABLE 12-3

HOW PROMOTION VARIES BY STAGE IN THE DIFFUSION PROCESS

Adopter Category	Promotional Approach
Innovator	Technical or scientific information about the innovation made available in special-interest or professional media and at trade meetings. Appeals should stress the excitement of trying something completely new and revolutionary. Salespeople should concentrate on people who are relatively young and who have high social status, incomes, and education.
Early adopters	Advertisements should emphasize the prestige of owning the item. Testimonials by respected people may be particularly effective.
Early majority	Appeals should concentrate on materials designed for this group's evaluation stage in the adoption process. Salespeople should stress that others, especially the relevant opinion leaders, have adopted the innovation. Make use of peer social pressure with the "house party" sales technique.
Late majority	Advertising appeals should overcome skepticism by making liberal use of such reassuring terms as: "Guaranteed by Good Housekeeping," "Produced by the makers of . . . ," or "Tested and approved by the . . . Laboratory." Salespeople are important and should concentrate on consumers whose income and social status are below average. Proper product demonstration is a must when this group is at the trial stage.
Laggards	Best to ignore them, in most instances

Source: Adapted from Gerald Zaltman, *Marketing: Contributions from the Behavioral Sciences*, pp. 51–53 © 1965 by Harcourt Brace Jovanovich, Inc., and reprinted with their permission.

consumer values and past experiences of adopters. Acceptance will be retarded for new products that are not compatible with consumers' norms.

Complexity refers to how difficult the innovation is to understand and use. Diffusion will tend to be slowed for more complex items.

Trialability (or divisibility) is the extent to which an innovation may be tried on a limited basis. Where an item cannot be sampled on a small, less expensive scale, diffusion is retarded.

Observability (or communicability) refers to the conspicuousness of the innovation. New products that are highly visible in social situations are those that will be communicated most readily to other adopters.

The marketing implications of these characteristics are readily apparent. First of all, an innovation should exhibit some clear-cut advantages. In addition, products might be designed so that they could be evaluated on a limited basis (for example, small trial sizes of a new toothpaste). With some products, however, such as automobiles and air conditioners, trial is more difficult. Nevertheless, auto test drives (or in some cases even extended car loans) and free home trials for appliances have been offered. Products should also be designed with minimum complexity and maximum compatibility (these also may make up part of the product's relative advantage). These features should then be stressed in promotional messages to potential adopters. If complexity and noncompatibility are inherent in the innovation, promotion should seek to overcome these limitations (for example, by stressing warranties or product-servicing facilities).

ARE THERE GENERALIZED INNOVATORS? It was concluded earlier that there is a moderate amount of opinion leadership overlap across product categories, with the greatest extent involving related product areas. A similar conclusion can be made with regard to innovators. There is no "superinnovator" who plays this part across a host of products. However, within a product category and perhaps between related product categories some innovative overlap can be expected to occur.[34]

MARKETING IMPLICATIONS OF PERSONAL INFLUENCE
In this section we shall suggest various marketing strategies to use effectively the process of personal influence. Two cautions are in order, however. First, it should be remembered that opinion leadership is not equally active for all products—some products are very prone to personal influence while others are not. Second, it may be difficult and expensive to control the process of personal influence.

Kotler and Zaltman suggest that the marketer will want to address several questions in targeting prospects for a new product: (1) the target market's innovative and early adoption propensities, (2) its heavy volume potential, (3) its susceptibility to influence, and (4) the cost of reaching this group. This will require a systematic procedure utilizing information from concept testing, product testing, test marketing, and so forth.[35] If the marketer finds that personal influence is potentially strong for the product, then he may desire to guide the process. There are several strategies which might be adopted: (1)

279

PERSONAL
INFLUENCE
AND
DIFFUSION OF
INNOVATIONS

identifying and using opinion leaders directly, (2) creating opinion leaders, (3) simulating opinion leaders, (4) stimulating opinion leadership, and (5) stifling opinion leadership.

Identifying and Using Opinion Leaders Directly

There are two major difficulties in pursuing this strategy. First of all, locating opinion leaders who are influential over a particular product is most complicated. Characteristics of opinion leaders, which were discussed earlier in this chapter, make it clear that they are not easy to isolate. Moreover, for the consumer-goods marketer the task is likely to be hard because of the large number of consumers. In order to identify them, the marketer would need to conduct difficult and expensive research on his own product. Second, there is evidence that in some cases opinion leaders may not be reached by certain advertising media any more effectively than the average consumer in a market.[36] Thus, direct appeal to personal influence may not always be the most effective approach.

If the direct approach is decided upon, however, the first step is to identify opinion leaders. There are several ways in which this may be done. One set of techniques involves measuring the degree of opinion leadership among consumers. Figure 12-4 presents a questionnaire that has been effectively used to ascertain the degree of consumers' opinion leadership through survey research. In this instance individuals would evaluate themselves on this characteristic.

Another approach to measuring opinion leadership involves the *sociometric* technique, which consists of asking group members to whom they go for advice and information about an idea. Finally, *key informants* in a group may be asked to designate the opinion leaders.

One of the best ways to identify those who may be influential for a company's product is to examine purchase records. For instance, many products today use a warranty card return system as in the General Electric clothes brush example cited earlier. With this approach the marketer could identify specific individuals who are early adopters of the product and the characteristics of these buyers. Of course, one disadvantage of relying exclusively on this approach is that not all buyers return these cards.

Study of past purchases may indicate which consumers are most likely to adopt new products. For example, by knowing that the most likely adopter of new telephone-system services, such as the videophone, would occur among those who had previously bought such equipment as Touch-Tone® phones, extension phones, and color phones, the telephone company might assess available records to determine the households in the service area which would have the greatest likelihood of adopting the new equipment.

Names and addresses of potential opinion leaders might be gathered not only from purchase records, but also from sponsorship of consumer contests, use of reader-service cards in magazines, and similar activities. Once names of potential opinion leaders have been secured, the marketer is in a position to utilize their influence effectively. For example, he could promote directly to them. They may be reached through direct-mail advertising, if the cost is not prohibitive. They could also be provided with inside information about new products so that they are in a strategic position to pass along this information to others.

Their purchasing habits might also be monitored so that trends and adoption patterns among this group are readily spotted. For example, Hollywood Vassarette has used this approach to predict fashion trends for women's intimate apparel.[37]

This group could also be provided with free samples (if an inexpensive product), discounts off the price of new products, or loan of the item (in the case of expensive durables). At one time, Chrysler Corporation offered one of its luxury automobile models for a trial period to professionals such as doctors and lawyers. Also Lincoln Continental dealers in one city recruited a select group of opinion leaders to drive the car at a premiere showing of the new model.[38]

Another approach that has been successfully used is to have opinion leaders model or sell the product. For example, many clothing stores have established "fashion advisory boards" on which high school or college opinion leaders are placed. These fashion leaders may act as retail salespeo-

281

PERSONAL
INFLUENCE
AND
DIFFUSION OF
INNOVATIONS

1. In general, do you like to talk about _____ with your friends?

    Yes _____   No _____

2. Would you say *you give very little information, an average amount of information,* or *a great deal of information* about _____ to your friends?

    You give very little information ...._____
    You give an average amount of information ...._____
    You give a great deal of information ...._____

3. During the *past six months,* have *you told anyone* about some _____?

    Yes _____   No _____

4. Compared with your circle of friends, are you *less likely, about as likely,* or *more likely* to be asked for advice about _____?

    Less likely to be asked ...._____
    About as likely to be asked ...._____
    More likely to be asked ...._____

5. If you and your friends were to discuss _____, what part would you be most likely to play? Would you *mainly listen* to your friends' ideas or would *you try to convince them* of your ideas?

    You mainly listen to your friends' ideas ...._____
    You try to convince them of your ideas ...._____

6. Which of these happens more often? Do *you tell your* friends about some _____, or do *they tell you* about some_____?

    You tell them about _____ _____
    They tell you about some _____ _____

7. Do you have the feeling that you are generally regarded by your friends and neighbors as a good source of advice about _____?

    Yes _____   No _____

FIGURE 12-4
Opinion leadership scale. (*Source:* Charles W. King and John O. Summers, "Overlap of Opinion Leadership Across Consumer Product Categories," *Journal of Marketing,* **7:**45, February 1970, published by the American Marketing Association.)

ple for the store or simply model the store's newest fashions for customers. These fashion board members may also appear in store advertising, which should generate additional opinion leadership, especially among the youth market.

Creating Opinion Leaders

When opinion leaders cannot be easily identified or used, it may be possible to "create" them. Such an approach is frequently attempted by aluminum siding and swimming pool manufacturers. Companies will typically select homeowners (especially those with central locations in their neighborhoods) and induce them to buy the product at a very low price if they will then demonstrate the product to others. The homeowner opinion leader is, in effect, being created by the company.

Another successful use of this technique was reported in the introduction of a new pop record. The task was to transform an unknown song recorded by an unknown singer into a hit. The initial step was to seek out social leaders among the relevant buying public—high school students. Names of class presidents, class secretaries, sports captains, and cheerleaders selected from geographically diverse high schools were obtained. Although these were social leaders, prior to the project these students would not likely have been classified as opinion leaders for records because of their low ownership of this item. Next, the students were contacted by mail and invited to join a select panel to assist a manufacturer in evaluating new records. They were to receive free records and were encouraged to discuss their choices with friends.

This inexpensive experiment provided very successful results. Several records reached the top ten charts in the trial cities, while failing to make the top ten selections in any other cities. Thus, without contacting any radio stations or record stores, records were pulled through the channels of distribution and made into hits.[39]

A number of companies have attempted to create opinion leadership by getting the product into the hands of people who have a great deal of public contact or exposure. Ford Motor Company has successfully utilized this approach. For example, when the Mustang was introduced, college newspaper editors, disc jockeys, and airline stewardesses were loaned Mustangs, largely on the presumption that they were influentials with regard to automobiles. Again, when the Pinto was launched, Ford placed the new car with numerous marketing professors and their classes across the country for the purpose of research projects to be conducted for Ford. This also tended to foster opinion leadership.

Numerous other examples could be cited, as indicated by the following:

During one year's model introduction Chrysler Corporation attempted to generate word-of-mouth advertising by rewarding 5000 cabdrivers in sixty-seven cities $5 if they asked "mystery" riders whether they had seen the new Plymouth.[40]

Some restaurants and bars provide cabdrivers and bellhops with meals and drinks at cost if they refer travelers to their establishments.[41]

Earl "Madman" Muntz, the TV tycoon, once hired 400 disc jockeys around the country to plug Muntz television sets.[42]

Adidas pays pro tennis players to wear its tennis shoes, and even outfits entire teams in other professional sports for free.[43]

Jewelry companies often select influential fraternity/sorority representatives to sell the companies' wares to members.

Party plan selling systems such as Tupperware and Mary Kay Cosmetics rely on opinion leader influence (usually exhibited by the neighbor hosting the party) for much of their effectiveness.

283

PERSONAL
INFLUENCE
AND
DIFFUSION OF
INNOVATIONS

Simulating Opinion Leadership

In this approach personal influence is simulated by various means, especially advertising. Advertisers frequently simulate opinion leadership by approximating the position of the disinterested and noncommercial speaker who would engage in word-of-mouth communication. By taking such a position the need for personal influence may be replaced to a certain extent by advertising.

There are several ways in which the marketer can simulate opinion leadership. One approach is that taken by many detergents, foods, laxatives, and other products in which a person (the simulated opinion leader) tells another person about the virtues of the sponsored item. Visual communication also is frequently used in commercials simulating opinion leadership whereby one shopper watches to see what another shopper (the opinion leader) purchases, and then is seen to buy the same item based on this visual recommendation. Commercials of the sort where a friend recommends the product to another often use nonprofessionals to enhance the believability and a script which is written in authentic consumer language based on focus-group research.

Often the advertiser simulates personal influence by using a *testimonial* approach in which the user of the product conveys a favorable experience or opinion about the item. Some testimonials feature a famous actor or athlete as the influencer. For example, in 1974 no fewer than sixty-four network television performers were appearing in commercials.[44] Well-known athletes such as Joe Namath, Billie Jean King, Bill Russell, and Bruce Jenner have also been effective influencers of opinion for all sorts of products. Of course, their greatest effectiveness undoubtedly occurs when recommending a product over which they may be perceived to have some believable relationship or expertise.

Another testimonial approach uses typical people in a seemingly unsolicited recommendation for the product. Commercials featuring man-on-the-street recommendations, hidden camera interviews, and similar techniques may serve to influence viewers through a simulation of opinion leadership. The success of the testimonial approach depends on several things, however. First, the customer must believe that the speaker is talking to the interviewer spontaneously and disinterestedly (that is, the speaker is not simply being paid to say it). Second, the speaker needs a believable relationship to the product. Third, the language which is used must sound authentic. In any event, it has been claimed that the use of a testimonial can increase advertising recall by 18 percent, while a celebrity's testimonial will boost it 75 percent.[45]

Stimulating Opinion Leadership

This strategy is designed to get people to talk about the product and thereby exert personal influence. One way this may be encouraged is by using a *teaser* promotional campaign. Such a technique provides only enough information about the new item to pique the customer's curiosity. One such tantalizing campaign was conducted for Trouble, a new men's cologne:

Atlanta and Denver were selected as test markets, and block advertisements were placed in local newspapers with headlines such as "Are you looking for Trouble?" and "Trouble is coming soon." Even the personal announcement columns of the paper carried messages mentioning Trouble. Banners were towed over the stadium during a pro football game between Atlanta and Denver with such statements as "Now you're going to have Trouble." In addition, a series of unidentified television and radio commercials using the same general theme were run, thus heightening the suspense. After consumers beseiged newspapers, television and radio stations in the two cities with calls wanting to know what was going on, the Mennen Company finally identified Trouble as a new cologne.

A second advertising strategy is to develop such highly entertaining campaigns that consumers engage in discussions about the product and its advertising. Volkswagen and Benson & Hedges have been very successful in such an approach. Some advertisers are even successful in having their slogans become adopted as part of the everyday language, such as Alka-Seltzer's "I can't believe I ate the whole thing," Avis's "We try harder," and Bic's "Flick your Bic."

Other advertising strategies encourage consumers to talk about the product. For example, Firestone's ads prompt the reader to "Ask a friend about Firestone." Minolta camera advertisements use the same approach. These and similar techniques attempt to instigate personal influence through having users disseminate product information and potential users request product information. Obviously, the marketer would desire only favorable word-of-mouth communications to be imparted about the product. This suggests that a monitoring system is needed to find out what present and potential customers are saying about the product and to help in the formulation of advertising strategies designed to react to word-of-mouth communication.

A final strategy is for the marketer to use in-store demonstrations and displays at favorable locations (such as in airport terminals) to secure consumer contact with the product. All of these approaches may be able to stimulate opinion leadership.

Stifling Opinion Leadership

There may be times when the marketer desires to stifle personal influence, rather than encourage it. Generally negative personal influence may be the result of rumor, a poor product, or misunderstandings among consumers.

One condition under which unfavorable personal influence should be retarded exists when a damaging rumor surfaces about the company or its product. Rumors abound in our society; they are part of people's fascination with the grotesque. For example, a popular rumor of recent years was that

Paul McCartney of the Beatles musical group had died. All sorts of bizarre "evidence" was offered to support it, and many clung to the idea until it became obvious that he was indeed alive. In the marketing sphere an example of a disastrous rumor that surfaced pertained to Bubble Yum bubble gum, produced by Life Savers, Inc.

285

PERSONAL
INFLUENCE
AND
DIFFUSION OF
INNOVATIONS

Bubble Yum was the hottest product to hit the chewing gum industry since sugarless gum. Suddenly rumors swept among kids from Los Angeles to New York that the gum caused cancer and/or had spider eggs in it. While sales plummeted, the company hired private detectives to investigate the origins of the rumor and placed full page ads in thirty newspapers stating, "Someone Is Telling Your Kids Very Bad Lies about a very Good Gum."[46]

In unfortunate cases such as this the marketer must take immediate action to stop negative word-of-mouth communication and build up a positive image.

When the product is obviously inferior, a campaign to slow personal influence may also be resorted to. For instance, the marketing strategy for a bad movie typically calls for mass advertising, to get into and out of town quickly before negative word-of-mouth has a chance to spread. An example of the contrasting case is shown by Director Stanley Kubrick for a recent movie. His approach involved a tasteful ad campaign, a limited-release pattern permitting good word-of-mouth communication to grow, then saturation bookings timed to coincide with expected Academy Award nominations.[47]

A final factor to be mentioned requiring slowing of personal influence is the result of consumer misunderstandings which could lead to poor word-of-mouth if not corrected. For example, consumers may be operating the product incorrectly, leading to malfunctions. Perhaps the item needs to be redesigned or instruction manuals rewritten to make them clearer. When the product is radically new, such problems are very likely to exist. In these cases demonstrations may be called for in stores and more explicit commercials showing the product in use. Once again the necessity of a system to monitor personal influence and word-of-mouth communication—both good and bad—is underscored.

SUMMARY

In this chapter we have examined the concept of personal influence and its role in gaining acceptance of innovations. First, we described the way in which personal influence operates and found it to be a significant factor in new product adoption. We next discussed three models of communication and influence flow—the one-step, two-step, and multistep processes—and found the latter conceptualization to have greater validity.

The process of opinion leadership in marketing was discussed by describing the characteristics of those who are marketing opinion leaders and citing the nature of the process. We determined that moderate marketing-opinion leadership overlap exists; that opinion leadership is situational; and that influencers as well as influencees have strong motivations to engage in word-of-mouth communication.

The adoption and diffusion processes were described and their significance for the marketer cited. The adoption process was seen to be an individual phenomenon—the stages through which an individual passes over a period of time in adopting a product. The innovation diffusion process, on the other hand, is a group phenomenon—it describes the categories of adopters who accept an innovation over a period of time. Both processes were related directly to the marketer through promotion strategy implications.

Finally, several marketing strategies were suggested to utilize the process of personal influence. The marketer may desire to identify and use opinion leaders directly, create opinion leaders, simulate opinion leadership, stimulate opinion leadership, and/or stifle opinion leadership.

DISCUSSION TOPICS

1. Describe the nature of personal influence. Why is it important to the marketer?

2. Describe the three models of communication discussed in the text. Which appears to be the most complete model of communication and influence?

3. Who are marketing opinion leaders? How do they differ from those they influence?

4. Think of a product or service about which you communicated by word-of-mouth recently. Were you the influencer or influencee? Which of the reasons for opinion leadership discussed in the text apply to this communication situation?

5. Locate several examples of new products (you might look in *Advertising Age, Business Week,* etc.). How would you classify each of these innovations in terms of their "newness"?

6. Pick one of the products discovered from question 5 and describe how you would market the item.

7. How might promotion differ as consumers move through the adoption process?

8. Describe the adopter categories.

9. Categorize your friends according to their position among the adopter categories. Which tend to be innovators, opinion leaders, laggards?

10. Suggest a plan for using the process of personal influence in the following marketing situations:

a. a campus clothing store
b. a new food product
c. a new, sophisticated quadraphonic receiver
d. a new sports car
e. a new novel

NOTES

1. Thomas S. Roberson, *Innovative Behavior and Communication,* Holt, New York, 1971, p. 170.
2. Deborah Sue Yeager, "Markdown Mecca," *The Wall Street Journal,* July 6, 1976, p. 1.
3. Ernest Dichter, "How Word-of-Mouth Advertising Works," *Harvard Business Review,* **44**:147, November-December 1966.

287

PERSONAL
INFLUENCE
AND
DIFFUSION OF
INNOVATIONS

4. George Katona and Eva Mueller, "A Study of Purchasing Decisions," in Lincoln H. Clark (ed.), *Consumer Behavior: The Dynamics of Consumer Reaction,* New York University Press, New York, 1955, pp. 30–87.

5. John R. Kerr and Bruce Weale, "Collegiate Clothing Purchasing Patterns and Fashion Adoption Behavior," *Southern Journal of Business,* **5**:126–133, July 1970.

6. "Desperation in Hollywood: Actor Jack Lemmon's View," *U.S. News & World Report,* August 22, 1977, p. 44.

7. Dale M. Elsner, "The Story in Brief Is Men's Underwear, and It's Full of Holes," *The Wall Street Journal,* June 3, 1975, p. 1.

8. Ralph Schoenstein, "It Was Just a Joke, Folks," *TV Guide,* May 8, 1974, pp. 6–7.

9. Johan Arndt, "Role of Product-Related Conversations in the Diffusion of a New Product," *Journal of Marketing Research,* **4**:291–295, August 1967.

10. Johan Arndt, *Word of Mouth Advertising: A Review of the Literature,* Advertising Research Foundation, New York, 1967, p. 25.

11. James H. Myers and William H. Reynolds, *Consumer Behavior and Marketing Management,* Houghton Mifflin, Boston, 1967, pp. 302–303.

12. Robertson, *Innovative Behavior,* pp. 126–127.

13. Robertson, *Innovative Behavior,* p. 175.

14. Myers and Reynolds, *Consumer Behavior,* p. 306.

15. Everett M. Rogers, *Diffusion of Innovations,* Free Press, New York, 1962, p. 241.

16. John O. Summers, "The Identity of Women's Clothing Fashion Opinion Leaders," *Journal of Marketing Research,* **7**:178–185, May 1970; and Fred D. Reynolds and William R. Darden, "Mutually Adaptive Effects of Interpersonal Communication," *Journal of Marketing Research,* **8**:449–454, November 1971.

17. Charles W. King, "Fashion Adoption: A Rebuttal to the Trickle Down Theory," in Stephen A. Greyser (ed.), *Toward Scientific Marketing,* American Marketing Association, Chicago, 1964, pp. 108–125.

18. Charles W. King and John O. Summers, "Overlap of Opinion Leadership across Consumer Product Categories," *Journal of Marketing Research,* **7**:43–50, February 1970.

19. David B. Montgomery and Alvin J. Silk, "Patterns of Overlap in Opinion Leadership and Interest for Selected Categories of Purchasing Activity," in Philip R. McDonald (ed.), *Marketing Involvement in Society and the Economy,* American Marketing Association, Chicago, 1969, pp. 377–386.

20. Elihu Katz, "The Two-Step Flow of Communication: An Up-to-Date Report on an Hypothesis," *Public Opinion Quarterly,* **21**:73, Spring 1957.

21. Dichter, "How Word-of-Mouth Advertising Works," pp. 148–152.

22. Robertson, *Innovative Behavior,* pp. 191–209.

23. Federal Trade Commission, "Permissible Period of Time During Which New Product May Be Described as New," *Advisory Opinion Digest,* no. 120, p. 1, April 15, 1967.

24. Federal Trade Commission, "Permissible Period."

25. William Lazer and William E. Bell, "The Communications Process and Innovation," *Journal of Advertising Research,* **6**:4, September 1966.

26. Gerald Zaltman and Ronald Stiff, "Theories of Diffusion," in Scott Ward and Thomas S. Robertson (eds.), *Consumer Behavior: Theoretical Sources,* Prentice-Hall, Englewood Cliffs, N.J., 1972, p. 426.

27. Thomas S. Robertson, "The Process of Innovation and the Diffusion of Innovation," *Journal of Marketing,* **31**:15–16, January 1967.

28. Robertson, *Innovative Behavior,* pp. 76–77.

29. Everett M. Rogers, "New Product Adoption and Diffusion," *Journal of Consumer Research,* **2**:290–301, March 1976.

30. Robertson, *Innovative Behavior,* p. 32.

31. See Rogers, *Diffusion of Innovations,* pp. 168–171; *The Adoption of New Products: Process and Influence,* Foundation for Research on Human Behavior, Ann Arbor, Mich., 1959, pp. 1–8; and Gerald Zaltman, *Marketing: Contributions from the Behavioral Sciences,* Harcourt, Brace & World, New York, 1965, pp. 45–51.

32. " 'Early Adopters' an Aid in New Product Success, GE Finds," *Marketing Insights,* April 24, 1967, p. 14.

33. Everett M. Rogers and F. Floyd Shoemaker, *Communication of Innovations,* Free Press, New York, 1971, pp. 137–157.

34. Thomas S. Robertson and James H. Myers, "Personality Correlates of Opinion Leadership and Innovative Buying Behavior," *Journal of Marketing Research,* **6**:164–168, May 1969; Robertson, *Innovative Behavior,* pp. 110–112; and James W. Taylor, "A Striking Characteristic of Innovators," *Journal of Marketing Research,* **14**:104–107, February 1977.

35. Philip Kotler and Gerald Zaltman, "Targeting Prospects for a New Product," *Journal of Advertising Research,* **16**:7–18, February 1976.

36. Douglas J. Tigert and Stephen J. Arnold, *Profiling Self-Designated Opinion Leaders and Self-Designated Innovators through Life Style Research,* University of Toronto School of Business, Toronto, June 1971, pp. 28–29.

37. James F. Engel, David T. Kollat, and Roger D. Blackwell, *Consumer Behavior,* 2d ed., Holt, New York, 1973, p. 429.

38. Myers and Reynolds, *Consumer Behavior,* p. 309.

39. Joseph R. Mancuso, "Why Not Create Opinion Leaders for New Product Introductions?" *Journal of Marketing,* **33**:20–25, July 1969.

40. *The Wall Street Journal,* September 27, 1962, p. 5.

41. Engel, Kollat, and Blackwell, p. 430.

42. "Would You Buy a Car from This Man?" *The Providence Sunday Journal,* December 21, 1975, p. F-10.

43. Frederick C. Klein, "Foot Race: Sneaker Makers Are Set to Pursue the Athletes at Summer Olympics," *The Wall Street Journal,* April 23, 1976, p. 20.

44. James P. Forkan, "From Soap Seller to Star and Back Again Proves Lucrative Mix for Actors," *Advertising Age,* September 2, 1974, p. 24.

45. "Ads Should Focus on Products, Not Themselves," *Marketing News,* August 12, 1977, p. 7.

46. John E. Cooney, "Bubble Gum Maker Wants to Know How the Rumors Started," *The Wall Street Journal,* March 24, 1977, p. 1.

47. "Kubrick's Grandest Gamble," *Time,* December 15, 1975, p. 72.

CASES

CASE 3-1   SUNSET, INC.

Sunset, Inc., a large California department store with numerous branches throughout the state, had its marketing research department conduct a study among its target market to determine the primary and consumption-related values of this group and assess the implications of these values for the organization's strategy.

The research resulted in the finding that patrons more strongly held the basic values of "imaginativeness," "independence," "an exciting life," "politeness," "cheerfulness," and "pleasure" than did nonpatrons. Related to these fundamental values, the researchers cited a number of consumption values held more strongly by patrons. The most important of these were "providing fast service on complaints," "responsiveness to consumer's true needs," "providing clear, accurate product information," "store location convenience," "ethical advertising," and "use of courteous, helpful salespeople."

Question

1. What implications might these findings have for store policies?

289

PERSONAL
INFLUENCE
AND
DIFFUSION OF
INNOVATIONS

CASE 3-2 CAMPBELL SOUP COMPANY[1]

Campbell Soup Company, which dominates the entire United States soup market, began overseas operations in 1958. However, its overseas activities were not as successful as its domestic operations and the company lost $30 million over a decade of foreign business. For example, several decisions by Campbell in England turned out to be unsuccessful. First, the concept of "condensed soup" was unusual to the British housewife, who could not justify the price for a small Campbell's can compared to the larger can of Heinz ready-to-eat soup. Second, the taste of the soup was not what the British were accustomed to. Third, the company's advertising was much too youthful and fanciful for the English consumer who was used to a more realistic and commonplace advertising approach for such products.

[1]Adapted from "The $30 Million Lesson," *Sales Management*, March 1, 1967, pp. 31–38.

Question

1. How could these mistakes have been avoided by Campbell?

CASE 3-3 KING SHOE COMPANY

King Shoe Company manufactures a broad line of athletic shoes for the entire family. The company has achieved national distribution mainly through small, higher-priced specialty clothing and shoe stores, but is searching for additional means of growth. Company management believes its brand of shoes has features that are superior to other brands of athletic shoes on the market, even though competitively priced.

Marketing research has identified the black and Spanish-American population as two segments containing much potential, which the company does not seem to have reached in the past. In order to increase the company's sales and profits, management would like to move to attract this segment, especially the youth in these groups, but executives are not sure what strategy might prove successful.

Question

1. Suggest a marketing strategy for King Shoe Company.

CASE 3-4 BORAX BROTHERS

Tilden and Reginald Borax, twin brothers, have recently inherited close to $3 million from the death of their father. The boys, age 23, are fifth-generation New Englanders who have recently graduated from a prestigious Ivy League university. They have always wanted to have their own business and so have decided to use their inheritances to open a large, new, warehouse-type furniture store. They realize they will be primarily dependent on the working-class consumer for patronage, due to the size of this market. However, in addition to this main target group, they believe it will be possible with the right marketing mix also to capture a predominant share of the middle- and upper-class buyers in the area by having one large store with "something for everyone." Although the metropolitan area has only 250,000 population, the market appears able to absorb the competition of a large store such as Borax Brothers.

Tilden and Reginald have carefully examined competitors' furniture offerings at the lower-class end of the market and feel they will have a strong advantage over these firms. As Reginald explains it, "These stores have really tacky tastes—things like overstuffed colonial sofas. Tilden and I think we have a much better feel for the community's needs. We'll be doing much of the buying for our new store ourselves and will therefore be helping to upgrade the working class's tastes in furniture with our product offerings. Of course, our background will also be beneficial in effectively marketing to the higher classes with this type store."

Questions

1. Evaluate Borax Brothers' philosophy.

2. Assume that Borax Brothers concentrates only on the working class. What guidelines can you offer for a marketing strategy for furniture aimed at this group?

CASE 3-5 MUELLER BREWERY, INC.[1]

Mueller's, a large mideast regional brewery, was established in 1826 and had since expanded its market to include an eight-state area. However, by 1972, the company began to experience a leveling of sales in some states with declines in others. Both national and regional breweries were making inroads into its markets. Mueller's market share position had declined from number two in the region in 1952 to number four by the end of 1971, with the potential of falling even farther during 1972 or 1973.

COMPANY BACKGROUND

Mueller's management had always been very conservative and very cautious. It wasn't until 1968 that they decided to introduce a second brand of beer, Little Queen, a 7-ounce bottle aimed at the female market.

Management did not believe it was necessary to conduct consumer research, since they felt that all consumers who drank beer wanted a good-tasting beer and that's what Mueller's was. The company had concentrated much of its promotional effort in the sales promotion area, providing supermarkets with banners and taverns with clocks, lighting fixtures, and other sales promotional materials. Until 1958, advertising had been restricted mostly to billboards, with some radio and newspaper ads.

In 1958, the impact of television advertising had become evident to management, so a local advertising agency was hired to handle all corporate advertising, including television. A typical Mueller television commercial in 1968 showed people sitting around a table laughing and talking, with the men drinking Mueller's and the women drinking Little Queen. Because of the company's cost consciousness, most television ads were shown at late hours when rates were lowest.

By 1972, management began to feel that their marketing effort needed to be reexamined. Although Mueller once had enjoyed strong loyalty among its distributors, this had declined lately, largely because it was easier for them to sell the more popular brands to their outlets.

Management concluded from information from their distributors that the problem was at the consumer level and that a greater promotional effort toward the consumer was needed. Advertising, they believed, held the key, and their current agency must not be getting the job done. Thus, in 1972, Mueller's invited a new ad agency—McClinton, Sharpe, and Kirkpatrick—to submit a proposal for their account. Charles Kirkpatrick, one of the three partners of the agency made the following presentation to Mueller's management:

"First, gentlemen, we must recognize that 72 percent of the beer consumed in your eight-state region is purchased by 28 percent of the beer-drinking population. And do you know who that 28 percent is? Blue-collar workers—the factory worker and the construction worker. That's who we must persuade to drink Mueller's. In that connection, we propose an advertising campaign that shows the typical blue-collar worker on the job with his hard hat on, and after work stopping off at the local tavern to have a Mueller's. In addition, because of the blue-collar, hard-hat patriotism for country, we'll show the American flag at the end of each commercial and say 'Mueller's—an all-American beer.' The blue-collar worker can identify with that kind of commercial. Mueller's will become the blue-collar beer. Of course, we won't say its a blue-collar beer; we'll refer to it by showing ads with their kind of people drinking Mueller's.

"Now, we can't forget about the future. The young people of America are the future beer drinkers. College and high school beer consumers constitute a significant market, but more importantly are the beer consumers of the future. I propose, gentlemen, that we aim a portion of our campaign at the college scene. High schoolers look up to college students, identify with them and wish to emulate them. Thus, part of our commercials will depict the college crowd drinking Mueller's.

"We get the best of both worlds. We attract the blue-collar worker with the 'hard-hat American' ad and the future beer drinkers with identification with 'Mr. Joe College.' It can't miss."

---

[1]Adapted from the original case, copyright © 1976 by M. Wayne DeLozier, which also appears in M. Wayne DeLozier (ed.), *Consumer Behavior Dynamics: A Casebook,* Merrill, Columbus, Oh., 1977. Used with permission of the author.

Questions

1. Evaluate the agency's presentation.

2. Do you feel the use of reference groups is a good approach in advertising a brand of beer? Why or why not?

3. If Mueller's management decided that using a reference group in its advertising campaign is a good approach, what reference group(s) would you recommend? Why?

CASE 3-6 SELLING SEDUCTIVE LINGERIE[1]

"This," says saleswoman Tiffany James, holding up a peach-colored wisp of diaphanous material, "is a nightie with a supersheer look."

"This next one," she continues, holding up another short and tiny garment in bold red, "is a baby doll with maribou trim at the bust. It's very cute and it's machine washable."

Toward the end of the demonstration, she holds up what looks like two minute triangles of black lace. "These," she says, "are crotchless panties, ladies. And if you're really innovative, you'll get two and wear one as a bra."

Gasp, giggle, shriek. The twenty-five women crowded into the suburban living room are transfixed. It is a scene repeated nearly every night of the week in the color-coordinated, vinyl-wallpapered living rooms of suburbia.

There is, of course, nothing new about the product—clothes of "a seductive nature." They have been sold through the mail for years. What is new and interesting is that these clothes, once snickered about in the same locker room breath as "kinky sex" and cheesecake, have been brought out of their plain brown wrappers to a new market—the solid suburban middle class. To some suburban women, Tiffany James's lingerie parties have become as popular as Tupperware and cut crystal punch bowls.

Before the show begins the guests all take a "sensuality test" to break the ice. There are about twenty questions on the test such as "If you've ever read *'The Sensuous Woman,'* give yourself 10 points." A lingerie prize goes to the winner.

Then, it's the moment of truth. "You're welcome to try anything on," James tells them. Although ten of the guests are middle-aged, another fifteen of them are younger—in their twenties and early thirties—slimmer, and much bolder. There is a brief moment of hesitation and looking around. Then a small group of women rushes into the upstairs bathroom with an armful of negligees and closes the door. Others shut themselves in the empty bedrooms. Only the teen-age daughter of the hostess and her friends are unabashed enough to parade the lingerie in front of the living room crowd. Others will only show theirs to one or two close friends.

By the end of the evening, some of the group will have tried on the items. Others, perhaps less bold, will not, but Tiffany James will have sold $300 worth of her supersheer, baby doll, lacy, satiny, backless, frontless, sideless, sexy and very naughty lingerie.

---

[1]Adapted from Manli Ho, "Peddling Naughty Lingerie . . . In Suburban Livingrooms," *Boston Globe,* March 2, 1976.

Questions

1. How would you explain the success of this party selling approach?

2. What market groups would you seek to appeal to in this situation? Why?

CASE 3-7 UNIVERSAL APPLIANCE COMPANY

During the annual marketing planning process in 1978, Frank Johnson, marketing manager for Universal, a large manufacturer of appliances, was analyzing the company's deteriorating market-share position in the small electric appliances category. During the past two years the company's share of the United States market had dropped from a dominating 45 percent down to 31 percent (and second place). If this trend continued, the company would soon be relegated to third place in the industry.

As the marketing planning and review process proceeded it became clearer that the fault was not with distribution, since this continued to be strong and loyal. Nor did the problem appear to be one of products not meeting consumers' needs, or of prices being out of line with product value or competition. The remaining area that might account for this precipitious drop in market share

293

PERSONAL
INFLUENCE
AND
DIFFUSION OF
INNOVATIONS

seemed to be the shift to a new advertising agency in 1976 and the resulting strategy that was adopted.

At that time the agency had proposed that a large share of the budget be used to promote to husbands directly. This decision was made on the basis of what appeared to be trends in the marketplace regarding changing marital roles. It was reasoned that with more working wives, there would be more housekeeping husbands, or at least, more husbands with interest in appliances to be used in the house. Thus, the feeling that both husbands and wives participated about equally in buying decisions for small electric appliances led to promotions aimed at husbands as much as at wives.

This decision had not been critically examined until now when Johnson discovered that a recent research study provided some insight into reported influences of each spouse in small appliance purchases. This information is presented below in Table 1.

TABLE 1

COMPARISON OF HUSBAND/WIFE INFLUENCE IN APPLIANCE PURCHASE DECISIONS

Purchases in past 12 months	Share of Influence					
Wife & husband influence on purchases = 100% (Read table across)	Purchase Decision Influence		Initiation		Information Gathering	
	Prod. Dec.	Brand Dec.	Prod. Dec.	Brand Dec.	Prod. Dec.	Brand Dec.
	Wife/Husb.	Wife/Husb.	Wife/Husb.	Wife/Husb.	Wife/Husb.	Wife/Husb.
Small appliances:						
Electric blender	59 41	53 47	67 33	50 50	53 47	52 48
Coffee maker	64 36	64 36	73 27	68 32	64 36	66 34
Vacuum cleaner	60 40	60 40	80 20	69 31	66 34	65 35

Table reads: Wives accounted for 59% of total influence on the decision to buy the last new electric blender purchased in the past 12 months, husbands 41%, etc.
Source: "Purchase Influence-Measures of Husband/Wife Influence on Buying Decisions," Haley, Overholser & Associates, New Canaan, Conn; 1975, p. 27.

Question

1. Based on the research presented above, what suggestions do you have for Universal's promotion strategy?

CASE 3-8   VIDEO INTERNATIONAL, INC.

Video International is a large electronics company which has pioneered in the development of video equipment for home use. One of its hottest new products is a videotape recorder (VTR) that utilizes cassettes and allows viewers to record television shows for replay at a later date. The machine not only allows one show to be recorded at the same time another is being watched, but with the built-in timer as standard equipment a person can record a show even when he is not at home.

The units range in price from $999 for the basic deck unit to $2295 for the deluxe console model, which features a 25-inch color television and includes a black-and-white video camera, microphones, and several tapes for making your own shows. Discounting has actively begun, with some retailers shaving the price to $750 for the economy model.

Although the market appears to be solidifying, there are several fundamental questions that face manufacturers of these units. For example, although Video's units have a tape cassette recording capacity of one hour, the newest competitive models are offering 2- to 4-hour recording capacities. With relatively minor modifications Video could double its present tape capacity. However, there are additional problems with standards between different manufacturers. Two types of tape recording systems are being used by all manufacturers. Whichever system becomes most widely accepted will probably displace the other system completely.

Another fundamental question concerns the potential introduction of videodisc recording units, which would accomplish the same thing but sell at much lower prices than videotape units. However, the apparent success of VTR has put videodisc research on the back burner for now.

A second new product of Video International is large-screen TV. The company manufactures sets ranging in screen size from 50 inches to 120 inches diagonally with prices ranging between $1500 and $4500. Each set consists of a screen that can stand on legs or be hung from a wall and a separate projection unit about the size of a small filing cabinet which must be placed *exactly* 8 feet away from the screen for proper operation.

The new giant-screen sets take some getting used to. Most viewers are accustomed to watching TV on screens that are bright enough to watch even in sunlight. At first glance, the large-screen set looks dim by comparison to regular TV, but is still several times brighter than what we see in movie houses (which are darkened). Thus, a low level of lighting is called for with giant-screen TVs.

Questions

1. What are the characteristics of an innovation that may retard its diffusion? Evaluate Video International's two innovations with regard to these criteria.

2. Recommend a marketing program to spread these innovations rapidly.

INDIVIDUAL DETERMINANTS OF CONSUMER BEHAVIOR

13. MOTIVATION 14. PERCEPTION 15. LEARNING
16. PERSONALITY AND SELF-CONCEPT
17. ATTITUDES 18. ATTITUDE CHANGE Cases for Part Four

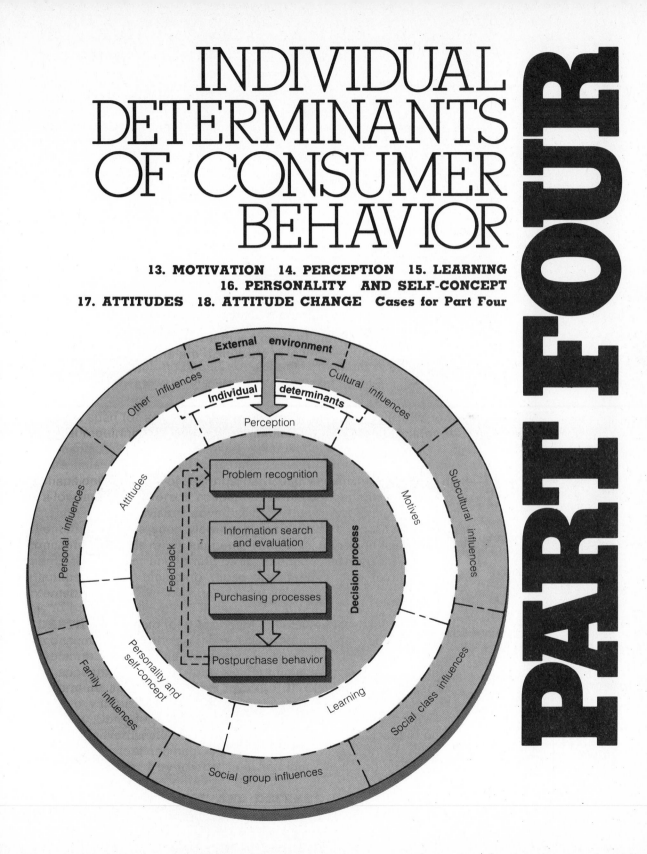

PART FOUR

MOTIVATION

MOTIVES DEFINED CLASSIFYING MOTIVES Physiological versus Psychogenic; Primary versus Selective; Rational versus Emotional; Conscious versus Unconscious; Positive versus Negative; Limitations of Classification Schemes MOTIVE AROUSAL Triggering Arousal; Tension and Arousal; Effects of Arousal MOTIVE STRUCTURE AND INFLUENCE Deprivation; Levels of Aspiration; Learning Influences; Motive Combinations; Self-Concept MOTIVE DIRECTION Selecting Goal Objects; Influencing Choice Criteria; Other Influences MOTIVATION RESEARCH

Anyone interested in consumers soon faces a very fundamental question: What energizes and directs their behavior? This question holds the interest of marketing managers for a wide variety of reasons. For example, product designers attempt to determine product features that will attract consumer interests. Advertisers are continually searching for appeals or themes to accomplish the same ends. In addition, retailers are very much interested in what directs consumers' shopping patronage toward particular establishments.

It would be quite surprising if any one variable could fully explain what activates and directs consumers' actions. Nevertheless, the concept of motivation has been offered as an explanation for much of this behavior. This chapter begins by defining motives, indicating their importance, and discussing some methods of classifying them. We shall then turn our attention to how motives are aroused and what factors influence their structure. Next, motivational influences on the direction our behavior takes are treated. Finally, we will review the usefulness of the area of motivation research in discovering consumers' motives.

MOTIVES DEFINED

A *motive* may be viewed as an inner state that mobilizes bodily energy and directs it in selective fashion toward goals usually located in the external environment.[1] This definition implies that motives involve two major components:

1. A mechanism to arouse bodily energy
2. A mechanism to provide some direction to that bodily energy

The arousal component activates a general state of tension or restlessness but does not provide any particular direction to this energy. This could be compared to the random thrashing about that an uncomfortable newborn baby shows. However, the directive aspect of motives focuses such aroused energy in a particular fashion—toward some goal that exists in the individual's environment. Thus, when our hunger is aroused, we are directed toward particular foods.

A number of writers make distinctions between motives and other related concepts such as needs, wants, and drives.[2] For our purposes, however, these distinctions are unnecessary and will be avoided.

Motives are important in influencing several facets of consumers' behavior. First, they activate and direct energy and thus help consumers identify their basic strivings such as achievement, affiliation with others, and security. Second, motives assist consumers in translating their basic strivings into desires for concrete products and services. For example, the achievement motive can influence the type of house, automobile, and vacation desired. A third and related motive influence is their effect on how consumers develop *choice criteria*—the specific factors used to evaluate products and services. Finally, motives may affect the other individual determinants discussed in the remaining chapters of this section. Although such influences are frequently subtle, their effect on the behavior of consumers is quite significant.

CLASSIFYING MOTIVES

Starting in the early 1900s many different motives were suggested to explain the diversity of human behavior. Often, they were named in terms of the goal objects that were apparently being sought. Love, sex, and esteem motives are examples of this tendency. Because so many motives were suggested, it became useful to classify them into common categories, several of which are particularly relevant to our study of consumer behavior.[3]

Physiological versus Psychogenic

One way to classify motives is with regard to the types of needs they are based on. *Physiological motives* stem directly from biological needs of the individual and include hunger, thirst, and pain-avoidance among others. Conversely, although *psychogenic motives* can result in satisfying biological needs, they are mainly oriented toward the satisfaction of psychological desires. Examples include the achievement, affiliation, and self-actualization motives.

Although general agreement exists about the number and nature of physiological motives, there is less consensus regarding their psychogenic counterparts. However, Bayton offered a scheme grouping psychogenic motives into three major categories.[4] These are listed below along with examples of how they have served as the basis for various promotional appeals.

1. *Affectional Motives*—those motives directed at forming and maintaining warm, harmonious, and emotionally satisfying relations with others
Figure 13-1 presents a Bell System advertisement linking use of the company's services to affectional motives. In another case, the Western Electric Corporation, which produces telephones and other communication equipment, has used the affectional theme, "We Make Things That Bring People Closer Together."

2. *Ego-Defensive Motives*—those directed at protecting the personality; to avoid physical and psychological harm; to avoid ridicule, "loss of face," and prevent loss of prestige; to avoid anxiety or achieve relief from it
A Doublemint Gum advertisement claims "It's A Natural For Fresh Breath." This appeals to ego-defensive motives by stressing that use of the product avoids the embarrassment of offending others with bad breath.

FIGURE 13-1
(opposite) Example of appeal to affectional motives. (Courtesy of American Telephone & Telegraph Company, Lone Lines Department.)

**Lots of people left impressions on your life.
Don't let them fade away.
Show them you still remember with Long Distance.
Give them a call.**

 Bell System

3. *Ego-Bolstering Motives*—those motives directed at enhancing or promoting the personality; to achieve, to gain prestige and recognition; to satisfy the ego through domination of others

Figure 13-2 presents an advertisement of the A. T. Cross Company which is aimed at retailers. Notice how the text of the ad encourages retailers to recognize and emphasize ego-bolstering motives which would draw ultimate consumers toward Cross writing instruments.

A common characteristic of most, if not all, psychogenic motives is that they are learned. The nature of this learning process is explored in Chapter 15. However, it is important to note here that we are primarily directed by motives that have been acquired through the learning process.

Primary versus Selective

Another way to classify consumer motives is according to the nature of their influence on the buying process. *Primary* buying motives are said to initiate buying behavior and direct it toward general product categories such as televisions or clothing. Curiosity, a desire for amusement, and a need to affiliate with others are examples.

Conversely, *selective* buying motives influence decisions between models and brands within a given product class, or the type of store chosen for a purchase. They would affect, for instance, a decision on whether to purchase a Sony or a Sanyo television set. Economy, status, safety, and achievement are examples of such selective motives.

Rational versus Emotional

Another classification scheme frequently used for buying motives is the rational/emotional dichotomy first offered by Copeland.[5] *Rational buying motives* are usually thought of as being related to some observable product feature that will affect its performance, such as size, purity, or price. Examples include efficiency in operation, durability, and reliability. Contrasted with these are *emotional buying motives* which are presumably related to subjective feelings or emotions such as the comfort, pleasure, or prestige that one expects to derive from the product or service. Since they are subjective in nature, the link between such motives and actual product features often is difficult to determine.

It is unlikely that any product or service is purchased for purely rational or purely emotional motives. Rather, these should be viewed as extreme points on a buying-motive continuum. Any product could then be positioned on this continuum, depending on the relative strength of rational and emotional buying motives influencing its purchase. Figure 13-3 portrays such a continuum with some suggested product positions.

When emotional motives are addressed in advertisements, emphasis is often placed on how possession of a product will influence a person's view of himself or how others will view him. This has led Levy and others to argue that many products have emotionally symbolic meanings more important to consumers than their functional/rational aspects.[6] Consequently, many marketers have developed strong symbols for their products or services. One example is the highly liberated-looking women used in Virginia Slims advertisements. Other cases are the rugged Marlboro men and the distinctive Englishman dressed in a Beefeater's uniform to promote Beefeater gin. Since gin is well known as an English drink the symbolism suggests the authenticity of the brand. As Figure 13-4 demonstrates, this Beefeater symbol has

WHEN YOUR CUSTOMERS ASK TO SEE YOUR FINE GIFT JEWELRY.

Most people know a Cross pen or pencil when they see one. And acknowledge the fine craftsmanship and quality materials that have earned us an enviable reputation of integrity. Plus a certain aura of prestige among discerning men and women throughout the world. We appreciate that. But you know our product is much more than a means of putting words on paper. Cross writing instruments are used, displayed, cherished and worn very much like fine jewelry. As a gift, they communicate the very personal sentiment of the occasion. And say something rather special about both people involved. So when your customers ask to see your fine gift jewelry, please include us. With just a hint from you, they'll recognize us for what we are.

CROSS®
SINCE 1846

Fine writing instruments for Ladies and Gentlemen from $7.50 to $300. Desk sets to $500. Suggested retail.

FIGURE 13-2
Example of appeal to ego-bolstering motive. (Courtesy of A. T. Cross Company)

gained such recognition that the brand name is not even mentioned in some advertisements

Consumers do not appear to consciously distinguish between rational and emotional motives. However, they can be quite sensitive regarding emotional motives and may actually attempt to disguise or hide them. Emotional appeals may therefore require more subtle marketing efforts than those based on rational motives. For example, a direct rational appeal such as "Datsun Saves Money" appears potentially much less offensive to consumers than a direct emotional appeal like "Cadillac Impresses Your Friends."

Conscious versus Unconscious

An important distinction that can be drawn between many motives is the degree to which they reach the consumer's awareness. Again, we could view all motives as fitting along a continuum ranging between completely conscious to completely unconscious. *Conscious* motives are those that consumers are quite aware of, whereas a motive is said to be *unconscious* when the consumer is not aware of being influenced by it.

As mentioned above, people are not conscious of some motives because they do not want to confront the true reason for their purchase. Thus, a consumer may not want to admit that one reason for purchasing a high-priced stereo is the esteem and interest that it will direct toward him or her by others. In other cases, consumers may simply not be aware of the true motives behind many of their purchases. For example, we really don't understand why we prefer certain colors over others.

Positive versus Negative

The final classification scheme to discuss suggests that motives can have either positive or negative influences on consumers. Positive motives lead consumers to approach desired goals, while negative ones direct them away from undesirable consequences. It appears that positive motives exert the predominant influence on consumers, but a few very important cases of negative motives do exist. One example—fear—plays an important role in some purchases, such as toothpaste to prevent decay and insurance to protect one's income and family. We shall examine appeals based on this motive in Chapter 18.

Limitations of Classification Schemes

Lists and classification schemes are useful in organizing motives and providing insight into potential appeals for products, services, and promo-

FIGURE 13-3
A rational/emotional buying motive continuum. (*Source:* Adapted from John G. Udell, "A New Approach to Consumer Motivation," *Journal of Retailing*, **40**:9, Winter 1964–65.)

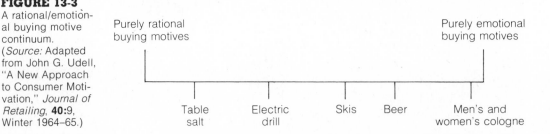

tional messages. However, merely listing and classifying motives leaves a number of unresolved issues relevant to using motivation in a marketing plan. Several of these issues are discussed below.[7]

RATIONAL VERSUS EMOTIONAL PROBLEMS Unfortunately, the rational/emotional classification scheme has led many to conclude mistakenly that emotional motives must be irrational in nature. As we have seen, this certainly was not the intent of the classification method. Consumers can operate on emotionally based motives just as rationally as they can on motives that are based on readily observable product differences. The problem is that emotional motives involve subjective evaluations and therefore are usually based on factors that only the individual consumer is aware of. Others unaware of these influences are unlikely to understand the consumer's actions and might mistake them for irrational behavior. For example, an individual may prefer one brand over a less expensive, but seemingly identical, alternative because he believes it to have an excellent reputation. This can be a perfectly rational decision even though it would confuse an observer who sees no objective difference between the two items. Because of this confusion, which the rational/emotional dichotomy has fostered, little use is made of the scheme today.

INFERRING MOTIVES FROM BEHAVIOR A number of motive lists have been generated by inferring motives from observed behavior. Since some of

Advertisement

"What'll it be?"

BEEFEATER® GIN IMPORTED FROM ENGLAND BY KOBRAND, N.Y. N.Y. 94 PROOF. 100% GRAIN NEUTRAL SPIRITS

FIGURE 13-4
Example of reliance on strong symbol recognition for Beefeater gin. (Courtesy of Kobrand Corporation.)

these lists have not been verified by critical testing, several problems can arise. One is that any given behavior of consumers can be instigated by a variety of motives. Therefore, by *merely observing* consumers we are *not* in a position to state which specific motives are influencing them. Also, since any one motive can influence consumers differently, knowing that a motive *can* direct consumers toward specific products does not necessarily enable us to predict that it *will* do so. This demonstrates that additional information is needed about motive strength and conditions affecting their directional influence.

OBSCURING OTHER DETERMINANTS Emphasis on consumers' motives has also been criticized because it tends to hide the effects of other variables. Motivated behavior is directed toward goal objects, but learning, attitudes, personality, and perception also provide significant guidance. Similarly, the specific situations that consumers confront can dramatically influence their behavior.[8] Accurate understanding of consumers requires that we do not credit motives for the influence of these other variables.

Overemphasis on motive classification schemes has also drawn attention away from their operational characteristics, such as how they are aroused, what influences their strength, why they persist over time, and the degree to which different motives can lead to different behaviors. Effective marketing use of the motivation concept requires that we have some appreciation of these operational elements.

MOTIVE AROUSAL

The arousal concept concerns what energizes consumers. Remember from our earlier discussion that although arousal activates bodily energy it offers little, if any, direction to behavior.

Triggering Arousal

A variety of ways exist to trigger motives into arousal and thereby activate behavior. The following triggers may work alone or in combination to set consumers into action.[9]

PHYSIOLOGICAL CONDITIONS One source of arousal is physiological in nature—satisfying our biological needs for food, water, and other life-sustaining necessities. Depriving these bodily needs gives rise to a state of tension. When tension reaches a sufficient strength, arousal occurs and this provides energy necessary to satisfy the need.

The consumer's previous experience and present situation will strongly influence the direction such heightened activity will take. For example, an aroused hunger motive could be directed toward popcorn in a movie theater or a hamburger while shopping in a mall. This illustrates that even when we know that a consumer's motive has been aroused, we often still cannot accurately predict which products or services will be desired.

SITUATIONAL CONDITIONS The particular situation confronting consumers may also trigger arousal. This can occur when the situation draws attention to an existing physiological condition, as when noticing an advertisement for Lipton iced tea suddenly makes you aware of being thirsty. Here, the need for liquids may have been present but not yet strong enough to trigger arousal. Seeing the advertisement draws attention to the condition and leads to activity. Again, the specific action taken will depend on past experience and present conditions.

Situational conditions can also work alone to generate motive arousal. This appears to occur as a result of consumers perceiving some disparity between their present state and a better condition. For example, a car owner may see a television commercial for a new type of spark plug that stresses how the plugs could result in considerable fuel economy. Such a message might, by itself, be responsible for triggering the aroused state.

COGNITIVE ACTIVITY Humans engage in considerable cognitive activity (thinking and reasoning) even when the objects of their thoughts are not physically present. This thinking, considered by some to be daydreaming or fantasy, can also act as a motive trigger. One way this occurs is when consumers deliberate about unsatisfied wants. For example, thinking about a lack of physical activity can arouse energy to remedy the situation. This energy can lead to a variety of actitivies and purchases ranging from golf clubs to seeds for a new garden.

Tension and Arousal

Historically, consumers have been viewed as tension reducers and avoiders who are influenced by the process of *homeostasis*—the tendency to maintain a state of biological and psychological equilibrium or balance. Disturbing this balance generates tension which, if strong enough, will lead to motive arousal. Behavior would then be directed at dissipating tension and restoring a state of balance to the body.

Our behavior with regard to food serves as a good illustration of the concept of homeostasis. Fasting results in a state of imbalance that generates tension within our system. When strong enough, the tension arouses behavior motivated toward food. Eating restores the balance and dissipates the tension.

It can be seen that the homeostatic view holds that consumers will not take actions that increase their tension levels. However, recent evidence suggests that in some situations this will actually occur. For example, one study indicated that consumers buy some new products merely for the change and not because they are dissatisfied with their present brand.[10] This behavior appears to derive from our innate curiosity and need to explore and master our environment.[11] It therefore seems that some changes in consumers' routine behavior can reduce boredom and result in actual enjoyment of some amount of tension.[12]

Effects of Arousal

As we have noted, arousal provides energy for consumers' actions. A second effect is to sensitize consumers' perceptual attention—that is, it can "open up" their perceptual receptors to information that previously may have been ignored. Realizing the importance of this informational "gatekeeper" role, marketers have developed various promotional appeals to generate arousal.

Table 13-1 lists just a small sampling of products and services which have appealed to the indicated motive in an effort to arouse consumers' attention.

Of course, a further result of motive arousal is a directional influence on consumers' actions. We now turn our attention to factors determining the relative strength of various motivational influences on consumer behavior.

MOTIVE STRUCTURE AND INFLUENCE

The concept of a *hierarchy* underlies many schemes offered to explain the relative strength of various motives in influencing behavior. This concept suggests that one could think of motives as being ranked according to their importance in influencing behavior. The most influential motive would enjoy the most dominant position, the second most influential would hold the second most dominant position, and so on through the entire list. To be useful, however, the hierarchy concept must also help explain what factors affect the ordering of motives.

Deprivation

One factor influencing ordering of the hierarchy is *deprivation.* That is, the longer a need goes unsatisfied the greater will be its strength in influencing

TABLE 13-1

A SAMPLE OF PROMOTIONAL AREAS EMPLOYING MOTIVES TO STIMULATE AROUSAL

Motive	Some Areas of Use and Illustrative Appeals
Affection	Areas: Telephones, liquor, greeting cards, insurance, writing instruments, charitable organizations, and vacation resorts
	Appeals: Campbell's soups—"Make someone feel a little warmer inside" Harvey's Bristol Cream Sherry—"When you care enough to give the very best" Kodak film—"For the times of your life"
Safety	Areas: Appliances, toys, air travel, batteries, toothpaste, burglar and fire alarms, and travelers' checks
	Appeals: Children's Tylenol tablets—"It works like children's aspirin . . . but it's safer" Allstate insurance—"You're in good hands with Allstate" Fisher-Price—"Fisher-Price makes toys you can trust with a baby"
Economy	Areas: Dishwashing liquid, automobiles, watches, rug cleaners, air travel, tools, and foods
	Appeals: AMC Gremlin—"More fun than a barrel of gas bills" Burnetts' gin—"British taste/American price" S & H Green Stamps—"Save a little . . . Live a little"
Achievement	Areas: Books, sporting equipment, lawn care products, calculators, colleges, magazines, and liquor
	Appeals: Seagram's V.O. Whiskey—"This sign tells you that you've arrived" Canon cameras—"Explore a world of your own creation" Bradley GT sports car kit—"You've made your mark. Now make your Bradley GT"

behavior. This is obvious to anyone who has been deprived of food or liquids for any significant period of time.

MASLOW'S HIERARCHY Perhaps the most widely known hierarchy was proposed by A. H. Maslow. His scheme classified motives and used the concept of deprivation to order a basic motive hierarchy.[13] Although his motive classification system is certainly relevant to our discussion at the first part of the chapter, its treatment has been reserved until now because of its importance to motive structuring.

Maslow proposed that motives could be classified into five basic categories: physiological, safety, love, esteem, and self-actualization. As depicted in Figure 13-5, he also suggested that for the average individual, the concept of *prepotency* arranges these motives in a hierarchical order as presented in the figure. That is, physiological motives are the lowest and most basic in the hierarchy while self-actualization enjoys the highest position.

Maslow argued that the basic physiological motives are necessary for survival and will exert the most influence on behavior until they are sufficiently satisfied. At that point, the next most prepotent motive—safety—would begin to dominate behavior. Here the consumer would become quite concerned with purchasing products to increase his safety, and safety would become an important evaluation criterion in selecting products. For example, auto safety bumpers, Underwriters Laboratory–listed electrical appliances, and nonskid soles on sneakers would perhaps be important product features. If the consumer is capable of sufficiently satisfying each succeeding motive, self-actualization would become prepotent and tend to dominate consumption behavior.

This pattern of motive domination is depicted in Figure 13-6. Here, it is

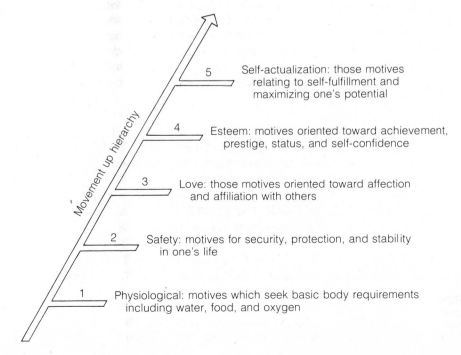

5   Self-actualization: those motives relating to self-fulfillment and maximizing one's potential

4   Esteem: motives oriented toward achievement, prestige, status, and self-confidence

3   Love: those motives oriented toward affection and affiliation with others

2   Safety: motives for security, protection, and stability in one's life

1   Physiological: motives which seek basic body requirements including water, food, and oxygen

Movement up hierarchy

FIGURE 13-5
Maslow's hierarchy of five basic motives.

graphically seen that the dominance pattern of each lower motive is superseded by the next higher motive in the hierarchy after it has been adequately satisfied. Thus, at points A through D in Figure 13-6 *although lower motives can still be quite influential,* higher motives will assume dominance over behavior. It is also important to note that even after being passed on the hierarchy, extensive deprivation of a motive can again lead to its temporarily dominating behavior. This was demonstrated in one study where subjects were placed on a semistarvation diet.[14] Food took on such an important concern that they became uninterested in previously motivating aspects of their lives.

Maslow also argued that as individuals progress to higher motives they grow psychologically and come to develop more wants and a greater variety of ways to satisfy particular motives. Thus, consumers primarily motivated by esteem or self-actualization would be expected to be interested in a greater variety of products and services than consumers primarily motivated by physiological needs.

Although Maslow provided a useful scheme for understanding motives, it does have limitations. Of particular concern is that consumers are constantly influenced by motives that they have apparently passed on the hierarchy. For example, even in our advanced economy, safety (second on the hierarchy) still motivates vast numbers of consumer decisions. Some suggest that Maslow accounted for such situations by indicating that motives could still

FIGURE 13-6
Diagram of the relative predominance of motives and the number and variety of wants recognized for each motive. (*Source:* Adapted from David Krech, Richard S. Crutchfield, and Egerton L. Ballachey, *Individual in Society,* McGraw-Hill, New York, 1962, p. 77.)

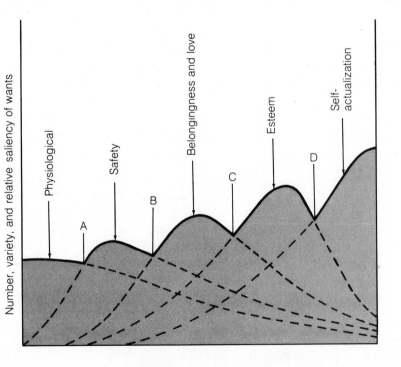

influence behavior even when they are not in a dominant position. However, others argue that he gave inadequate attention to how consumers are influenced by rising levels of aspiration.[15]

Levels of Aspiration

A *level of aspiration* may be thought of as a fluctuating goal the individual sets and attempts to achieve. It is not static and can be influenced by a number of factors to change either *up* or *down* over time. Therefore, as consumers approach a given goal they could still be influenced by the same motive structure but strive for even higher levels of achievement. Similar to Alice in Wonderland, the goal moves upward so that we run faster and faster to attempt to achieve it. For example, hunger can easily be satisfied by very basic foodstuffs such as beans or milk, but achieving this level leads most consumers to "set their sights" higher for foods such as Big Macs and Howard Johnson fish fries.

Included among the factors that influence consumers' levels of aspiration are the following:[16]

1. *Achievement*—success yields rising aspiration levels while failure tends to result in a decline in such goals.

2. *Reality orientation*—usually aspirations are set to reflect the individual's assessment of what levels of achievement are within reach.

3. *Group influences*—consumers' aspirations are influenced by individuals in membership and reference groups. In addition to pressures to "keep up with the Joneses," this provides consumers with reference points as to what levels of achievement exist for various activities and interests.

These characteristics of aspiration levels demonstrate that consumers' wants are insatiable and attempts to achieve them through purchases in the marketplace have led to a very advanced economic system in the United States. However, some suggest that it also has created serious resource shortages and a degradation of our environment, as well as other problems.[17]

Learning Influences

Another important influence on the structuring of motives is learning. As indicated earlier, consumers can acquire (learn) new motives from dealing with their environment. The addition of such learned or *secondary* motives results in a restructuring of the hierarchy. This occurs because secondary motives are often quite strong and therefore have a great influence on behavior. Consider, for example, how the learned need for social approval so strongly influences purchase decisions from personal-care products to automobiles.

Motive Combinations

It is convenient to discuss motives separately as if they influence consumers independently and one at a time. Actually, they often interact, leading to a combined influence on consumers or to situations where they conflict and exert opposing influences on behavior.[18]

MOTIVE LINKING Since motives can differ in how specific they are, it is possible for a linking to occur at various levels of generality. For example, safety may actually be made up of more specific motives, including those relating to security and protection. Therefore, achievement of some specific motive can be a *means* of approaching a more general motive which is viewed as the *goal.* This is referred to as the *means-end linking* of motives. A linking that might exist to influence a purchase of a door-lock is depicted in Figure 13-7. Here we see that safety has been linked to the more specific motives of protection and security. In turn, these have been linked to strength, dependability, and durability propereties of the product. All of these factors can exert a combined influence on the consumer.

MOTIVE BUNDLING A given product can also satisfy various motives at the same approximate level of specific influence. This results in the *bundling* or combining of influences on the consumer's decisions. For example, one study identified a bundle of motives, including financial security for loved ones and savings, as influencing life insurance purchases.[19] Also, for an automobile purchase, a desire for transportation can link with motives for achievement, social recognition, safety, and economy.

Motive bundling and linking suggest product and promotional strategies to increase or sustain consumers' attraction toward a firm's offering over a period of time. For example, the energy crisis of the 1970s resulted in changing both automobiles and their accompanying promotional strategies to emphasize fuel economy. Also, Sears has promoted their radial tires at various times as appealing to the economy motive (long-lasting), safety (superior handling), and again later in terms of economy (better mileage).

MOTIVE CONFLICT Motives can also conflict with each other to affect how consumers interact with the marketplace. A major contributor to the topic of motive conflict is Kurt Lewin.[20] He viewed motives as influencing the attracting or repelling forces of goals in the individual's environment. The degree to which a product or service satisfies a motive will therefore determine its attracting (positive) force, and how adverse it is to a motive will influence its repelling (negative) force.

In Lewin's view, conflict is most likely when motives are approximately of

FIGURE 13-7
A means-end linking for a door lock purchase. (*Source:* Adapted from John A. Howard and Jagdish N. Sheth, *The Theory of Buyer Behavior,* Wiley, New York, 1969, p. 107.)

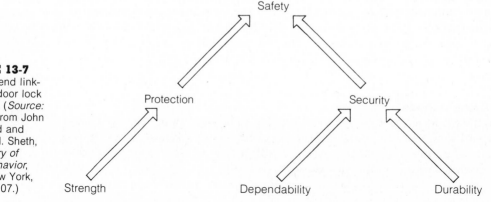

equal strength. Three specific cases are possible: *approach-approach, avoidance-avoidance,* and *approach-avoidance* conflict. Actually, these terms refer to psychological tendencies for attraction or repulsion. Although consumers may also exhibit physical movement in such conditions, this is not necessary.

Approach-Approach Conflict This is a situation where conflict exists between two desirable alternatives, as when a consumer must decide how to allocate purchasing dollars between a tennis racket and an electronic calculator (see Figure 13-8). These situations can lead to a period of temporary indecision and vacillation between alternatives. Permanent indecision is rare, however, because approach-approach conflict is said to be unstable. This occurs because the pull toward a positive goal increases as one approaches it, and declines as one moves away.[21] Therefore, a slight tendency to accept one alternative can lead to resolving the conflict quickly. Such resolution can occur through exposure to information useful in evaluating the alternatives. Promotional literature and salespeople's comments can therefore play a crucial role in this process.

Resolution of approach-approach conflict can also occur through reassessment of goals that might lead to a decision that achieving one goal is more important than the other. Again, comments of salespeople can be quite influential. Of course, a third resolution involves attempts to achieve modified versions of both goals. In our example, this could occur through purchase of less expensive models of the calculator and tennis racket.

Avoidance-Avoidance Conflict This situation occurs when consumers face choices between two alternatives, both of which are perceived as being negative in nature. For example, when the television set with which a family has been perfectly happy becomes seriously ill, the alternatives may be a hefty repair bill or the large expense of a replacement set (See Figure 13-8). Such situations are characterized as stable since consumers tend to vacillate between undesirable alternatives. This occurs because approaching a negative alternative leads to a stronger repulsion by it. Such situations often lead to considerable search for information (window shopping, literature review, and inquiries) but stop short of a commitment.

Approach-Avoidance Conflict This term describes situations where consumers are in conflict between a positive and negative alternative. Such situations often occur in decisions regarding a single product where both positive and negative aspects are involved in the purchase. For example, (see Figure 13-8) to acquire an attractive product such as a car, consumers must part with a sizable number of scarce purchasing dollars. Such cash outflows can generate considerable avoidance, as demonstrated by the frequent auto sales slumps that occur.

Approach-avoidance conflict also tends to be stable, since both attracting and repelling forces increase as the goal object is approached; but the repelling force increases more sharply. This results in the consumer being attracted by goal objects but experiencing increasing resistance to them as they are approached. Recognizing this problem, many marketers have developed means to reduce the avoidance aspect of such conflicts. Banks offer loans where you "borrow in June and start paying in September" and major airlines offer "fly now, pay later" programs. The availability of credit cards and financing arrangements also contributes to the ease of making large expenditures.

Approach-avoidance conflict also happens in more subtle ways as when consumers are faced with choosing between alternative brands of a given product where, compared to one another, each brand has both positive and negative features. For example, choosing a Ford over a Chevrolet because of its styling also means sacrificing the traditionally higher trade-in value of Chevrolets. When faced with such important choices, consumers frequently exhibit considerable conflict and indecision. Consequently, salespeople have developed *closing techniques* to encourage customers to make a decision. The following is just a sampling of such methods:

Advantage/disadvantage close—negative and positive features of each alternative are summarized to assist the customer in determining which alternative appears to be the better choice.

Critical feature close—stress is placed on one or a few "critical" features of one brand that the other does not possess.

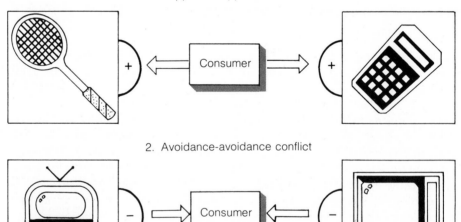

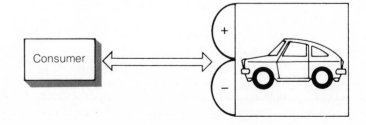

FIGURE 13-8
A typology of motive conflict situations. (*Source:* Derived from Kurt Lewin, *A Dynamic Theory of Personality*, McGraw-Hill, New York, 1935.)

Critical time close—in cases where one brand is in short supply, or where a special offer is about to end, emphasizing the immediacy of the decision can convince the consumer to purchase.

Self-Concept

Although a consumer's motive structure varies over a period of time due to changes in situations, roles, and life-styles, there remains a central theme or organization to the structure. One factor influencing this organization is the individual's *self-concept*. That is, consumers possess a certain image of themselves, and this self-concept exerts an organizing influence on their motives.

One important influence of the self-concept on motives is reflected in the types of goods purchased. Consumers appear to make purchases that are consistent with their self-concepts.[22] Thus, we would expect to see an individual who views himself or herself as a successful businessperson drive cars, own homes, join clubs, and interact with social groups that reflect this self-image. This topic will be more fully discussed in Chapter 16.

MOTIVE DIRECTION

It has been continually emphasized in this chapter that, in addition to their energizing aspects, motives also provide direction to consumers' actions. Some additional comments on the nature of these directional influences are warranted.[23]

Selecting Goal Objects

Although there are exceptions, consumers often see products or services as the means to achieve their motives.[24] In fact, consumers often think of a product as the actual goal that they are trying to achieve, without realizing that it is only a means to satisfy a motive.

This directional push toward products as goal objects is of great interest to marketers, particularly since it appears that it can be influenced. Certainly the features designed into a product can affect the degree to which it is accepted as a goal or means for achieving some goal. Much effort is also spent on developing promotions that persuade consumers to consider products as objects useful in achieving some motive. For example, the advertisement in Figure 13-9 effectively suggests that use of the product will lead to certain motive satisfactions.

Influencing Choice Criteria

Motives also assist consumers in developing criteria for evaluating products. That is, consumers evaluate products in terms of their ability to satisfy particular motives. Thus, for a car buyer strongly influenced by the convenience motive, features such as electronic speed control, electric door locks, and easy-servicing requirements would be more important choice criteria than styling or mileage.

It appears that marketers are also capable of influencing consumer's choice criteria. In some cases this occurs because consumers are not consciously aware of their own motives. For example, a salesperson for air conditioners may remark that one model is more efficient than others, thereby making the consumer realize that economy actually is important to his selection of a unit. In other cases consumers may be aware of their motives but unsure of the criteria to use in their evaluation. For example, safety is a highly conscious motive influencing most purchases of infant car

Very convincing.

The perfect gift for a sensuous man. A very different musk that comes across with unmistakable intentions. Deep, mysterious and long-lasting. And above all, definitely male.

Old Spice
MUSK FOR MEN
SHULTON

cologne

after shave lotion
in unbreakable bottle

FIGURE 13-9
Example of motive directional influence. (Reproduced by permission of Shulton, Inc.)

seats. However, many are probably unaware of the need for such seats to have side-wall protection against sideways movement during crashes. A manufacturer can therefore use promotion to inform consumers of the importance of this criterion and how well the company's product meets it.

A sound understanding of how motives can influence purchases may also suggest product modifications to provide new features relevant to such motives. The introduction of remote control television tuners, shatterproof eyeglasses, and energy-saving switches on frost-free refrigerators are illustrative of this approach.

Other Influences

At a more fundamental level, motives affect the individual determinants of perception, learning, personality, and attitudes. This also results in directional influences on behavior. For example, motives influence the perceptual process, which in turn regulates how we interpret and respond to our environment. These influences are discussed in greater detail in the remaining chapters of this section.

MOTIVATION RESEARCH

We have noted that many consumers are unaware of the motives influencing their purchase behavior. That is, some motives may not reach the consumer's consciousness and others may be repressed because they are uncomfortable to deal with. This presents difficulty to the marketer who needs to understand consumers in order to design the most effective mix of marketing offerings. Any direct attempts to determine such motives, say by asking consumers, may only yield "surface" explanations or rationalizations that hide their true motives.

The concept of motivation research has been offered as a means of determining consumers' true, underlying purchase motives. An introduction to this field and its methods was made in Chapter 3, and it would be useful to refer back to it at this point. Briefly, the methods involve disguised and indirect techniques in an attempt to probe consumers' inner motives without arousing defense mechanisms, which can yield misleading results.

In practice, motivation research has yielded provocative and sometimes strange conclusions. For example, explanations for various consumer actions include the following:

Many men don't like to fly because they fear that if the plane crashes they will be blamed by their family for not being killed in a decent fashion, such as in a car crash.

When baking, a woman is unconsciously and symbolically reenacting the process of giving birth.

Rice and tea are considered feminine while coffee and potatoes are considered masculine, and oranges and roast chicken are seen as bisexual.

Men who use suspenders have an unresolved castration complex.[25]

The novelty of these interpretations is at least partially explained by the heavy influence of Freudian thinking on some motivation researchers. The central role of fantasy, unconscious antisocial strivings, and sex in Freudian psychology have apparently strongly influenced conclusions drawn from many motivation research studies. The extent to which these interpretations are valid is open to question.

There have also been a number of other criticisms leveled at motivation researchers.[26] For one, sample sizes are frequently small because of the costly nature of depth interviewing. This has created problems with regard to making conclusions about the entire population of consumers. Secondly, motivation research studies have generated inconsistent findings, and this leaves the marketer in a quandary as to what action should be taken. Further, some findings are difficult for the marketer to capitalize on. For example, of what practical use is it to know (assuming it is true) that suspender wearers have a castration complex? Finally, and perhaps most importantly, motivation researchers have been criticized for improperly employing research techniques borrowed from psychologists. In psychology these techniques are used in conjunction with knowledge of a patient's history and normal standards of behavior as references. The lack of such standards in marketing makes it difficult to determine whether many motivation research findings are truly representative of most consumers.

Despite its potential limitations, motivation research has been a valuable research tool in a number of situations. For example, in a now classic study, Haire discovered evidence suggesting that initial resistance to Nescafé instant coffee may have been due to more than its taste characteristics. Projective methods revealed that women believed users of the instant product were lazy and not particularly good wives. Thus, it was argued, they would not be quick to adopt it themselves.[27] Other studies, pioneered by Dichter and others, have provided data for marketing decisions of major industrial giants such as Alcoa, Colgate-Palmolive, General Mills, and Chrysler Corporation.[28] Therefore, it appears that when employed with other information, properly conducted motivation research studies can provide valuable information about consumers.

SUMMARY

This chapter introduced the first of several individual determinants of consumer behavior. Motives were defined as an inner state that mobilizes and directs bodily energy toward goals located in the environment. After several schemes for classifying motives were reviewed, the concept of arousal was treated. Here we learned that the major ways motives can be triggered are through physiological conditions, situational conditions, and cognitive activity. Although the concept of tension is central to motive arousal, the primary goal of consumers is not always to reduce tension. Sometimes they seek increases in tension levels, perhaps due to curiosity or a need for a certain amount of stimulation.

The concepts of motive hierarchies and levels of aspiration were seen to be central to an understanding of motive structuring. However, a practical view of such structuring must consider that motives interact to combine their influence or conflict with each other.

The directional influence of motives was discussed next. Their potential effects on selecting goal objects, specifying choice criteria, and influencing individual determinants of behavior were treated.

Finally, the topic of motivation research was briefly reviewed. It appears that after an early flush of popularity, perhaps associated with overzealous application, the discipline has matured to a point where its valid contributions can be usefully combined with other methods to explore consumers' motives.

DISCUSSION TOPICS

1. What is a motive? Indicate the various roles motives play in influencing behavior.

2. Find two examples of advertisements that appeal to each of Bayton's three psychogenic motive categories. Be prepared to discuss the appropriateness of the association between the product and the motive category.

3. Discuss the problems unconscious motives pose for implementing the marketing concept.

4. What general factors can trigger motive arousal? Cite at least two examples of each type.

5. It has been argued that motives can be aroused by decreasing consumers' tension levels as well as increasing them. Review this argument and demonstrate how the marketer might be able to capitalize on each situation.

6. Briefly review Maslow's motive hierarchy and the concept of prepotency. Cite at least three products that might appeal to an individual at each stage of the hierarchy. Can you suggest any product for which the marketer might be able to appeal to at least three of the stages at the same time?

7. Of what interest is the concept of levels of aspiration to the marketer? What relevance does this concept have to the problem of energy shortage and depletion of resources?

8. Review the concepts of motive linking and motive bundling. Show how they can apply to the purchase of a jogging suit.

9. Define each of the four types of motive conflict and cite a personal experience that fits each of these situations. Be sure to indicate the specifics involved, including any relevant products, the duration of the conflict, and how it was resolved.

10. Relate a personal experience where you were strongly influenced by a particular motive and how this influenced the choice criteria you employed for a purchase.

NOTES

1. Theodore M. Newcomb, Ralph H. Turner, and Phillip E. Converse, *Social Psychology,* Holt, New York, 1965, p. 22.
2. See Joe Kent Kerby, *Consumer Behavior: Conceptual Foundations,* Dun-Donnelley, New York, 1975; and C. Glenn Walters, *Consumer Behavior: Theory and Practice,* 3d ed., Irwin, Homewood, III., 1978.
3. For a recent and quite comprehensive scheme, see William J. McGuire, "Some Internal Psychological Factors Influencing Consumer Choice," *Journal of Consumer Research,* **2**:302–319, March 1976.

4. James A. Bayton, "Motivation, Cognition, Learning—Basic Factors in Consumer Behavior," *Journal of Marketing,* **22**:282–289, January 1958.

5. Melvin T. Copeland, *Principles of Merchandising,* A. W. Shaw, New York, 1924, pp. 155–167.

6. Sidney J. Levy, "Symbols for Sale," *Harvard Business Review,* **37**:117–124, July-August 1959.

7. Some of this discussion follows James F. Engel, David T. Kollat, and Roger D. Blackwell, *Consumer Behavior,* 2d ed., Holt, New York, 1973, pp. 28–29.

8. See Russell W. Belk, "Situational Variables and Consumer Behavior," *Journal of Consumer Research,* **2**:157–164, December 1975.

9. Much of this section follows David Krech, Richard S. Crutchfield, and Egerton L. Ballachey, *Individual In Society,* McGraw-Hill, New York, 1962, pp. 84–87.

10. Elihu Katz and P. F. Lazarsfeld, *Personal Influence,* Free Press, New York, 1955; and G. H. Haines, "At Study of Why People Purchase New Products," in Raymond M. Hass (ed.), *Science, Technology and Marketing,* American Marketing Association, Chicago, 1966, pp. 685–697.

11. Robert W. White, "Motivation Reconsidered: The Concept of Competence," *Psychological Review,* **66**:297–333, 1959.

12. See John A. Howard and Jagdish N. Sheth, *The Theory of Buyer Behavior,* Wiley, New York, 1969, pp. 27–28 and 163–164, for a discussion of this view described as the "psychology of complication."

13. A. H. Maslow, "A Theory of Human Motivation," *Psychological Review,* **50**:370–396, 1943.

14. H. S. Guetzkow and P. H. Bowman, *Men and Hunger: A Psychological Manual for Relief Workers,* Brethen Press, Elgin, Ill., 1946.

15. Frederick Herzberg, "Retrospective Comment," in Howard A. Thompson (ed.), *The Great Writings in Marketing,* Commerce, Plymouth, Mich., 1976, pp. 180–181.

16. George Katona, *The Powerful Consumer,* McGraw-Hill, New York, 1960, p. 130.

17. See John Kenneth Galbraith, *The Affluent Society,* Houghton Mifflin, Boston, 1958.

18. Some of this section follows Howard and Sheth, *The Theory of Buyer Behavior,* pp. 105–118.

19. Katona, *The Powerful Consumer,* p. 117.

20. Kurt Lewin, *A Dynamic Theory of Personality,* McGraw-Hill, New York, 1935.

21. Bernard Berelson and Gary Steiner, *Human Behavior: An Inventory of Scientific Findings,* Harcourt, Brace & World, New York, 1964, p. 273.

22. See E. Laird Landon, Jr., "Self Concept, Ideal Self Concept, and Consumer Purchase Intentions," *Journal of Consumer Research,* **1**:44–51, September 1974.

23. Portions of this section follow discussion in Howard and Sheth, *The Theory of Buyer Behavior,* pp. 105–118.

24. One exception is the case of anxiety where consumers suffer from a lack of direction to their arousal.

25. See Ernest Dichter, *Handbook of Consumer Motivations,* McGraw-Hill, New York, 1964, for these and other interesting motivation research findings.

26. See N. D. Rothwell, "Motivational Research Reinstated," *Journal of Marketing,* **19**:150–154, October 1955.

27. Mason Haire, "Projective Techniques in Marketing Research," *Journal of Marketing,* **14**:649–656, April 1950.

28. Roger Ricklefs, "Ernest Dichter Thrives Selling Firms on Hidden Emotions," *The Wall Street Journal,* November 20, 1972, p. 1.

PERCEPTION

CHARACTERIZING PERCEPTION SENSATION AND SELECTIVE ATTENTION Awareness Thresholds; Differential Thresholds; Selective Attention—Stimulus Factors; Selective Attention—Individual Factors INTERPRETATION Organization; Categorization RESPONSE MARKETING IMPLICATIONS Product Perception; Price Perception; Company and Store Image Perception; Advertising Perception

Consider for a moment the following actual case histories:

The alcoholic content of many liquors is decreased, and very few consumers notice the change.

After intensive testing, Consolidated Cigar Corporation plans to market a cigar having the aroma of a pipe.

Consumers reject a new brand of catsup and the problem is diagnosed as the product tasting too much like the real thing—natural tomatoes. After adjusting production to overcook and scorch the catsup, it is reintroduced to the market and sales soar!

These situations have one common theme: consumer behavior is strongly influenced by perception.

A brief overview of the perceptual process will serve as a useful introduction to this chapter. We will then consider factors influencing consumers' selective attention to only certain aspects of their surroundings. Next, the manner in which consumers interpret and respond to aspects of their environment is treated. Finally, application of these principles to actual marketing decisions is reviewed.

CHARACTERIZING PERCEPTION

Generally, perception may be thought of as the process of receiving and deriving meaning from stimuli present in our internal and external environment. More specifically, we can say that:

To perceive is to
$\begin{cases} \text{see} \\ \text{hear} \\ \text{touch} \\ \text{taste} \\ \text{smell or} \\ \text{sense} \\ \text{internally} \end{cases}$
some
$\begin{cases} \text{thing} \\ \text{event} \\ \text{or} \\ \text{relation} \end{cases}$
and to
$\begin{cases} \text{organize} \\ \text{interpret and} \\ \text{derive meaning} \\ \text{from the} \\ \text{experience}[1] \end{cases}$

This definition correctly suggests that perception is actually a *process,* made up of several interrelated activities, which results in the consumer deriving meaning from some experience. Figure 14-1 shows the major activities involved in this perception process and will serve as a framework for our discussion.

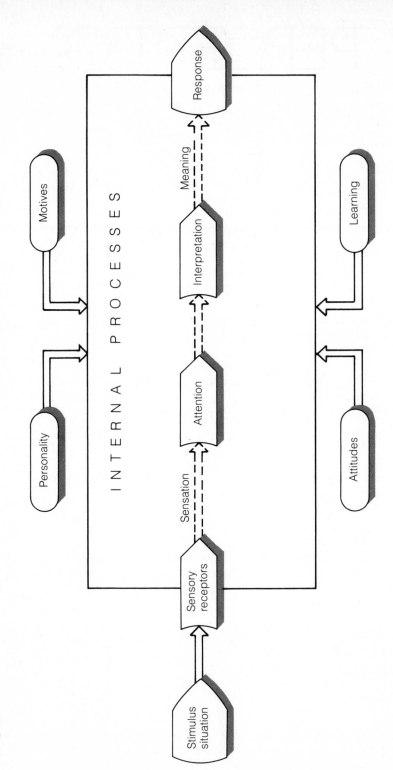

FIGURE 14-1
A diagram of the perceptual process.

Perception is activated by a stimulus situation which is made up of a variety of *stimuli*—units of energy, such as light and sounds, which can stimulate our sensory receptors. We have receptors for internally produced stimuli as well as for the commonly known five senses of taste, touch, smell, vision, and hearing.

Our perceptual receivers are constantly bombarded by an almost infinite number of stimuli. Two mechanisms reduce this "blooming confusion" to manageable proportions, however. First, our receptors have limited sensitivity and produce sensations for stimuli only within their range of operation. Secondly, we selectively attend to only a small proportion of the resulting sensations and literally ignore the rest.

Interpretation includes several functions to derive meaning from sensations reaching our attention. One activity involves organizing the sensations into some meaningful pattern. The activity of categorization then compares this organized pattern to past experiences in order to derive meaning from it. The entire process of interpretation is influenced by a number of individual determinants and operates so automatically that it rarely reaches conscious thought. In addition, the process is quite subjective in nature, which indicates that perception involves selective distortion of information as well as selective attention to it.

The end product of the perceptual process is some response. One type of response involves no overt behavior but fosters changes in internal factors. For example, a consumer may react to a television advertisement by remembering certain information and changing her attitude toward the product involved. Of course, the marketer is also concerned with consumers' overt responses to stimuli since they are more easily measured and can result in purchases.

Figure 14-1 also depicts the influence of major individual determinants on perception. Throughout this chapter we shall be able to demonstrate their significant impact on each stage of the perceptual process.

SENSATION AND SELECTIVE ATTENTION

In this section the processes by which consumers become aware of only a portion of the stimuli they confront is examined in more depth. First, we shall explore the limits of perceptual awareness and then discuss selective attention.

Awareness Thresholds

Any given stimulus may be either too small or weak to notice or so great that it also escapes awareness. Consumers' zones of stimulus awareness can therefore be identified by defining two thresholds:

Absolute Threshold—The minimum value of a stimulus capable of being consciously noticed

Terminal Threshold—The maximum value of a stimulus capable of being consciously noticed

To illustrate, the average person's absolute and terminal thresholds for sound pitch are about 20 and 20,000 cycles per second, respectively. Those familiar with stereo equipment will notice that this is the exact range manufacturers concentrate on when designing their equipment.

The threshold concept implies that we can determine precise values which mark the boundaries of stimulus awareness. This is actually misleading, since these limits for any given stimulus differ among individuals and even for the same individual over a period of time. Therefore, thresholds must be viewed as being somewhat variable, and are usually defined by the stimulus value that goes undetected 50 percent of the time.

MARKETING RELEVANCE OF ABSOLUTE THRESHOLDS Consumers' absolute thresholds are often of more interest to marketers than terminal thresholds because of their greater relevance to product designs. For example, the average individual's ability to detect that a light source is flashing is about 60 flashes per second for very bright lights, and considerably less for dimmer sources. Knowledge of this absolute threshold has enormous practical application to product designs as illustrated below:

Common household light bulbs pulsate at 60 cycles per second but appear to have a constant intensity.

Home movie projectors show 18 frames of film per second without appearing to flicker.

Television sets produce an apparent full screen image by rapidly scanning the entire screen with a narrow beam of light.

In another application, consider the following characteristics of absolute taste thresholds:

Absolute taste thresholds are high (not sensitive) at a very early age, and sensitivity increases as the individual matures.

For some substances, people differ considerably in their taste sensitivities, while for others little variability exists.

Consumers' relative lack of taste sensitivity at an early age has been of considerable concern to those marketing baby foods. Historically, many producers deemed it necessary to salt and sweeten their products to pass parents' sensitive taste tests, even though infants are unable to taste these flavorings in the amounts added.[2] Mounting evidence regarding the possible health disadvantages of this approach has led Beechnut and other producers to offer many foods without these flavorings. Informational promotions have also been implemented to explain babies' insensitive tastes to parents so that they will accept the product changes.

The conclusion that taste sensitivity can vary significantly between adult consumers is also important input to product designers. One area of application is the beer industry, where experts have segmented the consuming public into three distinct groupings: (1) discriminating individuals mainly concerned with the taste of beer, (2) discriminating individuals influenced by price and other variables, and (3) nondiscriminating consumers.[3] Marketing strategies directed at such segments could differ significantly.

Differential Thresholds

Many sellers have made changes in their offerings only to find that they went unnoticed in the marketplace. This suggests that consumers also have limited sensitivity for noticing differences between different stimulus values. The *differential threshold* defines this sensitivity as the smallest detectable difference between two values of the same stimulus. For example, a soft drink producer interested in whether consumers can detect a difference in sweetness in two different sugar concentrations in a drink would need to examine consumers' differential threshold for sweetness.

To measure the differential threshold for a stimulus, one commonly changes its intensity in very small amounts, as in a hearing test. The consumer's threshold exists where he first notices that the stimulus has changed. The difference between this value and the starting value is often referred to as the *just noticeable difference (jnd)*.

WEBER'S LAW As in the case of absolute thresholds, consumers also differ in their ability to detect differences between stimulus values, and this sensitivity varies with conditions. However, numerous studies have revealed a general relationship known as Weber's Law which states that the stimulus change needed to reach the differential threshold (produce a just noticeable difference) is a constant *proportion* of the starting stimulus value. Weber's Law can be expressed as:

$$\frac{\Delta s}{S} = K$$

where S = the initial stimulus value
Δs = the smallest change in the stimulus
capable of being detected—the jnd
K = the constant of proportionality

Expressing the equation as $\Delta s = K \cdot S$ suggests that if we know the values of K and S, we could predict how large a change in the stimulus is necessary before consumers detect the change. To illustrate, assume that through testing we found that 1 ounce ($\Delta s = 1$) had to be added to a 10-ounce package ($S = 10$) before consumers detected a change in its weight. This would yield a constant of proportionality of $K = 1/10 = 0.1$, allowing us to predict that:

Consumers will not detect a change in the weight of a 50-ounce box of detergent unless at least 5 ounces are added to or removed from it.

Consumers will be able to detect a 3-pound addition to a 20-pound portable television.

Two points should be noted with regard to Weber's Law: (1) there are different constants of proportionality for different stimuli such as weight, color, and size and (2) the law is not universal in its applicability because individuals differ and because it does not predict well near absolute and terminal thresholds. However, refinements have been made to the basic law and it appears to hold fairly well over the majority of stimulus range.

APPLYING WEBER'S LAW Marketers can apply Weber's Law to predicting how consumers will respond to differences between marketing variables or changes in these variables.[4] Sometimes the goal is to have consumers detect differences, and in other cases it is to have differences escape their attention. For example, because the cost of candy ingredients fluctuates widely there is a constant search for more stably priced substitutes. According to one report, this led to the discovery by Peter Paul, Inc., that tasters could not distinguish between one chocolate made with vegetable oil and another made with traditional cocoa butter.[5] However, a second firm found that most consumers could detect a difference between a chocolate substitute and the real thing.

A second way to hold prices constant in times of changing costs is to change the size or amount of the product slightly. For example, over a 23-year period the Hershey Foods Corporation changed the price of its basic milk chocolate bar only three times but varied its weight fourteen times.[6] It should be noted that many of these changes escaping consumers' awareness were weight *increases* allowed by declining costs. Similar changes (increases as well as decreases) have occurred in numerous packages and products, including newspapers, bathroom tissues, and soft drinks.

Another application of Weber's Law lies in the battleground of brand competition. Here producers of major brands such as A. T. Cross pens and Tide detergent seek to distinguish their products as quite different from those of private competitors. However some competing firms seek to produce similar products using less costly ingredients that might escape consumers' notice, thereby obtaining a differential price advantage. Also, packages of some privately labeled grocery products bear a striking resemblance to those of major brands.[7] Presumably, this discourages shoppers from detecting any noticeable differences existing between the brands. Exhibit 14-1 presents examples of this situation.

Pricing decisions may also make use of Weber's Law. For example, many merchants have noted that price reductions of at least 15 percent are usually needed to attract consumers to sales. This experience is supported by experimental evidence suggesting that consumers do possess awareness thresholds for price changes.[8]

Selective Attention—Stimulus Factors

The above discussion suggests that consumers' limited ability to receive stimuli is one aspect of their perceptual selectivity. Another aspect is their selective attention to only a fraction of the sensations that are produced. Certain characteristics of stimuli themselves influence this attention process. Several particularly important to promotion are treated below.

COLOR Considerable evidence indicates that color advertisements attract more attention than those presented in black and white. One reason may be that, especially in newspaper advertising, color stands out because of its infrequent use.[9] However, even though color can attract more attention, its higher cost may result in capturing less attention per advertising dollar spent.[10] Also, as television has demonstrated, wider use of color may diminish its attention-attracting power. Thus, as the use of color becomes commonplace, new and unique combinations of colors as well as increases in their intensity may be necessary to obtain high attention value.[11] The psychedelic colors used in television advertising for Levi's jeans demonstrate this approach.

NOVELTY AND CONTRAST Stimuli that stand out sharply against their background are known to attract attention. In fact, this may be a major reason for the attention-attracting power of color advertisements.[12] Greater impact is often attempted in the promotion field by the use of novelty and various contrasts. Novelty can be achieved through unique shapes, sounds, colors, and themes. Figure 14-2 illustrates the use of this approach to attract attention.

Contrast also attracts attention and facilitates definition of objects. In print media, complementary colors such as yellow and blue, and reversals (white lettering on a black or color background) are frequently used to achieve contrast. However, because reversals are more difficult to read, the message involved should be kept short.

In television and radio, volume levels have been both raised and lowered to achieve contrast between promotional messages and program content. It has also been suggested that the first few seconds of an advertisement could be completely silent to heighten contrast with the following message and thus attract attention.

EXHIBIT 14-1
Examples of package similarity. (*Source:* Candace E. Trunzo, "Checkout-Counter Lookalikes." Reprinted from the May 1976 issue of MONEY Magazine by special permission; © 1976, Time Inc. All rights reserved. pp. 71–72.)

SIZE AND POSITION Studies of newspaper and magazine advertising reveal that the size of an advertisement affects its power to attract attention. However, attention does not vary directly with size but seems to change in relation to the square root of the ad's area. Thus to double its attention-attracting power, the size of an advertisement would have to be quadrupled.

The position of an advertisement also appears to influence its attention-

FIGURE 14-2
Use of novelty to attract attention. (Courtesy of Levi Strauss & Co. and Foote, Cone & Belding/Honig. Original art by Jozef Sumichrast.)

attracting power. The following examples in print media are offered to illustrate. First, in terms of layout, ads with vertical splits (pictures on one side and copy on the other) and haphazard arrangements of pictures appear to discourage at least some readers.[13] Second, there seems to be little difference whether an advertisement appears on the right-hand or left-hand page.[14] Moreover, in terms of placement on a page, position does not seem to have an effect unless many ads share the page, in which case the upper right-hand corner appears advantageous.[15] Third, there appears to be an attention advantage for magazine ads placed in the first ten pages or next to related editorial matter, but due to high page traffic, position within a newspaper is not as critical.[16]

A wide variety of other stimulus factors, such as "scratch-and-sniff" strips in printed promotions and signs with moving parts, have been employed to attract consumers' attention. The interested reader is referred to retailing and advertising texts for a more detailed presentation of these techniques.

Selective Attention—Individual Factors

In addition to stimulus characteristics, individual attributes of consumers themselves also influence whether a given stimulus will be noticed. Some of these individual factors are discussed below.

ATTENTION SPAN One way to define an attention span is by its breadth—how many items can be attended to at any instant in time. The average attention span for adults is about seven items, but this narrows for complex material requiring concentration. The most important implication of this for advertisers is to "keep the message simple."

The time dimension of consumers' attention span is also rather short, perhaps only a matter of seconds, particularly when interest in the material is at a low level. Therefore, if consumers are to concentrate on something even as short as a television advertisement they must constantly renew their attention. Because such viewing is quite passive, not involving significant concentration, this rarely happens. Therefore, to design television advertisements that attract and briefly hold attention, advertisers use a variety of stimulus factors, including those discussed above, to heighten viewers' interest.[17]

ADAPTATION Prolonged exposure to constant levels of stimulation results in consumers not noticing them. This gradual adjustment to stimuli is called *adaptation*. For example, when we walk into an air-conditioned building it first appears quite cool, but a short time later we have adapted to the temperature and become less aware of it. Similarly, consumers appear to adapt to various marketing stimuli such as price levels and advertising messages. Consider, for example, how audiences have become used to color television advertisements, a factor that minimizes their attention-attracting power. Such situations help explain why marketers search for fresh advertising approaches and try to offer new and improved products.

PERCEPTUAL VIGILANCE AND DEFENSE The concept of *perceptual vigilance* explains consumers' heightened sensitivity to stimuli that are capable of satisfying motives. This suggests that higher motive arousal should lead consumers to pay increased attention to marketing stimuli relevant to the aroused motive. Based on this concept, it has been suggested that less expensive, small or medium-sized print advertisements may be more economically effective than large ones in reaching the attention of motivated consumers.[18] The rationale is that although the smaller ads might not be noticed by some consumers, they still will capture the attention of those who are aroused by relevant motives.

Individuals are also capable of *perceptual defense,* that is, decreasing their awareness to threatening stimuli. For example, one study found that only 32 percent of a sample of smokers consistently read articles relating smoking to lung cancer, while 60 percent of a group of nonsmokers read the articles.[19] Apparently, smokers feel threatened by such information and their perceptual defense mechanism allows them to ignore it.

The topic of perceptual defense has relevance in advertising, particularly to the use of fear appeals in commercial messages. Fear appeals have potential for promoting products such as burglar alarms, seat belts, and underarm deodorants. They have also been used in so-called anticommercials, including ones to reduce cigarette smoking and others to promote ecological concern. Of course, the danger of these fear appeals is that they may be threatening to consumers and lead to perceptual defenses against the message. For example, an advertisement showing burned children to draw viewers' attention to the need for home fire alarms would probably fail because consumers want to avoid thinking of such a tragedy.

INTERPRETATION

The process of interpretation involves deriving meaning from sensations produced from a stimulus situation. As mentioned earlier, we can view interpretation as involving two subprocesses: organization and categorization. *Organization* involves mentally arranging sensations into some unified whole while *categorization* involves comparing this pattern to similar past experiences in an attempt to derive meaning from it. Although these two processes are affected by the individual's past experiences and present conditions, some generalizations across individuals can be made.

Organization

We usually perceive an automobile not as a large number of pieces of glass, plastic, and steel but as a unified whole. That is, perception organizes sensations into some coherent pattern which is often called a *gestalt* (pronounced guh-shtalt´). In fact, this process has been the prime interest of gestalt psychologists, and much of this section is based on their work. Although visual examples are primarily used, many of the principles can be applied to other stimuli as well.

FIGURE-GROUND This is one of the most basic and automatic organizational processes perceivers impose on their world. Two properties of this innate perceptual tendency are: (1) the figure appears to stand out as being in front of the more distant background and (2) the figure is perceived to have form and be more substantial than the ground. An example of the way in which the figure-ground process operates is shown in Figure 14-3. Most individuals organize this stimulus situation as a white goblet (figure) on a black ground rather than as two faces (figure) with a white ground separating them. Print advertisements frequently employ figure-ground techniques to attract readers' attention to portions of an advertisement the marketer deems most important.

PROXIMITY In this organization process items close to each other in time or space tend to be perceived as being related, while separated items are viewed as being different. The uses of proximity in promotions are widespread. Mentholated cigarettes are shown in beautiful green, springlike settings or against a deep blue sky to suggest freshness. Soft drinks and fast foods are usually shown being enjoyed in active, fun-oriented settings, and sporty cars are frequently placed at racetracks or in other competitive situations. Also, in comparative advertising, the promoted brand is usually shown in the good company of other respected brands and separated from supposedly inferior alternatives.

SIMILARITY Assuming no other influence, items that are perceived as being similar to one another tend to be grouped together. This in turn can influence the pattern one perceives in a conglomeration of items. Figure 14-4 illustrates this point. Here, since similar elements form columns, there is a tendency to view the entire figure as a grouping of columns rather than a grouping of rows.

The principle of similarity has been used in various ways to influence consumers' perceptions. For example, Ford's advertising of the Granada has shown its similarity in appearance to the Mercedes in an effort to convince

FIGURE 14-3
Example demonstrating figure-ground perception.

consumers that the cars have similar attributes in performance as well as styling.

APPARENT MOTION Sometimes we organize our perceptions so as to produce the appearance of motion. For example, the rapid presentation of still pictures, each slightly different than the other, leads to the perception of motion. Use of the apparent motion technique in advertising no longer seems very dramatic, but it represents one of the most insightful and extensive applications of perception in marketing.

CLOSURE Frequently, consumers organize incomplete stimuli by perceiving them as complete figures. In other words, a figure such as an opened circle, would tend to be filled in by the individual to result in perception of a whole.

Research suggests that under certain conditions this tendency toward closure can be an effective advertising device because it motivates consumers to become involved in completing the message.[20] This involvement can attract attention and facilitate learning and retention. In fact, the closure concept has been employed by leading producers of consumer products. For example, the Kellogg Company showed its name on the far right-hand side of one billboard ad with the last "g" missing.[21] Also, Salem cigarettes were first advertised heavily in television employing the often quoted jingle:

"You can take Salem out of the country but—
You can't take the country out of Salem."

The verse was repeated several times with a bell ringing between the two halves of the message. Finally, only the first half of the jingle was sung, ending with the bell and leaving the listener compelled to complete the message. Figure 14-5 shows another use of the closure concept to facilitate retention of an important message.

It should be mentioned that not all such incomplete advertising messages

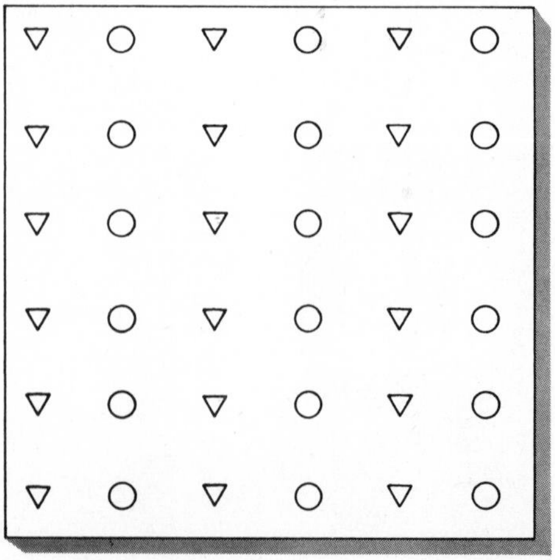

FIGURE 14-4
Example of the influence of similarity on perception.

appear to be remembered better than completed ones. Further investigation of closure is needed to determine both the nature and effectiveness of its role in advertising.

Categorization

Deriving meaning from stimuli involves some type of categorization process in which essential elements of a stimulus situation are stored in memory. Several influences affecting categorization are discussed below.

A Public Service of This Magazine & The Advertising Council.

Repeat after me, "Only you..."

LEARNING INFLUENCES Learning influences consumers' ability to categorize stimuli by developing their abilities to identify stimulus attributes used in discrimination and leveling. In *discrimination,* consumers learn those attributes useful in distinguishing between items in order to categorize them differently. For example, we learn to distinguish fresh from stale bread and traditional from contemporary furniture. Of course, there is no guarantee that all consumers will learn valid methods of discrimination. It depends on their prior experiences, as in the case where consumers rejected a new, quiet food mixer because they incorrectly perceived it as having less power than older, noisier models.[22] This was perhaps a result of their experience with powerful and noisy appliances in the past.

Learning also influences perceptual *leveling* whereby similar but not identical stimuli are classified into the same perceptual category and therefore generate the same response. For example, when instant coffee was first introduced, many families made clear distinctions between it and perk or drip coffee. However, over time leveling has taken place to the extent that frequently when coffee is now offered no distinction is made as to its type.

Marketers are interested in these learning influences because they want to provide consumers with information, product cues, and promotional symbolism designed to influence how their product is categorized. In terms of product cues, consider the case where a major producer of chickens for the Northeast feeds his poultry marigold petals and corn so that they develop the yellow skin that consumers of the region have learned to associate with succulent chicken.[23] The strategy of *positioning* can also influence consumers' categorization process by manipulating symbols, slogans, and other variables. The goal is to establish a unique perceptual category for the brand in consumers' minds. Examples are promotions that categorize Michelob as the first-class "weekend" beer and Marlboro cigarettes as a full-flavor brand with its "Come to where the flavor is" theme.

Learning also influences categorization through the development of *perceptual constancies* which are very stable perceptions of objects across a variety of situations in which they are encountered. For example, consumers realize the actual size of a pen is constant even though it appears much smaller when further away. Perceptual constancies simplify our world because we do not have to make new judgments every time we encounter these familiar objects in different contexts. In addition, they can serve as standards to judge other, less familiar stimuli. Thus, pens, cigarette packs, and other familiar objects are often used in advertisements as a frame of reference to judge the size of the product being promoted.

PERSONALITY AND MOTIVATIONAL INFLUENCES Consumers' personality characteristics also influence the perceptual meaning they derive from stimuli. For example, one study found that consumers who find it difficult to tolerate uncertain situations tend to be influenced by seals of approval, such as those of Good Housekeeping or Underwriters Laboratory, to a greater degree than do other consumers.[24] In addition, other research suggests that individuals can be categorized as having risk-avoiding or risk-seeking personalities, and these differences can lead to divergent perceptions of products and marketing communications.

The meaning individuals derive from stimuli is also influenced by their motivational state. This was demonstrated in one study where hungry subjects "saw" more food-related items in ambiguously shaped stimuli than did subjects who were not hungry. This type of finding helps explain why certain products may be highly valued by some groups of consumers and deemed rather useless by others.

ADAPTATION LEVEL Our discussion of selective attention noted that consumers tend to adapt to rather constant stimulus levels. This process leads to the formation of *adaptation levels,* which are standards of reference used to judge new stimulus situations. To demonstrate, assume that two individuals must judge the heaviness of this textbook. Prior to the test, however, one is required to sort envelopes and the other is assigned to moving office furniture. It seems reasonable that, due to their different standards of reference, the mail sorter will judge the text to be heavier than would the furniture mover. In fact, results of a large series of experiments have verified this expectation.[25] They have also demonstrated that adaptation levels can be influenced to *move* by exposing the individual to different stimulus values. This means that the frame of reference is a sliding scale which can change over time.

The concept of an adaptation level serving as a sliding frame of reference suggests that consumers adapt to levels of service, products, and other marketing variables, and these become standards by which new situations are judged. As a case in point, food-flavor experts have long recognized that consumers have adapted to the taste of packaged foods to such an extent that they now serve as taste standards. This led one food flavor chemist to remark: "We've moved away from the utilization of fresh flavor—it isn't familiar anymore." In another case, consider the United States energy problem and our recent inflationary period. In the early 1970s when gasoline prices averaged between 30 and 40 cents a gallon, a price of 50 cents would have been judged extremely expensive. However, after adapting to gradually increasing gasoline prices, 50 cents would now be judged as a great bargain![26]

A basic conclusion of our discussion of interpretation is that consumers' perceptions are subjective. They can derive meaning from stimuli only by interpreting them in relation to the present situation, their experiences, and their physical and psychological states. This presents both problems and opportunities to the marketing manager. Problems are encountered because it cannot be assumed that consumers will perceive products and other marketing variables in the same way that the marketer does. Opportunities arise from determining how consumers perceive these variables and using this insight to design more competitive offerings.

RESPONSE

We have noted that consumers' response to perceived stimuli may be nonobservable as well as overt. One important nonobservable response is the retention of perceptual experiences in memory. This retention is selective in nature and is influenced by how relevant the stimuli are to the individual. For example, when we recount shared experiences with friends, each person seems to remember different aspects of the situation. The perceptual experiences that are retained can affect the interpretation of subsequent stimuli and future actions.

Of course, marketers are also highly interested in consumers' overt responses to marketing stimuli, the most obvious of which is the purchase or nonpurchase of products. In addition, techniques have been developed to measure less apparent overt responses because they can be useful in assessing changes in internal conditions. One such technique, the *eye-movement camera,* records an individual's eye movements as he or she views an advertisement. This allows assessing which aspects of the ad are most effective in attracting consumers' attention. Still another method known as *pupilometrics* measures how much an individual's pupil enlarges while viewing an advertisement. This can be used as a measure of the reader's interest in various types of ads.

MARKETING IMPLICATIONS

Although numerous applications of the perceptual process to marketing and consumer behavior have already been cited, a wealth of additional evidence exists. This section summarizes some of the implications of perception to specific marketing variables.

Product Perception

The influence of perception on consumers' product evaluations has already been mentioned in this chapter. Some of this influence is the result of consumers' attempts to directly evaluate product attributes (often called product cues) such as size, shape, and grade of ingredients. Evidence suggests that, for many goods, buyers can have difficulty in distinguishing between brands on the basis of these direct product attributes. For example, some studies reveal that smokers have little success in identifying brands of similar types of cigarettes in "blind" taste testing (a blind test is one where identifying marks on the brands are concealed by the researcher).[27] Other studies suggest that beers must differ significantly for consumers to detect differences between them.[28] And finally, for soft drinks, recent evidence suggests that consumers can discriminate between Pepsi-Cola and Coca-Cola in blind tests but have difficulty distinguishing them from Royal Crown Cola.[29] Such evidence led to a serious promotional war in 1976 when Pepsi ads, stressing taste differences between Coke and Pepsi, tried to woo loyal Coke customers.[30]

The above evidence suggests that differences between at least some brands may not exceed consumers' differential thresholds even when they are attempting to "tune in" their discriminatory powers. Further, even experts are frequently unable to detect important but subtle product differences, as a recent wine scandal in France has demonstrated. Testimony about the scandal revealed that using chemicals to change the wine's taste apparently fooled even expert wine tasters as well as consumers.[31]

For other products, consumers may be quite capable of discriminating differences between brands but unable to determine whether these differences are important in predicting which brand will provide greater satisfaction. For example, how many consumers would be capable of identifying the best grade of carpeting without expert help? The consequence of such problems is that consumers frequently find they are not qualified to judge products directly on the basis of their physical characteristics.

Given these problems in product evaluations, it is not surprising to find that consumers' perceptions of products are often influenced by more subtle factors. To illustrate, studies have shown that adding a faint, not consciously noticeable, perfume scent to women's hose can lead consumers to strongly prefer them over identical but unscented alternatives.[32] A substantial amount of other evidence indicates that for many products consumers' brand preferences are based on nonproduct characteristics. These are often called *surrogate indicators* because they are not physical attributes of the product. To demonstrate the influence of just packaging materials, consider that one group of housewives perceived bread wrapped in cellophane to be fresher than bread wrapped in waxed paper, even though both were identical in freshness![33] A considerable amount of other evidence confirms the strong influence of promotions, brand names, and other marketing variables on consumers' product evaluations.[34]

PERCEPTUAL MAPPING The above discussion suggests that consumers' perceptions of products are developed in a complex way and are not easily determined by the marketer. However, a rather new technique known as perceptual mapping holds promise in exploring consumers' product perceptions. Since products can be perceived on many dimensions (such as quality, price, and strength) the technique is *multidimensional* in nature. That is, it allows for the influence of more than one stimulus characteristic on product perceptions. Typically, consumers fill out measuring scales to indicate their perceptions of the characteristics or similarities of competing brands. Computer programs analyze the resulting data to determine those product characteristics which are most important to consumers in distinguishing between competing brands. Results of this analysis can be plotted in terms of perceptual "maps," which display how consumers perceive the brands, and their differences, on a coordinate system.

Figure 14-6 presents a two-dimensional map for consumers' actual perceptions of beers. The most important characteristics to consumers' evaluations here were found to be lightness versus heaviness and prestige price versus popular price. The points labeled with brand names and letters indicate how consumers located actual brands in the perceptual space. Notice that in the prestige price range Schlitz and Budweiser are both perceived to be somewhat heavy compared to the relative lightness of Miller. On the other hand, Hamms occupies a central position in terms of heaviness.

The study also asked consumers to indicate their perception of their ideal beer. The numbered circles show how they tend to cluster together in their responses. The size of the circles indicate the proportion of consumers in each cluster. It can be seen that the largest segments of the market are being shared by the brands just mentioned.

These data provide insight to the marketer in terms of segmentation and brand positioning strategies. For example, one strategy might be to introduce a new, relatively light-tasting, popularly priced beer to capture clusters 3, 5, and 8. Promotional efforts would have to be consistent with such a strategy. Alternatively, producers of Brand D may wish to consider product and/or promotional changes to move their brand more centrally into cluster 4. A variety of other strategy decisions can be aided by this perceptual mapping technique.

Price Perception

Traditional microeconomic theory as reviewed in Chapter 2 has apparently influenced many marketers to assume that consumers use price only as an indicator of product cost. However, recent evidence suggests that the meaning consumers derive from the price variable may be considerably more complex in nature.[35]

PSYCHOLOGICAL PRICING Much discussion has focused on the concept of "psychological pricing" which suggests that there is greater consumer demand at certain prices, and this demand decreases at prices above *and* below these points. One aspect of psychological pricing is the frequently observed retail practice of *odd-pricing.* Here it is said that prices ending in an odd number (such as 5, 7, or 9) or just under the round number (like 96 or 98) generate higher demand than related round-numbered prices. However, this argument is usually based on retailers' experiences and has not yet been confirmed by rigorous testing.

PRICE AND PRODUCT QUALITY Another important price perception topic is the price-quality proposition, which holds that consumers tend to use price as an indicator of product quality or worth because they lack confidence or ability to judge products directly. To argue that consumers may judge the worth of products by their price is not unreasonable. For example, previous purchase experiences may lead to an awareness that higher-quality products tend to cost more. Adages such as "You get what you pay for" also act as a

FIGURE 14-6
A two-dimensional perceptual map of beer brands. (*Source:* Adapted from Richard M. Johnson, "Market Segmentation: A Strategic Management Tool," *Journal of Marketing Research*, **8:**16, February 1971, published by the American Marketing Association.)

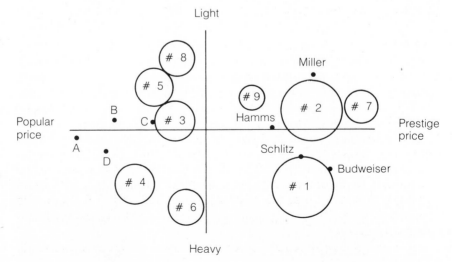

reinforcement. Given the uncertainty arising from attempts to directly evaluate today's technically complex products, consumers may rely on these previous experiences to conclude that higher-priced products are of higher quality.

Early price-quality research investigated situations where price was the only differential information available to subjects. These studies found that respondents tended to prefer the higher-priced brand, especially when brands were expected to differ considerably in quality. Further studies determined that the price-quality relationship varied across products, and was highest where consumers faced risky situations, and where their confidence in directly judging the quality of products was low.[36]

A number of more recent studies have used various products and perhaps more realistic shopping situations. The findings are that price may not be the most important influence on quality perception, especially when brand names are known and experience with the product is great.[37] Most likely, perception of price combines with judgments of actual product characteristics to form an overall perception of product quality.[38]

Several tentative conclusions are possibly based on these and other price-quality studies. Price appears to be used as an indicator of product quality when little differential information is available about products or when the consumer's confidence in judging them is low and the risk involved is high. This may occur for relatively similar products where brand differentiation is not strong. Also, these circumstances may exist for new products or for new purchase experiences with unfamiliar product classes. For relatively inexpensive grocery products and beverages, brand image and product features possibly dominate or interact with the influence of price on perceptions of product quality. For apparel, however, there appears to be a strong price-quality relationship although it may not always dominate the influence of brand image. The influence of price perceptions on technically sophisticated durable goods involving large expenditures (such as appliances and television) has not yet been well studied.[39]

Company and Store Image Perception

Astute marketers have long realized that, in addition to brand image, their company image can strongly influence consumers' behavior toward their enterprise and its products. A company's image is the perception consumers have of its character as a result of their experiences with it and their knowledge and beliefs about it.

IMPORTANCE OF AN IMAGE A strong and clear company image can increase consumers' confidence in its products and their predisposition to purchase them. This is demonstrated by results of a study where a sample of women were 14 percent more likely to try a new product offered from Heinz than from a large but unspecified food company.[40] Such evidence has led many corporations to invest considerable sums in promoting a favorable image or symbol. For example, the Humble Oil and Refining Company is reported to have spent over $100 million to change its trademark and company name to Exxon.[41]

Consumers' patronage of a particular retail store is also significantly influenced by their perception of its image or "personality." Store image may be defined as "the way in which the store is defined in the shopper's mind, partly by its functional qualities and partly by an aura of psychological attributes."[42] This implies that perception of store image is derived not only from so-called functional attributes of price, convenience, and selection of merchandise but also from the influence of variables such as architecture, interior design, and colors.

MEASURING STORE IMAGES Although a variety of methods (including perceptual mapping) exist to measure store images, the one most frequently used is the *semantic differential profile* that was described in Chapter 3. Consumers familiar with the store can indicate on semantic differential scales their perceptions of a variety of its tangible and intangible characteristics. This can also be done for competing stores. Average responses can then be calculated to yield an image profile for each store. Figure 14-7 serves as an illustration by portraying image profiles found for two competing department stores in the Los Angeles area.

These profiles indicate that store A is perceived more favorably than store B, although not by a great degree. It appears to have a rather high-price image, but compared to store B, consumers still perceive it as providing good value for the money. Ratings on attractiveness and neatness also reveal a potential problem to which managers of store B may wish to address their attention.

It should not be concluded from the above discussion that measurement of store image reveals only positive/negative image information. For example, one store may be perceived as progressive and another as conservative, neither of which is necessarily a good or bad trait. Research has also revealed a number of other interesting findings, particularly the fact that stores do have distinguishable images or personalities. Also, different stores appear to attract specific socioeconomic segments, and consumers in different social classes or stages of the family life cycle are likely to perceive a given store differently.[43] All of these findings suggest that stores may be more successful in appealing to specific target segments as opposed to the mass market.

Advertising Perception

Applications of perception to advertising have been cited throughout the chapter. However, two other areas that draw considerable attention are the use of sex in advertising and the controversy over subliminal advertising.

SEX IN ADVERTISING The use of sexually attractive models and sexually suggestive themes in advertising has a long history. It is therefore surprising that little is generally known about the specific effect or effectiveness of these measures in promoting products. The few studies that are generally available raise questions regarding the wisdom of employing sexual themes, at least in some circumstances.

One study indicates that a slight majority of the public believe that too much use is made of sexual appeals in advertising.[44] Further, since feminists and older individuals appear to hold this belief to a greater degree than others, sexual themes can have a negative impact on a substantial portion of the market. Other evidence suggests that the market is made up of different groups who react to sex in advertising in quite varied ways. For example, sexual-romantic themes and nonsexual themes appear to capture many consumers' attention more than does nudity.[45] These rather complex results suggest that a sexually suggestive theme may attract some viewers' attention but not be effective for many others.

Of course, attracting attention is only one purpose of advertising. Consumers must also remember the brand name and advertising message in a favorable manner. Interestingly, one study found that brand names accompanied by sexual illustrations were correctly recalled *less* often than those not accompanied by such illustrations.[46] Also, recall was even less for those who held unfavorable attitudes regarding the use of sexual content. Similar results have been noted in actual practice. For example, an ad for an office copier received much greater reader attention when the bikini-clad model standing beside it was removed.[47] These results suggest that sexually oriented devices may actually rob attention from the brand name or advertising message.

Although not great in number, the above studies point to the need for

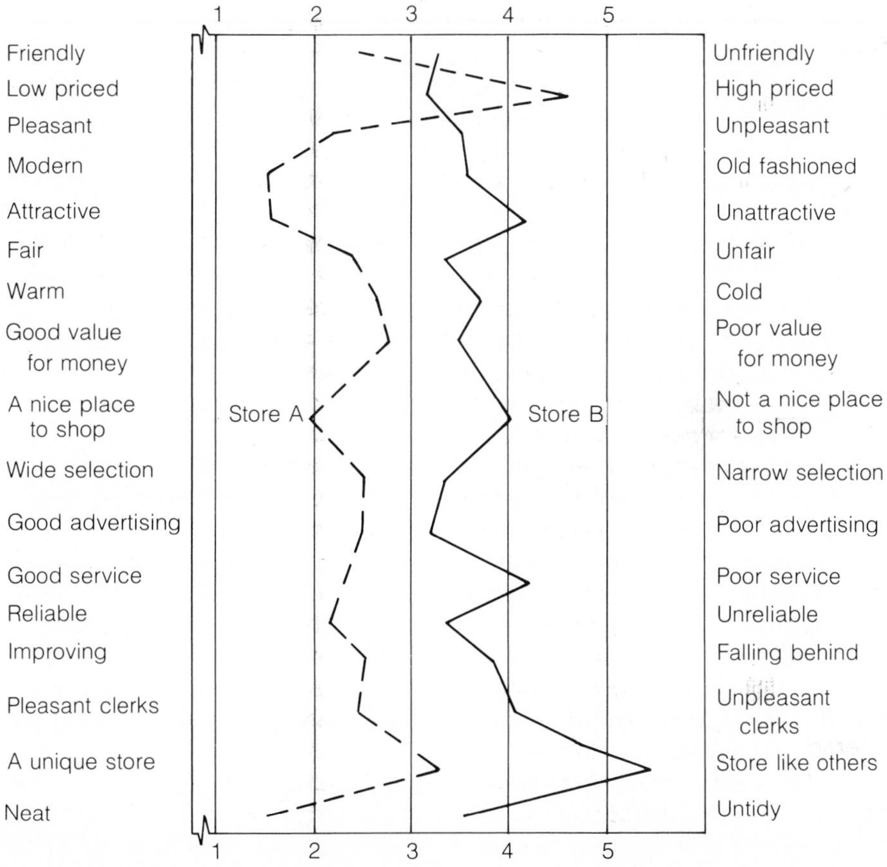

FIGURE 14-7
Semantic differential profiles of two competing department stores. (*Source:* Burton H. Marcus, "Image Variation and the Multi-Unit Retail Establishment," *Journal of Retailing*, **48**:39, Summer 1972. Adapted with permission of the *Journal of Retailing*, New York University.)

sound evaluation of sexual content before it is employed to promote any specific product. This is especially true in today's era of attitudes against sexual exploitation.

SUBLIMINAL ADVERTISING The perceptual technique called subliminal advertising has sparked considerable controversy in promotional and scientific fields. Recall from earlier discussions that the absolute threshold identifies the minimum value of a stimulus capable of being consciously noticed. Since this is also referred to as a "limen," the term "subliminal perception" actually means perception of stimuli that are below the level needed to reach *conscious* awareness. The purported benefit of using such a technique in advertising is that a subliminal message will not be strong enough to arouse consumer defense mechanisms and selective attention, but it will have enough strength to influence consumers at an unconscious level.

The first widely known test of subliminal advertising was conducted by Vicary during the 1950s.[48] During movie theater tests over 45,000 unsuspecting viewers were presented filmed messages every 5 seconds at speeds said to be 1/3000 of a second in duration. The two messages employed were "Eat Popcorn" and "Drink Coca-Cola." By comparing sales receipts during the test period to those from a previous period it was reported that popcorn sales increased 58 percent and Coca-Cola sales rose 18 percent.

These results quickly generated considerable concern regarding unethical use of subliminal methods. However, closer examination of Vicary's research raised questions as to its validity. As one review stated, "There were no reports . . . of even the most rudimentary scientific precautions, such as adequate controls, provision for replication, etc. . . ."[49] The lack of information on these provisions does not generate much confidence in the validity of the results.

Other efforts to subliminally influence television audiences have not been able to generate the positive effects reported by Vicary.[50] Experiments also suggest that while subliminal messages may arouse such basic drives as increased thirst and hunger, specific motives that would direct consumers toward brands appear to remain relatively unaffected.[51]

In summary, a number of experiments lead to the conclusion that under certain conditions subliminal perception may occur. However, the technical problems of developing subliminal advertising messages in a commercial setting are considerable. First, the speed of the message must be determined. Also, the message itself must be brief and simple, since anything more than a few words would probably be too complex to comprehend. Further, we have seen how consumers' motives, personality, and other individual determinants influence selective perception of stimuli above the absolute threshold. There is no guarantee that these factors would not operate on subliminal stimuli. Thus, the subliminal message "Drink Coke" could be distorted into "Stink Coke" or some other meaning not highly desired by the marketer.

Further, since subliminal messages appear to arouse only basic drives, they may initiate behavior not always beneficial to the advertiser. That is, a subliminal message for Pepsi may increase a consumer's thirst enough for a trip to the refrigerator for a glass of Dr. Pepper or some other liquid refreshment.

Finally, it seems rather safe to conclude that subliminal advertising will not turn customers into automatons at the mercy of marketers. Present technical difficulties and unknown consequences of the technique give little reason for advertisers to wholeheartedly embrace it.

SUMMARY

This chapter examined the perceptual process and its role in influencing consumer behavior. First, an overview of perception was presented. The next major section examined the process of selective attention. The sensitivity of consumers' perceptual receivers and absolute and differential thresholds were explored. Stimulus and individual factors influencing attention were also treated. Some implications of selective attention to various marketing applications were discussed.

The process of interpretation was then addressed by considering how consumers organize and categorize stimuli. Following this, a brief section was devoted to responses and some means of measuring them. These sections of the chapter provided a basis for appreciating the complexity of the perceptual process.

The next major section provided a review of the perceptual meaning consumers derive from selected marketing variables. Here we found that consumers have difficulty evaluating many products and their evaluations can also be influenced by nonproduct attributes. Price may be one of these surrogate indicators of product quality to at least some consumers but this influence can be quite complex in nature.

The effect of company and store characteristics on consumers' perception of the "personality" of these enterprises was also discussed. Attention then turned to advertising perception, which briefly treated the apparently complex effect of sexual themes in promotion. The discussion also focused on the controversy over subliminal advertising. It was concluded here that considerable obstacles appear to minimize the effectiveness of this technique.

DISCUSSION TOPICS

1. What is perception? Distinguish between the various activities that comprise the perceptual process.

2. It is often said that perception is selective in nature. In what way is this so, and what implications does this have for understanding consumer behavior?

3. It has been established that the tips of the fingers are eight times as sensitive to the touch as the legs, and eighty-three times as sensitive as regions of the foot. Discuss any implications this has for designing products such as men's and women's hosiery or pants.

4. The resemblance of certain private-brand packaging to those of nationally known brands has been so close at times that they have been described as "look-alikes." Visit a supermarket and bring back two packaged products to demonstrate this. Also, while there, make an effort to determine the prevalence of this phenomenon. In what ways might it influence the behavior of consumers?

5. Assume that consumers have heightened awareness of the following prices for various models in a product line—$11.70, $15.21, $19.77. Using Weber's Law, predict the next highest price in the line which would generate heightened awareness.

6. Bring to class two print advertisements which use each of the following techniques for gaining perceptual attention or influencing interpretation. Be prepared to assess how effectively the techniques have been employed.

a. novelty
b. figure-ground
c. proximity
d. color

7. Write up a procedure you would employ for conducting a taste test to determine (1) if your fellow students can discriminate between three brands of cola and (2) if they have a preference for any particular cola based on taste alone. Indicate the variables that might influence the results and how you would design the experiment to minimize their influence.

8. Choose any two restaurants or pubs that are frequented by students at your school. Measure their image profiles by designing a number of semantic differential items and administering them to a random sample of your fellow students. What conclusions can you draw from your data?

9. Find several examples of magazine advertisements that employ sexual themes or illustrations to capture readers' attention or influence perceptual interpretation. How appropriate do the methods appear to be for the target market involved? How effectively do the devices appear to accomplish their apparent goals? Can you foresee any possible problems the advertiser might encounter as a result of using the methods?

NOTES

1. Suggested by Paul Thomas Young, *Motivation and Emotion: A Survey of the Determinants of Human and Animal Activity,* Wiley, New York, 1961, pp. 298–299.

2. See Lynn Langway and Michael Reese, "Baby's Business," *Newsweek,* March 21, 1977, p. 72.

3. "Does Taste Make Waste?" *Forbes,* June 1, 1974, p. 24.

4. Some of the following discussion follows Richard Lee Miller, "Dr. Weber and the Consumer," *Journal of Marketing,* **26**:57–61, January 1962; and Steuart Henderson Britt, "How Weber's Law Can Be Applied to Marketing," *Business Horizons,* **18**:21–29, February 1975.

5. L. Paul Gilden, "Sampling Candy Bar Economics," *The New Englander,* **22**:32, January 1976.

6. "Hidden Costs," *The Wall Street Journal,* February 15, 1977, p. 1.

7. See "Checkout Counter Look-alikes," *Money,* May 1976, pp. 71–72.

8. Joseph Uhl, "Consumer Perception of Retail Food Price Changes," paper presented at First Annual Meeting of the Association for Consumer Research, 1970.

9. "What Stirs the Newspaper Reader?" *Printer's Ink,* June 21, 1963, pp. 48–49.

10. J. W. Rosenberg, "How Does Color, Size Affect Ad Readership," *Industrial Marketing,* **41**:54–57, May 1956.

11. Rafael Valiente, "Mechanical Correlates of Ad Recognition," *Journal of Advertising Research,* **13**:13–18, June 1973.

12. Samuel B. Cousley, "The Impact of Color Contrast on Advertising Effectiveness," in Henry W. Nash and Donald P. Robin (eds.), *Proceedings of the Southern Marketing Association Conference,* 1976, pp. 249–251.

13. Stephen Baker, *Visual Persuasion,* McGraw-Hill, New York, 1961.

14. "Position in Newspaper Advertising: 2," *Media/Scope,* March 1963, pp. 76–83.

15. "Position in Newspaper Advertising: 1," *Media/Scope,* February 1963, p. 57. This finding is contrary to much previous research; see Melvin S. Hattwick, *How to Use Psychology for Better Advertising,* Prentice-Hall, Englewood Cliffs, N.J., 1950, pp. 145–150.

16. See Hattwick, *Psychology for Better Advertising,* p. 155; and "Position in Newspaper Advertising: 1," p. 57.

17. Allan Greenberg and Charles Suttoni, "Television Commercial Wearout," *Journal of Advertising Research,* **13**:47–54, October 1973.

18. See Alvin J. Silk and Frank P. Geiger, "Advertisement Size and the Relationship between Product Usage and Advertising Exposure," *Journal of Marketing Research,* **9**:22–26, February 1972, which credits this hypothesis to Leo Bogart.

19. Charles F. Cannell and James C. MacDonald, "The Impact of Health News on Attitudes and Behavior," *Journalism Quarterly,* **33**:315–323, July-September 1956.

20. Norman Heller, "An Application of Psychological Learning Theory to Advertising," *Journal of Marketing,* **20**:248–254, January 1956; and Dev Pathak, Gene Burton and Ron Zigli, "The Memory Impact of Incomplete Advertising Slogans," in Henry Nash and Donald Robin (eds.), *Proceedings of the Southern Marketing Association Conference,* 1977, pp. 269–272.

21. James H. Myers and William H. Reynolds, *Consumer Behavior and Marketing Management,* Houghton Mifflin, Boston, 1967, p. 21.

22. Robert Froman, "You Get What You Want," in J. H. Westing (ed.), *Readings in Marketing,* Prentice-Hall, Englewood Cliffs, N.J., 1953, p. 231.

23. William Copulsky and Katherin Marton, "Sensory Cues, You've Got to Put Them Together," *Product Marketing,* January 1977, pp. 31–34.

24. Thomas L. Parkinson, "The Use of Seals of Approval in Consumer Decision-Making as a Function of Cognitive Needs and Style," in Mary Jane Schlinger (ed.), *Advances in Consumer Research,* **2**:133–140, Association For Consumer Research, Chicago, 1975.

25. Harry Helson, *Adaptation-Level Theory: An Experimental and Systematic Approach to Behavior,* Harper & Row, New York, 1964.

26. See Albert J. Della Bitta and Kent B. Monroe, "The Influence of Adaptation Levels on Subjective Price Perceptions," in Scott Ward and Peter Wright (eds.), *Advances in Consumer Research,* **1**:359–369, Association for Consumer Research, Urbana, Ill., 1973; and Anthony N. Doob, et al., "Effect of Initial Selling Price on Subsequent Sales," *Journal of Personality and Social Psychology,* **11**:345–350, April 1969.

27. R. W. Husband and J. Godfrey, "An Experimental Study of Cigarette Identification," *Journal of Applied Psychology,* **18**:220–251, April 1934; and C. K. Ramond, L. N. Rachal, and M. R. Marks, "Brand Discrimination among Cigarette Smokers," *Journal of Applied Psychology,* **34**:282–284, August 1950.

28. Ralph I. Allison and Kenneth P. Uhl, "Influences of Beer Brand Identification on Taste Perception," *Journal of Marketing Research,* **1**:36–39, August 1964; and Jacob Jacoby, Jerry C. Olson, and Rafael A. Haddock, "Price, Brand Name, and Product Composition Characteristics as Determinants of Perceived Quality," *Journal of Applied Psychology,* **55**:570–579, December 1971.

29. F. J. Thumin, "Identification of Cola Beverages," *Journal of Applied Psychology,* **46**:358–360, October 1962.

30. "The Cola War," *Newsweek,* August 30, 1976, p. 67.

31. Nan Robertson, "Experts at French Wine Trial Explode Some Vintage Myths," *The New York Times,* November 1, 1974, pp. 1+.

32. D. A. Laird, "How the Consumer Estimates Quality by Subconscious Sensory Impressions," *Journal of Applied Psychology,* **16**:241–246, June 1932; and *Women's Wear Daily,* January 28, 1961, p. 15.

33. Robert L. Brown, "Wrapper Influence on the Perception of Freshness in Bread," *Journal of Applied Psychology,* **42**:257–260, August 1958.

34. See Steven Miller, William Saigh and Harvey Sundel, "An Experimental Study of Consumer Perceptions of Selected Grocery Products under Manufacturer Brands and

Private Brands," in Henry Nash and Donald Robin (eds.), *Proceedings of the Southern Marketing Association Conference,* 1976, pp. 23–25; Charles Schaninger, "The Emotional Value of Different Color Combinations," in Barnett Greenberg and Danny Bellenger (eds.), *Contemporary Marketing Thought,* American Marketing Association, Chicago, 1977, pp. 23–25; and Allison and Uhl, "Beer Brand Identification."

35. For review of this research see Kent B. Monroe, "Buyers' Subjective Perceptions of Price," *Journal of Marketing Research,* **10**:70–80, February 1973, on which much of this section is based.

36. See Benson Shapiro, "Price as a Communicator of Quality: An Experiment," unpublished doctoral dissertation, Harvard University, 1970; and Zarrel Lambert, "Price and Choice Behavior," *Journal of Marketing Research,* **9**:35–40, February 1972.

37. See for example, Robert A. Peterson, "Consumer Perceptions as a Function of Product Color, Price, and Nutrition Labeling," in William D. Perreault, Jr., (ed.), *Advances In Consumer Research,* **4**:61–63, Association for Consumer Research, Atlanta, 1977.

38. Jacoby, Olson, and Haddock, "Price and Product Composition Characteristics."

39. An exception is P. S. Raju, "Product Familiarity, Brand Name, and Price Influences on Product Evaluation," in William D. Perreault, Jr., (ed.), *Advances in Consumer Research,* **4**:64–71, Association for Consumer Research, Atlanta, 1977.

40. National Probability Sample in Great Britain, Market and Opinion Research International Cooperative Image Study, Spring 1970, reported by Robert Worcester, "Corporate Image Research," in Robert Worcester (ed.), *Consumer Market Research Handbook,* McGraw-Hill, London, 1972, p. 508.

41. "Humble 'Exxon' In; and 'Esso' Out," *National Petroleum News,* June 1972.

42. Pierre Martineau, "The Personality of the Retail Store," *Harvard Business Review,* **36**:47–55, January-February 1958.

43. See William Lazer and Robert G. Wyckham, "Perceptual Segmentation of Department Store Marketing," *Journal of Retailing,* **45**:3–14, Summer 1969.

44. Gordon L. Wise, Alan L. King, and J. Paul Merenski, "Reactions to Sexy Ads Vary with Age," *Journal of Advertising Research,* **14**:11–16, August 1974.

45. Bruce John Morrison and Richard C. Sherman, "Who Responds to Sex in Advertising?" *Journal of Advertising Research,* **12**:15–19, April 1972.

46. Major Stedman, "How Sexy Illustrations Affect Brand Recall," *Journal of Advertising Research,* **9**:15–19, March 1969.

47. Baker, *Visual Persuasion.*

48. See H. Brean, "What Hidden Sell Is All About," *Life,* March 31, 1958, pp. 104–114.

49. James V. McConnell, Richard L. Cutter, and Elton B. McNeil, "Subliminal Stimulation: An Overview," *American Psychologist,* **13**:230, May 1958.

50. See M. Mannes, "Ain't Nobody Here but Us Commercials," *Reporter,* October 17, 1957, pp. 35–37; and "Subliminal Ad Okay if It Sells: FCC Peers into Subliminal Picture on TV," *Advertising Age,* **28**, 1957.

51. Del Hawkins, "The Effects of Subliminal Stimulation on Drive Level and Brand Preference," *Journal of Marketing Research,* **7**:322–326, August 1970.

LEARNING

One characteristic of consumer behavior is that it is constantly changing. Much of this change is a result of consumers learning to adapt to a changing environment. Consequently, knowledge of learning principles can be useful in understanding how consumers' wants and motives are acquired and how their tastes are developed. At a more specific level, the learning process can aid our understanding of topics ranging from why some consumers may remain loyal to particular brands to why it may be beneficial for marketers to produce television advertisements that are slightly irritating to viewers.

This chapter begins by defining learning and describing what it is that we learn. Second, major elements of the learning process are reviewed. Next, several ways by which consumers can learn are described and characterized, followed by a number of additional learning topics particularly useful for understanding the behavior of consumers. Finally, consumers' memory and the process of forgetting are addressed.

CHARACTERIZING LEARNING

Before going further, it is useful to adopt a definition of learning. Several introductory comments concerning the nature of learned material will also provide a beneficial foundation.

Learning Defined

Very simply, learning can be viewed as a relatively permanent change in behavior occurring as a result of experience. The implications of this definition are fairly subtle and, therefore, require some explanation.

First, as before, the term behavior is used to refer to nonobservable cognitive activity as well as overt actions. Therefore, it is very possible for learning to occur without any change in observable behavior. Changes in consumers' attitudes resulting from exposure to new information about a brand demonstrate this point. Secondly, learning results in relatively permanent changes in behavior. This excludes changes brought about by fatigue or other short-lived influences. Third, since our definition of learning stresses experience, we must exclude the effects of physical damage and natural human growth. It is interesting to note, however, that much of our early learning experiences are controlled by the degree of physical development needed to make practice of an activity possible.

Types of Learned Behavior

Nearly every type of behavior we exhibit as humans has been learned. The following paragraphs provide some specific examples.

PHYSICAL BEHAVIOR Generally, we learn many physical behavior patterns useful in responding to a variety of situations faced in everyday life. For example, all healthy humans learn to walk, talk, and interact with others. As consumers we also learn methods of responding to various purchase situations. These may take the forms of learning to act dissatisfied when hearing the first price quote on a car, or learning to read closely the fine print in purchase contracts.

Children also learn certain physical activity through the process termed *modeling* in which they mimic the behavior of their parents. One aspect of controversy relating to this is the growing concern that children who are exposed to violent television programs may learn undesirable behavior patterns.[1] This suggests the important influence of learned physical behavior.

SYMBOLIC LEARNING AND PROBLEM SOLVING People learn symbolic meanings that enable highly efficient communication through the development of languages. Symbols also allow marketers to communicate with consumers through such vehicles as brand names (Kodak and Sony), slogans ("Progress Is Our Most Important Product"), and signs (McDonald's Golden Arches). As mentioned previously, the marketer intends for these symbols to connote positive images of the company to consumers in addition to keeping the firm's name familiar to them.

One can also engage in problem solving learning by employing the processes of *thinking* and *insight*. Thinking involves the mental manipulation of symbols representing the real world to form various combinations of meaning. This often leads to insight, which is a new understanding of relationships involved in the problem. As we have noted, many consumer efforts can be viewed as problem-solving behavior. For example, consumers are constantly engaged in deliberating about how satisfaction of their various wants and needs can be improved by acquisition of new or different products or services. Thinking and problem-solving behavior, therefore, enables consumers to evaluate mentally a wide variety of products without having to purchase them.

AFFECTIVE LEARNING Humans learn to value certain elements of their environment and dislike others. This means that consumers learn many of their wants, goals, and motives as well as what products satisfy these needs. Learning also influences consumers' development of favorable/unfavorable attitudes toward a company and its products. These attitudes will affect the tendency to purchase various brands.

As we discovered in earlier chapters, consumers' interactions within a social system can have a significant influence on their learning of tastes. This is quite obvious for products such as scotch and tobacco, where it is said that one has to "acquire a taste" for the product. However, the same process is at work regarding the vast majority of foods, clothes, and other goods. The process that influences such learning includes sanctions and social pressure by group or family members.

The discussion of what we learn could easily fill the remaining pages of this chapter. It is more appropriate, however, that we now direct our attention toward the principal elements of learning and other issues of importance to the understanding of this process.

PRINCIPAL ELEMENTS OF LEARNING

As will be demonstrated shortly, consumers learn in several basic ways. However, four elements seem to be fundamental to the vast majority of situations: motive, cue, response, and reinforcement.[2] The exact nature and strength of these components influence what will be learned, how well it will be learned, and the rate at which learning will occur.

Motives

As noted in Chapter 13, motives arouse individuals, thereby increasing their readiness to respond. This arousal function is essential, since it activates the energy needed to engage in learning activity. In addition, any success at achieving the motivating goal, or avoiding some unpleasant situation, tends to reduce arousal. Since this is reinforcing, such activity will have a greater tendency to occur again in similar situations. Thus marketers strive to have their brand or its name available when relevant consumer motives are aroused because it is expected that consumers will learn a connection between the product and motive. For this reason, we see advertisements for Prestone antifreeze shortly before winter and Coppertone suntan lotion during the summer.

As noted in Chapter 13, motives can also be learned. It will be remembered that *primary* motives are based on innate physiological states such as hunger and thirst. Conversely *secondary* motives are psychological in nature and are acquired through the process of learning. Actually, secondary motives influence considerably more consumer behavior than do primary motives. Examples include strivings for money, social approval, and achievement.

Cues

Cues may be viewed as weak stimuli not strong enough to arouse consumers, but capable of providing *direction* to motivated activity. That is, they influence the manner in which consumers respond to motives. The shopping environment is packed with cues such as promotions and product colors which consumers can use to choose between various response options in a learning situation. For example, when hungry we are guided by certain cues such as restaurant signs and the aroma of food cooking because we have learned that these stimuli are associated with food preparation and consumption.

It is interesting to note that consumers frequently learn such strong bonds between certain cues and products that they are highly reluctant to purchase when these cues are absent. For this reason sellers make sure that the appropriate cues are present in their products. For example, many prepared foods have artificial coloring added to stimulate purchase. An orange coloring is frequently added to whole oranges because consumers have learned to expect oranges to have such coloring. In yet another case, Heinz ketchup still continues to be packaged in a narrow-neck, hard-to-pour bottle because the producer realizes that consumers have learned to associate the slow-moving thickness of the product with quality.[3]

Response

A response may be viewed as some mental or physical activity the consumer makes to a stimulus situation. Responses appropriate to a particular situation are learned over a period of time through experience in facing the situation. As we have noted, the occurrence of a response is not always observable. Therefore, it must again be emphasized that our inability to observe responses does not necessarily mean that learning is not taking place.

Chapter 13 introduced the concept of a motive hierarchy, and a similar situation exists for responses. Before learning occurs, our innate characteristics order responses to a stimulus from the most likely to least likely response. Thus, a hungry baby is more likely to cry or exhibit sucking behavior than other responses. Over some time learning will modify the response hierarchy so that other responses have a greater chance of occurring. In this way consumers are able to adapt to changing environmental conditions which confront them.

Reinforcement

Perhaps the most widely acceptable view of *reinforcement* is anything that follows a response and increases the tendency for the response to reoccur in a similar situation.[4] Because reinforced behavior tends to be repeated, consumers can learn to develop successful means of responding to their needs or changing conditions.

One important type of reinforcement is achieved through reducing motive arousal. This occurs through removing a *negative reinforcer* (something that generates discomfort and is avoided) or receiving a *positive reinforcer* (something that generates pleasure and is sought). In either case, reducing motive arousal is reinforcing to the consumer. For example, drinking Seven-Up on a hot day or purchasing a Norelco smoke detector to lessen the dangers of a home fire can both reduce motive arousal for the consumer.

In still other situations, punishment through mental or physical discomfort is applied as a negative reinforcer. Such circumstances usually result in learning to avoid something or to discontinue some behavior pattern. All of these situations demonstrate that reinforcement is a general term that involves more than just receiving or giving rewards.

It should be noted here that a number of learning experiments have not introduced positive or negative reinforcers.[5] In some cases it appears that just the accomplishment of a learning task is by itself a reinforcing experience. Thus consumers may learn about products merely by mentally evaluating their relevance to solving consumption problems. Window-shopping activity and informal discussions with friends or salespeople may be aspects of such learning behavior.

It should also be mentioned that our behavior can be reinforced so subtly that we may not even be aware that it has occurred.[6] Simple social gestures such as a nod, smile, or frown are often deceptively powerful in their influence. This suggests that consumers can develop attitudes and patterns of behavior toward brands without becoming aware that such changes are occurring.

CLASSIFYING LEARNING

Various theories have been developed to explain different aspects of learning.[7] These theories, however, can be grouped into several major categories for the focus of our present discussion. As Figure 15-1 depicts, the first major division is between the connectionist and cognitive schools of thought. While *cognitive* interpretations place emphasis on the discovery of patterns and insight, *connectionists* argue that humans learn connections between stimuli and responses. The connectionist school can be further subdivided on the basis of the type of conditioning employed. Each of these subdivisions will be discussed in turn.

Learning Connections

Some learning theorists maintain that learning involves the development of *connections* between a stimulus and some response to it. That is, the association of a response and a stimulus is the connection that is learned. Some members of this group minimize the importance of reinforcement to learning while others stress its crucial role. We shall sidestep this debate by adopting the reinforcement viewpoint because of its attractiveness in explaining consumers' learning behavior.[8] Reinforcement is employed in conjunction with two fundamentally different methods of learning connections: classical and instrumental conditioning.

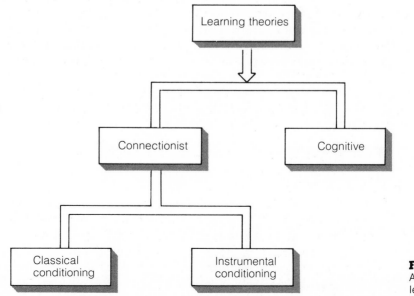

FIGURE 15-1
A classification of learning theories.

CLASSICAL CONDITIONING Essentially, classical conditioning pairs one stimulus with another that already elicits a given response. Over repeated trials, the new stimulus will also begin to elicit the particular response.

To appreciate the process involved, it is useful to review the experiment conducted by Pavlov, who pioneered classical conditioning.[9] Pavlov reasoned that since food already caused his dog to salivate, it might be possible to link a previously neutral stimulus to the food so that it too would be able to make the dog salivate. This would demonstrate that the dog had learned to associate the neutral stimulus with the food. Pavlov used a bell as the neutral stimulus. His experiment is diagrammed in Figure 15-2.

The term "unconditioned stimulus" is used for the food because conditioning is not required for it to cause the dog to salivate. This built-in stimulus-response connection is represented by the solid arrow. Since the salivating response also does not require learning it is termed the "unconditioned response." The bell is referred to as the "conditioned stimulus" because conditioning is required to learn a connection between it and the food. Pavlov accomplished this by ringing the bell every time he presented the dog with food. After a significant number of conditioning trials, the dog learned a connection between the bell and the food. In fact, the association was strong enough so that the bell alone was then capable of causing the dog to salivate. The dotted arrow connecting the bell and the food symbolizes the learned connection between the two stimuli, and the second dotted line indicates that the bell can now cause the dog to salivate.

In this situation a natural reflex of salivating to food was employed as the unconditioned stimulus. It is important to note, however, that classical conditioning does not require reflexive stimuli, and the dog could now be conditioned to a new stimulus by using the bell as the unconditioned stimulus. Learning new associations between stimuli in this manner is termed "second order conditioning." Since evidence suggests that humans are capable of even further levels of conditioning, this concept is more generally referred to as higher-order conditioning.[10]

Higher-order conditioning can be useful in understanding how consumers acquire secondary motives. Here, goals that once had no motivating abilities can become associated with reinforcing stimuli and take on motivating properties themselves. For example, the achievement motive may be ac-

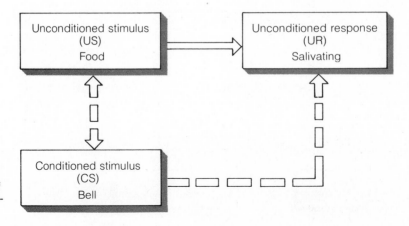

FIGURE 15-2
A representation of classical conditioning.

quired by a child because rewarding praise was given to him or her for accomplishing certain tasks. Later this achievement motive can influence the purchase of various products to assist in accomplishing tasks.

INSTRUMENTAL CONDITIONING The method of instrumental conditioning also involves developing connections between stimuli and responses, but the process involved differs from classical conditioning in several important respects. While classical conditioning relies on an already established stimuli-response connection, instrumental conditioning requires the learner to discover the appropriate response.

The principles of this type of learning can best be illustrated by employing the same "box" that B. F. Skinner made famous with his pioneering work in the area.[11] Assume that we place a pigeon into a box. On one wall is a button which when pressed will deliver food to the pigeon. In this case the button is the conditioned stimulus. When placed in the box the pigeon will respond in a variety of ways shown as R_1 through R_n in Figure 15-3. Eventually it will push the button (R_3), receive the food, and eat it with great enjoyment. Here, the food, which represents a positive reinforcer, is the unconditioned stimulus.

Most likely the pigeon will not immediately associate pushing the button with receiving the food. Other responses will occur but only a push of the button will lead to reinforcement. Therefore, over a number of reinforced trials the pigeon will learn a connection between the stimulus (button) and response (pushing). This can lead to very rapid repetition of the process— perhaps until the bird becomes ill from consuming too much food—which, as we know, also leads to learning.

DISTINCTIONS BETWEEN CONDITIONING METHODS A number of distinctions can be made between classical and instrumental conditioning. Three of the most important ones are summarized in Table 15-1. Note that while classical conditioning is dependent on an already established connection, instrumental conditioning requires the learner to discover the appropriate response. For this reason instrumental conditioning involves the learner

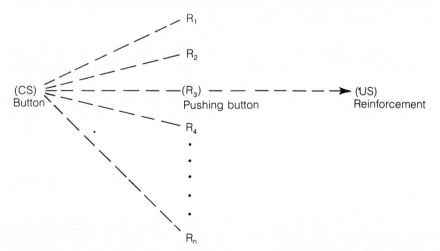

FIGURE 15-3
A representation of instrumental conditioning.

TABLE 15-1

IMPORTANT DISTINCTIONS BETWEEN CLASSICAL AND INSTRUMENTAL CONDITION-ING

Classical Conditioning	Instrumental Conditioning
1. Involves an already established response to another stimulus.	No previous stimulus-response connection necessary. Learner must discover appropriate response.
2. The outcome is not dependent on learner's actions.	The outcome is dependent on learner's actions.
3. Influences development and changes in opinions, tastes, and goals.	Influences changes in goal-directed behavior.

Source: Based on David Krech, et al., *Psychology: A Basic Course,* Knopf, New York, 1976, pp. 50–61.

at a more conscious and purposeful level than does classical conditioning.

A second distinction between these two methods concerns the outcome of the learning situation. In classical conditioning the outcome is not dependent on the learner's actions, but with instrumental conditioning a particular response can change the learner's situation or environment. The response then is actually *instrumental* in producing reinforcement or making something happen in the environment, hence the name for this type of conditioning.

Because of the above differences, each conditioning method is suited to explaining different types of learning. Learning to adapt and control one's environment is better explained by instrumental conditioning because it requires that the learner discover the response that leads to reinforcement. Alternatively, classical conditioning better explains how we acquire or change opinions, tastes, and goals. This occurs through their association with stimuli that already elicit favorable or unfavorable experiences.

Cognitive Interpretations

Instead of viewing learning as the development of connections between stimuli and responses, cognitive theorists stress the importance of perception, problem-solving, and insight. This viewpoint contends that much learning occurs not as a result of trial-and-error or practice but through discovering meaningful patterns which enable us to solve problems. These meaningful patterns are termed "gestalts," and cognitive theories of learning rely heavily on the process of insight to explain the development of gestalts.

Wolfgang Kohler's work with apes provides an interesting example to understand better this view of learning.[12] In one experiment a chimpanzee was placed in a cage with a box, and bananas were hung from the top of the cage beyond reach, even if the ape jumped. After failing to reach the food, the problem was solved when suddenly the chimp placed the box under the bananas and jumped from it to reach the food. This suggested that the ape's learning was not a result of trial-and-error but a consequence of deliberation and sudden insight into a problem solution. This feeling of insight is familiar to all of us when we suddenly "see" the solution to a problem situation (the "ah ha" effect).

In many problem-solving situations there does not appear to be a reward associated with problem solution. For example, no observable reward is present when the student solves a math problem. However, the concept of *closure* is viewed as having important reinforcing properties in the cognitive viewpoint. As long as an individual has not solved a problem, a state of incompleteness produces tension to motivate continued search for a solution. Problem solution results in closure, which reduces the motivating tension and is reinforcing.

Applying Alternative Learning Concepts to Consumer Behavior
We should not be dismayed by alternative explanations of how consumers learn. In fact, it is useful to have these alternatives, since the nature of what consumers learn probably influences the method they use to learn it.

As we have noted, cognitive interpretations stress problem-solving behavior and the learner's active understanding of situations confronting him. It is not "blind" or rote learning, as the learning of connections can be. This view of learning is therefore most useful in understanding how consumers learn which stores, methods of shopping, or products will best meet their needs. For example, it can take the form of learning about the uses and benefits of products new to the market, especially if they represent significant innovations. It can also explain how consumers learn about existing products for which they have developed a recent interest or need. In either case, the *position* consumers learn for a product vis-à-vis other products can dramatically influence its success. That is why marketers develop promotional messages and symbols to influence this learning process. A good case in point is Seven-Up's "un-cola" campaign to position their drink as an attractive alternative to colas, as opposed to an also-ran in direct competition with them. Whether successful or not, we see that the emphasis in such campaigns is to influence purposeful problem-solving learning behavior which occurs at a very conscious level.

Connectionists' theories of learning are appropriate to understanding a variety of other aspects of consumer behavior. As already noted, classical conditioning is useful in explaining how consumers acquire tastes and motives. Advertisers also employ the concept by showing their brands in selected surroundings. For example, Kentucky Fried Chicken is shown being enjoyed in fun-filled family gatherings, Salem cigarettes are shown against lush green forests, and Belairs are constantly depicted against deep blue skies. By repeating these themes, it is expected that consumers will associate the brands with fun, freshness, or other intended meanings.

Significant consequences can result from consumers learning associations between stimuli. Consider the case of Brown-Forman distillers' introduction of Frost 8/80 to the market in 1971. The product was a unique "dry-white" whiskey with what appeared to be a great market potential. Unfortunately, uniqueness was actually the problem—the drink was clear like vodka but tasted like whiskey. This so contradicted consumers' learned color association regarding liquor that the product was rejected, forcing its removal from the market. It is interesting to note that Heublein distillers has apparently learned well from Brown-Forman's failure. This company's new Hereford's Cows drink is loaded with cues of color, texture, and packaging that are consistent with the creamy liquid consumers expect from a product bearing such a name.

Certain types of habitual behavior are also explained through classical conditioning. For example, many consumers automatically purchase particular brands such as Scotch tape and Bayer aspirin because they have developed strong associations between the brand name and the generic product. This is often an advantage accruing to marketers who first develop a product that dominates the market. In still other cases, consumers habitually purchase particular brands such as Campbell's soups merely because their parents did. Here, such a strong association has been made between a particular brand and some activity or need that little consideration may be given to its actual suitability.

Instrumental conditioning is useful in understanding consumer learning where conscious choices resulting in positive or negative reinforcement are made. The obvious case is consumers' purchase and evaluation of products. Favorable experiences will result in positive reinforcement of the particular choice. Of course learning to avoid certain products due to negative reinforcement from bad experiences with them is also possible. This is strong justification for the marketer's stress on satisfying the customer.

Promotions depicting satisfied customers can also result in consumers learning a connection between a brand and favorable experiences. Other types of promotional efforts such as free product samples, trial periods, or low introductory prices make further use of instrumental learning. In these situations the goal is to provide consumers with a rewarding experience through use of the product.

Many other applications of both cognitive and connectionist learning could be cited. However, we now turn our attention to other useful concepts of consumer learning.

ADDITIONAL CONSUMER LEARNING TOPICS

A number of other aspects of consumer learning are of special interest. Although the following topics by no means exhaust the list of useful concepts, they are representative of the potential applications of learning theory to understanding consumer behavior.

Discrimination Learning

Learning to discriminate between various stimuli is important to consumers' ability to adapt to their environment. Discrimination is learned over a period of time when the same response to two similar but different stimuli leads to different consequences (reinforcement).

Consumers make frequent use of discrimination learning. New or different brands as well as different models within the same producer's line must be distinguished, even though they might differ by only a few features. Products that provide rewarding service must also be distinguished from those that are relatively inferior. Of course, a great deal of marketing effort encourages such discrimination learning. Here the goal is to reinforce consumers' attention to the uniqueness of a brand. In fact, the concept of a brand name is itself quite useful in this regard, but unique colors, shapes, and packages are also employed. In another quite different and interesting case, patrons of a small retail shop were personally telephoned and thanked for shopping at the store. Reaction to this distinctive reinforcement was quite favorable—sales increased 27 percent during the test period.[13] This attests to the impact of consumers' discrimination learning.

Stimulus Generalization

When a given response to a stimulus has been learned it will tend to be elicited not only by the original stimulus involved in the learning situation but also by stimuli that are similar to it. This process, called *stimulus generalization,* appears to occur *automatically* unless stopped by discrimination learning.[14] Stimulus generalization simplifies the consumer's life since it means that learning a unique response to every stimulus is not necessary. One response can be used for similar stimuli unless there is some important reason to learn to discriminate between them.

The *gradient of generalization* relates the degree of similarity between two stimuli to the likelihood that both will generate the same response. It has been found that the greater the resemblance between a given stimulus and another that already causes a response, the greater the chance that it will also generate the same response.[15] Conversely, the more dissimilar two stimuli are, the smaller the likelihood of stimulus generalization occurring. As noted in Chapter 14, some producers of private brands make use of the gradient concept by packaging products to closely resemble national brands in appearance. In other cases, firms "ride the coattails" of success of pioneering companies by offering highly similar products.[16] The sudden appearance of a variety of low-tar cigarettes and sugarless gums are cases in point.

The generalization gradient also helps us understand the marketing approach of introducing "new" products that often bear a considerable resemblance to their predecessors. This encourages consumers to generalize learned attitudes and preferences from the old product to the new model. The *family brand* strategy employs similar methods. Here, the family brand name is prominently associated with the new product as in the case of a General Motors car, a Wilson football, or a Panasonic radio. The intention is that consumers' favorable perceptions and attitudes about the family name will be generalized to the new product. Of course the danger of such a strategy is that unfavorable experiences on the part of consumers with one product in the family line may lead to a generalizing of poor impressions to the entire group of products.

Rate and Degree of Learning

In general, learning of all but the simplest tasks appears to follow a rather common pattern which has become known as a *learning curve.* A typical curve is displayed in Figure 15-4 where the amount learned is measured on the *y* axis and the number of practice trials is shown on the *x* axis. The characteristic shape of this curve demonstrates that the rate of learning is quite rapid during initial stages. However, in later stages as the amount learned accumulates, the *rate* of additional learning per trial decreases. This demonstrates the highly effective nature of practice in early stages of learning and its diminishing effect in later trials. It also demonstrates that even though the rate of learning is high initially, many practice trials are needed to ensure a large amount of total learning.

It is important to note that in many cases, repetition of an advertisement leads to a learning curve similar to the one Figure 15-4 depicts.[17] In these cases, the number of times the advertising message is repeated is measured along the *x* axis and the extent of consumers' learning of the message is measured along the *y* axis. Of course, marketers must determine whether this general pattern actually fits their particular products and situations.[18] If so, there are several implications regarding the use of advertising to encourage consumer learning. First, as the curve demonstrates, the marketer must be willing to repeat an advertising message a significant number of times. This is also why a brand name may be repeated several times in just one advertisement. Second, the curve demonstrates that after repeating messages many times the marketer is paying for quite small increases in consumer learning. Further, since many repetitions of the same ad can result in boredom and a decrease in consumers' willingness to learn, the marketer might be tempted to stop advertising after a period of time.[19] However, as will be demonstrated shortly, if a message is not repeated consumers forget most of it quite rapidly. This suggests the need to repeat advertisements merely to *maintain* consumers' level of learning. In addition, other evidence indicates that repetition can actually increase consumers' preference for a product and their intention to purchase it.[20] This suggests that marketers should repeat the basic content of an advertising message while periodically changing the method of doing so to maintain consumers' interest. Means of accomplishing this include using different spokespeople, using different beginnings and endings to the ads, and similar methods. Close attention to advertisements will demonstrate that such techniques are actually being employed.

Although the above general patterns of consumer learning do exist, a

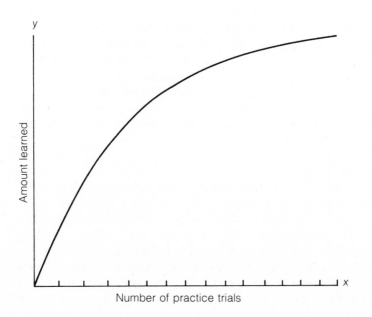

FIGURE 15-4
Graph of typical
learning curve.

number of variables influence the rate and strength of the process. Three of these factors are briefly reviewed below.

LEARNING ABILITY Individuals differ considerably in their abilities to learn, and intelligence is a primary factor influencing this ability. Intelligence appears to be normally distributed within the population with some consumers being much higher than average and others being considerably below normal. Highly intelligent consumers are capable of learning more quickly and are often interested in learning different types of information about products than consumers of lower intelligence. In addition, they tend to be more critical of unsubstantiated advertising claims and often have different readership habits than do other consumers. For example, readers of *National Geographic, Scientific American,* and *Saturday Review* tend to have higher intelligence levels than readers of many other magazines. Such differences in learning abilities require marketers to consider carefully intelligence levels of their target market before designing the content of promotional messages.

SCHEDULES OF REINFORCEMENT It is not necessary to reinforce every "correct" response in order for learning to occur. Different reinforcement schedules, however, lead to different patterns of learning. *Continuous reinforcement* schedules, which reward every correct response, yield quite rapid learning. Conversely, *partial reinforcement* schedules yield a slower rate, but also result in learning that is more resistant to change. This may at least partially explain why consumers' negative attitudes toward brands are usually highly resistant to change.[21] Negative attitudes can be acquired through partial reinforcement because a few unsatisfactory experiences with a brand can occur over some period of time. This can result in consumers being highly resistant to positive information about the brand, especially if the marketer is the source of such information.

PRACTICE SCHEDULES If only the time actually spent at a learning task is considered, periods of practice separated by rest intervals achieve much more efficient learning in many situations than do learning periods with no rest. The term *distributed practice* refers to learning sessions with rest periods, while learning without rest periods is known as *massed practice.* Aside from its obvious relevance to students' study habits, practice schedules have implications regarding the proper scheduling of advertising messages over time. Given that distributed practice is an effective learning technique, the marketer is interested in the optimum time interval to allow between advertising repetitions in order to generate the greatest amount of consumer learning. This has sparked a considerable amount of research in the advertising field.[22]

RETAINING LEARNED MATERIAL

As everyone's experience has demonstrated, learning is not necessarily permanent. Rather, a number of processes are at work which can result in the loss of learned material. These processes are of particular interest to marketers who strive to have consumers retain brand names and information about products. The challenge is also great when one considers that about 23,000 different brands are advertised on a national or regional scale in the United States alone.[23] In a very real sense each of these brands, as well as many local ones, vie for a prominent place in consumers' memory. Although consumers' retention of a brand name or information about it certainly does not ensure a sale, it is considered to be a very important step toward that goal.

In this section we shall discuss two factors affecting the loss of learned information: extinction and forgetting. Both processes, but especially forgetting, are of most immediate concern to those in the area of marketing communication.

Extinction

We can "unlearn" material or behavior that has been previously learned. This unlearning process is termed "extinction" and occurs when, over a period of time, a learned response is made to a stimulus but reinforcement does not occur. The greater the number of nonreinforced trials the less likely the response is to occur, but complete extinction is rare. Also, *spontaneous recovery*—the sudden reappearance of an extinguished response—reduces the chance of complete extinction. Resistance of extinction also increases when:

impelling motives are strong

the number of previously reinforced trials are large

the amount of reward during learning is large

reward is delayed during the learning process

a partial reinforcement schedule was used in the learning process

Resistance to extinction at least partially explains why consumers are slow to change many tastes, shopping patterns, and consumption habits. For example, many find it difficult to reduce or eliminate sweets, coffee, or smoking. Similarly, others who have developed strong brand or store loyalties over time resist making changes even if their regular brands or stores are not currently providing the rewards they once did. This poses a great challenge to marketers attempting to draw patronage away from competition.

Forgetting

It is important to distinguish extinction from the process of forgetting. *Extinction* will occur when a previously learned response continues to be made but is no longer reinforced. *Forgetting* can be defined as the loss of retained material due to nonuse or interference from some other learning task. As can be implied from this definition, *retention* is the amount of previously learned material that is remembered.[24]

The process of forgetting and how it can be minimized has been of more concern to marketers than has extinction. This is so not only because it is a more significant problem, but also because marketers can influence the process by repeating advertising messages to encourage consumers' retention. To determine the extent of their success, various measures of advertising retention are employed. The two most commonly used methods are:

Recall—the consumer relates to an interviewer the advertisement he remembers seeing recently. He may not be prompted at all (unaided recall), or may be given some guidance (aided recall), such as the product category involved.

Recognition—the consumer is presented with an advertisement or series of advertisements and is asked to indicate which ones he has seen recently.

Both methods of measuring retention are used frequently, but as shown in Figure 15-5 the level of retention as measured by recognition is typically greater than indicated by the recall method. Of course, the most appropriate technique will depend on promotional goals and the specific situation, such as the type of product involved. However, the marketing manager must be aware of which technique is being employed to evaluate properly the success of the promotional effort.

Note from Figure 15-5 that regardless of the measure of retention used, the fastest rate of forgetting occurs soon after learning has occurred. As the time since learning increases, forgetting continues but its rate slows considerably. This was dramatically demonstrated in one marketing experiment where the percentage who could remember a specific advertisement dropped by 50 percent only 4 weeks after the last repetition.[25]

This characteristic shape of retention curves demonstrates the marketer's concern for repeating advertisements to combat the forgetting process.

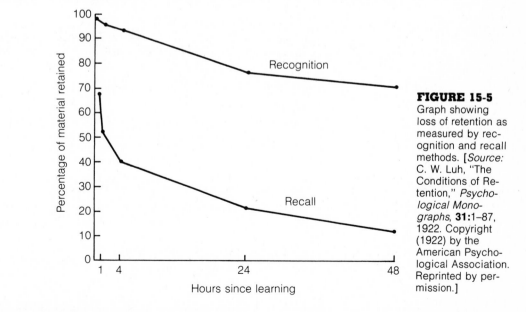

FIGURE 15-5
Graph showing loss of retention as measured by recognition and recall methods. [*Source:* C. W. Luh, "The Conditions of Retention," *Psychological Monographs*, **31:**1–87, 1922. Copyright (1922) by the American Psychological Association. Reprinted by permission.]

However, designing effective methods to minimize forgetting requires some understanding of human memory. We now turn our attention to this topic.

Memory A number of recent studies suggest that it is useful to view the consumer's memory system as being composed of three categories: sensory, short-term, and long-term memory. As shown in Figure 15-6, for the consumer to remember information for any significant period of time, it must pass through the sensory and short-term memory systems and be stored in long-term memory. However, at each stage of this process the information is also capable of being forgotten. Table 15-2 summarizes some of the major characteristics of each of these memory registers in order to assist our understanding of the forgetting process.[26]

Information reaching consumers is first received by their *sensory memory* system. This register has a very limited time span, lasting only a fraction of a second. Its capacity, however, is very large—capable of briefly storing all that perceptual sensors transmit. It also appears to store faithfully this information in a form that closely resembles the actual stimuli. A good illustration of the nature and duration of sensory memory is the after-image we "see" in our "mind's eye" immediately after observing some object and closing our eyes. Actually, this sensory memory exists for each of our senses and forgetting occurs as the result of the rapid fading of these after-images. Such fading of memory with the passage of time is referred to as the *decay* method of forgetting.

Information retained by sensory memory becomes the input to *short-term memory*. Although the duration of this memory register is considerably longer than sensory memory, it still is quite short, lasting less than one minute. In addition, the capacity of short-term memory is quite limited. Approximately seven items or groups are all that can be stored at any one time. The system can therefore be viewed as having two functions. First, it serves as a temporary holding place for information so that it can be acted upon. This occurs when we look up a telephone number and remember it long enough to dial it. Secondly, short-term memory is the source of information for long-term memory.

The material stored in short-term memory does not bear a one-to-one

FIGURE 15-6
Diagram of the memory systems. (*Source:* Based on Nancy C. Waugh and Donald A. Norman, "Primary Memory," *Psychological Review*, **72**:89–104, March 1965. Copyright (1965) by the American Psychological Association. Reprinted by permission.)

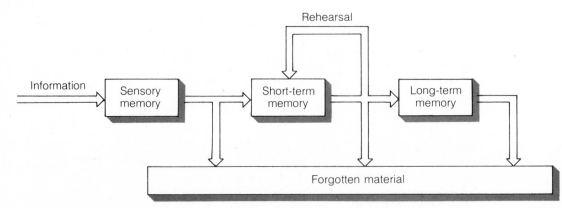

TABLE 15-2

361

LEARNING

SUMMARY OF MEMORY SYSTEMS CHARACTERISTICS

Memory System	Duration	Capacity	Type of Coding	Major Forgetting Mechanism
Sensory memory	Fraction of a second	All that perceptual sensors can deliver	Quite direct representation of reality	Decay
Short-term memory	Less than one minute	Approximately seven items	Indirect— chunking	Decay
Long-term memory	Up to many years	Almost unlimited	Indirect— clustering via meaningfulness	Interference

Source: Adapted from David Krech et al., *Psychology: A Basic Course,* Knopf, New York, p. 83. Copyright © Alfred A. Knopf, Inc.

correspondence with the real world. Instead, the process of coding organizes material into a more easily remembered format. One method of coding is termed "chunking." Here, a series of items is organized into a smaller number of chunks or groups to facilitate memory. For example, the social security number 038269746 can be organized as 038-26-9746 to simplify its retention. It appears that to employ the chunking process the individual must be prepared to receive the incoming information. For example a radio advertisement involving a telephone number should alert consumers that a number will be given so that they will be prepared to chunk it into an exchange plus a four digit number. Without such preparation, the material may be forgotten before chunking can be used. In addition, the telephone number should be announced in chunked form to facilitate memory.

As Figure 15-6 demonstrates, for material to have even a brief stay in short-term memory it must be rehearsed. This often is as simple as repeating an address to ourselves to remember it long enough to write it down. If such rehearsal does not occur, the information will be lost through the decay process. Continued rehearsal will transfer information to long-term memory.

The *long-term memory* system has the capacity to store an almost unlimited amount of information for as short as a couple of minutes or for as long as many years. The key to coding material in this highly efficient system appears to be *meaningfulness.* That is, material tends to be grouped or clustered into patterns that have meaning for the individual. This happens regardless of how the material is received. For example, consumers seem to remember product names according to how they relate to each other, as opposed to remembering them in some alphabetical or chronological order. Therefore any device that helps consumers in discovering meaningful relationships in material will assist them in remembering it.

As opposed to just decaying over time, material appears to be lost from long-term memory as a result of other learning *interfering* with retention of the material. The interference concept holds that material can be forgotten in two ways. In *retroactive inhibition* new learning interferes with material in long-term memory and the material in memory is forgotten. This could occur, for example, when attempts to learn material in this chapter result in forgetting material on the perceptual process. In *proactive inhibition,* material already in memory interferes with remembering new material. In either case, the greater the similarity between two sets of material, the more they will interfere with each other. However, several approaches can serve to minimize such forgetting. These are discussed below.

APPLICATIONS TO ADVERTISING A number of topics regarding forgetting have significant implications for the field of advertising.[27] The following conclusions represent only a sampling of the useful guidelines available. Selections have been confined to the long-term memory system, and while some guidelines are directly drawn from our previous discussion, others represent extension of that material.[28]

1. *Unique advertising messages have a greater potential for being remembered*—This occurs because highly unusual material is least affected by the interference process of forgetting. This is one factor that motivates advertisers to search for novel approaches and themes for their messages.

2. *The order in which material is presented influences how well it will be retained, with the middle portion of the material being the most easily forgotten*—This apparently occurs because the beginning and ending of messages stand out the most and interfere with remembering material in between (retroactive and proactive inhibition). The implication is that the most important parts of advertising messages should be placed at the beginning or end or both. Conversely, some direct-mail advertisers bury the price of their merchandise in the middle of a long letter so as to minimize its negative impact on a purchase decision.

3. *Messages that encourage immediate rehearsal of material stimulate its retention*—Rehearsal increases the chances that material will stay in short-term memory. Continued rehearsal will also encourage the transfer of the material to long-term memory. This is why some radio and television advertisements encourage listeners to repeat a telephone number or address several times during the duration of the message.

4. *Memory is cue-dependent and presentation of relevant cues will stimulate recall*[29]—Apparently certain cues present during learning, or shortly thereafter, become associated with the material in memory. Their presentation at a later date facilitates recall of the learned material. This process can be very effectively employed by designing packages and point-of-purchase displays to contain the same cues used in advertising the product. For example, a picture of Ed McMahon placed in a store reminds many consumers of Budweiser, Mr. Wipple reminds others of Charmin, and just the word "gusto" or "weekends" reminds still others of Schlitz and Michelob. Another use of this device is the advertisement that actually tells consumers to link two words together— indigestion and Pepto-Bismol—and advises, "When You Get One Take The Other."

5. *Repetition facilitates learning and increases the chances of retaining the material*—Continued repeating of an advertisement will assist consumers in learning the message content. Additional repetition strengthens the learning

bond and minimizes forgetting. However, as we noted, continued repetition of the same message can lead to consumer boredom and discourage retention. For this reason repeating the basic theme with some variety is most effective. Advertisements, such as those for Clorox bleach, using various situations or introductions, are examples of this technique. An additional benefit of repetition is that it appears to help increase brand preference and intention to purchase—especially for new brands about which little is known.[30]

6. *Material that is meaningful to the individual is learned more quickly and therefore has a greater chance of being retained than nonmeaningful material*[31]—Apparently meaningful material actively involves the individual's mental capacities and this leads to its greater retention. Therefore, the strong recommendation that has been made for some time is to design advertisements that stimulate consumers' mental involvement, thereby making messages meaningful to them. However, the marketer should develop the specific meaning he wishes for the message rather than rely on chance for consumers to determine what meaning they will derive from it themselves. Some methods of accomplishing this are listed below. Of course, the specific situation will dictate the degree to which they are appropriate.

a. *Interactive imagery*—Use of pictures, symbols, and other visual devices that depict how two concepts or properties relate to each other can be a highly effective aid to consumers' memory.[32] Such imagery can be used to link a specific brand to particular needs or to a general product group. A splendid example is using the image of the sun kissing an orange for the Sunkist brand of oranges.

b. *Showing mistakes*—When demonstrating mechanical skills, performance, or decision making, it is often useful to show how things should *not* be done as well as how they should be done.[33] The Midas muffler commercial that depicts a car owner's trauma when attempting to get his muffler replaced at service stations is such an example. An additional technique, which also heightens involvement, is to simulate situations as if the viewer were actually experiencing them. The Fram television commercial for oil filters where the repairman talks directly to viewers about the costly results of not regularly changing oil filters employs this strategy.

c. *Incomplete messages*—Leaving some messages open-ended so that consumers must become involved to complete them has been found to increase retention.[34] This may be quite overtly done by simply not completing the entire message, as in the commercial for Salem cigarettes cited in the last chapter, or it may be more subtly accomplished by having the announcer ask a question or pose a decision problem which is left to the viewer to answer.

d. *Mnemonic techniques*—The art of mnemonics (ne-mon′-ics) concerns developing a pattern for a series of seemingly unrelated facts so that they can be more easily remembered. Therefore, any technique that allows consumers to "see" some pattern for associating otherwise meaningless facts will usually be helpful. Where possible, one such device is to provide word associations for telephone numbers. For example, some cities have reserved the telephone number HELP (4357) for their emergency hotlines. A number of private firms have employed a similar technique. In other cases, a melodic pattern can be employed. The singing jingle Sheraton hotels devised to promote consumers' memory of their toll-free reservation number (800-325-3535) is a good illustration. In a similar fashion, a narrative or song can sometimes be devised to promote retention of other information. An excellent example is: "Two all-beef patties, special sauce, lettuce, cheese, pickles, onions on a sesame-seed bun." The proportion of Americans that remember these product characteristics for the Big Mac hamburger is probably astounding.

Again it should be stressed that the above list of general guidelines regarding consumers' memory is not by any means exhaustive. In addition, the specific situation must be considered before employing any of them. However, the list is illustrative of the potential benefits of applying learning concepts to the design of marketing communications.

SUMMARY

This chapter dealt with one of the fundamental methods by which consumers are able to adapt to their environment. The influence of the learning process was seen to be pervasive, affecting factors from consumers' basic likes and dislikes to typical methods of shopping. After some introductory comments, attention turned to principal learning elements—motive, cue, response, and reinforcement. Next, some of the basic methods by which consumers learn were introduced. Distinctions between cognitive and connectionist schools of thought were highlighted and the usefulness of each of these concepts to understanding consumer learning were addressed. Cognitive theories appear best-suited to understand problem-solving behavior, while classical conditioning is useful in explaining rote, unconscious learning. Instrumental conditioning falls between these extremes.

Attention then turned to a number of additional learning topics including generalization and discrimination, the rate and degree of learning, and factors influencing these variables. The last major topic dealt with consumers' memory systems and the process of forgetting. It appears most useful to view memory as being comprised of three separate and distinct systems—sensory, short-term, and long-term. Finally, a number of guidelines useful for advertisers concerned with maintaining consumers' long-term memory were offered.

DISCUSSION TOPICS

1. What is learning? Briefly indicate its importance to understanding consumer behavior.

2. What method of learning (classical conditioning, instrumental conditioning, or cognitive) seems best able to explain each of the following:

a. smoking cigarettes
b. purchasing an air conditioner primarily for reducing the humidity in a hot, humid room
c. writing Scotch tape on a shopping list instead of cellophane tape

3. What are stimulus generalization and discrimination learning and how are they important to the marketer?

4. Draw a learning curve and discuss its implications for repeating a given advertising message to consumers.

5. Add a typical retention curve to the learning curve drawn for question 4. Discuss the implications of these curves for advertisers.

6. Suggest some circumstances when an advertiser would be more interested in using the recall method for measuring retention than the recognition method. Do the same for the recognition method as opposed to the recall method.

7. Officials of the federal government have decided that the United States will "go metric." They are now concerned with how to promote learning of the metric system among the citizenry. Suggest methods and programs to assist in accomplishing this goal.

8. Compare and contrast the sensory, short-term, and long-term memory systems. Indicate the relevance of each to advertising strategies.

9. Cite some suggestions you would give to advertisers who were concerned with consumers remembering the following:

a. to start a rotary lawn mower safely one should make sure that (1) the deflector chute or grass bag is attached, (2) no objects or debris are next to the mower, (3) the left foot is placed on the mower, and (4) the right foot is placed well back.
b. choose a brand name for earth-moving equipment which contractors will remember and associate with their need for such equipment.
c. have consumers learn how to pronounce the airline name Alitalia so that they will not be reluctant to ask for it on their trips to Europe.

NOTES

1. See "From Bugs to Batman, Children's TV Shows Produce Adult Anxiety," *The Wall Street Journal,* October 19, 1976, p. 1, for one of a series of articles reviewing the effects of this and other issues concerning the influence of television.

2. Much of this section is based on John Dollard and Neal Miller, *Personality and Psychotherapy,* McGraw-Hill, New York, 1950, pp. 25–47.

3. See William Copulsky and Katherin Marton, "Sensory Cues, You've Got to Put Them Together," *Product Marketing,* January 1977, pp. 31–34.

4. Winfred F. Hill, *Learning: A Survey of Psychological Interpretations,* Chandler, San Francisco, 1963, p. 225.

5. Hill, *Learning,* pp. 100–112.

6. Leonard Krasner, "Studies of the Conditioning of Verbal Behavior," *Psychological Bulletin,* **55**:148–170, 1958.

7. See Ernest R. Hilgard and Gordon H. Bower, *Theories of Learning,* 3d ed., Appleton-Century-Crofts, New York, 1966, for a comprehensive review of these theories.

8. The two schools of thought are referred to as the reinforcement and contiguity advocates. See Hill, *Learning,* pp. 31–89, for a review of their differences and many similarities.

9. Ivan Pavlov, *Conditioned Reflexes. An Investigation of the Physiological Activity of the Cerebral Cortex,* edited and translated by G. V. Anrep, Oxford University Press, London, 1927.

10. Clark L. Hull, *Principles of Behavior,* Appleton-Century-Crofts, New York, 1943, p. 94.

11. B. F. Skinner, *The Behavior of Organisms: An Experimental Analysis,* Appleton-Century-Crofts, New York, 1938.

12. Wolfgang Kohler, *The Mentality of Apes,* Harcourt, Brace & World, New York, 1925.

13. J. Ronald Carey et al., "A Test of Positive Reinforcement of Customers," *Journal of Marketing,* **40**:98–100, October 1976.

14. Bernard Berelson and Gary A. Steiner, *Human Behavior: An Inventory of Scientific Findings,* Harcourt, Brace & World, New York, 1964, pp. 138–139.

15. C. I. Hovland, "The Generalization of Conditioned Responses: I.," *Journal of General Psychology,* **17**:125–148, 1937.

16. James H. Myers and William H. Reynolds, *Consumer Behavior and Marketing Management,* Houghton Mifflin, Boston, 1967, p. 59.

17. See Hubert A. Zielske, "The Remembering and Forgetting of Advertising," *Journal of Marketing,* **23**:239–243, January 1959.

18. Michael L. Ray, Alan G. Sawyer, and Edward C. Strong, "Frequency Effects Revisited," *Journal of Advertising Research,* **11**:14–20, February 1971.

19. C. Samuel Craig, Brian Sternthal, and Clark Levitt, "Advertising Wearout: An Experimental Analysis," *Journal of Marketing Research,* **13**:365–372, November 1976.

20. See Alan G. Sawyer, "Repetition and Affect: Recent Empirical and Theoretical Developments," in Arch Woodside, Jagdish Sheth, and Peter Bennett (eds.), *Consumer and Industrial Buyer Behavior,* North-Holland, New York, 1977, pp. 229–242.

21. Myers and Reynolds, *Consumer Behavior,* pp. 54–55.

22. See Edward C. Strong, "The Use of Field Experimental Observations in Estimating Advertising Recall," *Journal of Marketing Research,* **11**:369–378, November 1974, for one recent investigation.

23. Leo Bogart and Charles Lehman, "What Makes A Brand Name Familiar?" *Journal of Marketing Research,* **10**:17, February 1973.

24. Howard H. Kendler, *Basic Psychology: Brief Version,* W. A. Benjamin, Menlo Park, Calif., 1977, p. 448.

25. Zielske, "Forgetting of Advertising."

26. Much of this discussion follows David Krech et al., *Psychology: A Basic Course,* Knopf, New York, 1976, pp. 76–81.

27. Also see Joel Seagert and Robert Hoover, "Learning Theory and Marketing: An Update," in Kenneth Bernhardt (ed.), *Marketing: 1776–1976 and Beyond,* American Marketing Association, Chicago, 1976, pp. 512–514.

28. For additional guidelines see Steuart Henderson Britt, "How Advertising Can Use Psychology's Rules of Learning," *Printer's Ink,* **252**:74+, September 1955; and Steuart Henderson Britt, "Applying Learning Principles to Marketing," *MSU Business Topics,* **23**:5–12, Spring 1975.

29. E. Tulving and Z. Pearlstone, "Availability vs. Accessibility of Information in Memory for Words," *Journal of Verbal Learning and Verbal Behavior,* **5**:381–391, 1966.

30. Sawyer, "Repetition and Affect."

31. Berelson and Steiner, *Human Behavior,* p. 166.

32. See Kathy A. Lutz and Richard J. Lutz, "The Effects of Interactive Imagery on Learning: Application to Advertising," University of California, Los Angeles Center for Marketing Studies, Paper no. 40, March 1976.

33. Britt, "Psychology's Rules of Learning."

34. See for example James T. Heimbach and Jacob Jacoby, "The Zeigarnik Effect in Advertising," in M. Venkatesan (ed.), *Proceedings of the Third Annual Conference,* Association for Consumer Research, College Park, Md., 1972, pp. 746–757.

PERSONALITY AND SELF-CONCEPT

Personality and self-concept are two notions that attempt to take a *total* view of a person's makeup. Our purpose in studying these variables is to determine their usefulness in understanding consumers' brand and store preferences, media usage, susceptibility to persuasion, and other behavioral aspects.

The chapter begins by examining various concepts of personality. One concept that has seen extensive marketing use is then assessed in terms of its usefulness in predicting and understanding consumer behavior. After briefly treating the relationship of personality theory to psychographics and its consumer-behavior relevance, attention will turn to the topic of consumers' self-concept and its importance to understanding consumption behavior.

PERSONALITY THEORIES AND APPLICATIONS

The study of personality and its relationship to human behavior can be traced back to the earliest writings of the Egyptians, Chinese, Greeks, and Europeans. People have always made judgments about other people's personalities as being aggressive, passive, adventuresome, compliant, sociable, charismatic, and so forth. Even though most of us believe that we have an intuitive grasp of what constitutes personality, behavioral scientists have been unable to agree on its precise definition. Most would agree, however, that it involves some organization of influences within the individual which affect his characteristic method of thinking and responding. These *general patterns* of responses which people make toward their environment offer a broad framework of what personality is. However, within this framework several theories and therefore definitions of personality have emerged, some of which are described below.[1]

Psychoanalytic Personality Theory

Freud, the father of psychoanalytic theory, proposed that every individual's personality is the product of a struggle among three interacting forces—the id, the ego, and the superego. According to Freud, the *id* is the source of strong inborn drives and urges, such as aggression and sex. The id operates on what is called the *pleasure principle,* that is, it acts to avoid tension and seek pleasure. However, it tends to operate at a very subjective and unconscious level and is not fully capable of dealing with objective reality. Also, many of its impulses are not acceptable to the values of organized society.

The *ego* comes into being because of the limitations of the id in dealing with the real world. Through learning and experience it develops the individual's capabilities of realistic thinking and ability to deal appropriately with his environment. It operates on what is called the *reality principle,* which is capable of postponing the release of tension until that time when it will be effectively directed at coping with the external environment. Because it serves as the organized focal point for effective action, the ego is said to be the executive of the personality.

The *superego* is the third component of personality. It constitutes the moral part of the individual's psychic structure through internalizing the values of society. It represents the ideal by defining what is right and good, and influences the individual to strive for perfection. Therefore, it acts to control basic strivings of the id which could disrupt the social system, and influences the ego to strive for socially approved goals rather than purely realistic ones.

The individual's total personality is determined by the relationships among the id, ego, and superego. The ego serves to administer the interaction between moral standards of the superego and the often socially unacceptable desires and attempted expressions of the id. This usually results in realistic compromises between very basic strivings and socially accepted behavior.

APPLICATIONS OF PSYCHOANALYTIC THEORY Marketers have sometimes used Freudian psychoanalytic theory as a basis for influencing consumers. Its proponents suggest that appeals to the id, disguised by a veiled appeal to the superego, will result in purchase behavior dictated by the ego that is also acceptable to the id and superego. This idea has been translated into advertising themes such as those found in early Miss Clairol hair color commercials. Here, advertisements show a lovely woman with the announcer asking, "Does she or doesn't she?"—a clearly sexual theme appealing to the id. The commercial next focuses on the woman's left hand which is obviously bearing a wedding band to satisfy the superego. The ego then reasons that sex and marriage are acceptable behavior and therefore the ad is acceptable. In advertising this is referred to as the "triple appeal" because the id is sexually stimulated, the superego is placated, and the ego arbitrates the acceptability of these two forms of expression to both the id and superego.

Marketers have made many other uses of sexual and aggressive symbols to appeal to the id, while avoiding those that are *directly* offensive to the superego. Thus, the id is stimulated while the superego is left either undisturbed or placated. For example, it has been said that the Ajax White Knight was perceived as a phallic symbol representing masculinity and strength to the id, while the theme of cleanliness was acceptable to the superego. Also, the Maidenform bra advertisement, "I dreamed I was dancing in the streets of London [Paris, etc.] in my Maidenform bra," supposedly appeals to women's unconscious need for exhibitionism. Presumably, *dreaming* of wearing a Maidenform bra in such situations symbolically satisfies this unconscious need while not disturbing the superego. In the area of packaging, the phallic symbol represented by Macho men's cologne is certainly very Freudian, as are the male- and female-shaped bottles for Jóvan men's and women's cologne.

Although most believe that Freudian applications to marketing are restricted to sex, there are many themes which are not. Wish fulfillment, fantasy, aggression, and escape from life's pressures are Freudian themes upon which some appeals are based. For example, a suburban real estate company might advertise to city dwellers with the theme, "Escape to country living." Also, sporting events are often promoted by showing aggression or violent scenes. The NFL previews and the "agony of defeat" befalling a ski jumper in the introduction to "Wide World of Sports" are excellent illustrations. And, in other cases, promotions for Bermuda, Las Vegas, the Bahamas, and other vacation resorts frequently employ themes stressing escape, freedom, and a chance to "let it all hang out."

Social Theories

Even though they were not in total agreement on an alternative, Adler, Fromm, and Horney were the first to reject Freud's id-based theory of personality. Instead, they reasoned that the individual develops a personality through attempts to deal in a social setting with others. These social theorists, sometimes called the neo-Freudian school, view the individual as striving to overcome feelings of inferiority and searching for ways to obtain love, security, and brotherhood. The argument is that childhood experiences produce feelings of inferiority, insecurity, and a lack of love, which motivate individuals to develop methods to cope with these anxieties. These methods result in overt and covert behavior which form the individual's personality.

The first major consumer behavior study using a neo-Freudian approach was conducted by Cohen using the Horney Classification System, which places people into three groups according to how they respond to others. The three groups are: (1) those who move toward people (compliant), (2) those who move against people (aggressive), and (3) those who move away from people (detached).[2] Results of the study indicated that different products and brands were used by individuals having different personality types. For example, Cohen found that "compliant" types prefer known brand names and use more mouthwash and toilet soaps; "aggressive" types prefer to use razors instead of electric shavers, use more cologne and after-shave lotions, and purchase Old Spice and Van Heusen shirts; and "detached" types appear to have the least awareness of brands. Although such findings are interesting, social personality theories have found little practical application in consumer behavior research.

Stimulus-Response Theories

Stimulus-response theories of personality are grounded on contributions from notable learning theorists such as Pavlov, Skinner, and Hull. Although there are differences among these concepts, there is an agreement that personality results from habitual responses to specific and generalized cues.

They theorize that complex behavior patterns, attitudes, etc., are learned from stimulus-response situations that are continually reinforced, either positively or negatively. The personality, therefore, is created and changed by reinforcement of these stimulus-response associations. However, because of the lack of measuring instruments to study these propositions critically, few if any consumer behavior studies have been conducted relating stimulus-response concepts of personality to purchase behavior.

Trait and Factor Theories

The most popular personality concepts used to explain consumer behavior have been trait and factor theories. *Trait theories* emphasize that (1) people exhibit relatively stable behavioral tendencies, (2) individuals differ in the degree to which they possess these common traits, and (3) when measured, these relative differences between individuals are useful in characterizing their personalities.[3] *Factor theories* are based on the quantitative technique of "factor analysis," which analyzes the results of various behavioral tests on a large number of individuals. The goal of the analysis is to identify common factors or characteristics useful in explaining differences in individual personalities and behavior.

The advantage of trait and factor theories is that they are based on a number of presently available measurement tests and analysis techniques. Some of the measurement instruments include the Gordon Personal Profile, the Edwards Personal Preference Schedule (EPPS), the Thurstone Temperament Schedule, and the California Personality Inventory.

APPLICATION OF TRAIT AND FACTOR THEORIES A large number of researchers have tried to find a relationship between personality as measured by trait and factor theories and the behavior of consumers. These attempts have met with various degrees of success. Several representative studies are reviewed below to give the reader some appreciation of the nature of research in this area.

Koponen, using the EPPS scale, collected data from almost 9000 consumer panel respondents. His results indicate a positive relationship between cigarette smoking and the traits of sex dominance, aggression, and achievement needs among males. He also found personality differences among smokers of filter and nonfilter cigarettes and between readers' preference of certain magazines.[4] However, in a later reanalysis of Koponen's data, Brody and Cunningham found that personality traits accounted for only a small number of the differences among these groups.[5]

Another study using the Gordon Personal Profile found associations between certain personality traits and use of alcoholic beverages, automobiles, chewing gum, mouthwash, and other products. Unfortunately, in this as in many other studies the associations were not very strong.

In what has now become a classic study, Evans employed the EPPS to determine if personality differences could be found between Ford and Chevrolet owners. His findings were that measurable personality differences were of little value in predicting whether a consumer would own a Ford or Chevrolet.[7] Numerous studies have reexamined this research and the basic conclusion appears to be that personality traits are not very helpful in predicting consumers' brand choice for automobiles. However, some evidence indicates that they may be useful in predicting preferences for the type of automobile (sedan versus convertible, for instance).[8]

Other more recent studies have attempted to relate personality differences to innovativeness and other consumer characteristics. As in previous cases, these studies have met with varying degrees of success.[9]

After reviewing over 200 personality studies that have been conducted in consumer research, Kassarjian concluded that the results can be described by a single word, "equivocal."[10] Although a few studies indicate a strong relationship between personality and aspects of consumer behavior, some indicate no relationship, and the vast majority suggest that if a relationship does exist, it is so weak that it is of little practical value to the marketer. Yet experts still contend that personality is a critical variable in influencing consumers' purchasing processes. They argue that the lackluster performance of previous studies is due to inappropriate research methods and an inadequate understanding of the role of personality in influencing consumers. Some of these criticisms are reviewed below to provide guidelines for evaluating future personality studies:

1. Personality tests have frequently been inappropriately administered in consumer studies. Often a standard test designed by psychologists to determine general personality traits is used to predict consumers' specific product or brand purchases. Since the test was not designed for such specific prediction, it is not surprising to find a low success rate in this use. Also, in some cases the tests are not carefully administered to consumers and frequently are arbitrarily modified.[11] Since this can seriously alter the usefulness of the measure, future personality tests should ideally be designed to meet the specific needs of consumer research.[12]

2. Many studies have been conducted without adequate prior thought regarding why or how personality should be related to certain consumer variables.[13] Such a careful examination of the specific situation in question may reveal that there is little reason to expect personality to be related to behavior.

3. It is often inappropriate to expect that personality has a strong direct effect on consumer behavior. We should understand that personality interacts with other individual determinants such as attitudes and perception. Also, the interaction of consumers' personalities with the situation they confront will strongly influence their behavior.[14] In fact, we even should expect consumers' personalities to undergo some change as they attempt to cope with their environment.[15]

4. An emphasis on specific traits has led many to lose sight of the importance of the whole personality to understanding consumer behavior. It must be remembered that traits are aspects of the entire personality. Therefore, individuals can best be understood by an appreciation of how various traits can combine to develop a complete personality structure. Frequently, this interaction of traits results in a whole personality that is different from the sum of its parts. This aspect of consumers' personality has not been adequately appreciated by many consumer researchers or marketers.[16]

One review concludes that because of the above limitations it is actually surprising that previous studies were able to find *any* relationship between personality and consumer behavior.[17] Future research must be more carefully designed and employ more relevant tests of consumers' personalities. One effort in this regard is the use of the personality concept as part of a larger research "package" to understand consumers. This reorientation has resulted in the psychographic profiling of consumers.

PSYCHOGRAPHICS

A number of studies demonstrating how psychographics could be used to segment markets were reviewed in Chapter 5. Because many psychographic questions probe for specific personality characteristics, this method has similarities to trait methods of personality assessment.

The use of psychographics has also proved fruitful in developing advertising strategy and copy. For example, based on extensive research, Tigert demonstrated that psychographic profiles of readers, viewers, and listeners of various media are more important to advertisers' selection of media than traditionally used demographic variables. He successfully argues that life-styles of product and brand users cut across demographic and socioeconomic segments. Media selection should therefore be based upon the appeal directed toward the selected target audience and its life-style.[18]

Psychographic studies have also benefited other consumer-related decisions including the design of marketing channels. Getting the goods and services consumers want to the best place for a profit is a goal of distribution systems. However, with changing life-styles affecting channels of distribution, psychographics can provide useful data for channel designs. For example, because women are increasingly desirous of employment, they have less free time for shopping and therefore demand more convenience in their purchase activity. It has been suggested that many purchase decisions will become more routine for reasons of efficiency. Therefore, strong advertising programs designed to build a brand's reputation can assist in moving certain sales transactions away from stores and toward more automatic order systems that can be used in the home.[19]

Psychographic data also has been shown to be useful to industrial designers in creating product designs that consumers want. For instance, one study involving industrial design compared the usefulness of demographics versus psychographic data to the styling of a clock radio. A class of industrial design students was given a paragraph describing either the demographic characteristics or the psychographic characteristics of a given market and asked to create the radio's design based solely on the paragraph of information given them. Interviewers returned to the subjects from whom they had originally obtained the demographic and psychographic data and asked them to state their preferences for each of the radio designs. They found that the radios designed from psychographic data were preferred to those designed from demographic data.[20]

As the previous examples illustrate, psychographic information can be useful in market segmentation, creation of advertising copy and strategy, media choices, channel selection, and product design.

PERSONALITY AND MARKETING: A SUMMARY

Personality research in general, and those studies related to consumer behavior in particular, have evolved through various stages and in several directions. The application of personality measurements to studying consumer behavior has produced many contradictory findings and often disappointing relationships. Ironically, of all the personality theories available, the one that has probably enjoyed the greatest popularity and use among business practitioners is psychoanalytic analysis, especially as used in the most highly subjective and least scientific area—motivation research.

Of the remaining personality viewpoints, trait theory has been used in consumer research more than any other concept. As noted previously, however, its ability to predict or explain consumer behavior has met with lackluster success. Its greater contribution has been in the area of psychographics. Instead of being used alone, personality traits are combined with descriptions of activities, interests, opinions, demographics, and other measurements to *profile,* not predict, consumers and their behavior.[21] Therefore, psychographics has emerged in the last decade as an approach to develop composite "pictures" of consumer types and to "humanize" the data that are collected from consumers. In the next section we look at another theory which takes a total view of consumers and attempts to relate it to their behavior.

SELF-CONCEPT

Self-concept (image) has become a popular approach in recent years to describe relationships between consumer self-images and brand images, store images, or advertising themes. An advantage of studying consumer behavior using the theory of self-concept is that consumers provide descriptions of themselves as opposed to descriptions made by outside observers. That is, each consumer describes his or her own view of himself or herself in contrast to personality tests that fit consumer responses into predetermined categories. This distinction is important since how a consumer perceives himself or herself might differ substantially from how the researcher sees or categorizes the consumer.

As defined by Newcombe, *self-concept* is "the individual as perceived by that individual in a socially determined frame of reference."[22] More simply, the self-concept may be thought of as "myself as I see myself." This self-perception is not confined to the physical being, but includes such characteristics as strength, honesty, good-humor, sophistication, justice, guilt, and others.[23]

Although the self-concept is highly complex, it is, nonetheless, well-organized, and works in a consistent way. To the outside observer, a person may appear irrational and inconsistent in his behavior; but to the individual taking such action, he is acting in the only way he knows, given his frame of reference. When this individual's point of view is known, it becomes clear that he is *not* acting in an inconsistent way. For example, we may think a consumer is irrational to patronize a store that charges higher prices than does its competition for identical products. However, the consumer may show this loyalty because of the good service or because the salespeople make her feel important. Therefore, when viewed through her eyes, the slightly higher cost for her store loyalty may be well worth the money.

How the Self-Concept Develops

Behaviorists have formed various theories of how people develop their self-concepts. Social interaction provides the basis for most of these theories. Four particular views of self-concept development are presented below.

SELF-APPRAISAL Some theorists believe that a person fashions a self-concept by labeling his own dominant behavior patterns according to what is socially acceptable and unacceptable behavior. For example, certain behaviors are classified as "social" and others are labeled as "antisocial." By observing his own behavior a person might begin to develop an awareness that his behavior falls into the general category, "antisocial." With repeated confirmation of this label, a portion of the person's self-concept emerges, playing a dominant role in how he views himself.

REFLECTED APPRAISAL A second theory of self-concept development is termed reflected appraisal or the "looking-glass self." Basically, this theory holds that appraisals a person receives from others mold self-concept. The extent of this influence depends upon characteristics of the appraiser and his or her appraisal. Specifically, greater impact on the development of a person's self-concept occurs when (1) the appraiser is perceived as a highly credible source, (2) the appraiser takes a very personal interest in the person being appraised, (3) the appraisal is very discrepant with the person's self-concept at the moment, (4) the number of confirmations of a given appraisal is high, (5) the appraisals coming from a variety of sources are consistent, and (6) appraisals are supportive of the person's own beliefs about himself or herself. Appraisals from "significant others" such as parents, close friends, trusted colleagues, and other persons the individual strongly admires influence self-concept development.

SOCIAL COMPARISON The reflected appraisal theory gives a rather depressing picture of self-concept development because it emphasizes that people are passive and merely reflect the appraisals of others. The social comparison theory, however, states that people's self-concepts depend on how they see themselves in relation to others. Thorstein Velben, the major proponent of this theory, was curious as to why people so strongly desired to acquire more goods and services than were necessary to meet their physical needs. The absolute amount of products, property, and services was not as important, he felt, as the *relative* amount accumulated; that is, in comparison with others. "The end sought by accumulation is to rank high in comparison with the rest of the community. . . . So long as the comparison is distinctly unfavorable to himself, the normal, average individual will live in chronic dissatisfaction."[24]

This theory has much more direct bearing upon the development of marketing strategies than have the theories discussed so far. In particular, this view of how people perceive themselves is dependent upon their perception of their relative status as compared to social class, reference groups, and other groups important to them. By determining which groups a person compares himself or herself to in the consumption of products and services, marketers can develop messages that communicate the group referent's use of particular products and brands. Purchases would then be seen by the person as a means to increase relative position in the group.

Festinger improved upon the social comparison theory by arguing that people need to affirm continuously that their beliefs and attitudes are correct and that they compare their beliefs and attitudes with others to determine the validity of their own.[25] If, for example, a person is asked whether he is conservative, romantic, or sociable, the answer will depend to a large extent on how the person perceives himself in comparison with others.

BIASED SCANNING The last theory we shall discuss is concerned with motivation and biased scanning. In essence, this theory views self-concept development in terms of identity aspirations and biased scanning of the environment for information to confirm how well the person is meeting his or her aspirations. It suggests that a person who aspires (is motivated) to be a good lawyer, for example, will seek out information that helps to confirm this aspiration and filter out information that contradicts it. Thus, perceptual scanning is biased toward seeing ourselves as we would like to be (that is, it is biased toward self-gratification).

As we can see, these theories of self-concept development take somewhat different views of how people see themselves. In reality, probably all of the theories are working to some extent. Our self-concepts are very likely shaped to varying degrees according to how we perceive ourselves relative to others, our levels of aspirations and biased selection of information about ourselves, the labeling of ourselves according to how we perceive society categorizes us, and the reflected appraisals of significant others.

Consistency of the Self

Although theories vary on the development of a self-concept, psychologists agree that a person's conception of self displays a high degree of consistency, particularly in the short run. This relatively fixed structure of self is due to two conditions. First, as with many systems, self has an inertial tendency, that is, it tends to resist change. Second, after the self has become established, change becomes less likely because of selective perception of environmental information. That is, the self tends to interpret concepts in terms of the self.[26] Thus, ideas formed from a new experience are easily absorbed into the existing organization of self when the experience is perceived as consistent with the existing structure. In contrast, ideas perceived as inconsistent with the present structure are either rejected or altered to fit into the self, since they pose a threat to the individual. As Lecky states, there is a continuous "compulsion to unify and harmonize the system of ideas by which we live."[27]

Further, he points out that the problem of maintaining harmony and internal consistency of the self is not objective at all, but purely subjective.

These ideas point to the necessity of explaining a person's behavior by understanding how she perceives herself and her environment. On the basis of a situation as the individual sees it, a researcher should be able to predict an individual's behavior. Marketers have conducted several studies using these self-theoretic notions, some of which are discussed below.

Self-Concept Studies of Consumers

Consumer-behavior studies using self-theoretic concepts have focused on describing and predicting consumer-choice behavior. Marketers have based their studies primarily on the following two self-theoretic concepts:

1. People strive to maintain and enhance their self-image.

2. People tend to maintain a harmonious and internally consistent self.

Within this theoretical framework, products and brands are considered as objects that consumers purchase either to maintain or to enhance their self-images. The choice of which brand to buy depends upon how similar (or consistent) the consumer perceives the brand to be with his or her self-image.

In an early study relating self-concept to purchase behavior, a random sample of 1963 automobile purchasers were asked to evaluate themselves, their own automobile, and eight other cars. It was learned that owners' self-perceptions were highly congruent with their perception of their own automobile as opposed to their view of the other eight cars.[28]

In another study Grubb, generalizing from a study of beer drinkers, reasoned that goods as symbols communicate meaning to individuals that directly affect their self-concepts and, therefore, their consuming behavior. Grubb's findings indicated that individuals' purchases are the result of their attempts to maintain or enhance their self-concept.[29] In a later study, Grubb and Hupp found that owners of a specific brand of automobile perceived their self-concepts as similar to those of others who own the same brand of automobile, but significantly different from those of owners of competing cars.[30] This study differed from others in that self-images of car owners were compared with stereotyped images they had of owners of the same brand versus those of competing brands, and *not* with images of brands of a product. The study suggests two things: (1) prospective buyers of a brand are aware of the class of consumers who own a particular brand of product and (2) their generalized stereotyping of various brand owners affects their purchase decision. The general findings were confirmed in a later investigation.[31]

In another study, Dolich found evidence indicating that (1) consumers' self-images are matched more closely to their images of brands they prefer most than to their images of those brands preferred least, (2) consumers' self-images were generally *less* congruent with products consumed in social settings than with privately consumed products, and (3) neither self-image nor ideal self-image was dominant in predicting brand preferences.[32]

In a further effort, the relations between consumers' self-images, ideal self-images, and product images were tested using nineteen different product categories. It was concluded that (1) self-image and ideal self-image tend to be positively related and (2) the purchase intentions for some products tend to be more closely related to self-image, while intentions for other products are more related to ideal self-images.[33] In addition, the study characterized people as being either "actualizers" or "perfectionists." It appeared that actualizers were more likely to show a high self-image/purchase-intention relationship than perfectionists who are more likely to display a higher ideal self-image/purchase-intention relationship. This finding makes sense in terms of self-theory because perfectionists are more likely to purchase products that help them *enhance* (move toward) their ideal self-image, whereas actualizers are satisfied to *maintain* self-image through the purchase of products.

Other investigators argued that previous studies may not have measured adequately self-image/brand image matchings since they used brands known to their subjects. This opinion was based on the argument that since the self acts to reduce inconsistencies, one would expect already preferred brands to be more congruent with the consumer's self- or ideal self-image. To avoid this potential bias, a test was conducted with brands of perfume and shampoo that were unfamiliar to the subjects. Results still confirmed that self- and ideal self-image measures are useful in predicting consumers' brand choice. Also the study suggested that over a period of time a closer matching does occur between initially preferred brands and self-images.[34]

A good summary of the relationship between self-theory and consumer behavior is provided in the following model:

1. An individual does have a self-concept of himself.

2. The self-concept is of value to him.

3. Because this self-concept is of value to him, an individual's behavior will be directed toward the furtherance and enhancement of his self-concept.

4. An individual's self-concept is formed through the interaction process with parents, peers, teachers, and significant others.

5. Goods serve as social symbols and, therefore, are communication devices for the individual.

6. The use of these good-symbols communicates meaning to the individual himself and to others, causing an impact on the intra-action and/or the interaction processes and, therefore, an effect on the individual's self-concept.

Prediction of the model:
7. Therefore, the consuming behavior of an individual will be directed toward the furthering and enhancing of his self-concept through the consumption of goods as symbols.[35]

Figure 16-1 portrays brand choice as a matching process between the consumer's perceived images of a set of brands and her self-image. The decision rule for the situation can be stated as: a consumer's most preferred brand among several alternatives is the brand whose image best matches her self-image. Brands whose images are less congruent will be preferred less.

MEASURING IMAGES TO PREDICT BRAND CHOICE How can marketers measure self- and brand images to predict brand choices? One approach is to use seven-point semantic differential scales like those described in Chapter 14 regarding the measurement of store images. However, in this case consumers are asked to indicate the degree to which various adjectives describe their images of alternative brands and their own self-image. If numbers are assigned to each response option, it will then be possible to evaluate the numerical distance between consumers' perceptions of each brand's image and their own self-images. This suggests the degree to which various brand images match consumers' self-images.

To take a specific example, assume that there are five image components thought to be relevant to perfume purchases. Assume further that a woman responds to five different seven-point semantic differential scales designed to measure these image components. On each scale she indicates her perception of the image of three brands of perfume and her own self-image. The numerical values of one through seven could then be assigned to the seven different response options. Table 16-1 presents the adjectives used to describe the ends of each scale and the numerical responses of the woman.

To measure "how close" the woman perceives each brand image to her own self-image, marketers can use the general distance formula found in solid geometry. Here it is referred to as the D measure, and it is expressed as $D_{ij} = \sqrt{\Sigma d_{ij}^2}$ where D_{ij} is the linear *distance* between the self-image and a brand image, and d_{ij} is the numerical *difference* between the two ratings.

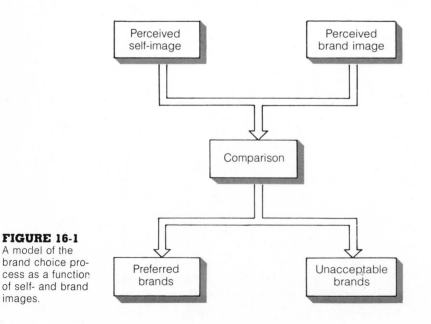

FIGURE 16-1
A model of the brand choice process as a function of self- and brand images.

TABLE 16-1

379

PERSONALITY
AND
SELF-CONCEPT

A WOMAN'S NUMERICAL RATINGS FOR SELF-IMAGE AND THREE BRANDS OF PERFUME

Scales	Concepts			
	Self-Image	Brand A	Brand B	Brand C
Sexy-reserved	2	7	1	3
Unadorned-sophisticated	1	2	2	6
Innocent-flirty	6	1	7	4
Sensitive-insensitive	2	4	1	3
Daring-cautious	2	6	1	4

Based on these scores, D measures can be computed to depict the matching between a consumer's self-image and her image of each brand. For example, the calculations for the distance between self-image and the image of Brand B for the woman described in Table 16-1 would be:

$$D_{SB} = \sqrt{(2-1)^2 + (1-2)^2 + (6-7)^2 + (2-1)^2 + (2-1)^2}$$

$$D_{SB} = \sqrt{1+1+1+1+1}$$

$$D_{SB} = \sqrt{5}$$

$$D_{SB} = 2.2$$

Similar calculations for self-image and brands A and C would yield D measures of $D_{SA} = 8.4$ and $D_{SC} = 5.9$. According to the decision rule stated above, marketers would predict that the woman would prefer Brand B since it is the shortest distance from her self-image. Developing these measures across many consumers could enable prediction of general market behavior.

Marketing Applications of the Self-Concept

It has been noted that several limitations of the self-concept notion can impede its usefulness in marketing applications.[36] In addition to problems of measurement common to many concepts, there is also lack of a clear-cut agreement on what is specifically meant by the "self." Different interpretations of the concept can create uncertainty regarding its use in understanding consumers. Further, the self-image concept stresses consumers' self-awareness at the conscious level and tends to minimize the importance of subconscious or unconscious levels of influence. As we have noted in Chapter 13 and earlier in this chapter, such deeper mainsprings of behavior can have an important influence on consumers' behavior.

In spite of these potential limitations, self-image is a powerful concept which has many implications and applications in the field of consumer behavior. The concept has been used in market segmentation, advertising, packaging, personal selling, product development, and retailing.

Some have suggested that companies can segment markets into more homogeneous sets of self-image profiles. These self-descriptions could then serve as "blueprints" useful to marketers in designing total marketing programs. It is argued that decisions based on markets segmented by consumer self-images operationalize the marketing concept by viewing the consumer from the consumer's point of view.[37]

The self-image concept is quite heavily used in a variety of aspects of promotion. This is clearly demonstrated in the area of clothing. For example, certain types of men's suits are shown being worn by distinguished, conservative-looking models, often with a touch of gray in their hair. Such suits are usually seen on bankers and businessmen who have achieved considerable success. Other suits, frequently those with continental styling, are shown being worn by younger men with longer hair, who appear much more contemporary. The setting for these advertisements frequently involves active, informal social settings where the model often is shown without a tie. Salespeople will often emphasize such self-image messages by telling customers they know that items are either consistent or not consistent with their self-images ("that suit is just not you").

In another promotional area, notice the differences between advertisements showing women using Dial and Camay bath soaps. Women using Dial are depicted as having very active days with a great deal of excitement and exercise. They are shown using Dial in invigorating, refreshing showers, and they generally seem to live life with gusto. Conversely, women who use Camay tend to be portrayed as considerably more feminine in nature. They seem to embrace the product for the delicate way in which it will treat their skin and the softness that it will yield. As opposed to taking refreshing showers they appear to desire the sensual experience of long, warm, relaxing baths. It is interesting to note how packaging of each product appears to support such distinctions in the image of each product.

In Chapter 14 we noted the importance for retailers to know the image of their store as perceived by customers. It should again be emphasized here that consumer segments with various self-images will probably exist within the trading area of any given store. It is quite possible that the store's image may not be consistent with some consumers' self-images. Therefore, it is essential for the retailer to determine the market segment to which the store is appealing.[38] Decisions must then be made on the appropriate target segments. This could entail adjustments of the store's image in order to coincide better with the self-images of target patrons.

Analysis of consumers' self-images and their images of brands can also aid marketers in developing products. New brands can be created based on consumer self-image profiles for which there are no "matching" brand images existing. Product categories having particular promise in this area include those that generate high ego involvement and have high social visibility. Examples include home furnishings, clothing, and automobiles, as opposed to such products as fingernail clippers and light bulbs. Therefore, measurement of consumers' product-image perceptions would involve more than just the assessment of product attributes as described in the perceptual mapping example in Chapter 14. Consumers' perceptions of nonphysical image components and the degree of their correspondence to self-image perceptions must also be assessed.

One final comment regarding the self-image concept is important to mention. Studies have suggested that self-image can be an important predictor of consumers' brand preferences. However, brand preferences are not necessarily translated directly into purchases. Constraining factors such as price and other individual or environmental influences can modify these brand preferences before they are acted upon.

SUMMARY

This chapter reviewed two broad concepts that attempt to take rather complete views of consumers. The concept of personality suggests that individuals possess quite stable and enduring properties which influence them to respond in certain characteristic ways. Several major concepts of personality, including psychoanalytic, social, and stimulus-response theories, were reviewed. However, the greatest amount of study regarding the relevance of personality to consumer behavior has involved trait and factor theories. After reviewing a number of the relevant studies in this area, it appears that even though research evidence has not yet offered much confirming support, experts believe that personality plays a significant role in influencing consumers.

After briefly reviewing the relevance of trait-related psychographic studies to several marketing-decision areas, attention next turned to the topic of consumers' self-concept. A discussion of how self-concepts develop and their consistency over a period of time led to consideration of representative self-concept studies in the field of consumer behavior. The evidence relating self-images to product and brand images certainly seemed worthy of further study. In addition, the chapter concluded by demonstrating the practical relevance of consumers' self-concepts to a variety of marketing decision areas including product designs, promotions, and market-segmentation strategies.

DISCUSSION TOPICS

1. Distinguish between the id, ego, and superego in the Freudian personality scheme. Suggest the basic influence each might exert on a purchase decision.

2. Of what relevance is the personality concept to understanding consumer behavior?

3. Describe the major characteristics of trait theories of personality, indicating their major advantages and disadvantages. Review their usefulness in explaining consumer behavior.

4. Find at least three examples of promotions that appear to be using Freudian concepts. Be specific in describing which concepts are involved and how you think they are being used.

5. Cite at least two product examples where it would appear that an understanding of consumers' psychographic profiles would be useful in describing their reaction to the products involved.

6. What are the significant limitations of the self-concept in explaining consumer behavior?

7. Of what usefulness is it for a marketing manager to know that the self tends to be consistent?

8. Why is it important for the marketer to understand the distinction between consumers' self-image and ideal self-image?

9. Choose two brands within the same product category that appear to be projecting different images. Characterize each image being projected by comparing and contrasting them. What methods or techniques are being used to project these images?

NOTES

1. Some of the following discussion follows Harold H. Kassarjian, "Personality and Consumer Behavior: A Review," *Journal of Marketing Research,* **8**:409–418, November 1971.

2. Joel B. Cohen, "An Interpersonal Orientation to the Study of Consumer Behavior," *Journal of Marketing Research,* **4**:270–278, August 1967. Also see Joel B. Cohen, "Toward an Interpersonal Theory of Consumer Behavior," *California Management Review,* **10**:73–80, Spring 1968.

3. Seymor Epstein, "Traits Are Alive and Well," in David Magnusson and Norman Endler (eds.), *Personality at the Crossroads: Current Issues in Interactional Psychology,* Lawrence Erlbaum Associates, Hillsdale, N.J., 1977, pp. 83–98; and David Krech et al., *Psychology: A Basic Course,* Knopf, New York, 1976, pp. 322–323.

4. Arthur Koponen, "Personality Characteristics of Purchasers," *Journal of Advertising Research,* **1**:6–12, September 1960.

5. Robert Brody and Scott Cunningham, "Personality Variables and the Consumer Decision Process," *Journal of Marketing Research,* **5**:50–57, February 1968.

6. William T. Tucker and John Painter, "Personality and Product Use," *Journal of Applied Psychology,* **45**:325–329, October 1961.

7. Franklin B. Evans, "Psychological and Objective Factors in the Prediction of Brand Choice," *Journal of Business,* **32**:340–369, October 1959.

8. See Alan S. Marcus, "Obtaining Group Measures from Personality Test Scores: Auto Brand Choice Predicted from the Edwards Personal Preference Schedule," *Psychological Reports,* **17**:523–531, October 1965; Gary A. Steiner, "Notes on Franklin B. Evans 'Psychological and Objective Factors in the Prediction of Brand Choice,'" *Journal of Business,* **34**:57–60, January 1961; Charles Winick, "The Relationship Among Personality Needs, Objective Factors, and Brand Choice: A Re-examination," *Journal of Business,* **34**:61–66, January 1961; and Ralph Westfall, "Psychological Factors in Predicting Product Choice," *Journal of Marketing,* **26**:34–40, April 1962.

9. See for example, Thomas S. Robertson, *Innovation and the Consumer,* Holt, New York, 1971; and Louis E. Boone, "The Search for the Consumer Innovator," *Journal of Business,* **43**:135–140, April 1970.

10. See Kassarjian, "Personality and Consumer Behavior," and Harold H. Kassarjian and Mary Jane Sheffet, "Personality and Consumer Behavior: One More Time," in Edward M. Mazze (ed.), *1975 Combined Proceedings,* American Marketing Association, Chicago, 1975, pp. 197–201.

11. William D. Wells, "General Personality Tests and Consumer Behavior," in Joseph W. Newman (ed.), *On Knowing the Consumer,* Wiley, New York, 1966, pp. 187–189.

12. See Kathryn E. A. Villani and Yoram Wind, "On the Usage of 'Modified' Personality Trait Measures in Consumer Research," *Journal of Consumer Research,* **2**:223–228, December 1975.

13. Kassarjian, "Personality and Consumer Behavior," p. 416.

14. Robert A. Peterson, "Moderating the Personality-Product Usage Relationship," in Ronald C. Curhan (ed.), *1974 Combined Proceedings,* American Marketing Association, Chicago, 1975, pp. 109–112.

15. Masao Nakanishi, "Personality and Consumer Behavior: Extensions," in M. Venkatesan (ed.), *Proceedings of the Third Annual Conference,* Association for Consumer Research, College Park, Md., 1972, pp. 61–65.

16. See Stewart Bither and Ira Dolich, "Personality as a Determinant Factor in Store Choice," in M. Venkatesan (ed.), *Proceedings of the Third Annual Conference,* Association for Consumer Research, College Park, Md., 1972, pp. 9–19; Robert A. Peterson and Louis K. Sharpe, "Personality Structure and Cigarette Smoking," in Barnett A. Greenberg (ed.), *Proceedings: Southern Marketing Association 1974 Conference,* Southern Marketing Association, 1975, pp. 295–297; and Larry Percy, "A Look At Personality Profiles and the Personality-Attitude-Behavior Link in Predicting Consumer Behavior," in Beverlee B. Anderson (ed.), *Advances in Consumer Research,* **3**:119–124, Association for Consumer Research, Cincinnati, Ohio, 1976.

17. Kassarjian and Sheffet, "Personality and Consumer Behavior."

18. Douglas J. Tigert, "Life Style Analysis as a Basis for Media Selection," in William D. Wells (ed.), *Life Style and Psychographics,* American Marketing Association, Chicago, 1974, pp. 173–201.

19. Calvin Hadock, "Use of Psychographics in Analysis of Channels of Distribution," in Wells (ed.), *Life Style and Psychographics,* pp. 215–216.

20. Robert W. Frye and Gary D. Klein, "Psychographics and Industrial Design," in Wells (ed.), *Life Style and Psychographics,* pp. 225–232.

21. William D. Wells, "Personality as a Determinant of Buyer Behavior: What's Wrong? What Can Be Done about It?" in David Sparks (ed.), *Broadening the Concept of Marketing,* American Marketing Association, Chicago, 1970, p. 20.

22. Theodore M. Newcombe, *Social Psychology,* Holt, New York, 1950, p. 328.

23. Donald Snygg and Arthur W. Combs, *Individual Behavior,* Harper, New York, 1949, p. 57; and William James, *Psychology,* Henry Holt and Company, New York, 1892, p. 176.

24. Thorstein Veblen, *The Theory of the Leisure Class,* Mentor Books, New York, 1958, p. 42; a reprint from Thorstein Veblen, *The Theory of the Leisure Class,* Macmillan, New York, 1899.

25. Leon A. Festinger, "A Theory of Social Comparison," *Human Relations,* **14**:48–64, 1954.

26. Snygg and Combs, *Individual Behavior,* p. 57.

27. Prescott Lecky, "The Theory of Self Consistency," in Chad Gordon and Kenneth J. Gergen (eds.), *The Self in Social Interaction,* Wiley, New York, 1968, p. 297.

28. A. Evans Birdwell, "Influence of Image Congruence on Consumer Choice," in George South (ed.), *Reflections on Progress in Marketing,* American Marketing Association, Chicago, 1965, pp. 290–303.

29. Edward L. Grubb, "Consumer Perception of 'Self Concept' and Its Relationship to Brand Choice of Selected Product Types," unpublished D.B.A. dissertation, University of Washington, 1965, pp. 120–124.

30. Edward L. Grubb and Gregg Hupp, "Perception of Self, Generalized Stereotypes, and Brand Selection," *Journal of Marketing Research,* **5**:58–63, February 1968.

31. Edward L. Grubb and Bruce L. Stern, "Self-Concept and Significant Others," *Journal of Marketing Research,* **8**:382–385, August 1971.

32. Ira J. Dolich, "Congruence Relationships between Self Images and Product Brands," *Journal of Marketing Research,* **6**:80–84, February 1969.

33. E. Laird Landon, Jr., "Self Concept, Ideal Self Concept, and Consumer Purchase Intentions," *Journal of Consumer Research,* **1**:50, September 1974.

34. Wayne DeLozier and Rollie Tillman, "Self Image Concepts—Can They Be Used to Design Marketing Programs?" *The Southern Journal of Business,* **7**:11, November 1972.

35. Reprinted from Edward L. Grubb and Harrison L. Grathwohl, "Consumer Self Concept, Symbolism and Market Behavior: A Theoretical Approach," *Journal of Marketing,* **31**:25–26, October 1967, published by the American Marketing Association.

36. See Kenneth E. Runyon, *Consumer Behavior and the Practice of Marketing,* Merrill, Columbus, 1977, pp. 257–258.

37. DeLozier and Tillman, "Self Concepts," p. 14.

38. For two endeavors of this nature see Joseph Barry Mason and Morris L. Mayer, "The Problem of the Self-Concept in Store Image Studies," *Journal of Marketing,* **34**:67–69, April 1970; and Ira J. Dolich and Ned Shilling, "A Critical Evaluation of 'The Problem of Self-Concept in Store Image Studies,'" *Journal of Marketing,* **35**:71–73, January 1971.

ATTITUDES

The study of attitudes is one of the most important topics in consumer behavior. The prevalence of attitude investigations among academicians and practitioners supports this statement. Attitude research forms the basis for developing new products, repositioning existing products, creating advertising campaigns, and predicting brand preferences and purchasing behavior. Understanding how consumer attitudes are developed, changed, and reinforced is essential to the success of any marketing program.

In this chapter, we explore how attitudes are formed and organized. The functions of attitudes in our daily lives and their relationship to purchase behavior are then discussed. Additionally, we describe several well-known attitude models and theories which help us to measure and predict consumer behavior. The chapter ends by exploring some marketing implications of attitude theories. These principles form a foundation for Chapter 18, which treats attitude change and the role of marketing communications in influencing consumers' attitude changes.

DEFINITIONS OF ATTITUDE

Social psychologists, unfortunately, do not agree on the precise definition of an attitude. In fact, there are over 100 different definitions of the concept.[1] However, four definitions are more commonly accepted than others. One conception is that an attitude is how positive or negative, favorable or unfavorable, pro or con a person feels toward an object.[2] This definition views attitude as a feeling or evaluative reaction to objects.

A second definition represents the thoughts of Allport, who views attitudes as "learned predispositions to respond to an object or class of objects in a consistently favorably or unfavorably way."[3] This definition is slightly more complicated than the first, since it incorporates the notion of a readiness to respond toward an object.

A third definition of attitude popularized by cognitively oriented social psychologists is: "an enduring organization of motivational, emotional, perceptual, and cognitive processes with respect to some aspect of the individual's world."[4] This views attitudes as being made up of three components: (1) the *cognitive* or knowledge component, (2) the *affective* or emotional component, and (3) the *conative* or behavioral-tendency component.

More recently, behaviorists have given more attention to a new definition of attitude which has generated much research and has been useful in predicting behavior. This definition treats attitudes as being multidimensional in nature, as opposed to the unidimensional viewpoint taken by earlier definitions. Here attitudes are seen to be a function of (1) the strength of each of several *beliefs* a person holds toward an object and (2) the *value* or importance he gives to each belief as it relates to the object.[5] A belief is the probability a person attaches to a given piece of knowledge being true.

The last definition has considerable appeal since consumers perceive a product (object) as having many attributes and form beliefs about each of those attributes. For example, a consumer may believe strongly that Listerine mouthwash kills germs, helps to prevent colds, gives people clean, refreshing breath, and prevents sore throats. If the consumer feels all four of these attributes are important to him, then according to the definition he would have a strongly favorable overall attitude toward the brand. On the other hand, another consumer might believe just as strongly as the first consumer that Listerine possesses all four of these traits; however, she may not feel that any of the attributes are important. Therefore, her overall attitude toward the brand would be less favorable. This idea will be discussed in more detail later in the chapter.

It has been important to provide all four definitions of attitudes since the majority of attitude studies have been based upon them. In fact, results of this research serve as the basis of this and the next chapter.

CHARACTERISTICS OF ATTITUDES

Attitudes have several important characteristics or properties, which are that (1) attitudes have objects, (2) attitudes have direction, intensity, and degree, (3) attitudes have structure, and (4) attitudes are learned.

Attitudes Have an Object

By definition attitudes must have an object. The object can be abstract as in the case of consumerism or it can be concrete in nature like a motorcycle. In addition, the object can be directed either at one person or a collection of people; and it can be either specific (Ford Mustang II) or general (Ford Motor Company). Furthermore, the attitude can be held by either an individual or a group of people.

Attitudes Have Direction, Degree, and Intensity

An attitude expresses how a person feels toward an object. It expresses (1) direction—the person is either favorable or unfavorable, for or against, the object; (2) degree—how much the person either likes or dislikes the object; and (3) intensity—the level of sureness, or confidence of expression about the object, or how strongly a person feels about his or her conviction.

Although degree and intensity might seem the same, and are actually related, they are not synonymous. For example, a person may feel that a Mercury outboard engine is very unreliable. This indicates that his attitude is negative and the *degree* of negative feeling is quite extensive. However, the individual may have very little *conviction* or feeling of sureness (intensity in attitude) that he is right. Thus, his attitude could be more easily changed in a favorable direction than a person who feels a strong conviction that Mercury engines are very unreliable.

The direction, degree, and intensity of a person's attitude toward a product provides marketers with an estimate of his or her "readiness to act toward," that is, purchase the product. However, a marketer must also understand how *important* the consumer's attitude is vis-á-vis other attitudes, and the constraints, such as ability to pay, that might inhibit the consumer from making a purchase decision.

Attitudes Have Structure

As explained below, attitudes display organization which means that they have internal consistency and possess interattitudinal centrality. They also tend to be stable, have varying degrees of salience, and are generalizable.

The structure of human attitudes may be viewed as a complex Tinker Toy set erected in some type of circular pattern. At the center of this structure are the individual's important values and self-concept. Attitudes close to the hub of this system are said to have a high degree of *centrality*. Other attitudes located further out in the structure possess less centrality.

Attitudes do not stand in isolation. They are associated (tied in) with each other to form a complex whole. This implies that a certain degree of *consistency* must exist between attitudes. That is, because they are related, there must be some amount of "fit" between them or conflict will result. Also, since more central attitudes are related to a larger number of other attitudes they must exhibit a greater degree of consistency than more peripheral attitudes.

Because attitudes cluster into a structure, they tend to show stability over a period of time. The length of time may not be permanent, but it is far from being temporary. Also, since attitudes are learned, they tend to become stronger, or at least more resistant to change, the longer they are held.[6] Thus, newly formed attitudes are easier to change and less stable than older ones of equal strength.

Attitudes tend to be *generalizable*. That is, a person's attitude toward a specific object tends to generalize toward a class of objects. Thus a man who wears very mod shirts and trousers might also be expected to wear bracelets, and necklaces. Moreover, a consumer who purchases a Porsche which develops mechanical difficulties may believe that all Porsches and Volkswagen products, and possibly all German-made products, are poorly constructed. Consumers tend to generalize in such a manner in order to simplify their decision making.

From among all of the attitudes in a person's attitudinal structure, some are more important or salient to her than others. For example, a consumer might feel that "buying American" is more important than saving energy. Therefore, she might purchase an American car that consumes more gasoline than a comparable foreign car that uses less. Also, the "buy American" attitude can be closely tied to attitudes of creating American jobs, keeping money at home, and others which thereby support it and increase its salience.

Attitudes Are Learned

Just as a golf swing, tennis stroke, and tastes are learned, so are attitudes. They develop from our personal experiences with reality, as well as from information from friends, salespeople, and news media. They are also derived from both direct and indirect experiences in life. Thus, it is important to recognize that learning precedes attitude formation and change, and that principles of learning discussed in Chapter 15 can aid marketers in developing and changing consumer attitudes.

FUNCTIONS OF ATTITUDES

Attitudes serve four major functions for an individual's personality: (1) the adjustment function, (2) the ego-defensive function, (3) the value-expressive function, and (4) the knowledge function.[7] Ultimately these functions serve people's need to protect and enhance the image they hold of themselves. In more general terms, these functions are the motivational bases which shape and reinforce positive attitudes toward goal objects perceived as need-satisfying and/or negative attitudes toward objects perceived as punishing or threatening. These situations are diagramed in Figure 17-1. The functions themselves can help us to understand why people hold the attitudes they do toward psychological objects.

The Adjustment Function

The adjustment function directs people toward pleasurable or rewarding objects and away from unpleasant, undesirable ones. It serves the utilitarian concept of maximizing reward and minimizing punishment. Thus, people acquire attitudes that they perceive as either helpful in achieving desired goals or useful in avoiding undesired goals. The development of these attitudes depends directly upon people's perceptions of what is need-satisfying and what is punishing.

Consumers perceive products, services, and stores as providing either need-satisfying or unsatisfying experiences. Depending upon their perceptions, consumers will develop either favorable or unfavorable inclinations toward brands and stores. In addition, there seems to be a relationship between the level of perceived need satisfaction and how favorable the attitude toward the object is. For example, where consumers perceive a department store as having pleasant decor, friendly and helpful salespeople,

FIGURE 17-1
Attitude development and function based on perceived need satisfaction or harm avoidance.

and good merchandise, the greater the likelihood that they will develop strong, positive attitudes toward the store and will be inclined to shop there.

ATTITUDES

The Ego-Defensive Function

Attitudes formed to protect the ego or self-image from threats perform the ego-defensive function. Actually, many outward expressions of such attitudes reflect the opposite of what the person perceives himself to be. For example, a consumer who has made a poor purchase decision or a poor investment may staunchly defend the decision as being correct at the time, or as the result of poor advice from another person. Such ego-defensive attitudes help us to protect our self-image and often we are unaware of them.

The Value-Expressive Function

Whereas ego-defensive attitudes are formed to protect a person's self-image, value-expressive attitudes enable the expression of the person's centrally held values. Therefore, consumers adopt certain attitudes in an effort to translate their values into something more tangible and easily expressed. Thus a conservative person might develop an unfavorable attitude toward bright clothing and be attracted toward pin-striped suits and a discreet Taurus bracelet that says "I am a stubborn and determined person."

Marketers should develop an understanding of what values consumers wish to express about themselves and design products and promotional campaigns to allow these self-expressions. Not all products lend themselves to this form of market segmentation, however. Those with the greatest potential for "value expressive" segmentation are ones with high social visibility. Parker pens, Saks Fifth Avenue clothes, Cadillac cars, and Sansui stereo receivers are examples.

The Knowledge Function

Humans have a need for a structured and orderly world and therefore seek consistency, stability, definition, and understanding. Out of this need develops attitudes toward acquiring knowledge and understanding as it relates to each person's own world; that is, the need to know tends to be specific. An individual who does not play golf, or wish to learn, is unlikely to seek knowledge or understanding of the game. However, people who believe that playing golf might enhance their chances to become successful in business will pay for golf lessons, learn about golf club swing weights, find out where the best courses are, and watch "how the pros do it" on television. This demonstrates that we all have a need to acquire knowledge, but the focus of the need differs among individuals. Out of the need to know comes attitudes toward what we believe we need or do not need to understand.

SOURCES OF ATTITUDE DEVELOPMENT

The preceding section not only discussed the functions of attitudes, but also provided us with an initial understanding of how and why attitudes develop. All attitudes ultimately develop from human needs and the values people place upon objects that satisfy those perceived needs. This section discusses sources that make us aware of needs, their importance to us, and how our attitudes develop toward objects that satisfy needs.

Personal Experience

People come into contact with objects in their environment every day. Some are familiar while others are new. We evaluate the new and reevaluate the old and this evaluation process assists in developing attitudes toward objects. For example, consider a homemaker who has searched 2 months for a new food processor only to have it break down 3 months after purchase. Through direct experience she will then reevaluate her earlier attitude toward the processor.

Our direct experiences with sales representatives, products, services, and stores help to create and shape our attitudes toward those market objects. However, several factors influence how we will evaluate such direct contacts.

NEEDS Because people's needs differ and also vary over time, they can develop different attitudes toward the same object. Thus, a consumer might be extremely favorable toward a Chevrolet over several years, then change her attitude toward the car in following years. A change in job status giving rise to different need conditions could be responsible for this shift in attitude toward the Chevy.

SELECTIVE PERCEPTION The way people perceive information about products, stores, etc. affects their attitudes. We have seen that people do not view reality but their interpretation of reality. Therefore, selective perception can strongly influence the development of attitudes toward objects.

PERSONALITY Personality is another factor that influences how people process their direct experiences with objects. How aggressive-passive, dominant-subservient, introverted-extroverted a person is affects what kind of attitudes he or she forms toward objects. A consumer who is very passive, for instance, may develop a negative attitude toward Remington rifles which can be used to kill deer and other animals, whereas the aggressive personality may develop strongly favorable attitudes toward the brand.

As we can see, although people develop attitudes from personal contact with products, their attitudes toward these products will differ because of several influential factors such as need state, selective perception, and personality.

Group Associations

All people are influenced to one degree or another by other members in the groups to which they belong. Attitudes are one target for this influence. For example, our attitudes toward products, ethics, warfare, and a multitude of other subjects are influenced strongly by groups that we value and with whom we do, or wish to, associate. Several particular groups, including family, work and social groups, and cultural and subcultural groups are quite important in affecting a person's attitude development.

THE FAMILY The family is perhaps the most influential group in shaping a person's attitudes. Parents, as authority figures, orient a child's thinking at the most susceptible point in a person's life. Fundamental attitudes toward food preferences, services, and various products are very similar between parent and child. Furthermore, the basic attitudinal structure of a child tends to carry over into adulthood. For example, because her mother uses Tide detergent, a newlywed daughter is likely to purchase the same brand. Knowing this, some advertisers utilize the mother/daughter, father/son relationships in their promotions. Advertisements for Lifesavers and Mc-Donald's are examples. Thus, a company's investment in its marketing effort today may affect its sales and profits for many years to come.

WORK AND SOCIAL GROUPS As children become adults, their work and social peers exert pressure upon them to conform to particular norms and standards. These norms and standards provide the benchmark for acceptable behavior and influence the development and modification of attitudes. This is often expressed in subsequent product preferences. For example, the fraternity or sorority students join in college can influence the brand of beer they drink—"It's the fraternity [sorority] beer"—the clothes they wear, and the colognes they use.

CULTURAL AND SUBCULTURAL GROUPS We have seen that cultural and subcultural inheritance is the result of the socialization process. This legacy results in an identification of who we are and strongly affects our attitudes about objects in our environment. For this reason many marketers try to use this cultural or subcultural "identification" as an appeal to use their brands. A developed identity with one's cultural and subcultural groups implies approval by them, and approval is a strong motivation to adopt the attitudes of our cultural heritage. It should be quite clear why cultural and subcultural groups, then, form more favorable attitudes toward certain products and brands that fit into their own patterns.

Influential Others

A consumer's attitude can be formed and changed through personal contact with influential persons such as respected friends, relatives, and experts. For this to happen, however, the person must be perceived to some degree as expert, trustworthy, likable, or prestigious. Opinion leaders are examples of people who are respected by their followers and who may strongly influence the attitudes and purchase behavior of followers.

To capitalize on this type of influence, advertisers often use actors and actresses who are similar or act similar to their intended audiences. People tend to like others who are similar to themselves since they believe that they share the same problems, form the same judgments, and use the same criteria in evaluating products.[8] As an example of the use of this approach, during the afternoon soap operas a brand of wax was advertised on television in which a beautiful and elegantly dressed woman was shown waxing her kitchen floor effortlessly in high heels. The typical female homemaker could not identify with this situation. Realizing this problem, advertisers began to use "average" looking women, dressed appropriately for waxing floors in an "average" looking kitchen. Another excellent use of this technique is the so-called slice of life commercial that has become quite popular. These ads show "typical" people confronting "typical" problems and finding solutions in the use of the advertised brand. Examples include ads for Alka-Seltzer ("I can't believe I ate the whole thing"), Aim toothpaste, ("Aim tastes good and Aim fights cavities"), and Midas mufflers.

Although they are sometimes viewed with a certain amount of suspicion, sales representatives can also positively influence consumers' attitudes when they express opinions similar to the consumer's viewpoint. A second condition for effective influence, however, is that the salesperson is also perceived by the customer as having some degree of expertise regarding the product.[9]

A pictorial summary of what we have learned so far is depicted in Figure 17-2. The model is a simple representation of the concepts that have been discussed in the previous sections. It shows that several sources provide consumers with information and influence about products, services, retail stores, and other objects. The individual selectively perceives and distorts the information according to his individual needs, values, and personality, and according to how well the information "fits" with currently held beliefs and attitudes. This processed information initiates either development, change, or confirmation in the consumer's beliefs about the product and the importance of each of the product's attributes to him and his current needs. Out of this process is synthesized a general attitude toward a product. Admittedly, this model is an oversimplification. However, it does reflect current understanding of attitudes, and presents a concise picture of the psychological and external elements involved in the process of forming attitudes toward products. Also, it should be pointed out that the process is dynamic; it continues to change over time.

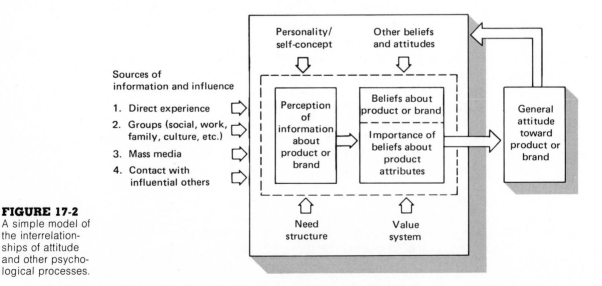

FIGURE 17-2
A simple model of the interrelationships of attitude and other psychological processes.

We now turn our attention to more specific theories and models of attitudes. Some of the models are descriptive, whereas others claim predictive abilities.

ATTITUDE THEORIES AND MODELS

This section describes attitude models and theories.[10] Although they can appear quite complicated, the essence of these theories is quite simple and useful in grasping the importance of attitudes' role in consumer-choice behavior.

Attitude theories primarily are concerned with how attitudes change. Three of the more popular viewpoints are founded on the general principle that *the human mind strives to maintain harmony or consistency among currently perceived attitudes.* If the mind perceives an inconsistency within its attitude structure, mental tension develops to return the structure to a consistent state. The three classical theories based upon the consistency principle are congruity, balance, and cognitive dissonance. Newer multiattribute attitude theories are discussed after a consideration of these traditional views.

Congruity Theory

A basic understanding of the congruity model can be gained through consideration of the following examples. Assume that a consumer holds attitudes toward entertainer Bob Hope (positive attitude of scale value +2) and Texaco (negative attitude of scale value −2) as illustrated in Figure 17-3. Also assume that the consumer sees Bob Hope appear in a television advertisement in which he makes positive statements about Texaco. Given the situation, the consumer will perceive that he holds inconsistent attitudes: "Bob, whom I like, said something nice about Texaco, which I don't like." In this case, the consumer is in a state of *incongruity.* This condition produces uncomfortable tension which must ultimately resolve the incongruous state. The congruity model would predict that a person in this situation would reduce his favorable attitude toward Bob Hope and decrease his unfavorable attitude toward Texaco as shown in part (b) of Figure 17-3. The model would

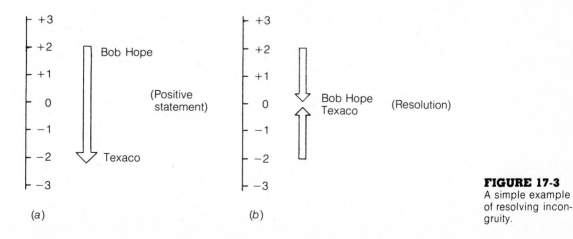

(a)   *(b)*

FIGURE 17-3
A simple example of resolving incongruity.

predict a movement of 2 units for each concept toward each other (the center in this case), because the consumer perceives both objects as being of equal strength but in opposite directions of the neutral point of 0.

Most of the time the resulting equilibrium point is not determined so simply. Figure 17-4 presents another situation of a consumer's perceived attitudes toward Bob Hope and Texaco. Note that the scale distance between the two concepts is 4 units as before. However, resolution is not the midpoint between the two concepts (+1) as we might expect. Instead, the model would predict that resolution would occur at +2 reducing the consumer's perceived attitude of Bob Hope by only 1 scale unit and increasing his attitude toward Texaco by 3 scale units.

Although the mathematics used to predict the resolution point will not be presented here, the greater shift for Texaco than for Bob Hope is intuitively understandable.[11] Strong attitudes are more difficult to change than weak or moderate ones. Thus, the consumer's stronger positive attitude toward Bob Hope exerts greater pull on his weaker negative attitude toward Texaco. This idea suggests that where consumers develop a strong dislike toward a brand, company efforts to improve consumer attitudes will require a tremendous marketing effort, which may not be worth the cost. The company might be better off in many cases either to (1) drop the brand and reintroduce it under another name, if promotional positioning were the problem, or (2) introduce a new reformulated brand if product quality, design, or formulation were the problem. Conversely, if the consumer holds an extremely positive attitude toward the brand, considerable unfavorable experiences and word-of-mouth influence would be required to deteriorate the attitude significantly.

It should be noted that although the model predicts resolution at a value of +2 in Figure 17-4 there are qualifications. First, if the consumer perceives the information he has heard to be totally unbelievable, he can reject it and no attitude change will occur. In this instance, the information would be totally discounted. Second, if the consumer experiences only some disbelief instead of total disbelief, his attitudes would change only slightly.[12] This qualification for disbelief adds further strength to the marketing examples previously mentioned. Specifically, consumers who hold an extremely negative attitude

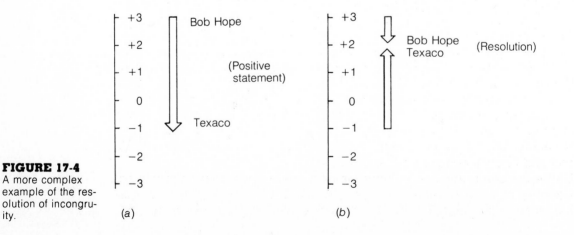

FIGURE 17-4
A more complex example of the resolution of incongruity.

toward a brand will not only be difficult to change, but will ignore or discount information to the contrary.

The congruity principle is used frequently in marketing.[13] Advertisers often use hired celebrities to endorse brands, services, organizations, and causes. Athletes speak against drug use among young people, movie actresses endorse various kinds of beauty aids, and race car drivers promote brands of tires, spark plugs, and other automobile accessories. Of course, the intent is that consumers who hold positive attitudes toward a source making such favorable statements toward an object will develop a positive value association between the source and the object.

Another way that marketers influence consumers' attitudes is by associating advertised brands with symbols toward which consumers have positive attitudes. The intent is that strong positive attitudes toward a brand will develop through its association with the symbol. For example, Schlitz advertisements depict a rampaging bull entering the scene immediately after an actor opens a can of Schlitz Malt Liquor. The bull is a symbol of strength to most people. The entire scene with the violent bull accompanied by an announcer with a deep masculine voice implies that the malt liquor is stronger than others. The association between the bull and the opening of a can of Schlitz Malt Liquor so impressed television viewers that the Federal Trade Commission warned Schlitz against showing the rampaging bull immediately after the actor ''popped'' the can. The bull now makes a delayed entrance.

In personal selling, a technique often used by salespeople is to allow customers to express their tastes by letting them pick out the model of a product in which they show interest. The salesperson then agrees with the customer's preference and good taste. This can result in the development of a positive attitude toward the salesperson because of his association with the customer's preference. Having gained a favorable attitude rating, the salesperson is now in a position to suggest other more sophisticated or expensive models of the same product.

As we can see, successful marketing principles and techniques can be derived from an understanding of the congruity model. In essence, marketers must associate with their brands people, symbols, settings, and surroundings that customers value.

Balance Theory

Several balance models have been developed, all of which are based upon the pioneer work of Fritz Heider.[14] According to balance theory, a person perceives his or her environment in terms of triads. That is, a person views himself or herself as being involved in a triangular relationship where all three elements (persons, ideas, or things) have either a positive (liking, favorable) or negative (disliking, unfavorable) relationship with each other. This relationship is termed *sentiment*. Figure 17-5 displays the eight balanced and unbalanced states that are possible.

Unlike the congruity model, there are no numerical values used to express the degree of unity between elements. Instead, the model is described as unbalanced if the multiplicative relationships among the three elements is minus, and in balance if the multiplicative relationship is positive. Thus, Figure 17-5(a) shows four balanced states, since the multiplicative relationships are all positive, and Figure 17-5(b) depicts four unbalanced states, since their multiplicative relationships are minus.

To illustrate the notion of balance in a marketing sense, consider the following example expressed as three statements: "I (concept) like (relationship) large, luxurious cars (concept)." "I do not like energy-wasting products." "But I believe large, luxurious cars waste energy." This situation is shown in Figure 17-6. The structure is not in balance since there is a positive relationship on two sides of the triangle and a negative relationship on the remaining side, and this results in a negative product.

Since the relationship presented in the example is unbalanced, it will produce tension for the consumer. It may be possible to "live with" the tension and do nothing to resolve it. However, if sufficient tension exists, it is likely that attitude change will occur regarding at least one element in the

FIGURE 17-5
Eight possible balanced and imbalanced states.

(a) Balanced states   (b) Imbalanced states

triad in order to restore balance to the system. These attempts at resolution can result in the consumer (1) disliking large, luxurious cars, (2) believing that large, luxurious cars are not really energy-wasting products, or (3) liking energy-wasting products (they create jobs, provide psychological satisfaction, for example). As we can see, *rationalization* can help to change our perceptions of relationships and thus our attitudes.

Cognitive Dissonance

The theory of cognitive dissonance was developed in 1957 by Leon Festinger.[15] Festinger describes cognitive dissonance as a psychological state which results when a person perceives that two cognitions (bits of information), both of which he believes to be true, do not "fit" together; that is, they seem inconsistent. The resulting dissonance produces tension which serves to motivate the individual to bring harmony to the inconsistent elements and thereby reduce psychological tension.

Dissonance can arise in three basic ways. First, any *logical inconsistency* can create dissonance. For example, "all candy is sweet; my candy is sour." A more dramatic example is a person who lies in the hot summer sun in a swimsuit for 10 hours and gets no sunburn.

Second, dissonance can be created when a person experiences an *inconsistency either between his attitude and his behavior or between two of his behaviors.* For example, Michael actively compliments Keds running shoes on many occasions and then purchases a pair of Adidas running shoes. This is an example of an inconsistency between two behaviors. On the other hand, a discrepancy between an attitude and behavior would exist where David strongly dislikes gambling but bets on the outcome of football games.

Third, dissonance can occur when a strongly held *expectation is disconfirmed.* To illustrate, Margaret expects to find significant savings at a sidewalk sale but finds only unstylish and damaged merchandise.

In all three cases, it is necessary that a person perceive the inconsistency; otherwise, no dissonance will occur. Some people are very capable of holding an attitude that contradicts their behavior without *perceiving* the contradiction. Therefore, they suffer no dissonance.

Regardless of its source, cognitive dissonance arises *after* a decision has been made. The decision, in effect, *commits* the person to certain positions

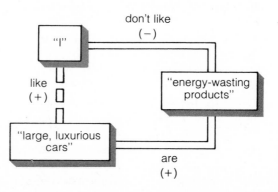

FIGURE 17-6
A graphic representation of attitudinal structure.

or attitudes where prior to that time he was capable of adjusting his attitudes or behavior to avoid dissonance.

Once an individual committed to a decision perceives an inconsistency in his attitude and/or behavior, with dissonance resulting, he has three major ways to reduce the dissonance and its accompanying tension. They are (1) rationalization, (2) seeking additional information that is supportive of or consistent with his behavior, and (3) either eliminating or altering some of the dissonant elements, which can be accomplished by either forgetting or suppressing dissonant elements or by changing his attitude so that it is no longer dissonant with another attitude or behavior. Each of these strategies may be used alone or in a combination.

To illustrate these methods, consider a consumer who has purchased a Nikon 35-mm, single-lens reflex camera for $450 after seriously considering other brands such as Pentax, Canon, and Minolta in the same general price range. Besides the investment of $450, the consumer also has invested much thought and searching time and a considerable amount of ego in the purchase decision. Therefore, the amount at stake in this purchase is considerable. After evaluating the pros and cons of each brand of camera, he selected the Nikon. Subsequent to the purchase the consumer found his camera hard to focus and difficult to change lenses; and the strap broke on the carrying case. He now begins to doubt the wisdom of his purchase. A tension arises from his two beliefs that (1) Nikons are well-constructed, precision cameras and (2) my Nikon is difficult to focus for clear pictures, takes too much time and effort to change lenses, and the strap on the carrying case broke.

The Nikon owner can reduce the tension arising from these two cognitions by *rationalizing* that any fine camera can have its faults and the retailer probably treated the carrying case with abuse causing the eventual strap break. Or he might *seek information* which reinforces his belief that Nikon cameras are among the very best in the world, thereby amplifying the strong points of the camera such as rapid film advancement, nice styling, and a solid shutter click indicating durability. Finally, a third option is to *change his opinion* toward Nikon cameras: "They are not good cameras. I should have purchased a Canon."

This example illustrates a very common type of marketing-related dissonance—*postpurchase dissonance.* Postpurchase dissonance occurs when a person makes a decision to buy one brand from among several alternative brands within a product category. The dissonance becomes particularly strong when the consumer makes a large commitment in the purchase. Such commitment refers not only to the amount of money, but also to the investment of time, effort, and ego as was illustrated in the previous example. Therefore, a purchase decision involving choice among brands of chewing gum at a supermarket check-out counter is unlikely to produce much perceptible dissonance. Goods requiring the consumer to commit much of himself or his money, however, are likely to generate considerable postpurchase dissonance. In general, therefore, durable and luxury goods are more likely to produce dissonance than convenience goods, since they usually require larger consumer investment in time, effort, ego, and money.

In a purchase decision, dissonance can result when the consumer recognizes that alternative brands have both positive and negative characteristics. Therefore, after this decision he realizes that he has acquired some *relatively* undesirable traits of the selected brand while forgoing some relatively desirable traits of the alternative brands. At this point, the consumer may even rate the unchosen alternatives *higher* than the brand he purchased. In his mind he emphasizes the positive attributes of the unchosen brands, and the negative characteristics of the chosen brand. This period of postpurchase process is called the *regret* phase, which fortunately is usually very brief. The next phase is termed the *dissonance reduction period.* In this stage the consumer is very likely to evaluate the chosen brand more positively than at the time of purchase, and evaluate the unselected brands less positively.

Multiattribute Models

In recent years marketers have begun to question the adequacy of earlier attitude models. One of their apparent limitations is that they inadequately consider that consumers' attitudes toward an object are determined by their reaction toward a variety of its different attributes or characteristics. That is, they fail to recognize the multiattribute basis for attitudes toward objects. Secondly, earlier models failed to consider that some attributes of an object may be unimportant to the consumer and have little or no influence on his attitudes, while others might have a strong influence. Therefore, the consumer will only form negative and/or positive evaluations of an object according to those attributes that he deems are important.

Rosenberg did the pioneering work in developing multiattribute models, followed by extensive research and model development by Fishbein.[1] The popularity of the Fishbein model among marketers is evidenced by the numerous studies that have used it as a basis for assessing attitudes.[17] In marketing applications the Fishbein multiattribute model is frequently expressed as:

$$A_0 = \sum_{i=1}^{n} I_i B_i$$

where A_0 = The consumer's overall attitude toward the object 0

I_i = the consumer's assessment of the importance of the ith attribute of the object

B_i = the consumer's evaluation of the object in terms of the ith attribute or his belief in the extent to which the object possesses the ith attribute

n = the number of attributes the consumer considers to be important regarding this object[18]

Mathematically the model states that a consumer's attitude toward a brand is equal to the sum of the products of his evaluation of the object regarding each attribute times his evaluation of the importance of each attribute. This suggests that the consumer's evaluation of various attributes can actually offset each other. For this reason the model is sometimes referred to as a *compensatory* model.

An example will reinforce our understanding of the model. Assume that we want to determine a consumer's attitude toward Nuance perfume, and we have been able to identify ten attributes of the perfume that she believes are important. We can next measure her assessment of the *degree* to which each attribute is important on a three-point scale where the value of 1 indicates high importance and a value of 3 indicates low importance.[19] Finally, assume that we employ a seven-point rating scale such as the semantic differential to determine her evaluation of the product according to each of the attributes involved. Table 17-1 presents results of these data collection efforts. As shown in the last column, the importance weights and evaluation scores are multiplied together for each attribute, and a sum of these products yields a total score of 61. This value represents the consumer's overall attitude toward Nuance perfume where scores can range between 210 and 10, with 10 being the most favorable score. Also, attitude scores for other brands could be similarly computed and compared to the score for Nuance.

It is interesting to note how differences in the individual's importance weights can influence her overall attitude toward the product. For example, the consumer in our example evaluated the perfume equally (+3) on the dignified—plain and prestigious—not prestigious dimensions. However, since prestige is a very important attribute to this consumer, and dignity is not, their contribution to the consumer's overall attitude toward the product differs considerably. This demonstrates the potential value in the multiattribute attitude model. Wilkie and Pessemier succinctly elaborate on this advantage:

The potential advantage of multi-attribute models over the simpler "over-all affect" approach (unidimensional model) is in gaining understanding of attitudinal structure. *Diagnosis* of brand strengths and weaknesses on relevant product attributes can then be used to suggest specific changes in a brand and its marketing support.[20]

TABLE 17-1

AN EXAMPLE OF HOW A CONSUMER'S ATTITUDE TOWARD A BRAND OF PERFUME CAN BE CALCULATED

Attributes of Importance	Importance weight (I_i)	Evaluation score (B_i)	Product (I_iB_i)
1. Enduring—not enduring	2	5	10
2. Delicate, sensitive—harsh, insensitive	2	2	4
3. Popular—acceptable	3	4	12
4. Sensual—modest	1	1	1
5. Dignified—plain, ordinary	3	3	9
6. Prestigious—not prestigious	1	3	3
7. Low in price—high in price	3	6	18
8. Appealing—unappealing	1	1	1
9. Natural—artificial	2	1	2
10. Attracts others—does not attract others	1	1	1

$$\text{Attitude score } (A_o) = \sum_{i=1}^{10} I_iB_i = 61$$

That is, the data generated by a multiattribute model, such as Fishbein's, provide the marketer with knowledge of which attributes are *most important* to the consumer's attitude toward the product and the degree to which the consumer evaluates the product according to those characteristics. This knowledge offers suggestions regarding potential changes in product attributes or where emphasis may be needed in a promotional campaign. Caution must be observed, however, in selecting the product attributes to be included in the study. Care must also be taken in determining how consumers might interpret the term "important," since several meanings are possible.

ATTITUDES AND PURCHASE BEHAVIOR

A considerable number of studies have explored the relationship between consumers' attitudes and their purchase behavior. Those conducted prior to the development of the Fishbein model, reflecting traditional unidimensional views of attitudes, have yielded mixed results.[21] Although a number of traditional studies have found positive relationships between attitude measures and behavior,[22] it is also true that many have not enjoyed great success.[23]

Because of these mixed findings, marketers have sought other means to predict behavior, and attention turned toward the Fishbein attitude model. However, Fishbein noted that his model was developed to measure a person's attitude toward an object and *not* toward performing specific behaviors.[24] Certain purchase constraints or needs can stand in the way of translating such an attitude into purchase behavior. Therefore, a distinction can be made between an attitude toward an object and an attitude toward behavior relating to that object. For example, a consumer may very positively evaluate a white Triumph TR-7 sports car that has an all-white interior and many attractive extras. However, limited funds or the fact that she lives in an area with many dirt roads could result in a low tendency to purchase the car.

As a result of these distinctions, Fishbein developed the following model for prediction of a person's attitude toward an act such as a purchase:

$$A\text{-act} = \sum_{i=1}^{n} B_i A_i$$

where A-act = the individual's attitude toward performing a specific act such as purchasing a specific brand

B_i = the individual's perceived likelihood or belief that performing the behavior will lead to some consequence i

A_i = the individual's evaluation of consequence i

n = represents the number of salient consequences involved.

A significant number of studies have been conducted using the Fishbein A-act model to predict consumer behavior.[25] The general results appear quite promising and additional testing of the model's ability to predict the behavior of consumers is under way. In addition, refinements and extensions are being made to Fishbein's model to further its ability to predict consumer behavior.[26]

MARKETING IMPLICATIONS

Attitude research can provide a number of basic clues useful to marketers in developing effective strategies. The specific guidelines can affect pricing decisions, product formulation, packaging, promotional strategies and channel-selection decisions.

Lutz suggests that three possible marketing strategies can be developed, based upon the Fishbein A-act model.[27] They are:

1. Change consumers' existing beliefs (B_i) about a brand. For example, use mass advertising to try to change consumers' perception about Top Flite golf balls ("they get up to 14 yards more distance than other golf balls").

2. Change consumers' evaluation of the value (A_i) of a particular attribute or consequence. For example, an advertisement for Scope mouthwash might stress that "mouthwash doesn't have to taste strong to be strong."

3. Introduce a new $B_i A_i$ combination. That is, add a new and important attribute to the advertised brand. One advertising use might be: "The larger Prince tennis racket yields a bigger 'sweet spot' to increase your chances of getting consistently better tennis shots."

Lutz's findings suggest that the first strategy of changing consumers' perceptions about a brand may be more effective than the second strategy of changing consumers' assessment of particular attributes. However, more work is needed to confirm this possibility.

Others who have studied attitudes suggest their relevance to five basic strategies with general marketing implications:

1. Affect those forces that strongly influence choice criteria consumers use for evaluating brands belonging to the product class;

2. Add characteristics to those already considered important for the product class;

3. Change consumers' attitudes regarding the importance of a relevant product characteristic;

4. Change consumers' perception of the company's brand with regard to some important product characteristic; or

5. Change consumers' perceptions of competitive brands with regard to some important product characteristic.[28]

With the first strategy a marketer attempts to affect consumers' attitudes toward an entire product class. "It's better to eat cereal than eggs for breakfast" is an example. Therefore, the firm tries to influence consumers' needs, values, and goals in order to change their choice criteria and bring them in line with the company's offerings.

The second strategy suggests the addition of important characteristics to consumers' choice criteria. This strategy can be particularly useful when a product is in its maturity stage. Some examples of this strategy are adding filters to cigarettes, adding vitamins to fruit drinks, and adding condenser microphones to cassette recorders.

Whereas strategy 2 attempts to add important characteristics to the consumers' choice criteria, strategy 3 tries to *change* their perceptions of the importance of existing characteristics. This strategy is particularly useful when a company's brand is rated higher than competitors' brands along a specific attribute which consumers presently feel is not very important. Therefore, it is necessary to make consumers believe that the attribute *is* important. For example, consumers might believe that egg substitutes are easy to prepare and have low cholesterol, but may not feel that a low-cholesterol intake is important. However, if marketers of the Egg Beaters brand are able to convince consumers of the importance of a low-cholesterol diet then the company might be able to achieve higher sales and profits.

Whereas strategy 1 deals with influencing consumer needs and values and strategies 2 and 3 are concerned with affecting consumer choice criteria, strategies 4 and 5 are aimed at changing consumers' brand perception sets. Strategy 4 attempts to change consumers' perceptions of the company's brand to bring it more in line with their image of the ideal brand. However, the company's brand must actually possess the characteristics that it promotes, and should try to emphasize those product attributes for which it has a relative advantage.[29]

Strategy 5 suggests a repositioning of competitors' brands by changing consumers' perceptions of them. An example of such a repositioning is the advertising campaign conducted by Beck's beer, stating, "You've tasted the German beer that's the most popular in America. Now taste the German beer that's the most popular in Germany." American consumers had incorrectly assumed that Lowenbrau was the most popular beer in Germany and therefore must be a good-tasting beer. However, Beck's advertising moved Lowenbrau out of that position and moved itself into that position in the minds of consumers.[30]

This model, with its various strategies, offers marketers a number of opportunities regarding the development of consumers' attitudes toward their products. It also is consistent with Fishbein's model in that emphasis is placed on developing consumers' *perceptions* about the product/brand, and influencing their evaluation of the *importance* of its attributes.

As we have consistently noted, a significant part of strategy development in marketing is the identification of market segments. Knowledge of consumers' attitudes have also proved useful in this regard. For example, attitudes appear useful in distinguishing innovators from noninnovators for new products.[31] They also have proved useful in segmenting a variety of product markets. Therefore, the use of attitude measurements to distinguish among classes of product users and for developing marketing strategies to penetrate those markets appears quite promising.

SUMMARY

This chapter introduced the concept of attitudes, described their basic characteristics, and reviewed their basic functions. The various sources of attitude development also served as a focus for discussion.

In the next major section, several theories and models of attitudes were depicted. Specifically the congruity, balance, and cognitive dissonance views of attitudes were treated. Although these viewpoints provide significant insight, recent attention has turned to multiattribute attitude models, especially those offered by Fishbein. The attraction of these newer models lies in their view of attitudes as having more than one dimension and being influenced by several attributes of a product which the consumer views as having importance.

Finally, this chapter concluded by suggesting some implications of attitude research for practical marketing strategies. A number of specific recommendations were offered which, depending on the particular situation, could prove beneficial to the marketer. In the next chapter we will pick up on this train of thought to develop more specific guidelines for marketing communications which attempt to change consumers' attitudes.

DISCUSSION TOPICS

1. A variety of definitions of attitude exist. What appears to be the emphasis of the more recent definitions?

2. What are the major characteristics of attitudes? Assume an attitude regarding a specific product and use this as an example to demonstrate each characteristic.

3. What are the functions of an attitude? Can you cite specific personal experiences that demonstrate each of these functions?

4. What are the sources of attitude development? Can you foresee how these sources might conflict with one another in their influence on developing attitudes? If so, cite an example to demonstrate your point.

5. Review the attitude theories of congruity, balance, and cognitive dissonance. Highlight their major characteristics.

6. Using your knowledge of attitudes, what celebrity would you recommend as a spokesperson for each of the following brands? Defend your choice.
a. Norelco smoke detectors
b. Trident sugarless gum
c. Head skis

7. Some advertisements make highly exaggerated claims for a brand which it probably cannot fulfill. Using your knowledge of cognitive dissonance, assess the wisdom of this technique.

8. Distinguish between the Fishbein attitude model and earlier attitude theories. What implications does this have for predicting consumer behavior?

9. Cite some actual examples of Lutz's suggested marketing strategies based upon the Fishbein A-act model.

NOTES

1. Martin Fishbein, "The Relationship between Beliefs, Attitudes, and Behavior," in Shel Feldman (ed.), *Cognitive Consistency,* Academic, New York, 1966, pp. 199–223.
2. The term object is used here to include abstract concepts such as enjoyment as well as physical things.
3. Gordon W. Allport, "Attitudes," in C. A. Murchinson (ed.), *A Handbook of Social Psychology,* Clark University Press, Worcester, Mass., 1935, pp. 798–844.
4. D. Krech and R. Crutchfield, *Theory and Problems in Social Psychology,* McGraw-Hill, New York, 1948.
5. Martin Fishbein, "A Behavior Theory Approach to the Relations between Beliefs about

an Object and the Attitude toward the Object," in Martin Fishbein (ed.), *Readings in Attitude Theory and Measurement,* Wiley, New York, 1967, p. 394.

6. T. M. Newcomb, R. H. Turner, and P. E. Converse, *Social Psychology,* Holt, New York, 1965, p. 115.

7. Daniel Katz, "The Functional Approach to the Study of Attitudes," *Public Opinion Quarterly,* **24**:163–204, 1960.

8. M. Wayne DeLozier, *The Marketing Communications Process,* McGraw-Hill, New York, 1976, p. 81.

9. Arch G. Woodside and J. William Davenport, "The Effect of Salesman Similarity and Expertise on Consumer Purchasing Behavior," *Journal of Marketing Research,* **11**:198–202, May 1974.

10. This section is based largely upon the works of Charles E. Osgood, George J. Suci, and Percy H. Tannenbaum, *The Measurement of Meaning,* University of Illinois Press, Urbana, Ill., 1957; Milton J. Rosenberg et al., *Attitude Organization and Change,* Yale, New Haven, Conn., 1960; Leon A. Festinger, *A Theory of Cognitive Dissonance,* Stanford, Stanford, Calif., 1957; and Roger Brown, *Social Psychology,* Free Press, New York, 1965.

11. For a thorough treatment of the mathematics involved in predicting the resolution of such cases see Osgood, Suci, and Tannenbaum, *Measurement of Meaning,* pp. 199–207.

12. See Jonathan L. Freedman, Jr., Merrill Carlsmith, and David O. Sears, *Social Psychology,* Prentice-Hall, Englewood Cliffs, N.J., 1970, p. 263; and Charles E. Osgood and Percy H. Tannenbaum, "The Principle of Congruity in the Prediction of Attitude Change," *Psychological Review,* **62**:42–55, 1955.

13. Some of the ideas in this section are attributable to Brown, *Social Psychology,* pp. 566–670.

14. Fritz Heider, "Attitudes and Cognitive Organizations," *Journal of Psychology,* **21**:107–112, January 1946.

15. See Festinger, *Cognitive Dissonance.*

16. See Milton J. Rosenberg, "Cognitive Structure and Attitudinal Affect," *Journal of Abnormal and Social Psychology,* **53**:367–372, November 1956; Martin Fishbein, "An Investigation of the Relationship between Beliefs about an Object and the Attitude toward That Object," *Human Relations,* **16**:233–240, 1963; and Martin Fishbein, "Attitudes and the Prediction of Behavior," in Martin Fishbein (ed.), *Readings in Attitude Theory and Measurement,* Wiley, New York, 1967, pp. 477–492. For more current insights see Martin Fishbein and Icek Ajzen, *Belief, Attitude, Intention, and Behavior: An Introduction to Theory and Research Reading,* Addison-Wesley, Reading, Mass., 1975.

17. Some examples are: Arch G. Woodside and James D. Clokey, "Multi-Attribute/Multi-Brand Models," *Journal of Advertising Research,* **14**:33–40, October 1974; Frank M. Bass and W. Wayne Talarzyk, "An Attitude Model for the Study of Brand Preference," *Journal of Marketing Research,* **9**:93–96, February 1972; Michael B. Mazis, Olli T. Ahtola, and R. Eugene Klippel, "A Comparison of Four Multi-Attribute Models in the Prediction of Consumer Attitudes," *Journal of Consumer Research,* **2**:38–52, June 1975; and James R. Bettman, Noel Capon, Richard J. Lutz, "Multiattribute Measurement Models and Multiattribute Theory: A Test of Construct Validity," *Journal of Consumer Research,* **1**:1–14, March 1975.

18. See as examples, Jagdish Sheth, "Brand Profiles from Beliefs and Importances," *Journal of Advertising Research,* **13**:37–42, February 1973; and Bass and Talarzyk, "Attitude Model for Study of Brand Preference."

19. Debate still exists regarding the most appropriate method to determine important attributes and how to measure them. See William L. Wilkie and Edgar A. Pessemier, "Issues in Marketing's Use of Multiattribute Attitude Models," *Journal of Marketing Research,* **10**:428–441, November 1973.

20. Wilkie and Pessemier, "Issues in Multiattribute Models," p. 428.

21. The development of the Fishbein model is used as a dividing line for reviewing these studies because of its rather dramatic departure from traditional means of measuring attitudes. This is not necessarily intended to imply that the Fishbein model is better at predicting brand-choice behavior.

22. See for example Alvin A. Achenbaum, "Knowledge Is a Thing Called Measurement," in Lee Adler and Irving Crespi (eds.), *Attitude Research at Sea,* American Marketing Association, Chicago, 1966, pp. 111–126; and Henry Assael and George S. Day, "Attitudes and Awareness as Predictors of Market Share," *Journal of Advertising Research,* **8**:3–10, December 1968.

23. See R. T. LaPiere, "Attitudes vs. Actions," *Social Forces,* **13**:230–237, 1934; and L. Festinger, "Behavioral Support for Opinion Change," *Public Opinion Quarterly,* **28**:404–417, 1964.

24. Martin A. Fishbein, "Some Comments on the Use of 'Models' in Advertising Research," in *Proceedings: Seminar on Translating Advanced Advertising Theories into Research Reality,* European Society of Market Research, Amsterdam, The Netherlands, 1971, p. 301.

25. See Masad Nakanishi and James R. Bettman, "Attitude Models Revisited: An Individual Level Analysis," *Journal of Consumer Research,* **1**:16–21, December 1974; Bass and Talarzyk, "An Attitude Model for Brand Preference"; Mazis et al., "A Comparison of Models in Prediction of Consumer Attitudes"; and Frederick W. Winter, "A Laboratory Experiment of Individual Attitude Response to Advertising Exposure," *Journal of Marketing Research,* **10**:130–140, May 1973.

26. See Martin Fishbein, "Attitude and the Prediction of Behavior," in Martin Fishbein (ed.), *Readings in Attitude Theory and Measurement,* Wiley, New York, 1967, pp. 477–492; and Michael J. Ryan and E. H. Bonfield, "The Fishbein Extended Model and Consumer Behavior," *Journal of Consumer Research,* **3**:118–136, September 1975.

27. Richard J. Lutz, "Changing Brand Attitudes through Modification of Cognitive Structure," *Journal of Consumer Research,* **1**:49, March 1975.

28. Harper W. Boyd, Jr., Michael L. Ray, and Edward C. Strong, "An Attitudinal Framework for Advertising Strategy," *Journal of Marketing,* **36**:27–33, April 1972.

29. Boyd, Ray, and Strong, "Framework for Advertising," p. 32.

30. Jack Trout and Al Ries, "The Positioning Era Cometh," reprinted in Robert F. Hoel (ed.), *Marketing Now,* Scott, Foresman, Glenview, Ill., 1973, p. 68.

31. Everett Rogers and J. David Stanfield, "Adoption and Diffusion of New Products: Emerging Generalizations and Hypotheses," paper presented at the Conference on the Application of Sciences to Marketing Management, Purdue University, July 12–15, 1966.

ATTITUDE CHANGE

THE COMMUNICATION PROCESS   SOURCE FACTORS   Source Credibility; The Sleeper Effect; Similarity with Audience; Communicator Attitudes toward Self, Message, and Receiver   MARKETING COMMUNICATION SOURCES   The Company; Sales Representatives; The Media; Hired Promoters; Retailers; Combined Source Effects   MESSAGE FACTORS   Message Structure; Message Appeals; Message Codes   RECEIVER FACTORS   Personality Traits; Sex Differences; Bases of Attitudes; Belief Types

This chapter builds on our previous discussion by focusing on marketers' attempts to change consumer attitudes toward their companies and brands. The reader should bear in mind that the degree of success of such efforts depends on how strongly consumers hold their existing attitudes. Strongly entrenched attitudes are extremely difficult to change, whereas neutral and weakly held attitudes are considerably easier to influence.

Changing consumers' attitudes is the function of the persuasive communication process. After reviewing a simplified model of this process the chapter treats several of its major components. First, various factors influencing the effectiveness of communication sources and the major types of marketing communication sources are reviewed. Next, the effect of various characteristics of the communication message itself are explored. Finally, characteristics of the audience which affect their receptivity and predisposition to be influenced by communication are examined from the point of view of attitude change.

THE COMMUNICATION PROCESS

In this chapter we are concerned with the persuasive communication process by which a person or group seeks to change the attitudes and ultimately the behavior of consumers.[1] A simplified model of this process as shown in Figure 18-1 allows a more concrete appreciation of some of its major elements.

The sender initiates a communication message. This individual or group has as an objective the transmission of some intended message to one or more individuals acting as receivers. In marketing, the sender usually represents a company or its brand and the intended message is usually conceived of as a mechanism to change consumers' attitudes toward the brand and hopefully their predisposition to purchase it.

The intended message is the meaning the sender wishes to convey to the receiver. In order to deliver this intended meaning, however, the message must be suitably formed for transmission in the channel selected to deliver the message. That is, the intended message must be *encoded* into symbols making up the actual message, which represents the thoughts of the sender. These symbols are usually words but often involve pictures and actions of the sender.

The sent (actual) message is transmitted over some channel of communication. In marketing the potential channel alternatives are quite varied, ranging from radio to in-store displays and personal messages. Therefore, considerable deliberation must be taken to select the channel with characteristics most appropriate to the message involved.

The sent message is acquired by one or more receivers. However, the received message is rarely identical to the sent message. Characteristics of the channel of transmission are one set of factors which can alter the message. For example, it is very difficult to reproduce accurately product colors and textures on television or in newspapers. Consequently the received message can differ significantly from the sent message.

The received message is transformed into a perceived message through the receiver's perceptual process. Here the received message is *decoded.* That is, the symbols received are transformed back into meaning or thoughts by the receiver. As we have seen, the individual's experiences as well as the context in which she perceives the message will influence the meaning she derives from it. The receiver then will change her attitude and/or action based on this perceived message.

The feedback loop in Figure 18-1 recognizes that the communication process involves a two-way flow. That is, individuals or groups are both receivers and senders of messages and they interact with each other. Therefore feedback can be viewed as the initiation of another communication where the receiver can now be construed as a message sender. This feedback process enables the original sender to monitor how well her

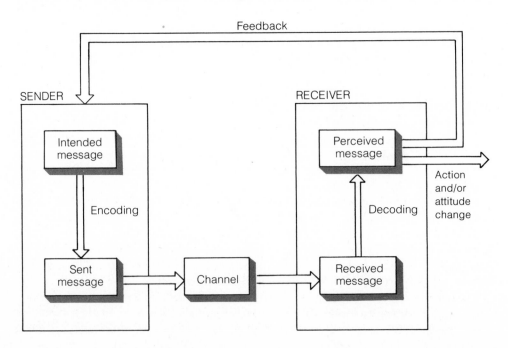

FIGURE 18-1
A model of the communication process.

intended meaning was conveyed and received. In many marketing situations communications are transmitted via mass media to widely distributed consumers, therefore accurate feedback information is very rare and difficult to obtain.

The concept of *noise* is frequently used to refer to some type of disruption in the communication process. We have seen that a variety of noise sources exist. The sender may have difficulty in formulating the intended message and further problems encoding it into a message to be transmitted. The channel of communication itself is also capable of interfering with the message. After receiving the message the receiver may introduce noise through the decoding process. Of course, the feedback loop may also contribute noise. Therefore, each stage of the communication process is susceptible to message distortion.

In order to study the persuasive communication process it is necessary to understand three general kinds of factors that operate to influence attitudes, beliefs, and behavior. They are source, message, and receiver factors.[2] These three sets of factors interact to produce intended and unintended communication effects. For simplicity, each set of factors is examined separately. However, the reader should continually bear in mind that the factors are interactive.

SOURCE FACTORS

What characteristics do certain individuals, companies, or groups possess that permit them to change more easily the views and attitudes of others? This section discusses the major characteristics of persuasive communicators. In a marketing context these communicators are salespeople, companies, hired promoters, the media, and other marketing sources of product and brand information.

Source Credibility

Perhaps the most important source factor in persuasion is credibility (believability). A long-held principle of persuasion, supported by a variety of research studies, has been that a communicator is more persuasive when the audience perceives him as being highly credible than when it perceives him as having low credibility. The important word in this general finding is *perceives* since it is not important whether the source *is* credible, but rather that the audience perceives him as being credible. As an example, consider the case where a very distinguished, French-looking gentleman is introduced to consumers as an expert on wine when in fact he is a dress designer having no expertise in wines. The extent to which the audience believes his false identity will affect his ability to influence them regarding the most important factors contributing to the taste of wines.

To most of us this general finding that a highly credible source will effect greater attitude change than one low in credibility may seem quite obvious and understandable. However, recent studies have begun to reveal that under certain conditions source credibility may not significantly influence the attitudes of receivers.[3] In addition, for cases where the marketer wishes to change consumers' behavior directly, and have this lead to later attitude change, a highly credible source may actually be a disadvantage.[4] Such a case could exist in situations where the marketer arranges for free brand trials or samples and advocates their use to encourage the development of favorable brand attitudes.

Given the above exceptions there still are a great number of situations where source credibility can significantly influence consumers' attitude change. But what makes a source appear credible? The major dimensions are (1) trustworthiness, (2) expertise, (3) status or prestige, (4) likability, and (5) an assortment of physical traits of the source.

TRUSTWORTHINESS A source will be perceived as credible if his audience views him as honest (trustworthy), and thus will be more persuasive than a person perceived as dishonest or untrustworthy.

A communicator's effectiveness as a trustworthy source will depend upon whether his audience perceives he has an *intention to manipulate* them. If the audience believes that the communicator, no matter how generally honest, has something to gain personally by his message, then his persuasive attempts will lose effectiveness. Thus, a principle of persuasion is that a source who is perceived as having nothing to gain from his argument is more persuasive than a source who is perceived to have something to gain from his persuasive attempts.

This idea suggests one reason why advertising and personal selling is generally less effective than a trusted friend in changing consumer attitudes. Advertisers have attempted to overcome this problem to some extent by using "candid interviews" with consumers who were not aware that they were giving testimony to a company's brand. Other similar approaches have been used by advertisers to reduce their perceived "intention to manipulate," such as the "disguised brand comparison test" used for Ivory Snow and others. A housewife is shown in a television commercial testing two unidentified brands of detergent on her infant's diapers. She expresses approval of how much better one of the brands performs in softening diapers. She is then informed that the brand she selected as the best is Ivory Snow. This approach tries to reduce the sponsor's perceived intention to manipulate an audience by use of "objective" test comparisons.

Another way to reduce the communicator's perceived intent to manipulate is to use the "overheard conversation." When one person overhears two other people talking, he is more likely to be influenced by the persuasive attempts of the speakers since he realizes he is not the intended receiver of the message. Therefore, he feels that the persuasive communicator has no intent to influence him directly. One use of the "overheard conversation" on television is the advertisements for E. F. Hutton stockbrokers. In a variety of different situations, the viewer is made to feel that he is about to overhear selected stock tips from a customer of the firm. The favorable image of the firm is reinforced when the viewer realizes that many others in the ad were also discreetly listening with great interest.

The general notion expressed here is that a communicator can increase his persuasiveness by having the audience perceive him as trustworthy, which in turn means being perceived as having no intention to manipulate message receivers for personal gain.

EXPERTISE Another dimension of source credibility is perceived expertise. That is, when an audience views a communicator as having higher qualifications than others to speak on a topic, she will be more persuasive than a person viewed as less qualified. In marketing, experts in a field related to a company's product often are used to promote its brands. However, the wisdom of using Joe Namath at one time to advertise Hanes pantyhose is somewhat questionable on expertise grounds.

STATUS/PRESTIGE A communicator whom an audience perceives as high in status or prestige is more persuasive than one whom an audience perceives as low in these attributes. As we have learned, society "confers" status and prestige upon individuals according to the roles they occupy. As examples, a physician is generally regarded as of higher status and prestige than a nurse, and a scientist usually has more prestige than an engineer. Marketers often attempt to obtain as endorsers of their products individuals who have obtained high status. Examples include using Art Linkletter as an endorser of a life insurance company and former astronaut Frank Borman as a spokesman for Eastern Airlines. It should be noted that although the concepts of prestige and expertise overlap, they are not synonymous.[5]

OTHER DIMENSIONS Although other dimensions of source credibility will not be discussed fully, some that are not obvious will be mentioned. For example, age, sex, color, dress, mannerisms, and voice inflections, as well as general attractiveness affect source credibility.[6] Regarding age, older people tend to be quite influential upon younger people. The tendency for youth to accept their elders' advice and influence might be due largely to the younger generation's perception of their elders' experience in life, thus viewing them as more "expert."

Other cues for assessing the expertise of a communicator are his voice, accent, dress, and mannerism. An announcer who speaks with an authoritative voice, dresses "like a millionaire," and uses confident nonverbal cues[7] can be very persuasive and influential upon his audience's attitudes in a "get-rich-quick" scheme, for example.[8]

THE LOW-CREDIBILITY COMMUNICATOR We have stated that a high-credibility source can be persuasive. However, research indicates that a source low in credibility can also effect attitude change under certain circumstances. Specifically, the low-credibility source can be persuasive when he argues against his own self-interests. By doing so the communicator appears to establish credibility because it becomes obvious to an audience that he has nothing to gain by arguing for someone else's position. For example, in one advertisement the spokesperson states that he is not getting "one red cent" for endorsing the product.

A low-credibility source also can increase his persuasiveness if he is identified *after,* rather than *before,* presenting his message. The reason is that the audience will attend to the message if they do not know he is a low-credibility source. Otherwise, they will selectively ignore the presentation if they strongly suspect his credibility.

The Sleeper Effect

Although a communicator high in credibility can influence attitude change in receivers, does the effect last? Research indicates that it dissipates rapidly, which is not surprising, given our understanding of the learning curve. However, a startling discovery is that an audience exposed initially to a low-credibility source develops opinions *more* closely in line with the communicator as time passes. That is, as time passes, an audience comes *more* in agreement with the low-credibility source and *less* in agreement with the high-credibility source. Figure 18-2 illustrates this phenomenon known as the "sleeper effect."

From the research conducted on the sleeper effect,[9] the following principle emerges: as time since exposure to a message passes, opinion change attributed to the high-credibility source decreases, whereas the opinion change attributed to the low-credibility source increases.[10] This phenomenon is puzzling at first, but does have a plausible explanation. Specifically, the explanation involves two factors that underlie opinion change. First, the receiver must *remember* the contents of the persuasive message, and second he must have some *motivation to accept* the communicator's arguments in the message. Based on these two concepts, the sleeper effect is explained because both audiences *forget the source* of the message more rapidly than they do the *content* of the message. Thus, the "enhancing" effects of the high-credibility source upon audience opinion change dissipates rapidly, and only the message content remains. Consequently, opinion change declines over a period of time among the audience exposed to the high-credibility source. The "depressing" effect of the low-credibility source also dissipates rapidly, but the content of the persuasive message remains.

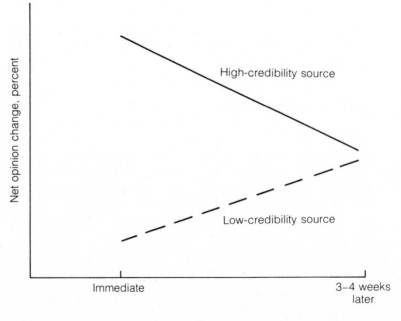

FIGURE 18-2
An illustration of the "sleeper effect."

Therefore, opinion change increases in the desired direction since the low-credibility source becomes disassociated with the content of the message.

If the low- and high-credibility sources are both "reinstated" (allowed to reintroduce their positions) at a later time, the effect is to restore both audiences' opinion levels to nearly the points they were right after the initial communications.[11] This is shown in Figure 18-3. Note how the solid lines indicate that with reinstatement the high-credibility source continues to hold a higher degree of attitude change than the low-credibility source. The dotted lines demonstrate, however, that without an opportunity to reintroduce his argument, the high-credibility source loses this advantage over time. This sleeper effect suggests that where a high-credibility source is used to promote a company's brand, constant reinforcement is required to maintain the positive opinion change. However, where a low-credibility source is used initially to promote a product, it is better not to reinstate the source.

Similarity with Audience

Another finding regarding communication sources is, "people are persuaded more by a communicator they perceive to be similar to themselves."[12] That is, people seem to trust others who are like themselves. Similarity can be perceived in a variety of ways, such as personality, race, interests, self-image, and group affiliations. This has led marketers to use so-called slice-of-life advertisements in many cases. For example, ads for Maxwell House Coffee, Calgon dishwasher detergent, and Crest toothpaste, as well as many other brands, attempt to show "typical" people finding satisfaction with their products.

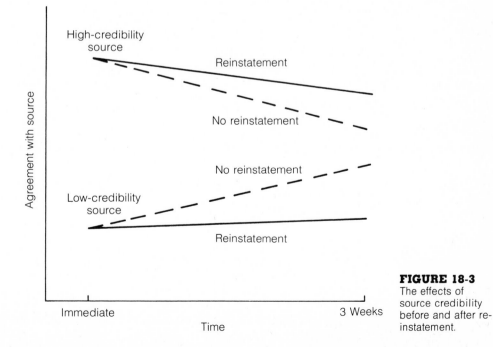

FIGURE 18-3
The effects of source credibility before and after reinstatement.

Communicator Attitudes toward Self, Message, and Receiver

A communicator is more persuasive if she has a positive attitude toward herself, her message, and her receiver.[13] Within a marketing context, a sales representative who has a positive attitude toward herself is one who has self-confidence. Her self-confidence is perceived by the prospective buyer and can influence the decision to buy.

Sales representatives are trained to show a positive attitude toward their product and sales presentation (their message). That is, they are trained to *believe* in the product they are selling and what they say about it. Thus, many sales training programs are designed to develop representatives' confidence in their company and the products they sell.

Regarding a positive attitude toward the receiver, a sales representative must demonstrate respect and admiration toward her prospective buyers to be successful. Customers quickly realize when they are being "talked down to" in a sales pitch. In such cases they will quickly react negatively to the sales presentation and the brand involved.

MARKETING COMMUNICATIONS SOURCES

Thus far, we have discussed several principles of persuasive communications related to the source. In marketing, several sources are perceived by consumers as influential upon their purchase decisions. In addition, these sources can interact to produce a combined source effect upon consumers. These marketing sources are described below.

The Company

Consumers perceive companies as sources of information, and some are seen as highly credible but others are viewed with suspicion. Most consumers feel that Procter & Gamble, for example, is a trustworthy company because P&G has built an excellent reputation by developing good products and spending considerable sums of money on advertising and consumer research. Because of its highly credible image, P&G is much more successful than many other companies in introducing new brands to the market.

Companies develop source credibility in a variety of ways, among which are: (1) producing dependable, need-satisfying products, (2) developing sound advertising and public relations programs, (3) providing reliable warranties and guarantees, (4) using friendly and helpful sales representatives, (5) providing dependable delivery, and (6) acting in a socially responsible manner. Building a good company reputation takes time, but it pays handsome dividends especially in the form of consumer loyalty.

Sales Representatives

Because of their face-to-face contacts with current and prospective customers, sales representatives are viewed by consumers as information sources. Also salespeople who are viewed as knowledgeable (expert) and trustworthy appear to be more persuasive than those not regarded as credible.[14] In addition, evidence suggests that consumers are more receptive to salespeople from highly credible companies such as the Prudential Insurance Company and Colgate-Palmolive than from unknown or low-credibility companies.[15] Thus the sales representative from the well-known company has an advantage over those from low-credibility companies regardless of her competence.

The Media

Consumers use media extensively for product information. Although media are actually channel links between companies and consumers (receivers), people view them as sources; thus it is important to understand their effects on persuading consumers to purchase products. *Good Housekeeping* and *Parents' Magazine* are examples of media that consumers perceive as credible sources of product information. Because of their product-screening processes and "seals of approval," they have built reputations as expert and trustworthy sources upon which consumers can rely.

Specialized print media also are very persuasive sources of information. Examples are *The Wall Street Journal, Popular Photography, Golf Digest,* and *Consumer Reports.* Consumers perceive these media as expert, trustworthy, and therefore credible sources for product information. They can create positive halo effects for products mentioned in them and can therefore increase the persuasive impact of the advertiser's message.

Hired Promoters

Companies frequently use hired promoters in their advertising. In fact, on-camera spokespeople were used in 37 percent of all television advertisements in 1976.[16] Effective hired promoters are ones who have established credibility for themselves, often in occupations unrelated to the advertised product. Arthur Godfrey became a trustworthy source in product advertising when he refused to advertise certain brands on his radio show. John Wayne, besides being a well-known actor, successfully battled cancer and now appears in advertisements for the American Cancer Society. Bob Hope over the years has established himself as an honest, sincere, and likable person. He has tremendous credibility among many consumers, particularly since people perceive that he has virtually nothing to gain financially from his commercial recommendations.

Frequently, people unknown to audiences are used in testimonial advertisements. This approach often takes the form of "candid" conversations with people on the street or in the supermarket. The purpose of using such unknowns in unrehearsed, unsolicited conversations is to improve the message credibility by showing people who have no intention to manipulate the audience and therefore nothing to gain by their endorsement of a particular brand. Producers of Sealtest ice cream have employed this approach when they show people on the street saying that the packaged product tastes as good as "ice cream parlor" quality ice cream. This approach can often be more persuasive than using celebrities whom audiences might perceive as doing it for the money.

Retailers

Retailers act as sources of messages at the local level. A department store that has a good local reputation can more easily sell unknown brands than less reputable stores. Also, specialty shops are successful in selling unknown brands because of their perceived expertise in the product line, such as cameras and stereo equipment. Thus a manufacturer who produces brands with low consumer awareness can benefit from using specialty outlets if he can convince the retailers to carry his line.

Combined Source Effects

Although we have described each marketing source separately, in reality there are combined source effects that interact to produce a persuasive impact on consumers. Therefore, a company must be careful in selecting hired promoters, media, and retailers to deliver a persuasive brand message. A bad selection can cancel the positive effects of the other message sources used. A company must view all the source components from a system's point of view to gain maximum effectiveness.

MESSAGE FACTORS

It is important to understand what components make up a persuasive message. This section discusses three sets of message factors: (1) message structure, (2) message appeal, and (3) message code.

Message Structure

Message structure refers to how the elements of a message are organized. Three structures that have been extensively studied are message sidedness, order of presentation, and conclusion drawing.

MESSAGE SIDEDNESS A message can be either one-sided or two-sided. A *one-sided message* is one in which only the strengths of the communicator's position are described. That is, a salesperson uses a one-sided message when describing only the good points of his company's products and does not mention their weaknesses, or the good features of competing products. For example, advertisements for Chevrolet automobiles only talk about their advantages and don't mention any of their possible weaknesses, or possible advantages of Fords. A *two-sided message,* on the other hand, presents the strengths of the communicator's position as in the one-sided message, but also either admits to weaknesses in the argument or admits to a few strengths in the opponent's position. In this case the salesperson either mentions one or two weaknesses in her company's products or admits to one or two strong features of competitor's products. However, the sales representative's product (or side) is always presented as stronger than the competitors'. Cases in point include the Avis Rent-A-Car campaign, "We're not number one but we try harder," and Listerine ads which suggest that the product does not have the greatest taste. Another example of a two-sided message is presented in Figure 18-4.

Two questions arise regarding message sidedness. The first is why would anyone want to admit to weaknesses in their own product or mention the strengths of competing products? Secondly, which approach is more effective? The answer to the first question lies in discussion of the second. Either approach can be more effective than the other, depending upon conditions under which the message is presented. The conditions are (1) the audience's initial opinion on the issue, (2) their exposure to subsequent counterarguments, and (3) the audience's educational level.

Regarding the first condition, a one-sided argument is more effective when the audience is already in agreement with the communicator's position, and a two-sided message is more effective when the audience initially disagrees with the communicator's position. The one-sided message is more effective for an audience that already agrees with the communicator's position since it reinforces what they already believe. A two-sided message

"The U.S. has 1.5 trillion tons of coal. We should use it."

With the world's oil and gas running low, where can we turn for energy? To coal? To uranium? What else? What energy sources offer the greatest near-term promise, the fewest problems?

Coal is already our leading source of electrical energy. Fortunately, it is abundant, readily available. We are researching ways to liquefy and gasify it affordably, to power cars, heat homes. True, burning coal can foul our air. Mining it—from both deep and surface mines can disrupt the land, can pollute our streams. But we are solving these problems. More complete solutions are being researched.

Meanwhile, some people see uranium as our most promising fuel. Nuclear plants do not pollute the air. They produce no noxious odors. The sites are clean. They have the potential to yield enormous energy from small quantities of fuel.

True, our nuclear history is short, the technology young, power awesome. But, present safety records are good, and safeguards elaborate. The risk so far seems acceptable.

We should continue to perfect our nuclear technology: breeder reactors that could insure centuries of energy from known fuel reserves. That could consume present fission wastes. Ultimately we may unlock the limitless energy of fusion.

But realizing full nuclear potential will take time. Before we reach nuclear self-sufficiency we may well run low on oil and gas. So we must continue to refine our coal technology. To develop affordable petroleum substitutes. To make coal cleaner, less disruptive. To buy time to research other energy forms: winds, tides, the sun, geothermal heat.

Coal may not be the ultimate solution. But it can keep things humming until that solution comes.

Caterpillar makes machines used in the development of energy, whatever the form.

There are no simple solutions. Only intelligent choices.

Caterpillar, Cat and ⒸⒷ are Trademarks of Caterpillar Tractor Co.

"Uranium power has great potential. Let's perfect it."

FIGURE 18-4
An example of a two-sided message. (Courtesy of Caterpillar Tractor Company.)

under this condition would serve only to place doubt in their minds. However, the use of a one-sided message for an audience *not* in initial agreement with the communicator's stance tends to be less effective since they will perceptually resist a view counter to their own. In this case, a two-sided message is more effective because the audience tends to view the communicator as more objective and honest (credible) since he admits to the merits of their position. The approach allows the communicator to get through the audience's perceptual filters, present his views, and thereby increase the likelihood of gaining some measure of attitude change.

A second condition that determines the effectiveness of one-sided and two-sided messages is whether an audience will later be exposed to opposite arguments. If an audience will be later subject to counterarguments, a communicator should use a two-sided rather than a one-sided message. By presenting a two-sided message, the communicator, in a sense, "immunizes" his audience against later counterarguments. Audience members tend to discount the counterargument because they have heard those points before. Using this technique, sales and spokespeople are often able to take the "wind out of their competitors' sails" (and sales) by presenting potential buyers with two-sided messages.

The third condition for determining whether to use a one-sided or two-sided message is the educational level of the audience. A two-sided message is more persuasive on better-educated audiences, whereas a one-sided message is more effective in changing the opinions of less well-educated audiences. Because better-educated people generally are more capable of seeing both sides of an argument anyway, a communicator should either admit the strengths of opposing views or weaknesses in his own position. In this way, the communicator is established as being more objective and credible in the minds of his audience. Less-educated people are less capable of seeing another side of an issue and therefore are more likely to accept the argument they hear. To present them with two sides might confuse them and they would find it difficult to know which side to accept.

Evidence of the effectiveness of one- and two-sided messages in advertising has been studied by Faison, who asked half of a 500-subject sample to listen to one-sided radio commercials for an automobile, a gas range, and a floor wax. Each commercial was "conventional" in the sense that it presented only positive product features. The second half of the sample was presented two-sided commercials comparable to the one-sided messages, except that some negative features were included. Among Faison's findings were the following:

1. Two-sided advertisements were more effective on higher-educated subjects, whereas one-sided advertisements were more effective on less-educated subjects.

2. Two-sided commercials were more effective on subjects who used competing brands, whereas one-sided commercials were more effective on subjects who used the brand featured in the commercial. In this case, a subject who used the advertised brand is similar to one who has initial agreement with the communicator. A subject who used the competing brand is similar to one who does not have initial agreement with the communicator.

3. The commercials' effectiveness in changing opinions appears to be influenced by characteristics of the product being promoted. For example, greater attitude change was created for the low-cost floor wax than the high-priced automobile. This finding can be explained in terms of the amount of commitment (or investment) a person has made in the product in terms of money, search time, and effort. With greater commitment, consumers hold more tightly to their purchase decision.

4. After 4 to 6 weeks, the subjects showed no diminishing effects in their attitudes toward the advertised brands. In fact, subjects exposed to the two-sided advertisements actually showed an increase in attitude toward the advertised brand.[17]

Perhaps unfortunately, many companies have generally rejected the idea of their spokespeople ever admitting to either a competitor's product's strengths or to their own product's weaknesses. However, in a number of situations this could be a very viable approach. First, where it is possible to segment consumers into loyal and nonloyal groups, it may be useful to direct one-sided messages toward loyal customers and two-sided ads toward the nonloyal group.[18] Of course this strategy requires that each group is capable of being isolated enough so that they are not inadvertently exposed to both messages. In personal selling, salespeople may also find it to their advantage to use a two-sided sales pitch either by admitting to minor weaknesses in their companies' brands or by mentioning one or two strengths of competitors' brands. Such a tactic may create a resistance in prospects' minds toward competitors' sales claims. Additionally, in an industrial selling situation, sales representatives usually are confronted by well-educated purchasing agents, consulting engineers, and others of similar education. In these cases, a two-sided sales pitch should prove more effective than a one-sided message. However, for door-to-door salespeople in a low-income (and therefore very likely poorly educated) neighborhood, a one-sided argument should be more effective.

ORDER OF PRESENTATION What is the best order in which to present persuasive arguments in an advertising message? Should the communicator present the most important parts at the beginning, the middle, or the end? In a two-sided message, should the communicator use a pro-con or a con-pro order? Does the first or second communicator have the advantage when presenting an opposing message? This section briefly addresses these questions and provides answers based upon current research in the area.

Climax versus Anticlimax Order To answer the questions above, it is necessary to define certain terms used in the order of presentation. A *climax order* refers to ordering message elements whereby the strongest arguments are presented at the end of a message. An *anticlimax order* refers to the presentation of the most important points at the beginning of a message. When the most important materials are presented in the middle of a message, it is referred to as a *pyramidal order.* Figure 18-5 graphically describes these three alternatives to message order.

Based on research findings, the following guidelines can be offered regarding the ordering of messages:

1. An anticlimax order tends to be most effective for an audience having a low level of interest in the subject being presented.

2. A climax order tends to be most effective for an audience having a high level of interest in the subject being presented.

3. The pyramidal order is the least effective order of presentation.

The first two generalizations can be explained in terms of audience interest. Where audience interest is low, the stronger, more interesting points in a message have the greater potential for gaining audience attention and therefore should be placed first (anticlimax order). In this way, a communicator is better able to get his message across and thus effect change in his audience. However, with this approach the communicator also must be careful of avoiding an audience "let down" when the weaker points in a message follow.

Where audience interest is high in the subject of the message, there is no need to present the stronger points first, because the audience will attend to the message out of interest. Therefore, the climax order should be used since points made at the end of the message exceed the expectations created by the points initially presented.[19]

The lesson marketers must learn from these statements is that for low-interest products, an anticlimax order should be used, and for high-interest products, a climax order appears effective. In addition, in some cases each method can perhaps be strengthened by presenting the important points at *both* the beginning and end of the message—in the form of an introduction and summary of important points. However, very little if any justification exists for a pyramidal order.

Recency and Primacy Effects In presenting a two-sided message, should the points favorable to the advertiser's product be presented first or last? If two competing messages are involved, does the first or last communicator have the advantage? Both of these questions involve the subject of primacy and recency effects. When material presented first produces the greater

FIGURE 18-5
Three orders of message presentation.

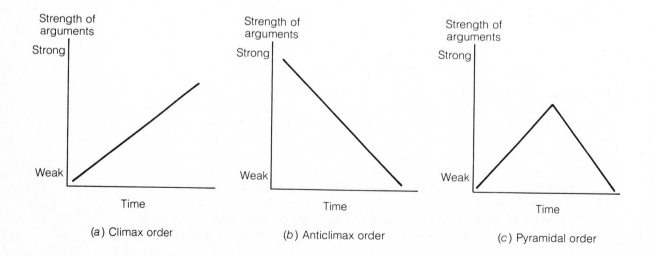

(a) Climax order   (b) Anticlimax order   (c) Pyramidal order

opinion or attitude change, a *primacy effect* has occurred. When material presented last produces the greater effect a *recency effect* is observed.

Research into the question of which order of presentation is more effective in changing audience attitudes is still not conclusive. It appears that sometimes primacy and sometimes recency is more effective. However, some tentative guidelines can be offered to the communicator. First, nonsalient, controversial topics, interesting subject matter, and highly familiar issues tend to generate a primacy effect. This suggests that such situations call for the important message points to be placed first. Second, salient topics, uninteresting subject matter, and moderately unfamiliar topics tend to yield a recency effect. In such cases the most important message points should probably appear last. Finally, other conditions (such as a strong argument or reinforcing actions) appear to generate *either* a primacy or recency effect depending on whether they are placed first or last in the message.[20]

These general conclusions require advertisers to explore carefully the audience's potential reaction to their message and the issues it raises before developing the structure of the promotional message. For example, because interest in detergents is usually not high, this might suggest that Procter & Gamble place the important parts of its promotions at the end of the message. However, an MGM advertisement for a new film about "Big Foot" which has already generated considerable public interest might most benefit from the important message points being placed first.

DRAWING A CONCLUSION Is it better to draw a conclusion for your audience at the end of a message or let them draw their own conclusions? Although the answer to this question is dependent upon several conditions, the most useful generalization is that communicators are more effective in changing opinions of an audience if they draw a conclusion for them.[21]

Investigations of this question have shown that a conclusion must be drawn for a less intelligent audience to achieve opinion change; otherwise they may draw either the wrong conclusion or no conclusion, and therefore the intended opinion change will not occur. For audiences of higher intelligence it usually makes no difference whether a conclusion is drawn, since they have the ability to reach the "correct" conclusion.[22] Therefore, to be safe, it is better generally to draw a conclusion at the end of a message regardless of the educational level of the audience.

Message Appeals

The above review summarized some of the major conclusions regarding the structuring of messages to achieve maximum attitude change. We now turn our attention to message appeals and how they can be used to enhance the persuasiveness of messages. Message appeals are requests for audiences to respond in ways that are desired by the communicator. Several kinds of appeals used by marketers are discussed in this section.

FEAR APPEALS In some situations it seems reasonable for marketers to consider using a fear appeal in their attempts to persuade consumers. That is, fear of physical danger, social disapproval, or other consequences seem potentially useful in influencing consumers' attitudes and/or behavior toward the advertised brand. In fact, fear appeals have been employed to promote the use of various goods from toothpaste to life insurance. Figure 18-6 presents an example of an advertisement capable of evoking fear among at least some readers.

The earliest fear research by Janis and Feshbach appeared to suggest that minimal fear appeals, as opposed to moderate or strong ones, are most effective in persuading audiences.[23] One explanation is that strong fear-evoking components of a message cause consumers to set up perceptual defenses and in doing so they also reject the rest of the message. The result of these and other early findings was that most advertisers became highly reluctant to use fear appeals to promote the use of their products or services.

Several years after these initial studies were reported, other investigators began to uncover results that appeared to contradict earlier findings.[24] That is, the more recent studies suggested that higher fear appeals could actually motivate *more* attitude change than mild fear appeals. However, after a lengthy review of the research, Ray and Wilkie noted that the studies may actually not contradict each other. They argued that the various investigators had probably found difficulty in controlling the amount of fear content in their messages and this led to the apparently contradictory, but actually consistent findings.[25] The result of this argument can be summarized as follows: low fear appeals generate little motivation for attitude change, and high fear appeals also yield little attitude change because they activate defense mechanisms against feared aspects which also screen out other parts of the message. Moderate fear appeals, which provide sufficient motivation but which do not activate perceptual defenses, appear most effective in generating attitude change.

More recently others have argued that it is probably inappropriate to draw general conclusions about any given level of fear because a number of factors may influence how audiences will respond to the appeal. For example, factors that appear to influence the persuasiveness of the fear appeal include (1) source credibility; (2) audience characteristics, including the receiver's ability to cope with fear, his self-esteem, and the extent to which he perceives himself as vulnerable to the feared consequence; (3) the type of fear appeal used; and (4) the context of the message presentation.[26] It appears that a higher fear appeal is more persuasive if delivered by a highly credible source to an audience high in self-esteem and ability to cope with tension, who also perceive themselves as not highly vulnerable to the feared consequences. Some evidence also suggests that fear of social disapproval may be more effective in influencing actual behavior change than an appeal based on fear of physical harm. In addition, certain conditions in the environment which can distract attention away from a strong fear appeal can increase message persuasiveness.

Certain promotional messages appear to be making use of these more recent findings regarding fear appeals. In such cases, the technique often appears to involve the inclusion of some means that makes it more easy for the audience to deal with the fear-arousing message. These include making light of the object involved or presenting it in a humorous way to lower its perceived fearfulness. For example, it has been suggested that recent ads that show humorous incidents confronting users of long cigarettes suggest that the potentially fearful product is actually laughable and nothing to be feared (from a health standpoint).[27] In other cases, advertisements may not *directly* confront the viewer but instead use an *indirect* technique to make a third party bear the brunt of the feared consequences. This can make the message easier to accept for the viewer. An example of an advertisement

**Transamerica
Insurance:**

**Help
when you need it.**

Property and Casualty Insurance
from Transamerica Corporation
T Transamerica Insurance Group Serving over 1,000,000 policyholders. Home Office: Los Angeles, CA 90015.
Transamerica Insurance Co./ Wolverine Insurance Co./Premier Insurance Co./Riverside Insurance Co./Canadian Surety Co./Automotive Insurance Co.

FIGURE 18-6
Example of an advertisement capable of evoking fear. (Courtesy of Transamerica Insurance Group.)

using both the humor and the third-party technique is presented in Figure 18-7.

DISTRACTION Some early studies and actual promotional experiences have suggested that pleasant forms of distraction can often work to increase the effectiveness of persuasive appeals in encouraging attitude change.[28] Sales representatives often practice this principle when they take clients out to dinner. Advertisers can also use such pleasant forms of distraction as music or background activity.

The explanation for the effectiveness of distraction on attitude change has

© 1977 New England Mutual Life Insurance Company, Boston. Affiliates: NEL Equity Services Corporation (mutual funds, variable annuities); Loomis, Sayles & Company, Inc. (investment counselors).

"My insurance company? New England Life, of course. Why?"
We also offer a finely tuned selection of mutual funds, variable annuities and investment counseling.

FIGURE 18-7
Example of using humor and third-party to reduce negative effects of fear-evoking message. (Courtesy of New England Mutual Life Insurance Company.)

been that it retards *counterargumentation.* That is, when a communication is inconsistent with the receiver's present attitudes he tends to develop a counterargument upon being confronted with the message. However, distraction tends to make the receiver lose his train of thought or forget to argue against the message. This, according to the explanation, results in greater acceptance of the message.[29]

Later studies, using various forms of distraction have been unable to find that distraction increases attitude change.[30] In fact, in some cases it may actually reduce viewers' attention to the message. Therefore, evidence is still not clear regarding the effectiveness of this method of increasing attitude change and the conditions that influence it.

PARTICIPATION As discussed earlier in the text, active participation is a means of gaining attention to and enhancing the learning of a message. Similarly, active participation can increase the effectiveness of a persuasive appeal.[31] Marketers have learned the value of giving product samples to prospective customers, encouraging trial use of their products, and providing coupons for trial purchase. In addition, they often develop television advertisements that place the viewer in the position of vicariously "trying" the product by using well-developed camera angles and other production techniques that make the viewer feel a part of the commercial.

HUMOR Recently humor has seen significant use in advertisements appearing in both print and electronic media. However, between 1974 and 1976 its use actually *decreased* on prime-time television ads.[32] As this seems to suggest, advertisers as well as consumer researchers hold diverse opinions regarding the effectiveness of this message appeal. On one hand advertisers for such brands as Benson & Hedges ("oh the disadvantages—"), Alka-Seltzer ("I can't believe I ate the whole thing"), and Volkswagen have made extensive use of humor. In many other cases, however, the appeal is never given serious consideration. Opponents of the technique argue that amusing circumstances are not universal in appeal, that they wear out quickly with repetition, and that they take up too much valuable advertising time or space.

We have already noted the possible effectiveness of humor to moderate the perceived threat of fear appeals. In reviewing other, often contradictory, evidence concerning the effectiveness of humor, Sternthal and Craig included the following conclusions:

1. Humorous messages can attract attention, but they may also have a detrimental effect on message comprehension.

2. Humorous appeals appear to increase the credibility of a source and may also increase audience liking for the source as well as create a positive mood toward it.

3. Although humorous appeals appear to be persuasive, they do not seem to be more persuasive than serious appeals.[33]

These findings indicate that much more needs to be generally known about the effectiveness of humor and conditions that make its use attractive.

EMOTIONAL VERSUS RATIONAL APPEALS Should marketers use emotional or rational appeals in promoting their products? As the reader might guess, experts are also divided on this question. Neither approach has been shown to be generally superior to the other. This seems understandable because, as suggested in the motivation chapter, the effectiveness of appeals is likely to be a function of the underlying motives consumers have for considering the product.

When emotional appeals do appear to be appropriate, the following points have been offered as guidance for constructing the appeal:

1. Use emotionally charged language, especially words that have high personal meaning to the target consumers.

2. If the brand or message is unfamiliar to the audience, associate it with well-known ideas.

3. Associate the brand or message with visual or nonverbal stimuli that arouse emotions. The advertisement for Kodak films in Figure 18-8 provides an excellent example of this technique.

4. The communication should be accompanied by nonverbal cues such as hand motions which support the verbal message.[34]

Message Codes

The way in which marketers assemble and use message codes can have an impact on the persuasiveness of their messages. Three broad classes of message codes are verbal, nonverbal, and paralinguistic codes.

VERBAL CODE The verbal code is a system of word symbols that are combined according to a set of rules as in the English language. Although a variety of alternatives exist for devising verbal code structures, advertisers tend to use modifier words, such as adjectives and adverbs, to elicit favorable emotions within a consumer. For example, the same factual information is conveyed by using either of the following advertising messages, but one conveys the facts with words higher in emotion.

1. The new plastic product resembling leather will soon be available to shoe manufacturers.

2. The fabulous new plastic product which out-leathers leather will soon replace all other products used in the manufacture of superior-quality shoes.[35]

Frequently the advertiser is likely to use the second statement because it expresses the same idea with highly charged modifiers.

NONVERBAL CODE Nonverbal codes are extremely important in persuasive communication and have not been given the attention they deserve in published research. For example, a communicator's facial expressions, gestures, posture, and dress can affect how a receiver perceives a message.

Sales representatives have found the study of nonverbal communications extremely helpful in better understanding prospective customers and in meeting sales resistance. For example, they can tell when a client is bored, receptive, doubtful, critical, interested, and so forth, by observing nonverbal cues such as crossed legs, body lean, hand gestures, and mannerisms.

Advertisers also are aware of the importance of nonverbal communications in television and print advertisements, particularly ones that use models. For example, Figure 18-9 shows how facial expressions enhance the effect of the verbal message in the advertisement for Downy Fabric Softener.

I think I'll write him a love letter. Just as soon as I learn to write.

Kodak film

Kodak film. For the times of your life.

FIGURE 18-8
Example of associating a brand to emotional visual stimuli. (Courtesy of Eastman Kodak Company.)

PARALINGUISTIC CODE The paralinguistic code is one which lies between the verbal and nonverbal code. It primarily involves two components—voice qualities and vocalizations.[36]

Voice qualities refer to such speech characteristics as rhythm pattern, pitch of voice, and precision of articulation. They can communicate urgency, boredom, sarcasm, and other feelings. *Vocalizations,* on the other hand, are sounds such as yawns, sighs, and various voice intensities which reflect certain emotions.

FIGURE 18-9
Example of using facial expressions to enhance verbal message. (Courtesy of Procter & Gamble Company.)

Advertisers are very careful to select models whose tonal qualities match the product message. As an example, Janitor in a Drum television commercials use a strong, male voice (paralinguistics) to describe the powerful cleaning action of the product. In addition, other nonverbal cues are used to connote the strength of the product, such as a scene depicting a large barrel of the product being lifted by a forklift truck and set down loudly on the floor. Another case in point is the American Tourister luggage advertising. Commercials show the luggage dropped from airplanes and rammed by locomotives to reinforce the actor's statement that it can withstand great abuse. Other examples include soaps, facial creams, and shampoos that are soft and gentle. These product themes usually are described by a woman with a gentle voice, as in the case of Nuance perfume, where the spokeswoman actually whispers.

RECEIVER FACTORS

To be a persuasive communicator and an effective marketer, it is important to adopt a ''know your audience'' attitude. This section deals with personal characteristics that make some people more susceptible than others to the persuasive attempts of communicators. Some of these characteristics involve people's personality traits and currently held attitudes and beliefs. Personality traits that are correlated with persuasibility are discussed first.

Personality Traits

Behavioral research has shed light on the relationship between personality traits and persuasibility. Among these traits are self-esteem, rich imagery, and intelligence.

SELF-ESTEEM Self-esteem refers to a person's feelings of adequacy and self-worth. In general, research has suggested that people who have low self-esteem tend to be more persuasible than those with high self-esteem.[37] This generalization appears to be particularly true in situations where people are motivated by social approval. Researchers believe that the reasons for their findings are that people who feel inadequate are more persuasible; they lack confidence in their judgments and therefore tend to rely upon the opinions of others. On the other hand, people with feelings of high self-worth have confidence in their abilities to make good judgments without accepting the opinions of others.

In a marketing study concerning the persuasibility of women subjects in a personal selling situation, Cox and Bauer found that women with medium self-esteem showed the greatest opinion change, while women at the high and low ends of the self-esteem spectrum were low in their susceptibility to the persuasive sales pitch. The researchers suggested that women with low self-esteem acted in an ego-defensive manner, such as to say ''I don't need help in making up my mind,'' while those with high self-esteem behaved as had subjects in previous experiments.[38]

The apparent contradiction of the Cox and Bauer findings to previous research may be due to the broader range of self-esteem of subjects in their sample. Also, differences in experimental settings may have influenced the results. Earlier studies used social approval to motivate subjects to change opinions, whereas the Cox and Bauer study and other later studies involved subjects in problem-solving situations.[39]

RICH IMAGERY People who are high in rich imagery or live out much of their lives through dream worlds and fantasy are more persuasible than those who are not high in rich imagery. Recall from an earlier example in Chapter 5 how Schlitz learned that one significant trait of the heavy beer drinker is that he is high in rich imagery. With this information, the company developed its advertising theme, "You only go around once in life," which other companies have subsequently borrowed.

INTELLIGENCE People of both high and low intelligence are susceptible to persuasion depending upon the message approach a communicator uses. Two general principles of persuasion which emerge from behavioral research on audience intelligence are the following:

1   Persons with high intellectual ability will tend—mainly because of their ability to draw valid inferences—to be *more* influenced than those with low intelligence when exposed to persuasive communications that rely primarily on impressive logical arguments.

2. Persons with high intelligence will tend—mainly because of their superior critical ability—to be *less* influenced than those with low intelligence by unsupported generalities or false, illogical, irrelevant arguments.[40]

A person's intellectual capacity is made up of three interacting components: (1) learning ability, which is the mental capacity to acquire and recall information; (2) critical ability, which is the ability to assess the rationality of information and to accept or reject it on a logical basis; and (3) ability to draw inferences, which refers to the ability to interpret information and to use facts to make sound implications. In the first principle stated above, the relationship between intelligence and persuasibility is based upon a person's ability to draw correct inferences; in the second principle, the relationship is based upon a person's critical ability.

In marketing, audiences can be segmented according to levels of intelligence, often by inference rather than through data collection. Physicians, engineers, business leaders, and other similar occupations generally are made up of people of high intellectual ability. Specialized media are available to advertise products that are pertinent to their fields and to them personally.

Sex Differences

Regarding the persuasibility of men versus women, a consistent finding among researchers is that in our society women are more persuasible than men.[41] The difference in persuasibility is not attributable to physiological differences, but rather to the sex-typed roles played by men and women. In our society, women have historically learned submissive and dependent roles, whereas men have learned that they must be dominant and independent. Thus, it should not be surprising that research has shown that women conform to others' opinions more than men. However, it should also be noted that women tend to be more persuasible on rather minor issues and not on subjects for which they have strongly held beliefs.[42]

Although research has found consistently that women are more persuasible than men, it is important to recognize that changes in the traditional sex-typed roles in our society will probably bring about a redirection in persuasibility differences between the sexes.

Bases of Attitudes

To be successful in changing a negative consumer attitude, it is necessary to understand the basis for the attitude. There are three bases for an attitude—factual, social, and personal.

FACTUAL BASIS A negative attitude toward a brand may be based upon a consumers' lack of factual information (or a false understanding) of the benefits of the brand. This can be countered by developing an advertising campaign that facilitates consumer learning of the necessary information. For example, if homemakers' negative attitudes toward Teflon-coated cookware are based upon lack of awareness of the greaseless, no-stick features of the product, then alterations must be made in the advertising campaign to facilitate their learning about those two features.

SOCIAL BASIS Consumers may have all the necessary facts about a brand, but may believe that its use is unacceptable to their social groups. Even though the product's features may have advantages, their negative attitude is based on the lack of the brand's acceptability to friends, neighbors, and other social groups. In this case the advertiser must show the social acceptability of using the brand and how consumers' peer groups (or other relevant social groups) will approve of their using the brand. As an example, some women might object to driving a sports car because they believe their neighbors would consider them to be "swingers." In such cases an advertisement showing how the neighbors might approve of such a purchase could be effective.

PERSONAL BASIS A third basis for an attitude is one on an individual level. This attitude is closely tied to a person's self-image and the role he or she plays. To return to the sports car example, the woman may feel that a sports car just does not fit her self-image. In this situation, an advertising campaign that suggests how the consumer might realistically think of herself in this new light—and the fun that might result from owning a sports car—could be effective.

Belief Types

As indicated in Chapter 17, and in the introduction to this chapter, a person's attitude or belief structure can be an opportunity for, or an obstruction to, persuasive marketing communications.[43] The three basic belief types appear to be central beliefs, derived beliefs, and central-free beliefs. *Central beliefs* are fundamental and basic to a person's life. They form the core of a person's cognitive structure. Because they are so deeply rooted in a person's cognitive system, they are the most difficult to change. For example, consumers' beliefs regarding freedom may be fundamental to their lives. Such beliefs are extremely difficult to change, and any advertising that directly attacks them will have very little chance for success.

Derived beliefs are an outgrowth of central beliefs. For example, "Retailers should be free to charge whatever prices they feel appropriate" is a belief derived from the central belief about freedom. As the name implies, *central-free beliefs* are not based upon central beliefs. Instead, they exist separate and apart from central and derived beliefs. "I believe that Al's market is the best in town" is an example of a central-free belief.

In order of difficulty, central beliefs are the hardest to change, derived beliefs are the next most difficult, and central-free beliefs the easiest to change. Marketers should avoid attacking central beliefs and instead should see them as opportunities. That is, messages that are aligned with central beliefs are readily acceptable, since they reinforce already strongly held attitudes. Similarly, beliefs derived from more central ones may be used as a basis for an advertising theme. In this way the beliefs are not attacked, but instead are used as a means of enhancing the value of the advertised brand. The lesson to be learned is that a consumer's psychological barriers should be avoided and turned into opportunities.

SUMMARY

This chapter focused on evidence relevant to the marketing communication goal of attitude change. The many relevant variables were categorized into several groupings. The category of source factors concerns properties or characteristics of message senders. In marketing these include salespersons, companies, hired promoters, media, and other marketing sources of product and brand information. A number of characteristics of the source including credibility and similarity to the audience were discussed. It was noted that, particularly with regard to the sleeper effect of source credibility, the influence of these variables on attitude change can be complex.

Attention then turned to message factors, including message structure, order of presentation, appeals, codes, and the drawing of conclusions for an audience. Again, although general guidelines could be offered, the influence of the particular situation was stressed.

Of course, particularly significant aspects of the situation include characteristics of the audience itself. This therefore became the next topic of interest. Here the audience characteristics of personality, sex, attitude bases, and beliefs were addressed. Strategies to handle situations arising from these characteristics were suggested.

DISCUSSION TOPICS

1. Who are the major marketing communicators of a firm?

2. What major factors assist a source in being perceived as credible? Cite specific advertising examples of the use of each factor.

3. What is the sleeper effect, and what implications does it have for the communicator?

4. What recommendations would you make to a communicator regarding the following aspects of message structure: (1) message sidedness, (2) order of presentation, and (3) message code?

5. What guidelines would you offer regarding drawing a conclusion in a marketing communication? Watch a number of television advertisements and try to determine the extent to which these guidelines are being followed.

6. What guidelines can you offer regarding the effective use of message appeals? Can you point out any specific advertisements that might not be following these guidelines?

7. What receiver factors influence consumers' susceptibility to persuasion? Cite specific examples of each factor.

8. If you were going to present a speech to United States business leaders on "The Declining Quality of America's Goods and Services," what guidelines could you employ from this chapter?

9. Design a specific advertisement for an actual product using material you have learned from this chapter.

NOTES

1. E. P. Bettinghaus, *Persuasive Communication,* 2d ed., Holt, New York, 1973, p. 10.

2. One might validly suggest that channel factors should be included in this list. However, for purposes of this chapter channel effects are included within the source, since consumers frequently view a medium as a source of information and influence.

3. See for example A. Eagly and S. Chaiken, "An Attribution Analysis of the Effect of Communicator Characteristics on Opinion Change: The Case of Communicator Attractiveness," *Journal of Personality and Social Psychology,* **32**:136–144, 1975; and Homer Johnson and Richard Izzett, "The Effects of Source Identification on Attitude Change as a Function of the Type of Communication," *Journal of Social Psychology,* **86**:81–87, 1972.

4. Ruby Roy Dholakia and Brian Sternthal, "Highly Credible Sources: Persuasive Facilitators or Persuasive Liabilities?" *Journal of Consumer Research,* **3**:223–232, March 1977.

5. For a more complete discussion see Bettinghaus, *Persuasive Communication,* p. 104.

6. See for example E. Aronson and B. Golden, "The Effect of Relevant and Irrelevant Aspects of Communicator Credibility on Opinion Change," *Journal of Personality,* **30**:135–146, 1962; also see Peter Bennett and Harold Kassarjian, *Consumer Behavior,* Prentice-Hall, Englewood Cliffs, N.J., 1972, p. 89.

7. For elaboration on the importance of nonverbal cues, see G. I. Nierenberg and H. H. Calero, *How to Read a Person like a Book,* Hawthorne, New York, 1971.

8. See for example Paul Friggens, "Pyramid Selling—No. 1 Consumer Fraud," *Reader's Digest,* March 1974, pp. 79–83.

9. See Carl Hovland and Walter Weiss, "The Influence of Source Credibility on Communication Effectiveness," *Public Opinion Quarterly,* **15**:635–650, 1951–1952; Herbert Kelman and Carl Hovland, " 'Reinstatement' of the Communicator in Delayed Measurement of Opinion Change," *Journal of Abnormal and Social Psychology,* **48**:327–335, 1953; and Carl Hovland, Arthur A. Lunsdaine, and Fred D. Sheffield, *Experiments on Mass Communications,* Princeton, Princeton, N.J., 1949, pp. 188–189.

10. M. Wayne DeLozier, *The Marketing Communications Process,* McGraw-Hill, New York, 1976, p. 77.

11. Kelman and Hovland, "Reinstatement of the Communicator."

12. M. Karlins and H. I. Abelson, *Persuasion,* 2d ed., Springer, New York, 1970, p. 128.

13. David K. Berlo, *The Process of Communications,* Holt, San Francisco, 1960, pp. 45–48.

14. Arch G. Woodside and J. William Davenport, "The Effect of Salesman Similarity and Expertise on Consumer Purchasing Behavior," *Journal of Marketing Research,* **11**:198–202, May 1974.

15. Theodore Levitt, "Communications and Industrial Selling," *Journal of Marketing,* **31**:15–21, April 1967.

16. Arthur Bellaire, "Bellaire Survey III Finds Music and Demo Up; Humor, Animation Decline in TV Ads," *Advertising Age,* January 3, 1977, pp. 17–18.

17. E. W. J. Faison, "Effectiveness of One-Sided and Two-Sided Mass Communications in Advertising," *Public Opinion Quarterly,* **25**:468–469, 1961.

18. DeLozier, *Marketing Communications,* p. 95.

19. C. I. Hovland, I. L. Janis, and H. H. Kelley, *Communication and Persuasion,* Yale, New Haven, Conn., 1953, p. 119.

20. R. L. Rosnow and E. J. Robinson (eds.), *Experiments in Persuasion,* Academic, New York, 1967, p. 101.

21. Hovland, Janis, and Kelley, *Communication and Persuasion,* pp. 103–105.

22. D. L. Thistlethwaite, H. de Haan, and J. Kamenetzky, "The Effects of 'Directive' and 'Nondirective' Communication Procedures on Attitudes," *Journal of Abnormal and Social Psychology,* **51**:107–113, 1955.

23. I. Janis and S. Feshbach, "Effects of Fear Arousing Communications," *Journal of Abnormal and Social Psychology,* **48**:78–92, 1953.

24. See L. Berkowitz and D. R. Cottingham, "The Interest Value and Relevance of Fear-Arousing Communication," *Journal of Abnormal and Social Psychology,* **60**:37–43, 1960; A. S. DeWolf and C. N. Governale, "Fear and Attitude Change," *Journal of Abnormal and Social Psychology,* **69**:119–123, 1964; H. Leventhal, R. P. Singer, and S. Jones, "Effects of Fear and Specificity of Recommendation upon Attitudes and Behavior," *Journal of Personality and Social Psychology,* **2**:20–29, 1965; and C. A. Insko, A. Arkoff, and V. M. Insko, "Effects of High and Low Fear-Arousing Communications upon Opinions toward Smoking," *Journal of Experimental Social Psychology,* **1**:254–266, August 1965.

25. Michael L. Ray and William L. Wilkie, "Fear: The Potential of an Appeal Neglected by Marketing," *Journal of Marketing,* **34**:54–62, January 1970.

26. Brian Sternthal and C. Samuel Craig, "Fear Appeals: Revisited and Revised," *Journal of Consumer Research,* **1**:22–34, December 1974.

27. John R. Stuteville, "Psychic Defenses against High Fear Appeals: A Key Marketing Variable," *Journal of Marketing,* **34**:39–45, April 1970.

28. M. Karlins and H. I. Abelson, *Persuasion,* 2d ed., Springer, New York, 1970, p. 15.

29. J. Allyn and L. Festinger, "The Effectiveness of Unanticipated Persuasive Communications," *Journal of Abnormal and Social Psychology,* **62**:35–40, 1961.

30. See Stewart W. Bither, "Effects of Distraction and Commitment on the Persuasiveness of Television Advertising," *Journal of Marketing Research,* **9**:1–5, February 1972.

31. See Hovland, Janis, and Kelley, *Communication and Persuasion,* pp. 228–237; also see W. Watts, "Relative Persistence of Opinion Change Induced by Active Compared to Passive Participation," *Journal of Personality and Social Psychology,* **5**:4–15, 1967.

32. Bellaire, "Bellaire Survey III," p. 17.

33. Brian Sternthal and C. Samuel Craig, "Humor in Advertising," *Journal of Marketing,* **37**:12–18, October 1973.

34. Bettinghaus, *Persuasive Communication,* pp. 160–161.

35. Bettinghaus, *Persuasive Communication,* pp. 152–153.

36. Bettinghaus, *Persuasive Communication,* pp. 121–122, in reference to G. L. Trager, "Paralanguage: A First Approximation," *Studies in Linguistics,* **13**:1–12, 1958.

37. See I. L. Janis, "Personality Correlates of Susceptibility to Persuasion," *Journal of Personality,* **22**:504–518, 1954; F. J. Divesta and J. C. Merivan, "The Effects of Need-Oriented Communications on Attitude Change," *Journal of Abnormal and Social Psychology,* **60**:80–85, 1960; and I. L. Janis and P. B. Field, "Sex Differences and Personality Factors Related to Persuasibility," in I. L. Janis and C. I. Hovland (eds.), *Personality and Persuasibility,* Yale, New Haven, Conn., 1959, pp. 55–68.

38. D. F. Cox and R. A. Bauer, "Self Confidence and Persuasibility in Women," *Public Opinion Quarterly,* **28**:453–466, Fall 1964.

39. R. A. Bauer, "Games People and Audiences Play," paper presented at Seminar on Communications in Contemporary Society, University of Texas, March 17, 1967.

40. Hovland, Janis, and Kelley, *Communication and Persuasion,* p. 183.

41. See T. Scheidel, "Sex and Persuasibility," *Speech Monographs,* **30**:353–358, 1963; H. Reitan and M. Shaw, "Group Membership, Sex-Composition of the Group, and Conformity Behavior," *Journal of Social Psychology,* **64**:45–51, 1964; J. Whitaker, "Sex Differences and Susceptibility to Interpersonal Persuasion," *Journal of Social Psychology,* **66**:91–94, 1965; and W. Carrigan and J. Julian, "Sex and Birth—Order Differences in Conformity as a Function of Need Affiliation Arousal," *Journal of Personality and Social Psychology,* **3**:479–483, 1963.

42. See D. Carment, "Participation and Opinion-Change as a Function of the Sex of the Members of Two-Person Groups," *Acta Psychologica,* **28**:84–91, 1968.

43. This discussion is based in part upon Bettinghaus, *Persuasive Communication,* pp. 59–61.

CASES

CASE 4-1   JIM'S BIKE SHOP

Jim Nessen owns and operates the only local motorcycle shop in a college town in Louisiana. In addition to the permanent population of 35,000 residents, college students add another 18,000 inhabitants. This often results in overcrowded roads and messy traffic conditions during busy hours of the day.

This situation began to make Jim realize that a market potential for mopeds might exist. A moped is a motorized bicycle that has been used for years in European countries and in many resort areas. It is very light in weight and is "powered" by a one-cylinder engine capable of generating a top speed of from 17 to 30 miles per hour on level roadway. Often this lack of power requires the driver to pedal to augment the engine. Recent legislation in the United States has been very favorable toward mopeds. In many places helmets, licenses, and insurance are not required for the operation of the slower models.

Jim's recent trip to Bermuda has sold him on the moped concept. The one he rented there got over 150 miles per gallon and he heard of others yielding 200 miles per gallon. In addition, he easily moved through congested traffic conditions and found the machine a "barrel of fun." A number of people he has talked to also gave the same reactions. One 47-year-old lady told him that "It's the most fun I've had since I tried downhill skiing." Further checking revealed that he could obtain the exclusive franchise for a popular brand which would retail between $300 and $600, depending on the model. Before committing himself Jim wants to consider his position and how he might be able to develop potential product appeals.

Questions

1. Can you suggest the motives that might influence a purchase in this situation?

2. How would you categorize these motives? Can they be appealed to at the same time, or must choices be made?

3. What factors other than motives might potentially influence such a purchase?

CASE 4-2 FISH-KING, INC.

Management of the Fish-King Company, producer of a line of small boats, has recently been considering entry into the bass-boat market. The basic construction of such a boat is a low-sided, sleek-looking, flat-bottomed hull having a 115-horsepower engine as the main power supply.

Able to seat only two people, the craft is crammed with sophisticated equipment to assist the angler in hooking his prey—freshwater bass. The powerful engine allows quick travel time (over 50 mph) for covering large lakes. A second, small electric motor is perfectly suited for quiet trolling. Two padded chairs are mounted on pedestals to allow easy casting and a good fighting position for the angler. The boat also has a water temperature gauge and sonar to help locate the prey, carpeting for comfort, and aerated holding tanks to keep any caught bass alive. A highly-sophisticated-looking master control panel is included, and a host of more specialized and expensive options are also available.

The cost of such a boat, which is uniquely designed for the bass fisherman, averages between $5000 and $8000. However, some sell for more than $11,000. Sales records indicate that many anglers are apparently willing to make such a purchase even if it entails spending up to a half a year's pay.

Mr. Miles, marketing director for Fish-King, is still somewhat skeptical about the venture. He knows that the boats are now highly popular and even have become a prestige item among some anglers. He is also aware that the industry currently has several competitors. In summing up his feelings he said, "I'm not sure what motivates fishermen to spend so much for such a specialized craft with basically one function. This knowledge could really help us define the market, determine whether we should enter it, and if so, help us to develop appeals to reach this group of fishermen."

Questions

1. Can you offer any suggestions as to possible motivational influences on the purchase of bass boats?

2. Can you make suggestions as to how these influences may be capitalized on by Fish-King in designing and promoting a bass boat?

CASE 4-3 STANTON CHEMICAL COMPANY[1]

Stanton Chemical Company produces Clo-White, a liquid laundry bleach, and distributes it on a regional basis. The company was founded in 1950 by its current president, Robert M. Stanton. From a modest beginning, the company has grown in size until it now has annual sales of over $6 million out of an estimated total industry sales in 1975 of $130 million. Stanton Chemical has its headquarters in a large southern city and operates several mixing and bottling plants in the Southeast.

The manufacture of bleach is simple, since it is merely sodium hypochlorite and water mixed together in a solution. All of the bleaches on the market contain 5.25 percent sodium hypochlorite and 94.75 percent inert ingredients (water), but bleach produced in this manner is subject to an "aging" problem. When first produced, laundry bleach has no odor and is at its highest potency level. However, once it has been on the shelf for a length of time (5 to 8 days), the solution begins to break down chemically. The chlorine in the mixture is given off as a gas; hence, the strong smell that certain bleaches exhibit. When a bleach breaks down in this manner, it loses some of its potential for whitening and stain removal, but smells "stronger" to the consumer.

Stanton has developed the capability to deliver its bleach quicker and more consistently than any of its competitors by locating mixing and bottling plants close to its markets. This quick, efficient delivery results in Clo-White's being able to outperform competing bleaches in stain removal power and whitening ability.

Despite the availability of detergents with bleach additives, homemakers still look to the chlorine-based laundry bleach as the means to remove stains and whiten clothes. Independent research studies suggest that the woman's attitude toward domestic activities and the degree of family orientation are primary determinants in brand selection. Women who possess a strong domestic orientation are more likely to perceive real or imagined differences in the quality of various bleaches, while women who possess weaker orientations will tend to rate all brands equal in quality and will prefer to shop for the lowest-priced brands.

CURRENT PROBLEM

Top management has expressed concern over the ability of Snowy-White, a regional competitor, to outsell Clo-White, particularly since price and promotional expenditures for both products are approximately equal. To find a remedy for the situation, Mr. Pearl, vice president of marketing, recommended that research be conducted to determine what consumers actually thought of Clo-White compared with other brands and, if possible, some reasons for the particular brand image.

A sample of 1000 homemakers was selected at random from several large southern cities where Clo-White enjoyed a large market share. They were asked to rank pairs of leading regional brands in terms of their perceived similarity, then to rank the brands according to their own individual preferences. Finally, respondents were asked to give reasons why they ranked the bleaches in that particular order. The data were analyzed by a multidimensional routine and are displayed as a perceptual map in Figure 1. The labeled axes represent the two main dimensions on which brands of bleach appear to have been evaluated. Consumers' perception of the ideal bleach is also indicated. Some of the typical comments received from respondents were:

"All the bleaches are the same. I just buy the cheapest one."

"There's not much difference in price, so I usually buy the stronger bleach. It gets my clothes cleaner and that's what I want."

"Well, you can take the cap off this one (Snowy-White), and smell the bleach."

"The other brands just don't have that kind of smell. I always buy the stronger bleach to get my clothes cleaner."

Composite brand ranking:

1. Snowy-White

2. Blue Sky

3. Clo-White

4. Dixie Day

5. Miracle-White

6. Quality

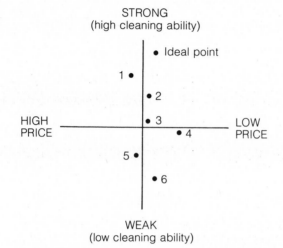

FIGURE 1
Relative brand-
image position.

Pearl feels that what most consumers want is the strongest bleach on the market and that they are willing to pay at least the competitive price for it. Thus, he feels that Stanton should mount an advertising campaign that "educates" the consumer about the superiority of Clo-White over its competitors. "Tell them the research results and tell them that smell doesn't make any difference. We must maintain our quality."

Mr. Lawrence, brand manager for Clo-White, feels that the research results indicate the importance consumers attach to smell as an indicator of strength. "Telling them that Clo-White is the strongest bleach won't convince them once they take the cap off and smell it. They just won't believe that kind of advertising." He believes that Stanton must allow its bleach to "age" to develop a stronger smell. "Most consumers go by the smell. Let's give them what they want." Lawrence's plan is to introduce "Clo-White Plus" and advertise it as a new and stronger bleach. "Shoot, we won't be lying to them; it will have a stronger smell and that's what they want. Gentlemen, we're dealing with consumer perceptions. How do you think Snowy-White got ahead of us?"

[1]Adapted from the original case by Daniel L. Sherrell appearing in M. Wayne DeLozier (ed.), *Consumer Behavior Dynamics: A Casebook,* Merrill, Columbus, Oh., 1977. Used with permission of the author and Charles E. Merrill Publishing Company.

Questions

1. What other alternatives might Stanton Chemical consider?

2. What would be the short- versus long-run effects of each strategy?

3. How important is olfactory perception in the consumer's evaluation of bleach and other similar products? How easy (difficult) would it be for a company to "educate" consumers about product characteristics that are contradictory to their own perceptions of the product?

4. Is Mr. Lawrence's suggestion unethical, or is he right in giving consumers what they "want"?

CASE 4-4 PILGRIM DEPARTMENT STORE

The Pilgrim Department Store was founded in a large eastern city in 1920. After the Depression, the company prospered, expanded, and took occupancy of a six-story granite structure in the heart of the downtown area.

Recent history has seen the rapid growth of suburban areas away from the central city and their attraction for the middle- to upper-income classes. The out-migration of these groups has left the urban area predominantly populated by lower-income families, many of whom are from minority ethnic groups. Recognizing these trends, and noticing a steady decline in sales of their downtown store, management of Pilgrim realized the potential attractiveness of providing their services to suburban shoppers. Therefore when a new shopping center opened in a major suburban area, Pilgrim became an anchor store in the mall with a large, contemporary, two-story structure. The downtown location still serves as the main headquarters for both stores. Major business functions, purchasing, and promotion all are still conducted from the main store. This arrangement was justified not only on the basis of operating efficiency but also on the need for maintaining a consistent and traditional image based on the store's long-time membership in the community. In addition to the centralized buying and merchandising activities, salespeople for both stores are trained by veteran members of the urban stores' staff. Emphasis has always been on being professional and acting "proper" with the customers.

Four years have passed since the opening of the mall store; and despite the high hopes of management, its sales growth has been disappointingly slow. In addition, sales in the city store have continued to slide. Clothing sales have been especially poor. With this information in hand, management sought the assistance of a retail consultant. The first step taken by the consultant was a study of the shopper profiles of the two stores. The major findings were that although the city store still attracted some long-time loyal shoppers who were older and had very high incomes, the vast majority of its clientele were lower-income city dwellers. Although these shoppers were fashion-conscious, their tastes were strongly oriented toward modern, informal fashions. In addition, they were highly value-oriented in terms of evaluating satisfaction for price paid. On the other hand, patrons of the suburban store were primarily middle- to upper-middle-income shoppers. They were also fashion-conscious but their tastes were directed toward much more sophisticated fashions. Additionally, they seemed to be considerably less value-oriented than city shoppers.

With this knowledge in mind, management sought to determine the image of each store as viewed by a sample of typical customers. Although many measures were used, the profiles of responses to nine important measures, as presented in Figure 1, are particularly relevant.

Questions

1. Discuss the results of the image profiles. What tentative conclusions can you draw from them and the background information presented in the case?

2. What additional information would be helpful to you in drawing your conclusions or recommending action?

3. What action, if any, might you be willing to suggest, based on available

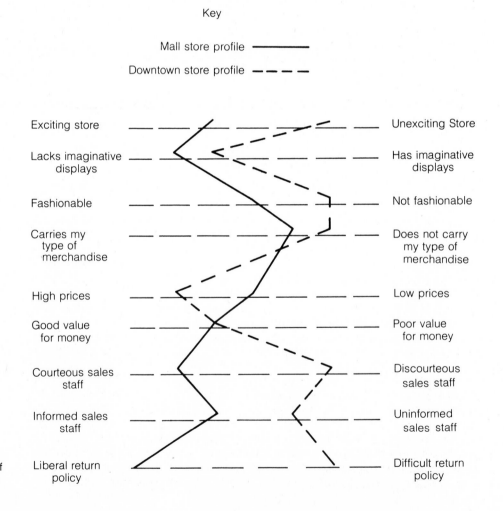

FIGURE 1
Image profiles of two stores.

information? Are there any potential dangers or limitations to your recommendations?

CASE 4-5 HOME-COMP

Home-Comp is a manufacturer of a relatively inexpensive line of computers designed for use in the home. The company was founded in 1975 by John Hanson and Biff Loftin, who were former classmates in a graduate electrical engineering program. With backing from several wealthy investors, they established a high technology manufacturing facility.

Their products belonged to a new generation of computers called microcomputers because they made use of the new microprocessor technology. This technology makes the small Home-Comp unit comparable to the huge "state of the art" machines of the late 1950s in terms of computing power and speed. In addition, the company has included several other advanced concepts in computer technology. Although these features require more user sophistication, they also yield a cost and computation advantage when compared to the competition.

Home-Comp's new products span a rather broad range and include kit packages for home assembly. Their basic unit sells for $350 in kit form and $750 fully assembled. The company's optional accessories and compatible components range from "floppy disc" memory units to videogame controls and telephone interface devices.

The preassembled Home-Comp unit is ready to use when unpacked and plugged into a TV set, which serves as a display screen. It is no larger than a typewriter and is very sleekly designed. Its uses range from storing vast amounts of information and quickly preparing taxes to regulating the function of many appliances and serving as a teaching machine for children. Predictions are that the household of tomorrow will be highly dependent on the computer.

At the start of their venture, Hanson and Loftin were very optimistic. Industry sources estimated that well over 30,000 units had already been purchased by individuals and over 300 retail outlets were available nationwide. Other evidences of consumer interest were the formation of about 150 computer clubs and a number of computer magazines. By 1979, however, after 2 years of market exposure, Home-Comp was far from achieving break-even volume. Although the company achieved wide retail distribution, retail sales had been quite disappointing.

At a meeting with their financial backers to assess the situation, Loftin and Hanson noted that they were quite perplexed by the firm's experience. Their machines were relatively sophisticated and less expensive than competitive units. Yet, they seemed to meet consumer resistance for some unknown reason.

James Irvine, a prime financial backer, felt that the problem arose because they were marketing a technical, high-learning product. He noted an industry estimate that the market of really knowledgeable "computer buffs" had been considerably saturated and most future sales would come from less sophisticated buyers. He noted another industry estimate that about one-half of the computers sold in kit form never got fully assembled. His strong suggestion was to carefully design a marketing strategy to conquer such an environment: "Your technical know-how has basically solved production problems, but you really have no marketing strategy to deal with consumers' reactions to a high-learning product. If you don't handle this problem, we'll probably all lose our shirts."

Questions

1. What do you think Mr. Irvine means by a "high-learning product," and why does Home-Comp seem to face this situation?

2. In what ways might your knowledge of the learning process be used to assist Home-Comp's managers in reducing consumer resistance to its product and stimulating sales?

CASE 4-6   LIONEL ELECTRONICS, INC.[1]

With the boom in citizen band (CB) radios, Lionel Electronics had increased sales from approximately $1 million in 1970 to nearly $24 million by 1975. Sales for 1976 were expected to total $67 million.

The company had achieved national distribution of its products, primarily in the CB line, but Frank Putnam, vice president of marketing, was concerned over competition in the expanding CB market as well as the long-term sales potential of this line. Putnam began to feel that Lionel must develop new products for new markets, not only to grow but also to weather the entry of competition from such powerful companies as RCA, GE, and Westinghouse.

Because Lionel had developed a strong reputation for superior, high-quality electronics, Putnam began to explore the possibilities of developing products that present Lionel customers might purchase. Since 85 percent of Lionel's business came from CB sales, he decided to survey the personality traits of CB owners to determine how they differ from nonowners. The idea to study personalities arose from his conversations with dealers who believed CB purchasers were interested in gadgetry and tended to be extroverted and outdoor types. Putnam believed that if he could identify the CB personality that he would know into which product lines to expand and also how to promote them.

Putnam hired ICON Associates, a market research firm specializing in the study of consumers' personalities, to determine whether CB owners had different personality traits from those not interested in purchasing a CB. Furthermore, ICON was commissioned to ascertain whether CB owners differed significantly in the kinds of products they were or might be interested in purchasing.

Personal interviews were conducted by ICON in five major cities and eight rural areas to collect data that would answer some of Lionel's questions. The following report was submitted:

"Our research into the personality characteristics of CB owners and potential owners (potential owners defined as those showing a strong interest in purchasing a CB within the next 12 months) versus nonowners reveals the following:

1. CB owners are very extroverted, where nonowners tend to be slightly introverted.

2. Those who own CBs tend to be highly achievement-oriented. Nonowners were significantly less achievement-oriented.

3. There were no significant differences in authoritarianism, dogmatism, responsibility, and detachment between owners and nonowners.

4. Although there were no apparent differences between owners and nonowners along the aggressiveness dimension, a follow-up, in-depth study revealed that owners desired to be more aggressive than they were and that nonowners were or wished to be.

5. CB owners tended to be more competitive than nonowners.

6. CB owners were significantly more risk-averse than nonowners.

7. CB owners were much more conservative than nonowners of CBs.

8. Along the dimension of persuasibility, CB owners were found to be more persuasible on issues of security, family, national issues, and business practices, but less persuasible on dress fashions and social change.

9. Although less sociable in large groups, CB owners tended to desire close relationships with a few people and to socialize in small groups.

10. Other results of the test showed a strong desire for dominance, great self-control, and a fascination with gadgetry among CB owners. Moreover, CB owners showed a strong desire for acceptance and approval seeking. CB owners exhibit a need for independence, yet show strong signs of dependence on others. They are very sympathetic, yet intolerant of others' imperfections."

---

[1]Adapted from the original case, copyright © 1976 by M. Wayne DeLozier, which also appears in M. Wayne DeLozier (ed.), *Consumer Behavior Dynamics: A Casebook*, Merrill, Columbus, Oh., 1977. Used with permission of the author.

Questions

1. Based upon the personality traits of CB owners and potential owners described in the case, what product-line extension alternatives would you recommend to Frank Putnam? Upon what do you base your recommendations? Which would you choose and why?

2. In what way would you promote Lionel CBs to potential CB owners? How would you promote your proposed product line(s) to present and potential CB owners?

3. What other product purchase decisions might be associated with CB owner personalities? Defend.

4. Are there any implications for product modifications for CB owners?

CASE 4-7 COMMUNITY-BASED FAMILY PLANNING[1]

In the United States "liberated" women are giving them to their husbands by the boxful. Condoms have also been advertised on television and are even being openly displayed on druggists' counters as opposed to their under-the-counter status of a few years ago. Many of these changes have coincided with the feminist movement and worries about the safety of other forms of birth-control devices, as well as a more open attitude toward venereal disease. However, in straitlaced Thailand, which faces a popualtion explosion, their use (along with other birth-control devices) has been met with conservative resistance.

Recently, however, family planning in Thailand has come under the influence of Mechai Viravaidya, head of a nonprofit organization dedicated to reducing the birthrate in his area of the world. Mechai's methods of accomplishing his goal are what many would consider unique. Consider, for example, his tactic when approaching large village crowds. Shouting "Balloons for everyone!" he hands out multihued condoms and encourages contestants to see who can inflate the largest "balloon." He constantly dispenses free condoms to everyone—from diplomats to farmers. In fact, his business card is a brightly colored condom attached to a mail-order form.

Mechai's influence does not stop here. He has managed to get birth-control mottos placed on soccer team jerseys. His witty family-planning sayings are also available on a nightly radio show, T-shirts, and bikini panties, where they draw considerable attention. In addition, Mechai has a cadre of approximately 5000 rice farmers, village elders, and others, who act as regional distributors of condoms, other contraceptive devices, and family planning information for remote regions of the country. It has even gotten to the point where bus fares can be paid for with—you guessed it.

[1]Adapted from "Family Planning Can Be Fun," *Forbes*, **116**:68, October 15, 1975; and Linda Matthews, "What Makes Mechai Run, or How to Curb Births of a Nation." *The Wall Street Journal*, September 15, 1976, pp. 1, 35.

Questions

1. Is there a method behind Mechai's madness? Evaluate his approach.

2. Suggest additional and/or alternative methods Mechai could effectively employ to accomplish his ends. Would your suggestions change if Mechai wished to institute a similar campaign in the United States?

CASE 4-8 FOOD FOR THOUGHT

At one time potatoes were thought to be poisonous. In colonial times lobsters were considered unclean and unfit for human consumption. Any that were caught by fishermen were thrown to the pigs. Now researchers and others concerned with the world food problem are attempting to change many long-held beliefs and attitudes toward certain underutilized food sources. For example, squid, octopus, eels, and what were formerly considered trash fish are now being viewed as potential sources of food for the general public.

The saltwater mussel is also being eyed by researchers and private enterpreneurs as an unexploited food source. These blue-black shelled creatures cling to rocks, piers, and other saltwater habitats by the millions. They are highly nutritious—having a protein content equivalent to steak, with many more carbohydrates and vitamins, while containing only 25 percent as many calories and a fraction of its fat. Also, they can be grown under controlled conditions to yield much more meat per cultivated area than beef.

Despite these advantages, Americans have never sought the mussel in great numbers. Some think they are poisonous, others don't like their looks, and many have been "turned-off" by the grit and sometime pearl that wild mussels contain. However, when mussels are cultured, these problems with grit and pearls are eliminated.

Many Europeans relish mussels. Spain, France, and the Netherlands alone harvest about 370,000 tons of the cultured variety. Famous recipes involve steaming them, frying them, or cooking them in rich wine sauces. However, the general American attitude toward mussels is not favorable. This presently prevents this rich food source from being exploited.

Questions

1. Can you suggest the reasons or sources for United States consumers' attitudes toward mussels?

2. How strongly held do you think these attitudes are? Why?

3. What suggestions would you give a government agency seeking means to change United States consumers' negative attitudes toward mussels as a food source? Defend your suggestions.

CONSUMER DECISION PROCESSES

19. PROBLEM RECOGNITION 20. INFORMATION SEARCH AND EVALUATION 21. PURCHASING PROCESSES 22. POSTPURCHASE BEHAVIOR

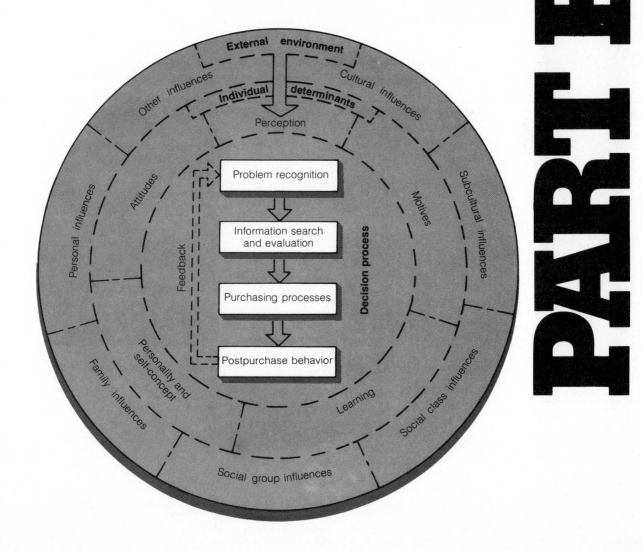

PART FIVE

PROBLEM RECOGNITION

TYPES OF CONSUMER DECISIONS   INTRODUCTION TO THE CONSUMER DECISION-PROCESS MODEL   PROBLEM RECOGNITION   Situations Leading to Problem Recognition; Results of Problem Recognition   MARKETING IMPLICATIONS OF PROBLEM RECOGNITION   Measurement of Problem Recognition; Utilizing Problem-Recognition Information

I n this chapter we shall examine the types of consumer decisions which are possible and shall see that these may range from very simple to quite complicated processes. Next, the basic model of steps involved in consumer decision making will be highlighted to set the stage for the remainder of this section. The bulk of this chapter will then discuss the nature of problem recognition, its determinants, and implications of this particular consumer decision stage to marketers.

TYPES OF CONSUMER DECISIONS

There are a myriad of decision options possible for the consumer in today's market economy. These options, however, may be distilled into five main types of decisions: (1) what to buy, (2) how much to buy, (3) where to buy, (4) when to buy, and (5) how to buy.

Deciding *what* to buy is one of the consumer's most basic tasks. No buying activity may take place unless this fundamental decision is made. A consumer's product or service decision may encompass not only the generic category of products desired, such as appliances, but more specifically, the narrower range of items, such as kitchen appliances. Consumers must even make decisions on brands, prices, and product features. For example, a homemaker may decide to purchase an Amana Radarange 675-watt microwave oven, Model RR-7, with digital controls, featuring timed self-defrost and automatic browning, for a price of $529. This is a specific decision as to what will be purchased, and with this particular decision finalized the consumer moves closer to completion of the overall purchase-decision process.

A second basic decision by the consumer relates to *how much* of the item will be purchased. For example, when shopping for groceries the consumer must determine whether three cans of Libby's green beans will be bought or perhaps a greater supply purchased.

Another determination to be reached by the consumer involves *where* he will purchase the selected product or service. This is a very important decision, which interacts thoroughly with the previous decision on what to buy. Two products, although physically the same, are likely to be perceived differently because of other facets associated with them. For example, consider an air conditioner sold with delivery, installation, and in-home servicing guaranteed by a full-service department store compared with the same model priced lower but sold on a no-frill basis, with none of the above services. Consumers clearly are likely to perceive these same air conditioners in quite different ways, based on the nature of the prices and services attached.

Consequently, what one purchases is closely related to decisions of where one decides to purchase. Not all sales outlets are alike, and consumers have many options concerning location (such as downtown or suburban stores), services offered (discount or full-service), merchandise lines (full versus narrow), prices (high versus low), and so on. Consumers must decide not only on the general type of store to purchase from but also determine the particular outlet. In fact, buyers may decide not to even visit a store, but to purchase from a catalog instead.

The consumer must also determine *when* to buy. Such a decision is influenced by such factors as urgency of the need and availability of the chosen item. Other elements such as store opening times, periods of sales and clearances, availability of transportation, and freedom of family members to shop all have a bearing on when one purchases.

Finally, the decision of *how* to buy is another complex issue. Many factors influence how the consumer buys. To indicate merely a few of the elements involved, consider some of the alternative strategies consumers use: shop extensively or buy from the first outlet, pay cash or charge it, have it delivered or take it home.

Numerous purchasing patterns occur in the marketplace with each consumer relying on whatever strategy seems to work well for himself. The problems that consumers must solve, however, could benefit from the cold logic of a computer rather than the "hit or miss" decision approach taken by some consumers. The next section outlines the general purchase-decision process followed by consumers.

INTRODUCTION TO THE CONSUMER DECISION-PROCESS MODEL

Consumer decision processes vary considerably in their complexity. Most of the decisions consumers are required to make are probably rather simple ones such as the purchase of staple foods (although a disadvantaged consumer might argue persuasively that merely buying food is difficult when one is functionally illiterate). However, consumers also must make decisions that are comparatively complicated, such as when buying durable goods. The range of difficulty of consumer decision processes extends even further to problem solving that may be characterized as being highly complex, such as might well typify the consumer's purchase of a very expensive item like a home.

The examples of consumer decision making cited above may be generalized toward a typical consumer problem-solving model consisting of four basic types of activities in the process of purchasing. The consumer's four steps are: (1) problem recognition, (2) information search and evaluation, (3) purchase decision, and (4) postpurchase behavior.[1] These activities are diagramed in Figure 19-1. In the remainder of this chapter the first stage in this problem-solving model, which is shown unshaded in Figure 19-1, will be further examined. The other processes will be discussed in detail in the following chapters.

PROBLEM RECOGNITION

Problem recognition results when a consumer recognizes a difference of sufficient magnitude between what is perceived as the desired state of affairs and what is perceived as the actual state of affairs.[2] As a consequence, the consumer becomes motivated to achieve the desired state. For example, an individual may have acid indigestion (actual state) and want relief (desired state). The result may be a motivation to visit a drugstore, purchase Pepto-Bismol, and use it in the recommended dosage.

Situations Leading to Problem Recognition

There are numerous situations that may cause consumer problem recognition to occur. Although discussion of all of the potential sources is impossible, we can present the most significant reasons and explain briefly how each one might arise.

DEPLETED OR INADEQUATE STOCK OF GOODS These are probably the most frequent reasons for consumers recognizing problems. In the first situation, the consumer uses up the assortment of goods she has and must repurchase in order to resupply her needs. As long as there still is a basic need for the item, problem recognition should result from its consumption.

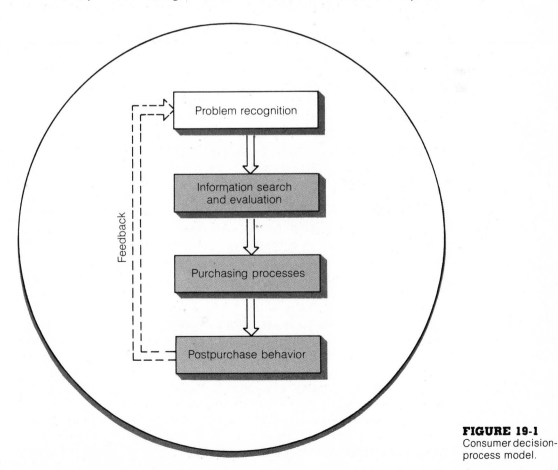

FIGURE 19-1
Consumer decision-process model.

The most obvious purchasing situations which result from this are caused by consumers running out of groceries, gasoline, health and grooming aids, and other similar convenience goods.

Sometimes the consumer's stock of goods is inadequate for even her everyday needs and may require a purchase. For instance, she may want to install a bracket for a hanging planter but finds that she doesn't have the necessary tools such as ruler, drill, and screwdriver.

DISCONTENTMENT WITH THE STOCK OF GOODS Frequently consumers become discontented with products they own and this leads to problem recognition. For example, men's ties and jacket lapels narrow and widen as fashion cycles progress. Consequently, men may feel their clothing is no longer stylish, and desire to update their wardrobes. Even though the old clothes might be perfectly serviceable, they may be an embarrassment to wear. As a result, this problem is resolved by purchasing some of the latest fashions.

The consumer's dissatisfaction with her present assortment of goods can also arise as the result of other decisions. For instance, consider the case of a family that remodels their 20-year-old home. After the work is completed and the house looks new again, then comes the letdown and dissatisfaction of having to move all the family's old hand-me-down furniture into the newly decorated rooms. The result of this problem recognition may be the purchase of new furniture to go with the remodeled house.

Finally, discontentment may lead the consumer simply to search for something new and different, to break out of a rut. Problem recognition in this case is really founded on a desire to do something novel for a change. One research study on new-product adoption has shown, for example, that one-third of those switching to a new brand did so simply because they desired a change, not because they were dissatisfied with their present brand.[3]

CHANGING ENVIRONMENTAL CIRCUMSTANCES Consumers sometimes encounter changes in their environmental circumstances which lead to problem recognition. One of the most significant of these situations is the family's changing characteristics. As we learned in earlier chapters, different life-cycle stages produce needs for different products. Consequently, as the family evolves, new problems are continually being recognized which result in different assortments of goods over time.

Another important force in the consumer's environment which leads to problem recognition is the influence of reference groups. As we identify with different reference groups, their standards are likely to influence our consumption patterns. For example, the code of dress among a college student's fraternity or sorority group may cause that student to recognize a problem with his or her current wardrobe. Several items of new clothing may be purchased so that the person fits in with this reference group.

CHANGING FINANCIAL CIRCUMSTANCES The financial status of the consumer has a very important relationship to problem recognition. The present or anticipated financial picture may trigger problem recognition as the consumer determines what purchases can be afforded. A consumer, for example, who inherits $50,000, or receives a $2000 salary increase, or receives an income tax refund of $800 may begin to consider alternative ways of spending or saving the money which had not been thought of before. The person may substantially alter his or her desired state in a positive direction based on a financial windfall. Problem recognition, in this case, may lead to purchasing a new car, a new boat, a dishwasher, or taking a vacation. If, on the other hand, the consumer expects to lose his or her job and livelihood, then the financial expectations and desired state will be altered in a negative direction.

MARKETING ACTIVITIES The marketer frequently precipitates problem recognition through promotional efforts aimed at the consumer. With such efforts the marketer seeks to have the consumer perceive a difference of sufficient magnitude between her desired state (ownership of the product) and her actual state (not owning it) to engage in search, evaluation, and purchasing activity for the marketer's brand.

Results of Problem Recognition

Once the consumer becomes aware of a problem, two basic outcomes are possible. One result is for the consumer, in effect, not to pursue any further problem-solving behavior, which might occur if the difference between the consumer's perceived desired and actual states is not great enough to cause him to act to resolve the difference. For example, assume that a consumer has a six-month-old, 19-inch color television set that works perfectly. One day he visits his neighbor who has just bought a 25-inch color TV, and sees how much larger the screen size is than on his set. Although our consumer's desired state may be to own a larger screen TV, there is not likely to be a difference of sufficient magnitude between that and his actual state (the 19-inch set) to cause him to purchase one. If, however, his set were to give out, then he might be motivated to purchase the larger model.

Another situation in which problem recognition may not lead to further stages of consumer decision-making occurs when certain environmental elements preclude it. For example, suppose the consumer from our previous illustration has his household belongings (including his TV) destroyed by a fire. In replacing his possessions, one of the first things he wants to buy is a new 25-inch television set, like his neighbor's. However, because his insurance policy does not cover the full replacement value of all his belongings, and other items are of greater urgency, he determines that he can get along well enough for a while without a TV. Thus, in spite of a difference of sufficient magnitude between the consumer's desired state (owning a TV) and actual state (not owning a TV) financial considerations restrict the consumer's ability to proceed further in the decision-making process.

Other constraints may similarly preclude further decision activity by the consumer. Factors such as time constraints, social class values, and differing family desires may all impede the process.

The second type of response that may occur from the problem recognition process is for the consumer to proceed into further stages of decision-making activity by engaging in information search and evaluation.

MARKETING IMPLICATIONS OF PROBLEM RECOGNITION

The significance to marketers of the problem-recognition stage of consumer decision making is that the process can be effectively measured and can be used to develop and evaluate marketing strategies.

Measurement of Problem Recognition

Consumer researchers have found that the best way to assess the problem-recognition process is through scaling techniques, which measure purchase intentions. Purchase intentions incorporate the consumer's attitudes toward the product and may be viewed as the mental forerunner of buying behavior. The continuum presented in Table 19-1 indicates attitudes that correspond to the various levels of buyer predisposition and are indicative (where positive) of a situation in which problem recognition has occurred and the consumer has some intention of resolving the problem.

Utilizing Problem-Recognition Information

The marketer may find information on buyer intentions to be useful in the following ways.

ANALYZING PURCHASE-INTENTION CATEGORIES From measurement of the speed, direction, and size of shifts in buying likelihoods for a product over several periods in various market segments, the marketer may discover what trends are taking place as well as the timing and size of their potential impact on sales.[4] For example, consider the kinds of comparisons that may be made based on Table 19-1.[5] From this table we can see that consumers who use either statement in Category 1 to describe their intentions are highly predisposed to buy. Consumers who describe their readiness in terms of

TABLE 19-1

RANGE OF CONSUMER'S PREDISPOSITIONS

Category	Predisposition	Attitudes
1	Firm and immediate intent to buy a specific brand.	"I am going to buy some right away." "I am going to buy some soon."
2	Positive intention without definite buying plans.	"I am certain I will buy some sometime." "I probably will buy some sometime."
3	Neutrality: Might buy, might not buy.	"I may buy some sometime." "I might buy some sometime, but I doubt it."
4	Inclined not to buy the brand but not definite about it.	"I don't think I'm interested in buying any." "I probably will never buy any."
5	Firm intention not to buy the brand.	"I know I'm not interested in buying any." "If somebody gave me some, I would give it away, just to get rid of it."
6	Never considered buying.	"I have never heard of the brand."

Source: Adapted from William D. Wells, "Measuring Readiness to Buy," *Harvard Business Review,* **39:**82, July-August 1961.

statements from Category 2 are favorably disposed, but are without immediate purchasing intentions. Consequently, a low Category 1 to Category 2 ratio means that there is a large reservoir of goodwill that needs to be converted into a stronger intention to buy. If this ratio increases over a period of time it suggests that consumers holding a favorable disposition toward the brand are increasing their intentions to purchase it. Deficiencies at the point of sale may be a reason for failure to convert predispositions into purchases. Perhaps price reductions or special promotional deals might be called for in such a situation.

Concentrations of respondents in Category 3 may not be unfavorable since these consumers are still psychologically accessible because their intentions are not yet firmly set. Of course, the marketer would want to shift these respondents into higher categories over a period of time. A strong, effective promotion campaign may be called for in this instance.

A concentration of persons in Category 5 is very undesirable. These respondents have strong, preformed negative intentions about the brand and are likely to be extremely difficult to convince to buy. If the marketer suspects that these attitudes could be the result of his promotion campaign, new and different appeals might be tried with this segment. Since laggards (the last adopter category) are likely to be in Categories 4 and 5, such changed appeals will probably be necessary. Personal selling may also be more heavily needed for this group.

Failure to shift respondents out of Category 6 (those who have never heard of the brand) into higher categories probably indicates lack of a sufficient program to establish ready brand recognition. Heavier advertising and free product sampling may be called for in this case in order to increase consumers' knowledge levels.

If the marketer fails to convince consumers that his brand is worth trying, this pattern will show up as a movement of respondents from Category 6 into 5, 4, or 3, rather than into the top two categories. Product or package improvements may be called for in this case. Product improvements are almost certainly in order if the marketer finds a shift into lower categories by those who have already used the brand.

ANALYZING CONVERSION OF PURCHASE INTENTIONS[6] The marketer may also find significant implications for his marketing strategy by investigating the relationships between purchasing intentions and buying behavior. Longitudinal analysis of intentions data allows the marketer to understand the dynamics of marketplace activity. He obtains a clearer picture of which brands are converting predispositions into buying action. This information can help him to determine the point at which marketing success or failure is occurring and isolate the reasons.

In order to conduct this analysis, data on purchase intentions and behavior over a period of time are necessary such as those contained in Figure 19-2. Assume that there are three national brands in a particular appliance category for which such data have been gathered from interviews conducted 12 months apart. Figure 19-2 indicates that 44 percent of those who stated a definite intention to buy a Brand A appliance actually bought an appliance during this period (we are not concerned at this moment with brand decisions, only generic product decisions). From Figure 19-2 it can be seen, therefore, that Brand A had a higher percentage of intenders making purchases than either Brands B or C.

A second very important aspect of these conversion patterns is the *brand intention-fulfillment rate.* Looking again at Figure 19-1 it may be seen that 68 percent of those who intended to buy Brand A actually did so, while 32 percent bought an alternative brand. According to the brand-fulfillment data in Figure 19-2, Brand A was most successful at converting brand-preference intentions, followed by Brand C and Brand B. Thus, Brand A appears to have the most effective marketing strategy, while Brand C is more effective than Brand B. Based on information such as this the manager of Brand B might seek to determine the reasons for his brand's disappointing sales by assessing the various elements in its marketing program.

SUMMARY

This chapter has initiated our discussion of consumer decision making. First, various types of consumer decisions were described to indicate the diversity and complexity of consumer purchasing processes. Next, the consumer decision-process model was introduced, and purchasing processes were seen to range from those that are rather simple and highly programmable to

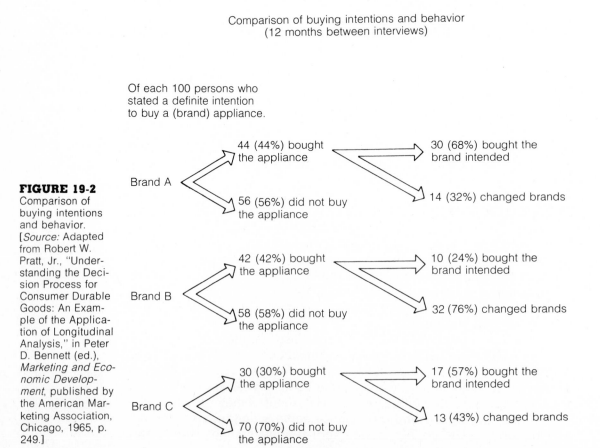

Comparison of buying intentions and behavior
(12 months between interviews)

Of each 100 persons who
stated a definite intention
to buy a (brand) appliance.

FIGURE 19-2
Comparison of
buying intentions
and behavior.
[*Source:* Adapted
from Robert W.
Pratt, Jr., "Under-
standing the Deci-
sion Process for
Consumer Durable
Goods: An Exam-
ple of the Applica-
tion of Longitudinal
Analysis," in Peter
D. Bennett (ed.),
*Marketing and Eco-
nomic Develop-
ment,* published by
the American Mar-
keting Association,
Chicago, 1965, p.
249.]

Brand A
44 (44%) bought the appliance → 30 (68%) bought the brand intended
56 (56%) did not buy the appliance → 14 (32%) changed brands

Brand B
42 (42%) bought the appliance → 10 (24%) bought the brand intended
58 (58%) did not buy the appliance → 32 (76%) changed brands

Brand C
30 (30%) bought the appliance → 17 (57%) bought the brand intended
70 (70%) did not buy the appliance → 13 (43%) changed brands

those that are extremely complicated. The remainder of this chapter was devoted to examining the first stage of the decision process, problem recognition.

Problem recognition amounts to a condition in which the consumer recognizes a difference of sufficient magnitude between what is perceived as the actual state and what is perceived as the desired state of affairs. Situations causing problem recognition were then described. The outcome of problem recognition could be for the consumer to continue into other stages of decision making or to be restrained by environmental circumstances from further purchasing behavior. The chapter concluded with a discussion of applications of problem-recognition information to marketing analysis.

DISCUSSION TOPICS

1. Why is it important to understand consumer decision making?

2. Describe the types of consumer decisions. Illustrate them with a recent decision of your own.

3. What is problem recognition?

4. Describe from your own recent experience what factors led to problem recognition in at least three different product or service situations (not necessarily purchases). Explain the similarities or differences that exist in these situations.

5. How can the marketer use purchase-intentions data?

NOTES

1. These stages follow the excellent consumer decision-process model developed by Engel, Kollat, and Blackwell. The material to be presented in this part is adapted from their model, but also extended and updated where possible.
2. James F. Engel, David T. Kollat, and Roger D. Blackwell, *Consumer Behavior,* 2d ed., Holt, New York, 1973, p. 352.
3. Elihu Katz and Paul Lazarsfeld, *Personal Influence,* Free Press, New York, 1955.
4. C. Joseph Clawson, "How Useful Are 90-Day Purchase Probabilities?" *Journal of Marketing,* **35**:43–47, October 1971.
5. William D. Wells, "Measuring Readiness to Buy," *Harvard Business Review,* **39**:81–87, July-August 1961.
6. This section is drawn from Robert W. Pratt, Jr., "Understanding the Decision Process for Consumer Durable Goods: An Example of the Application of Longitudinal Analysis," in Peter D. Bennett (ed.), *Marketing and Economic Development,* American Marketing Association, Chicago, 1965, pp. 244–260.

INFORMATION SEARCH AND EVALUATION

THE INFORMATION-SEEKING PROCESS Nature of the Consumer's Search Activities; Amount of Information Seeking by Consumers; Factors That Influence the Search Process; Types of Information Sought; Sources of Information **THE INFORMATION-EVALUATION PROCESS** Evaluating Alternatives; Factors Influencing the Amount of Evaluation; Results of Evaluation **MARKETING IMPLICATIONS** Researching the Information-seeking Process; Influencing the Consumer's Evoked Set; Influencing Consumers' Evaluation; How Much Information for the Consumer?

Once a consumer has recognized the existence of a problem, and assuming there are no constraints preventing further behavior, the next stage in the decision-making process involves a search for and evaluation of information. This step is shown in Figure 20-1.

In this chapter we shall first examine what the information-seeking process entails and the many ways it is influenced. Next, the process of evaluation will be discussed. Finally, some marketing implications will be presented to indicate how the marketer may seek to influence consumer search processes.

THE INFORMATION-SEEKING PROCESS

In this section we shall examine the search process engaged in by consumers and the factors that influence it.

Nature of the Consumer's Search Activities

For our purposes *information* may be considered to be knowledge obtained about some fact or circumstance. And in the context in which we are dealing within this chapter such knowledge is to be used in a consumer-behavior situation.

The term "search" refers to mental as well as physical information seeking and processing activities which one engages in to facilitate decision making regarding some goal-object in the marketplace.[1] Consequently, search may be undertaken in order to find out about products, prices, stores, and so on, related to the product. Search may be active or passive, internal or external. *Active* search could involve visiting stores to make product and price comparisons, while *passive* search may entail only reading a magazine advertisement with no specific goal in mind or thinking about the features of a desired product.

The processes of internal and external search consist of different activities. These activities are described in detail below.

INTERNAL SEARCH This is the first stage to occur after the consumer experiences problem recognition. It is a mental process of recalling and reviewing information stored in memory that may relate to the purchase situation. For instance, a consumer may recall that a friend made very negative comments about a particular brand of coffee maker (which the consumer is now considering buying) while playing bridge several months ago. Notice that these derogatory comments were stored in the consumer's memory and now have come into play by affecting her attitudes unfavorably toward the brand. Thus, the consumer relies on any attitudes, information, or past experiences that have been stored in memory and can be recalled for application to the problem at hand. The recall may be immediate or may

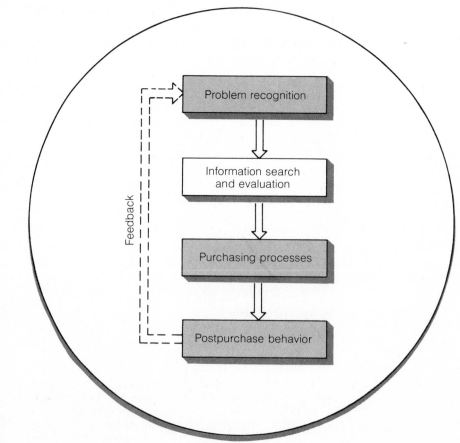

FIGURE 20-1
Consumer
decision-process
model.

occur slowly, as a conscious effort is made to bring the information to mind. Once recalled, the information may be used in the evaluation process as the consumer seeks to resolve the purchase decision confronting her.

The result or outcome of internal search and alternative evaluation may be that a consumer (1) makes a decision and proceeds to engage in purchase behavior, (2) is constrained by certain environmental variables (such as a determination that his checking account cannot stand the purchase), or (3) determines that insufficient or inadequate information exists in his memory to make a decision now, so that external search is undertaken.[2]

EXTERNAL SEARCH This refers to the process of obtaining information from other sources in addition to that which can be recalled from memory. Some sources from which such information might be obtained are advertisements, friends, salespeople, store displays, and product-testing magazines. Whereas internal search is always passive, external search may be either passive or active.

During external search the brand alternatives to the buyer's product-choice decision are identified. Although there may be many brands in existence in the product category (which we may call the *total* set of brands), the consumer is not likely to be aware of all of them. Thus, some brands will not be considered by the consumer because of this unawareness. Consequently, the marketer seeks to make consumers aware of the availability of his brand and to supply them with sufficient information to evaluate it and, hopefully, purchase it.

Even among brands of which the consumer is aware, however, are some that he would not consider purchasing for several reasons:

1. He may feel they are beyond his reach.

2. They are not perceived as adequate for his motives.

3. He has insufficient information on which to evaluate them.

4. He has tried and rejected them.

5. He is satisfied with his current brand.

6. He has received negative feedback from advertising or word-of-mouth communication.[3]

It has been suggested, therefore, that there actually exist three subsets of brands within the awareness set of alternatives: (1) evoked set, (2) inert set, and (3) inept set.[4]

The *evoked set* consists of the few select brands evaluated positively by the consumer for purchase and consumption. The *inert set* consists of those brands that the consumer has failed to perceive any advantage in buying; that is, they are evaluated neither positively nor negatively. Perhaps the consumer has insufficient information on which to evaluate them, or she simply may not perceive them as better than the brands in her evoked set. The *inept set* is made up of brands that have been rejected from purchase consideration by the consumer because of an unpleasant experience or negative feedback from others. Thus, the brands in this set are evaluated negatively by the consumer and will not be considered at all in their present form.

Knowledge of consumers' awareness sets of brands is valuable to marketers because they are interested in moving their items into their evoked set. Only if consumers are aware of the brand and have evaluated it positively will it be purchased. Later in this chapter we will discuss alternatives for moving a brand into consumers' evoked sets.

Now that we have a better understanding of the nature of search activities engaged in by the consumer, it is time to examine some of the factors that influence the process.

Amount of Information Seeking by Consumers

Consumers appear to engage in a rather limited information search when making purchase decisions. Marketer-supplied information such as that obtained from advertisements or retail stores is not actively used by all consumers. The findings presented in this section are illustrative of this pattern.

USE OF ADVERTISEMENTS Several research studies have indicated that consumer use of advertisements is not very great. Consider the following conclusions:

Only about one shopper in ten checks advertisements before shopping for shoes and personal accessories.[5]

Of consumers buying food products only 19 percent were able to recall obtaining information from advertisements.[6]

Of consumers purchasing small electrical appliances, such as radios, hair dryers, toasters, and coffee makers, only 25 percent consulted newspaper advertising, 15 percent read magazine advertising, 14 percent saw television advertising, and 7 percent listened to radio advertising before buying.[7]

It can be seen from this that consumers generally are not active users of advertising, although this varies by product and among individuals.

INFORMATION OBTAINED FROM RETAIL OUTLETS Another source of marketer-supplied information is the retail store. Here consumers are able to see and assess products, and this facilitates their evaluation process. Two aspects of the usage of store-provided information are relevant here: the number of stores visited and the amount of information secured within stores.

Number of Stores Shopped Table 20-1 presents findings from several research studies in which consumers were asked the number of stores they visited before purchasing the items listed. It is clear from this table that very often consumers do not visit more than one store in order to obtain information before purchasing. It should also be noticed that the number of stores visited differs according to the product. Thus, most consumers appear

TABLE 20-1

463

INFORMATION
SEARCH
AND
EVALUATION

NUMBER OF STORES CONSUMERS VISIT BEFORE PURCHASE

	Percentage of Purchases by Number of Stores Visited			
Product	Don't Know or None	One Store	Two Stores	Three or More Stores
Toys*		87.4	6.1	6.5
Small electrical appliances†	2.0	60.0	16.0	22.0
Refrigerators‡		42.0	16.0	42.0
Living room furniture§	2.4	22.0	13.4	62.1
New cars and major appliances¶		49.0	26.0	23.0

Source: *Alderson and Sessions, Inc., "Basic Research Report on Consumer Behavior," in Ronald E. Frank, Alfred A. Kuehn, and William F. Massy, (eds.), *Quantitative Techniques in Marketing Analysis,* Irwin, Homewood, Ill., 1962, pp. 129–145.
†Jon G. Udell, "Prepurchase Behavior of Buyers of Small Electrical Appliances," *Journal of Marketing,* **30:**50–52, October 1966.
‡William P. Dommermuth, "The Shopping Matrix and Marketing Strategy," *Journal of Marketing Research,* **2:**128–132, May 1965.
§Bruce LeGrand and Jon G. Udell, "Consumer Behavior in the Market Place—An Empirical Study in the Television and Furniture Fields with Theoretical Implications," *Journal of Retailing,* **40:**32, Fall 1964.
¶Joseph W. Newman and Richard Staelin, "Prepurchase Information Seeking for New Cars and Major Household Appliances," *Journal of Marketing Research,* **9:**249–257, August 1972.

to have little need for securing information from several different stores during their search process. But what about their in-store information-seeking? Is this also minimal?

Amount of In-Store Search Of course neither the number of stores visited nor the number of visits per store by consumers may be truly indicative of the amount of information-seeking that takes place within retail stores. Unfortunately, there is relatively little research on consumers' in-store search activities. Thus, marketers have little insight into how much information-seeking really goes on inside retail stores.

One measure of the amount of in-store information search is the number of brands consumers compare in making a purchase decision. One study showed that there was considerable variation by product, with 41 percent of the shoppers evaluating only one brand of refrigerator, with 49 percent for television sets, 61 percent for washing machines, 65 percent for electric irons, and 71 percent for vacuum cleaners. It was also found that only 29 percent compared four or more brands of refrigerators, while 9 percent shopped four or more brands of irons.[8]

Another measure of the amount of in-store information search is the extent to which consumers consider products in other price ranges and seek information on product features. A study of this found that 46 percent of buyers of durable goods did not consider items in other price ranges. The study also measured the extent to which consumers sought information on such product features as quality, performance, style, operating cost, service and guarantees. Omitting price and brand, 27 percent did not consider any features; 34 percent considered one feature; 18 percent considered two features; and 17 percent considered three or more.[9]

In conclusion it can be seen that consumers generally do not seek large amounts of information. Clearly, their search process is highly selective. This does not necessarily mean, however, that consumers entering the market-place are uninformed. The studies referred to do not really address the question of information *quality,* only certain aspects of information *quantity.* It is possible that buyers, although visiting only one store, are able to obtain large amounts of helpful information from that one source. They may examine the product, check prices, practice using the item, talk with the salesperson, read product literature, and study the package.

It is also possible that many consumers begin their external search processes with large amounts of relevant information stored in memory, which therefore requires that little additional data be gathered. Consumers are continuously gathering information from advertising, personal conversations, observation, and so forth. Some of this may later become relevant to a purchase-decision situation.

In any event, more research needs to be done before we have a clear idea of how much search consumers *actually do* or *should do* for purchasing decisions. Later in this chapter some of the public policy implications of information search and processing activities will be offered.

Factors That Influence the Search Process

There are quite a few variables that determine the amount of search consumers undertake. The following factors are not mutually exclusive, however.

COSTS VERSUS BENEFITS OF SEARCH ACTIVITY There are many potential benefits from engaging in search activity. Yet there are also costs associated with information seeking that may partially counteract the perceived benefits. Hence consumers may tend to apply the principle of *marginality* in search activities. That is, additional search activity may be engaged in if the added benefits are perceived to be greater than the additional costs involved. These benefits and costs could take several forms.

One benefit to be derived from search is the possibility of making a "better" purchase decision—at least as the consumer perceives it. Shopping can provide consumers with information on the best product features, warranties, service, and prices, for example. As support for the benefit of shopping, it has been found that consumers are more willing to shop for higher-priced than for less expensive items, since the potential gains to be realized are greater.[10]

Another benefit of search is the sheer pleasure of the shopping experience for many consumers. Most people like to buy new things, and thus shopping and buying become an excellent way to get out of a rut. Many consumers find shopping to be an enjoyable activity, one of the pleasurable parts of their day, and sometimes an escape mechanism from their cares.[11] Thus, search is more likely to be undertaken when viewed as a pleasurable activity.

Search activity is usually not without costs, however.[12] There are several types of costs that may or may not be explicitly recognized by consumers. First, there is the direct cost associated with traveling to various stores and parking. It is questionable whether consumers carefully consider this cost. However, higher costs of travel in the future may increase consideration given to it. At least one study has found that consumers make more comparisons between stores when this requires little expense and effort.[13]

A second cost involves time. Search frequently entails visits to retail stores to gather information. Such shopping excursions often turn into all-day adventures. For example, there is the time involved in traveling between home and the place of shopping, time spent parking, time spent walking from the car to store and back and from store to store, and the time spent selecting and paying for goods in each store.[14] Thus, the use of one's time for search as opposed to a game of tennis or watching television may represent a cost to many consumers. This is particularly true for those who work because they may more readily equate their time with money that might be earned in alternative pursuits. As one study concluded, "Today's shopper must weigh the opportunity cost involved in expending time for prolonged search against the probable benefits to be derived from it. Relative to total income, the time involved may outweigh potential economic benefits."[15] Consequently, if the time pressure or opportunity cost is great to the consumer, extensive search is less likely.

A third searching cost to the consumer is the resultant delay in enjoying ownership of the product. Some consumers may be unwilling to engage in extensive search because this forestalls their satisfaction from using the product. Hence, where delay in making a decision is unattractive, less extensive search will result.

A final cost exacted by external search is its toll on the consumer's psyche. Although the consumer may look forward to shopping as a pleasurable activity, it sometimes turns out to be a nightmare, as during holiday sales. The shopper may pay a high price in terms of frustration and anger. Thus, the psychological costs involved in search may be high, which will tend to reduce the intensity of the process.

TYPE OF PRODUCT The nature of the product has an important influence on the amount of information seeking. Traditionally, marketers have recognized three types of products and shopping patterns.[16] *Convenience goods* are classified as those that the customer usually purchases frequently, immediately, and with a minimum of effort in comparison and buying. *Shopping goods* are those that, in the process of selection and purchase, customers usually compare on such bases as suitability, quality, price, and style. Finally, *specialty goods* are those with unique characteristics and/or brand identifications for which a significant group of buyers are habitually willing to make a special purchasing effort.

The type of product, therefore, can be seen to affect the nature and amount of search undertaken. This factor relates also to our previous discussion of search cost and benefit. The probable gain from comparing price and quality of shopping goods is significant enough to lead to more extensive search activities, whereas such would not be the case for convenience goods.[17] A number of research studies have affirmed that consumers do engage in more information seeking when their purchases are more expensive.[18]

PERCEIVED RISK Risk or uncertainty regarding the most appropriate purchase decision or the consequences of the decision is a third variable influencing the total amount of information gathered by consumers.

It is important to recognize that risk is subjective. That is, the risk involved in a purchase decision is *perceived* by the consumer and may or may not bear a strong relationship to what actually exists. For example, an objective observer may not evaluate the purchase of a canned ham as involving much risk. However, the choice may involve considerable risk in terms of the impression a housewife wishes to make when she is purchasing the ham for a dinner party she is having for her husband's boss.

Situations Influencing Risk There are several situations that influence the consumer's perception of uncertainty or consequences and thus the perception of risk:

1. Uncertainty regarding buying goals. For example, should a new sport jacket be purchased for more formal occasions or for very informal get-togethers?

2. Uncertainty regarding which alternative (such as product, brand, or model) will best match or satisfy the purchase goals. That is, if private transportation to school is desired, what should be purchased: car or motorcycle; Ford, Chevrolet, or Plymouth; two-door or four-door?

3. The consumer can perceive possible undesirable consequences if the purchase is made (or not made) and the result is failure to satisfy buying goals.[19]

If any of these situations are sensed by the consumer, then he or she is said to perceive risk in the situation.

Types of Risk As one may expect, there are also several kinds of risk that consumers may perceive in a purchase situation.[20]

1. *Financial Risk*—The consumer may lose money if the brand doesn't work at all, or costs more than it should to keep it in good shape.

2. *Performance Risk*—The brand may not work properly.

3. *Physical Risk*—The brand may be or become harmful or injurious to one's health.

4. *Psychological Risk*—The brand may not fit in well with the consumer's self-image or self-concept.

5. *Social Risk*—The brand may negatively affect the way others think of the consumer.

6. *Time Loss Risk*—The brand may fail completely, thus wasting the consumer's time, convenience, and effort getting it adjusted, repaired, or replaced.

Thus, overall risk is a combination of several factors as perceived by consumers when buying a product.

How Consumers Deal with Risk Since most purchase behavior appears to involve at least some risk, consumers may take various steps to handle the problem. In most cases this results in attempts to reduce risk. Consumers develop various strategies to relieve perceived risk, including the following:

1. Buy the brand whose advertising has endorsements or testimonials from typical consumers, from a celebrity, or from an expert on the product.

2. Buy the brand that the consumer has used before and has found satisfactory.

3. Buy a major, well-known brand, and rely on its reputation.

4. Buy the brand that has been tested and approved by a private testing company.

5. Buy the brand offering a money-back guarantee with the product.

6. Buy the brand that has been tested and approved by some branch of the government.

7. Buy the most expensive and elaborate model of the product.[21]

Thus as some of the approaches on the above list indicate, consumers may reduce risk through information acquisition aimed at reducing uncertainty. Several consumer research studies have confirmed this process.[22] Information acquisition can also be used to help reduce the perceived consequences of a decision, as can reduction of the amount at stake (for example, purchasing a smaller size), reducing expectations about how perfect the product will be, or minimizing the consequences (such as a cigarette lighter slogan that states, "For 99 cents it's a pretty good lighter").

LEARNING AND EXPERIENCE The consumer's past experience with a product and the amount and nature of information learned will affect the extent of search.[23] A particular purchase may become routine or habitual when the customer repeats the buying behavior frequently and if the consumption experience has been pleasurable, thus reinforcing the behavior. Because the consumer feels that her previous experience is sufficient, she is likely to perceive less need for additional search activity.

Various research studies have confirmed the role of learning from previous experience as an important variable in consumer search. The relevant dimensions of the information stored by consumers that bears upon their search patterns are its amount and appropriateness.

Amount of Information The amount of information that has been stored by the consumer will depend on his or her length and breadth of experience. Thus, the occurrence and extensiveness of search activity undertaken by a consumer will be greater to the extent that he or she has a shorter and narrower range of purchase experience with brands in a product category.[24]

Appropriateness of Information Appropriateness of the consumer's stored information depends on several factors. First, satisfaction with past purchases will affect search. If the consumer has achieved great satisfaction in the product's consumption, she is likely to engage in less search when the problem is recognized again.[25] Second, appropriateness is determined by the similarity perceived between problems. If the present consumer problem is seen to be the same as an earlier situation that was satisfactorily resolved, then the consumer is likely to rely on the previous solution (i.e., buy the same brand) and thus engage in less external search.[26]

A third variable affecting the appropriateness of stored information involves changes in the alternatives available on the market. Products come and go from the marketplace, prices change, and retail stores open and close. The extent to which these variables are altered affects the appropriateness of the consumer's stored information such that she is likely to engage in search to up-date her knowledge.[27]

Changes in the mix of market alternatives are very likely to occur with the passage of time. Thus, time between purchases is a final factor affecting information appropriateness. As interpurchase time increases, the consumer is more likely to engage in search activity.[28]

There are several other determinants of information search that have been suggested. The following are indicative of the more important ones and the direction of their influence.

RECOGNITION AND INTENSITY OF NEED It appears that consumers' product needs are often not well defined before shopping. Because of this the retail store serves as an important information source in meeting their search needs. As they shop, they gather information and their needs become more clearly defined. Therefore, if consumers have not identified their needs before shopping they will tend to engage in more search.[29]

If a consumer has an urgent need, then the chances are that search activity will be reduced in order to satisfy that need.[30] However, the greater the consumer's intensity of need for a particular product, the more likely she is to engage in extensive search for that product.[31]

PERSONALITY AND SELF-CONCEPT Certain personality types appear to be more information-sensitive than others, hence, to engage in greater search activities.[32] It has also been suggested that the extent to which a woman sees herself as being a deliberate searcher, the more extensive her search to obtain any given product.[33]

Types of Information Sought

It would be important for the marketer in planning promotional campaigns and merchandising strategies to know what types of information consumers look for in search activities. It has been suggested that consumers need three types of information. First, they need information about the existence or availability of a product or brand before they can purchase it; that is, they must be aware. Second, they need information that will give them reason to become interested in the product (assuming they must be interested in an item before they will consider it for purchase). Third, consumers need information that will help them evelute a product in terms of its ability to satisfy their needs.[34]

Evaluative information includes information about the product itself, such as cost, characteristics, functions, variations, performance, and so on; about products or brands that compare to it; and about the psychological and social consequences of buying the product. It has been found that the type of product appears to determine to some extent the type of information people seek.[35]

Sources of Information

The consumer has three sources of information in purchase-decision making: (1) marketer-dominated channels of communication, (2) consumer channels, and (3) neutral sources. Each of these sources offers certain advantages to consumers who might use it.[36]

MARKETER-DOMINATED SOURCES This source of information is under the direct control of the marketer and includes such means of communication as the product itself, packaging, pricing, advertising, sales promotion, personal selling, displays, and distribution channels.

The advantages favoring consumer use of this source are (1) the information is readily available, (2) it is obtainable with little effort on the consumer's part (i.e., it is low in cost), and (3) it is perceived as competent and technically accurate information. However, consumers may also believe that there are drawbacks to using this source: (1) superficial information may be provided, (2) the information may not be perceived as trustworthy, and (3) all information may not be provided.

CONSUMER SOURCES Consumer-oriented channels of communication include all interpersonal sources of information that are not under the direct control of the marketer. These sources are valued for the following reasons: (1) flexibility; that is, the information can be tailored to meet the consumer's needs, (2) trustworthiness, and (3) large amounts of information are available from them. Certain factors hinder the use of this channel by consumers, however. The primary disadvantages are: (1) the information is not always correct and (2) the information may have to be sought out, which means that it may be high in cost. The nature of this influence process was discussed extensively in Chapter 12.

NEUTRAL SOURCES Neutral sources include such means as newspaper and magazine articles, government reports, research agencies, and publications by testing groups such as Consumers Union (publisher of *Consumer Reports*). These groups provide product information but are supposedly not directly influenced by either the marketer or consumer. The perceived advantages of using neutral sources are the following: (1) the source is perceived as competent and trustworthy and (2) information is perceived as factual and unbiased.

Utilization of neutral sources (particularly product-testing information) is hindered, however, by the fact that (1) the information may be incomplete (for example, not all brands may be tested and reported on), (2) securing information may be time-consuming or expensive, (3) information may be outdated or incomplete, (4) consumers may need rather highly developed intellectual skills in order to use some of the lengthy and technical product-test information (such as appears in *Consumer Reports*), and (5) consumers may disagree with the emphasis on "rational" performance-related evaluative criteria as opposed to how well the product may satisfy certain social or psychological needs.[37]

DETERMINANTS OF INFORMATION SOURCE USAGE Although consumers have access to various sources of information, these sources may have varying degrees of influence.

In terms of exposure, marketer-dominated sources are usually the most important. With regard to the influence criterion, however, consumer and neutral sources are most effective. Which sources consumers choose are determined by the following factors:

1. *Type of information sought.* Consumers usually rely on marketer-dominated sources when searching for information on the availability of alternatives and their attributes. Consumer-dominated sources tend to be relied on more heavily at the evaluation stages of decision making.

2. *Previous experience with product.* If the consumer has had experience with the product, this will affect his reliance on sources of information. For example, if he has previously purchased the item and been satisfied with its use, he is likely to rely simply on the retail store for information rather than on other sources.[38]

3. *Perceived risk.* When perceived risk is high, consumers appear to try to reduce this risk, often through personal sources of information. Consumers have also been found to use neutral sources of information such as seals and certifications (e.g., *Good Housekeeping, Parents' Magazine,* Underwriters' Laboratory, U.S.D.A. Choice) more when there is a high degree of perceived risk.[39]

4. *Type of product.* Consumer-dominated sources appear to be of great importance for many types of products purchased. For example, in a summary of the information sources for a number of studies on different products it was found that consumer-dominated sources were by far the most important for major appliances. They were also somewhat more important than the next source for new cars, small electrical appliances, new grocery and household items, and clothing. The marketer-dominated retail store was found to be second in overall importance as a source of information. Newspaper ads were also found to be important where style and fashion are important considerations.[40]

THE INFORMATION-EVALUATION PROCESS

As the consumer is engaged in search activity, he or she is also actively engaged in information evaluation. Evaluation involves those activities undertaken by the consumer to carefully appraise, on the basis of certain criteria, alternative solutions to market-related problems. The search process determines what the alternatives are, and in the evaluation process they are compared so that the consumer is ready to make a decision.

Evaluating Alternatives

How do consumers perform the product-evaluation process? One of the most thorough explanations is that offered by Donald Cox, which is briefly described below.[41]

Cox observes that a product can be conceived of as an array of cues including such information as price; product color, taste or feel; friends' suggestions; and salesmen's opinions. The consumer's task is to use these cues as the basis for making judgments about the product. Cox's thesis is that when presented with an array of cues, the consumer will value some more highly than others. In addition, the more the consumer values a cue, the more likely the consumer is to utilize that cue as the primary basis for evaluating the product. Thus, the consumer is seen as selective in use of information about a product, and tends to base the evaluation mainly on high-value information or cues.

How do consumers establish the value of cues? Cue value is established on two dimensions: their predictive value and their confidence value. *Predictive value* is the consumer's assessment of the probability that a cue seems associated with (predicts) a specific product attribute. For example, when shopping for a stereo receiver consumers are likely to be very much interested in the product attribute of "good quality." Some product features then, such as well-constructed internal components, or a 10-year guarantee will be high in predictive value for this product attribute. Other product features, however, such as the looks of the unit, will probably be perceived as being low in their predictive value of quality.

The second dimension of cues is their *confidence value,* which is a measure of how certain the consumer is that the cue is what he or she thinks it is. For example, consider the cases of an engineer who works at a radio station and a homemaker, both of whom are evaluating the quality of a stereo receiver. For both shoppers the nature of internal components is a high predictive value cue. That is, if they were certain that the components were good, they would also be relatively certain that the receiver itself was good. The engineer is likely to be able to ascertain with a high degree of confidence (from inspection and reading the specification sheets) that the internal components *are* of high quality. For this consumer the cue has both high predictive value and high confidence value. The homemaker, on the other hand, may be unable to determine with any confidence that the receiver does have good internal components. Consequently, for her the cue has a low confidence value in spite of its high predictive value.

Let us consider how the evaluation process might work for a novice stereo buyer such as the homemaker mentioned above. In determining whether a stereo receiver is high, medium, or low quality in sound reproduction performance, for instance, the brand will be sorted into one of these attribute categories on the basis of the following rule:

Sort the product into the attribute category, using the criterion category with the highest predictive value (provided that cue also has a high confidence value). Otherwise, sort the product into the attribute category indicated by the criterion category with the next highest predictive value (provided it can be assigned with a high degree of confidence).[42]

Our consumer, therefore, would first attempt to sort the stereo receiver into one of the attribute categories (either high, medium, or low quality of sound reproduction) on the basis of internal components, assuming this criterion has the highest predictive value. However, because our consumer has a low confidence value in her ability to discriminate stereo innards she will discard this criterion. The next highest criterion in terms of predictive value might be price. Since our consumer can determine the price of the receiver with a high degree of confidence, she will, therefore, decide whether the receiver is low, medium, or high quality on this basis. In fact, this is the approach which many consumers take when confronted with a mass of bewildering cues such as in the purchase of sophisticated electronic equipment like stereos. Inability to evaluate these cues confidently often results in their reliance on price as an indicator of quality. This is exactly what our homemaker has done.

Factors Influencing the Amount of Evaluation

The same factors that were discussed earlier with regard to the extent of search activity will determine the amount of evaluation that occurs. For example, at least to some extent, the following guidelines are true:

1. The more urgent the need, the less evaluation will take place.

2. The more significant the product is to the buyer (e.g., a house, car, boat), the greater the amount of evaluation.

3. The more complex the alternatives, the more evaluation will take place.

Results of Evaluation

The appraisal of information produced during search may have several possible results, depending on the extent to which the buyer reconciles his desired and available alternatives. One outcome is for the consumer to stop searching because he has found an acceptable product which satisfies the recognized problem. At this point, assuming no further constraints, the consumer would purchase the item. A second possibility is for the consumer to discontinue search because no acceptable product has been identified. A third possible outcome is for the consumer to continue searching even though no acceptable alternative has yet been found. At this point he obviously feels that the benefits of continued search outweigh the costs involved.

MARKETING IMPLICATIONS

There are a number of marketing implications that flow from this exposition of search and alternative evaluation processes. In this section we shall examine some of the significant ramifications of this process for the marketer's task.

Researching the Information-seeking Process

In order for the marketer to influence the process of search and alternative evaluation, he first must have information about it among his market segments. There are several pieces of the information processing puzzle that he should seek to fill in (assuming that search activity is engaged in by a significant segment of his market). First, he needs to determine what sources of information are actually used by consumers. Next, he must determine each source's influence.

DETERMINING SOURCES OF INFORMATION Two useful approaches for the marketer involve the use of warranty registration cards and more in-depth questioning approaches.

Warranty Cards Where appropriate, many marketers use warranty registration cards to gather data on the information seeking activities of their customers. These questionnaires enable the respondent to check the source of information as well as the place of purchase for a product. However, these cards are often so small, in order to be machine-processed, that the amount of information obtainable on them is rather limited. Thus, such questions as where the consumer shopped (as opposed to purchased) and which information source was the most important are usually left for the company to speculate about. As a result, this type of research approach, although useful, leaves many unanswered questions for the marketer attempting to make distribution or promotion decisions.

In-Depth Research The marketer may also utilize cross-sectional or longitudinal research approaches to obtain information on consumer search processes. While cross-sectional approaches may be acceptable for products with relatively short decision times, longitudinal studies may be more useful, especially when the decision time for a product is long.

In formulating questionnaires to be used in such studies, it is suggested that the influence of information sources can be obtained by asking several types of questions:[43] (1) *specific influence* questions about the decision process itself (rather than specific sources), such as "How did you learn about this new product?" or "Why did you decide to buy this brand?" (2) questions *assessing overall influence,* such as, "Overall, what was the most important thing in causing you to purchase this product?" and (3) questions about *exposure* to various sources of information, such as checklists like those used on warranty cards.

DETERMINING SOURCE INFLUENCE We learned in the previous chapter that analysis of purchase intentions and fulfillment rates over time could help to pinpoint weaknesses in marketing strategy. One of the variables that need to be assessed to determine its strength or weakness is the influence of information sources on brand-purchase intentions and fulfillment.

Building on the discussion in the last chapter we can see the type of analysis that might be necessary in order for the marketer to secure greater intention-fulfillment rates. Several steps of analysis are required. First, the marketer should determine the effectiveness of information sources to which consumers of each brand are exposed. This necessitates gathering data for each brand and each information source with regard to whether that source was effective for consumers, and the degree of its effectiveness. Once this information is known, brands can then be compared on the basis of how effective each information source is. It may be found, for example, that one brand's word-of-mouth and television advertising is especially ineffective when compared to other brands.

Several other facets of analysis would be helpful in isolating the problem.

For example, analysis of information source effectiveness by type of customer (demographic or psychographic bases) would help to determine which consumers are being effectively or ineffectively influenced. Of course, once the weak link in the information search and evaluation process is known (such as poor word-of-mouth advertising), the reasons for the poor performance must still be determined and corrected.

Influencing the Consumer's Evoked Set

It is also beneficial for the marketer to determine whether his brand is perceived as being in the consumer's evoked, inert, or inept set.[44] The marketer can conduct research among a sample of consumers to determine all the brands they are aware of, the brand names that they do and do not consider buying, as well as the reasons for this. Using this approach, the marketer can learn what percentage are aware of his brand and which awareness set it primarily falls into. From such study it is likely that the marketer will find that although consumers are aware of many brands in a product category they generally hold only a few brands in their evoked and inept sets. If the marketer determines that a large share of the market is unaware of his brand, this would indicate the need for an intensified advertising campaign. Reasons for a brand's position within consumers' awareness sets may also be learned by assessing information on their evaluative beliefs regarding the brand. This information may help explain why certain brands are in the evoked set while others are in the inept set. For instance, it may be learned that many consumers reject the marketer's brand because of its physical characteristics, or dislike the brand's advertising, or do not have adequate information with which to evaluate the brand. Thus, the marketer might rectify these problems by modifying the physical features of the brand, changing the ad copy, or utilizing comparative advertising and free samples. As a result of such strategies a brand currently in consumers' inept set may be able to move into their inert or evoked sets.

Influencing Consumers' Evaluation

The marketer may decide to change his brand's image upon finding that his brand suffers from continued existence in consumers' inept or inert sets. If he pursues this change he has a choice between two main strategies. He may alter the characteristics of dominant cues, and/or he may alter the information value of the cues.[45]

ALTERING CUE CHARACTERISTICS Changing the characteristics of a dominant cue can have a dramatic effect on the product image. This is particularly important in the many cases where brands are perceived very similarly. The marketer may be able to move his brand from the inert or inept set into the consumer's evoked set by a very minor change in some cue (for example, making an electric food mixer slightly noisier so that it seems more powerful to consumers). A "just noticeable difference" between brands can be accomplished by emphasizing a minor (but easy to evaluate with high confidence) difference in product, price, or package. Moreover, such changes appear to be more effective than claiming a large and nearly unbelievable (that is, difficult to evaluate with confidence) brand difference (such as, "This electric food mixer is powerful enough to churn concrete.").

ALTERING INFORMATION VALUE Rather than changing the characteristics of a cue, the marketer may attempt to change the way consumers evaluate a product. For instance, rather than change the sound of the mixer in the above example, consumers could be educated to base their evaluation of power on another cue (such as horsepower rating or wattage). Thus, the marketer may seek to increase the degree of association in the mind of the consumer between horsepower rating and actual mixer power (a change in the predictive value of the cue). This might be accomplished through advertising and personal selling efforts. At the same time the marketer may attempt to teach consumers how to be sure that a given horsepower rating was adequate or inadequate for a mixer (an increase in the confidence value of the cue).

How Much Information for the Consumer?

It is felt by many in legislative, regulative, and judicial circles that the consumer does not have adequate information on which to base decisions. Critics of current marketing practices claim that much factual information relevant to consumer choice is simply unavailable and that this results in higher prices, "artificial" brand differences, and a stress on frills that represent no real value to consumers. Marketers, on the other hand, rebut these claims by noting that in many of the cases where product promotions contained numerous facts there has been little positive effect on sales. In addition, marketers feel that if consumers really wanted and would use more product information, our system of competition would provide it.[46]

In any event, there is growing pressure for businesses to provide more and better quality information so that more rational or better decisions can be made by consumers. A result of this belief has led to a number of consumer information programs.

UNIT PRICING Unit pricing means that the retailer not only displays the total price of the item, but also displays the price per relevant unit of the product (such as dollars per pound, fluid ounce, and so forth). The basis for this program arose from consumerists who alleged that consumers could not identify the most economical item in a product class because of the large variety of brands, package sizes, and quantity sizes (e.g., jumbo, super, giant, large economy size, and so on), and the poor presentation of quantity information on packages. Even educated shoppers sometimes find it difficult to identifiy the most economical items.

The results of studies on usage of unit pricing have not been consistent, however. Most have found higher usage among higher socioeconomic categories rather than the lower-income groups who might appear really to benefit most from them. Research generally indicates a high awareness among consumers of unit pricing but much variability with regard to claimed usage and effectiveness.[47] There are at least two reasons for such findings. First, even with access to unit price information consumers may not necessarily buy the most economical item because of such factors as brand quality differences and the convenience of smaller but more expensive sizes (such as to a single elderly buyer). Second, the method of unit price information presentation varies considerably. Some unit price programs have been very effectively introduced and run, while others meet the letter of the law without really facilitating consumers' usage.

NUTRITIONAL LABELING With the growing concern over dietary deficiencies among the American public (particularly among young people) and the increasing demand to know what really goes into the foods we eat, manufacturers have been under pressure to increase their nutritional labeling.[48] Yet whether consumers are able to understand and thus use such additional information is questionable. It has been shown that some consumers would refer to additional nutritional information and could buy more nutritious products as a result.[49] But just how much information should be provided is not clear. One study showed that consumers preferred labels with moderate levels of nutritional information compared with those with either the least or the most information.[50]

As with research on unit pricing, most studies on nutrient labeling have found that consumers in lower socioeconomic categories are less likely to use such information.

OPEN DATING This is the practice whereby dates are printed on packaged food products to inform consumers of their freshness. Consumers appear to desire this information more than unit pricing or nutrient labeling. However, studies conducted on open dating indicate that only a rather small percentage of consumers are able to interpret the dates. Moreover, the system of dating used in most programs is the one least preferred by consumers.[51]

TRUTH-IN-LENDING The effects of federal truth-in-lending legislation (which requires full disclosure of the rate of finance charges and other aspects of a consumer credit transaction) are also rather unclear. One study showed that although the practice of making such information available apparently improves consumer knowledge of credit rates and charges, it has been found to do little to change credit behavior because of the importance of the retailer in the credit decision. Moreover, it was shown that most consumers (particularly those with lower incomes and education) remained uninformed about interest rates; and many did not even understand the concept of interest, nor could they calculate it in dollars. Thus, this study concluded that consumers must not simply be provided with information but should also be taught to understand it and use it.[52]

ARE CONSUMERS OVERLOADED WITH INFORMATION? Many of the foregoing research studies on consumer-information programs indicated that consumers do not heavily use them. What causes this lack of use? Some researchers suggest that the problem may be the result of information overload. That is, there are limits to the amount of information that consumers can process; hence, too much information is dysfunctional for them.[53]

The first systematic study of the information overload phenomenon was done by Jacoby and his colleagues, in which subjects were asked to make decisions on product brands with varying quantities of information.[54] The researchers concluded that as the amount of information increased, consumers were less able to select the brand best for them; yet the information had beneficial effects on the consumer's degree of satisfaction, certainty, and confusion regarding his selection. That is, subjects appeared to feel better with more information while actually making worse purchase decisions! This result was taken to mean that an information-overload phenomenon had been identified. Similar results were found in a succeeding study in which information overload was observed to be related to an increase in the number of brands. It was found, however, that increased information per brand resulted in better decisions.[55]

How does the consumer cope with information overload? There may be several strategies employed to reduce the amount of information actually used in purchase decision making so as not to be overwhelmed by the great amount available. It has been suggested that consumers base their decisions on the most important three to five product-attribute dimensions rather than on all of the information available.[56] Another suggestion is that consumers organize and integrate the separate information bits into larger information "chunks," as described in the learning chapter. For example, a brand name may serve as the consumer's basic device for summarizing the impressions and comparisons that exist among brand alternatives in the marketplace.[57]

Although few definitive statements can yet be made, the concept of information overload may become an extremely important issue among marketers, consumerists, legislators, regulators, and others who seek to provide even more information to the consumer.[58] The "more information is better" argument, however, may result in American shoppers feeling better but making worse purchase decisions.

For the marketer to provide more information than he now does may also prove to be uneconomical. For instance, industry experience indicates that a 30-second television commercial is economically superior to a 60-second ad both in terms of recall and sales (except in the case of new products). Thus, if the marketer were compelled to run a longer commercial in order to provide more information to the consumer this would be uneconomical from the brand's own standpoint, although perhaps justifiable from the position of industry's obligation to the consumer. Perhaps it is possible to restructure ads to provide more of the "right kind" of information within the same time limit. In order to resolve this potential problem, more advertising research will be needed.[59]

SUMMARY

This chapter has expanded our discussion of consumer decision processes by examining search and alternative evaluation. First, the meaning of information search was discussed and it was found that consumers may engage in active or passive, and internal or external search activities.

The information-seeking process was then described. Although consumers do not appear to rely to any great extent on marketer-dominated sources of information, the true extent of search activity is not well known. The amount of information-seeking activity was seen to be determined by a number of factors. The types of information sought as well as the major sources of consumer information were also discussed.

Consumer evaluation was extensively discussed and conceptualized according to the "sorting-rule" model by which consumers utilize the predictive value and confidence values of cues in determining which products to buy. Finally, several marketing implications of search and evaluation activities were presented.

DISCUSSION TOPICS

1. Distinguish between active and passive, internal and external search.

2. "Consumers should read more advertisements and visit more retail stores during the information-gathering stage of the decision process." Evaluate this statement.

3. What are the benefits and costs of search activity?

4. What types of risk might consumers perceive in a purchase situation? How might consumers deal with these risks? How could the marketer seek to minimize each type?

5. Read several recent product rating reports contained in *Consumer Reports* and evaluate the rating system used. What other information would you find helpful?

6. Design a product warranty registration card that you think would provide insight into the information search and evaluation process.

7. Debate this statement: "Government should provide consumers with more information in their purchase decisions."

8. Visit a supermarket and select one aisle of products to obtain the following information:

a. Number of products
b. Number of brands
c. Number of sizes in each brand

Based on this experience do you think there is information overload? Why or why not?

NOTES

1. Robert F. Kelly, "The Search Component of the Consumer Decision Process—A Theoretic Examination," in Robert L. King (ed.), *Marketing and the New Science of Planning*, American Marketing Association, Chicago, 1968, p. 273.

2. James F. Engel, David T. Kollat, and Roger D. Blackwell, *Consumer Behavior*, 2d ed., Holt, New York, 1973, p. 375.

3. Chem L. Narayana and Rom J. Markin, "Consumer Behavior and Product Performance: An Alternative Conceptualization," *Journal of Marketing*, **39**:2, October 1975.

4. Narayana and Markin, "Consumer Behavior," p. 2.

5. Louis P. Bucklin, "The Informative Role of Advertising," *Journal of Advertising Research*, **5**:11–15, 1965.

6. George Fisk, "Media Influence Reconsidered," *Public Opinion Quarterly*, **23**:85, 1959.

7. Jon G. Udell, "Prepurchase Behavior of Buyers of Small Electrical Appliances," *Journal of Marketing*, **30**:51, October 1966.

8. William P. Dommermuth, "The Shopping Matrix and Marketing Strategy," *Journal of Marketing Research,* **2**:130, May 1965.

9. George Katona and Eva Mueller, "A Study of Purchasing Decisions," in Lincoln H. Clark (ed.), *Consumer Behavior: The Dynamics of Consumer Reaction,* New York University Press, New York, 1955, pp. 30–87.

10. Louis P. Bucklin, "Testing Propensities to Shop," *Journal of Marketing,* **30**:22–27, January 1966.

11. Ernest Dichter, *Handbook of Consumer Motivations,* McGraw-Hill, New York, 1964, pp. 82–83.

12. Wesley C. Bender, "Consumer Purchase-Costs—Do Retailers Recognize Them?" *Journal of Retailing,* **40**:1–8, 52, Spring 1964.

13. Bucklin, "Testing Propensities to Shop."

14. Anthony Downs, "A Theory of Consumer Efficiency," *Journal of Retailing,* **37**:7, Spring 1961.

15. William P. Dommermuth and Edward W. Cundiff, "Shopping Goods, Shopping Centers and Selling Strategies," *Journal of Marketing,* **31**:32, October 1967.

16. Melvin T. Copeland, "Relation of Consumers' Buying Habits to Marketing Methods," *Harvard Business Review,* April 1923.

17. Richard H. Holton, "The Distinction between Convenience Goods, Shopping Goods, and Specialty Goods," *Journal of Marketing,* **23**, July 1958.

18. Dommermuth and Cundiff, "Shopping Goods"; Katona and Meuller, "A Study of Purchasing"; Bucklin, "Testing Propensities to Shop"; and Udell, "Prepurchase Behavior."

19. Donald F. Cox (ed.), *Risk Taking and Information Handling in Consumer Behavior,* Division of Research, Graduate School of Business, Harvard University, Boston, 1967, pp. 5–6.

20. The first five risks listed were suggested in Jacob Jacoby and Leon Kaplan, "The Components of Perceived Risk" in M. Venkatesan (ed.), *Proceedings of the Third Annual Conference of the Association for Consumer Research,* Association for Consumer Research, Chicago, 1972, pp. 382–393. The sixth risk was suggested in Ted Roselius, "Consumer Rankings of Risk Reduction Methods," *Journal of Marketing,* **35**:56–61, January 1971.

21. Roselius, "Consumer Rankings," pp. 57–58.

22. See Dommermuth and Cundiff, "Shopping Goods"; Dommermuth, "The Shopping Matrix"; and Jagdish N. Sheth and M. Venkatesan, "Risk-Reduction Processes in Repetitive Consumer Behavior," *Journal of Marketing Research,* **5**:307–310, August 1968.

23. John A. Howard, *Marketing Management: Analysis and Planning,* rev. ed., Irwin, Homewood, Ill., 1963, p. 58.

24. See for example George Katona, *The Mass Consumption Society,* McGraw-Hill, New York, 1964, pp. 289–290; Paul E. Green, Michael Halbert, and J. Sayer Minas, "An Experiment in Information Buying," *Journal of Advertising Research,* **4**:17–23, September 1964; and G. David Hughes, Seha M. Tinic, and Philippe A. Naert, "Analyzing Consumer Information Processing," in Philip R. McDonald (ed.), *Marketing Involvement in Society and the Economy,* American Marketing Association, Chicago, 1969, pp. 235–240.

25. Katona and Mueller, "A Study of Purchasing"; Joseph Newman and Richard Staelin, "Multivariate Analysis of Differences in Buyer Decision Time," *Journal of Marketing Research,* **8**:192–198, May 1971; Peter D. Bennett and Robert Mandell, "Prepurchase Information Seeking Behavior of New Car Purchasers—The Learning Hypothesis," *Journal of Marketing Research,* **6**:430–433, November 1969; and John E. Swan, "Experimental Analysis of Predecision Information Seeking," *Journal of Marketing Research,* **6**:192–197, May 1969.

26. Swan, "Experimental Analysis"; Katona, *The Mass Consumption Society;* and Frederick E. May, "Adaptive Behavior in Automobile Brand Choices," *Journal of Marketing Research,* **6**:62–65, February 1969.

27. George Katona, *Psychological Analysis of Economic Behavior,* McGraw-Hill, New York, 1951, pp. 67–68.

28. Katona, *The Mass Consumption Society,* pp. 289–290.

29. David T. Kollat, "A Decision-Process Approach to Impulse Purchasing," in Raymond M. Haas (ed.), *Science, Technology and Marketing,* American Marketing Association, Chicago, 1966, pp. 626–639; and Bucklin, "Testing Propensities to Shop."

30. Katona and Mueller, "A Study of Purchasing."

31. Kelly, "The Search Component," p. 277.

32. Paul E. Green, "Consumer Use of Information," in Joseph W. Newman (ed.), *On Knowing the Consumer,* Wiley, New York, 1966, p. 76.

33. Kelly, "The Search Component," p. 277.

34. Donald F. Cox, "The Audience as Communicators," in Stephen A. Greyser (ed.), *Toward Scientific Marketing,* American Marketing Association, Chicago, 1963, pp. 58–72.

35. Bruce Le Grand and Jon G. Udell, "Consumer Behavior in the Market Place," in *Journal of Retailing,* **40**:32–40, 47, Fall 1964; Newman and Staelin, "Multivariate Analysis"; and Katona and Mueller, "A Study of Purchasing."

36. Cox, "The Audience as Communicators."

37. See Hans B. Thorelli, Helmut Becker, and Jack Engledow, *The Information Seekers,* Ballinger, Cambridge, Mass., 1975, p. 19.

38. Newman and Staelin, "Multivariate Analysis."

39. Thomas L. Parkinson, "The Influence of Perceived Risk and Self-Confidence on the Use of Neutral Sources of Information in Consumer Decision-Making," in Barnett A. Greenberg (ed.), *Proceedings: Southern Marketing Association 1974 Conference,* pp. 298–301.

40. Joseph W. Newman and Bradley D. Lockeman, *Consumers' Information-Seeking Processes for Fashion Goods: A Literature Review,* Bureau of Business Research, University of Michigan, Ann Arbor, Mich., 1972, p. 88.

41. Donald F. Cox, "The Sorting Rule Model of the Consumer Product Evaluation Process," in Donald F. Cox (ed.), *Risk Taking and Information Handling in Consumer Behavior,* pp. 324–369.

42. Cox, "The Sorting Rule Model," p. 335.

43. Engel, Kollat, and Blackwell, *Consumer Behavior,* p. 423.

44. Narayana and Markin, "Consumer Behavior."

45. Cox, "The Sorting Rule Model," pp. 365–368.

46. William L. Wilkie, *Public Policy and Product Information: Summary Findings from Consumer Research,* National Science Foundation (RANN), Washington, D.C., 1975, p. vii.

47. See for example Kent B. Monroe and Peter J. La Placa, "What Are the Benefits of Unit Pricing?" *Journal of Marketing,* **36**:16–32, July 1972; and Monroe Peter Friedman, "Consumer Responses to Unit Pricing, Open Dating, and Nutrient Labelling," in M. Venkatesan (ed.), *Proceedings,* pp. 361–369.

48. Warren A. French and Hiram C. Barksdale, "Food Lebelling Regulations: Efforts toward Full Disclosure," *Journal of Marketing,* **38**:14–19, July 1974.

49. Raymond C. Stokes, "The Consumer Research Institute's Nutrient Labelling Research Program," *Food Drug Cosmetic Law Journal,* **27**:263–270, May 1972.

50. Edward H. Asam and Louis P. Bucklin, "Nutrition Labelling for Canned Foods: A Study of Consumer Response," *Journal of Marketing,* **37**:32–37, April 1973.

51. Friedman, "Consumer Responses."

52. George S. Day and William K. Brandt, "Consumer Research and the Evaluation of Information Disclosure Requirements: The Case of Truth in Lending," *Journal of Consumer Research,* **1**:21–32, June 1974.

53. G. A. Miller, "The Magical Number Seven, Plus or Minus Two: Some Limits on Our Capacity for Processing Information," *Psychological Review,* **63**:81–97, 1956; and Richard N. Cardozo, "Customer Satisfaction: Laboratory Study and Marketing Action," in L. George Smith (ed.), *Reflections on Progress in Marketing,* American Marketing Association, Chicago, 1964, pp. 283–289.

54. Jacob Jacoby, Donald E. Speller and Carol A. Kohn, "Brand Choice Behavior as a Function of Information Load," *Journal of Marketing Research,* **11**:63–69, February 1974.

55. Jacob Jacoby, Donald E. Speller, and Carol Kohn Berning, "Brand Choice Behavior as a Function of Information Load—Replication and Extension," *Journal of Consumer Research,* **1**:33–42, June 1974.

56. Fleming Hansen, "Consumer Choice Behavior: An Experimental Approach," *Journal of Marketing Research,* **6**:436–443, November 1969; and Jerry Olson and Jacob Jacoby, "Cue Utilization in the Quality Perception Process," in M. Venkatesan (ed.), *Proceedings,* pp. 167–179.

57. Jacoby, Speller, and Berning, "Brand Choice Behavior."

58. For critiques of Jacoby's work see William L. Wilkie, "Analysis of Effects of Information Load," *Journal of Marketing Research,* **9**:462–466, November 1974; John O. Summers, "Less Information Is Better?" *Journal of Marketing Research,* **11**:467–468, November 1974; and J. Edward Russo, "More Information Is Better: A Re-evaluation of Jacoby, Speller, and Kohn," *Journal of Consumer Research,* **1**:68–72, December 1974.

59. John A. Howard, "Conceptualizing the Adequacy of Information," in M. Venkatesan (ed.), *Proceedings,* pp. 99–100.

PURCHASING PROCESSES

CHOOSING A STORE Factors Determining Store Choice; The Effect of Store Image on Purchasing; Shopper Profiles; Store Loyalty **IN-STORE PURCHASING BEHAVIOR** Merchandising Techniques; Personal Selling Effects **IN-HOME PURCHASING PROCESSES** Significance of In-Home Shopping; Characteristics of Purchasers; In-Home Shopping Motivations; Marketing Implications **PURCHASING PATTERNS** Brand Loyalty; Impulse Purchasing

I n this chapter we shall be looking at the actual purchasing process of consumers, seeking to build a better understanding of how consumers make their purchases. Figure 21-1 presents the consumer decision model and highlights the purchasing-process stage. Purchasing processes involve not only the purchase decision but activities directly associated with the purchase. The purchase-decision stage itself involves selecting a course of action based on the preceding evaluation process. Some of the elements of the purchasing process stage, such as choosing a store, may actually be viewed as part of search and evaluation activities. However, because they are more directly connected with making a purchase, they are best discussed at this point. Thus, we are considering in this chapter the various facets of the consumer purchase environment of which the marketer should be aware in order to attract his chosen segments successfully.

The first topic to be discussed in this chapter is the matter of consumer store choice. This will be followed by a presentation of research findings regarding both in-store and out-of-store purchasing behavior. Finally we shall examine some repeat purchasing patterns. Implications of these topics to the marketer will be discussed throughout the chapter.

CHOOSING A STORE

We all like to think of ourselves as intelligent shoppers, as the cartoon in Figure 21-2 illustrates. But how do consumers actually make store-choice decisions? Basically, the consumer has certain evaluative store criteria established in her mind and compares these with her perception of a store's characteristics. As a result of this process, stores are categorized as either acceptable or unacceptable and hence will be patronized on that basis. If the resulting shopping experience is favorable, the consumer is reinforced in her learning experience and the matter of store choice will become largely routinized over a period of time.

Factors Determining Store Choice

There are several important factors that influence consumer store-choice behavior. Although the influence of these elements differs, depending on such variables as the type of product purchased, the type of store (such as discount, department, or other), and the type of consumer, the factors discussed in this section have been found to exert general influence on store choice. They include store location, physical design, assortment, prices, advertising, sales promotion, personnel, and services.

STORE LOCATION Location has an obvious impact on store patronage. Generally the closer consumers are to a store the greater their likelihood to purchase from that store. The further away consumers are from a store, the greater the number of intervening alternatives and thus the lower the likelihood to patronize that store. Research on the influence of location on store choice has taken several directions described in the following sections.

Intercity Choice Marketers have long been interested in the factors that cause consumers outside metropolitan areas to choose city A rather than city B in which to shop. Reilly and Converse conducted research on the drawing power of urban areas on consumers located near these cities. Believing that population and distance were not the causes of consumer store choice but could be used as good substitute variables for all the factors influencing

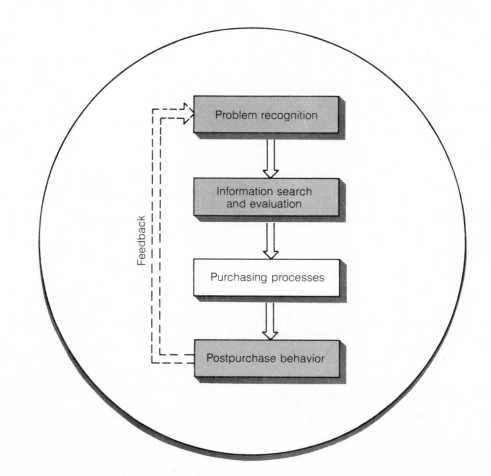

FIGURE 21-1
Consumer decision-
process model.

consumers, Reilly developed a "law of retail gravitation" to explain the strength of one city's attraction on consumers living near it:[1]

$$\left(\frac{B_a}{B_b}\right) = \left(\frac{P_a}{P_b}\right)\left(\frac{D_b}{D_a}\right)^2$$

where B_a = the proportion of retail trade from the intermediate town attracted by city A.

B_b = the proportion of retail trade from the intermediate town attracted by city B.

P_a = the population of city A.

P_b = the population of city B.

D_a = the distance from the intermediate town to city A.

D_b = the distance from the intermediate town to city B.

In effect, this law states that two cities attract retail trade from an intermediate city or town in the vicinity of the breaking point (that is, where 50 percent of the trade is attracted to each city) approximately in direct proportion to their population and in inverse proportion to the square of the distances from these two cities to the intermediate town. Reilly tested this law by computing the breaking point between thirty pairs of cities. The predictions were very close to results of actual field studies in which the breaking point was measured.

In applying the laws of retail gravitation it should be kept in mind that they were meant to apply only to two large cities. In addition, the laws apply only to the division of shopping goods trade, and particularly to fashion goods

"Reflecting pool, reflecting pool in the mall, who's the sharpest shopper of them all?"

FIGURE 21-2
How we view ourselves as shoppers. (*Source: Better Homes and Gardens*, December 1974, p. 128.)

(often referred to as style or specialty goods) because a large part of convenience and bulk goods is purchased locally.[2] Although the work by Reilly and Converse has helped marketers to conceptualize intermarket behavior, these laws are incomplete as explanations for store-choice behavior because they ignore such factors as income levels, the character of retailing in the two cities, and consumer preferences.

While the above approach has taken a macro orientation to the examination of intermarket patronage, others have taken a micro approach, which rests on the assumption that consumers have different characteristics and therefore have a differential predisposition to forego secondary costs such as time, money, and effort in selecting one trade area over another. Studies have found that consumers do frequently shop out-of-area *(out shoppers),* and they can be distinguished from non-outshoppers by certain demographic and psychographic characteristics.[3]

Intracity Choice As shopping centers developed during the period since 1950, researchers began to investigate their influence on the shopping behavior of consumers. These suburban alternatives to the central downtown shopping district introduced new wrinkles in explaining store choice.

To determine the factors that influence store choice within urban areas, some studies have examined the role of driving time on shopping center preference. Travel times longer than 15 minutes appear to be a barrier to many shopping center patrons.[4] Those who are willing to drive longer times seem to be attracted by the size of the shopping center.[5]

Other work in the area of shopping center preference has been done by Huff, who developed a model to determine the retail trade area for a shopping center.[6] The model estimates the probability that shoppers in homogeneous geographical segments (such as census tracts or neighborhoods) will visit a particular shopping center for a particular type of product purchase. The two fundamental variables associated with probability of patronage are square feet of floor space in the shopping center and travel time to the center. These variables substitute for population and distance used in Reilly's model.

Although Huff's model achieves a higher level of sophistication than Reilly's, it nevertheless fails to adequately incorporate variables that may influence consumer store preferences. The use of travel time and shopping center size, although important, are not the only factors that influence store choice.[7]

Interstore Choice Store location can also be very influential in shopper choice among competing stores, especially through its effect on store image. For example, stores in attractive surroundings are more likely to be patronized than those in unattractive surroundings. The remainder of this section looks at other components of a store's image and the way in which these factors affect store choice.

STORE DESIGN As we noted in Chapter 14, the design characteristics of a store visibly reflect its image and can dramatically influence patronage.[8] Many consumers appear to "size up" a store based on its outward appearance of architecture and signs and hence are drawn to the store or repelled by it, based on their perception of whether this store looks "right" for them. Interior design continues the image-fostering process.

MERCHANDISE ASSORTMENT The product variety and assortment of a store has been found to influence store choice. Consumers prefer stores that offer either a wide variety of product lines, brands, and prices, or substantial depth to their assortment, such as in size, colors, and styles, over stores with only medium depth or breadth of assortment.[9]

PRICES Evidence on the influence of price on store choice behavior is mixed. For example, among supermarket shoppers some studies indicate that price is very important, while others find it relatively unimportant.[10] The same is true for discount store shoppers.[11] Department store shoppers report that price is not a very high-priority reason for selecting a particular store.[12] In the face of such ambiguous research results, no firm conclusions may yet be made about the significance of price on store-choice behavior.

ADVERTISING AND SALES PROMOTION Retail advertising does not have a consistent impact but instead appears to vary in influence, depending on product and store type. Nevertheless, it is certainly true that retail advertising can be important in fulfilling any of its three goals: (1) to inform consumers, such as for a new store opening, (2) to persuade consumers that they should patronize a certain store or buy a particular brand, and (3) to remind customers of the store that they are appreciated. As we also have learned, advertising can be highly influential in cultivating a store image in consumers' minds.

The effect of sales-promotion activities on store choice also appears to be rather inconsistent. One of the primary means of sales promotion for stores has been the use of trading stamps. Stamps had a history of growth until the early 1960s and then declined, so that in 1970 only 37 percent of supermarkets offered trading stamps.[13] Although some consumers place great importance on stamps, they rarely seem to have enough significance to be a dominant factor in choice.[14]

PERSONNEL Employees of a retailer also are very instrumental in influencing the store's image. Consumers generally desire to trade where store personnel, particularly salespeople, are helpful, friendly, and courteous.[15]

If salespeople are not properly selected and well-trained, the results may be devastating for sales. One estimate has it that 70 percent of all consumers who stop patronizing a particular store do so because of employee attitude. In fact, one study found that some salespeople often preferred to purchase in competing stores because they considered their coworkers to be too uncooperative.[16]

CUSTOMER SERVICES Retail stores may offer numerous services in order to attract customers. One scheme classifies services according to those which (1) increase product satisfaction (such as credit, alterations, installation, and shopper information), (2) increase convenience (such as delivery, telephone ordering, and parking), and (3) provide special benefits (such as gift wrapping, product returns, and complaint offices).[17]

The extent of the effect of customer services on store choice is unclear. Generalizations are difficult in view of the conflicting evidence, and appear to vary considerably across products and consumers.

The Effect of Store Image on Purchasing

Store image is a complex of tangible or functional factors and intangible or psychological factors that a consumer perceives to be present in a store. The various determinants of store choice just discussed are intimately related to a store's image and influence its attracting power. Consequently, retailers need to understand what evaluative criteria consumers use in store choice, how important each criterion is, what image consumers have of the retailer's store, and how this image compares to an ideal image and to competitors' images. Berry has suggested the model presented in Figure 21-3 as being useful for retailers making image decisions. Specific programs similar to this reflect the need for store managers to determine the unique market segments they want to attract and then develop a store image useful in influencing patronage by those segments. The need to review periodically desired market segments and the consistency of store image to those segments is also stressed. Such activities should prove useful in satisfying consumer needs and in maintaining the vitality of the organization.

Shopper Profiles

It has been found that consumers tend to shop at different stores, depending partly on their demographic characteristics and their attitudes toward shopping.

One source summarizes numerous studies investigating socioeconomic characteristics of store patrons and finds that they arrive at quite similar discoveries:

1. Department and specialty stores attract a disproportionately large share of consumers over 40 to 45 years of age. A larger proportion of younger shoppers are attracted by department store chains, discount stores, and variety stores.

2. Department and specialty stores attract upper-income consumers while department store chains, discount stores, and variety stores tend to attract middle- and lower-income shoppers.

3. Department and specialty stores attract families without children, while families with children tend to shop in discount stores.[18]

Although each of the above groups of consumers may shop in all of the stores cited, the stores, nevertheless, tend to attract disproportionately large shares of certain types of shoppers.

Shopper attitudes and orientations are also helpful in understanding store choice. One of the most useful approaches to establishing a customer typology on this basis was that suggested by Stone. Based on his research, Stone was able to identify four types of shoppers: (1) economic, (2) personalizing, (3) ethical, and (4) apathetic.[19] Although probably no single consumer

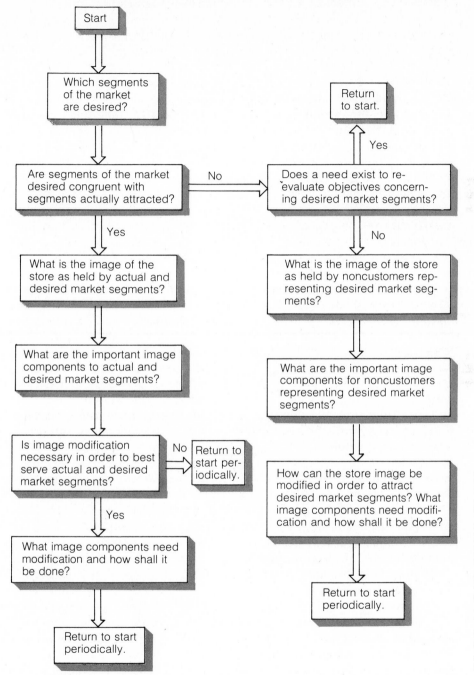

FIGURE 21-3
Image-decision
program for depart-
ment stores.
(*Source:* Leonard L.
Berry, "The Com-
ponents of Depart-
ment Store Image:
A Theoretical and
Empirical Analy-
sis," *Journal of Re-
tailing*, Spring
1969, p. 18. Repro-
duced by permis-
sion of *Journal of
Retailing*, New York
University.)

is adequately described by any of the models, they do represent composites of actual consumers and their characteristic role orientations.

The *economic consumer* is a close approximation to the classical economist's "economic man." She is quite sensitive to price, quality, and assortment of merchandise. Clerical personnel and the store are viewed merely as instruments of her purchase of goods.

The *personalizing consumer* shops where she is known by name. Strong personal attachments are formed with store personnel, and this personal, often intimate, relationship is crucial to her store-patronage decision.

The *ethical consumer* shops where she feels she "ought" to. That is, she is willing to sacrifice low prices or wide merchandise selection in order to "help the little guy out" or because "the chain store has no heart or soul." She sometimes forms strong attachments with personnel and store owners.

The *apathetic consumer* shops only because she "has" to. Shopping is viewed as an onerous task and one to be completed quickly. Convenient location is her crucial store selection criterion; and since she is not interested in shopping, she minimizes her expenditure of effort in purchasing products.

What is particularly interesting is that each of these consumer types was characterized by a distinctive pattern of social position and community identification. For example, economic consumers were lower-middle-class housewives with little allegiance to the area. Personalizing consumers had lower social status and a positive allegiance to the local area. Ethical consumers were relatively high in social status and long-time residents in the area, while apathetic consumers were characteristically older women who were also long-time residents. Thus, Stone's research found that economic and personalizing shopping orientations were more often exhibited by housewives new to the area, while ethical and apathetic orientations were adopted by women who had lived in the area for a long time. Although formulated in the 1950s, Stone's typology has been supported by more recent empirical research.[20] Other consumer taxonomies have been developed on the basis of shopping orientations and research is continuing in this field.[21]

Although care must be used in generalizing on the basis of findings from small samples, limited geographical areas and product types, further research may hold great promise for retailers attempting to segment shoppers in their market. Thus, store managers should conduct research to determine the percentage of each shopper orientation that exist in their areas. Such information can be very helpful in planning the store's marketing mix.

An understanding of demographic as well as life-style characteristics of each shopper-orientation category can also provide valuable data in making marketing (particularly promotion) decisions. For instance, by understanding the shopping predispositions of groups that constitute high potential, the retailer can enhance his promotion aimed at these groups. Economic shoppers, for example, will be drawn by a product and promotional mix stressing an optimal price and quality balance. For apathetic shoppers aspects of the retail mix that accommodate fast, easy shopping should be emphasized, such as easy credit purchases, shopping by phone or mail, home delivery, wide and deep assortments, branch store locations nearby, and attractive store hours.

Personalizing shoppers, who may be the largest segment in a market, could also be quite important to attract. Strategies aimed at this segment might stress that the store is a friend to the consumer. Such an atmosphere could be portrayed in the store's advertising and used in slogans. Store personnel could also be trained to treat customers in a warm, friendly manner.

The particular strategy chosen, however, should be consistent with the image that the store wants to project. It would probably be a mistake, for example, if an upper-status department store actively sought lower-status personalizing shoppers. To do so might alienate more attractive consumer segments and be inconsistent with the store's fundamental image.

For manufacturers who must make market segmentation decisions and select channels as a result of these decisions it is important to know whether a particular shopper orientation predominates among their customers. If purchasers are primarily apathetic consumers, then a channel oriented toward ease of shopping should be selected. Convenience goods and impulse items, for instance, might fit this pattern. If buyers tend to be personalizing shoppers, however, channel members able to provide the friendly, intimate assistance necessary to please this group should be selected. Of course, dual or multiple distribution channels may be necessary if purchasers exhibit two or more of these shopping orientations.

The next section discusses attempts to segment the market on the basis of store loyalty.

Store Loyalty

The term "store loyalty" refers to the consumer's inclination to patronize a given store during a specified period of time. Because consumer patronage results in revenue, store loyalty can be a very important factor influencing the company's profits. Loyal customers will tend to concentrate their purchases in the store and therefore may represent a very profitable market segment if they can be readily identified. Consequently, an important question for the marketer concerns the wisdom and ease of attracting this segment.

First of all, it is known that store loyalty among consumers can be measured in the marketplace. It is also known that store loyalty may be diminishing. According to a recent study, 41 percent of the housewives in 1954 shopped in one supermarket exclusively. In 1975, however, only 10 percent were that loyal.[22]

Second, it appears that the financial benefit to the retailer of pursuing the store-loyal consumer may be very significant. With regard to supermarket customers, for example, one writer states that the greatest opportunities lie in attracting the best possible mix of customer loyalties for the traffic that the store will carry. Particularly when many competitors exist, a store's best bet for holding and increasing sales volume is to improve the quality of its customer loyalty mix.[23] In support of this, one research study found that more loyal consumers allocate much larger proportions of their expenditures to their first choice store than do less loyal consumers, and that stores with the largest number of loyal customers have the largest market share. Moreover, loyal customers were found to be no more expensive to serve than nonloyal customers.[24]

Several studies have examined the demographic, socioeconomic, and psychographic characteristics of store-loyal food shoppers and found that there are patterns of personal characteristics. Although space precludes their review here, the interested reader can refer to the specific studies.[25] It should also be mentioned that store loyalty may vary by store type as well as consumer type. For example, some evidence indicates that although store loyalty may be high for supermarkets, little loyalty appears to exist for department stores.

Store loyalty seems to represent a potentially profitable approach to market segmentation for at least some stores, although research findings have been limited and not altogether consistent. The remainder of this section explores some marketing implications of store loyalty.

In order to capitalize on store loyalty, the retailer needs to know a significant amount about his loyal customers. However, since loyalty is not a strongly inherent consumer trait and cannot be identified in advance of shopping behavior, the retailer must seek to identify loyal patrons by the frequency of their shopping activity. Interviews could then be held with these patrons to determine the extent of their loyalty to the store, their particular wants and needs, and purchase behavior patterns such as their mass media exposure, store hour preferences, and credit card usage.

Not only should the marketer seek to understand the store loyalty characteristics and patterns of her own customers but also of her competitors' customers. Generally, it is important to learn as much as possible about why these families buy where they do. One element of the research should involve measuring the store's image in relation to the images of competitors. As a result of this kind of research, the marketer will be able to identify specific marketing programs to attract more store-loyal customers.

IN-STORE PURCHASING BEHAVIOR

Once consumers have selected the stores they will patronize, they must then proceed to consummate the purchase. A number of factors influence consumers' behavior within the store environment. In this section we shall examine some of the important variables affecting consumer shopping activities within stores.

Merchandising Techniques

A number of topics are discussed under the umbrella of merchandising techniques, including store layout, displays, product shelving, pricing strategies, branding, and promotional deals.

STORE LAYOUT AND TRAFFIC PATTERNS A store's interior is organized in such a manner as to accomplish the firm's merchandising strategy. Much of the research on store layout and its effect on consumers has been done in supermarkets. For example, supermarkets are traditionally organized on the basis of the following principles:

1. Spread major departments and demand items as widely as possible in order to expose more customers to more products.

2. Place service and perishables departments adjacent to work areas to reduce time and effort for servicing them.

3. Place high-margin, high-impulse departments and categories in the flow of traffic before demand products. As a result impulse purchases are made before planned purchases.[26]

Figure 21-4 presents an example of a contemporary approach to store layout showing traffic pattern data.

Traffic pattern studies are very popular with retailers in order to determine where good or bad sales areas are within the store. Supermarkets especially conduct such research in order to determine optimum layout and placement of goods. Shopper activity is diagramed on these layouts for both density and main direction of traffic for each aisle and for buying rates within the aisles. From these statistics it can readily be seen that shoppers shop a store in different ways. There are also differences in the times spent in the store among different patrons. Consequently, depending on the type of shopper and the length of time spent shopping, different expenditures result.[27]

Although use of passing, buying, and passing-buying ratios can be helpful in visualizing *what* consumers did, they fail to explain *why* these patterns exist. Thus, further research would need to be conducted by the retailer to understand why such passing and buying ratios exist and how a change in store layout could alter these patterns.

DISPLAYS An effective combination of good store layout and attractive displays can change a humdrum retail environment into one that not only is more exciting but also produces more sales.

Special displays are used in stores in order to attract shopper attention to one or more products. The use of displays and store signs has grown so that in 1976 national advertisers spent well over $2.2 billion for these materials. It is also known that 88 percent of all retail outlets use promotional displays. In a study of chain drug stores, supermarkets, full-line discount stores, and home improvement centers, it was found that drug stores use the most displays (96 percent of stores) and home improvement centers use the least (74 percent). Moreover, 36 percent of store managers say they are now using more promotional displays than they were in 1974.[28]

The bulk of published research conducted on the effectiveness of displays has come from the supermarket and drugstore fields. Numerous examples of the effectiveness of displays in attracting consumer attention could be cited. The following are representative of the findings:

1. Of 2473 supermarket shoppers interviewed, 38 percent had purchased at least one brand or item they had never before bought. The reason cited most frequently (25 percent) for a first-time purchase was that it had been displayed.[29]

2. A study of 5215 customers in supermarkets, variety stores, drugstores,

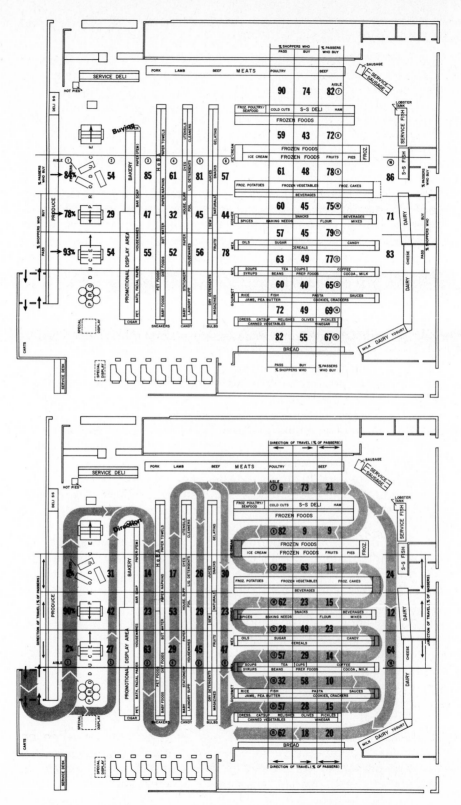

FIGURE 21-4
Contemporary supermarket layout. (*Source:* "Consumer Behavior in the Super Market—Part III," *Progressive Grocer*, January 1976, pp. 70–71. Reprinted with permission.)

hardware stores, liquor stores, and service stations found that one-third had purchased at least one of the displayed items.[30]

3. Interviews with 2803 shoppers in 16 drugstores spread across the United States discovered that 30 percent of those who decided to try a new brand after entering the store did so because of displays.[31]

While displays can have quite positive results, they must be used correctly in order to achieve their potential. A series of studies conducted by *Progressive Grocer* yielded the following conclusions regarding various methods employed:

1. Advertisement tie-ins boosted product sales 194 percent when only shelf signs were used. When shelf signs and special displays were used, sales were up 629 percent over normal.

2. Making full use of available storewide point-of-purchase and decorative tie-ins resulted in 153 percent more sales than in stores that did the same advertising but used minimal in-store tie-ins.

3. Special displays of unadvertised items resulted in sales 420 percent higher than normal.

4. The addition of signs to displays increased their sales by 112 percent over displays without signs.

5. Shelf signs are very effective in moving merchandise. "As advertised" signs resulted in 124 percent more sales than stores not using signs; cents-off signs created 23 percent more sales; slogans (e.g., "save more") resulted in 5 percent sales increase; product identification signs created 18 percent more sales than normal; and full information signs resulted in 33 percent more sales than normal.

6. Related items displayed side-by-side resulted in 170 percent more dollar sales than when the same items were displayed separately.

7. Display selling power declines 47 percent in the second week, and 74 percent by the third week unless the item has great seasonal appeal or some other sustaining feature.[32]

It is clear from these results that displays are effective in increasing sales. A legitimate question by the reader may be whether the display takes sales away from ordinary shelf sales. It has been found that displays do tend to reduce normal shelf sales. However, net sales of display and shelf combined are usually so far above normal that use of displays appears to be strongly substantiated. Moreover, tests show that there is a rapid return to normal shelf sales once the item is removed from display. This would indicate that customers are not simply stocking up on the item but are actually consuming more. Thus displays have much evidence to support their continued strong usage as a merchandising tool.

PRODUCT SHELVING Product shelving has an important influence on consumer behavior. Both the height at which products are displayed and the number of rows presented (facings) can influence sales of products. In addition, the use of shelf signs and extenders can affect sales.

Shelf Height When it is realized that the average shopper selects only 35 of the available 7000 or more grocery products during the average 27-minute shopping trip, it is easy to see why manufacturers clamor for the most visible eye-level shelf position.

Tests conducted by *Progressive Grocer* indicate that the most favorable shelf position is generally at eye level, followed in effectiveness by waist level, and knee or ankle level. It has been calculated from *Progressive Grocer* data that sales from waist-level shelves were only 74 percent as great, and sales from floor-level shelves were only 57 percent as great as sales from equivalent space allocations on eye-level shelves.[33]

Beyond the physical impossibility of stocking all products at eye level, there are also valid arguments for placing products on lower shelves. Actually, the shelf height dictated for an item is a function of its package size, its normal movement, whether or not it is being advertised, and its market target.

Shelf Space It is crucial for a product to be given enough shelf space to attract the buyer's attention. In order to help ensure this, the science and industry of packaging has mushroomed. Yet all of the manufacturer's careful packaging efforts can be counteracted by an insufficient amount of shelf space in the store. Without adequate shelf facings the item will be lost in the mass of 22,000 other facings lining the average supermarket's shelves.

There have been a number of experiments on *shelf space elasticity,* that is, the ratio of relative changes in unit sales to relative change in shelf space. The result of these experiments is that there is a small positive relationship between shelf space and unit sales. However, the relationship is not uniform among products, or across stores or intrastore locations.[34] *Progressive Grocer's* tests have concluded that products can have too many as well as too few facings, with both situations resulting in wrong use of space.

An adequate number of facings is especially important for new products. Tests show that doubling shelf facings on new items during their first 2 to 3 weeks in stores produced sales increases from 85 percent to 160 percent over stores that stocked the items but did not make any facing adjustments. In addition fast-moving items tend to react much more dramatically to changes in shelf space than slow-moving products.

IN-STORE INFORMATION PROGRAM Although the factors to be discussed here are not strictly merchandising strategies, they most definitely can have an influence on where consumers shop and which brands they choose. Many shoppers are dissatisfied with their regular supermarket on this score. In fact, a survey among one magazine's readers found that 51 percent of the respondents thought that information in the store to help make buying decisions was inadequate.[35] Figure 21-5 provides a general overview of consumers' familiarity, evaluation of usefulness, and usage of three major consumer-information programs, according to a survey by *Progressive Grocer.*

In spite of the attractiveness of instituting various information programs for consumers in order to help them make more intelligent shopping decisions, there is some question about the effectiveness of such practices.

Consequently, more research needs to be conducted on ways to make information programs more beneficial not only to consumers but also as a competitive technique for the retailer.[36]

It seems clear that well-thought-out programs of information carefully provided to the consumer can pay dividends for manufacturers or retailers in attracting consumers. Consumers may well switch to companies that provide more helpful information to them. Whether or not consumers make better decisions because of the increased amount of information is not known since it is difficult to define what a "better decision" is. It would help to answer this question if we knew how much time and money consumers saved because of these programs, how much better their nutritional levels were because of diet changes, and what levels of satisfaction are achieved by users.

PRICING STRATEGIES We have already discussed the microeconomic view of consumer reactions (Chapter 2) and the way in which consumers' perceptual processes influence their evaluation of prices (Chapter 14). There

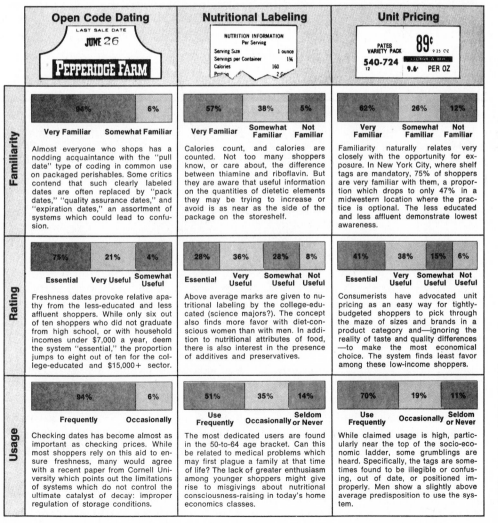

FIGURE 21-5
How consumers view information programs. (*Source:* Robert F. Dietrich, "Some Signs of Our Times on the Road to Smarter Shopping," *Progressive Grocer*, November 1976, p. 43. Reprinted with permission.)

are other elements of pricing which can affect consumers in their shopping activities. This section presents two of those influencing strategies.

Price Awareness Although consumers have a critical attitude toward the general price level and supermarket prices in particular, they apparently have little specific knowledge about actual product prices. For example, only about one shopper in twelve can name the exact price of even one out of a broad range of common food store items.[37] Since price is one of the most important criteria in food store choice it is important for most supermarket operators to achieve a low-price image. Yet at the same time it is obvious that shoppers are not at all clear what constitutes a "good" price for even popular items, much less those that are bought infrequently. Consequently, an appropriate strategy to achieve a low-price image among consumers would be to concentrate price advertising for only the most popular items where consumers would be most cognizant of price differences. This is often accomplished by the use of *loss leaders*—products that are sold slightly above cost to draw traffic into the store and create an impression of low prices. Moreover, as many supermarkets do, the regular or competitor's price could be cited along with the special or store's price in both media advertising and in-store materials.

Multiple-Pricing This refers to the technique by which retailers price items in multiple quantities such as 2 for 25 cents, 3 for 49 cents, and so on. The basic idea of multiple-pricing is to offer the customer a "cents-off" deal on a quantity purchase. However, the technique has long been complained about by some consumerists as a device that confuses customers more than it saves them money, and one that causes them to buy more than they had planned. Nevertheless 74 percent of supermarket customers usually buy items priced in multiple-units.[38] For the marketer additional sales can result from pricing items in such a way, but several factors need to be considered:

First, the price must be easy for customers to comprehend. Consumers will tend to buy the full multiple or the segments most easily figured when confronted by a multiple too complicated for easy division—e.g., 3 for 79 cents or 7 for $1.

Second, when units are priced in multiples exceeding $1, customers appear to become very resistant.

Third, products that are slow to consume or highly perishable do not do well in multiple-unit offerings, while seasonal items do.

Fourth, availability of different sizes will influence the effectiveness of the price depending on which is the best buy.

Fifth, brands with the greatest acceptance show greater increases from multiple pricing than less popular brands.

Finally, a significant number of incorrect prices are rung by checkers who cannot divide multiples correctly. Incorrect prices rung too low will hurt the store's profits, while those rung too high may alienate customers.[39]

In conclusion, marketers who use the technique are advised to (1) properly train checker personnel, (2) clearly mark products and perhaps inform customers of breaks within the multiple, (3) avoid complicated multiples, (4) use multiples selectively, and (5) explain this pricing policy to their customers.

BRAND CHOICE—NATIONAL VERSUS PRIVATE For a number of years now there has been a "battle" between manufacturers' national brands and distributors' private brands for brand predominance in certain product categories. To the winner go greater product sales and profits. Consequently, it is important, particularly from the marketer's viewpoint, to know whether there are any distinguishing characteristics between private and national brand customers which might make possible their effective market segmentation.

Position of Private Brands The competitive position of private brands differs from industry to industry. For example, although they account for less than 10 percent of sales in portable appliances, private brands control over 50 percent of the market in shoes. In grocery and drug stores private brands have less than a 30-percent share of the market. As for the number of consumers who purchase private label merchandise, the figures are quite large. Research by A. C. Nielsen found that 80 percent of buyers of grocery products have purchased private brands.[40] Nevertheless, based on the evidence available, no significant swing away from national brands to private brands is expected to occur.[41]

Characteristics of Private-Brand Buyers Although it has been shown that consumers view private and national brands differently, it is not clearly known what consumer characteristics differentiate between private- and national-brand users.[42] Thus, more research is needed to determine the extent to which such buyers are different, how they can be reached, and what the best marketing approaches might be.

SALES PROMOTION Sales promotion techniques used by manufacturers and retailers can be very effective. Couponing for instance, has expanded tremendously. In 1962, 5.2 billion manufacturer cents-off coupons (excluding retailer in-ad coupons) were distributed compared to 35.7 billion in 1975 (with about 3 billion redeemed). The number of manufacturers offering coupons has also risen from perhaps 350 in 1962 to 970 in 1975.

During 1975, 65 percent of United States households used coupons. Supermarket redemptions account for a significant share of coupon volume. *Progressive Grocer* estimates that almost 8 percent of all supermarket transactions involve coupon redemptions. Significant, too, is the fact that redeemers shop longer in the store (by an average six minutes) and spend one-third more than do nonusers.[43]

Characteristics of Deal-prone Consumers In order to understand better whether certain customers react more favorably to deals such as coupons, several studies have been conducted in an attempt to segment "deal-prone" consumers. Unfortunately very few socioeconomic variables are consistent predictors of this behavior.[44]

Because deal-prone consumers are not yet able to be effectively differentiated, segmentation on this basis is difficult. Nevertheless, couponing continues to grow and prosper. For retailers and manufacturers who desire to attract customers in certain important market segments, couponing is a valuable tool which can be effectively used.

Personal Selling Effects

We have been primarily discussing in-store purchasing behavior for grocery items that are sold via self-service. However, there are also many product purchase situations in which customers interact with salespeople.

Personal selling in which a salesperson interacts with a consumer is referred to as a "dyad." Such an influence may be very strong, as seen in our earlier discussion of interpersonal influence and social group behavior. From a consumer-behavior viewpoint, however, little is known about what factors make this process a success. Studies of salespeople have generally sought to learn what main characteristics lead to success, and have assumed homogeneity among prospects. Usually, researchers point to a bundle of personality variables as predictors of good sales performance. More recently, however, researchers have begun to view selling as dyadic interaction in terms of not only the characteristics of the salesperson but also the buyer, and how the two parties react to each other.[45]

Figure 21-6 presents a conceptual framework of buyer-seller interaction. This figure (which can explain industrial as well as consumer selling) illustrates four possible outcomes based on the compatibility of style and content of communication between the parties. For example, if the customer and salesperson are compatible with respect to style (such as the format, ritual, or mannerisms) of communication but not content (that is, the substantive aspects or the purposes of communication), the sale may not be consummated because of differences in product expectations. Either discussion is terminated or negotiations take place to change each other's product expectations. Other outcomes are possible as a result of different buyer-seller communications.

As this recent research suggests, it appears that rather than focusing merely on the salesperson's traits, the marketer would do well to also consider the customer's traits. Careful research into market-segment characteristics and needs may result in more effective sales management. By hiring salespeople who match desired customers better and preparing them better to perform effectively in the dyadic interaction process, the firm may achieve more success in the market.

IN-HOME PURCHASING PROCESSES

While the vast bulk of consumer purchasing processes take place in stores, there is a growing amount of in-home shopping such as with Sears' Catalog or Avon cosmetics. This section examines the significance of in-home purchasing and the factors that influence the process.[46]

Significance of In-Home Shopping

According to U.S. census retail trade statistics, in-home buying is increasingly urban and has been growing appreciably faster than total store sales and general merchandise sales for some time. Due to classification and measurement problems of the census, however, there is not a clear picture of the significance of this activity. Estimates of nonstore buying range from 2 to 12 percent of total retail sales.

Catalog shopping is one of the rapidly growing segments of this industry. The number of catalog companies (excluding department stores) rose 20 percent to 6500 by 1975. Today's catalogs are a far cry from the first catalog offering only a handful of items, issued in 1872 by Montgomery Ward to serve rural areas in the Midwest. Sears, for example, now issues 19 catalogs in 24 different editions for a total of 300 million books annually. The major catalogs have 150,000 items in them.[47]

What amounts to an avalanche of largely unsolicited mail might appear to turn consumers off. However, according to the A. C. Nielsen Company, three out of four people open catalogs received by mail; and 67 percent of those

FIGURE 21-6
A conceptual framework of buyer-seller interaction. [*Source:* Jagdish N. Sheth, "Buyer-Seller Interaction: A Conceptual Framework," in Beverlee B. Anderson (ed.), *Advances in Consumer Research,* **3**:383, Cincinnati, Association for Consumer Research, 1976.]

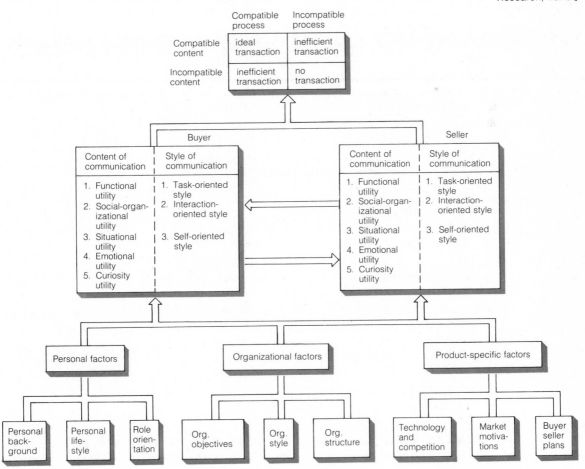

who bother to do so end up making a purchase.[48] Other studies have found similar results.[49] However, in-home buying still amounts to only a small fraction of total household purchases.[50]

Characteristics of Purchasers

There are a number of differences that are notable between in-home shoppers and other shoppers. These differences may be classified according to socioeconomic status, race, wife's employment status, and geographic location. It must be pointed out that, because of methodological differences between studies and the limited amount of research, these results are not conclusive.

1. *"Upscale" Households*—With few exceptions, in-home shoppers are described as above-average in socioeconomic status. These differences increase with in-home shopping intensity, and are especially pronounced among households utilizing several in-home shopping modes.

2. *Racial Patterns*—It appears that black and white households differ little on total in-home shopping expenditures or frequency. However, shopping mode differences do exist. For example, blacks do less mail-order buying than do whites at similar income levels.

3. *Working Wives*—It might be expected that working women restricted in shopping time flexibility, would be especially likely to take advantage of in-home shopping. However, this relationship has not been supported so far. In fact, some studies have found employed women even more willing to shop in stores than women not employed outside the home.

4. *Geographic Location*—There is limited evidence that geographical location within a trading area influences in-home shopping, with those in rural areas utilizing it more than their urban counterparts. Its use seems to be higher where there is greater retail inaccessibility and inadequacy.

In-Home Shopping Motivations

There are several motivational and life-style factors which influence in-home buying. The most important ones are discussed in this section.

CONVENIENCE Shopping convenience is probably the most important motivator in consumer decisions to shop at home and is the one so often stressed by the industry. High convenience orientation does explain some but not all in-home shopping motivation. For example, phone shoppers seem especially convenience-oriented, while catalog buyers not only want shopping convenience, but also merchandise assortment and uniqueness, competitive prices, and useful descriptive shopping information. Mail order's strength today seems to lie less in its shopping convenience than its ability to offer new, unique, personalized products.

RISK OF BUYING In spite of the obvious advantages of shopping at home, the high perceived risk that is associated with buying by description partially explains why many consumers are hesitant to use this particular technique. Research on telephone and mail-order shopping supports this hypothesis.

LIFE-STYLE Active in-home buyers are more cosmopolitan, style- and value-conscious, convenience-oriented, and generally are more demanding shoppers than other consumers. They are more flexible in shopping style, visit stores more frequently, and view shopping and shopping risk more positively. Their in-home buying is discretionary, often impulse- or convenience-oriented, and they use a variety of in-home buying methods and sources.

Personality characteristics found among in-home shoppers indicate that they tend to be more self-assured, venturesome, and cosmopolitan in outlook and in shopping behavior.

Marketing Implications

The home shopper segment is becoming an increasingly attractive and competitive market. Especially with the growing revolution in technology and the possibilities it brings for in-home marketing is the future of this area sure to be exciting. At present, however, not nearly enough is known about such shoppers.

Many companies not presently active in in-home marketing will have to assess the cost/benefit potential of serving this market. Once a firm makes a positive decision to pursue this group, it is necessary to locate important customer segments. In some cases this may be relatively easy. The frequent catalog buyer, for instance, may be reached by direct mail through the use of zip codes related to geographic areas having the greatest potential, as defined by this segment's demographic profile (such as upscale consumers), or by using mailing lists based on this pattern of discriminating demographic characteristics.[51]

Designing a promotional mix appealing to at-home shoppers is a challenging task. The themes and copy should be consistent with this group's life-style, such as emphasizing their venturesome, self-assured, and cosmopolitan orientation. Both in message design and layout, catalogs and circulars offered to this group should be carefully developed so as to be congruent with the images the marketer wants to project. To overcome hesitancy among buyers due to perceived risk associated with at-home shopping, promotional materials should provide buyers with sufficient information about products offered (perhaps including testimonials from satisfied users where appropriate) and safeguard the purchaser by offering easy, guaranteed return privileges.

PURCHASING PATTERNS

The final section of this chapter focuses on two important purchasing patterns. We shall examine (1) the extent to which consumers develop repeat purchasing patterns and (2) the extent to which purchases are unplanned. These subjects will be discussed in the context of brand loyalty and impulse purchasing.

Brand Loyalty

Brand loyalty is a topic of much concern to all marketers. Every company seeks to have a steady group of unwavering customers for its product or service.

NATURE OF BRAND LOYALTY An important question for the marketer has been whether there is a tendency for consumers to be "brand loyal," that is, to purchase a particular brand time after time. An early affirmative answer was given to this question based on results of data from a *Chicago Tribune* consumer purchase panel for nine products. This study of repeat purchase behavior suggested that there were four brand loyalty patterns, as follows:[52]

1. *Undivided loyalty* is exhibited by families purchasing Brand A in the following sequence: A A A A A A.

2. *Divided loyalty* is exhibited by the family purchasing Brands A and B in the following sequence: A B A B A B.

3. *Unstable loyalty* is shown by the family buying Brands A and B in the following sequence: AAA BBB.

4. *No loyalty* is shown by families buying Brands A, B, C, D, E, and F in the following sequence: A B C D E F.

On the basis of the products studied, it was concluded that the majority of consumers tend to purchase a favorite brand or set of brands.

Although the degree of loyalty varied by product, the percentage of consumers exhibiting some brand loyalty was rather high. Efforts to group products by some type of merchandise classification (for example, foods and nonfoods) showed no relationship to brand loyalty, although a definite relationship was discovered between strength of brands and nature of the loyalty shown. Loyalty appears to be high for well-established products where little or no changes have occurred, and low where product entries are frequent.

Various other studies have used these and other measures of brand loyalty and have generally concluded that brand loyalty exists and is a relatively widespread phenomenon.[53] Most studies, however, suffer from a lack of comparability because of differing conceptions of brand loyalty. Until consumer-behavior researchers agree on a common definition, there will continue to be difficulty synthesizing results. Engel, Kollat, and Blackwell have suggested a useful definition of brand loyalty that recognizes that true brand-loyal consumers should exhibit not only a high degree of repeat purchasing but also a *favorable attitude* toward the purchased brand. Their extended definition states that it "is the preferential attitudinal and behavioral response toward one or more brands in a product category expressed over time by a consumer (or buyer)."[54]

WHAT FACTORS EXPLAIN BRAND LOYALTY? Numerous studies attempting to explain brand loyalty have been largely inconclusive to this point. The following results appear to be indicated:

1. Some socioeconomic, demographic, and psychological variables are related to brand loyalty (when extended definitions are used) but tend to be product-specific rather than general across products.

2. Loyalty behavior of an informal group leader influences the behavior of other group members.

3. Some consumer characteristics are related to store loyalty, which in turn is related to brand loyalty.

4. Brand loyalty is positively related to perceived risk and market structure variables such as the extensiveness of distribution and market share of the dominant brand, but inversely related to the number of stores shopped.[55]

EFFECT OF OUT-OF-STOCK CONDITIONS A potentially important influence on brand loyalty is the possibility of brand substitution. It has been found that between 19 percent and perhaps as much as 33 percent of shoppers presold by an advertising campaign change their minds and switch to another brand when they get inside the supermarket.[56] An important reason for brand substitution is an out-of-stock condition. To appreciate the impact out-of-stock conditions may have on the retailer, consider that for a moderate-sized supermarket these costs have been estimated to run between $13,000 and $15,000 per year.[57]

Although the result of out-of-stock conditions appears to be very significant, little research has been done on its effect on brand loyalty. The A. C. Nielsen Company, however, has provided some indication of the extent of brand substitution in the supermarket. A large survey of shoppers found that 25 percent left the store with some portion of their wants unsatisfied because of out-of-stock conditions among desired brands or package sizes. Although 42 percent of the consumers refused to accept a substitute brand, 58 percent were willing to do so. The proportion of consumers refusing to accept a substitute brand varied among products studied, from 23 percent for toilet tissue to 62 percent for toothpaste. Among consumers who failed to find their desired package size, 52 percent bought another size of the same brand, while 30 percent bought another brand, and 18 percent would not accept a substitute.[58]

MARKETING IMPLICATIONS Several marketing implications flow from our discussion of brand loyalty. The first question, of course, for the marketer attempting to attract more brand-loyal customers is the feasibility of segmenting this group. That is, are these consumers identifiable? As we have just seen from the correlates of brand loyalty, those customers generally do not appear to differ significantly from other customers on most segmentation bases. The marketer may be more successful, however, in discerning unique characteristics of customers loyal to his particular brand or product. The results of such an analysis may provide him with useful insights for developing attractive marketing strategies.

Certainly, the marketer would desire to attract more brand-loyal customers and also increase the level of loyalty among his present customers. These various goals of the marketer may necessitate different marketing strategies. For instance, increasing brand loyalty of present customers may necessitate better after-sale service, while attracting new customers to become steady users may require certain inducements such as price discounts. Thus, the varying ranges of brand loyalty that the marketer faces point to different competitive actions. For less highly committed consumers a catchy advertising message, coupon offer, free sample, point-of-purchase display, or attractive package could cause a switch to the marketer's brand. This is the reason we see so much of these sorts of activities and the resultant brand switching in certain product groups (e.g., foods, soaps, and detergents). The packaged consumer goods field can generally be considered highly dynamic in this regard.

In order to induce brand switching among customers who are more highly loyal, the marketer is likely to require more fundamental changes in consumer perceptions and attitudes. Therefore, significant revisions in product image are often necessary, frequently accomplished through revamped promotional programs.

Advertising decisions are usually geared to the loyalty situation that confronts the brand. It is suggested that if brand loyalty is high, the advertiser has a good case for "investment" expenditures where large amounts are expended over short periods of time to attract new users, since continued purchases after the advertising has been curtailed will "amortize" the advertising investment. Where a low degree of brand loyalty exists in the product class, advertising expenditures should be made at a fairly steady rate on a pay-as-you-go basis, with demonstrated returns in extra sales equal to or greater than the extra advertising costs.[59]

Finally, it is clear that both retailers and manufacturers need to strive to avoid out-of-stock conditions, which might lead not only to reduced sales but also to less store and brand loyalty.

Impulse Purchasing

Impulse buying, or as some marketers prefer to call it—unplanned purchasing—is another consumer purchasing pattern. As the term implies, the result or purchase was not specifically planned. In this section we will find that the process is rather widespread and may have significant implications for the marketer.

NATURE OF IMPULSE PURCHASING It is difficult for marketers to agree on a definition of impulse buying. Stern cites four types of impulse purchases:

1. *Pure Impulse*—a novelty or escape purchase which breaks a normal buying pattern.

2. *Reminder Impulse*—a shopper sees an item and is reminded that the stock at home needs replenishing, or recalls an advertisement or other information about the item and a previous decision to purchase.

3. *Suggestion Impulse*—a shopper having no previous knowledge of some product sees the item for the first time and visualizes a need for it.

4. *Planned Impulse*—a shopper enters the store with the expectation and intention of making some purchases on the basis of price specials, coupons, etc.[60]

EXTENT OF IMPULSE BUYING There are several studies which have indicated the significant and growing trend toward unplanned purchasing. Here are some of the conclusions on the extent of impulse buying:

Over 33 percent of all purchases in variety and drugstores are unplanned.[61]

One-half of buying decisions in supermarkets are unplanned.[62]

Only 41 percent of grocery shoppers use a shopping list. However, list users are more intensive shoppers and bigger spenders than nonusers.[63]

Thirty-nine percent of all department store shoppers and 62 percent of all discount store shoppers purchased at least one item on an unplanned basis.[64]

These factors are somewhat deceiving in that no distinction is made between the various kinds of impulse purchases possible for consumers. The picture painted is one of consumers running around somewhat out of control making irrational decisions on the spur of the moment in the store. Actually, although most consumers may not use a shopping list, their product and brand purchases are certainly rational (as we have defined it) and most probably fit into the reminder and planned impulse categories rather than the pure and suggestion impulse types.

FACTORS INFLUENCING IMPULSE PURCHASES The rather limited amount of research on unplanned purchases indicates that there are several product, marketing, and consumer characteristics which appear to be related to the process. Product characteristics that may influence greater impulse purchasing are those low in price, for which there is a marginal need, having a short product life, small in size or light in weight, and easy to store. Marketing factors include mass distribution in self-service outlets with mass advertising and point-of-sale materials, and prominent display position and store location.[65] Consumer personality, demographics, and socioeconomic characteristics have not been shown to be related to the rate of impulse buying. However, the percentage of unplanned supermarket purchases appears to increase with: (1) size of the grocery bills, (2) number of products purchased, (3) major shopping trips, (4) frequency of product purchase, (5) absence of a shopping list, and (6) number of years married.[66]

MARKETING IMPLICATIONS The unplanned nature of much purchasing behavior today places a greater burden on manufacturers and retailers. The extent to which shoppers buy on impulse and without written lists puts a strong emphasis on the various kinds of in-store merchandising and personal selling stimuli which the marketer may use.

Managers of retail outlets need to understand better the types and extent of occurrence of impulse purchases in order to better plan store layout, merchandise and display location and allocation, and so on. Manufacturers also could benefit from an improved understanding of impulse purchasing by determining how much in-store product information may be necessary to provide on or with their products.

SUMMARY

This chapter began with an explanation of the nature of the purchasing process, which was found to involve not only the purchase decision but activities directly associated with the purchase. We then examined the influence of various factors on the consumer's store choice decision. Factors such as location, store design, merchandise assortment, prices, advertising and sales promotion, personnel, and services are all very important influencing variables. Taken together these and other elements form a store's image to the consumer that is of fundamental importance in store selection decisions. We also profiled various types of shoppers and discussed the significance and implications of store loyalty.

In-store purchasing behavior was described in detail. Merchandising techniques and personal selling efforts were discussed to provide a better understanding of effective techniques which the marketer might utilize.

In-home consumer purchasing processes were also discussed. This growing market is expected to have much significance for the marketer as we enter the electronic era and a period of diminished driving.

Finally, we examined two often-used purchasing approaches: brand loyalty and impulse purchases. Both of these have important implications to the marketer and several strategies were suggested.

DISCUSSION TOPICS

1. Visit competing discount houses, supermarkets, department stores, or specialty shops in your area and describe the image you have of each store. What factors account for the image differences?

2. For the poorest image store in question 1 design a strategy for upgrading its image.

3. Visit a supermarket and observe the extent to which displays are used and whether they conform to the guidelines suggested in this chapter.

4. Does this supermarket appear to conform to the text's guidelines on multiple-pricing?

5. Keep a record of your product purchases for a period of time. How brand loyal are you? What factors seem to explain your degree of brand loyalty? How does your pattern and explanation differ from other students in the class?

6. Which of the above purchases were bought on impulse? Categorize them as to price, reminder, suggestion, or planned impulse purchases.

NOTES

1. William J. Reilly, *The Law of Retail Gravitation,* William J. Reilly, New York, 1931.

2. Paul D. Converse, "New Laws of Retail Gravitation," *Journal of Marketing,* **14**, October 1949.

3. See for example Robert O. Herrmann and Leland L. Beik, "Shoppers' Movements Outside Their Local Retail Area," *Journal of Marketing,* **23**:45–51, October 1968; John R. Thompson, "Characteristics and Behavior of Outshopping Consumers," *Journal of Retailing,* **47**:70–80, Spring 1971; and Fred D. Reynolds and William R. Darden "Intermarket Patronage: A Psychographic Study of Consumer Outshoppers," *Journal of Marketing,* **36**:50–54, October 1972.

4. James A. Brunner and John L. Mason, "The Influence of Driving Time upon Shopping Center Preference," *Journal of Marketing,* **32**:57–61, April 1968.

5. William E. Cox, Jr. and Ernest F. Cooke, "Other Dimensions Involved in Shopping Center Preference," *Journal of Marketing,* **34**:12–17, October 1970.

6. David L. Huff, "A Probabilistic Analysis of Consumer Spatial Behavior," in William S. Decker (ed.), *Emerging Concepts in Marketing,* American Marketing Association, Chicago, 1962, pp. 443–461.

7. For a discussion of problem areas in the Huff model, see David L. Huff and Richard R.

Batsell, "Conceptual and Operational Problems with Market Share Models of Consumer Spatial Behavior," in Mary Jane Schlinger (ed.), *Advances in Consumer Research,* vol. 2, Association for Consumer Research, Chicago, 1975, pp. 165–172; Joseph Barry Mason, "Retail Market Area Shape and Structure: Problems and Prospects," in Schlinger (ed.), *Advances;* and Louis P. Bucklin, "The Concept of Mass in Intra-urban Shopping," *Journal of Marketing,* **31**:37–42, January-February 1958.

8. See Pierre Martineau, "The Personality of the Retail Store," *Harvard Business Review,* **36**:47–55, January-February 1958.

9. Wroe Alderson and Robert Sessions, "Basic Research on Consumer Behavior: Report on a Study of Shopping Behavior and Methods for Its Investigation," in Ronald E. Frank, Alfred A. Kuehn, and William F. Massy (eds.), *Quantitative Techniques in Marketing Analysis,* Irwin, Homewood, Ill., 1962, pp. 129–145.

10. "Consumer Behavior in the Supermarket," *Progressive Grocer,* October 1975, p. 37.

11. "How Housewives See the Discount Store Today," *Discount Merchandiser,* March 1970, pp. 77–90; and "Why Shoppers Choose Discount Stores vs. Downtown Stores," *Discount Merchandiser,* December 1971, pp. 31–32.

12. Stuart U. Rich and Bernard D. Portis, "The 'Imageries' of Department Stores," *Journal of Marketing,* **28**:10–15, April 1964.

13. "38th Annual Report of the Grocery Industry," *Progressive Grocer,* April 1971, p. 65.

14. T. Ellsworth, D. Benjamin, and H. Radolf, "Customer Response to Trading Stamps," *Journal of Retailing,* **33**:165–169, 206, Winter 1957–1958.

15. Rich and Portis, "The 'Imageries' "; and David J. Rachman and Linda J. Kemp, "Profile of the Discount House Customer," *Journal of Retailing,* **39**:1–8, Summer 1963.

16. E. D. Fraser, "Inside Information on Retailers," *Journal of Retailing,* **30**:21 ff, Spring 1954.

17. C. Glenn Walters, *Consumer Behavior: Theory and Practice,* rev. ed., Irwin, Homewood, Ill., 1974, p. 425.

18. James F. Engel, David T. Kollat, and Roger D. Blackwell, *Consumer Behavior,* 2d ed., Holt, New York, 1973, p. 457.

19. Gregory P. Stone, "City Shoppers and Urban Identification: Observations on the Social Psychology of City Life," *American Journal of Sociology,* **60**:36–45, 1954.

20. William R. Darden and Fred D. Reynolds, "Shopping Orientations and Product Usage Rates," *Journal of Marketing Research,* **8**:505–508, November 1971; and Louis E. Boone et al., " 'City Shoppers and Urban Identification' Revisited," *Journal of Marketing,* **38**:67–69, July 1974.

21. See for example P. Ronald Stephenson and Ronald P. Willett, "Analysis of Consumers' Retail Patronage Strategies," in Philip R. McDonald (ed.), *Marketing Involvement in Society and the Economy,* American Marketing Association, Chicago, 1969, pp. 316–322; William R. Darden and Dub Ashton, "Psychographic Profiles of Patronage Preference Groups," *Journal of Retailing,* **50**:99–112, Winter 1974–1975; and George P. Moschis, "Shopping Orientations and Consumer Use of Information," *Journal of Retailing,* **52**:61–70, 93, Summer 1976.

22. Robert F. Dietrich, "Know Thy Consumer: A Quiz That Shows How Well You Do," *Progressive Grover,* March 1975, p. 55.

23. Ross M. Cunningham, "Customer Loyalty to Store and Brand," *Harvard Business Review,* **39**:137, November-December 1961.

24. Ben M. Enis and Gordon W. Paul, " 'Store Loyalty' as a Basis for Market Segmentation," *Journal of Retailing,* **46**:42–56, Fall 1970.

25. Enis and Paul, " 'Store Loyalty,' " pp. 51, 53; and Fred D. Reynolds, William R. Darden, and Warren S. Martin, "Developing an Image of the Store-Loyal Customer," *Journal of Retailing,* **50**:79, Winter 1974–1975.

26. "Consumer Behavior in the Super Market—Part III," *Progressive Grocer,* January 1976, p. 68.

27. "Consumer Behavior in the Super Market—Part I," *Progressive Grocer,* October 1975, p. 40.

28. Howard Stumpf, "P-O-P State-of-the-Art Review," *Marketing Communications,* September 1976, pp. 53, 76.

29. Stumpf, "P-O-P," p. 75.

30. *Awareness, Decision, Purchase,* Point-of-Purchase Advertising Institute, New York, 1961, p. 14.

31. *Drugstore Brand Switching and Impulse Buying,* Point-of-Purchase Advertising Institute, New York, 1961, p. 14.

32. These conclusions are from "Merchandising Guide for the 70's," *Progressive Grocer,* 1971.

33. Ronald C. Curhan, "Shelf Space Allocation and Profit Maximization in Mass Retailing," *Journal of Marketing,* **37**:56, July 1973.

34. Curhan, "Shelf Space," p. 56.

35. Robert F. Dietrich, "New Survey Shows In-Store Information Tops Shoppers' Needs," *Progressive Grocer,* September 1976, p. 33.

36. Jacob Jacoby, Robert W. Chestnut, and William Silberman, "Consumer Use and Comprehension of Nutrition Information," *Journal of Consumer Research,* **4**:119–128, September 1977; J. Edward Russo, "The Value of Unit Price Information," *Journal of Marketing Research,* **14**:193–201, May 1977; and J. Edward Russo, Gene Krieser and Sally Miyashita, "An Effective Display of Unit Price Information," *Journal of Marketing,* **39**:11–19, April 1975.

37. Walter H. Heller, "What Shoppers Know—and Don't Known about Prices," *Progressive Grocer,* November 1974, pp. 39–41.

38. "Multiple-Pricing Makes the Most of the Moment of Purchase," *Progressive Grocer,* March 1964, p. C128.

39. "How Multiple-Unit Pricing Helps . . . and Hurts," *Progressive Grocer,* June 1971, pp. 52–58.

40. D. R. McCurry, "Shifts in Supermarket Buying Patterns, 1975," *The Nielsen Researcher,* no. 2, 1975, p. 7.

41. Joseph S. Cayce, "Are Brand Names Losing Their Luster? A Respected Consumer Watcher Says 'No, But . . .' " *Progressive Grocer,* October 1976, pp. 64–65.

42. See for example John G. Myers, "Determinants of Private Brand Attitude," *Journal of Marketing Research,* **4**:73–81, February 1967; Ronald E. Frank and Harper W. Boyd, Jr., "Are Private-Brand-Prone Grocery Customers Really Different?" *Journal of Advertising Research,* **5**:27–35, December 1965; and James T. Rothe and Lawrence M. Lamont, "Purchase Behavior and Brand Choice Determinants," *Journal of Retailing,* **49**:19–33, Fall 1973.

43. Richard H. Aycrigg, "A New Look At Coupons," *The Nielson Researcher,* no. 1, 1976, pp. 2–13; and "Consumer Behavior in the Super Market—Part I," p. 46.

44. William F. Massy and Ronald E. Frank, "Short Term Price and Dealing Effects in Selected Market Segments," *Journal of Marketing Research,* **2**:171–185, May 1965; Frederick E. Webster, Jr., "The 'Deal-Prone' Consumer," *Journal of Marketing Research,* **2**:186–189, May 1965; and David B. Montgomery, *Consumer Characteristics and 'Deal' Purchasing,* Marketing Science Institute, Cambridge, Mass., 1970.

45. Franklin B. Evans, *Dyadic Interaction in Selling: A New Approach,* Graduate School of Business, University of Chicago, Chicago, 1964, p. 25.

46. This section is based largely on Peter L. Gillett, "In-Home Shoppers—An Overview," *Journal of Marketing,* **40**:81–88, October 1976.

47. Stanley H. Slom, "While Retail Sales Have Ups and Downs Catalog Shopping Gains in Popularity," *The Wall Street Journal,* June 6, 1975, p. 30.

48. Slom, "While Retail Sales," p. 30.

49. Peter L. Gillett, "A Profile of Urban In-Home Shoppers," *Journal of Marketing,* **34**:42, July 1970.

50. Gillett, "A Profile of Urban In-Home Shoppers."

51. Fred D. Reynolds, "An Analysis of Catalog Buying Behavior," *Journal of Marketing,* **38**:51, July 1974.

52. George H. Brown, "Brand Loyalty—Fact or Fiction?" *Advertising Age,* January 26, 1953, p. 75.

53. See for example Ross M. Cunningham, "Brand Loyalty—What, Where, How Much?" *Harvard Business Review,* **34**:116–128, January-February 1956; Lester Guest, "A Study of Brand Loyalty," *Journal of Applied Psychology,* **28**:16–27, 1944; Lester Guest, "Brand Loyalty—Twelve Years Later," *Journal of Applied Psychology,* **39**:405–408, 1955; and

Lester Guest, "Brand Loyalty Revisited: A Twenty-Year Report," *Journal of Applied Psychology,* **48**:93–97, 1964.

54. Engel, Kollat, and Blackwell, *Consumer Behavior,* pp. 551–552.

55. Engel, Kollat, and Blackwell, *Consumer Behavior,* pp. 557–558.

56. Gerald O. Caballo and M. Lewis Temares, "Brand Switching at the Point of Purchase," *Journal of Retailing,* **45**27–36, Fall 1969.

57. F. H. Graf, "The Logistics of Grocery Products," presented to the National Association of Food Chains, 55th Annual Meeting, A. C. Nielsen Co.

58. J. O. Peckham, Sr., "The Wheel of Marketing," *The Nielsen Researcher,* 1973, pp. 9–11.

59. Brown, "Brand Loyalty," p. 76.

60. Hawkins Stern, "The Significance of Impulse Buying Today," *Journal of Marketing,* **26**:59–60, April 1962.

61. Vernon T. Clover, "Relative Importance of Impulse Buying in Retail Stores," *Journal of Marketing,* **15**:66–70, July 1950.

62. *Consumer Buying Habits Studies,* E. J. duPont de Nemours and Co., Wilmington, Del., 1965.

63. "Consumer Behavior in the Super Market—Part I," p. 44.

64. V. Kanti Prasad, "Unplanned Buying in Two Retail Settings," *Journal of Retailing,* **51**:3–12, Fall 1975.

65. Stern, "The Significance of Impulse," pp. 61–62.

66. David T. Kollat, "A Decision-Process Approach to Impulse Purchasing," in Raymond M. Haas (ed.), *Science, Technology, and Marketing,* American Marketing Association, Chicago, 1966, pp. 626–639.

POSTPURCHASE BEHAVIOR

BEHAVIOR RELATED TO THE PURCHASE Decisions on Product Payment; Decisions on Product Set-up and Use; Decisions on Related Products or Services; Marketing Implications **POSTPURCHASE EVALUATION** Consumer Satisfaction/Dissatisfaction; Postpurchase Dissonance

Consumer decisions do not end with the act of purchase but continue as the consumer uses the product and evaluates his or her purchase decision. In this chapter we shall examine the nature of consumer postpurchase behavior. This stage in the consumer-decision model is highlighted in Figure 22-1. We will first discuss the types of behavior that may be exhibited as a result of and related to the purchase. Next, the concept of postpurchase evaluation and the significant implications it holds for marketing strategy will be examined.

BEHAVIOR RELATED TO THE PURCHASE

Once the consumer makes a decision to purchase a product there can be several types of additional behavior associated with that decision. Three activities are of primary importance: (1) decisions on financing the purchase; (2) decisions on the product's installation and use; and (3) decisions on products or services related to the item purchased.

Decisions on Product Payment

Although many small purchases are made for cash, our society is increasingly run on credit. The consumer's access to numerous credit avenues such as Master Charge, Visa, oil company and department store credit cards, means that for a vast number of purchases, especially expensive durables, a major decision involves the nature of payment to be used in the purchase. Such payment decisions may be very simple, reflexive decisions in which the consumer may instinctively pay cash or reach for her Visa card, for example. Other decisions to use credit may be classified as extended problem solving. For instance, a consumer may shop around for the most favorable credit terms, thus considering numerous alternatives.

Decisions on Product Set-up and Use

All consumers who have purchased consumer durables are familiar with the need to have their product set up or installed. The product must be made ready for the buyer to use, as with a car, for example. Many other durables could be cited which necessitate some set-up in order for them to be properly used. Televisions, stereos, furniture, clothes washers, air conditioners, for example, all must be carefully set up if the consumer is to find satisfaction from their use.

Many other types of products require very little in the way of set-up, however. Even apparently simple products, though, can be very complicated and frustrating in their set-up processes. For example, many a parent can tell horror stories about simple assembly of products for their children on Christmas Eve which turned out to be all-night exercises.

Of course, another element of product set-up and use concerns instructions given to the buyer for assembly and operation of the item. Products such as autos, calculators, microwave ovens, and so forth may require detailed explanations as to methods of operation. In order to ensure buyer satisfaction, such brochures (even books for some products) must be carefully developed to provide sufficient instructions.

Decisions on Related Products or Services

It often happens that a buyer of one item becomes a candidate for all sorts of related products or services. For instance, a 35-mm camera buyer may become interested in numerous optional lenses, a camera bag, dust brush, filters, a slide projector and trays, photo developing equipment, and even

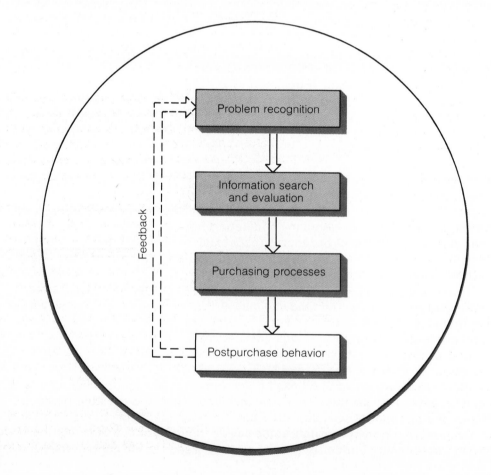

FIGURE 22-1
Consumer decision-
process model.

photography lessons. Similarly, a camping enthusiast may begin with a tent and buy a wide range of related products such as a stove, lantern, sleeping bag, and backpack.

Marketing Implications

Some very important marketing implications flow from these consumer postpurchase decisions. First of all, marketers clearly must make the arrangement of payment as easy as possible. Retailers have moved to ease the payment decision in numerous ways. For instance, making store checkouts easier facilitates the consumer's payment process. The use of electronic scanners at the point of checkout combined with compatible credit cards should also make the payment decision process easier and quicker. Moreover, retailers generally offer numerous payment alternatives in order to meet consumers' needs.

Banks have also joined the move to facilitate purchase-payment decisions. Not only are numerous bank cards and loan plans available, but even after regular banking hours, electronic funds transfers may be effected in order to obtain the necessary credit, or cash with which to pay for purchases. Since consumers from different social classes use bank credit cards for different purposes (upper classes use them for convenience, while lower classes use them as installment credit) it may be helpful to incorporate appeals appropriate for each group in a bank's or retailer's advertising of its credit plans.[2] Certainly retailers and financial institutions need to research their chosen market segments to determine their desired financing alternatives and if possible offer and promote these alternatives.

A second set of implications flows from decisions on product set-up and use. As mentioned previously, products such as televisions, ranges, washers, and so forth requiring set-up must be carefully installed and explained to the user. Unless such activities are conscientiously undertaken, consumer dissatisfaction is likely to result, and the consequence of consumer dissatisfaction, as we have seen, is likely to be poor word-of-mouth communications about the product, the retailer, or both. Thus, manufacturers need to select carefully retailers as members of their distribution team who will provide the kind of quality after-sale installation or warranty service that will enhance the manufacturer's image. The retailer needs to be considerate of such activities for the same reasons—that it can be an important factor in generating a favorable image and repeat customers.

The importance of information on product set-up and use becomes even more critical in today's self-service economy. Consumers are buying many complicated products from self-service discount outlets which may offer very little product knowledge or installation assistance. As a result, they must rely almost exclusively on whatever literature comes with the product. Such a situation provides an added impetus for manufacturers to assess their product literature and make sure it is readable and understandable. The consumer who fails to follow instructions with her microwave oven is likely to blame the manufacturer rather than herself.

Even more fundamental than the provision of information to consumers is the marketer's first understanding how his product is used by the consumer, and how this product fits into the consumer's "consumption system." For example, the marketer needs to know how his product is used by consumers not only to make improvements in its quality and functions but also to suggest new uses for it (as done by Jell-O and Arm & Hammer Baking Soda). If marketers were to research more thoroughly the use environment and behavior of their products prior to full-scale launching, we would undoubtedly see fewer failures and products more carefully attuned to consumers' life-styles.

It is also important for the marketer to understand the user's consumption system, that is, the manner in which the consumer performs the total task of whatever she is trying to accomplish when using the product whether it is washing clothes or cooking a meal.[2] By understanding how this product (let's say a washing machine) fits in with other products (e.g., dryer, iron, and detergents) in terms of consumption behavior, new marketing opportunities may arise.

A third factor for the marketer to consider with regard to postpurchase activities concerns buyers' interests in related products and services. This is another area of potential profit that should be actively cultivated.

Since buyers may become interested in related items, they need to be made aware of the potential products that exist. Thus, literature enclosed with a product could present other products in the line. For example, camera manufacturers do an excellent job of presenting their full line of attachments and accessories in this way. Also appliance manufacturers such as Whirlpool and Hotpoint frequently feature a number of their major appliances in one advertisement, since the buyer who purchases a clothes washer may soon be interested in a matching dryer. Another example of this practice is the packing of Tide detergent and Bounce fabric softener in certain makes of washers and dryers. Buyers of these appliances may be very susceptible to brand switching at this time. Consequently, new customers may be gained through such sampling.

In order to capitalize on the sales potential of related items, many marketers have diversified their operations. Gillette sells razors, shaving cream, hair spray, and deodorants; Starcraft makes boats and motor homes; Coleman produces coolers, tents, trailers, and other camping gear. Thus, the marketer's task is to determine what product mix is most appropriate to the firm. This is largely a function of applying the marketing concept to identify products that may be related in nature and can be effectively marketed.

POSTPURCHASE EVALUATION

In addition to the overt types of behavior that result from purchase, the consumer also engages in an evaluation of the purchase decision. Because the consumer is uncertain of the wisdom of his decision, he rethinks this decision in the post-purchase stage. There are several functions which this stage serves. First, it serves to broaden the consumer's set of experiences stored in memory. Second, it provides a check on how well he is doing as a consumer in selecting products, stores, and so on. Third, the feedback that the consumer receives from this stage helps to make adjustments in future purchasing strategies.[3]

Consumer Satisfaction/Dissatisfaction

Satisfaction is an important element in the evaluation stage. According to Howard and Sheth, *satisfaction* refers to the buyer's state of being adequately rewarded in a buying situation for the sacrifice he has made. *Adequacy* of satisfaction is a result of matching actual past purchase and consumption experience with the expected reward from the brand in terms of its anticipated potential to satisfy the consumer's motives.[4] Figure 22-2 presents a diagram of the process.

The concept of satisfaction is one about which there are presently few agreed-upon definitions or approaches to measurement. Nevertheless, Hunt has summarized the concept in the following statement:

Satisfaction is a kind of stepping away from an experience and evaluating it. . . . One could have a pleasurable experience that caused dissatisfaction because even though pleasurable, it wasn't as pleasurable as it was supposed or

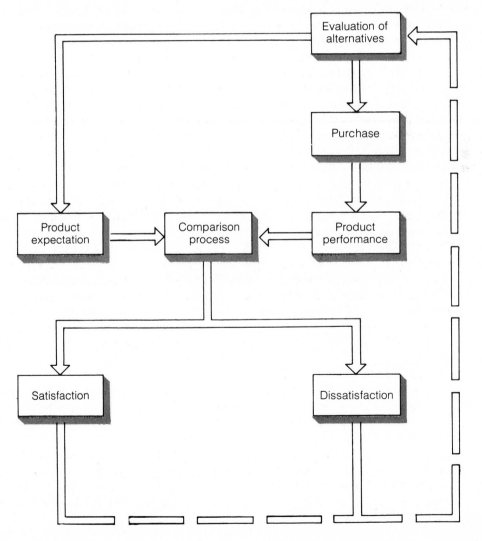

FIGURE 22-2
Purchase evaluation process.

expected to be. So satisfaction/dissatisfaction isn't an emotion, it's the evaluation of an emotion.[5]

Consumers form certain expectations prior to the purchase. These expectations may be about (1) the nature and performance of the product or service (that is, the anticipated benefits to be derived directly from the item), (2) the costs and efforts to be expended before obtaining the direct product or service benefits, and (3) the social benefits or costs accruing to the consumer as a result of the purchase (that is, the anticipated impact of the purchase on significant others).[6]

The result of satisfaction or reward to the consumer in the purchase of a product is that the same behavior is likely to be exhibited in a similar purchasing situation. That is, attitudes can be learned in the same way as habit, by reinforcement.[7] Thus as long as positive reinforcement takes place the consumer will tend to continue to purchase the same brand. It is true, however, that consumers will sometimes not follow these established patterns, but will purchase differently simply for the sake of novelty.[8]

Postpurchase Dissonance

As we learned earlier, consumers may become dissonant over their purchase behavior. As explained by Festinger, cognitive dissonance occurs as a result of a discrepancy between a consumer's decision and the consumer's prior evaluation. Consider the illustration in Chapter 17 of the Nikon camera buyer who encounters some problems with the brand he has purchased. This is a typical situation leading to postpurchase dissonance. Festinger's theory was derived from two basic principles: (1) dissonance is uncomfortable and will motivate the person to reduce it and (2) dissonant individuals will avoid situations that produce more dissonance. Let us examine this concept more closely to see what factors lead to dissonance, how the consumer deals with the conflict, and what marketing implications are embodied in the concept.

CONDITIONS LEADING TO DISSONANCE From a review of research findings on cognitive dissonance, Engel, Kollat, and Blackwell suggest that dissonance is likely to occur under the following conditions:

1. Once a minimum threshold of dissonance tolerance is passed. That is, consumers may tolerate a certain level of inconsistency in their lives until this point is reached.

2. The action is irrevocable. For instance, when the consumer purchases a new car, there is little likelihood that he will be able to reverse his decision and get his money back.

3. Unselected alternatives have desirable features. In our camera example earlier, the Pentax, Canon, and Minolta (brands not selected), all had attractive features.

4. There are several desirable alternatives. Today's car buyer, for example, has an abundance of choices among similar attractive models.

5. Available alternatives are quite dissimilar in their qualities (i.e., there is little

cognitive overlap"). For instance, although there are many automobile models, each one may have some unique characteristics.

6. The buyer is committed to his decision because it has psychological significance. A large and important living room furniture purchase is likely to have great psychological significance to the buyer because of its dramatic reflection of one's decorating tastes, philosophy, and life-style. Ego involvement will be quite high.

7. There is no pressure applied to the consumer to make the decision. If the consumer is subjected to outside pressure, he will do what he is forced to do without letting his own viewpoint or preference really be challenged.[9]

It is clear that dissonance is likely to be strongest for the purchase of durables, although it can exist for almost every purchase. The factors cited above and others are illustrated in Table 22-1 which presents conditions under which high or low dissonance would be expected.

DISSONANCE REDUCTION There are several major ways in which the consumer strives to reduce dissonance. He may (1) change his evaluation of the alternative, (2) seek new information to support his choice, or (3) change his attitudes.

Changing Product Evaluations One of the ways consumers seek to reduce dissonance is to reevaluate product alternatives. This is accomplished by the consumers' enhancing the attributes of the products selected while decreasing the importance of the unselected products' attributes. That is, consumers seek to polarize alternatives in order to reduce their dissonance.[10]

Another approach to reducing dissonance is for the consumer to reevaluate product alternatives to view them as being more alike than was thought at the purchase stage; that is, to establish or imagine that cognitive overlap exists. As a result of viewing the alternatives as essentially the same, it makes little difference which one is chosen; hence, little dissonance would be experienced.

In addition, selective retention may operate to allow the consumer to forget positive features of the unselected alternative and negative features of the chosen product while remembering negative attributes of the unchosen item along with favorable features of the chosen alternative.

Seeking New Information A second way consumers may reduce dissonance is by seeking additional information in order to confirm the wisdom of their product choice. According to Festinger's theory, dissonant individuals would be expected to actively avoid information that would tend to increase their dissonance and seek information supporting their decision. It seems reasonable to assume that consumers would seek out advertisements for products they have purchased and tend to avoid competing ads. Research on this topic, however, has failed to support this hypothesis. Although it is widely documented that consumers experiencing dissonance do seek additional information, there is no evidence to substantiate either a general preference by consumers for supportive over nonsupportive information or a greater information-seeking/avoidance tendency by high-dissonance consumers.

TABLE 22-1

DISSONANCE AND BUYING SITUATIONS

Factors Affecting Dissonance	Buying Situation	Conditions with High Dissonance Expectation	Conditions with Low Dissonance Expectation
1. Attractiveness of rejected alternative	A high-school graduate decides which of several pictures to order.	Three of the proofs have both attractive and desirable features.	One of the proofs clearly is superior to the rest.
2. Negative factors in chosen alternative	A man chooses between two suits of clothing.	The chosen suit has the color the man wanted but not the style.	The chosen suit has both the color and style the man wanted.
3. Number of alternatives	A teacher shops for a tape-recorder.	There are eight recorders from which to choose.	There are only two recorders from which to choose.
4. Cognitive overlap	A housewife shops for a vacuum sweeper.	A salesman offers two similarly priced tank types.	A salesman offers a tank type and an upright cleaner.
5. Importance of cognitions involved	A child buys a present for her sister.	The sister has definite preferences for certain kinds of music.	The sister has no strong tastes for certain records.
6. Positive inducement	Parents decide to buy a photo-enlarger for their son.	The son already has hobby equipment and does not need the enlarger.	The son never has had a true hobby and needs something to keep him occupied.
7. Discrepant or negative action	A man purchases an expensive watch.	The man had never before paid more than $35 for a watch.	Fairly expensive watches had been important gift items in the man's family.
8. Information available	Housewife buys a detergent.	The housewife has no experience with the brand purchased—it is a new variety.	The housewife has read and heard a good deal about the product, and has confidence in the manufacturer.
9. Anticipated dissonance	A small boy buys a model airplane.	The boy anticipates trouble at home because of the cost of the model.	The boy expects no trouble at home relative to the purchase.
10. Familiarity and knowledge	A family buys a floor polisher.	The item was purchased without much thought.	The item was purchased after a careful selection process.

Source: Robert J. Holloway, "An Experiment on Consumer Dissonance," *Journal of Marketing,* the American Marketing Association, **31**:40, January 1967.

Consumers sometimes seek consonant information to support their choice, sometimes seek discrepant information to refute it, and sometimes merely look for useful information, no matter what the content. It appears to depend on the amount of information gathered before his decision and whether he perceives that he has made a wise choice. Thus, if the consumer gathered much evidence before purchase to support his decision and if he strongly believes he made a wise selection, he will feel free to seek out exposure to discrepant as well as consonant information.[11]

Unfortunately, the research findings in this area have numerous methodological problems; so at present it cannot be concluded that dissonance factors have any effect on the consumer's postpurchase information-seeking behavior.[12] Nevertheless, the fact that individuals do engage in selective exposure to marketing information and may at the same time be dissonant does have some implications for the marketing manager; these will be examined shortly.

Changing Attitudes As a result of dissonance the consumer may change his attitudes to make them consonant with his behavior. For example, when the marketer secures new product trial among target customers who initially have an unfavorable attitude toward the item (let's say they purchased it because of a coupon offer, or were given a free sample), this situation is likely to produce dissonance. That is, unfavorable attitudes toward the product are inconsistent with the behavior of product trial. Motivation to achieve consonance will likely take the form of attitude change because that is easier than renouncing the purchase and returning the product. By reevaluating the product and adopting a positive attitude toward it, attitudes and behavior are now consistent and consonance is achieved.

MARKETING IMPLICATIONS There are several marketing implications that arise from our discussion of cognitive dissonance. Most of these suggestions relate to the promotional variable.

Confirming Expectations When the purchase confirms the consumer's expectations, reinforcement takes place. When expectations are not confirmed, however, cognitive inconsistency develops and the consumer will likely reduce the dissonance by evaluating the product (or store) negatively. Thus, where a product fails to measure up to the consumer's expectations or guidelines for evaluation, the result may be no initial sale, no repeat sale, or unfavorable word-of-mouth communication.[13]

It is important, therefore, for the product to confirm expectations. Similarly, it is imperative that the marketer not build up expectations unrealistically. Marketers should first design products that will fulfill consumers' expectations insofar as possible. As our scientific progress advances, people come to expect fewer technical deficiencies in products. These expectations may be set unrealistically high, with resultant dissatisfaction when they are not fulfilled, as when the product breaks down for some reason. In order to reduce this occurrence, products should be carefully developed with the consumer in mind. A clear understanding of how the product will be used and how it fits into the consumer's life-style is necessary.

Much of the advertising done today may appear to be harmless exaggeration or puffery, but it may actually be contributing unwittingly to less satisfaction on the part of buyers. Promotions that promise more than products can possibly deliver may be destined for problems. Dissatisfied customers can spread unfavorable word-of-mouth communications and refuse to purchase the item again.

How can the advertiser counter this potential problem? One way is to develop promotions that are consistent with what the product can reasonably deliver. A number of recent ad campaigns have adopted this approach. Not only are positive product attributes mentioned, but some of the deficiencies are also cited. For example, a Buick Opel advertising headline proclaims

"Thrilling conclusion of Buick Opel 5-Car Showdown. Opel finishes . . . uh . . . 2nd." This approach is more consistent with what the consumer might accept than proclaiming that Opel beats every small car on the market. Such two-sided approaches to advertising can be very effective.

For the marketer interested in conducting consumer analysis, surveys may be undertaken to find out what consumers like and dislike about a product. Ford Motor Company conducts thousands of interviews with its buyers to learn what they like and do not like about their Fords. In addition, consumer expectations should be measured to determine how well the firm's product is meeting these expectations. Both manufacturer and dealer promotion should be assessed to determine if either is promising more than can be delivered.

A large-scale survey focusing on satisfied as well as unsatisfied product users might yield several important types of information:

—areas for improvement of the physical product

—ideas for promotional copy to create favorable attitudes toward the firm's brand

—promotional copy illustrating why our brand is better, based on competitive product failures

—guidelines for developing warranties or other kinds of guarantees[14]

Thus, to prevent cognitive dissonance from arising, marketers would be well advised not to create unrealistic expectations in the minds of consumers.

Inducing Attitude Change We saw earlier that when attitudes are inconsistent with purchase behavior, they are likely to change. Consequently, the marketer may seek to induce behavior changes in consumers through various means. Promotional tools including free samples and cents-off coupons are frequently used by the marketer to accomplish this. By offering these deals to consumers they may be enticed to try the item and as a result adopt the product or switch brands. However, the size and nature of the inducements should be carefully considered.

There is some evidence that the smaller the incentive the greater the consumer's dissonance and the greater the attitude change.[15] That is, small inducements force the consumer to confront his purchase behavior without a ready explanation for it, whereas large inducements may allow the consumer to simply rationalize his behavior. Therefore, a coupon worth 25 cents off on an item may produce more attitude change than one for 50 cents off.

In the case of free samples, however, it has been suggested that acceptance of the brand may never take place because the consumer could fail to fully expose herself to attitude change from use of the sample.[16] Thus, there may very well be an optimum value range over which promotional techniques produce the desired attitude and behavior change; beyond that point (either too low or too high) they may be relatively ineffective.

Reinforcing Buyers Although it has not been proved that consumers engage in postpurchase information-seeking behavior to reduce dissonance, it may nevertheless be the prudent marketing approach to proceed on this supposition. Such an approach may pay handsome dividends to the company undertaking some promotion aimed at new buyers. It could be especially important in the case of a company launching an innovation.

The marketer may not have to develop special ads aimed at new buyers. Much of his regular advertising may be sufficient to reinforce buyers about their decision. Buyers are likely to be looking for the kind of support stressed in ads featuring the product's major sales features. Nevertheless, if a sufficient advertising budget can be mustered, some ads specifically designed to reduce dissonance among buyers could be developed. Besides, the marketer may find that the kind of advertisement designed to attract customers may not be very effective in reducing dissonance among present buyers. Thus, ads more specifically tailored for new buyers may be necessary. Ford, for instance, aims certain advertisements specifically at new buyers for this reason.[17]

There are many illustrations of marketing strategies that appear to be logical approaches to reducing dissonance, in spite of the lack of substantiation in the published literature. For example, the marketer should supply sufficient dealer literature, which could provide new buyers with reinforcement. Moreover, instruction manuals should not only tell how to install and operate the product properly but also seek to convince the buyer of the wisdom of his selection. Information about warranties, guarantees, and where and how to secure service should help reduce postpurchase dissonance. These materials should be packed with the product. In addition, some firms spend huge sums to promote the availability and quality of their aftersales service in order to forestall dissonance.

Manufacturers and retailers may inaugurate correspondence with the new buyer as part of a dissonance-reducing campaign. For instance, auto companies publish magazines that are sent to new car buyers telling them how to gain more enjoyment from their purchase. Retailers have also learned that postpurchase messages to buyers can be beneficial. One study found that individuals receiving posttransaction letters from a retailer reinforcing their purchase decision experienced less dissonance.[18] Another study found that automobile buyers who received favorable postpurchase reinforcement from car salespeople had significantly lower back-out or cancellation rates.[19] Thus, marketers may develop several effective informational programs aimed at reducing cognitive dissonance in buyers.

SUMMARY

This chapter has examined the postpurchase stage of consumer behavior. Postpurchase behavior refers to those behaviors exhibited subsequent to the purchase decision. Consumers generally make several types of decisions related to the purchase, including financing, installation, and purchase of other related items.

In the postpurchase evaluation stage we discussed the concepts of consumer satisfaction, postpurchase dissonance, and the feedback mechanism. Satisfaction was seen to be an essential ingredient of this stage and one that determines future purchasing behavior.

Postpurchase or cognitive dissonance occurs as a result of a discrepancy between a consumer's decision and his prior evaluation. The conditions leading to dissonance were discussed, as well as ways consumers attempt to reduce dissonance. Because of methodological and conceptual limitations of dissonance research studies, definite statements about the applicability of dissonance theory to consumer behavior are difficult to make. Nevertheless, the evidence is substantially in favor of it (except as noted with regard to postpurchase information-seeking behavior). Marketing implications of cognitive dissonance were explored in order to suggest numerous ways in which promotional strategies could be used to offset dissonance and achieve a more favorable evaluation of the marketer's brand.

DISCUSSION TOPICS

1. Why should the marketer be concerned with postpurchase behavior?

2. Discuss the concept of satisfaction/dissatisfaction.

3. What is postpurchase dissonance, and what conditions lead to it?

4. How do consumers reduce cognitive dissonance?

5. Why should the marketer be concerned about consumer expectations in purchasing? What strategy implications are there in connection with expectation confirmation?

6. How can marketers reinforce buyers after the purchase?

NOTES

1. H. Lee Mathews and John W. Slocum, Jr., "Social Class and Commercial Bank Credit Card Usage," *Journal of Marketing,* **33**:71–78, January 1969.

2. Harper W. Boyd, Jr., and Sidney J. Levy, "New Dimension in Consumer Analysis," *Harvard Business Review,* **41**:129–140, November-December 1963.

3. C. Glenn Walters, *Consumer Behavior: Theory and Practice,* rev. ed., Irwin, Homewood, Ill., 1974, pp. 559–560.

4. John A. Howard and Jagdish N. Sheth, *The Theory of Buyer Behavior,* Wiley, New York, 1969, p. 145.

5. H. Keith Hunt, "CS/D—Overview and Future Research Directions," in H. Keith Hunt (ed.), *Conceptualization and Measurement of Consumer Satisfaction and Dissatisfaction,* Marketing Science Institute, Boston, 1977, pp. 459–460.

6. Ralph L. Day, "Toward a Process Model of Consumer Satisfaction," in Hunt (ed.), *Conceptualization,* pp. 163–167.

7. Howard and Sheth, *The Theory of Buyer Behavior,* p. 146.

8. M. Venkatesan, "Cognitive Consistency and Novelty Seeking," in Scott Ward and Thomas S. Robertson (eds.), *Consumer Behavior: Theoretical Sources,* Prentice-Hall, Englewood Cliffs, N.J., 1973, pp. 354–384.

9. James F. Engel, David T. Kollat, and Roger D. Blackwell, *Consumer Behavior,* 2d ed., Holt, New York, 1973, pp. 536–537.

10. See William H. Cummings and M. Venkatesan, "Cognitive Dissonance and Consumer Behavior: A Review of the Evidence," in Mary Jane Schlinger (ed.), *Advances in Consumer Research,* 2d ed., Association for Consumer Research, Chicago, 1975, pp. 21–31; and Leonard A. LoSciuto and Robert Perloff, "Influence of Product Preference on Dissonance Reduction," *Journal of Marketing Research,* **4**:286–290, August 1967.

11. Engel, Kollat, and Blackwell, *Consumer Behavior,* pp. 538–539.

12. Cummings and Venkatesan, "Cognitive Dissonance." Also see William H. Cummings and M. Venkatesan, "Cognitive Dissonance and Consumer Behavior: A Review of the Evidence," *Journal of Marketing Research,* **13**:303–308, August 1976, for a review of the methodological problems.

13. Richard N. Cardozo, "An Experimental Study of Customer Effort, Expectation, and Satisfaction," *Journal of Marketing Research,* **2**:244–249, August 1965.

14. John E. Swan and Linda Jones Combs, "Product Performance and Consumer Satisfaction: A New Concept," *Journal of Marketing,* **40**:33, April 1976.

15. Thomas S. Robertson, *Consumer Behavior,* Scott, Foresman, Glenview, Ill., 1970, p. 58.

16. Engel, Kollat, and Blackwell, *Consumer Behavior,* p. 535–536.

17. George H. Brown, "The Automobile Buying Decision within the Family," in Nelson N. Foote (ed.), *Household Decision-Making,* New York University Press, New York, 1961, pp. 193–199.

18. Shelby D. Hunt, "Post-Transaction Communications and Dissonance Reduction," *Journal of Marketing,* **34**:46–51, July 1970.

19. James H. Donnelly, Jr. and John M. Ivancevich, "Post-Purchase Reinforcement and Back-Out Behavior," *Journal of Marketing Research,* **7**:399–400, August 1970.

CASES

CASE 5-1 TASTY FOODS, INC.

Tasty Foods, Inc., is a national producer of fresh and refrigerated fine bakery products, such as breads, cakes, and cookies. In 1978 management determined that because of the rising criticism of many nutritionists toward "junk food," a large segment of their business might come under increasing pressure and face the possibility of stagnant or even declining sales in the years ahead. Consequently, a decision was made to diversify into other food product areas. One of the most lucrative new food areas appeared to be frozen pizza. Since the firm already produced refrigerated biscuits and rolls, a frozen pizza line seemed to be a related and logical extension. Also, a recent test of fast-food chains by an independent testing agency had identified pizza as being the most nutritious of the alternatives. Therefore management saw pizza as a product that would have a favorable nutritional image among concerned consumers.

Six months after introducing the new pizza line, which was offered in several varieties, the company was assessing the results of the new venture. Sales had been mediocre, at best, although blind taste tests revealed a strong preference for Tasty Pizza compared with other leading brands. In order to gauge future sales and determine whether the new product should be scrapped, executives commissioned a marketing research firm to conduct an extensive study and provide them with some measure of consumers' predispositions toward the brand. The results from a representative sample of consumers are as follows:

Response Category	Description	Percent of Consumers
1	Firm and immediate intention to buy Tasty	5
2	Positive intention without definite buying plans	25
3	Neutral—might buy, might not buy Tasty	25
4	Inclined not to buy Tasty, but not definite about it	10
5	Firm intention not to buy Tasty	10
6	Never heard of Tasty	25
		100

In addition, a survey of supermarket shoppers found that of those consumers stating a definite intention to buy a Tasty Pizza prior to shopping, 70 percent actually purchased pizza, but only 44 percent of these purchased Tasty.

Questions

1. Based on this information, what would you recommend to Tasty management?

2. What additional research information would be useful?

CASE 5-2   BRANDS MART[1]

When choosing audio equipment, most people develop pounding hearts, shaking hands, and full-fledged inferiority complexes. As a result of this situation, executives at Brands Mart, a closed-door discount retail chain selling merchandise, including sound equipment, to members of unions and other groups, think they have found a way to cure these symptoms in stereo shopping. They claim that the traditional approach to merchandising for most audio equipment, at best, intimidates and, at worst, excludes a large segment of the potential market. Realizing that most people feel they have to be either hi-fi buffs

FIGURE 1
The Sound Gallery

or electronic engineers in order to fathom the complexities of component systems, the company decided an entirely new approach to merchandising and consumer education was needed.

The result is "The Sound Gallery," recently opened in the company's Cambridge, Massachusetts, outlet, offering a futuristic sound environment and audio education exhibitions. (See Figure 1.) Prospective audio equipment buyers see and hear presentations entitled: "The Shiny Vinyl Canned Grand Canyon Tour" and "Speakers and Spaces."

The "grand canyon" is actually the groove of a phonograph record, magnified thousands of times. The prospective buyer is taken step-by-step through the vinyl record groove walls until he understands the exact nature of sound, how it is produced and reproduced, and what pleasure it can give in its unadulterated state.

The second presentation deals with all aspects of speakers. In about one-half hour, the listener-viewer has learned a considerable amount about sound reproduction and audio equipment and has had fun doing it.

The goal with The Sound Gallery is to present uninitiated listeners with the chance to experience the pleasure of high-quality sound reproduction without making them feel inferior in terms of technical know-how.

[1]Adapted from "The Sound Gallery, Brands Mart's New Approach to Stereo Equipment Merchandising Aims to Change Nervous Novices into Savvy Shoppers," *Marketing News,* May 7, 1976, p. 6, published by the American Marketing Association.

Questions

1. Evaluate the usefulness of this approach to the consumer during the information search and evaluation process. Can you suggest any changes and/or additions?

2. How may The Sound Gallery influence consumers at the problem-recognition and purchasing-process stages?

CASE 5-3   W. T. GRANT[1]

In 1975 W. T. Grant was a retailing giant—the seventeenth largest in the nation, with almost 1200 stores. Today it doesn't exist, a victim of bankruptcy. Although the chain was relatively profitable until 1973, it closed in 1976 as a result of several years of questionable management, poor merchandising, and internal bickering.

Grant expanded rapidly from 1963 to 1973, opening not only many new stores but oversized ones. Apparently each district tried to see which could add the most stores. However, expansion of store management was not able to keep up with the expansion of stores, and mediocrity began to show up. In order to fill the larger stores with merchandise, Grant added major appliance and furniture lines. It also began emphasizing its own label (which had a poor recognition level) on such big-ticket items as TVs, major appliances, and power tools. In order to sell these new lines, extremely lenient credit policies were adopted, which ultimately resulted in a tremendous bad-debt loss.

As the firm broadened its merchandise selection excessively, it found it impossible to cope with the resulting inventory problems. The result was that as styles, seasons, and tastes changed, stale merchandise was being sold in new stores; yet management was reluctant to use markdowns to move the items off the shelves and out of inventory.

There was much dissension among company management over whether to become like K Mart or to go after Ward and Penney. In effect the company took a middle position. Grant stores were not standardized but came in large and small sizes, some in shopping centers and others not, with different interiors and exteriors, and different merchandise assortments. Related to this was the fact that Grant's real estate people not only selected store sites but also laid out the interiors. In a typical store the men's apparel sections were the first encountered by shoppers, although most of Grant's customers were women.

[1]Adapted from "How W. T. Grant Lost $175-million Last Year," *Business Week,* February 24, 1975, pp. 74–76; and Stanley H. Slom, "Man on the Spot," *The Wall Street Journal,* December 4, 1975, pp. 1, 28.

Question

1. How might an understanding of consumer behavior and the consumer decision-making process have helped Grant's management?

CASE 5-4 NATIONAL APPLIANCES, INC.

National Appliances, Inc., manufactures a wide line of major home appliances including clothes washers, dryers, refrigerators, ranges, dishwashers, trash compacters, and air conditioners. Until recently the company was among the three largest United States manufacturers in this market. However, while sales have been increasing, the company has begun to slip in its market share. Marketing research indicates that there has been a general rise in consumer dissatisfaction with major appliances among all companies in the industry. However, the rise for National Appliances has been greater than the other leading producers. This appears to be largely a result of National's greater concern with what happens before the sale than after it. The marketing research department has suggested that more careful consideration be given to postpurchase behavior by consumers. Top management has requested that the marketing department prepare a report on important facets of postpurchase behavior which the company needs to understand more clearly, and to recommend a course of action that will help National achieve its former position.

Questions

1. What aspects of postpurchase behavior may be important to National in resolving this problem?

2. How may findings about postpurchase evaluation be used by National in developing effective marketing strategies? Assuming the company currently has no coordinated program of after-sales strategy, recommend a course of action for National.

CASE 5-5 NED BUCKLEY'S BIKE[1]

When his Raleigh 3-speed bike was stolen from his garage, Ned Buckley had to face the rest of the summer without his favorite mode of transportation. It had been purchased 2 years before at a yard sale, largely because the price was right. Ned had not even been looking for a bike, but when he came across one in good condition for only $30 he decided to buy it.

Ned and his roommate, Bob Hill, were working toward their bachelor's degrees in business administration. They resided in a small New England college town which was also a summer resort. Living in a tourist area meant traffic jams and parking problems, which Ned and most of his friends avoided by riding bicycles.

Ned gave the police a chance to recover his bike, but it was never found; by the following April he was ready to start looking around for a new one. Over the winter he had read a few articles on biking and had even checked out some consumer rating magazines. He knew that this time he wanted a 10-speed even though one consumer magazine seemed to be trying to discourage him. It said that 10-speeds were expensive and that most riders basically don't need what a 10-speed provides—for a pleasure ride on a Sunday afternoon, a finely tuned, expensive 10-speed bike isn't necessary—a 3-speed will do just fine. However, Ned was sure he'd put a 10-speed to a lot of good use.

He and Bob (who owned a 10-speed Columbia) were talking about different brands of bikes one day when Bob suggested that Ned should consider a Columbia instead of a Raleigh, particularly because of the price. He also mentioned that he understood the university biking team used them as practice bikes, which Bob thought was a good recommendation. Although Ned acknowledged that he would look into Columbia, he was actually thinking to himself that while Columbias might be good and sturdy, and while Bob liked his, they were not very "classy." Besides, they seemed to be featured in every discount house in town and were always offered as a price special—which didn't sound like much of a recommendation. Ned had been happy with his Raleigh and thought that they probably had quite an edge over Columbias in sleekness and design and that he most likely would buy another one—only this time, a 10-speed.

The next day Ned and Bob went to look at bikes. Their first stop was at a motorcycle and bicycle shop downtown that carried Raleigh, Columbia, and Schwinn. However, the shop emphasized motorcycles and had a disappointing selection of 10-speeds. The salesperson was also a disappointment. He looked as if he'd never even ridden a bike and seemed just to be giving them the standard sales spiel. Ned asked him to explain about the different brands of derailleurs (gear-changing mechanisms) available on 10-speeds, particularly the Raleighs.

"Raleigh doesn't make derailleurs, so their bikes are equipped with those from another manufacturer. This one is a Simplex, which is very lightweight and is designed primarily for racing. The gear-changing levers and ratchets are all plastic. Sun Tour derailleurs are available on Raleighs also, and they are made of a heavy gauge metal."

"So, if I'm not interested in speed, then a Sun Tour derailleur would probably be better for me?"

"Yes, if you don't really plan on doing any racing."

After Bob purchased some derailleur lubricant, which he had noticed on a counter display, they left that shop and decided to go to the other one in town.

The second shop only carried the Fuji line, but Ned and Bob decided that they might be able to get some comparative information on Raleighs anyway. The salesperson at this store looked as if she had been repairing bikes, so they felt more comfortable with her as a source of information.

Upon meeting them the woman went into a Fuji sales pitch, but with probing from Ned the subject turned to Raleigh bikes. She didn't seem to be able to say anything bad about them, so when they left the store Ned felt confident about his decision to buy a Raleigh.

The Yellow Pages listed one more store in the area that was an authorized

Schwinn and Motobecane dealer but which also carried some Raleighs, and since it was a 45-minute ride Ned decided to call them. A friendly sounding salesperson told him, "The Raleigh Record is $179.95 and comes in metallic blue or red."

"Do you have them in stock, and can I get one with a Sun Tour derailleur?"

"Yes, sir. And I can have it assembled for you in an hour if you'd like. I should also mention that our price includes handlebar taping in the color of your choice and a free 100-mile tuning and adjustment service."

"Well, I'm still shopping around, but thanks."

Ned hadn't really checked prices at the local Raleigh shop, so he called back and found that a Raleigh Record was $180.00.

At his statistics class the next day Ned met Jim Stevenson whom he had known for some time but saw only infrequently, even though they usually got along very well together. It was then that Ned recalled that Jim was really "into" 10-speed biking. After bringing up the subject, Ned asked Jim if he could spend some time schooling him on what to look for in bikes. They made a date to talk after Friday's class.

On Friday they grabbed some coffee at the Student Center and Jim began his "lesson."

"First, you have to understand that any brand of bike is really a collection of a number of pieces of equipment that the manufacturer usually 'packages' on the frame. Take my Peugeot, for example. It has a derailleur made by one company, while the brakes and brake handles are made by two other companies, as are the seat and pedal cranks. The trick, of course, is to get the best package of these components for the lowest price. That's what shopping for a 10-speed is all about."

This made a lot of sense to Ned, and he was becoming sort of excited about the idea of owning a 10-speed.

"Look, Jim, you can really help me because I know nothing about bikes—don't even know where to start in deciding how to buy one. First, I'm going to ask a really dumb question—What's a Peugeot?"

"Oh, a Peugeot is a French-made bike that's really quite a machine. It comes in various price ranges but sort of has this status image—at least to me."

"Are French bikes good?"

"Definitely. Brands like Peugeot and Motobecane really have good names. Don't forget, bike racing is big in Europe, especially in France, so they have a lot of experience in designing and manufacturing fine machines. Come on over to my apartment and I'll show you my bike and point out features you should look for."

Ned was really quite impressed with how clean, sleek, and precision-made Jim's bike appeared. He realized that he had never before been impressed by the looks of a bike, but seeing the brilliant blue tubing contrasting with the silver handlebars, crankset, and rims all of a sudden made him appreciate why Jim frequently referred to them as "finely-tuned machines."

"Man, that really looks like a jewel," Ned blurted.

"Yeh, Peugeots are quite the thing, especially if you're willing to spend a little extra."

"Why, how much did that set you back—if you don't mind my asking?"

"No, I don't mind. The total price with set-up and adjustment and a few extras was $425."

"My Gosh! That's surely out of my league."

"Well, you don't have to spend anywhere near that to get a nice bike. Here, let me give you a few pointers on some things to look for. First, the lighter the bike the better, because that means less pedaling effort for you. What you find, however, is that price rises in some kind of direct proportion to lightness. You don't need a really light machine, but I would recommend something weighing 29 pounds or less. Also, make sure you get one that carries at least 70 pounds of air pressure in the tires."

Ned noticed how Jim was getting excited and realized that he was going to get hit with more information than he could easily digest.

"Hold it, Jim, give me a pad so I can get all of this down, okay?"

"Sure. Now I did quite a bit of research on bikes before I bought, and let me tell you what components I decided would make the best total package in a bike. First, I was looking for a good derailleur, and to me that meant Simplex. Next in importance were the brakes, which had to be Mafac center pulls with two-position handles."

Jim described what he meant by center pull brakes and demonstrated their advantages.

"Next, I wanted alloy wheel rims and a Uniglide gold chain for strength while being light. I also was looking for a Maillard gear cluster, a Campagnolo crankset, Phillipe alloy handlebars, and Michelin tires. I had to make a couple of compromises, but I got most of what I wanted."

Jim continued his monologue of brand names for various parts of the bike and also went further, on occasion, to point out the construction details which distinguish a better 10-speed from a less expensive one. Much of this became an information blitz to Ned, and he began to feel as if his brain were going to short-circuit. But he dutifully took notes, hoping these could provide a checklist for him when he was ready to make his purchase.

That night Ned read his notes to draw some conclusions as to what action to take. They were quite incomplete, but one thing that he did notice was that there was a predominance of brand names to look for but very few reasons as to why one brand was to be preferred over another. This made Ned feel somewhat insecure, because in several previous purchases—including that of a stereo set, when he had selected primarily on the basis of brand names—he later felt that perhaps he had not made the best choice.

After giving his purchase decision some further thought he decided that his best bet might be to buy a Peugeot. After all, Jim knew a lot about 10-speeds and was very happy with his. He grabbed the Yellow Pages to look up the nearest Peugeot dealer, but the only one listed was a two-hour drive away. That seemed to have the potential of a nightmare in terms of servicing and parts replacement. He then decided that since Motobecanes were French made, and Jim spoke highly of them, he would visit the Motobecane dealer that he had called previously.

Early Saturday, armed with his notes, Ned set out for the bike shop while grumbling under his breath about the increasingly congested traffic conditions in town. Arriving at the dealership he was first impressed by the size of the store and its very large selection of bikes and accessories. No salesperson approached him immediately even though several were not busy. He found the 10-speed bikes and narrowed in on the Motobecane section. The first thing that hit him was that there were over six different models of the brand. They all looked quite sleek and were displayed in a way that seemed to accentuate their beauty. Ned began to get that feeling he experienced whenever he became enamored of a new "toy." This usually meant that his willingness to spend money was rapidly increasing. A salesperson approached him. He was about 20 years old, wearing jeans, and seemed to have the look of a savvy cyclist. Ned also noted that he wore some type of cycling emblem on his shirt.

"Hi, May I help you in any way?"

The approach and tone of voice were very low-key and friendly, which immediately made Ned feel comfortable.

"Yes, I was interested in looking at the 10-speed Motobecanes."

"Well, we have most of their models displayed here, from the Nomade on up. Were you interested in a touring bike or a racing machine?"

"I'm not really sure," Ned responded, as he tried to figure out the difference without displaying his ignorance. Finally he decided to level with the salesperson, especially since he seemed willing to help.

"I really don't know much about these things; maybe you can help me decide which models I should be looking at."

"Oh, well, let me ask you this. Do you want a bike primarily for racing in competitive meets or for more general riding?"

"General riding."

"Okay. Now, do you expect that most of your riding will be around town with occasional long trips or mostly cross-country jaunts and a little riding around town?"

"Mostly I want the bike for basic transportation around town, but I guess I would also like the capability to take an occasional longer trip."

"Fine, now may I ask whether you had a specific price range in mind?"

"Well, not really, although I have done some looking in the $170-$180 range."

"Our Nomade sells in that price bracket. Let me see, it looks as though a 25-inch frame would fit you."

"No, my old bike was a 23-incher," said Ned.

"That sounds a little small, but here, jump on this 23-incher and we'll see."

Ned obliged him and after some switching between the 23- and 25-inch frame bikes he was surprised to find that he agreed with the salesperson. The 25-inch frame was more suited to his 6'1" height and his leg length.

"What is the weight of this one?" Ned inquired.

"The Nomade is slightly over 29 pounds."

Ned remembered what Jim had said about weight and asked to see something lighter.

"Well, our Mirage is listed at 28³/₄ pounds."

"Let me see that one."

Ned found himself sitting on a brown Mirage and liking the feel and look of the bike enough not to be dissuaded by its $210 price.

"What kind of derailleur does it have?"

"A Sun Tour" the salesperson responded.

"Oh, I was really interested in a Simplex," said Ned as he remembered Jim's recommendation. "How about the brakes?"

"They're Weinmann center-pulls; the cluster is Maillard; it has Lyotard pedals; and as you can see, the chain is a black Sedis. But may I ask why you are specifically interested in the brand names?"

"Well, a friend of mine who knows quite a bit about bikes gave me a few pointers and recommended certain brands."

"Look, let me give you some advice. The Motobecane company is topflight, and it's not going to ruin its name by putting inferior components on its frames. Besides, the difference between a Sun Tour and Simplex derailleur in a given price category is minimal, if it exists at all. Also, to show you how good it is, the derailleur on this Mirage is exactly the same as the one offered on our $300 model. I think you should be more concerned with how light but sturdy the bike is, what features it has for the price, and how reputable the company is that stands behind it.

"For example, the Mirage is fairly light but has features that make it quite strong. It also comes with 90-pound pressure gum tires, a quick-release front wheel, and quick-release brakes which allow you to quickly change a blowout. The crankset and handlebars are made of a strong but very light metal alloy."

The salesperson went further to explain the gear ratios, the quality of the saddle, how Motobecane really pays attention to finer construction details, and how this has gained the firm an enviable reputation. He concluded by saying, "I sincerely believe that it is a great bike. In fact, I own a Motobecane and so do most of the members of my cycling club. But don't take my word for it—take it for a spin around the block."

This quickly made Ned realize that he had not yet ridden any of the bikes he had considered. Taking the bike out gave him an opportunity to get the feel of it, and it really impressed him in terms of smooth, effortless operation. It responded like a precision machine, and he was surprised at the speed he could achieve.

The test ride also allowed Ned to reflect on the salesperson's advice, and it made a lot of sense. Upon returning his only comment was, "Sold."

"Fine, and since things are slow right now I can have the guys in the back set one up for you while you wait. What color would you like?"

"I'll take the blue one, and can I have it with blue tape on the handlebars?"

"Sure thing." The salesperson disappeared only to return a moment later.

"Bad news, I'm afraid. We don't have any more blue Mirages in stock—only brown. But if you're really hot on the color, I can sell you a Super Mirage for $225. It weighs 27½ pounds, has alloy wheel rims instead of steel, and I think it is generally a better bike than the Mirage."

Ned looked over the blue Super Mirage that was on the floor, noticed its ticket price of $235, and quickly agreed to the deal.

While waiting for the bike the salesman suggested that Ned might be interested in a security chain and combination lock. In addition to those, Ned spotted tire pumps and chose one of the less expensive models. The salesperson threw in a free can of lubricant.

While waiting for the bill Ned noticed a tire pressure gauge and added this to the list. Since these additional items totaled $21.50, Ned decided not to get the touring bags that he had spotted, but he made a mental note to consider them at some future date. The total bill was $246.50 before tax, and while this made a large dent in Ned's checkbook he was happy with his purchases. He was excited about getting out on the road with his new, brilliant blue machine.

Given the trouble Ned had getting his bike home without a car rack he decided to look into one the next time he was near a bike shop. He then proceeded to take his first ride on his new machine and enjoyed it immensely. The bike was fast, responded very well, and he loved going by all the cars waiting in traffic lanes.

Running into Jim on Sunday gave Ned an opportunity to show off the bike. Jim's reaction was quite favorable, but a couple of times he did mention that the bike had components other than those that he previously mentioned a preference for. The second time Ned responded, "I don't think that the difference between brands in this price class is really noticeable." However, the tone of Jim's comment left him with less than perfect confidence in his statement.

It took Ned less than a week, however, to realize that he had made two mistakes. First, he should have purchased the lighter security cable instead of the heavy chain. Also, he should have spent a little more and gotten a pump with the convenient built-in air pressure gauge. He also noted that there were a couple of scratches in the paint on the frame.

The next Saturday he returned to the bike shop to seek an exchange on the chain and pump. A different salesperson waited on him. He allowed the exchange on the security chain but said he couldn't exchange the pump. Ned thought that he would try to sell it on campus and then get the one with the built-in pressure gauge.

He also mentioned the scratches and was told that they would be touched up free of charge at the 100-mile servicing. The salesperson suggested that Ned might want to also keep some blue touch-up paint himself, so he got a $2.50 bottle of the manufacturer's official color.

While in the store, Ned also looked at the car racks and found that the least expensive decent-looking one cost $22.00. While leaving he noticed an application form for a local bicycle touring club which planned weekend trips as a group. He took one home with him.

After several weeks Ned was using his bike more and more for basic transportation as opposed to recreational rides. He had noticed this but reasoned that the end-of-semester pressures were keeping his free time to a minimum. He was sure that once the semester ended there would be more longer pleasure trips. He made a mental note to find that touring club application form he had dropped somewhere in his room.

---

[1]This case was prepared by the authors and Linda Hemphill.

Questions

1. What stages of the decision process can you identify in this case? How would your own decision process for a bike differ from Ned's? Why?

2. Explain which of the following environmental influences have applicability in this case: culture, subculture, social class, family, social group, personal influence, and situational conditions. Be specific.

3. Explain which of the following individual determinants have applicability to the decision process in this case: motives, perception, learning, attitudes, personality, and self-concept. Be specific.

4. If Ned were typical of a large consumer segment, what implications are there for bicycle manufacturers and retailers with regard to their marketing programs?

INDEX

INDEX